Lecture Notes in Artificial Intelligence   13088

Subseries of Lecture Notes in Computer Science

Series Editors

Randy Goebel
University of Alberta, Edmonton, Canada

Wolfgang Wahlster
DFKI, Berlin, Germany

Zhi-Hua Zhou
Nanjing University, Nanjing, China

Founding Editor

Jörg Siekmann
DFKI and Saarland University, Saarbrücken, Germany

More information about this subseries at https://link.springer.com/bookseries/1244

Bohan Li · Lin Yue · Jing Jiang · Weitong Chen ·
Xue Li · Guodong Long · Fei Fang ·
Han Yu (Eds.)

Advanced Data Mining and Applications

17th International Conference, ADMA 2021
Sydney, NSW, Australia, February 2–4, 2022
Proceedings, Part II

Springer

Editors
Bohan Li
Nanjing University of Aeronautics
and Astronautics
Nanjing, China

Jing Jiang
University of Technology Sydney
Sydney, NSW, Australia

Xue Li
University of Queensland
Brisbane, QLD, Australia

Fei Fang
Carnegie Mellon University
Pittsburgh, USA

Lin Yue
University of Queensland
Brisbane, QLD, Australia

Weitong Chen
University of Queensland
Brisbane, QLD, Australia

Guodong Long
University of Technology Sydney
Sydney, NSW, Australia

Han Yu 🆔
Nanyang Technological University
Singapore, Singapore

ISSN 0302-9743   ISSN 1611-3349 (electronic)
Lecture Notes in Artificial Intelligence
ISBN 978-3-030-95407-9   ISBN 978-3-030-95408-6 (eBook)
https://doi.org/10.1007/978-3-030-95408-6

LNCS Sublibrary: SL7 – Artificial Intelligence

This Springer imprint is published by the registered company Springer Nature Switzerland AG
The registered company address is: Gewerbestrasse 11, 6330 Cham, Switzerland

Preface

The 17th International Conference on Advanced Data Mining Applications (ADMA 2021) was held in Sydney, Australia, during February 2–4, 2022. Researchers and practitioners from around the world came together at this leading international forum to share innovative ideas, original research findings, case study results, and experienced insights in advanced data mining and it's applications. With the ever-growing importance of appropriate methods in these data-rich times, ADMA has become a flagship conference in this field.

ADMA 2021 received a total of 116 submissions. After a rigorous review process, 61 regular papers were accepted to be published in the proceedings. Of these, 26 were selected to be delivered as oral presentations in the conference, and 35 were selected as poster presentations. This corresponds to a full oral paper acceptance rate of 22.4%. The Program Committee (PC), composed of international experts in relevant fields, did a thorough and professional job of reviewing the papers submitted to ADMA 2021, and each paper was reviewed by at least three PC members. With the growing importance of data in this digital age, papers accepted in ADMA 2021 covered a wide range of research topics in the field of data mining, including machine learning, text mining, graph mining, predictive data analytics, recommender systems, query processing, analytics-based applications, and privacy and security analytics.

There are a number of important aspects to the ADMA 2021 conference worth mentioning. First, due to the impact of COVID-19, the conference date was postponed from December 2021 to February 2022 to allow for in-person gathering and networking. Second, the submission system was switched from EasyChair to CMT, which provided a smoother submission process. Third, we have witnessed an overwhelming trend of deep learning that has profoundly influenced or reshaped many research and application domains, thus, many submissions to ADMA 2021 explored deep learning technology to solve various data mining problems. Fourth and finally, the organizing committee was composed of an international team from prestigious universities and research institutes, such as Carnegie Mellon University (USA), Stanford University (USA), the University of Washington, (USA), Nanyang Technological University (Singapore), the University of Queensland (Australia), the University of Technology Sydney (Australia), the University of Western Australia (Australia), and the University of Alberta (Canada).

We would like to express our gratitude to all individuals, institutions, and sponsors that supported ADMA 2021. We also thank the PC members for completing the review process and providing valuable comments within tight schedules. The high-quality program would not have been possible without the expertise and dedication of our PC members. Moreover, we would like to take this valuable opportunity to thank all authors who submitted technical papers and contributed to the tradition of excellence at ADMA. We firmly believe that many colleagues will find the papers in this proceedings exciting and beneficial for advancing their research. We would like to thank Microsoft for providing the CMT system that is free to use for conference organization, and thank Springer for the long-term support and sponsorship of the conference.

We are grateful for the guidance of the steering committee members, Xue Li and Jianxin Li, and the great support from the general co-chairs, Fang Chen, Osmar Zaiane, and Mohammed Bennamoun. With their leadership and support, the conference has run smoothly in a well-organized manner.

We also would like to acknowledge the support of the other members of the organizing committee. All of them helped to make ADMA 2021 a success. We appreciate local arrangements from the local co-chairs, Jing Jiang and Weitong Chen, the time and effort of the publication co-chairs, Lin Yue and Bohan Li, and the effort on advertising the conference by the publicity co-chairs, Lu Liu, Miranda Li, Yanjun Zhang, and Sonali Agarwal. We would like to give very special thanks to the web chair, Xueping Peng, for creating a beautiful website and maintaining the information. We also want to thank Chiyu Wang for her contribution in managing the registration system. Finally, we would like to thank all other co-chairs who have contributed to the conference organization.

November 2021

Guodong Long
Fei Fang
Han Yu

Organization

General Co-chairs

Fang Chen   University of Technology Sydney, Australia
Osmar Zaiane   University of Alberta, Canada
Mohammed Bennamoun   University of Western Australia, Australia

Program Committee Co-chairs

Guodong Long   University of Technology Sydney, Australia
Fei Fang   Carnegie Mellon University, USA
Han Yu   Nanyang Technological University, Singapore

Steering Committee

Xue Li   University of Queensland, Australia
Jianxin Li   Deakin University, Australia

Tutorial Co-chairs

Franck Vidal   Bangor University, UK
Tao Shen   University of Technology Sydney, Australia
Tianyi Zhou   University of Washington, USA

Publication Co-chairs

Lin Yue   University of Queensland, Australia
Bohan Li   Nanjing University of Aeronautics and Astronautics, China

Publicity Co-chairs

Lu Liu   University of Technology Sydney, Australia
Miranda Li   University of New South Wales, Australia
Yanjun Zhang   University of Queensland, Australia
Sonali Agarwal   Indian Institute of Information Technology, Allahabad, India

Workshop Co-chairs

Huaxiu Yao   Stanford University, USA
Sunil Aryal   Deakin University, Australia

Local Co-chairs

Jing Jiang   University of Technology Sydney, Australia
Weitong Chen   University of Queensland, Australia

Volunteer and Virtual Co-chairs

Xianzhi Wang   University of Technology Sydney, Australia
Qin Zhang   Shenzhen University, China
Xuyun Zhang   Macquarie University, Australia

Web Chair

Xueping Peng   University of Technology Sydney, Australia

Program Committee

A. M. Kayes   Swinburne University of Technology, Australia
Bin Zhao   Nanjing Normal University, China
Bo Ning   Dalian Maritime University, China
Bohan Li   Nanjing University of Aeronautics and
                                Astronautics, China
Chang-Dong Wang   Sun Yat-sen University, China
Chee Keong Wee   Department of Health, Australia
Chun Wang   University of Technology Sydney, Australia
Debajyoti Bera   IIIT-Delhi, India
Dong Huang   South China Agricultural University, China
Farhana Choudhury   University of Melbourne, Australia
Guangyan Huang   Deakin University, Australia
Haiyan Zhao   University of Technology Sydney, Australia
Han Zheng   University of Technology Sydney, Australia
Hongzhi Wang   Harbin Institute of Technology, China
Indika P. K. Dewage   Tilburg University, The Netherlands
Jiajie Xu   Soochow University, China
Jianxin Li   Deakin University, Australia
Jie Ma   University of Technology Sydney, Australia
Jing Zhang   Changchun University of Science and
                                Technology, China

Ke Niu	Beijing Information Science and Technology University, China
Ke Deng	RMIT University, Australia
Krzysztof Goczyta	Politechnika Gdańska, Poland
Lei Li	University of Queensland, Australia
Li Li	Southwest University, China
Lin Guo	Changchun University of Science and Technology, China
Lina Yao	University of New South Wales, Australia
Lu Chen	Swinburne University of Technology, Australia
Lu Liu	University of Technology Sydney, Australia
Lukui Shi	Hebei University of Technology, China
Manqing Dong	University of New South Wales, Australia
Md. Musfique Anwar	Jahangirnagar University, Bangladesh
Meng Wang	Southeast University, China
Ningning Cui	Anhui University, China
Noha Alduaiji	Majmaah University, Saudi Arabia
Peiquan Jin	University of Science and Technology of China, China
Peng Yan	University of Technology Sydney, Australia
Philippe Fournier-Viger	Shenzhen University, China
Priyamvada Bhardwaj	Otto von Guericke University Magdeburg, Germany
Qin Zhang	Shenzhen University, China
Quan Z. Sheng	Macquarie University, Australia
Quoc Viet Hung Nguyen	Griffith University, Australia
Saiful Islam	Griffith University, Australia
Sayan Unankard	Maejo University, Thailand
Shan Xue	Macquarie University, Australia
Shuiqiao Yang	University of Technology Sydney, Australia
Tao Shen	University of Technology Sydney, Australia
Tarique Anwar	Swinburne University of Technology, Australia
Tong Chen	University of Queensland, Australia
Wei Chen	University of Auckland, Australia
Weiwei Yuan	Nanjing University of Aeronautics and Astronautics, China
Xiangmin Zhou	RMIT University, Australia
Xianzhi Wang	University of Technology Sydney, Australia
Xiaowang Zhang	Tianjin University, China
Xueping Peng	University of Technology Sydney, Australia
Xuming Han	Jinan University, China
Xuyun Zhang	Macquarie University, Australia

Yajun Yang	Tianjin University, China
Yanda Wang	Nanjing University of Aeronautics and Astronautics, China
Yang Li	University of Technology Sydney, Australia
Yanjun Zhang	University of Queensland, Australia
Yanmei Hu	Chengdu University of Technology, China
Ye Yuan	Beijing Institute of Technology, China
Ye Zhu	Deakin University, Australia
Yucheng Zhou	University of Technology Sydney, Australia
Yue Tan	University of Technology Sydney, Australia
Yuhai Zhao	Northeastern University, China
Yunjun Gao	Zhejiang University, China
Yurong Cheng	Beijing Institute of Technology, China
Yuwei Peng	Wuhan University, China
Zhi-Hong Deng	University of Technology Sydney, Australia
Zhuowei Wang	University of Technology Sydney, Australia
Zonghan Wu	University of Technology Sydney, Australia

Contents – Part II

Text Mining

Multimedia and Time Series Data Mining

Classification, Clustering and Recommendation

Contents – Part I

Others

Pattern Mining

SMIM Framework to Generalize High-Utility Itemset Mining

Siddharth Dawar, Vikram Goyal, and Debajyoti Bera[✉]

Indraprastha Institute of Information Technology (IIIT-Delhi), New Delhi, India
{siddharthd,vikram,dbera}@iiitd.ac.in

Abstract. In high-utility itemset mining (HUIM), the utility of a set of items is calculated as the sum of the utilities of the individual items. In this paper, we describe scenarios where utility may be less than this sum for multi-item itemsets. To overcome the limitation of the current itemset mining algorithms for such scenarios, we introduce the SMIM framework for itemset mining in which utilities are constrained to be non-negative subadditive and monotone functions over itemsets. SMIM generalizes HUIM, can be used to analyse transaction databases with multi-item discount schemes, and can further be used to mine interesting patterns in a social network dataset. Finally, we explain how to design algorithms for SMIM with any general subadditive monotone utility function.

1 Introduction

High-utility itemset mining (HUIM) involves a transactional database, in which every transaction consists of a set of weighted items, and the objective is to identify a set of items (*aka.* itemsets) whose total weight in the entire database crosses a threshold [7,22]. The weight of an itemset $X = \{x_1, x_2, \ldots, x_k\}$ in the database $\mathcal{D}$ is the sum of the weights of X in all transactions of $\mathcal{D}$ that contain X, and the weight of X in such a transaction T, usually denoted $u(X, T)$ for utility, has been *traditionally computed as the sum* of the weights (or utilities) of the individual items of X in T, denoted $u(x, T)$.

$$u_{\mathcal{D}}(X) = \sum_{T \subset \mathcal{D}, X \subseteq T} u(X, T) = \sum_{T \subset \mathcal{D}, X \subseteq T} \mathrm{Sum}_{x \in X} u(x, T) \qquad (1)$$

Current state-of-the-art algorithms employ highly optimized data structures to process a large number of transactions at breathtaking speed on modest hardware. However, they are unsuitable in the scenarios where utility of an itemset in a transaction is *not* defined as the sum of the itemized weights, but some different function.

For example, consider a utility function that defines the utility of an itemset as the sum of its individual utilities discounted by the lowest utility:

B. Li et al. (Eds.): ADMA 2021, LNAI 13088, pp. 3–15, 2022.
https://doi.org/10.1007/978-3-030-95408-6_1

$u(\{x_1, x_2, \ldots x_k\}, T) = \sum_{i=1}^{k} u(x_i, T) - \min\{x_1, \ldots, x_k\}$. This situation can arise during discount seasons ("buy 1 shirt and 1 trouser, get the lowest free"), or when hampers are created consisting of items of different nature. Even though HUIM algorithms were proposed for transactions consisting of discounted items, the discounts considered were applicable on only single items ("buy 2 toothpastes, get another toothpaste free") [2,11]. These algorithms are difficult to extend to the former scenario where utility is no longer a simple *sum* of itemwise utilities. Ad-hoc adjustments to HUIM become difficult if the discount schemes are numerous, complex, and use complicated formulæ involving many items.

The focus of this work is not HUIM for discounted transactions, but how far can the idea of a "non-addition" utility function be pushed? Quite far, as can be seen in the list of contributions below.

- We propose an itemset mining problem named SMIM in which the utility function is not necessarily *Sum*, but any subadditive and monotone (SM) function on itemsets. This means that the utility of an itemset X in some transaction T cannot decrease when a new item from T, say a, is added to X, and when it increases, it does so by at most the utility of a in T.
- We show that SM utility functions have mathematically helpful properties, and can model HUIM, as well as multi-item discounted itemsets in retail transactions. Further, they can be used to identify active and popular users in a Twitter dataset. Treating a Twitter dataset as transactional is easy (e.g., each transaction can include the users active on each day), but identification of complex patterns requires more general utility functions than *Sum*.
- We design an algorithm named SM-Miner for SMIM where $u(\cdot, T)$ is given as a blackbox. We show how to adapt the existing HUIM algorithms for SMIM, but empirically show that SM-Miner delivers better performance.

One novelty of our solution is that SM-Miner is a single algorithm for *any utility function* that can be proved to be subadditive and monotone.

Our framework for SMIM allows us to capture extraneous interactions among the items in an itemset in their joint utility which is not possible in the HUIM framework. Another novelty of our solutions for SMIM is the use of the superfast HUIM algorithms [7] which show that they are still relevant and applicable towards non-trivial utility functions. Future improvements on HUIM algorithms can possibly speedup SMIM too.

2   Problem Statement

Consider a set $\mathcal{U}$ of items where each item has a positive real weight (we do not consider "negative utility") denoted $w(x)$.

Definition 1 (subadditive and monotone function). *A function $f : \mathcal{U} \to \mathbb{R}+$ is defined as subadditive if $\forall X, Y \subseteq \mathcal{U}$, $f(X \cup Y) \leq f(X) + f(Y)$, and is defined as monotone if $\forall X \subseteq Y \subseteq \mathcal{U}$, $f(X) \leq f(Y)$.*

The $Sum()$ function, defined as $Sum(X) = \sum_{x \in X} w(x)$, is a well-known example of such a function. However, $Min(X) = \min_{x \in X} w(x)$ is not monotone (e.g., say $X = \{x_1, x_2\}$, $w(x_1) = 4$ and $w(x_2) = 2$).

Now, let T be some transaction in a database $\mathcal{D}$ with positive weights on items that are denoted $w_T(x)$. We define the utility of a singleton itemset $\{x\}$ as $u(\{x\}, T) = w_T(x)$. We consider the general scenario where utility over the items in T is some monotone and subadditive function over T, denoted $u(X, T)$. The utility of an itemset X in the entire database $\mathcal{D}$, denoted $u_{\mathcal{D}}(X)$, is defined as the sum of $u(X, T)$, summed over all T that contains X. We do not require the monotone and subadditive property to hold for $u_{\mathcal{D}}(.)$.

The SMIM problem considers a transaction database $\mathcal{D}$, and a utility function $u(\cdot, \cdot)$ defined as above, and wants to know the itemsets whose utility over $\mathcal{D}$ is at least a given threshold θ. SMIM generalizes HUIM since Sum is an SM function, and variations of HUIM that were studied by Yao [21] for similar reasons.

3   Related Work

Several algorithms have been proposed in the literature for HUIM [1,5,6,10,13, 20]. Broadly these algorithms vary in terms of the number of stages they run for (one phase and two-phase), their database representation (tree, utility list, and projected database) and other data structures and heuristics used to prune non-high-utility itemsets effectively. All the HUIM algorithms explore itemsets in a branch-and-bound manner; however, to limit the number of database scans, they use upper bounds functions on the utility function to prune itemsets and decide exploration branches [14,15]. All the above techniques work for a specific utility function, $\sum_{x \in I} u(\{x\}, T)$ to be precise, and do not generalize to arbitrary (or even subadditive monotone) utility functions. The research community has contributed significantly to improving the efficiency of high-utility itemset mining algorithms in the last few years. One of our objectives is to identify protocols to adapt these algorithms to the SMIM framework. Our SMIM algorithms are designed in a similar manner, but with modifications to the upper bound function that are necessitated by the non-Sum nature of SMIM utility functions.

Declaration constraint programming has been used to generalize various notions of itemset mining. In this approach the constraints are expressed in a high-level language and a separate solver is used to identify the appropriate itemsets. Silva et al. [16] proposed a framework for constraint pattern mining that allowed anyone to organize and analyze different algorithms based on the properties of constraints like anti-monotonicity, monotonicity, succinctness, etc. Guns et al. [9] introduced a declarative framework named MiningZinc that can express HUIM. Coussat et al. [4] defined the problem of HUIM in uncertain tensors, and showed that an algorithm called multidupehack [3] could be deployed for a version of the high-utility itemset mining problem where the utility of an item is more general than in HUIM. However, both MiningZinc and multidupehack define the utility of an itemset as the sum of utility of individual items, akin to HUIM, and cannot be generalized to the SMIM scenario.

Subadditive monotone set functions have appeared in quite a few works on identifying important groups of entities, however, we are aware of only one work that is somewhat related to that of ours, but involves sequences of items. Tschiatschek et al. [18] introduced a utility function over a sequence of items, which is further defined using a submodular monotone function, that captures the ordered preferences among items over arbitrarily long ranges. They proposed a greedy algorithm for selecting a sequence of items under sequence length constraints and showed an application of their algorithm for the task of recommending a sequence of movies to a user.

Our approach is similar to that adopted by Yao et al. [21]. They unified several forms of "utility" measures proposed for itemset mining until 2006, including the ones used in FIM (frequent itemset mining) and HUIM, using a common framework and then identified common mathematical properties that can be used to design efficient pruning strategies. We not only generalize all those utility measures, but go far beyond and present interesting examples along with a case-study that can identify patterns in a social network.

4   Examples of SMIM

We show two scenarios that can be modelled using SMIM.

Example 1 – Discount Scheme: First, consider a retail store that is running this multi-product discount scheme: "Buy 1 pencil (P), get 1 eraser (E) free". Observe that utility of any itemset that does not contain both pencil(s) and eraser(s) is once again the sum of the itemwise utilities; for the other itemsets, its utility depends on the quantities of pencils and erasers. Let c_p and c_e denote the costs of 1 pencil and 1 eraser, respectively; let n_p and n_e denote the number of pencils and erasers in T, respectively. We can express the utility function on any transaction T as

$$u(X,T) = \begin{cases} Sum(X,T) & \text{if } \{P,E\} \not\subset T \\ Sum(X \setminus \{P,E\}, T) + n_p \times c_p & \text{o/w, if } n_p \geq n_e \\ Sum(X \setminus \{P,E\}, T) + n_p \times c_p + (n_e - n_p) \times c_e & \text{o/w, if } n_p < n_e \end{cases}$$
$$(2)$$

We now prove that the above $u(X,T)$ is subadditive and monotone under the reasonable assumption that $c(E) \leq c(P)$. Note that if there are n_p pencils in T, and X contains pencils, then the quantity of pencils in X is also n_p; in other words, X cannot contain a partial amount of some items.

To show that $u(X,T)$ is monotone, consider some $y \notin X$, and define $Y = X \cup \{y\}$. Now, if y is not a pencil or an eraser, then $u(Y,T) = u(X,T) + u(y,T) \geq u(X,T)$. When y is a pencil or eraser, $u(Y,T)$ may be different depending on whether X already had the other. However, since the cost of 1 eraser is at most that of 1 pencil, the total cost of Y cannot be less than that of X (even when there is an unequal number of pencils and erasers).

A similar line of arguments is used to prove subadditivity for which it is sufficient to consider two disjoint sets of items X and Y. Now, the only situation when $u(X \cup Y, T)$ would be different from $u(X, T) + u(Y, T)$ is when, *wlog.*, X contains pencil(s) and Y contains eraser(s). However, in that scenario, the combined utility $u(X \cup Y, T)$ would be less than $u(X, T) + u(Y, T)$ since 1 or more erasers would now be given for free.

Even though we discuss only one discount scheme, we are hopeful that many other common discount schemes can also be brought into the folds of SMIM.

Example 2 – Transactions along with a Relationship Graph: For the second scenario consider a Twitter dataset containing tweets and retweets of many users and their followers, over a period of several months. We construct a transaction database, denoted $\mathcal{D}$, by fixing (say) 3-h intervals to construct each transaction that represents the active users during this time period. The weight or utility (denoted $u(x, T)$) of a user x is set to the number of tweets posted by that user in that period. Next, we constructed a directed follower-followee graph, denoted $\mathcal{G}$, on the users by adding a directed edge from a user A to user B if B has retweeted at least one tweet posted by A in any of the time intervals.

Observe that identifying itemsets with high frequency or high utility in $\mathcal{D}$ would fail to account for the "following" relationship exhibited by the retweets. To incorporate this, we use the graph-theoretic notion of coverage of a set of nodes in G which is defined as $Co(X) = |X \cup \bigcup_{x \in X} \text{neighbor}(x)|$ in which the neighbours of x are those users that retweeted at least one tweet of X. We interpret $Co(X)$ as a measure of the *collective influence* of X. We proved that $Co()$ is an SM function and can be used in SMIM; however, $Co()$ does not capture temporal behaviour.

To further identify groups of users who are both "active and possess large influence as a group", an obvious utility function is the following: $sumcov(X) = \sum_{x \in X} u(x, T) \times Co(\{x\})$. *sumcov* defines the itemset utility as sum of values for each item, and just like *Sum* in HUIM, is subadditive and monotone.

TID	Transaction	$u(A) =$ $ucov(A)$	$u(C) =$ $ucov(C)$	$u(AC)$	$ucov(AC)$
T_1	$(A:5)(C:10)(D:2)$	5	10	15	$5Co(AC) + 5Co(C) = 35$
T_2	$(A:10)(C:6)(E:6)(G:5)$	10	6	16	$6Co(AC) + 4CO(C) = 36$
T_3	$(A:10)(B:4)(D:12)(E:6)(F:5)$	10	0	0	0
T_4	$(A:5)(B:2)(C:3)(D:2)(H:2)$	5	3	8	$3Co(AC) + 2Co(A) = 18$
T_5	$(B:8)(C:13)(D:6)(E:3)$	0	13	0	0
T_6	$(B:4)(C:4)(E:3)(G:2)$	0	4	0	0
T_7	$(F:1)(G:2)$	0	0	0	0
T_8	$(F:4)(G:3)$	0	0	0	0
	Total utility in database	30	36	39	89

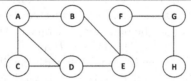

Fig. 1. Comparative illustration of traditional HUIM and SMIM. $u(I)$ denotes the utility of an itemset I as defined in traditional HUIM, whereas $ucov(I)$ denotes its utility whose computation involves both the transaction database and an external graph given below.

To illustrate the ability to create interesting utility functions, we designed another utility function towards the same objective. For this, it will be helpful to recall that $u(\{x\}, T)$ indicates *activity* of x. Let T be a transaction in $\mathcal{D}$ in which q_i denotes the utility of x_i in T, and the items are ordered such that $q_i \leq q_{i+1}$ for all i. Let $X = \{x_1, x_2, \ldots x_k\}$ be an itemset from T. The *coverage utility* of X in T is defined as $ucov(X, T) = q_1 \times Co(X) + \sum_{j=2}^{k}(q_j - q_{j-1}) \times Co(\{x_j \cdots x_k\})$. Figure 1 illustrates $ucov()$ and compares it with $u()$ on an example dataset. For example, $ucov(ACD, T_1)$ in the database in Fig. 1 is 37 and $sumcov(\{ACD\}, T_1) = 5 \times Co(\{A\}) + 10 \times Co(\{C\}) + 2 \times Co(\{D\}) = 5 \times 4 + 10 \times 3 + 2 \times 4 = 58$.

We further analysed a Twitter dataset using $ucov$ and $sumcov$ and showed that the former may be a suitable utility function (see the full version for details). However, it may not be easy to identify high-utility patterns based on a complicated function like $ucov$. Our strategy for this is to first prove that $ucov$ is subadditive and monotone, and then use the generic algorithms in the next section that operate on any SM utility function. Proving $ucov$ as subadditive and monotone turned out to be quite involved. The proofs are included in the full version of this paper[1]. We discuss the algorithms in the next section.

5   Algorithmic Framework for SMIM

Like the specialized HUIM algorithms where the utility function is Sum, specific algorithms have to be designed for specific SM utility functions. Here we lay down a general framework to design SMIM algorithms by adapting HUIM algorithms only relying on the fact that a utility function is subadditive and monotone.

Existing HUIM algorithms can be categorized into list-based, tree-based, and projection-based. These algorithms devise strategies to upper bound certain utility values and employ efficient data structures to explore the space of itemsets with clever pruning strategies using those upper bounds. We show that for SMIM too similar data structures and exploration algorithms can be designed with appropriate upper bound functions. The proofs of the claims in the section are available in the full version of this paper.

5.1   Projection-Based Algorithms

An essential step in the projection-based algorithms like EFIM [23], D2HUP [12], and MAHI [17] is merging two identical transactions to reduce the costly database scans during the construction of a projected database for an itemset. We explain why this should not be done for arbitrary utility functions.

Let $T = \{(A_1 : q_1), \ldots (A_n : q_n)\}$ and $S = \{(A_1 : r_1), \ldots (A_n : r_n)\}$ be two transactions with the same items in them, but with possibly different weights. Merging T and S to create a transaction $M = \{(A_1 : q_1 + r_1), \ldots (A_n : q_n + r_n)\}$ does not change the utility of the itemset $J = \langle A_1, A_2, \ldots A_n \rangle$ in the database

---

[1] http://www.iiitd.edu.in/dbera/docs/2021-smim.pdf.

for the $Sum()$ utility function that is used for HUIM. However, utility of J may not satisfy the same for an arbitrary SM utility function. For example, $ucov(\{F, G\}, T_7) = 7$ and $ucov(\{F, G\}, T_8) = 15$ for the transactions T_7 and T_8 in Fig. 1, but if we merge them to a single transaction $M = \{(F : 5), \ldots (G : 5)\}$, then we get $ucov(\{F, G\}, M) = 20$. Therefore, transaction merging should be disabled when adapting projection-based algorithms to SMIM.

5.2   Tree-Based Algorithms

A tree-based algorithm like UP-Growth and UPGrowth+ [19] creates a tree data structure from a transaction database which is then used to find potential high utility candidates. They create a global tree structure before starting the mining process. Every node of this tree stores an itemset, a pointer to its parent node, its support, an upper-bound of its utility (like transaction-weighted utility (TWU)), and pointers to its child nodes which are extensions of the itemset by one more item. As the algorithm recursively visits a node, local trees are created and used for recursively exploring its child nodes. An itemset X is unpromising in a transaction database if $TWU(X)$ is less than the minimum utility threshold θ. Unpromising itemsets are removed, thereby pruning the search space, during both the global and local tree creation; removing unpromising items has an added advantage of deriving better estimates during exploration.

The general idea can be extended to SM utility functions. The unpromising items can be removed during a global tree creation with an additional step to recompute the utility of a transaction after removing the unpromising items (this is easy for Sum). However, removing unpromising items during local tree creation may not give correct upper-bound estimates for an arbitrary function, even though it works for the Sum function. Imagine a tree-based algorithm at an intermediate stage and let Y denote the path to a node in the tree. Further, consider the case where an item A appears on the path to Y and, at that intermediate stage, A was found to be unpromising. The tree-based algorithms at this point remove A from the local tree and re-adjust the utility upper bounds of all the nodes on the path to Y. To update the utility upper bound of some node, say Z, the algorithm simply subtracts from it $\sum_T u(\{A\}, T)$ summed over all transactions that contain A. This happens to be correct when $u = Sum$ since the $Sum(Z \setminus \{A\}, T) = Sum(Z, T) - Sum(\{A\}, T)$, but may not necessarily hold for other utility functions. If we nevertheless use the same method and update $u(Z \setminus \{A\}, T) = u(Z, T) - u(\{A\}, T)$, we may incorrectly prune itemsets with high-utility; this is since subadditivity only guarantees that $u(Z \setminus \{A\}, T) > u(Z, T) - u(\{A\}, T)$ which clearly shows that the updated value, which appears on the right-hand side, could be lesser than the actual utility value of the left.

Let $T = \{(A_1 : q_1), \ldots (A_n : q_n)\}$ be some transaction, X denote the itemset $X = \{A_1\}$ and Y denote the itemset $\{A_2, \ldots, A_n\}$ with $n - 1$ items. Suppose it happens that the item A_1 is unpromising, i.e., $TSMWU(A_1) < \theta$; thus, A_1 cannot be a part of any high-utility itemset. It can be easily verified that $u(X, T) + u(Y, T) = u(X \cup Y, T)$ when $u(\cdot)$ is the $Sum(\cdot)$ defined for HUIM.

Therefore, $u(Y,T) = u(X \cup Y,T) - u(X,T)$ gives a correct bound for HUIM. However, computing tighter utility estimates by removing unpromising items can result in incorrect upper bound estimate i.e. resulting in false negatives for those functions where $f(X,T) + f(Y,T) > f(X \cup Y,T)$. We found that the tree-based algorithms for HUIM can be adapted for arbitrary subadditive monotone function without any change but for the removal of the unpromising items during local tree creation.

We identified an additional optimization to speed things up. The transaction utility (TU) of a transaction is the *sum* of the utilities of its items. TWU of an itemset X is the sum of TU for transactions that contain X. The *transaction-weighted downward closure* property of TWU ensures that if $TWU(X)$ is less than the threshold, then X and its super-sets cannot be high-utility itemsets [14]. We define related terms for SM functions.

Definition 2 (TSMU and TSMWU). *The transaction subadditive monotone utility of a transaction T is defined as $TSMU(T) = u(T,T)$. The transaction subadditive monotone weighted utility (TSMWU) of an itemset X is the sum of $TSMU(T)$ for all the transactions containing X.*

For example, consider transaction T_1 from Fig. 1. TU for T_1 (using *ucov* for utility) is equal to $ucov(\{A\},T_1)+ucov(\{C\},T_1)+ucov(\{D\},T_1)$ which evaluates to $20 + 30 + 8 = 58$. However, $TSMU(T_1) = ucov(\{ACD\},T_1) = 37$.

Observe that $TSMU(T) = TU(T)$ and $TSMWU = TWU$ when $Sum()$ is used as the utility function (as in HUIM). Like TWU, we were able to show that $TSMWU$ satisfies the downward-closure property; further, it turns out be a tighter bound compared to TWU for an arbitrary $u(\cdot,\cdot)$.

Lemma 1. *If $TSMWU(X)$ is less than the threshold, then X and its supersets cannot be high-utility itemsets. Further, $TSMWU(X)$ is a tighter upper-bound compared to $TWU(X)$.*

5.3   SM-Miner Algorithm

The list-based HUIM algorithms [6,13] use the exact-utility (EU) and remaining-utility (RU) bounds that are tighter compared to the TU bound explained earlier. These algorithms process items according to some fixed order, and the items in each transaction are sorted accordingly. Let X be some itemset that is being processed, T be some transaction containing X and T/X be the *items appearing after X in T* (note that $X \cup (T/X)$ is not T, e.g., items appearing in T before X in the processing order are not in T/X). The exact utility $EU(X,T)$ is the *sum* of the utilities of the items in X in T and the remaining utility $RU(X,T)$ is defined as the *sum* of the utilities of the items in T/X. It can be shown that X and its extensions (according to the processing order) cannot be high utility if $EU\_RU(X) = \sum_{T \supseteq X} EU(X,T) + RU(X,T)$ is less than the threshold [13]; this fact is used in HUIM algorithms to decide whether to examine extensions of the currently explored itemset X. Towards this purpose, they maintain a utility-list consisting of triples $\langle$Transaction id (TID), Exact-utility $(EU(X,T))$, Remaining-utility $(RU(X,T))\rangle$ with each itemset X. They scan the transaction database to construct the utility-list for promising items, i.e., items with TWU no less than the minimum utility threshold. The utility-list for a $\{k\}$-itemset (an itemset consisting of k items) is constructed by intersecting lists of two $\{k-1\}$ itemsets with the same prefix. The algorithms also store two mappings $sumEU(X)$ and $sumRU(X)$ that store the sum of $EU(X,T)$ and $RU(X,T)$ for all transactions that contain an itemset X.

We show how to define a tighter bound for utility functions that are arbitrary, not necessarily Sum, but subadditive and monotone.

Definition 3 (Combined utility (CU)). *Given an itemset X and a transaction T with $X \subseteq T$, the combined utility of X is defined as $CU(X,T) = u(X \cup T/X, T)$ and $CU(X) = \sum_{T \supseteq X} CU(X,T)$.*

Note that $CU(X) = EU\_RU(X)$ when Sum is used as the utility function (as in HUIM). We were able to prove the following properties which show that we can use $TSMWU$ in place of TWU and CU in place of EU_RU to design our SM-Miner algorithm. The proof of the lemma is included in the full version of the paper.

Lemma 2. *If $CU(X)$ is less than a threshold, any extension X' of X in the processing order of items is not a high-utility itemset. Further, $CU(X)$ is a tighter upper-bound compared to $EU\_RU(X)$.*

Our algorithm uses a data structure called SMI-list to store a list of triples of the form $\langle$Transaction Id (TID), Current Weighted Itemset (CWI), Remaining Weighted Itemset (RWI)$\rangle$ with each itemset X. Here CWI stores the item-quantity information for all items in X present in the transaction given by TID and RWI stores the items with their quantities which appear *after* X in a transaction. We associate with each item X two variables $SumEU(X)$ and $SumCU(X)$ that accumulate the EU and CU values during the construction of the inverted-list for X. A variable combined-utility (CU) stores $CU(X)$ with the utility-list for every itemset X. The construction of an SMI-list is described in Algorithm 1 in which we do not scan the SMI-list of the prefix while constructing the list for a k-itemset (unlike HUIM algorithms like HUI-Miner and FHM [6,13]) since an SMI-list for X stores the quantity information for all items in X as well as extensions of X in a transaction. We illustrate these bounds in our example transaction database presented in Fig. 1 for *ucov*.

SM-Miner has an initialization phase in which the database is scanned to compute the TSMWU of the items; TSMWU is computed since it is a tighter bound compared to TWU (Lemma 1). Another database scan is then performed to remove from the database the items with TSMWU less than θ (Lemma 1), and alongside, construct the SMI-lists of individual items that remain in the database. SM-Miner is then called on each of the items, along with the corresponding list, and its procedure is described in Algorithm 2. When called on an itemset I, it explores the search space in a depth-first manner to identify

Table 1. Illustration explaining Algorithm 1 on the dataset in Fig. 1.

	TID	CWI	RWI
	1	$\{(A:5)\}$	$\{(C:10),(D:2)\}$
SMI list of $\{A\}$	2	$\{(A:10)\}$	$\{(C:6),(E:6),(G:5)\}$
	3	$\{(A:10)\}$	$\{(B:4),(D:12),(E:6),(F:5)\}$
	4	$\{(A:5)\}$	$\{(B:2),(C:3),(D:2),(H:2)\}$

	TID	CWI	RWI
	3	$\{(B:4)\}$	$\{(D:12),(E:6),(F:5)\}$
SMI-list of $\{B\}$	4	$\{(B:2)\}$	$\{(C:3),(D:2),(H:2)\}$
	5	$\{(B:8)\}$	$\{(C:13),(D:6),(E:3)\}$
	6	$\{(B:4)\}$	$\{(C:4),(E:3),(G:2)\}$

	TID	CWI	RWI
SMI-list of $\{A,B\}$	3	$\{(A:10),(B:4)\}$	$\{(D:12),(E:6),(F:5)\}$
	4	$\{(A:5),(B:2)\}$	$\{(C:3),(D:2),(H:2)\}$

Algorithm 1. Construct-SMI-List of a $\{k\}$-itemset from SMI-Lists of two $\{k-1\}$-itemsets with common prefix

---

Input: L_{Ix}: SMI-List of a $\{k-1\}$-itemset Ix
Input: L_{Iy}: SMI-List of a $\{k-1\}$-itemset Iy
Global: Tables $SumEU$ and $SumCU$
Output: L_{Ixy}: SMI-List of $Ixy = Ix \cup Iy$
1: $Ixy = [\ ]$
2: **for** each triple Ex in L_{Ix} **do**
3:      **if** $\exists Ey \in Iy$ such that $Ex.Tid = Ey.Tid$ **then**
4:          $Exy = \langle Ex.TID, Ex.CWI \cup Ey.CWI, Ey.RWI \rangle$
5:          Append Exy to L_{Ixy}
6:          $sumEU(Ixy)\ +=\ u(Ex.CWI \cup Ey.CWI, Ex.TID)$
7:          $sumCU(Ixy)\ +=\ u(Ex.CWI \cup Ey.CWI \cup Ey.RWI, Ex.TID)$
8:      **end if**
9: **end for**
10: Return L_{Ixy}

---

the complete set of high-utility itemsets with prefix I; alongside it constructs the promising extensions of I in the form of their SMI-Lists using Algorithm 1. Pruning of an itemset Ix happens if $SumCU(Ix)$ is less than the utility threshold θ since Ix and its supersets/extensions cannot be high-utility as per Lemma 2; we use $SumCU$ instead of EU_RU since it gives a tighter bound (Lemma 2).

5.4 Empirical Observations

The objective of our experiments was to identify if there is any change in the performance trend in SMIM compared to HUIM for a complex utility function. In the absence of any existing algorithm for SMIM, we report the performance of our tree-based, projection-based and list-based algorithms for SMIM (listed in Table 2) using $ucov$, on two sparse and two dense datasets, namely Chainstore, Kosarak, Mushroom, Accidents [8]. Due to the lack of real-life networks on the corresponding items, we synthetically constructed graphs (for computing coverage) by taking the items present in a database as vertices and linking them by edges randomly such that the average degree of a vertex in a graph is four. The detailed results are available in the full version of this paper.

Algorithm 2. SM-Miner with threshold θ

Input I: Prefix itemset I
Input $\mathcal{L}_{I+}$: Set of SMI-Lists of Ix for all items x
Output: the set of high-utility itemsets with I as prefix
1: **for** SMI-List L_{Ix} in $\mathcal{L}_{I+}$ **do**   ▷ Ix denotes itemset I and item x
2: **if** $sumEU(Ix) \geq \theta$ **then**
3:   Output Ix as a high-utility itemset
4: **end if**
5: **if** $sumCU(Ix) \geq \theta$ **then**   ▷ Recursively explore extensions of Ix
6:   $L_{Ix+} = \{\ \}$
7:   **for** SMI-List L_{Iy} after L_{Ix} in $\mathcal{L}_{I+}$ **do**
8:    $L_{Ixy} = \text{Construct} - \text{SMI} - \text{List}(L_{Ix}, L_{Iy})$ ▷ Algorithm 1
9:    $\mathcal{L}_{Ix+} = \mathcal{L}_{Ix+} \cup L_{Ixy}$
10:   **end for**
11:   $SM - Miner(Ix, \mathcal{L}_{Ix+}, \theta))$
12: **end if**
13: **end for**

Table 2. Implementations of SMIM

SMIM algorithm	Adaptation of (HUIM algorithm)	Type
SM-Miner	(this work)	List-based
UPG+SM	UP-Growth+ [19]	Tree-based
EFIMSM	EFIM [23]	Projection-based
D2HUPSM	D2HUP [12]	Projection-based

The most prominent observation is that the performance trend of the SMIM algorithms with the *ucov* utility function is completely different from the HUIM scenario. Projection-based HUIM algorithms are known to perform an order of magnitude better than the other algorithms on dense and sparse datasets; for example, D2HUP performs the best on the sparse datasets and EFIM performs the best on the dense datasets. However, we observe that for SMIM, the tree-based and the list-based algorithms perform better compared to the projection-based algorithms on the sparse datasets. Further, SM-Miner competes with EFIMSM for the best performance on the dense datasets. Our investigations revealed that much of this behaviour is attributed to the number of utility function calls, and the tightness of the various bounds discussed earlier. In fact, the total execution times of the algorithms appear to be more correlated with the number of utility function calls than to the number of candidates generated, unlike HUIM.

Acknowledgements. This work was supported in part by Infosys Centre for Artificial Intelligence, Indraprastha Institute of Information Technology, Delhi (IIIT-Delhi), and Visvesvaraya Ph.D. scheme for Electronics and IT.

References

1. Ahmed, C.F., Tanbeer, S.K., Jeong, B., Lee, Y.: Efficient tree structures for high utility pattern mining in incremental databases. IEEE Trans. Knowl. Data Eng. **21**(12), 1708–1721 (2009)
2. Bansal, R., Dawar, S., Goyal, V.: An efficient algorithm for mining high-utility itemsets with discount notion. In: Kumar, N., Bhatnagar, V. (eds.) BDA 2015. LNCS, vol. 9498, pp. 84–98. Springer, Cham (2015). https://doi.org/10.1007/978-3-319-27057-9_6
3. Cerf, L., Meira, W.: Complete discovery of high-quality patterns in large numerical tensors. In: 2014 IEEE 30th International Conference on Data Engineering (2014)
4. Coussat, A., Nadisic, N., Cerf, L.: Mining high-utility patterns in uncertain tensors. Procedia Comput. Sci. **126**, 404–412 (2018)
5. Dawar, S., Goyal, V., Bera, D.: A hybrid framework for mining high-utility itemsets in a sparse transaction database. Appl. Intell. **47**(3), 809–827 (2017). https://doi.org/10.1007/s10489-017-0932-1
6. Fournier-Viger, P., Wu, C.-W., Zida, S., Tseng, V.S.: FHM: faster high-utility itemset mining using estimated utility co-occurrence pruning. In: Andreasen, T., Christiansen, H., Cubero, J.-C., Raś, Z.W. (eds.) ISMIS 2014. LNCS (LNAI), vol. 8502, pp. 83–92. Springer, Cham (2014). https://doi.org/10.1007/978-3-319-08326-1_9
7. Fournier-Viger, P., Chun-Wei Lin, J., Truong-Chi, T., Nkambou, R.: A survey of high utility itemset mining. In: Fournier-Viger, P., Lin, J.C.-W., Nkambou, R., Vo, B., Tseng, V.S. (eds.) High-Utility Pattern Mining. SBD, vol. 51, pp. 1–45. Springer, Cham (2019). https://doi.org/10.1007/978-3-030-04921-8_1
8. Fournier-Viger, P., et al.: The SPMF open-source data mining library version 2. In: Berendt, B., et al. (eds.) ECML PKDD 2016. LNCS (LNAI), vol. 9853, pp. 36–40. Springer, Cham (2016). https://doi.org/10.1007/978-3-319-46131-1_8
9. Guns, T., Dries, A., Nijssen, S., Tack, G., Raedt, L.D.: MiningZinc: a declarative framework for constraint-based mining. Artif. Intell. **244**, 6–29 (2017)
10. Jaysawal, B.P., Huang, J.W.: DMHUPS: discovering multiple high utility patterns simultaneously. Knowl. Inf. Syst. **59**(2), 337–359 (2019). https://doi.org/10.1007/s10115-018-1207-9
11. Lin, J.C., Gan, W., Fournier-Viger, P., Hong, T., Tseng, V.S.: Mining high-utility itemsets with various discount strategies. In: 2015 IEEE International Conference on Data Science and Advanced Analytics (DSAA) (2015)
12. Liu, J., Wang, K., Fung, B.C.M.: Mining high utility patterns in one phase without generating candidates. IEEE Trans. Knowl. Data Eng. **28**(5), 1245–1257 (2016)
13. Liu, M., Qu, J.: Mining high utility itemsets without candidate generation. In: Proceedings of the 21st ACM International Conference on Information and Knowledge Management (2012)
14. Liu, Y., Liao, W.k., Choudhary, A.: A fast high utility itemsets mining algorithm. In: Proceedings of the 1st International Workshop on Utility-based Data Mining (2005)
15. Liu, Y., Liao, W., Choudhary, A.: A two-phase algorithm for fast discovery of high utility itemsets. In: Ho, T.B., Cheung, D., Liu, H. (eds.) PAKDD 2005. LNCS (LNAI), vol. 3518, pp. 689–695. Springer, Heidelberg (2005). https://doi.org/10.1007/11430919_79
16. Silva, A., Antunes, C.: Constrained pattern mining in the new era. Knowl. Inf. Syst. **47**(3), 489–516 (2015). https://doi.org/10.1007/s10115-015-0860-5

17. Sohrabi, M.K.: An efficient projection-based method for high utility itemset mining using a novel pruning approach on the utility matrix. Knowl. Inf. Syst. **62**(11), 4141–4167 (2020). https://doi.org/10.1007/s10115-020-01485-w
18. Tschiatschek, S., Singla, A., Krause, A.: Selecting sequences of items via submodular maximization. In: Proceedings of the Thirty-First AAAI Conference on Artificial Intelligence (2017)
19. Tseng, V.S., Shie, B., Wu, C., Yu, P.S.: Efficient algorithms for mining high utility itemsets from transactional databases. IEEE Trans. Knowl. Data Eng. **25**(8), 1772–1786 (2013)
20. Tseng, V.S., Wu, C.W., Shie, B.E., Yu, P.S.: UP-growth: an efficient algorithm for high utility itemset mining. In: Proceedings of the 16th ACM SIGKDD International Conference on Knowledge Discovery and Data Mining (2010)
21. Yao, H., Hamilton, H., Geng, L.: A unified framework for utility based measures for mining itemsets. In: 2nd International Workshop on Utility-Based Data Mining (2006)
22. Zhang, C., Han, M., Sun, R., Du, S., Shen, M.: A survey of key technologies for high utility patterns mining. IEEE Access **8**, 55798–55814 (2020)
23. Zida, S., Fournier-Viger, P., Lin, J.C.-W., Wu, C.-W., Tseng, V.S.: EFIM: a fast and memory efficient algorithm for high-utility itemset mining. Knowl. Inf. Syst. **51**(2), 595–625 (2016). https://doi.org/10.1007/s10115-016-0986-0

TKQ: Top-K Quantitative High Utility Itemset Mining

Mourad Nouioua[1,5], Philippe Fournier-Viger[1(✉)] [iD], Wensheng Gan[2], Youxi Wu[3], Jerry Chun-Wei Lin[4], and Farid Nouioua[5]

[1] Harbin Institute of Technology (Shenzhen), Shenzhen, China
`philfv@hit.edu.cn`
[2] Jinan University, Guangzhou, China
[3] Hebei University of Technology, Tianjin, China
[4] Western Norway University of Applied Sciences (HVL), Bergen, Norway
`jerrylin@ieee.org`
[5] University of Bordj Bou Arreridj, Bordj Bou Arreridj, Algeria

Abstract. High utility itemset mining is a well-studied data mining task for analyzing customer transactions. It consists of finding the sets of items purchased together that yield a profit that is greater than a *minutil* threshold, set by the user. To find more precise patterns with purchase quantities, that task was recently generalized as high utility quantitative itemset mining. But an important drawback of current algorithms is that finding an appropriate *minutil* value is not intuitive and can greatly influence the output. A too small *minutil* value may lead to very long runtimes and finding millions of patterns, while a too high value, may result in missing many important patterns. To address this issue, this paper redefines the task as top-k quantitative high utility itemset mining and proposes a novel algorithm named TKQ (**Top K Quantitative** itemset miner), which let the user directly specify the number k of patterns to be found. The algorithm includes three strategies to improve its performance. Experiments on benchmark datasets show that TKQ has excellent performance.

Keywords: High utility itemset mining · Quantitative itemsets · Top-k Pattern mining

1 Introduction

Nowadays, a large amount of data is collected about customer purchases in online stores, brick and mortar stores. To analyze the behavior of customers and gain insights into their habits, a popular data mining task is high utility itemset mining (HUIM) [3,6,15]. The objective of that task is to enumerate all the high utility itemsets. A high utility itemset (HUI) is a set of items (products) that yields a profit that is greater or equal to a parameter called the minimum utility threshold (*minutil*). Finding HUIs in transactions is useful to understand customer habits. For instance, it can reveal that customers buying {*chocolate, cake*}

B. Li et al. (Eds.): ADMA 2021, LNAI 13088, pp. 16–28, 2022.
https://doi.org/10.1007/978-3-030-95408-6_2

together is highly profitable. However, a major problem is that HUIs do not provide information about the purchase quantities of items (e.g. how many chocolate bars a customer may purchase with how many cakes).

To give more detailed information about HUIs to users, HUIM was recently generalized as the task of high utility quantitative itemset mining (HUQIM) [7, 8,11,14]. The goal is to find patterns called high utility quantitative itemsets (HUQIs) that are profitable and also include the quantity information. For example, a HUQI is *"chocolate: 2, cake: 4-6"*, which indicates that buying 2 chocolate bars with 4 to 6 cakes yields a high profit. HUQIs are more informative than HUIs. The added information about quantities can be useful for marketing [7,8,11]. But finding HUQIs is much more difficult than mining HUIs. The reason is that not only different items must be combined together to form HUQIs but also different quantities may be considered.

Several algorithms have been developed to mine HUQIs such as HUQA [14], VHUQI [8], HUQI-Miner [7], and FHUQI-Miner [11]. These algorithms adopt various data structures and strategies to reduce the search space and find all HUQIs. However, an important drawback of those algorithms is that finding an appropriate *minutil* value is not intuitive and can greatly influence the output. If the user chooses a too small *minutil* value, then an algorithm may run for hours and find millions of patterns. But if *minutil* is too high, few patterns may be discovered. Hence, users typically set this parameter by trial and error, which is time-consuming.

To address this issue, this paper redefines the task of HUQIM as top-k HUQIM and proposes a novel algorithm named TKQ (**T**op **K** **Q**uantitative itemset miner), which let the user directly specify the desired number k of patterns to be found without having to define *minutil* before starting the mining process. The algorithm then finds exactly k patterns, and relies on three strategies to improve its performance. Experiments on benchmark datasets show that TKQ has excellent performance and can be a suitable alternative to find HUQIs giving only the desired number of HUQIs k.

The rest of this paper is organized as follows. Section 2 describes related work. Section 3 presents preliminaries and the problem definition. Section 4 introduces the designed TKQ algorithm. Section 5 reports results from the experimental evaluation. Finally, Sect. 6 presents the conclusion.

2 Related Work

Research on pattern mining algorithms has started almost three decades ago by initially focusing on finding patterns that appear frequently in data such as frequent itemsets [4]. To efficiently find frequent itemsets in transactions, the property that the support is anti-monotonic is widely used. It says that the support (occurrence frequency) of an itemset cannot be greater than that of its supersets.

Though, frequent itemset mining (FIM) is useful, frequent itemsets are not always the most important for users. To find patterns that meet other interestingness criteria such as the profit, FIM was generalized as the problem of high utility itemset mining (HUIM) [5,10,12] where both quantities and unit profits are taken into account. HUIM is harder than FIM because the utility function for selecting patterns is neither monotonic nor anti-monotonic. As a solution, HUIM algorithms apply various upper bounds on the utility that are anti-monotonic to reduce the search space such as the TWU [10] and the remaining utility upper bound [9].

To address the problem that HUIs do not provide information about quantities, HUIM was extended as HUQIM. HUQA is the first HUQIM algorithm [14]. It introduced the concept of candidate quantitative itemsets as well as a search space pruning property based on a k-support bound measure. Then, a more efficient algorithm named VHUQI was designed [8], it relies on a vertical database representation to reduce the cost of database scans. Thereafter, to further reduce the search space, the HUQI-Miner algorithm was designed [7], which relies on both a *remaining utility* and a TWU-based upper bound to eliminate low utility quantitative itemsets (LUQIs). Recently, an improved version of this algorithm named FHUQI-Miner was proposed [11]. Besides, additional search space pruning strategies were introduced to reduce the search space. FHUQI-Miner is the state-of-the-art HUQIM algorithm [11].

3 Preliminaries and Problem Definition

This section first introduces the problem of HUQIM, and then the novel problem of top-k HUQIM is presented.

Let there be a finite set of N distinct items (products), $I = \{I_1, I_2, \ldots, l_N\}$. A positive number p_i is assigned to each item $i \in I$ called *external utility*, which represents its unit profit. A *quantitative transaction database* is a finite set of transactions, $D = \{T_1, T_2, \ldots, T_M\}$. Each transaction $T_d \in D$ ($1 \leq d \leq M$) has a unique identifier d and it contains a set of exact Q-items, $T_d = \{x_1, x_2, \ldots, x_k\}$. An *exact Q-item* x is a pair (i, q) indicating that q units of item $i \in I$ have been purchased. For example, Table 1 shows a transaction database with four transactions (T_1 to T_4) and four items (A to D). The transaction T_2 contains two exact Q-items $(B, 4)$ and $(C, 3)$, which indicates that a customer has purchased four units of item B and three units of C. Table 2 gives the external utility values of items. For example, $p_A = 3$ indicates that a profit (external utility) of 3\$ per unit is gained by selling product A. The transaction database presented in Table 1 will be used as a running example in the rest of this paper.

Table 1. A transaction database

T_{id}	Transaction
T_1	(A, 2) (B, 5) (C, 2) (D, 1)
T_2	(B, 4) (C, 3)
T_3	(A, 2) (C, 2)
T_4	(A, 2) (B, 6) (D, 1)

Table 2. External utility of items

Item	A	B	C	D
Profit	3	1	2	2

HUQIM contains two kinds of Q-items, exact Q-items and range Q-items. Range Q-items do not exist explicitly in the database but they are obtained using the combination process. A *range Q-item* is a triple (i, l, u) indicating that an item i is purchased with a quantity that is at least l and no more than u. The interval size of (i, l, u) is calculated as $u - l + 1$ and it is called a *Q-interval*. For instance, $(B, 4, 6)$ is a range Q-item with a Q-interval of size 3. Note that, any exact Q-item, (i, q), can be expressed as a range Q-item as (i, q, q). A set X of Q-items is called a *Q-itemset*. A Q-itemset with k items is called a *k-Q-itemset*. A Q-itemset containing at least one Q-item with a Q-interval size greater than 1 is called a *range Q-itemset*. For example, $[(B, 5)(C, 5, 7)]$ is a range 2-Q-itemset.

A range Q-item $y = (j, l, u)$ *contains an exact Q-item* $x = (i, q)$ if $i = j$ and $q \in [l, u]$. Furthermore, y *contains a range Q-item* $z = (j', l', u')$ if $j' = j$, $l \le l'$ and $u \ge u'$. As example, the range Q-item $(B, 2, 4)$ contains the exact Q-item $(B, 3)$ and the range Q-item $(B, 2, 3)$.

The goal of HUQIM is to find all Q-itemsets that have a high utility (e.g. yield a high profit) [8]. The *utility of an exact Q-item* $x = (i, q)$ in a transaction T_d is defined and denoted as $u(x, T_d) = p_i \times q$. The *utility of a range Q-item* $x = (i, l, u)$ in a transaction T_d is defined as $u(x, T_d) = \sum_{j=l}^{u} u((i, j), T_d)$. The *utility of a Q-itemset* X in a transaction T_d is defined as $u(X, T_d) = \sum_{x \in X} u(x, T_d)$. For instance, $u((B, 4), T_2) = 1 \times 4 = 4$, $u((B, 3, 4), T_2) = u((B, 3), T_2) + u((B, 4), T_2) = 0 + 4 = 4$ and $u([(A, 2)(B, 6)], T_4) = 6 + 6 = 12$.

The utility of a Q-itemset X in a database D is denoted and defined as $u(X) = \sum_{T_d \in OCC(X)} u(X, T_d)$ [8]. Where $OCC(X)$ is the *occurrence set* of X [7,8,11]. For instance, $u([(B, 4, 5)(C, 2, 3)]) = 9 + 10 = 19$.

The *utility of a transaction* T_d is $TU(T_d) = \sum_{y \in T_d} u(y, T_d)$, that is the sum of the utility of its Q-items. The total utility of a database D is defined as $\sigma = \sum_{T_d \in D} TU(T_d)$, that is the sum of the utility of its transactions. For instance $TU(T_3) = u((A, 2), T_2) + u((C, 2), T_2) = 6 + 4 = 10$ and $\sigma = TU(T_1) + TU(T_2) + TU(T_3) + TU(T_4) = 17 + 10 + 10 + 14 = 51$.

The task of **High Utility Quantitative Itemset Mining (HUQIM)** aims to find all the *high utility quantitative itemsets* (HUQIs) in a database D given some user-defined *minimum utility threshold* $(0 \le minutil \le \sigma)$. A Q-itemset X is a HUQI if $u(X) \ge minutil$. Otherwise, X is a *low utility quantitative itemset* (LUQI) [8]. For example, if $minutil = 13$, the Q-itemset $[(A, 2)(B, 5)(C, 2)]$ is a HUQI because $u([(A, 2)(B, 5)(C, 2)]) = 15 \ge 13$.

HUQIM is a hard problem for three reasons: First, the utility function is neither *anti-monotonic* nor *monotonic*, i.e., a Q-itemset may have a utility that is greater, smaller or equal to that of its supersets [8]. Hence, the utility cannot be directly used to reduce the search space and other strategies must be used. Second, one item in HUIM can form several Q-items in HUQIM. Third, from each itemset, many range Q-itemsets may be formed which makes the search space larger than the case of HUIM.

HUQIM algorithms adopt two main operations, namely join operation and merge operation [7,11]. The join operation starts from small itemsets and recursively adds items to these itemsets to find larger itemsets. The merge operation is used to find range Q-itemsets which are produced by combining a set of Q-items that have consecutive quantities. More precisely, some pairs of LUQIs may be combined to obtain a range HUQI. But the combination process is limited with a parameter called ($qrc > 0$) (Quantitative Related Coefficient). The qrc controls Q-intervals of produced range Q-itemsets to avoid obtaining range Q-itemsets having large Q-intervals. Moreover, The combination of Q-itemsets can be done using three methods, named $Combine\_Min$, $Combine\_Max$ and $Combine\_All$ [2,7].

Top-k High Utility Quantitative Itemset Mining (Top-k HUQIM). Top-k HUQIM consists of finding a set γ of k Q-itemsets such that there are no other Q-itemsets not in γ that have a higher utility. For example, the top-3 HUQIs found in the database of the running example are: $[(A, 2)(C, 2)]$, $[(A, 2)]$ and $[(A, 2)(B, 5)(C, 2)(D, 1)]$ with utilities 20, 18 and 17, respectively.

4   The TKQ Algorithm

To efficiently perform the task of top-k HUQIM, a novel algorithm is designed, called TKQ (Top-K Quantitative itemset miner). In contrast with traditional HUQIM where the user has to set the $minutil$ threshold before starting the mining process, the $minutil$ value is unknown in top-k HUQIM. Thus, $minutil$ is initially set to zero. However, it is impracticable to start the itemset search with $minutil = 0$ because this may lead to consider many Q-itemsets that are not promising which will negatively affect the performance of the algorithm. To overcome this problem, it is desirable to apply some effective *threshold raising strategies* to raise $minutil$ to higher values without missing any top-k HUQIs. For this purpose, TKQ adopts three effective threshold raising strategies. The first two raising strategies, named RIU and CUD, are adapted from strategies used for top-k HUIM [1,13] so as to be used for top-k HUQIM. These strategies are applied before starting a depth-first search. The third raising strategy is used during the depth-first search to raise $minutil$ based on the current list of top-k HUQIs. In the following, the Q-item utility-list structure is first introduced and then the pruning strategies are used by TKQ to reduce the search space. Finally, the TKQ algorithm is described, integrating the three raising strategies.

Q-items Utility-Lists. As for FHUQI-Miner, TKQ is also a utility-list based algorithm. A utility-list is a structure that is used to represent each pattern (Q-itemset) of the mining problem. It allows to quickly calculate the utility of its associated Q-itemset without requiring to scan the database [9,11]. Besides, each utility-list contains two important records named $SumEutil$ and $SumRutil$. $SumEutil$ represents the exact utility of a its associated pattern in the database. Whereas, $SumRutil$ gives the remaining utility of its associated pattern and it is used to prune unpromising Q-itemsets using the remaining utility pruning strategy.

Pruning Strategies. TKQ adopts three pruning strategies to efficiently mine HUQIs. The first two pruning strategies are *the TWU pruning strategy* and *the remaining utility pruning strategy* [9]. These strategies are frequently used in HUIM and they are adopted for HUQIM [7,11]. The third strategy is *Co-occurrence pruning strategy* which allows to eliminate LUQIs with their transitive extensions without even the need to construct their utility-lists. It is based on *the TQCS structure* which contains all pairs of Q-items that have co-occured in the database with their utility information [11]. The reader is referred to [11] for a detailed explanation of the pruning strategies used by TKQ.

The Algorithm. This section describes the main steps of TKQ to find top-k HUQIs including the raising strategies that are used. The TKQ algorithm (Algorithm 1) takes four parameters as input: The transaction database D, the desired number of patterns k, the combining method CM and the quantitative related coefficient qrc. TKQ outputs the top-k HUQIs in D. TKQ starts by scanning the database to calculate the TWU and the exact utility of each Q-item in D (line 1). Then, TKQ applies the first raising strategy based on the exact utilities of Q-items using the RIU raising strategy (line 2).

Algorithm 1: The TKQ algorithm

Input : D: The quantitative transaction database, k: The desired number of patterns, CM: The combining method (*Combine_Min*, *Combine_Max* or *Combine_All*), qrc: The quantitative related coefficient.
Output: The top-k HUQIs.

1 First database scan to calculate the TWU and utility of each Q-item;
2 Raise $minutil$ to the kth largest utility value; // RIU raising strategy
3 Create initial set of promising Q-items P^* such that $\forall x \in P^* : TWU(x) \geq \frac{minutil}{qrc}$ and discard unpromising Q-itemsets; // TWU pruning strategy
4 Second database scan to create utility-lists of promising Q-items $ULs(P^*)$ and build the TQCS structure;
5 Raise $minutil$ to the kth largest utility value in TQCS; // CUD strategy
6 Create a priority queue to store the top-k Q-itemsets;
7 **foreach** $x \in P^*$ **do**
8   **if** $UL(x).SumEutil \geq minutil$ **then**
9   Q=Update_Queue(Q,x);
10         $H = H \cup x$;
11   **else**
12   **if** $UL(x).SumEutil + UL(x).SumRutil \geq minutil$ **then** $E = E \cup x$;
13   **if** $\frac{minutil}{qrc} \leq UL(x).SumEutil \leq minutil$ **then** $C = C \cup x$;
14 Discover High Utility range Q-itemsets (HR) using CM and C;
15 **foreach** $x \in HR$ **do**
16   Q=Update_Queue(Q,x);
17 $QI_s \leftarrow sort(H \cup E \cup HR)$;
18 Recursive_Mining_Search($\emptyset$, QI_s, $ULs(QI_s)$, P^*, qrc, CM, k,Q,$minutil$);

Real Items Utilities Threshold Raising Strategy (RIU). The RIU raising strategy is based on the utility calculation of all Q-items in the database. Let $q = \{q_1, q_2, \ldots, q_n\}$ be a set of n Q-items in the database D, and $L_1 = \{u(q_1), u(q_2), \ldots, u(q_n)\}$ be the list of utilities of Q-items in q. If $n \geq k$, then $minutil$ can be raised to the kth largest value in L_1. In the running example, if $k = 5$, then $minutil$ is raised to the 5th largest utility which is $u(B, 5) = 5$.

Based on the raised $minutil$ and using the TWU pruning strategy (property 1), TKQ identifies promising Q-items and removes unpromising Q-items to reduce the search space (line 3). Then, TKQ scans again the database to construct the utility-lists of promising Q-items and to build the TQCS structure (line 4) which will be used not only to reduce the search space during the recursive search for patterns, but also to raise again the *minutil* threshold to a higher value using the CUD raising strategy (line 5).

Co-occurrence Threshold Raising Strategy (CUD). The CUD raising strategy uses the utilities of 2-Q-itemsets stored in TQCS to raise *minutil*. Note that, utilities of 2-Q-itemsets are easily calculated during the second database scan. Formally, suppose that the TQCS structure contains h tuples of the form (a_i, b_i, c_i, d_i) where $1 \leq i \leq h$. From these tuples, the list $L_2 = \{d_1, d_2, \ldots, d_k, \ldots, d_h\}$ is created which contains the utilities of all 2-Q-itemsets that co-occurred in the database. The utilities of these patterns are sorted in descending order. If $h \geq k$ and if the kth largest utility in L_2, denoted as d_k, is larger than the current *minutil* then *minutil* is raised directly to d_k. Continuing with the previous example, the CUD raising strategy raises *minutil* to $u[(B,4)(C,3)] = 10$ which is the 5th largest utility in L_2.

After applying the CUD raising strategy, TKQ creates a priority queue Q that is used to store the top-k HUQIs (line 6). Moreover, TKQ checks the utility of each promising Q-item. If the utility of the current Q-item is not less than *minutil*, this Q-item is inserted in Q using the *Update_Queue* procedure(lines 8–10). Otherwise, TKQ performs two tests to put this Q-item either in the set of candidate Q-items (C) or the set of Q-items to be explored (E) (lines 11–13). If the candidate set C is not empty, TKQ will perform the combination process (line 14). At this point, TKQ calls the recursive mining search procedure (line 18) which is illustrated in Algorithm 2.

Algorithm 2: *Recursive_Mining_Search*

Input : P: The prefix Q-itemset, QI_s: The Q-itemsets list, $UL_s(QI_s)$: Utility lists of Q-itemsets, P^*: The list of promising Q-itemsets, qrc: The quantitative related coefficient, CM: The combining method, k: The desired number of patterns, Q: A priority queue of k Q-itemsets sorted by ascending utility, *minutil*: The internal minimum utility threshold

Output: The set of HUQIs with respect to prefix P.

```
1  foreach [Px] such that x ∈ QIₛ do
2      QIₛ ← ∅; P* ← ∅;
3      foreach [Py] such that y ∈ P* and y ≻ x do
4          Apply EQCPS or RQCPS pruning strategies.
5          Z ← [Pxy]; UL(Z) = Construct(x, y, P);
6          if U ≥ minutil/qrc then
7              P* = P* ∪ Z;
8              if UL(Z).SumEutil ≥ minutil then
9                  Q=Update_Queue(Q,x);
10                 E = E ∪ Z;
11             else
12                 if UL(Z).SumEutil + UL(Z).SumRutil ≥ minutil then  E = E ∪ Z;
13                 if minutil/qrc ≤ UL(Z).SumEutil ≤ minutil then  C = C ∪ Z;
14     Discover High Utility range Q-itemsets HR using CM and C;
15     foreach x ∈ HR do
16         Q=Update_Queue(Q,x);
17     QIₛ ← (H ∪ E ∪ HR);
18     Recursive_Mining_Search(Px,QIₛ,ULₛ(QIₛ),P*,qrc,CM,k,Q,minutil );
```

The TKQ recursive search algorithm is a depth-first search algorithm which is similar to that used in FHUQI-Miner [11] with changes to find the top-k HUQIs. Note that, the reason for choosing FHUQI-Miner as a basis for TKQ is that FHUQI-Miner is the most efficient HUQIM algorithm [11]. The TKQ recursive search procedure has two more parameters which are the desired number of patterns k and the priority queue Q that will contain the top-k HUQIs. TKQ differs from FHUQI-Miner in that $minutil$ in TKQ is not fixed. In fact, TKQ gradually raises the $minutil$ value based on the HUQIs found during the depth-first search (line 9 and line 16). This raising process is done using the third raising strategy named $Update\_Queue$.

$Update\_Queue$ allows to maintain the queue Q of the k Q-itemsets that have the highest utility until now. More precisely, once a new HUQI is found, it is inserted in Q (line 1). Then, $minutil$ is raised to the new k^{th} highest value in Q (line 3). Finally, each Q-itemset in Q having a utility less than $minutil$ is deleted from Q (line 4). As more HUQIs are found, the internal $minutil$ threshold is raised based on Q, which allows to reduce the search space. When no more patterns can be generated, the top-k HUQIs are returned to the user.

5   Experiments

Experiments have been carried out to evaluate the performance of TKQ. They were done on a workstation having an Intel(R) i7-8700 processor, 16 GB RAM, and the Windows 7 operating system. The performance of TKQ was compared with FHUQI-Miner, and both were implemented in Java.

Datasets. Four benchmark datasets were utilized, which were obtained from the SPMF data mining library [2]. These datasets are often used in the HUQIM literature to evaluate algorithms, and have various characteristics. *Foodmart* is a sparse dataset with 4,141 transactions and 1,559 distinct items. *Retail* is a sparse dataset having 88,162 transactions and 16,470 items. *Mushroom* is a dense dataset with 8,416 transactions and 128 items. Lastly, *BMS* is a sparse dataset with 7,751 transaction and 23,340 items. The first dataset has real utility values, while the three others have synthetic values [11].

Influence of the RIU and CUD Strategies on the Runtime. A first experiment was done to evaluate the benefits of using the designed raising strategies in TKQ. TKQ was compared with two modified versions named TKQ-RIU and TKQ-CUD, where only the RIU and CUD strategies were used, respectively. The runtimes of the three algorithms for k values ranging from 10 to 5,000 are shown in Fig. 1. It can be observed that, generally TKQ is faster than TKQ-RIU and TKQ-CUD on the four datasets. For Retail, it can be clearly seen that, TKQ is faster than the two other algorithms especially when k is increased. Moreover, it can be seen also from Fig. 1 that, for small k values, the runtime of TKQ and TKQ-RIU is quite similar. However, as k is increased, TKQ becomes faster than both the TKQ-RIU and TKQ-CUD algorithms.

To gain more insights into the effectiveness of each strategy, Fig. 2 shows how much each strategy raised the $minutil$ threshold as a percentage of the optimal

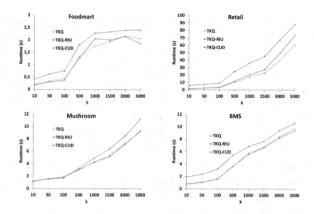

Fig. 1. Influence of the CUD and RIU strategies on runtime

minutil value. It is found that for small k values, RIU can raise *minutil* more than CUD. However, for larger k values, CUD can raise *minutil* more than RIU. Hence, it is desirable to jointly use the two strategies to raise *minutil*.

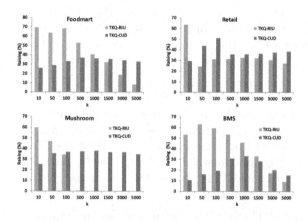

Fig. 2. Comparison of RIU and CUD's effectiveness to raise the *minutil* threshold

Runtime Comparison with FHUQI-Miner for the Optimal *minutil* **Threshold.** In a second experiment, TKQ's performance was compared with the state-of-the-art FHUQI-Miner HUQIM algorithm. To be able to compare both algorithms, FHUQI-Miner was set with an optimal *minutil* value that results in obtaining the same k patterns as TKQ. It should be noted that, this comparison is unfair as TKQ has to start searching from *minutil* = 0 while FHUQI-Miner directly knows the optimal *minutil* value and use this information to reduce the search space. However, this comparison is still interesting to see how close the performance of TKQ can be to that of FHUQI-Miner.

Table 3 compares the runtimes of TKQ and FHUQI-Miner for different k values on the four datasets. FHUQI-Miner is generally faster than TKQ. This was expected as FHUQI-Miner directly uses the optimal *minutil* threshold. However, it can be found that the performance of TKQ is very close to that of FHUQI-Miner. This indicates that, TKQ is efficient as the added cost for using the k parameter is generally small. Moreover, this is a good result considering that in real-life, the user is unlikely to set the optimal *minutil* threshold for FHUQI-Miner to obtain a given number of patterns as it will be demonstrated in the next experiment. From Table 3, it can be seen that the results of both algorithms on the Foodmart dataset are very close. For Retail, the difference between FHUQI-Miner and TKQ increases for large values of k. This result is expected since the task of top-k HUQIM becomes harder as k is increased, especially for large datasets such as Retail. However, it is worth noticing that, this difference is small and the performance of the two algorithms remains close. The results for the Mushroom and BMS datasets confirm again that the performance of TKQ is very close to the performance of FHUQI-Miner.

Table 3. Comparison of TKQ with FHUQI-Miner on Foodmart and Retail

k	Foodmart			Retail		
	minutil	TKQ	FHUQI-Miner	minutil	TKQ	FHUQI-Miner
10	26908	0.159	0.146	9781812	1.337	1.298
50	22725	0.236	0.237	2589300	2.485	1.549
100	22051	0.268	0.187	1603476	2.788	1.964
500	19843	0.644	0.358	445120	9.726	6.625
1000	18767	1.185	0.24	299264	14.869	10.791
1500	18015	0.945	0.255	230398	19.276	14.442
3000	16546	1.324	0.315	148950	32.713	25.82
5000	15422	1.222	0.348	117991	43.737	35.572
k	BMS			Mushroom		
10	1227600	0.75	0.713	3345705	1.073	1.045
50	735335	1.089	0.995	1645875	1.695	1.675
100	491940	1.375	1.257	1254574	2.104	2.066
500	246822	3.152	2.324	779980	3.196	2.821
1000	246723	3.898	2.291	617934	3.72	3.345
1500	246678	4.282	2.671	524151	4.078	4.045
3000	246606	5.328	2.585	389360	5.344	4.738
5000	246554	5.845	2.502	307956	6.206	5.559

Benefits of Using TKQ Instead of FHUQI-Miner. The third experiment is performed to illustrate the benefits of using TKQ instead of FHUQI-Miner.

Generally, if a user wants to find k patterns using FHUQI-Miner, the user must guess a *minutil* threshold value to find k HUQIs. But the user does not know beforehand how many patterns (HUQIs) will be found for a given *minutil* value. If the user sets *minutil* lower than the optimal *minutil* value, a very large number of patterns will be found, and runtime may be very long. Conversely, if the user sets *minutil* higher than the optimal *minutil* value, none or few patterns may be found. This experiment is designed to assess how likely a user is to select the optimal *minutil* value using FHUQI-Miner to get exactly the desired number of patterns k. To evaluate this, TKQ was run for different values of k on the four datasets, and the optimal *minutil* values were recorded. Based on the recorded *minutil* values, the average size between the *minutil* values for each pair of consecutive k values $[k_1, k_2]$ was calculated. Given that the user can choose *minutil* from the range $[0, total\ utility]$, the interval size is the percentage of the difference between optimal *minutil* values for obtaining k_1 and k_2 versus the total utility of the database (σ). The average sizes for the four datasets are presented in Table 4. Note that, due to the space limitation, only the interval sizes are shown without giving the optimal *minutil* for each value of k.

Table 4. Probability to find HUQIs between $k1$ and $k2$

k_1–k_2	Interval size(%)			
	Foodmart	Retail	BMS	Mushroom
10–50	0,015	0,515	0,316	0,588
50–100	0,002	0,070	0,072	0,135
100–500	0,008	0,082	0,088	0,164
500–1000	0,003	0,010	0,030	0,056
1000–1500	0,002	0,004	0,017	0,032
1500–3000	0,005	0,005	0,025	0,046
3000–5000	0,004	0,002	0,015	0,028

It can be seen that the interval sizes are very small which shows the difficulty of selecting the optimal *minutil*. For example, the optimal *minutil* to find 50 HUQI for Foodmart is 22725 while the optimal *minutil* for 100 HUQI is 22051. The difference between these thresholds is thus 674, that is only 0.002% of the whole range of selection which is from 0 to the total utility (σ), i.e., $[0, 27027840]$. This means that using FHUQI-Miner, to obtain top-k HUQIs where $k \in [50, 100]$, the user should select *minutil* in a very small interval that represents only 0.002% from the whole range of selection. Thus, the selection of an optimal threshold for FHUQI-Miner is unlikely. It can be seen also that for some datasets such as Mushroom and Retail, the interval size decreases as k_1 and k_2 are increased.

From these results, it is concluded that, although FHUQI-Miner is slightly faster than TKQ, it is strongly recommended to use TKQ instead of FHUQI-Miner to obtain a desired number of HUQIs. Using TKQ allows the user to avoid spending time on fine-tuning the *minutil* threshold to find just enough patterns. And the runtime difference between TKQ and FHUQI-Miner is very small considering that users may need to run FHUQI-Miner multiple times to find an optimal *minutil* value.

6 Conclusion

To address the difficulty of setting the *minutil* threshold in HUQIM, this paper has redefined the task as top-k HUQIM. An algorithm named TKQ was designed to efficiently discover the top-k HUQIs. The algorithm adopts a depth-first search and integrates several pruning and raising strategies to improve its performance. An experimental evaluation with several datasets has shown that TKQ is efficient and has a performance that is generally close to the state-of-the-art HUQIM algorithm knowing that TKQ addresses a more difficult problem.

In future work, other optimizations will be developed. Moreover, it is planned to develop a distributed version of TKQ to mine patterns in very large datasets.

References

1. Duong, Q.H., Liao, B., Fournier-Viger, P., Dam, T.L.: An efficient algorithm for mining the top-k high utility itemsets, using novel threshold raising and pruning strategies. Knowl. Based Syst. **104**, 106–122 (2016)
2. Fournier-Viger, P., Gomariz, A., Gueniche, T., Soltani, A., Wu, C.W., Tseng, V.S.: SPMF: a java open-source pattern mining library. J. Mach. Learn. Res. **15**(1), 3389–3393 (2014)
3. Fournier-Viger, P., Chun-Wei Lin, J., Truong-Chi, T., Nkambou, R.: A survey of high utility itemset mining. In: Fournier-Viger, P., Lin, J.C.-W., Nkambou, R., Vo, B., Tseng, V.S. (eds.) High-Utility Pattern Mining. SBD, vol. 51, pp. 1–45. Springer, Cham (2019). https://doi.org/10.1007/978-3-030-04921-8_1
4. Fournier-Viger, P., Lin, J.C.W., Vo, B., Chi, T.T., Zhang, J., Le, H.B.: A survey of itemset mining. Wiley Interdisc. Rev. Data Min. Knowl. Discov. **7**(4), e1207 (2017)
5. Fournier-Viger, P., Wu, C.-W., Zida, S., Tseng, V.S.: FHM: faster high-utility itemset mining using estimated utility co-occurrence pruning. In: Andreasen, T., Christiansen, H., Cubero, J.-C., Raś, Z.W. (eds.) ISMIS 2014. LNCS (LNAI), vol. 8502, pp. 83–92. Springer, Cham (2014). https://doi.org/10.1007/978-3-319-08326-1_9
6. Gan, W., Lin, J.C.W., Fournier-Viger, P., Chao, H.C., Tseng, V.S., Yu, P.S.: A survey of utility-oriented pattern mining. arXiv preprint arXiv:1805.10511 (2018)
7. Li, C.H., Wu, C.W., Huang, J., Tseng, V.S.: An efficient algorithm for mining high utility quantitative itemsets. In: 2019 International Conference on Data Mining Workshops (ICDMW), pp. 1005–1012. IEEE (2019)
8. Li, C.H., Wu, C.W., Tseng, V.S.: Efficient vertical mining of high utility quantitative itemsets. In: 2014 IEEE International Conference on Granular Computing (GrC), pp. 155–160. IEEE (2014)
9. Liu, M., Qu, J.: Mining high utility itemsets without candidate generation. In: Proceedings of the 21st ACM International Conference on Information and Knowledge Management, pp. 55–64 (2012)

10. Liu, Y., Liao, W., Choudhary, A.: A two-phase algorithm for fast discovery of high utility itemsets. In: Ho, T.B., Cheung, D., Liu, H. (eds.) PAKDD 2005. LNCS (LNAI), vol. 3518, pp. 689–695. Springer, Heidelberg (2005). https://doi.org/10.1007/11430919_79
11. Nouioua, M., Fournier-Viger, P., Lin, J.C.W., Gan, W.: FHUQI-Miner: fast high utility quantitative itemset mining. Appl. Intell. **51**, 1–25 (2021). https://doi.org/10.1007/s10489-021-02204-w
12. Peng, A.Y., Koh, Y.S., Riddle, P.: mHUIMiner: a fast high utility itemset mining algorithm for sparse datasets. In: Kim, J., Shim, K., Cao, L., Lee, J.-G., Lin, X., Moon, Y.-S. (eds.) PAKDD 2017. LNCS (LNAI), vol. 10235, pp. 196–207. Springer, Cham (2017). https://doi.org/10.1007/978-3-319-57529-2_16
13. Ryang, H., Yun, U.: Top-k high utility pattern mining with effective threshold raising strategies. Knowl. Based Syst. **76**, 109–126 (2015)
14. Yen, S.-J., Lee, Y.-S.: Mining high utility quantitative association rules. In: Song, I.Y., Eder, J., Nguyen, T.M. (eds.) DaWaK 2007. LNCS, vol. 4654, pp. 283–292. Springer, Heidelberg (2007). https://doi.org/10.1007/978-3-540-74553-2_26
15. Zhang, C., Han, M., Sun, R., Du, S., Shen, M.: A survey of key technologies for high utility patterns mining. IEEE Access **8**, 55798–55814 (2020)

OPECUR: An Enhanced Clustering-Based Model for Discovering Unexpected Rules

Sadeq Darrab[1][✉], Priyamvada Bhardwaj[1], David Broneske[2],
and Gunter Saake[1]

[1] Otto von Guericke University, Magdeburg, Germany
{sadeq.darrab,Gunter.Saake}@ovgu.de, priyamvada.bhardwaj@st.ovgu.de
[2] German Centre for Higher Education Research and Science Studies,
Hannover, Germany
broneske@dzhw.eu

Abstract. Rare association rules gained importance since they are widely used in critical real-life domains, such as medicine, fraud detection, malware attacks, recommender systems, and weather forecasting. In order to extract actionable rules that can be used in real-life scenarios, user confidence and an easy-to-use model with as few as possible tuning knobs are required. On top of this, an inherent imbalance of the data (e.g., in the medical domain, there are fewer ill people compared to healthy people) poses a severe challenge, which complicates the finding of rare patterns. Recently, an unsupervised clustering model was proposed to discover interesting rare rules. However, the performance of this model degrades in terms of time and accuracy. In this paper, we propose an efficient model to recover interesting rare rules. In this model, we employ machine learning-based classifiers to assess the performance of the generated rules. To evaluate the proposed model, we experiment with three real-life medical datasets. The experimental results show that our model outperforms the state-of-the-art model in terms of time and accuracy. Furthermore, we generate more accurate results, which means that the user is only confronted with the most important and compact rules. This reduces a user's effort on postprocessing of associating rules significantly.

1 Introduction

Frequent itemset mining is the process of finding a set of items (known as pattern or itemset) that co-occur in a given dataset. If a strong relation between items can be inferred, they form an association rule. An inferred association rule is represented as X → Y, where X and Y are a set of itemsets. For example, in market basket analysis, a rule milk → bread represents that if a customer buys milk, the customer also tends to buy bread as well. Generating association rules from a dataset is called association rule mining (ARM). ARM gains special importance due to its advantages in many domains, such as market basket analysis, medical diagnosis, and web usage mining [1,2]. The primary goal of ARM

© Springer Nature Switzerland AG 2022
B. Li et al. (Eds.): ADMA 2021, LNAI 13088, pp. 29–41, 2022.
https://doi.org/10.1007/978-3-030-95408-6_3

is to produce rules that are sensible and beneficial to the user. However, a vital shortcoming of ARM is that it usually generates many rules (i.e. for an itemset with d items, there are $2^d - 1$ rules that can be generated [20]). Extracting such a large number of association rules degrades the performance, making it challenging for a decision-maker to analyze the produced rules. Hence, the resulting rules require extensive downstream analysis. To overcome these shortcomings, it is practical to produce fewer and more meaningful rules for the user.

One of the most frequently used techniques for the simplification of rules is called clustering association rules [10,15,19]. Clustering association rules generate a condensed representation of association rules and, thus, less rules compared to those generated by conventional methods. Therefore, extracting compact and understandable rules leads to more accurate classifiers and produces a manageable number of rules for the end-user for further investigation. There is a plethora of work proposed for clustering association rules [6,10,15]. Most of these methods focus on generating rules from frequent patterns. However, the generated rules represent common events and are, thus, usually expected and unsurprising. Therefore, analyzing the data at hand for more meaningful and unexpected patterns is desirable to reveal unknown knowledge in many real-life applications. To this end, discovering unexpected association rules (also known as rare itemset mining) came into focus [8]. To reveal such knowledge, the state of the art is to use an unsupervised machine learning method, DBSCAN-based clustering [5], to extract unexpected association rules. Although this method finds unexpected rules, it comes with the following shortcomings. First, it is costly in terms of time and memory since it utilizes the Apriori algorithm to generate the complete set of rules [18]. Second, adjusting the parameters properly (i.e., ϵ, $minPts$ for DBSCAN) is challenging since DBSCAN as a clustering-based method may fail to identify unexpected rules when choosing improper parameters. Lastly, the F1-score of a classifier was utilized in the DBSCAN-based model to evaluate the quality of generated rules. However, the reported score was observed only for a single class (i.e., minority class), leading to ambiguity when used on data with class imbalances [12]. For instance, an improved F1-score of a class might also mean that the classifier improved its prediction at the cost of other class scores in imbalanced data (i.e., predicting that everyone is ill).

Due to these shortcomings, designing an efficient model to address these three gaps is still a critical research problem. This paper deals with these limitations by developing an efficient model, *OP*TICS-based clustering of *EC*LAT-generated *U*nexpected *R*ules (OPECUR), to find unexpected association rules efficiently and accurately. The main contribution of this paper is as follows.

- To generate the whole set of association rules, we employ FP-Growth and ECLAT algorithms to extract the complete set of association rules efficiently.
- For the clustering task, we utilize a density-based clustering algorithm, OPTICS, to avoid the problem of extensive hyperparameter tuning. OPTICS can also detect clusters of different densities efficiently leading more precise unexpected association rules.

- We utilize three different machine learning classifiers for the classification task in the evaluation process: Support vector machines (SVM), Random forest (RF), and Neural network-based multi-layer perceptron (MLP).
- The experimental results show that the F1-score and area under the curve (AUC) of our OPECUR model are constantly better than the state-of-the-art DBSCAN-based model. Furthermore, our experimental results show that our model recovers association rules much faster than the state of the art and generates more interesting unexpected association rules.

The remainder of this paper is structured as follows. In Sect. 2, we provide background on association rules and present related work in Sect. 3. In Sect. 4, our proposed method adopted in the paper is explained. Our evaluation strategy, performance criteria, and variations are discussed in Sect. 5. We end the paper with a conclusion in Sect. 6.

2 Background

This section briefly presents important fundamental knowledge for discovering unexpected rules. One primary data mining task is association rule mining aiming at discovering hidden valuable knowledge from a dataset. The main step of ARM is to find a set of items (known as patterns or itemset) that co-occur in the dataset. Hence, association rule mining requires the following two main steps:

1. The complete set of interesting patterns is extracted.
2. The association rules are generated from the set of desired patterns that have been mined in the first step.

We describe the problem of association rule mining and its related concepts, such as frequent and unexpected (rare) patterns with the following definitions. Let DB be a dataset of m transactions such as $DB = \{T_1, T_2, \ldots, T_m\}$ and I represents the set of unique n items in DB, $I = \{i_1, i_2, \ldots, i_n\}$. Some common definitions are defined below to illustrate the concept of association rule mining.

Definition 1 (Support of a pattern). Given a pattern X, its support (Sup) is defined as the number of transactions in DB containing the pattern X such that $Sup(X) = \frac{Sup(X)}{|DB|}$, where $|DB|$ represents the size of the dataset, DB.

Definition 2 (Frequent and Rare Patterns). A pattern X whose support satisfies a user-specified support threshold, $minSup$, is called frequent pattern such that $sup(X) \geq minSup$. In contrast, the pattern X that does not satisfy $minSup$ is called a rare pattern.

Definition 3 (Strong Association Rule). An association rule X → Y is called strong if its support and confidence measures satisfy a specified minimum support threshold $(minSup)$ and minimum confidence threshold $(minConf)$.

Definition 4 (Unexpected Association Rule [16]**).** A rule $X \rightarrow Y$ is an unexpected rule w.r.t. a known rule $A \rightarrow B$ if the following conditions hold:

1. The antecedents of rules (i.e., A and X) statistically hold on DB. Besides, they are similar according to a statistical measure (i.e., cosine similarity exceeds a given threshold).
2. The consequences of rules (i.e., B and Y) contradict each other.

In this paper, we focus on discovering unexpected association rules that satisfy Definitions 3 and 4.

3   Related Work

Association Rule Mining (ARM) identifies interesting relations among patterns in a dataset. ARM gains vital importance since it helps to turn data into useful knowledge in various domains such as fraud detection, disease diagnosis [3], and road traffic accident prediction [13]. There is a plethora of methods presented to recover the complete set of association rules [1,11,14,21]. The Apriori and FP-Growth algorithm [18] and their extended versions are well-known methods that are extensively used for ARM. These methods work well for recovering the complete set of association rules, but generate too many rules leading to a scalability issue. Besides, producing a massive amount of rules makes it challenging for a decision-maker to analyze the produced rules.

To this end, clustering techniques can produce fewer, more concise rules in many models by grouping similar rules into clusters [6,10,15,19]. In [19], a method has been presented to prune undesired association rules and group similar rules into clusters. They use the concept of a rule cover to prune uninteresting rules and then apply clustering to get fewer, more concise rules. Further methods are the "BitOp" algorithm [15], or the usage of conditional market-basket difference (CMBP) and conditional market-basket log-likelihood (CMBL) to group association rules by utilizing agglomerative clustering [10]. The latter generates association rules that are grouped based on a normalized distance metric. In [6], Dhabi et al. group association rules into disjoint clusters using K-means. All these approaches use frequent itemsets.

Rare rules can capture hidden patterns in data that may be important in rare disease diagnosis and credit card fraud detection. Instead of generating the whole set of rules, there are several algorithms that generate rare rules [7,8]. Although these methods produce interesting rare association rules, they have some limitations, such as 1) finding the rare items before the mining process is challenging and 2) they generate many rare rules. To address these shortcomings, a clustering-based model has been proposed to mine unexpected rare rules by utilizing DBSCAN to cluster rare rules [5]. After clustering association rules, the DBSCAN based model checks whether rules are noise rules or unexpected rules based on a contradiction check. Although this model finds unexpected rules, it comes with notable limitations. First, its performance is not optimal since it employs the Apriori algorithm to mine the rules. Second, the interesting unexpected rules may be missed since the DBSCAN algorithm suffers from the problem of not detecting nested cluster structures [4]. Lastly, the hyperparameters of the DBSCAN algorithm are crucial to the clustering results and greatly influence the overall results. Hence, setting up proper hyperparameters is challenging. In this paper, we propose a model to address these challenges as in the following section.

4   Proposed Method: OPECUR Model

This paper proposed a clustering model, the OPECUR model, to discover valuable unexpected rare association rules. Figure 1 shows the workflow of the model to obtain the unexpected rare rules. The model first derives all the association rules from a dataset. The minimum support is kept low for generating the rules so that the chance of missing important rare rules can be eliminated. Furthermore, all the association rules are converted to feature vectors using the correlation of items/attributes present in a dataset. Next, the contradiction check function, which we describe at the end of the clustering algorithm section, is applied to the noise points marked by the clustering algorithm to determine the final unexpected association rules. Our proposed model consists of two main phases (i.e., Association rules generation and clustering process see Fig. 1). In the first phase, the complete set of association rules is generated by utilizing efficient methods such as FP-growth and ECLAT. The second step explains the process of generating unexpected rules by utilizing the OPTICS clustering technique [4].

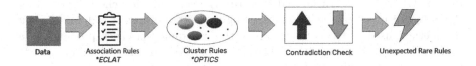

Fig. 1. OPECUR workflow to generate unexpected rare rules

4.1   Generating Association Rule

The state of the art approach [5] generates the whole set of association rules using the Apriori algorithm. However, Apriori has the shortcoming of a huge amount of candidates generated and it has to take multiple passes over the dataset. Our proposed model, OPECUR, addresses these limitations by employing faster, more scalable, and more efficient algorithms (i.e., FP-Growth and ECLAT algorithms) to generate association rules. The FP-Growth [11] algorithm uses a tree structure called FP-Tree to hold all necessary information for the mining process without a candidate and test generation process. FP-Growth scans a dataset at most twice. In the first scan, the FP-Tree is constructed by adding transactions (i.e., after removing useless items) one by one. After the tree is built, the mining process starts by employing a divide-and-conquer approach. The ECLAT algorithm [21] uses a depth-first search approach to generate the whole set of patterns. ECLAT works vertically and does not require multiple passes over the data. Moreover, it applies intersections to find the support count of the generated patterns.

4.2   Clustering Algorithm

Our proposed model groups similar association rules together using a density-based algorithm *OPTICS* [4]. The OPECUR algorithm sorts the data points based on the reachability distance of a point p to all other points. Reachability distance is the largest value between the distance between two points and the point's core distance. The core distance of a point is the largest distance between its n neighbors, where n is *minPts*. This enables the data points which are within the reachability distance of each other to stay together. Furthermore, the concept of reachability distance reduces the necessity of providing an *eps* value since it is automatically calculated based on *minPts*. This helps in dealing with different densities within a cluster and discovering nested clusters. As it can be seen in Fig. 2 and Fig. 3, the OPECUR model generates more clusters. Since *eps* is calculated automatically in the OPTICS algorithm, it is able to discover the clusters which are not available with a given value of *eps* like in DBSCAN. Notably, red points in Fig. 2 and Fig. 3 are noise points. To recover unexpected rules, we investigate the noise rules that may contain interesting unexpected rules. To identify whether a noise rule is an unexpected rule or not, we use a similar approach as used in [5] with the following difference. We first run the OPECUR algorithm and then run the contradiction check function on the potential noise rules to find interesting unexpected rules. It is different from the method used in [5] as they employ the contradiction check property as a part of the clustering algorithm. Thus, the contradiction check function affects the results since adding multiple parameters to tune at once making it harder and undesirable. In contrast, OPECUR model generates noise rules for a *minPts* value and then runs the contradiction check function. Hence, our model reduces the chances of missing the most informative unexpected rules.

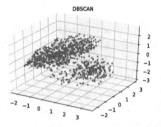

Fig. 2. Clusters on breast cancer dataset using DBSCAN

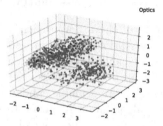

Fig. 3. Clusters on breast cancer dataset using OPECUR

As per the contradiction check function, if there exists two rules X → Y and X' → Y' the following conditions are checked:

1. Y != Y'
2. Cosine similarity of X and X' is high
3. Confidence of both rules is high
4. Rule X→ Y is a noise point

The noise rule X→Y is compared to the cluster rules and it is marked as an unexpected rule in contradiction to a frequent rule X' → Y' if all of the above conditions are satisfied.

5   Experimental Evaluation

In this section, our proposed model's performance is compared with the state-of-the-art model introduced in [5]. In the following, we introduce the evaluation setup and then explain the results of our conducted experiments.

5.1   Experimental Setup

We compare our model, OPECUR, with the state-of-the-art model introduced in [5] by utilizing three real-life medical datasets. The datasets are Breast Cancer, Cleveland Heart Disease, and Hepatitis obtained from the UCI repository [9]. In Table 1, we summarize the main characteristics of the datasets. The Cleveland heart disease dataset has four target variables for prediction, 0 (absence) and 1, 2, 3, 4 (presence)[1]. Hepatitis and Cleveland datasets consist of real-valued and categorical attributes. Breast Cancer and Hepatitis datasets have a non-uniform distribution of instances 29% and 25% respectively in the minority classes. The skewed data distribution of the instances in the classes poses a significant challenge in finding fewer representative and meaningful rare rules from the datasets.

To test the efficiency and effectiveness of our new approach, we execute three experiments. In the first experiment, we compare our proposed OPECUR model with the DBSCAN-based model in terms of time required to generate the complete set of rules in order to assess its scalability. In order to test the quality of our clustering, the second experiment compares found clustered association rules from our OPECUR with the DBSCAN-based model. Besides, we evaluate the quality of generated rare rules from our clustering algorithm OPTICS with the DBSCAN algorithm by training a classifier with the representation of the rules. This will assess whether the generated rules are meaningful for decision making (i.e., identifying ill or healthy people). All the experiments ran on Google Colab with a limited 12 GB of RAM to test the scalability and easy-to-use nature of the models. The results are presented in the following subsections.

---

[1] It is converted to binary classification, 0 (absence), and 1 (presence) for simplicity.

Table 1. Dataset details

Dataset	Instances	Class	Attributes	%MinorityClass
Breast cancer	286	2	9	.29
Hepatitis	155	2	20	.25
Cleveland	303	2	14	.44

*All the Datasets are taken from UCI Machine Learning Repository.

5.2 Experiment 1: Execution Time Comparison

This section evaluates the execution time of our proposed OPECUR model with the state-of-the-art model using DBSCAN for generating the complete set of association rules. While the DBSCAN-based model utilizes Apriori, we also test here FP-Growth and ECLAT algorithms to generate the whole set of rules. For all experiments, the minSup is varied from 0.01 to 0.04. These algorithms generate the exact same set of rules.

Figure 4, 5 and 6 shows the performance of the algorithms on all datasets. As it can be seen, FP-Growth and ECLAT consume less time compared to the Apriori algorithm. This is not totally surprising, because FP-Growth and ECLAT algorithm outperformed the Apriori algorithm for frequent itemset mining in various studies [18]. However, compared to higher minSup values in frequent pattern mining, it can be seen that even with low minSup, FP-Growth and ECLAT algorithms recover patterns faster. This is crucial in generating the complete set of rules, including interesting rare ones. Hence, our algorithm relies on the usage of ECLAT algorithm to generate the complete set of rules since it shows better performance when mining itemsets with a low support threshold.

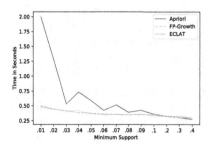 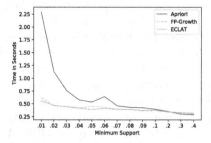

Fig. 4. Runtime performance on breast cancer dataset

Fig. 5. Runtime performance on cleveland heart disease dataset

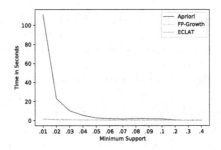

Fig. 6. Runtime performance on hepatitis dataset

5.3 Experiment 2: Clustering Process Comparison

In this experiment, we compare the results of the clustering process using our proposed model, OPECUR, with the state-of-the-art DBSCAN-based model. To reach comparable results, we set the parameters for the whole experiment similar to the compared model, DBSCAN-based [5] (i.e., minPts to 10, delta1 and delta2 of the contradiction check to 1 and −1, respectively). Table 2 shows the post clustering statistics from the OPECUR and DBSCAN-based algorithms. The results show that our model generates more unexpected rare rules than those generated by the DBSCAN algorithm. Hence, our model successfully recovers the interesting rare rules, whereas the DBSCAN model misses these unexpected rare rules. This is because the OPECUR model automatically calculates the minEps parameters and can find more clusters in the data than the DBSCAN algorithm, resulting in lesser noise rules. Hence, experimental results show that our proposed model can find more interesting unexpected rare rules that may be missed by the state-of-the-art DBSCAN-based model. However, the question whether these are meaningful is still open and will be evaluated.

To evaluate the quality of unexpected rare rules generated by our proposed OPECUR model, we adopted a similar evaluation strategy as in [5]. At its heart, they measure the impact of rare rules through using machine learning-based classifiers. We adhere to their assumption that if a rule improves the performance of a classifier by refining its decision boundary, then the rule indeed is beneficial. Beyond these assumptions, we change the evaluation procedure in the following way: As the first revision, in the evaluation procedure, we perform a 3-fold cross validation on the datasets to train and test the model instead of the independent hold-out method. Hence, the rules in two folds are used as a training dataset, whereas the remaining third fold is used as a test dataset. The process is repeated until each fold has served as an independent test set to be evaluated. We report the average scores of the models after cross validation for a better estimate of the generalization error. For the classification task, we utilize Random Forest (RF), Support Vector Machine (SVM), and Multi-Layer Perceptron (MLP) classifiers implemented in Sklearn library [17] with default classifier parameters. We report F1 and AUC metrics of the classifiers for the evaluation metric. F1 score considers precision and recall of the classifier, and AUC (Area under the curve) gives a better idea of the balance between true-positive and false-positive rates.

Figure 7 and Fig. 8 show the performance of our proposed model, OPECUR, and the state-of-the-art model, DBSCAN-based, on all three datasets. For both measures, our proposed model, OPECUR, shows consistently better performance compared to the state-of-the-art DBSCAN-based model [5], on all three datasets. This is due to the fact that OPECUR can find more clusters and generate fewer valid noise rules that pass the contradiction check. This is a clear advantage compared to the DBSCAN model, which only finds a limited number of the actual amount of clusters. Hence, rules that should ideally be marked as noise will still be assigned to a cluster by DBSCAN and, thus, be considered as a frequent rule. Thus, our proposed model is able to generate more unexpected rare rules and gains better performance in terms of F1 and AUC score.

Table 2. Comparison of clustering algorithms

Algorithm	Noise	Rare	Clusters
Breast Cancer Dataset			
DBSCAN	748	3	20
OPTICS	386	23	54
Cleveland Dataset			
DBSCAN	17269	415	4
OPTICS	15291	1650	17
Hepatitis Dataset			
DBSCAN	11925	0	3
OPTICS	7289	4	10

*Values are based on minpoints = 10 for all the datasets. The table describes the number of clusters, noise rules and rare rules generated by each algorithm on all the datasets.

Notably, our OPECUR methods shows the highest performance for the Hepatitis dataset. This is due to the fact that it contains more attributes, which benefits the identification of correlations in these attributes. Furthermore, our in-depth analysis of the rules and clusters shows that this dataset is a challenge for DBSCAN as nested clusters in the Hepatitis dataset have not been identified.

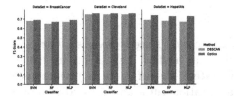
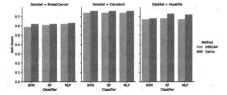

Fig. 7. F1 Score (F1-Score and AUC-Score of the three classifiers on the datasets when using the rules from DBSCAN or OPECUR (SVM = Support Vector Machine, RF = Random Forest, MLP = Multi-Layer Perceptron).)

Fig. 8. AUC Score (F1-Score and AUC-Score of the three classifiers on the datasets when using the rules from DBSCAN or OPECUR (SVM = Support Vector Machine, RF = Random Forest, MLP = Multi-Layer Perceptron).)

5.4 Experiment 3: Evaluation of Unexpected Rules

In this section, we evaluate the generated unexpected rules by two criteria. Firstly, we evaluated them by utilizing the contradiction check approach that used in the compared model [5] with same parameters. According to this property, our model generates more interesting unexpected association rules. For instance, a rule **'age = 50–59'**, **'breast = left'**, **'deg-malig = 3'**, **'irradiat = no'**, **'menopause = ge40'**, **'tumor size = 30–34'**→ **class = yes** is marked as unexpected rule by OPECUR. The rule is in contradiction to the following two rules:

- 'age = 50–59', 'breast = left', 'irradiat = no', 'menopause = ge40' → **class = no.**
- 'breast = left', 'irradiat = no', 'menopause = ge40''→ **class = no.**

Secondly, we compare the unexpected rules generated by the rare-pre-post-order algorithm, RPP [7]. RPP algorithm is proposed recently to discover the whole set of rare rules. The results show that the a set of unexpected association rules generated by our proposed model, OPECUR, is a subset to the rare rules generated by the RPP algorithm, providing meaningful and concise information.

For example, a rare rule generated by RPP algorithm is the following: **'tumor size = 30–34'**, **'inv-nodes = 3–5'**, **'node-caps = no'**, **'menopause = ge40'**, **'deg-malig = 3'**, **'irradiat = no'** → class = yes. The rule states that if a patient has a tumor of diameter 30–34, 3–5 auxiliary lymph nodes, node caps is no, degree of malignancy of the node is 3, and patient is menopausal without any history of radiation therapy taken, then the chances of recurrence of cancer are higher. In comparison, our model marks the following rule as rare: **'menopause = ge40'**, **'inv-nodes = 3–5'**, **'node-caps = no'**, **'irradiat = no'**→ class=yes. Hence, the same information generated by our model in this rules is also generated by the RPP algorithm. Thus, the results show that the unexpected association rules generated by our model are informative and meaningful.

6   Conclusion

Discovering unexpected (rare) rules gains attention since it reveals interesting hidden knowledge from various domains such as medical diagnosis, fault detection, and fraud detection. However, the state-of-the-art model's performance degrades when generating unexpected association rules and fails to generate the whole set of unexpected association rules. To address these limitations and discover unexpected rules, we designed a clustering-based model, OPECUR, to recover unexpected association rules from real datasets. The proposed model addresses the state of the art's shortcomings to efficiently generate the complete set of rules. Besides, our proposed model generates more interesting unexpected rules due to its capability to set parameters automatically during the clustering process. Hence, our model can find more clusters, resulting in more unexpected rules that helped improve the decision boundary of a machine learning classifier. The discovered unexpected rules are assessed based on several criteria: contradiction check property, classifiers' performance, and the RPP algorithm's results. The experimental results show that our model is scalable and generates more trustworthy unexpected rules. In the future, we intend to investigate this model further on streaming data.

References

1. Agrawal, R., Srikant, R.: Fast algorithms for mining association rules in large databases. In: VLDB, pp. 487–499. Morgan Kaufmann Publishers Inc. (1994)
2. Ahmed, M., Barkat Ullah, A.S.S.M.: Infrequent pattern mining in smart healthcare environment using data summarization. J. Supercomput. **74**(10), 5041–5059 (2018). https://doi.org/10.1007/s11227-018-2376-8
3. Altaf, W., Shahbaz, M., Guergachi, A.: Applications of association rule mining in health informatics: a survey. Artif. Intell. Rev. **47**(3), 313–340 (2016). https://doi.org/10.1007/s10462-016-9483-9
4. Ankerst, M., Breunig, M.M., Kriegel, H.P., Sander, J.: Optics: ordering points to identify the clustering structure. SIGMOD Rec. **28**(2), 49–60 (1999). https://doi.org/10.1145/304181.304187
5. Bui-Thi, D., Meysman, P., Laukens, K.: Clustering association rules to build beliefs and discover unexpected patterns. Appl. Intell. **50**(6), 1943–1954 (2020). https://doi.org/10.1007/s10489-020-01651-1
6. Dahbi, A., Mouhir, M., Balouki, Y., Gadi, T.: Classification of association rules based on K-means algorithm. In: CiST, pp. 300–305. IEEE (2016). https://doi.org/10.1109/CIST.2016.7805061
7. Darrab, S., Broneske, D., Saake, G.: RPP algorithm: a method for discovering interesting rare itemsets. In: Tan, Y., Shi, Y., Tuba, M. (eds.) DMBD 2020. CCIS, vol. 1234, pp. 14–25. Springer, Singapore (2020). https://doi.org/10.1007/978-981-15-7205-0_2
8. Darrab, S., Broneske, D., Saake, G.: Modern applications and challenges for rare itemset mining. IJMLC **11**(3), 208–218 (2021). https://doi.org/10.18178/ijmlc.2021.11.3.1037
9. Dua, D., Graff, C.: UCI machine learning repository (2017). http://archive.ics.uci.edu/ml

10. Gupta, G.K., Strehl, A., Ghosh, J.: Distance based clustering of association rules. Intell. Eng. Syst. Artif. Neural Networks **9**, 759–764 (1999)

11. Han, J., Pei, J., Yin, Y., Mao, R.: Mining frequent patterns without candidate generation: a frequent-pattern tree approach. Data Min. Knowl. Discov. **8**(1), 53–87 (2004). https://doi.org/10.1023/B:DAMI.0000005258.31418.83

12. Jeni, L.A., Cohn, J.F., De La Torre, F.: Facing imbalanced data-recommendations for the use of performance metrics. In: International Conference Affect Computing Intelligence Interact Workshops, pp. 245–251 (2013)

13. Joshi, S., et al.: Pattern mining predictor system for road accidents. In: Hernes, M., Wojtkiewicz, K., Szczerbicki, E. (eds.) ICCCI 2020. CCIS, vol. 1287, pp. 605–615. Springer, Cham (2020). https://doi.org/10.1007/978-3-030-63119-2_49

14. Kamepalli, S., Bandaru, S.: Weighted based frequent and infrequent pattern mining model for real-time e-commerce databases. Adv. Model. Anal. B **62**(2–4), 53–60 (2019). https://doi.org/10.18280/ama_b.622-404

15. Lent, B., Swami, A., Widom, J.: Clustering association rules. In: ICDE, pp. 220–231 (1997). https://doi.org/10.1109/icde.1997.581756

16. Padmanabhan, B.: A belief-driven method for discovering unexpected patterns. In: KDD, pp. 94–100. AAAI Press (1998)

17. Pedregosa, F., Varoquaux, G., Gramfort, A., Michel, V., Thirion, B., Grisel, O., et al.: Scikit-learn: machine learning in Python. JMLR **12**, 2825–2830 (2011)

18. Singh, A.K., Kumar, A., Maurya, A.K.: An empirical analysis and comparison of apriori and FP-growth algorithm for frequent pattern mining. ICACCCT, pp. 1599–1602 (2015). https://doi.org/10.1109/ICACCCT.2014.7019377

19. Toivonen, H., Klemettinen, M., Ronkainen, P., Hätönen, K., Mannila, H.: Pruning and Grouping Discovered Association Rules. In: Workshop on Statistics, Machine Learning, and Knowledge Discovery in Databases, pp. 47–52 (1995)

20. Zaki, M.J.: Generating non-redundant association rules. In: SIGKDD, pp. 34–43. Association for Computing Machinery (2000). https://doi.org/10.1145/347090.347101

21. Zaki, M.J., Parthasarathy, S., Ogihara, M., Li, W.: New algorithms for fast discovery of association rules. In: KDD. AAAI Press (1997)

Tourists Profiling by Interest Analysis

Sonia Djebali, Quentin Gabot, and Guillame Guérard[✉]

Léonard De Vinci, Research Center, 92 916 Paris La Défense, France
{sonia.djebali,guillame.guerard}@devinci.fr, quentin.gabot@edu.devinci.fr

Abstract. With the recent digital revolution, analyzing of tourists' behaviors and research fields associated with it have changed profoundly. It is now easier to examine behaviors of tourists using digital traces they leave during their travels. The studies conducted on diverse aspects of tourism focus on quantitative aspects of digital traces to reach its conclusions. In this paper, we suggest a study focused on both qualitative and quantitative aspect of digital traces to understand the dynamics governing tourist behavior, especially those concerning attractions networks.

Keywords: Data mining · Measure of interest · Profiling · Big data · Social network · Tourism

1 Introduction

Nowadays, tourism industry is considered as one of the largest and fastest growing industries [9]. In 2019, *World Tourism Organisation* UNWTO[1] has recorded 1.5 billion international tourists, 4% more than the previous year.

With the recent booming of digital tools and mobile internet technology, alternative sources of data to understand tourism behaviors and to capture tourists' experiences have emerged. Users of social networks, tend to share openly and frequently photos, videos, reviews and recommendations of their travels and their experiences. Thus, when users share photos or reviews, geographical information is included. These geo-located data represent tourism and sociological views [7]. These social networks constitute an interesting observation field to analyze tourists' behavior evolution through time and space.

In social networks, graph models are widely used to represent an interaction between entities and their relations. A graph model allows to understand both local phenomena (i.e. node level) as well as global phenomena (i.e. graph level). One of an interesting way mostly used to analyze movement networks is to evaluate and detect community structure [20]. Detecting communities in networks provides a means of coarse-graining interactions between entities and offers a more interpretable summary of a complex network.

---

[1] International tourism Growth continues outpacing the global economy: edition 2020.

Q. Gabot—Research Student.

© Springer Nature Switzerland AG 2022
B. Li et al. (Eds.): ADMA 2021, LNAI 13088, pp. 42–53, 2022.
https://doi.org/10.1007/978-3-030-95408-6_4

In literature, studies carried out on social networks use a quantitative dimension of digital traces as a research hypothesis [14]. Models developed focus on the question of the number of tourists without considering a qualitative analysis and the interest of users to make a given action. Interest analysis allows us to identify trends that are not perceptible with quantitative analysis. Being able to define another kind of relationship between two places visited in a city will not give the same result as observing flows of tourists between these two places.

To better understand tourists' movements and their interest to consider this movements, we propose in this paper to detect tourist communities to perform tourist profiling based not on the quantitative aspect but also on the qualitative aspect i.e. the interest of the tourists to make movements or visits. Our study takes advantage of existing quantitative methods to analyze how of tourists perform an action. Then, we enhance them with qualitative methods to analyze why tourists perform this action. Thanks to a community detection and profiling, stakeholders will be able to better identify behaviors and thus target communities by proposing adapted excursions at the best places.

Our key contributions can be summarized as: (1) an automatic Graph Movement extraction methodology dedicated to graph of interest, (2) the Measure of Interest using an interest measure as weighted in a graph. This measure is not dependent on frequency or probability based on number of tourists, (3) Spheres of influence to compare a neighborhood of each visited place to determine a similarity matrix, (4) Community detection by a clustering on the similarity matrix provide profiles. A thorough study of tourists' profiles is compared to tourism management works.

In this paper, we will first relate in Sect. 2 comparable works on community detection network analysis. In Sect. 3 we formalize our graph data model. In Sect. 4 we present our approach to perform a community tourist detection and tourist profiling. Our model is implemented and is subject of a case study on a TripAdvisor dataset in Sect. 5. Finally, the Sect. 6 concludes this paper.

2   State of the Art

Social networks are a social structure where a set of social actors are connected by relationships. Due to the size of social networks with numerous and heterogeneous relationships, it has been becoming difficult to analyze them. Therefore, several algorithms and graph theory concepts are used to study a structure of social networks [16]. Most researches aiming at analyzing social networks enable to understand different social phenomena including social structures evolution, to measure an importance of nodes, to detect communities of nodes [1] that share some characteristics by looking metrics at the whole network cohesion [17], etc.

Social networks are paradigmatic examples of graphs with communities. The word community itself refers to a social context. The concept of community has no unified definition [18], most of the researchers have reached a consensus that communities in a network indicate groups of nodes, such that nodes within a group are connected more often than those across different groups [30]. Detecting community in networks is very hard and not yet satisfyingly solved, despite an huge effort of a large interdisciplinary community of scientists working on it over the past few years.

In the literature, several researches have been interested to detect of community in social networks to analyze and understand tourist behaviors. To detect tourists community, social networks are modeled as a directed graph with a weight attached to each edge. These values of weights can be represented, for example, frequencies of movement of tourists, probabilities value, rules metrics, etc. Based on this graph model, a detection community method and approach exposed below have been studied by many research fields.

Graph Partitioning: This method consists to divide a graph into groups of predefined size, such that the number of links in a cluster is denser than the number of edges between the clusters [10]. The disadvantage of this method is to define the size of clusters in a relevant way.

Hierarchical Clustering. Hierarchical clustering techniques are based on a nodes similarity measure [12]. These techniques don't need a predefined size and number of communities. Hierarchical clustering techniques can be categorized into two classes. *Agglomerative algorithms* starts by considering each node of a graph as a separate cluster and iteratively merge them based on high similarity and ends up with a unique community. And *Divisive algorithms* start by the entire network as a distinct cluster and iteratively splits it by eliminating links joining nodes with low similarity and ends up with unique communities.

Modularity Optimisation Based. Modality, is a quality function introduced by Newman and Girvan [19] to measure the quality of a partition of graph nodes. The larger the modularity value the better is the partition. The best-known methods within are: *Greedy method of Newman* is an agglomerative method. Initially, each node belongs to a distinct module, then they are merged iteratively based on the modularity gain. And *Blondal's Louvain algorithm* is an heuristic greedy algorithm for uncovering communities in complex weighted graphs [8]. It is based on the modularity optimization.

Statistical Inference-Based Methods. These methods deduct properties of datasets, starting from a set of observations and model hypotheses. If the dataset is a graph, based on hypotheses on how nodes are connected to each other, the model has to fit the actual graph topology [10]. These methods attempt to find the best fit in a model to the graph, where the model assumes that nodes have some sort of classification, based on their connectivity patterns.

All the methods cited above are used to detect communities on network models as a directed weighted graph. Where weights values represent frequencies, probabilities, labels, vectors, etc. The probability weights is deduced from frequencies or is computed, thanks to data mining, by considering relation between nodes as rules. Those methods implement a measure like support, confidence or lift and return rules which satisfy some constraints. To determine communities, one can analyze a graph as a Markov Chain [2] Most advanced methods use adapted clustering or partitioning such as spectral clustering [29], label propagation [23].

In the tourism research field, methods used for community detection are focused on detecting community based of the quantitative dimension i.e. frequencies movement of individuals or flows in a graph. These methods form clusters based on clustering metrics (Silhouette, Dunn, etc.). However, the interpretation of clustering contents is unrepresentative of a community sharing a same interest or a profile but rather a mass of data. In this study, we will focus on detection community to extract tourist profiling base on the interest of tourists to make a movement or visit by integrating the notion of overtourism [5].

3   Tourism Movement's Data Model

To model tourism movement, we must consider visited locations, users information and their interactions. To study interactions on locations, we propose to model tourist data by a graph of movement. Graphs rely on links between users and locations through their reviews.

Data Types. Our database is composed of users, reviews, and geo-located locations. A location is composed of longitude and latitude coordinates, type of location (hotel, restaurant, attraction) and a rating. Each location has been aligned with administrative areas (GADM)[2]. A user is identified by nationality, age and is described by a timeline. A user timeline represents a chronological set of reviews from its first reviews to its last reviews. This timeline allows computing intermediate properties like time between two consecutive reviews i.e. consecutive visited places. A review represents a note given by a user on a location at a given time.

3.1   Sequences Dataset

To study tourists' movement of a given destination, we need to target tourists. For this, we focus only on users who visit at least one destination. Then we extract all their reviews to gather their circulation all over the world. Tourists review several locations during their trip. A trip is a succession of days when a tourist writ at least one review per day, i.e. as soon as there is a day when a tourist does not write a review, its trip is considered broken. However, a tourist may not review during a limited period during the same trip. The break can be canceled between two trips that took place in the similar country by a user. We consider a sequence is composed of reviews written at most at 7 days apart [13]. The method consists of merging two trips if they satisfy the following conditions: $\Delta B \leqslant \Delta T_i$ and $\Delta B \leqslant \Delta T_j$ and $L_{T_i} = F_{T_j}$. Where $\Delta B \leq 7$ represents break's duration, ΔT_i and ΔT_j present i^{th} and j^{th} trip's duration, F_{T_j} represents the first country visited during j^{th} trip and L_{T_i} represents the last country visited during i^{th} trip. For each tourist, we build a set of trips based on its reviews. Each trip corresponds to sequence and presents a succession of locations in a temporal order of visit during a trip.

---

[2] GADM: https://gadm.org/index.html. $386,735$ administrative areas (country, region, department, district, city, and town).

3.2 Sequential Rule Mining

Based on sequences dataset, we use a sequential rules mining algorithm to discover and to extract all existing rules in the dataset. The input structure is a set of sequences, and the output structure is the rules. A sequential rule is a rule of the form $X \longrightarrow Y$ where X and Y are items. In our case a rule $X \longrightarrow Y$ is interpreted as, if location X occurs then it will be *directly followed* by the location Y. To exploit the sequential rules, two measures are predominantly employed, *support* and *confidence*. The support of a rule $X \longrightarrow Y$ is how many sequences contains the location from X followed directly by the location Y. The confidence of a rule $X \longrightarrow Y$ is the support of the rule divided by the number of sequences containing the location X.

To discover sequential rules appearing in sequence dataset, we use a *TRule-Growth* algorithm [11] for its performance. The TRuleGrowth algorithm uses a pattern-growth approach for discovering sequential rules such that it can be much more efficient and scalable. After, extracting all the rules from the sequences dataset, we use an *Interest measure* to value interesting and useful rules for an effective decision making.

3.3 Measure of Interest

To value interesting rules, there exist several measures developed in diverse fields such as machine learning, social science, statistics, data mining, etc. Selecting a right measure for a given application is difficult because many measures may disagree with each other. Each measure has several properties that make them unsuitable for other applications. In our case, the key properties one should consider selecting an accurate measure are:

1. The measure must distinguish the movement between location X and Y with that between location Y and X. The measure must be **asymmetric**.
2. To understand the interest of tourists to perform a given movement, the measure must be **antisymmetry** to express the positive and the negative correlation resulting of the movement between two locations.
3. The measure must have a positive value if there is a positive correlation and equals zero if items are **statistically independent**.
4. Considering size of the dataset, the measure must be easy to implement, readable, editable and context-free with a **limit scale**. The measure must have an upper bound and a lower bound.
5. The quantity dimension mustn't be ignored. The measure will scale in a limited way with it.

The measure respects and corresponds to all these properties is *Klosgen* [15]. The Klosgen measure is a normalization of the *Added Value measure*, also called *Pavillon Index* or *Confidence*, [25]. For a given rule $X \longrightarrow Y$ Added Value $AV(X \Rightarrow Y)$ measure quantifies how much the probability of Y increases when conditioning on the transactions that contain X: $AV(X \Rightarrow Y) = confidence(X \Rightarrow Y) - support(Y)$. Where, $confidence(X \Rightarrow Y) = \frac{|X \Rightarrow Y|}{|X|}$ and

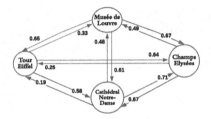
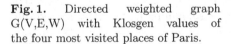
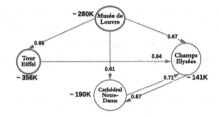

Fig. 1. Directed weighted graph G(V,E,W) with Klosgen values of the four most visited places of Paris.

Fig. 2. Weighted graph of the top 2 mainstream nodes with a Klosgen threshold at 0.6.

$support(X) = |X|$. $|X|$ denotes the frequency of X in the database. The Added Value of a rule can be positive, negative or zero. The rules with a high Added Value are considering as interesting rules. Since the Added Value vary greatly depending of the support of the antecedent X and the consequent Y, we normalize the Added Value measure by multiplying it by its squared root which gives Klosgen measure. Then, we compute the Klosgen measure for each rule as follows: $Klosgen(X \Rightarrow Y) = \sqrt{supp(X \Rightarrow Y)} * AV(X \Rightarrow y)$

Using the Klosgen measure has two main advantages. The first is that, the influence of support or confidence is lowered, which means that very low or very high support of the antecedent or the consequent have a low influence on the value of the measure (unlike lift or confidence) [27]. The second is that the Klosgen measure is not a complex measure, which makes its meaning relatively clear, since it is presented as the normalization of the Added Value. The Added Value being itself part of the basic objective interest measures.

3.4 Graph Movement Model

Based on the set of rules and their interest value calculated by Klosgen, we build a movement graph of tourists. The movement graph $G(V, E, W)$ is a weighted directed graph. The nodes V are a set of the antecedents and the consequent of the rules. These nodes present the locations visited by the tourists. The arcs E are the association of the rules and present two direct consecutive locations. The weighted W of the arcs is the values of the *interest* measure of rules that represent interest of the tourists to move between two places i.e. two nodes. The Fig. 1 shows an example of graph of movements of tourist fours most visited place in *Paris*.

4   Community Detection

Based of our graph model, to detect community, we first identify a **mainstream nodes**, the nodes having a most influential and strong attractiveness. Secondly, we define a **neighborhood** of mainstream nodes. The neighbors of a node consist in a set of nodes that are connected to this node up to a *certain distance*, i.e., the number of steps between a source node and its neighbors. Then, for each mainstream node we build a **Sphere of Influence**. Finally, we define a **similarity measure** between spheres of influence, this measure is used to create **clusters** and then detect communities.

4.1   Mainstream Nodes

We will define two kinds of nodes, *mainstream nodes* having the most influential on the graph and *secondary nodes* the other remaining nodes. Based on graph of tourist movements $G(V, E, W)$, for each node of V we calculate its support (i.e. number of occurrences) on the sequences dataset, described in Sect. 3.1. We select a subset of node V' having a K maximum value of support. The value of k is fixed according to the number of nodes in the graph and the distribution of the support amount all the nodes. We note $V'' = V \setminus V'$ the secondary nodes as the rest of the nodes which are not mainstream.

Once mainstream nodes and secondary nodes are defined, to perform community detection, we extract a subgraph $G'(V, E', W)$ formed with $V = V' \cup V''$, and arcs $E' \subseteq E \wedge ((v1, v2) \in E \to W_{v1,v2} > threshold)$. A low weight presents a low interest of movement while the most significant weights present the interest of moving from one node to another.

The Fig. 2 presents subgraph of the graph in Fig. 1. Where the bold nodes *Musée de Louvre* and *Tour Eiffel* are the mainstream nodes with their respective support value of $280k$ and $356K$. The Klosgen value threshold is taken at 0.6.

4.2   Spheres of Influence

In graph theory a sphere of influence of the graph assigns, for each node, a ball centered at that node of neighbors distance D equal to a definite value. In this study, we create a sphere of influence to all mainstream nodes. A sphere of influence of a mainstream node is an aggregation of its neighboring nodes (mainstream and secondary).

The neighbor distance D of an influence sphere equals to the average length of sequences in the sequences dataset minus one. To process a sphere of influence for a mainstream node $S_m i$, we create an array A_i for each mainstream node m_i. The array contains all neighbors of distance 1 to D from m_i. The Table 1 shows the result of creating the influence spheres of two mainstream nodes $m_{Tour\ Eiffel}$ and $m_{Musee\ du\ Louvre}$ the graph Fig. 2.

4.3   Similarity Measure

Once all influence spheres are created, we will compare them in pair. Comparing two influence spheres consist to analyze all the nodes composing them and report the percent of similitude into a matrix.

Let M be the matrix of similarity of size $|V'|$, referring to the number of mainstream nodes. The value $M(i, j)$ equal to the percent of nodes in $S_m i$

Table 1. Sphere of influence of the two mainstream nodes of Fig. 2.

Mainstream node	$m_{Musee\ du\ Louvre}$	$m_{Tour\ Eiffel}$
Neighbors at distance $= 1$	$A_{Musee\ du\ Louvre} =$ {Tour Eiffel, Cathédral Notre-Dame, Champs Elysées }	$A_{Tour\ Eiffel} =$ {Champs Elysées}
Neighbors at distance $= 2$	none	$A_{Tour\ Eiffel} =$ {Champs Elysées, Cathédral Notre-Dame}

(i.e. the influence sphere of a mainstream node m_i) that are also present in nodes $S_{m}j$ (i.e. the influence sphere of a mainstream node m_j). Thus, the matrix is non-symmetric. $M(i, j) = 1$ means that all the nodes in $S_{m}i \subseteq S_{m}j$ and $M(i, j) = 0$ means that $S_{m}i \cap S_{m}j = 0$. Let us take for example the results in Table 1. The matrix of similarity M is as follows:

$$M = \begin{matrix} m_{Musee\ du\ Louvre} \\ m_{Tour\ Eiffel} \end{matrix} \begin{matrix} m_{Musee\ du\ Louvre} & m_{Tour\ Eiffel} \\ \begin{pmatrix} - & 0.66 \\ 1 & - \end{pmatrix} \end{matrix}$$

4.4 Profiling

Based on the similarity matrix, we detect community for purpose to create a tourism profile. The matrix is seen as a graph for the profiling process. In this study, we are looking for a community detection based on high similarity values and high density of arcs inside communities compared to that of arcs connecting to outside communities. This distinction between arcs inside the communities and outside is called *modularity*. Then we must optimize the modality in order to have the best possible grouping into communities. To achieve this, we use the *Louvain clustering* [4] which maximizes modularity for each community.

5 Experiments

We conducted experiments on reviews posted by tourists between 1st January 2013 to 31th December 2016 in `Tripadvisor` focused on Paris, French regions. After cleaning and pre-processing the data, we obtain $1'666'584$ trips of more than 3 reviews, with an average length of stay of 2.5 days and an average number of reviews per stays at 4.14 with close to $40'000$ places of Paris.

5.1 Measure of Interest

In our study, values of weights of the graph are computed using *Klosgen (Kl)* measure. To compare our results with others methods, we also provide the following measures: *Support (Supp)*: depends on the number of occurrences of the rule $X \longrightarrow Y$, *Confidence (Conf)*: is a ratio between the support of the rule on the support of X, as a probability of a Markov chain, *Lift*: provides a value showing how different of a random process the rule is, *Certainty Factor (CF)*: a high Certainty Factor means Y is dependent of X and not another node, $J - Measure$ $(cross - entropy)$ (J): computes the cross-entropy, i.e. the information contain in the rule over all the rules and *Conditional Entropy (CE)*: compute the correlation between X and Y based on the entropy value.

The Table 2 presents the top 3 rules based on Support and top 3 rules based on Klosgen. Nodes representing a monuments *Tour Eiffel, Musée du Louvre, Cathédrale Notre-Dame* and other well-known monuments will be over-represented with Support. Confidence and Lift highest values are a combination of a high support node with one with a very few support. Same for Certainty Factor, the values between the highest support nodes or node presents in few rules are very low. J-Measure are closed to zero for all rules since rules are numerous for a fixed X or a fixed Y. Moreover, the large majority of Conditional Entropy are closed to zero.

As shown, Klosgen measure is not influenced by the support of nodes, nor by the number of nodes (entropy tends to zero). Since the value is between 0 to 1, Klosgen measure is easily readable and understandable. This measure fits perfectly with the notion of *interest*.

5.2   Mainstream Monuments

To select K mainstream monuments of Paris, we initially order monuments by decreasing order of support and then we compute the cumulative number of reviews per monument of Paris. The curve displays an elbow which distinguishes on the left side mainstream monuments to secondary monuments. We set the number of mainstream monuments when the elbow start at $K = 111$ which represents approximately 73% of all reviews.

5.3   Sphere of Influence

To create influence spheres, we first start in mainstream monuments then aggregate the neighbors nodes with distance of $D = 3$, average length of sequences

Table 2. Measures' results on a sample from the database.

Rules	Kl	$Supp$	$Conf$	$Lift$	CF	J	CE
Tour Eiffel ⟶ Musée du Louvre	0.33	**49565**	**0.18**	0.58	−0.18	**0.03**	**0.68**
Tour Eiffel ⟶ Cathédrale Notre-Dame	0.57	**26129**	0.09	0.51	−0.11	**0.02**	**0.45**
Cathédrale Notre-Dame ⟶ Tour Eiffel	0.18	**23092**	**0.20**	0.45	−0.43	**0.04**	**0.71**
Le Bataclan ⟶ Place de la République	**0.86**	300	0.09	**2.53**	**0.06**	0	0.44
Hôtel Plaza Athénée ⟶ Hotel George V	**0.85**	297	0.05	**4.40**	**0.04**	0	0.29
Arc de Triomphe ⟶ Sacré-Coeur	**0.85**	1285	0.05	**1.47**	**0.02**	0	0.27

in the dataset, in our case 4, minus one. The similarity matrix and the Louvain clustering are compute on the 111 corresponding nodes with a Klosgen's threshold = 0.1. Since the graph have about 40'000 nodes, with 111 mainstream nodes, we do not provide a figure presenting the result. Concerning the similarity matrix, its size is 111 * 111, thus we can't show it in this paper.

5.4   Clustering Analysis

After applying the Louvain clustering algorithm, we obtain 4 clusters of similar size, around twenty nodes. We do not regard the 5 clusters of size less than 3 and clusters with singleton. We note that tourist's profiles are bounded to an unique cluster and they do not overlap.

Cluster [1] contains mainly architectural monuments, some can be visited but they are principally known for their aspect like the *Pyramide du Louvre*, *Grand Palais* or *Opéra Garnier*. This cluster contains the main bridges of Paris and typical district like *Montmartre* or *Le Marais*. One monument radically differs is the famous tearoom *Ladurée*. But this restaurant is very close to the monuments of this cluster, which can explain its presence. The profile of this cluster is *Architectural tourism* [26] and *Photography tourism* [22].

Cluster [2] contains architectural monuments and cultural monuments like museums (mostly about history of the country). Some of those monuments also have a religious context like the *Cathédrale Notre-Dame* or *Basilique Sacré-Coeur*. The outsiders are *Tour Eiffel* and *Jardin du Luxembourg*, those monuments are most recent than the others but have a strong cultural aspect. The profile of this cluster is *Heritage tourism* [21] and *Religious tourism* [24].

Cluster [3] contains mostly sport complexes, stadium and cabarets. The outsiders are the restaurant *Le Perchoir*, the train stations *Gare de Lyon* and *Gare de l'Est*. The profile of this cluster is *Sport and Event tourism* [6] and *Recreation tourism, Urban tourism* [28].

Cluster [4] contains the *Grands Magasins de Paris* (Paris department stores), luxury stores and luxury hotels. This cluster clearly refers to shopping and the luxury of Paris, which is a significant attractive aspect of the city. The outsiders are restaurants, but are referred as gastronomic restaurants which refer to luxury. Obviously, this cluster refers to the profiles of *Luxury tourism* and *Culinary tourism* [3].

5.5   Discussions

Impact of Klosgen's Threshold. Since the Klosgen's threshold determines if an arc is kept in the graph, an upper value increases the number of clusters and the number of singleton. When increasing the threshold value, the nodes in a cluster remains together or are split into two or more clusters. The threshold does not modify the profiles but only the number of profiles found.

Clustering Without Computing Spheres of Influence. When we compute the Louvain algorithm to the mainstream monuments with Klosgen values without doing the spheres of influence, we obtain 4 clusters (and some singleton).

Some trends can be extract to each cluster, with several outsiders. The trends are in order: *Cultural tourism (Heritage)*; *Cultural tourism (Modern Art)* and *Luxury tourism*; *Sport and Event tourism*; *Luxury tourism*. The profiles are less distinct without computing the spheres of influence and some kind of tourist's profiles are present in many clusters.

Clustering with Other Measures. We also implement the method with support, confidence and lift measures instead of Klosgen measure. The clusters do not have any main trend but are mostly influenced by the metro lines and other public transports of Paris. Clusters reflect also the overtourism in Paris with a cluster with the top 23 most visited monuments of Paris.

6 Conclusion

When scientists study tourism thanks to social networks data, they used measure based on the frequency to understand the tourists' behaviors. We provide a method to extract tourism behaviors using an interest Klosgen measure and by adapting the notion of neighborhood used in social graph to the tourism industry. Our method returns significant results, already observed by tourism management studies in a more limited scale. In future work, we have to enhance our method to refine the profiling, by using a fuzzing clustering to improve the clusters' knowledge discovery. We will additionally use the method to other cities and a vaster area of France to confirm the validity and efficiency of the proposed method.

References

1. Arenas, A., Danon, L., Díaz-Guilera, A., Gleiser, P.M., Guimerá, R.: Community analysis in social networks. Eur. Phys. J. B **38**(2), 373–380 (2004). https://doi.org/10.1140/epjb/e2004-00130-1
2. Ben Baccar, L., Djebali, S., Guérard, G.: Tourist's tour prediction by sequential data mining approach. In: Li, J., Wang, S., Qin, S., Li, X., Wang, S. (eds.) ADMA 2019. LNCS (LNAI), vol. 11888, pp. 681–695. Springer, Cham (2019). https://doi.org/10.1007/978-3-030-35231-8_50
3. Batat, W.: The role of luxury gastronomy in culinary tourism: an ethnographic study of Michelin-starred restaurants in France. Int. J. Tourism Res. **23**(2), 150–163 (2021)
4. Blondel, V.D., Guillaume, J.L., Lambiotte, R., Lefebvre, E.: Fast unfolding of communities in large networks. J. Stat. Mech. Theor. Exp. **10**, P10008 (2008)
5. Capocchi, A., Vallone, C., Pierotti, M., Amaduzzi, A.: Overtourism: a literature review to assess implications and future perspectives. Sustainability **11**(12), 3303 (2019)
6. Chalip, L., Costa, C.A.: Sport event tourism and the destination brand: towards a general theory. Sport Soc. **8**(2), 218–237 (2005)
7. Chareyron, G., Cousin, S., Da-Rugna, J., Gabay, D.: Touriscope: map the world using geolocated photographies. In: IGU meeting, Geography of Tourism, Leisure and Global Change (2009)

8. Clauset, A., Newman, M.E., Moore, C.: Finding community structure in very large networks. Phys. Rev. E **70**(6), 066111 (2004)
9. Cooper, C., Hall, C.M.: Contemporary Tourism. Routledge, Milton Park (2007)
10. Fortunato, S.: Community detection in graphs. Phys. Rep. **486**(3–5), 75–174 (2010)
11. Fournier-Viger, P., Wu, C.-W., Tseng, V.S., Nkambou, R.: Mining sequential rules common to several sequences with the window size constraint. In: Kosseim, L., Inkpen, D. (eds.) AI 2012. LNCS (LNAI), vol. 7310, pp. 299–304. Springer, Heidelberg (2012). https://doi.org/10.1007/978-3-642-30353-1_27
12. Friedman, J., Hastie, T., Tibshirani, R., et al.: The Elements of Statistical Learning. Springer Series in Statistics, vol. 1. Springer, New York (2001). https://doi.org/10.1007/978-0-387-21606-5
13. Gössling, S.: Tourism, tourist learning and sustainability: an exploratory discussion of complexities, problems and opportunities. J. Sustain. Tourism **26**(2), 292–306 (2018)
14. Kaufmann, M., Siegfried, P., Huck, L., Stettler, J.: Analysis of tourism hotspot behaviour based on geolocated travel blog data: the case of qyer. ISPRS Int. J. Geo Inf. **8**(11), 493 (2019)
15. Klösgen, W.: Problems for knowledge discovery in databases and their treatment in the statistics interpreter explora. Int. J. Intell. Syst. **7**(7), 649–673 (1992)
16. Knoke, D., Yang, S.: Social Network Analysis, vol. 154. Sage Publications, Thousand Oaks (2019)
17. Kolaczyk, E.D., Csárdi, G.: Statistical Analysis of Network Data with R, vol. 65. Springer, New York (2014). https://doi.org/10.1007/978-1-4939-0983-4
18. Lancichinetti, A., Fortunato, S.: Community detection algorithms: a comparative analysis. Phys. Rev. E **80**(5), 056117 (2009)
19. Nicosia, V., Mangioni, G., Carchiolo, V., Malgeri, M.: Extending the definition of modularity to directed graphs with overlapping communities. J. Stat. Mech. Theor. Exp. **03**, P03024 (2009)
20. Palla, G., Derényi, I., Farkas, I., Vicsek, T.: Uncovering the overlapping community structure of complex networks in nature and society. Nature **435**(7043), 814–818 (2005)
21. Park, H.Y.: Heritage Tourism. Routledge, Milton Park (2013)
22. Picard, D., Robinson, M.: The Framed World: Tourism, Tourists and Photography. Routledge, Milton Park (2016)
23. Raghavan, U.N., Albert, R., Kumara, S.: Near linear time algorithm to detect community structures in large-scale networks. Phys. Rev. E **76**(3), 036106 (2007)
24. Rashid, A.G.: Religious tourism-a review of the literature. J. Hospitality Tourism Insights (2018)
25. Sahar, S., Mansour, Y.: Empirical evaluation of interest-level criteria. In: Data Mining and Knowledge Discovery: Theory, Tools, and Technology, vol. 3695, pp. 63–74. International Society for Optics and Photonics (1999)
26. Specht, J.: Architectural Tourism: Building for Urban Travel Destinations. Springer, Wiesbaden (2014). https://doi.org/10.1007/978-3-658-06024-4
27. Tan, P.N., Kumar, V., Srivastava, J.: Selecting the right objective measure for association analysis. Inf. Syst. **29**(4), 293–313 (2004)
28. Tribe, J.: The Economics of Recreation, Leisure and Tourism. Routledge, Milton Park (2020)
29. Von Luxburg, U.: A tutorial on spectral clustering. Max Planck Institute for Biological Cybernetics. Technical Report (2006)
30. Xia, X., Zhu, S.X.: A survey on weighted network measurement and modeling. TELKOMNIKA Indonesian J. Electr. Eng. **11**(1), 181–186 (2013)

Extracting High Profit Sequential Feature Groups of Products Using High Utility Sequential Pattern Mining

Priyanka Motwani[⊠], C. I. Ezeife, and Mahreen Nasir

School of Computer Science, University of Windsor,
401 Sunset Avenue, Windsor, ON N9B3P4, Canada
{motwanip,cezeife,nasir11d}@uwindsor.ca

Abstract. Creating a set of product features obtained through mining users' opinions helps retailers identify the attributes (features or aspects) more accurately and discover the most preferred features of a certain product. High Profit Feature Groups are created by extracting such product feature groups such as '{*batterylife, camera*} of a smartphone,' which results in higher profit for manufacturers and increased consumer satisfaction. The accuracy of opinion-feature extraction systems can be improved if more complex sequential patterns of customer reviews are included in the user-behavior analysis to obtain relevant feature groups. An existing system referred to in this paper as HPFG19_HU uses High Utility Itemset Mining and Aspect-Based Sentiment Analysis to obtain high profit aspects considering the high utility values, but it does not consider the order of occurrences (sequences) of features formed in customers' opinion sentences that help distinguish similar users and identify more relevant and related high profit product features. This paper proposes a High Profit Sequential Feature Groups based on the High Utility Sequences (HPSFG_HUS) system, which identifies sequential patterns in features. It combines Opinion Mining with High Utility Sequential Pattern Mining. This approach provides more accurate high feature groups, sales profit, and customer satisfaction, as shown by the retailer's graphs of extracted High Profit Sequential Feature Groups. Experiments with evaluation results of execution time and evaluation metrics show that this system generates higher revenue than the tested existing systems.

Keywords: Social network · Sentiment classification · Opinion mining · Data mining · High utility sequential pattern mining · Feature extraction

1 Introduction

'Do you like this product? Is this worth purchasing? What other people think of this product?'. Customers and manufacturers of products rely on opinions.

C. I. Ezeife—This research was supported by the Natural Science and Engineering Research Council (NSERC) of Canada under an Operating grant (OGP-0194134) and a University of Windsor grant.

© Springer Nature Switzerland AG 2022
B. Li et al. (Eds.): ADMA 2021, LNAI 13088, pp. 54–67, 2022.
https://doi.org/10.1007/978-3-030-95408-6_5

The Internet has significantly enhanced the way customers share their opinions. The web has become a hub of online review websites [9]. E-Commerce review sites like Epinions, Amazon and social networking websites like Twitter, IMDB, Facebook have a significant impact on their users when sharing their thoughts, reviews, ratings, likes, and dislikes about a particular topic, relevant field, or product [4].

The rapid growth of online review websites and lots of customers' reviews bring up the need for an automated way of obtaining opinions - *Opinion Mining.* Therefore, it can be drawn to attention that Opinion Mining has come out as an emerging and explorable research direction for increasing customer experiences and providing them useful recommendations [4].

Data Mining techniques perform a vital role in customer behavior analysis and are used to extract product features from the opinions/reviews mined from online review websites. These methods include Association Rule Mining [2], Frequent Itemset Mining [2], Sequential Pattern Mining [2], etc. Utility-Based mining is a modern improvement over traditional Itemset and Sequential Pattern Mining in which pattern filtering parameters depend on the pattern's utility rather than just frequency metrics where utility represents both some quantitative (e.g., number of items) and qualitative (e.g., unit profit) features of items. High Utility Patterns are beneficial in various fields, including market basket analysis and web usage mining [3].

1.1   Opinion Mining (OM) and Sentiment Analysis (SA)

Opinion Mining (OM) is defined as the process of converting unstructured and textual data into positive, negative, and neutral or good, poor, and average results in order to evaluate any product or service [10]. The computational examination of ideas, sentiments, emotions, and attitudes conveyed in texts about a certain entity is known as Sentiment Analysis (SA). In some ways, the development of the term 'Sentiment Analysis' is similar to that of 'Opinion Mining'.

Example: Consider following set of reviews from Amazon.com for a product with User ID (UID), Review ID (RID) and product text (Product reviews)

Table 1. Product reviews of 'iphone 11 Pro'

UID	RID	Product reviews
U1	R1	The phone has an amazing batterylife and an outstanding camera quality
U2	R2	It has a horrible voice quality!!!. Not worth of a purchase
U3	R3	No doubt colour accuracy and Touch response are good, but not that sharp

Table 2. Components of opinion

Opinion target	iphone 11 Pro
Opinion polarity	R1: Positive; R2: Negative; R3: Neutral
Features	R1: batterylife, camera quality; R2: voice quality; R3: colour accuracy, touch response
Opinion words	R1: amazing, outstanding; R2: horrible; R3: good, sharp
Opinion source	U1, U2, U3

Feature-Opinion Extraction: Given sequence of terms $T = <t_1, ..., t_q>$ that corresponds to a sentence, a set of features $F = \{f_1, ..., f_n\}$, and a set of sentiment terms $S = \{s_1, ..., s_k\}$ extracted from T, feature-sentiment matching generates tuples (f_i, s_j, sc), such that s_j is the sentiment of feature f_i with sentiment score sc [3]. Note that this score can be either positive or negative as in conventional Sentiment Analysis. The base score is basically associated with the sentiment term, but it may be modified due to enhancers or negators in the sentence. For example, <*Iphone 11 Pro has a long batterylife, but the cost is high*> the output of the feature-sentiment matching process is (batterylife, long, 2), (price, high, −1).

1.2 High Utility Sequential Pattern Mining (HUSPM)

High Utility Sequential Pattern Mining [13] is an emerging topic in the data mining community and is an extension to Sequential Pattern Mining [2]. The concept of "utility" is introduced into pattern mining to mine patterns of high utility by considering the quality (such as profit) and quantity (such as the number of items purchased) of itemsets which indicates business value and impact.

Table 3. A Q-sequence database

SID	Sequence with internal utility	Sequence utility ($)
S1	a(3) {a(2) b(6) d(2)} f(1) a(5) d(1)	130
S2	e(3) {a(2) b(5)} d(1) c(4)	85
S3	{c(1) f(2)} b(3) {d(1) e(4)}	74
S4	a(2) {b(7) d(4)} {a(6) b(3)} e(5)	180

Table 4. A profit table

Item	a	b	c	d	e	f
Profit ($)	5	7	3	10	6	8

Preliminary and Key Properties of the Problem of High Utility Sequential Pattern Mining [13]: A Quantitative Sequence Database is shown in Table 3. which displays the sequences of items purchased having Sequence ID as SID. Table 4 shows the profit values associated with each item. High Utility Sequential Patterns are extracted as shown.

Input: A Quantitative (Q) Sequence Database (Table 3), Profit Table (Table 4)

Output: High Utility Sequential Patterns

Internal Utility: Quantity of items: iu(b, S1) = 6, iu(a, S1) = 3 + 2 + 5 = 10.

External Utility: Profit values of items: eu(b) = 7.

Sequence Utility of Item: Product of internal utility and external utility of the given item: su(b, S1) = 6 × 7 = 42

Sequence Utility of Sequence in a Transaction: Sum of Sequence Utility of Sequence X in a given transaction: Sequence *ab* has two distinct occurrences in S4. Hence, su(ab, S4) = (2 × 5 + 7 × 7) + (6 × 5 + 3 × 7) = 26 + 48 = 110.

Sequence Utility of a Transaction: Sum of products of internal (iu) and external (eu) utilities of each item (which is sequence utility) in a transaction: su(TS1) = su(a, S1)+su(b, S1)+su(d, S1)+su(f, S1) = 50 + 42 + 30 + 8 = 130.

Sequence Utility of a Sequence X in SDB: Sum of Sequence Utility of sequence X in all the transactions of SDB: Sequence *a(bd)a* has two occurrences in SDB: su(a(bd)a, SDB) = su(a(bd)a, TS1)+su(a(bd)a, TS4) = 102 + 129 = 231.

Sequence Utility of the Whole SDB: Summation of all Sequence Utility values of each Transaction: su(SDB) = 130 + 85 + 74 + 180 = 469.

Minimum Sequence Utility Threshold δ: Percentage of Sequence Utility value of SDB: If δ is 30% or can be expressed as 0.3, minSeqUtil = 0.3 × 469 = 140.

High Utility Sequential Pattern: A sequence X is a High Utility Sequential Pattern if su(X) ≥ minSeqUtil. For minSeqUtil = 140, *a(bd)a* is a High Utility Sequential Pattern as su(a(bd)a) = 231.

1.3   Problem Definition

Given a set of reviews R of a product P as an input, the problem being addressed in this paper is to identify P's features (shape, size, color, quality, or price) and their opinions. Then, these features are grouped to form feature-sets and generate potentially High Utility/Profit Sequential Feature groups from the extracted features.

1.4   Contributions

In this paper, we propose a system called High Profit Sequential Feature Groups based on High Utility Sequences (HPSFG_HUS) which is an enhancement of an existing system referred in this paper as HPFG19_HU [3]. This existing system used Aspect-Based Sentiment Analysis and High Utility Itemset Mining (HUIM) using FHN algorithm [5] to mine frequent high utility patterns with positive and negative unit profit values. Since this system performs HUIM [12] in a transaction database of features, which does not take the order of occurrences of feature words into account. There may be frequent occurrences of these feature-groups or individual features that can form sequences or patterns. These sequential patterns provide a better chance to identify important product features that can be related to other aspects in the form of price, importance, customer preference, etc. Hence we propose a system that combines Opinion Mining and High Utility Sequential Pattern Mining to obtain High Profit Sequential Feature Groups.

HPSFG_HUS Feature Contributions.

1. The proposed approach will form Q-Sequences based on utility values and the itemsets of features. The utility values are obtained by calculating sentiment score and adding '+5' to this score to get positive values. These sequences are formed based on the order of occurrences of feature words in the sentences.
2. After forming Q-Sequences, the proposed methodology will perform High Utility Sequential Pattern Mining using USpan algorithm on the sequence of features and obtain High Profit Sequential Feature Groups.

The rest of the paper is organised as: Sect. 2 discusses the Related Work, Sect. 3 discusses the Proposed System, Sect. 4 explains the Experimental Evaluation and Sect. 5 discusses the Conclusion and Future Work.

2   Related Work

This section discusses the recent studies that integrate some data mining approaches with Opinion Mining in order to achieve good accuracy for extracting relevant product features from customer opinions or reviews.

1. **SPM and ARM with Opinion Mining** [9]:
   The authors [9] tried to compare two important and renowned algorithms of Association Rule Mining [2] and Sequential Pattern Mining [2] for frequent features and opinion words extraction from customers' opinions obtained from a social networking website. For this comparison, they used the Apriori algorithm [2] and the Generalized Sequential Pattern (GSP) algorithm [2] on the review's dataset to find out an efficient algorithm for extracting features and opinions.
2. **Sequential Pattern Rules with Opinion Mining** [8]:
   The research to study the impact of Sequential Pattern Mining [2] in the context of Opinion and Feature extraction was done by the authors [2]. Their methodology had a major focus on the features (aspects) that are present in the opinions of customers' reviews. The authors in [8] focused only on explicit features and using the PrefixSpan algorithm [7], sequential patterns are generated; certain rules were specified by analyzing sequential patterns produced during the first step on the basis of the correlation between aspect and opinion terms. The explicit aspects were extracted in the last part using the sequential rules generated.
3. **HPFG19_HU System combining Opinion Mining and HUIM** [3]:
   The authors [3] proposed a method that performed Aspect-Based (Feature-Based) Sentiment Analysis, triples-to-transactions transformation, and High Utility Itemset Mining [12] to extract feature groups. The input to the system is a set of product reviews and the output is a set of feature groups that yield high profit considering the utility factor. Aspect-Based Sentiment Analysis helps in identifying the aspect, sentiment and corresponding sentiment score of the aspect. Triples are formed of (aspect, sentiment, sentimentscore) and these are transformed into transaction where the aspect is considered as item and sentiment score as internal utility value and external utility values are considered identical i.e. equals 1. In this way, itemsets are formed and high utility itemsets are obtained using FHN algorithm [5].

3 Proposed High Profit Sequential Feature Groups Based on High Utility Sequences (HPSFG_HUS) System

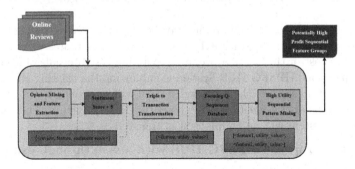

Fig. 1. Overall architecture of the proposed HPSFG_HUS System

---

Algorithm 1: High Profit Sequential Feature Groups based on High Utility Sequences (HPFSG_HUS)

Input: Online product reviews dataset
Output: High Profit Sequential Feature Groups
1 **BEGIN**
2 **Stage 1. Feature Based Opinion Mining:**
3 Collect product reviews dataset of a Product P from an online reviews' website:
   R ← Reviews. Initialize T ← ∅
4 **for** *each review r in R* **do**
5   Perform data cleaning and preprocessing steps on the product reviews
   dataset R
6   Extract features f_i, Opinions o_i, calculate Sentiment Scores sc and form
   triples: $TR \leftarrow ExtractTriples(r)$
7   Triples formed for each review r in R are unioned in $T \leftarrow T \cup TR$

8 **Stage 2. Modify Sentiment Score:**
9 Modify each sentiment score for each triple by adding "+5" to convert it into a
   positive value
10 **Stage 3. Triples-to-Transaction Transformation:**
11 Construct a Transaction Database D of itemsets with the modified triples [3] D
   $\leftarrow ConstructTransactionDatabase(TG)$
12 **Stage 4. Forming Q-Sequences from Transaction Database:**
13 Construct a Q-Sequence database from the sequence of itemsets and calculate
   sequence utility for each sequence
14 Given D, Group transactions based on the occurrence of sentences in a review
15 $S \leftarrow ConstructQ\text{-}SequenceDatabase(D)$
16 **Stage 5. High Utility Sequential Pattern Mining:**
17 $HPSFG \leftarrow ApplyUspan(S)$
18 **END**

The major goal of proposing High Profit Sequential Feature Groups based on High Utility Sequences (HPSFG_HUS) System is to extract High Profit Sequential Feature Groups (HPSFG) by forming Q sequences of features and performing High Utility Sequential Pattern Mining on the mined features and opinions. Figure 1 shows the overall architecture of the proposed system. The overall method is presented in Algorithm 1, where each step is represented in general terms. In the rest of this section, we are explaining the internals of each phase. Since the proposed HPSFG_HUS System is enhancing the existing HPFG19_HU System [3], certain steps of the proposed system will be similar to the algorithms proposed by authors [3] mentioned in the HPFG19_HU System. The changes of the proposed system will be highlighted in the steps.

Steps in the proposed HPSFG_HUS with a walkthrough example:

Input: Set of Reviews Dataset for Product P (Table 5)

Output: High Profit Feature Groups based on High Utility Sequences.

Table 5. Product reviews dataset

RID	Review text
1	The iphone11 pro has an amazing batterylife. It has a good quality. For such an outstanding battery life, the price is great!
2	The phone comes with 3 lens and has beautiful camera quality. The charger is fast. It makes battery life longer in a good price
3	I just dont like the shape because I was always bumping it and Siri kept popping up and it was irritating
4	People who speak with me say voice quality great. Battery life is good as well as the price is good
5	These make using the home button easy. I like the longer battery life. Well worth the price

STAGE 1: FEATURE BASED OPINION MINING

All the steps of this stage are similar to the steps mentioned in the existing HPFG19_HU System [3].

Step 1.1: Data Preprocessing of each Review: Parse each review present in the product reviews data set (Table 5) and perform the data cleaning and preprocessing steps. At the end of this step, we get cleaned text without any unwanted special characters, stopwords (is, the was, etc.), whitespaces, punctuation, and emoticons [1]. Lemmatization, Stemming and Tokenization tasks [1] are performed to get the preprocessed reviews as shown in Table 6.

Table 6. Cleaned and preprocessed reviews

RID	Review text
1	pro amazing batterylife good quality outstanding battery life price great
2	phone come lens beautiful camera quality charger fast make battery life longer good price
3	dont like shape always bump siri keep pop irritate
4	people speak say voice quality great battery life good well price good
5	make use home button easy like long battery life well worth price

Step 1.2: Extracting Features, Opinions and calculating Sentiment Score: In this step, we extract nouns (e.g., quality), noun phrases (e.g., camera quality), and nouns having possessive forms (e.g., phone's charger) as features. Extract the corresponding sentiment words (adjectives, adverbs) with the features as sentiments and its corresponding sentiment score using a sentiment lexicon (SentiStrength) [10]. Form Feature-Opinion pairs for each co-occurring noun and sentiment pairs.

Step 1.3: Forming Triples: In this sub-step, triples (feature, opinion, sentimentscore) are formed with noun/noun phrases, sentiments and sentiment score extracted from the previous step.

STAGE 2: MODIFIED SENTIMENT SCORE
In HPFSG_HUS system, we modify the sentiment score by adding '+5' to sentiment score of each review in order to normalize the score and get a positive value as '+5' is the highest sentiment score value. This positive value will be helpful because we are interested in High Profit Groups as the final result. Table 7 shows the triples formed after Step 1.2, 1.3 and Stage 2.

Table 7. Triples with modified sentiment score

RID	Features-opinions
1	{batterylife, amazing, 6}, {quality, good, 7}, {batterylife, outstanding, 9}, {price, great, 9}
2	{quality, beautiful, 7}, {cameraquality, beautiful, 7}, {batterylife, long, 8}, {price, good, 5}
3	{shape, like, 3}, {shape, irritating, 2}
4	{quality, great, 9}, {voicequality, great, 9}, {batterylife, good, 7}, {price, good, 7}
5	{button, easy, 6}, {homebutton, easy, 6}, {batterylife, long, 8}, {price, well, 6}

STAGE 3: TRIPLES-TO-TRANSACTION TRANSFORMATION
This transformation is made according to the transformation mentioned in the existing HPFG19_HU System [3] except that we do not group triples and just

form itemsets by considering features as items and modified sentiment scores as internal utility value and external utility value is considered identical (equals 1).

Table 8. Transaction database D of itemsets

TID	Features-opinions
1	{(batterylife: 6), (quality: 7), (batterylife: 9), (price: 9)}
2	{(quality: 7), (cameraquality: 7), (batterylife: 8), (price: 7)}
3	{(shape: 3), (shape: 2)}
4	{(quality: 9), (voicequality: 9), (batterylife: 7), (price: 7)}
5	{(button: 6), (homebutton: 6), (batterylife: 8), (price: 6)}

STAGE 4: FORMING Q-SEQUENCE DATABASE

In this stage a Q-Sequence database[13] as shown in Table 9 is constructed based on the order of occurrences of features in each sentence of each review. All the features occurring in one sentence of review will have their corresponding itemsets in one sub-sequence and all such sub-sequences combine to form one sequence for each review. Sequence Utility (SU) value is calculated for each sequence as shown in Sect. 1.2. Calculate Total Sequence Utility (TSU) value at the end for the entire Sequence Database. **(TSU)** = 31 + 29 + 5 + 32 + 26 = 123

Table 9. Q-sequence database

SID	Q-sequences	SU
1	<(batterylife: 6), (quality: 7), [(batterylife: 9), (price: 9)]>	31
2	<[(quality: 7), (cameraquality: 7)], [(batterylife: 8), (price: 7)]>	29
3	<(shape: 3), (shape:2)>	5
4	<[(quality: 9),(voicequality: 9)], [(batterylife: 7), (price: 7)]>	32
5	<[(button: 6), (homebutton: 6)], (batterylife: 8), (price: 6)>	26

STAGE 5: HIGH UTILITY SEQUENTIAL PATTERN MINING

Set the minimum utility threshold with respect to TSU value of Q-Sequence database and obtain High Profit Sequential Feature Groups HPSFG, by applying the USpan Algorithm [13]. For example, min_util = 10% = 0.1 * 123 = 12.3

High Profit Feature Groups Based on High Utility Sequential Patterns: For Q-Sequence, <[(batterylife), (price)]>, the utility values of this sequence = 9 + 9 = 18 >12.3

Final Output of High Utility Sequences: <[(quality), (cameraquality)]>, <[(batterylife), (price)]>, <[(quality), (voicequality)]>

4   Experimental Evaluation

4.1   Dataset and Implementation Details

We used Amazon product data [6] for the experiments. For bifurcation, we took the reviews having rating >3 as positive and discarded the negative reviews because we are only interested in High Profit Feature Groups. The implementation is done in JAVA programming language v8 using Eclipse IDE and for USpan algorithm [13], we used open-source SPMF [11] data mining library.

Table 10. Dataset statistics

Number	Dataset	Source	Number of reviews
D1	Cellphones and accessories	Amazon	194439
D2	Musical instruments	Amazon	10261

4.2   Comparison Analysis of HPSFG_HUS System

We have compared the results obtained by the proposed HPSFG_HUS System with the existing HPFG19_HU System and baselines as mentioned in [3].

Aspect-Based Sentiment Analysis (ABSA): We analyze the utilities provided by the aspects' sentiment scores corresponding to one item's high utility patterns. This gives single feature as an output based on the sentiment score.

Frequent Itemset Mining (FIM): We analyze the utilities provided by the itemsets of frequent feature sets that appear together in the database.

One-item Frequent Itemset: We analyze the performance of frequent single features in terms of utility gain.

Extracting Feature Groups HPFG19_HU: We analyze the itemsets obtained as feature sets in terms of utility gain.

Extracting Sequential Feature Groups HPSFG_HUS (Proposed System): We analyze the sequential patterns obtained as high profit feature sets in terms of utility gain.

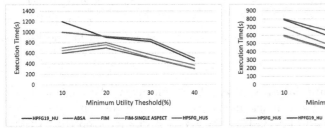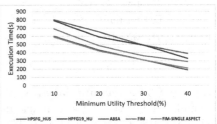

Fig. 2. Execution time v/s minimum utility threshold

Effect of Minimum Sequential Utility Threshold on Execution Time:
We evaluated the execution time of proposed HPSFG_HUS System with respect
to different values of minimum utility thresholds in comparison to the baseline
algorithms. The total number of transactions for D1 and D2 are 117894 and 8378
respectively while the total number of unique features for D1 and D2 are 411 and
461 respectively. From the graphs, it can be observed that the execution time
of proposed HPSFG_HUS system is more for both the datasets. This is because
extra work is required in forming Q-Sequences and the major performance time
is required by USpan to generate high profit sequences in comparison to the time
required for extracting the features or aspects.

Evaluation Metrics for HPSFG_HUS System: We evaluated the performance of HPSFG_HUS system on the basis of metrics shown in Table 11. The
datasets are divided in the ratio of 80:20 for training and testing, respectively.
The evaluation metrics for the baselines ABSA and FIM-Single Aspect show
significantly better results because only single features/aspects are obtained as
a result rather than High Profit Feature Groups. The HPSFG_HUS system outperforms the previous HPFG19_HU system by giving High Profit Sequences of
Features instead of High Profit Itemsets of features for all datasets.

Table 11. Evaluation results of HPSFG_HUS system

Cellphones and accessories (Metrics in %)				
Algorithms	Accuracy	Precision	Recall	F1-score
Aspect-Based Sentiment Analysis (ABSA)	79.123	78.657	74.967	76.306
Frequent Itemset Mining (FIM)	77.532	76.122	73.124	76.989
One-item Frequent Itemset	78.980	77.456	75.145	75.989
HPFG19_HU System	75.673	74.547	75.222	74.695
Proposed HPSFG_HUS System	77.672	76.129	75.489	75.807
Musical instruments (Metrics in %)				
Algorithms	Accuracy	Precision	Recall	F1-score
Aspect-Based Sentiment Analysis (ABSA)	84.563	83.123	82.784	82.345
Frequent Itemset Mining (FIM)	82.895	81.023	81.234	81.322
One-item Frequent Itemset	83.989	82.783	81.673	81.234
HPFG19_HU System	81.524	81.012	79.306	78.123
Proposed HPSFG_HUS System	83.234	81.481	80.456	80.965

Analyzing the Accumulated Utility Performances: We compared the
accumulated utilities' values under an increasing number of top patterns for
each algorithm as shown in Fig. 3. The HPSFG_HUS develops top High Utility
Sequences with the USpan method with an increasing number of accumulated

utility values in contrast to existing HPFG19_HU and other algorithms that yield itemsets of features. Since, the transaction count is the same for all reviews, the number of high utility sequences exhibits essentially identical behaviour to itemset patterns for the top 25 positive utility patterns. The top sequential patterns extracted have individual sequence features and groups of multiple sequential features that clarify the interestingness (what people have talked about the most in reviews) of feature denoting High Profit values of top feature sets in terms of sequences.

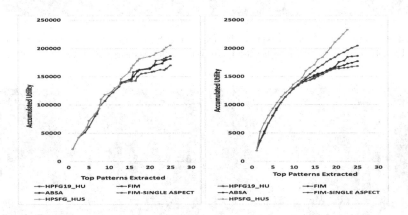

Fig. 3. Top patterns extracted with accumulated utility values

Support v/s Utility Values for Top Sequential Feature Groups: We plotted the top 15 high utility feature sequences with their support and utility values in this experiment as shown in Fig. 4 and Fig. 5. We can see from the graphs that the top patterns extracted for the existing system are itemsets of features, which are mostly single items. The sequences of features are obtained as results in the proposed system. The features will be similar, but the proposed system extracts sequential patterns of features rather than single items or numerous feature items in a single itemset. Hence, single-item top feature groups suggest that there are specific features that bring great consumer satisfaction. The feature groups with high support value but lower utility value, may indicate that they have been discussed frequently, but the expressed sentiments are either not particularly strong or inconsistent (i.e., there are both positive and negative sentiments). Feature groups with low support but high utility, have a higher potential and aren't discussed often, but carry a lot of sentiment values.

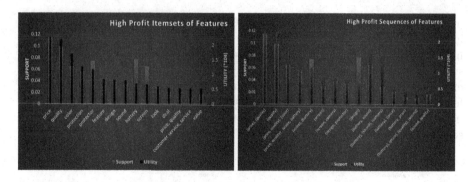

Fig. 4. Comparison of feature-sets of HPFG19_HU System [3] (left side) and proposed HPSFG_HUS System (right side) for Cellphones and Accessories dataset

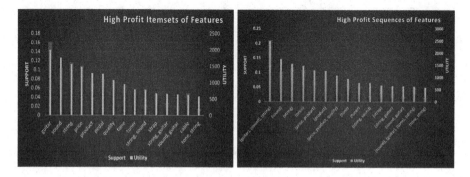

Fig. 5. Comparison of feature-sets of HPFG19_HU System [3] (left side) and proposed HPSFG_HUS System (right side) for Musical Instruments dataset

5   Conclusion and Future Work

In this paper, we presented a method for extracting High Profit Sequential Feature Groups for a given product family by combining Social Network Opinion Mining and High Utility Sequential Pattern Mining. On the same datasets, we compared the proposed HPFSG_HUS system against current system such as the HPFG19 HU system and baseline Frequent Itemset Mining techniques. We attempt to improve the existing HPFG19_HU [3] system by obtaining relevant high profit sequences and frequent features rather than high profit itemsets that act as high profit features that raise sales-profit. The number of extracted feature sets suggested is even higher. For future work, the system can be extended to cope with both positive and negative utility values, resulting in sequential feature groups having high profit and high loss values.

References

1. Aggarwal, C., Zhai, C.: Mining Text Data, 1st edn. Springer Science & Business Media, New York (2012)
2. Agrawal, R., Srikant, R.: Fast algorithms for mining association rules. In: 20th International Conference Very Large Data Bases, VLDB 1215, pp. 487–499 (1994)
3. Demir, S., Alkan, O., Cekinel, F., Karagoz, P.: Extracting potentially high profit product feature groups by using high utility pattern mining and aspect based sentiment analysis. In: Fournier-Viger, P., Lin, J.C.-W., Nkambou, R., Vo, B., Tseng, V.S. (eds.) High-Utility Pattern Mining. SBD, vol. 51, pp. 233–260. Springer, Cham (2019). https://doi.org/10.1007/978-3-030-04921-8_9
4. Ejieh, C., Ezeife, C.I., Chaturvedi, R.: Mining product opinions with most frequent clusters of aspect terms. In: 34th ACM/SIGAPP Symposium on Applied Computing, pp. 546–549. Association for Computing Machinery, New York (2019)
5. Lin, C.-W., Fournier-Viger, P., Gan, W.: FHN: an efficient algorithm for mining high-utility itemsets with negative unit profits. Knowl. Based Syst. **111**, 283–298 (2016)
6. McAuley, J.: Amazon Data (2016). https://jmcauley.ucsd.edu/data/amazon/
7. Pei, J., et al.: PrefixSpan: mining sequential patterns efficiently by prefix-projected pattern growth. In: Proceedings 2001 International Conference Data Engineering (ICDE 2001), pp. 215–224. Heidelberg (2001). Accessed 11 June 2021
8. Rana, T., Cheah, Y.: Sequential patterns rule-based approach for opinion target extraction from customer reviews. J. Inf. Sci. **45**(5), 643–655 (2019)
9. Rashid, A., Asif, S., Butt, N.A., Ashraf, I.: Feature level opinion mining of educational student feedback data using sequential pattern mining and association rule mining. Int. J. Comput. Appl. **81**(10), 31–38 (2013)
10. Sentistrength. http://sentistrength.wlv.ac.uk/. Accessed 12 Apr 2021
11. SPMF. https://www.philippe-fournier-viger.com/spmf/. Accessed 13 June 2021
12. Yao, H., Hamilton, H.J., Butz, C.J.: A foundational approach for mining itemset utilities from databases. In: SIAM International Conference on Data Mining, pp. 482–486. Orlando, FL (2004)
13. Yin, J., Zheng, Z., Cao, L.: USpan: an efficient algorithm for mining high utility sequential patterns. In: 18th ACM SIGKDD International Conference on Knowledge Discovery and Data Mining, pp. 660–668 (2012)

Game Achievement Analysis: Process Mining Approach

Martin Macak[(⊠)][iD], Lukas Daubner[iD], Julia Jamnicka, and Barbora Buhnova

Faculty of Informatics, Masaryk University, Brno, Czech Republic
{macak,daubner,jamnicka,buhnova}@mail.muni.cz

Abstract. Data-oriented techniques are currently standardly used in the video game domain, providing an interesting insight into the players' behaviour. However, the game can be seen as a set of steps that are performed for its completion. Therefore, these steps form a process. Process mining is a discipline with a focus on process analysis which can help to bring additional insights to the analysts. Hence this work explores the potential of a process-oriented approach in this context. We chose the game achievement log as the dataset as it contains valuable information about the player's steps in the game. Furthermore, it is publicly available, and therefore, anyone, not only game developers, can perform the process analysis. The dataset and the analysis source code used in this work were made publicly available.

Keywords: Process mining · Game achievements · Data analysis

1 Introduction

As the popularity of video games rises [15], so does the amount of data showing player in-game behaviour [5]. The field of game analytics focuses on analyzing said data to improve game development and design. Data mining is commonly used for game analysis; however, in contrast to traditional data-centric approaches, process mining [1] involves both data and end-to-end processes in the analysis, offering unique benefits for the analysis results [6]. As the game can be viewed as the set of steps that are performed for its completion, process mining can be an ideal candidate to provide additional insights to the analysts about the players' progression through a game. We chose the game achievement log as the dataset as it contains valuable information about the player's steps in the game. The other benefit is that this log is publicly available, and therefore, anyone, not only game developers, can perform the process analysis.

This paper explores the potential of process mining analysis in this context. Therefore it demonstrates and discusses four identified use cases in game analytics, taking a process-oriented approach and utilizing the process mining techniques. We used publicly available achievement data from the Steam platform[1].

---

[1] https://store.steampowered.com/.

© Springer Nature Switzerland AG 2022
B. Li et al. (Eds.): ADMA 2021, LNAI 13088, pp. 68–82, 2022.
https://doi.org/10.1007/978-3-030-95408-6_6

Our focus is on the typical playthrough of players, comparing player behaviour from different groups, e.g., those who finished playing the game versus those who did not or players who rated the game positively versus negatively. The work also aims to discover bottlenecks, i.e., game parts the players spent the longest time advancing through, and suggest improvement of pace and difficulty based on the result. Detection of anomalous behaviour is also a subject of this analysis.

The paper is organized as follows. Section 2 provides basic understanding of the topic. Section 3 outlines the related work. Section 4 presents the data set, classification and choice of games for analysis. Section 5 demonstrates the considered use cases. It is followed by Sect. 6 which discusses the results and suitability of various types of games for the mentioned analyses. Finally, Sect. 7 concludes the paper.

2 Background

This section provides the technical background on process mining and achievements, to build the elementary understanding needed for the rest of the paper.

2.1 Process Mining

Process mining techniques [1] aim to understand and analyze processes, providing more data interpretation perspectives. They are helping with challenging tasks in many domains, such as healthcare [11], manufacturing [13] and education [10]. In this work, they are used to extract knowledge from achievement logs to provide a better understanding of the game playing process. Moreover, all its technique types are used in this work, namely 1) *process discovery*, which aims to find a descriptive model of the underlying process from event logs, 2) *conformance checking*, which inspects whether the execution of the process conforms to the corresponding reference process model, and 3) *process enhancement*, which, in our case, extends the process model with time perspective, allowing us to inspect bottlenecks.

2.2 Achievements

Game achievements (also called trophies) form a system of rewards in video games. They operate on a layer separate from the actual game [4] and have no effect on the in-game progress of the player [12].

The purpose of the achievements is to provide extrinsic motivation to ensure greater player participation [3]. Whether they have this effect and what possible problems their use can cause have been a subject of various studies [3,4,7].

While different platforms may present achievements in a slightly different form, some components are always present. Concretely, *Title*, a unique identifier of the achievement and an *Icon*, a visual representation of the achievement. Other common features are the *Description* which usually offers hints on how the achievement can be unlocked, and *Timestamp* specifying the date and time when the player unlocked the achievement. Additionally, *Points* can be awarded to the player after the achievement is unlocked.

3   Related Work

Data mining is suited for analysis of large datasets and allows for effective analysis of game telemetry data [5]. Several studies that focus on video games, and specifically on video game achievements, use data mining techniques for analysis.

Apperly and Gandolfi [2] use Steam achievements to analyze behaviour of players in the game NieR: Automata (PlatinumGames, 2017). Dividing the game's achievements into several categories, the authors discover the percentage of players that gained the individual achievements. Their focus is therefore purely data-centric and is not interested in the game as a process.

Heeter et al. [8] use achievements (among other variables) as game metrics to measure meaningful player behaviour; the goal is to analyze differences in gameplay of two types of players, specifically the fixed-mindset and growth-mindset players. While fixed-mindset players believe that gaming skills cannot be improved and avoid hard challenges, growth-mindset players believe that their skills can be developed further precisely by challenging themselves. The study confirms that there are significant differences in the in-game behaviour of the two types of players. However, the focus of the study is exclusively on learning games, as well as purely data-centric.

Siquera et al. [18] aim to deduce World of Warcraft (Blizzard Entertainment, 2004) player profiles by using various data mining methods. The results divide players into categories according to their game behaviour, based on their time spent playing the game. Furthermore, based on the relevant game metrics, the authors are able to predict the probability of a player renewing their subscription. This study does not use achievements as game metrics.

While data mining offers many benefits in the field of game analytics, it does not consider a *process*, i.e. a sequence of activities executed in order, in its analyses, nor is the focus of data mining on improving said processes [14]. Since player behaviour can be considered to form a process, process mining can be suited to various types of game analysis.

There are few studies focused on games that use process mining. Uhlmann et al. [19] focus specifically on non-digital learning games and board games, and therefore cannot consider automatically logged achievements in the study. Ramadan et al. [16] focus on logged gaming data; however, the data was collected from a game created specifically for the study, and it did not contain achievements.

4   Data Preparation

Achievement data of a large number of players is needed for any meaningful analysis of video game achievements. One of the ways to obtain the data is through Steam, a video game platform that provides APIs for downloading data. This section provides overview of the data set, its preparation and preprocessing. We made the used dataset, including its process mining analysis, publicly available[2].

---

[2] https://github.com/lasaris/Game-Achievements-for-Process-Mining.

4.1   Steam Achievements Extraction

Steam Web API offers interfaces and methods to download data from the platform. From the Steam APIs interfaces available, we use the `ISteamUserStats`[3], containing methods for querying game statistics data, including achievements.

However, Steam Web API does not contain any method that would return a list of users that have played a particular game. A solution we found is to make a Store API[4] call to download a list of user reviews of a game, since every review contains the Steam ID of the author. As the number of reviews is large, the results are paginated and accessed by the parameter `cursor`. The method also returns other statistics, e.g., the total time the user spent playing the game, the last time the user played the game, whether the review was positive or negative, and the text of the review itself.

4.2   Conversion to Event Log

In order for the data to be usable in process mining analysis, it has to have mandatory fields for an event log. Concretely, those are *case id*, *activity* and a *timestamp*, which need to be extracted from the achievement data.

The case id identifies the case, i.e., an instance of the process, and in our data corresponds to a user's Steam ID. The individual events that belong to a particular case are identified by the activity, represented by an unlocked achievement's name. Any commas in an achievement's name are deleted since we use a comma as a separator later. Finally, since the events need to be ordered, the timestamp is included, representing the time when achievement was unlocked.

The event data are saved to a CSV file in the following format:

steam_id , achievement_name , unlock_timestamp

Additional player data are saved into a JSON file in the following format:

```
<steam id>: {
    "playtime":              <num minutes played>,
    "left_positive_review":  <left positive review>,
    "review":                <review text>,
    "collected_all":         <has all achievements>
}
```

4.3   Game Categorization

For the purposes of this study, we established three types of game categories that bear relevance to our analysis. The description of the categories are as follows:

Game Linearity. Games can be divided according to the linearity. We discern *linear games* which a clearly defined storyline that a player has to follow in a

---

[3] https://partner.steamgames.com/doc/webapi/ISteamUserStats.

[4] Details can be found at: https://partner.steamgames.com/doc/store/reviews.

given order, with little variation allowed. Another type is *slightly linear games*, which usually have a main storyline, but also allow greater freedom for players to explore (e.g., open-world games, or games where the players may follow divergent storylines). The last type, *non-linear games*, encompass all other types of games, e.g., games with no storyline or games that are played repeatedly in rounds.

This category is important to consider when attempting to discover its process model. A linear game should have a clear, concise process model with far less variation (since players must follow a clear-cut path). On the other hand, a non-linear game might produce a complex process model, which would be hard to understand, and therefore, more advanced processing of data might be needed.

Achievement Types. We divide achievements into *progress achievements* and *optional achievements*. Progress achievements are awarded for crossing a certain point in a game, usually finishing or starting a level; everyone that plays the game will be awarded these achievements so that they act as milestones of player progression. On the other hand, optional achievements are usually awarded for the completion of special tasks or side-quests, and only a certain percentage of players will be able to unlock these achievements. Therefore, the games can be divided into those that contain only progress achievements, those with only optional achievements, and that contain a combination of both.

This category is as important as the previous one. Even if a game is linear, the absence of progress achievements will make it more difficult to discover a fitting process model. Games with a combination of progress and optional achievements seem to be the most viable for analysis since the progress achievements will clearly mark levels/milestones, while the optional achievements bring enough variation to offer interesting information. The games with only progress achievements should have a simple and easily discoverable model. Although, variations are expected for the players that did not finish the game.

Rating. The rating of the game is determined by the amount of positive and negative reviews a game has received on Steam ranging from *Overwhelmingly Positive* to *Overwhelmingly Negative*. The rating is used as an indicator of popularity, which indirectly influences various factors, such as the percentage of people who finished the game or the number of reviews. Therefore it is expected that games with more positive rating should have more relevant and complete data for purposes of this study.

4.4   Selected Games

The games used in our analyses were chosen to represent different game categories. Games with a negative rating were not considered due to generally insufficient data. Within the paper, the games are referred to by labels G1–G8 specified in Table 1, which also contain their respective categories.

Table 1. Summary of selected games for the study, with their respective categorization.

	Game	Game Linearity	Achievement Types	Rating
G1	Gris (Nomada Studio, 2018)	L	P(5), O(12)	OP
G2	Hades (Supergiant Games, 2018)	SL	P(5), O(44)	OP
G3	TIS-100 (Zachtronics, 2015)	NL	O(10)	OP
G4	Per Aspera (Tlön Industries, 2020)	SL	P(5), O(27)	M
G5	Oxygen Not Included (Klei Entertainment, 2017)	NL	O(35)	OP
G6	Friday the 13th: The Game (IllFonic, 2017)	NL	O(53)	MP
G7	Witcher 3: The Wild Hunt (CD Projekt, 2015)	SL	P(8), O(70)	OP
G8	Black Mirror (King Art Games, 2017)	L	P(16), O(5)	M

L — linear, SL — slightly linear, NL — non-linear
P — progress achievements (count), O — optional achievements (count)
OP — overwhelmingly positive, MP — mostly positive, M — mixed

4.5 Data Filtering

Prior to the analysis, the event log is checked for errors caused by faulty event logging and filtered accordingly. Incorrect logging of the unlocked achievements can be caused by the Steam client, as by playing a game with Steam in offline mode can record wrong unlocking time or not logging at all. Another possibility is a bug in the game or dishonest player using a tool[5] to unlock Steam achievements without unlocking them in the game.

Within this study, three rules are considered. Cases that matches any of the rules are filtered out. However, it might be desirable to analyze these traces further. While games without progress achievements cannot be easily checked for these types of errors, they could also contain erroneous cases. A solution to this problem is suggested in Sect. 5.4. The rules are:

- Progress achievements that were unlocked out of order. Since the progress achievements mark passing a level in the game, they should be unlocked in the same specific order by every player.
- Progress achievements that were unlocked at the same time. While game can allow for multiple achievements to be unlocked at the same time, this should not be the case with progress achievements.
- Achievements with timestamp to 2008. Since achievements were introduced to Steam in 2008 [9].

5 Analysis of Game Achievements

In this section, the four use cases of process-focused game analytics utilizing process mining are demonstrated. These are of particular interest for game designers offering valuable insight into player behaviour, and should serve as an inspiration

---
[5] For example: https://github.com/gibbed/SteamAchievementManager.

for analyses in the game industry. Each analysis is performed in Python using the PM4Py[6] library.

5.1 Typical Playthrough

Typical playthrough refers to the mainstream behaviour of players in a game. *Playthrough* can be defined as the act of playing a game from start to its end. Since some games do not have a clearly defined ending point, the playthrough in this context is the act of playing a game from the first achievement unlocked to the last achievement unlocked.

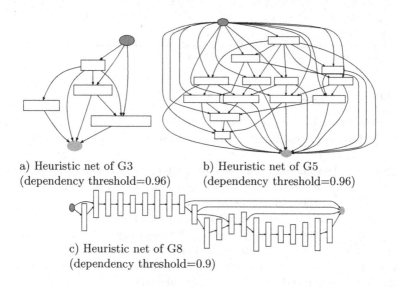

a) Heuristic net of G3
(dependency threshold=0.96)

b) Heuristic net of G5
(dependency threshold=0.96)

c) Heuristic net of G8
(dependency threshold=0.9)

Fig. 1. Process models discovered by Heuristics miner.

A selection of the discovered process models is shown in Fig. 1 (their nodes and transitions do not contain captions because of readability issues). Noticeably, the discovered process models of games G3 and G5 look vastly different from the process model of G8. As G8 is a highly linear game, the process model is straightforward and easy to understand. Interestingly, the behaviour of players as shown in the G3 model is less straightforward despite G3 being a linear game. This is caused by the absence of progress achievements, as G3 contains optional achievements exclusively. Furthermore, it is interesting to point out that even though G5 is a non-linear game, its process model does not contain any cycle, which means the achievements have some virtual ordering.

For the discovery of typical playthrough Heuristic miner was used, with dependency threshold adjusted accordingly so that the infrequent behaviour is

---

[6] https://pm4py.fit.fraunhofer.de/.

filtered out. The threshold also has to be adapted according to the linearity of a game. However, it seems setting the value at 0.96 produces a fitting process model for the majority of games. Concerning further parameters, the minimum activity count was set to 33.3% and the cleaning threshold to 0.5.

Process discovery can also help us with getting the most frequent trace variant in an event log. It can be discovered by using the variant filter and setting the percentage parameter to 0 (only the most frequent variant is kept). In the case of G1, the most frequent variant corresponds to a full playthrough of a game, which is an exception when compared to the other games. It shows that a high percentage of players (~17%) had exactly the same playthrough. On the other hand, the most common variant of G2 contains only the first progress achievement. However, since it represents only 18 players (<2%), it cannot be considered as representative behaviour. Instead, it means that the optional achievements were unlocked in a more random order that cannot be simply generalized. However, while the most common variant of G3 also contains only the first progress achievement, it actually represents the common behaviour well, since 204 of players (~30%) truly obtained only a single, trivial achievement.

5.2 Comparing Player Behaviour

Player behaviour can be compared in multiple important aspects, e.g., whether they finished the game or not, whether they have a positive or negative experience from the game, and based on the version of the game they played. In this demonstration, we show the first case.

We compare the behaviour of players who finished the game with the behaviour of players that did not because it is useful to have insight into the reasons why players quit the game before the finish. Two different event logs are prepared by including/excluding traces that do not contain the game's end achievement, and two process models are discovered on them. Additionally, the event log containing the game's end achievement was further filtered to contain only achievements gained before reaching the end of the game to exclude behaviour on replays.

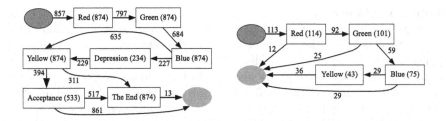

Fig. 2. Comparison of two process models of game G1, the left one showing behaviour of players that finished the game, while the model on the right shows behaviour of players that did not. Dependency threshold was set to 0.96 and cleaning threshold was set to 20% for both models. (Color figure online)

Two such process models of G1 are in Fig. 2. There are significant differences between the finished model (model of finished traces) and the unfinished model (model of unfinished traces). The first observation is before which achievements the players quit in the unfinished model. As players get further in the game, the probability that they will not finish the game rises, which is depicted by the transitions from the individual level achievements to the end node of the model. While only 12 of the 114 players quit after achieving *Red*, i.e., during the first level, the number doubles in the second level and triples by the last level. Interestingly, unlocking optional achievements was not common among the players who quit, suggesting they did not explore the game as much as players who finished playing it.

Another observation are the interplay of optional achievements. Concretely, *Depression* was commonly unlocked after *Blue*, i.e., during the third level, while *Acceptance* was unlocked as the last achievement before the end achievement, i.e., during the ultimate level. Since we discovered that 75 quitting players reached *Blue* and only 43 quitting players reached *Yellow*, it can be assumed that the low percentage of unlocked optional achievements was caused by the loss of players in the former levels.

Note that even though we filtered the events to contain only traces with the *The End* achievement and filtered out the achievements unlocked later, the process model of the finished game ends in 13 cases with *Acceptance*. It is caused by the threshold parameters of the discovery algorithm that were used, specifically in cases where there are many activities between *Acceptance* and *The End*.

5.3   Game Level Analysis

Good level design is important part of a game's success [17]. This section of the analysis focuses on discovering bottlenecks in the game, i.e., finding out which game levels took players the longest time to pass. Additionally, a correlation between level duration and the number of players that quit the game during the respective levels is explored. Since this analysis focuses on game levels, only games with progress achievements (i.e., achievements that are unlocked by passing through a certain point in the game) are suitable.

Finding Bottlenecks. For the bottleneck analysis, the models need to be enhanced with information about *performance* by an aggregate function of the elapsed time between the unlocking of two achievements. Two functions are applicable, the mean and the median. However, using the mean lengthens the duration significantly since the few players who took month-long breaks from the game skew the numbers. The median produces the more suitable level duration that corresponds closely to the actual time players spent passing the level.

Since only the level duration is relevant, the game event log can be filtered by keeping only the progress achievements. The time between two achievements in the model corresponds to the time spent in the corresponding level. For the filtered event log, a directly-follows-graph is sufficient and supported by PM4Py for performance visualization.

The chosen models are in Fig. 3, where the transitions between activities, i.e., levels' starting points, contain information about the median level duration. The activity duration does not apply since achievements contain only the time when they were unlocked. Note that the first progress achievement actually marks the start of a second level, not the first one, since none of the games contains an achievement signifying the game start. In this case, determining the duration of the first level is not possible, but for the sake of clarity, the actual second level is referred to as the first one when describing models.

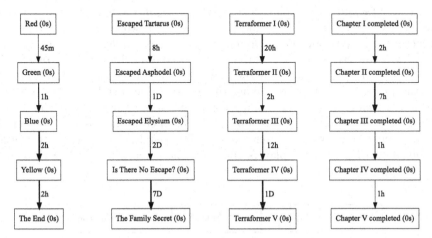

a) Perfomance model of G1   b) Perfomance model of G2   c) Perfomance model of G4   d) Perfomance model of G8

Fig. 3. Performance models showing the median level duration.

By analyzing the models, G1 shows the least amount of variation in the level duration. The first level *Red* lasting 45 min and the last level *Yellow* lasting $2 h^7$, with the last two levels being very slight bottlenecks in comparison. A clear upward trend in the level duration can be observed. The same upward trend can be seen in G2. However, the variation in the level duration is more pronounced, ranging from 8 h in the first level to the 7 days in the last level (longest duration in all games). The clear bottleneck in the game is, therefore, the level starting with the achievement *Is There No Escape?*, and to a much lesser degree, the level preceding it, with the median duration of two days.

Neither G8 nor G4 show the upward trend of the level duration. G8 contains a bottleneck in the level preceding the *Chapter III completed* achievement, with the level duration at 7 h, a major increase when compared to the other levels. The last game, G4, does not conform to the trend of the first levels' relatively short duration that can be observed in the other games. While slightly shorter than the last level, the first level can also be considered a bottleneck with a median

---

[7] At the time of writing this paper, PM4Py cannot adjust the duration accuracy.

duration of 20 h. The last level starting with the *Terraformer IV* achievement is the largest bottleneck with a 1 day duration.

Correlation with Player Statistics. If the bottlenecks correspond to the levels where most players left the game, it can signal a bad level design. Cross-checking the findings with negative reviews offers even more information about the individual game levels.

Particularly interesting is G4, which breaks the pattern of all of the other games, specifically the increase of players quitting the game at every further level. Instead, 30% and 36% of players stopped playing in the first and the last level, respectively, which is markedly more than the other two levels. This corresponds exactly to the two bottlenecks found in the process model in the first and the last level, suggesting that the players experience difficulties in these two levels.

It is further corroborated by the number of negative reviews. More than half of the players who stopped playing the game in the first level left a negative review, which is an extreme number compared to the other games. The reviews from the level mention various bugs and broken storyline, issues that seem to have been mostly fixed in later patches. The last level also seems to contain problems, although fewer players that quit the game while passing through it wrote a negative review.

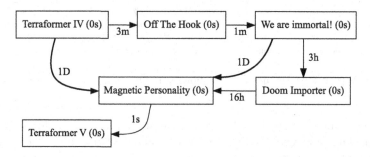

Fig. 4. Performance model of the last level of the game G4. Discovered as a directly-follows-graph with 80% of variants shown.

Focusing solely on the last level, the performance model in Fig. 4, the last bottleneck that the reviews mention corresponds to the achievement *Magnetic Personality*, which is a prerequisite of finishing the game and, based on the model, a clear bottleneck. All this points towards a problem that discouraged a significant number of players from finishing the game.

5.4   Noise Detection

Following analysis focusing on all anomalous behaviour, regardless of the cause being bugs or cheating players, makes the anomalies easier to detect. The aim is finding behaviour that does not represent the common player behaviour.

However, in cases of having the knowledge of the game and its achievements more deeply, we can use a similar technique to find behaviour that is not desired, i.e. caused by bugs or cheating. This would be done by constructing the reference process model by hand, not discovering it.

Table 2. Fitness of selected process models as discovered by the token replay algorithm.

	Fitness
Figure 1(a)	0.798
Figure 1(b)	0.782
Figure 1(c)	0.990
Figure 2 (left)	0.941
Figure 2 (right)	1

The conformance checking is utilized to find inconsistencies in the traces that might successfully filter out unwanted logged behaviour. In our case, first, the process model is discovered, using Heuristics miner algorithm, as it filters out infrequent behaviour [20]. As the token replay algorithm is utilized for conformance, the model must be a Petri net, but a heuristic net can be converted into one for this purpose. Then, the discovered Petri net and the original event log are put as an inputs to token replay algorithm, which outputs evaluation of fitness. Concretely, the values for the models in Figs. 1 and 2 are in Table 2.

To determine the accuracy of the token replay, we can compare its results with the manually found incorrect traces (described in Sect. 4.5). Ideally, we want to find a significant overlap between incorrect and unfit traces. Naturally, no such check can be done for games with no progress achievements.

Out of the total 1,002 traces, we have found 59 unfit traces through conformance checking, while 71 traces are classified as incorrect by manual filtering. Noticeably, out of the 59 unfit traces, 58 were classified as incorrect manually, leaving only one unfit trace that was not caught by the manual filtering. In the case of cheating traces, 5 out of the 6 are classified as unfit. Overall, the conformance checking discovered a large percentage (81.69%) of anomalous traces.

6   Discussion

We have shown how process mining techniques can be utilized in the context of video game analysis based on achievement data. In this setting, four use cases were shown. Table 3 shows which categories of games are appropriate for the specific use case.

The discovery of a process model that shows common player behaviour was demonstrated as not being limited by the game linearity. We have further shown that a variety of questions can be answered by examining the process model

Table 3. Appropriate types of games for specific analyses.

	Game linearity		
	Linear (P+0)	Slightly Linear (P+0)	Non-linear
Typical playthrough	✓	✓	✓
Comparing player behaviour (Un/finished)	✓	✓	✗
Game level analysis	✓	?	✗
Noise detection	✓	✓	?

with the aim of game improvement. For example, if there is a suspicion that specific activity in the game is causing problems, we can examine the activities and behaviour that players exhibited after passing it.

Furthermore, we showed usage of process mining for comparing behaviour of selected player groups. Concretely, players who did and did not finish a game. While this specific comparison is possible only for games with progress achievements, there is virtually no limitation on the type of players that can be compared. For example, players who have written a positive/negative review, players who did and did not unlock a particular achievement in the game, players who spent more/less time playing than a specified time limit. However, if the process model needs to contain all of the behaviour found in the event log, the dependency threshold should be set to −1.

Conformance checking, specifically token replay, was used to verify the appropriate fitness of the discovered process models. We applied token replay to both the linear and non-linear games. While the approach was sufficiently accurate for the linear games, there is not enough information about the non-linear games to determine the accuracy of the approach, mandating further research.

Lastly, we have shown that suggestion to level design can be based on the bottleneck analysis when the additional player statistics are also considered. The analysis is also limited to games that contain progress achievements.

7   Conclusion

This paper presented four use cases for process-focused game analytics, based on game achievement data. Within this setting, the usability of process mining techniques was demonstrated as a viable way to get much-needed insight for game design and beyond. Moreover, we categorized the games and showed their influence on the applicability of process mining.

All analyses were performed with a particular use case in mind, which we believe will ease possible adoption in the game industry. Specifically, player behaviour was observed in the process models, together with the demonstration of the possibility to compare between players groups. Furthermore, aiming at the purpose to improve level design, bottleneck analysis was performed, with the possibility of in-depth analysis. Taking the results into account, cross-check with other player statistics was recommended. Lastly, conformance checking was utilized to discover faulty traces in an event log to identify bugs or cheating players. In summary, the applicability and utility of process mining in game design were clearly illustrated.

References

1. van der Aalst, W.: Process Mining: Data Science in Action, 2nd edn. Springer, Heidelberg (2016). https://doi.org/10.1007/978-3-662-49851-4
2. Apperley, T., Gandolfi, E.: Evaluating gamer achievements to understand player behavior. In: Data Analytics Applications in Gaming and Entertainment (2019)
3. Baek, Y., Touati, A.: Exploring how individual traits influence enjoyment in a mobile learning game. Comput. Hum. Behav. **69**, 347–357 (2017)
4. Cruz, C., Hanus, M.D., Fox, J.: The need to achieve: players' perceptions and uses of extrinsic meta-game reward systems for video game consoles. Comput. Hum. Behav. **71**, 516–524 (2017)
5. El-Nasr, M., Drachen, A., Canossa, A.: Game Analytics: Maximizing the Value of Player Data. Springer, London (2016). https://doi.org/10.1007/978-1-4471-4769-5
6. Ghasemi, M., Amyot, D.: From event logs to goals: a systematic literature review of goal-oriented process mining. Requirements Eng. **25**(1), 67–93 (2019). https://doi.org/10.1007/s00766-018-00308-3
7. Groening, C., Binnewies, C.: "Achievement unlocked!" - the impact of digital achievements as a gamification element on motivation and performance. Comput. Hum. Behav. **97**, 151–166 (2019)
8. Heeter, C., Lee, Y.H., Medler, B., Magerko, B.: Conceptually meaningful metrics: inferring optimal challenge and mindset from gameplay, p. 36, March 2013
9. Jakobsson, M.: Achievement anatomy. In: Debugging Game History: A Critical Lexicon, p. 1 (2016)
10. Macak, M., Kruzelova, D., Chren, S., Buhnova, B.: Using process mining for git log analysis of projects in a software development course. Educ. Inf. Technol. **26**, 1–31 (2021)
11. Mans, R.S., Van der Aalst, W.M., Vanwersch, R.J.: Process Mining in Healthcare: Evaluating and Exploiting Operational Healthcare Processes. Springer, Cham (2015). https://doi.org/10.1007/978-3-319-16071-9
12. Montola, M., Stenros, J., Waern, A.: Pervasive Games: Theory and Design. CRC Press, Boca Raton (2009)
13. Myers, D., Suriadi, S., Radke, K., Foo, E.: Anomaly detection for industrial control systems using process mining. Comput. Secur. **78**, 103–125 (2018)
14. Nikitina, K.: Educational game analysis using intention and process mining. Master's thesis, National Research University Higher School of Economics (2020)
15. Prot, S., McDonald, K.A., Anderson, C.A., Gentile, D.A.: Video games: good, bad, or other? Pediatr. Clin. **59**, 647–658 (2012)
16. Ramadan, S., Ibrahim Baqapuri, H., Roecher, E., Mathiak, K.: Process mining of logged gaming behavior. In: 2019 International Conference on Process Mining (ICPM), pp. 57–64 (2019)
17. Shaker, N., Yannakakis, G.N., Togelius, J.: Digging deeper into platform game level design: session size and sequential features. In: Di Chio, C., et al. (eds.) EvoApplications 2012. LNCS, vol. 7248, pp. 275–284. Springer, Heidelberg (2012). https://doi.org/10.1007/978-3-642-29178-4_28

18. Siqueira, E., Castanho, C., Rodrigues, G., Jacobi, R.: A data analysis of player in world of warcraft using game data mining. In: 2017 16th Brazilian Symposium on Computer Games and Digital Entertainment (SBGames), pp. 1–9, November 2017
19. Schaedler Uhlmann, T., Alves Portela Santos, E., Mendes, L.A.: Process mining applied to player interaction and decision taking analysis in educational remote games. In: Auer, M.E., Langmann, R. (eds.) REV 2018. LNNS, vol. 47, pp. 425–434. Springer, Cham (2019). https://doi.org/10.1007/978-3-319-95678-7_47
20. Weijters, A., van der Aalst, W.M., De Medeiros, A.A.: Process mining with the heuristics miner-algorithm. Technische Universiteit Eindhoven, Technical report WP 166, pp. 1–34 (2006)

A Fast and Accurate Approach for Inferencing Social Relationships Among IoT Objects

Abdulwahab Aljubairy[1,2(✉)], Ahoud Alhazmi[1,2], Wei Emma Zhang[3],
Quan Z. Sheng[1,2], and Dai Hoang Tran[1,2]

[1] Macquarie University, Sydney, NSW 2109, Australia
{abdulwahab.aljubairy,ahoud.alhazmi,dai-hoang.tran}@hdr.mq.edu.au,
michael.sheng@mq.edu.au
[2] Intelligent Computing Laboratory (ICL) Lab, Macquarie University,
Sydney, Australia
[3] The University of Adelaide, Adelaide, SA 5005, Australia
wei.e.zhang@adelaide.edu.au

Abstract. The Internet of Things (IoT) has recently moved towards the "object-object" interaction model where things look for other things to provide composite services for the benefit of human beings, leading to the birth of the Social Internet of Things (SIoT) paradigm. Investigating the social dimension in IoT objects offers great opportunities to increase social awareness among IoT objects. To achieve this goal, recurrent spatio-temporal meetings among IoT objects could be exploited to enable smart objects to understand the co-presence with other smart objects. Therefore, we target to explore the social dimension by determining if any two IoT objects have met at a particular place for a period of time. In this paper, we develop a novel approach, named Social Relationships Inference (*SociRence*), based on computational geometry to calculate the co-presence among IoT objects efficiently. We conduct experimental studies on real-world SIoT datasets to evaluate the efficacy of our approach. The results demonstrate that our approach can calculate the spatio-temporal co-presence at a much higher speed than the baseline computation methods.

Keywords: Social Internet of Things · Social structure · Social relationships · Social awareness

1 Introduction

The Internet of Things (IoT) has become a critical component in a variety of daily living scenarios. The massive amounts of data streaming through IoT sensors have accelerated the development of new applications in a variety of fields, including industrial plant management, logistics, and transportation supply chains, e-health, and smart buildings [4]. This paradigm has eased the development of IoT applications by bringing together the diverse services provided by

© Springer Nature Switzerland AG 2022
B. Li et al. (Eds.): ADMA 2021, LNAI 13088, pp. 83–94, 2022.
https://doi.org/10.1007/978-3-030-95408-6_7

these smart objects [7–9]. The IoT paradigm, on the other hand, is predicted to be overpopulated by a large number of objects, with intense interactions, heterogeneous connections, and millions of services [1,8]. As a result, several challenges concerning service discovery, availability, and scalability would arise.

The Social Internet of Things (SIoT) is a recently proposed paradigm that aims to integrate the social dimension into IoT objects along with connectivity and sensing capabilities [2]. The objective of this paradigm is to boost the discovery, selection and composition of services, and ensure the information provided by objects in a distributed manner. Moreover, it can enhance resource availability, objects' reputations assessment, and exchanging experience [1,4]. In addition, SIoT enables IoT objects to establish new acquaintances and expand their social circle, collaborate to achieve common goals, and exploit other objects' capabilities. SIoT also aims to help steer the interaction among the billions of objects which will crowd the future Internet. Within a given social network of objects, these objects can publish information/services, find and discover novel resources to better implement services. This can be achieved by navigating a social network of "friend" objects [2].

The main perception of the SIoT paradigm is to establish and boost social awareness among IoT objects and exploit this awareness as a means to turn communicating objects into autonomous decision-making entities [1,4]. The new social dimension is supposed to enable IoT objects to create relationships with other peer objects. Hence, they can establish social structure and utilize each other's capabilities. Therefore, establishing a social structure among IoT objects is the cornerstone of the SIoT paradigm. Thus, building this structure will definitely increase the social awareness of the objects. To achieve the establishment of the social structure among objects, a set of relationships should be created among IoT objects. In the literature, several studies proposed various types of static and dynamic relationships [2,4,5]. Atzori et al. [2] discussed that IoT objects can be able to establish relationships based on social interaction. They define the social interaction as objects that may come into contact sporadically or continuously. In other words, objects could be in close proximity on several occasions. They labelled this type of relationship as social object relationship (SOR). Such a relationship is essential relationship since it is dynamically created among objects. The creation of the social structure in the SIoT context is largely based on simulation tools [1,4], and most studies investigated other aspects of the SIoT have relied on these tools. Therefore, there is a need to develop an approach that can establish the social structure among objects using real data generated from the objects.

This paper addresses the following research question "how IoT objects could create a social relationship with each other when they have been approximately on the same geographical location at the same time on multiple occasions?" Benefiting from the computational geometry algorithms, Sweep Line is a key technique in computational geometry and is widely applied to design geometric algorithms in Euclidean space [3]. This technique can be used to enhance performance and reduce the computation time when solving a variety of different problems. Thus, we propose to develop a novel mechanism to identify co-occurrence in time and space among IoT objects. Since there is a large number of IoT objects, computing these meetings becomes very complex. Consequently, our approach should be efficient in dealing with large-scale interactions.

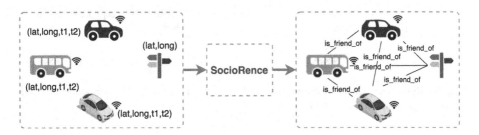

Fig. 1. Inferring relationships among IoT objects using spatio-temporal co-occurrences.

We propose **Soci**al **R**elationships Infer**ence** (*SociRence*) algorithm based on the sweep line technique. The idea of *SociRence* is to calculate the number of co-occurrence among IoT objects based on geographic coincidences. The core idea is to use a conceptual sweep line (often a vertical line as shown in Fig. 2), which is moved across the plane, stopping at some points. Figure 1 shows several objects that stayed at a particular place for some time. These objects are not aware of each other. *SociRence* mines their stay data to infer friendship relationships among them. In the future, these objects could utilize their friendships in order to share their experiences and exchange information of interests.

This paper makes several noteworthy contributions to the effectiveness of our approach, which can establish social structure among IoT objects using spatio-temporal co-presence. We implement SociRence, a novel sweep line-based algorithm that can efficiently address the introduced problem. SociRence is fast, adaptable, viable, and stable. We also conduct comprehensive experiments using SIoT real-world datasets to demonstrate the efficiency of our approach.

2   Problem Formulation and Basic Definitions

In this section, we first formally define some basic notions used in this paper. Then, we formulate the problem at hand.

2.1   Basic Definitions

– **Definition 1 (Stay):** Let $\mathcal{O}$ denotes a set of unique IoT object identifiers, $\mathcal{L}$ denotes a set of locations where IoT objects stayed at (each location is represented by $(long, lat)$), $\mathcal{T}$ denotes the time interval IoT objects stayed at that location (each time interval is represented as (t_s, t_e) where t_s is the start time and t_e is the end time of the stay). So, a **stay** can be represented as a triple $(o, l, t) \in \mathcal{O} \times \mathcal{L} \times \mathcal{T}$ which indicates the IoT object o has stayed at location l for some time t. Figure 2 shows an example of a stay.

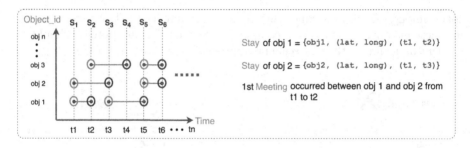

Fig. 2. Illustrating the definitions. Red and green circles indicate the start and the end of the stays, respectively. (Color figure online)

– **Definition 2 (Meeting):** A meeting represents a social interaction that occurs between any two IoT objects. So, a meeting can occur if and only if there is an overlap between the stay intervals of intended IoT objects when they are in close proximity. Figure 2 shows an example of a meeting.

$$\texttt{Meeting(a, b)} = \begin{cases} 1, & \text{if } distance(a,b) \leq \tau \ \& \ \max(ts_a, ts_b) < \min(ts_a, ts_b) \\ 0, & otherwise \end{cases}$$

– **Definition 3 (Social Object Relationship (SOR)):** It is a relationship that can be established between any two IoT objects they reach a particular threshold of *meetings*.

$$\texttt{SOR(a, b)} = \begin{cases} 1, & \text{if } \texttt{Meeting(a, b)} \geq X \text{ times} \\ 0, & otherwise \end{cases}$$

– **Definition 4 (Social Structure).** It is an undirected graph denoted as $\mathcal{G} = (\mathcal{V}, \mathcal{E})$ where $\mathcal{V}$ represents the set of IoT objects in the graph and $\mathcal{E}$ represents the set of *SOR* among IoT objects. Each *SOR* represents social relationship that created between any two IoT objects.

2.2 Problem Statement

Suppose that there is a set of IoT objects $\mathcal{O} = \{o_1, ..., o_n\}$. Some of these objects are mobile and can visit several places. As IoT objects can be able continuously to move, there is a high chance they can meet other IoT objects (sometimes they can meet other static IoT objects where their locations are stationary).

Our hypothesis is that some of these objects could be at the same location for a period of time. Therefore, let $\mathcal{S}$ be a collection of stays (Definition 1) and $o_i \in \mathcal{O}$ an IoT object, then the set $S_{o_i} := (o, l, t) \in \mathcal{S}$ is the set of stays of IoT object o_i. Given a set of stays $\mathcal{S} = \{S_{o_1}, ..., S_{o_n}\}$ of IoT objects where S_{o_n} set of stays for object n, the goal is to determine if there are some meetings (Definition 1) that occurred among IoT objects using their set of stays. Based on the meeting occurring among IoT objects, the social structure (Definition 4) is established according to the *SOR* relationship (Definition 3).

3   *SociRence*: The Proposed Approach

A straightforward way to determine the *meetings* that occurred among IoT objects is to employ a naive technique for comparing every stay in S with every other. This iterative process continues until the end of the set of stays S. As can be seen, the computational cost of such a method increases exponentially with the number of stays in S. The computational cost is $O(n^2)$.

One way to overcome the high cost of computation is to devise an approach that efficiently avoids unnecessary comparison among stays, specifically, stays of objects that do not overlap. For that, we develop a novel approach called *SociRence* that is based on the sweep line technique. The goal is to determine if there are meetings (Definition 2) occurred among IoT objects. The core idea is to move a conceptual vertical line to sweep (i.e., scan) stays (Definition 1) from left to right. During the scanning process of the stays, *SociRence* determines if IoT objects have met. In other words, *SociRence* capture and report meetings occurred among IoT objects using their stay information. Figure 2 depicts the idea of how the sweep line scanning all stays from left to right. Later, we explain the whole process in detail with giving vivid examples.

There are two types of events that happen while the imaginary line scans the stays. The events that *SociRence* needs to deal with which are the *start event* and the *end event*. Hence, *SociRence* employs a data structure to maintain the status of the sweep line while scanning. The *start event* is when the sweep line (dotted line) hits the start of a stay (red color circles), and the *end event* is when the sweep line hits the end of a stay (green color circles) as shown in Fig. 2. At each type of event, the status of the sweep line changes. If the event type is a *start*, then insertion operation is invoked. That means the endpoint of that stay is added to the status data structure of the sweep line. If the event type is an *end*, then two types of operations are invoked. First, meeting checking is conducted to determine if there are some meetings that occurred. Second, deletion operation is invoked for that stay. That means the sweep line is finished from scanning the stay, so it deletes the corresponding start endpoint of that stay.

Algorithm 1 describes our approach in further details. The input of this algorithm is a set of stays S of IoT objects. The output is a list of identified meetings that occurred among IoT objects. In this algorithm, there are two main steps. In the first step, *SociRence* employs two data structures to store all the required information of the stays and to keep track of the sweep line status while moving to scan the stays (line 2–3). Thus, a priority queue Q is used to store endpoints of the set of stays S in sorting order. Since each endpoint represents an event, each stay consists of two events (start and end) as discussed previously. We store each stay record twice to represent the start and the end of the stay (*i.e.*, [ts, status=``start'', (ts, te), object_id]) and [te, status=``end'', (ts, te), object_id]) where ts and te are the start and end time of the stay respectively, status refers to status record if it is start points or endpoints, (ts, te) is the interval of the stay, and object_id. Second, an empty list *Sweepline_Status* is used for maintaining the status of the sweep line when scanning the stays from left to right.

Algorithm 1: SociRence

    Input : $S = \{s_1, s_2, ..., s_n\}$
    Output: $Meetings = \{m_1, m_2, \ldots, m_n\}$
1 **begin**
2   Let **Q** be a priority queue to store stays' events together with other metadata of stays.
3   Let **Sweepline_Status** an empty list to maintain the sweep line status.
4   **while** *(Q is not empty)* **do**
5   currentEvent ← pull element from **Q**
6   **if** *(currentEvent is a start)* **then**
7 | Sweepline_Status.insert(currentEvent)
8   **else**
9   Meetings.insert(Check_Meetings(Sweepline_Status, currentEvent))
10   Sweepline_Status.remove(currentEvent)

11   **return** Meetings = $\{m_1, m_2, \ldots, m_n\}$

The second step runs the sweep line (line 4–11) to scan the stays and handle the two possible events as mentioned above. As the imaginary sweep line moves and stops at each endpoint, this is represented by getting the stays' endpoints from Q one by one. When the sweep line detects the start of the stay, it adds it to the *Sweepline_Status*. Also, when it detects the end of the stay (in this case, the sweep line finished from scanning the stay), it checks for potential meetings with the endpoints in *Sweepline_Status*. If it is the start of this stay, then the algorithm removes the stay from *Sweepline_Status* with no action. If the last element in *Sweepline_Status* is not the start of the finished stay, then an overlap or more have been detected between this stay and other active stays in the *Sweepline_Status*.

We present a visual illustration to clarify the entire process of our method. Figure 3 depicts a more in-depth illustration of how our *SociRence* technique is implemented. It depicts how object stay intervals are displayed, with the x-axis representing the timestamp and the y-axis representing the object ids. This figure illustrates six stays for objects obj_1, obj_2 and obj_3. Because each stay consists of two endpoints (events), *SociRence* stores these 12 events in a priority queue data structure as points sorted according to the x-axis. Along with the endpoint, *SociRence* stores metadata about the stays, such as the object id and whether the endpoint is the start or end of the stay. Figure 3(a) illustrates how the sweep line scans intervals from left to right. Because the first event detection happened at time t_1, the sweep line status will include the events that were detected because they indicate the beginning of the two remaining stays. Figure 3(b) indicates that the second event detection occurred at time t_2, and hence an overlap check is undertaken, as the detected event signifies the end of obj_1's stay. After that, the stay of that event is then removed from the sweep line status. Simultaneously, the sweep line status will put the detected event of obj_3's stay into its status because it signals the start of the stay. Finally, Fig. 3(c) explains the *ith* detection occurred at time t_6,

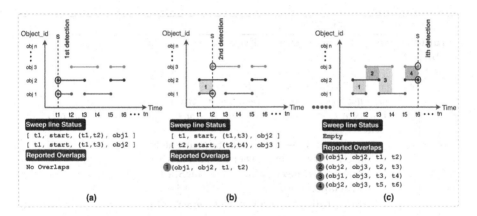

Fig. 3. Depicting the idea of *SociRence* algorithm.

and because these two points indicate the end of the two stays, an overlap check is performed for each stay. Then, the stays associated with these two endpoints are removed from the sweep line's status, and so on. As may be seen, multiple instances of overlap have happened and have been reported. Additionally, this figure illustrates how the sweep line's status changes while the intervals of stays are scanned from left to right.

Algorithm 2 checks for the possible meetings occurred among IoT objects. This algorithm is invoked when the sweep line hits the event of type end. In this case, the sweep line finished from scanning the stay, but before removing the stay from its status, it checks for possible meetings occurred. Hence, it calculates distance (d) between two IoT objects using Eq. (1), where r is given and represents the radius of the sphere (earth), θ_1, θ_2 are the latitude of the stays records of IoT objects, λ_1, λ_2 are longitude of the stays records of IoT objects.

$$d = 2r.sin^{-1}\left(\sqrt{sin^2(\frac{(\theta_2 - \theta_1)}{2}) + cos(\theta_1).cos(\theta_2).sin^2(\frac{(\lambda_2 - \lambda_1)}{2})}\right) \quad (1)$$

If the distance is less than a threshold τ, it starts to compute the meeting duration, and then it returns the results to Algorithm 1. There are $2n + k$ events where $2n$ is the number of endpoints of n stays and k is the number of meetings identified, so the overall time complexity is $O((n + k)logn)$.

4   Experiments

We evaluated the effectiveness and efficiency of our approach based on comprehensive experiments. The experiment was conducted using Python language that runs on a Mac mini with a 6-Core Intel Core i7 3.2 GHz, 64 GB RAM and macOS Big Sur version (11.4). This section introduces the settings of our experiments, including the SIoT datasets employed and baselines. Then, it discusses the performance evaluation and the effect of distance and duration parameters.

Algorithm 2: Check_Meetings

Input   : Sweepline_Status, current_Event
Output: Overlaps

1 **begin**
2   **for** *(event in Sweepline_Status)* **do**
3   **if** *(distance(event, current_Event)* $\leq \tau$*)* **then**
4   **if** *(event.ts < current_Event.te)* & *(current_Event.ts < event.te)* **then**
5   meetingStart ← max(event.ts , current_Event.ts)
6   meetingEnd ← min(event.te, current_Event.te)
7   Duration ← meetingEnd - meetingStart
8   **Overlaps**.insert(`current_Event.objID, event.objID,`
        `meetingStart, meetingEnd, Duration`)

9   **return** Overlaps

4.1 Datasets Description

We used the SIoT datasets [4], which are based on real IoT objects available in the city of Santander, Spain. They include stay data of public and private IoT objects. The total number of IoT objects is 16,216 where 14,600 objects are owned by private users and 1,616 are owned by the city. The public mobile dataset contains 150 mobile devices and has 125,020 stays records. The private mobile dataset contains stay data of 8,520 devices and has around 290,705 stays records. Each device is described as (`id, lat, long, timestamp_start, timestamp_stop`). We also used public and private static devices. The private and public static devices datasets contain 6,080 and 1,466 stationary objects respectively. These datasets show the geographical locations of the devices, and each device is described as (`id, lat, long`). We performed preprocessing on the datasets to ensure that the records contained correct data. We discovered that some records in the mobile objects datasets (public and private) reveal that the timestamp_end of the stay is less than the timestamp_start of the stay, and this is not reasonable. We could have treated them as outliers and subsequently deleted them, but we chose to flip the values to benefit from these records.

4.2 Baselines

To assess the efficacy of the *SociRence* algorithm, we compare its performance against baselines. We built three algorithms using three powerful techniques to serve as baselines. The first algorithm, **BrutForce**, uses brute force, which is a common problem-solving method that compares each stay record sequentially to all others. The second algorithm, **Div&Conqr**, is based on the divide and conquer strategy. To make this strategy works, the list of stays must first be arranged by the start timings of each stay. The third algorithm, **Greedy**, uses the greedy approach. A greedy strategy selects the locally optimal decision at each stage. In our case, the best local method is to compare the following stay if the start time is earlier than the finish time.

4.3   Performance Evaluation

Because of the magnitude and dynamics of the IoT objects, the overall performance of the technique is critical. We compared *SociRence*'s running time performance to that of the (*Brutforce*, *Div&Conqr*, and *Greedy*). Figures 4(a) and 4(d) compare *SociRence*'s performance against that of *Brutforce*. As these figures show, *SociRence* outperforms *Brutforce* significantly. What stands out in these two figures is the steady performance of the *SociRence*. In contrast, the computational cost of the *Brutforce* exponentially increased since it conducted unnecessary computations. For example, when the number of stays reached 80,000, *Brutforce* took over 150 min (2+ h) to complete, whereas our approach only took 6.3 s. In addition, we compared *SociRence* with *Div&Conqr* and *Greedy*. We used two different scenarios to demonstrate the effectiveness of our strategy. The first scenario would be to have a list of stays already sorted ascending by start time. Therefore, there is no need to sort the data, and this is the best-case scenario for comparing *SociRence* to *Div&Conqr* and *Greedy*. Figures 4(b) and 4(e) illustrate our method's performance versus these baselines for public and private datasets, respectively. Although the running times of all three approaches are comparable, *SociRence* runs faster than any of these two methods. The second scenario would

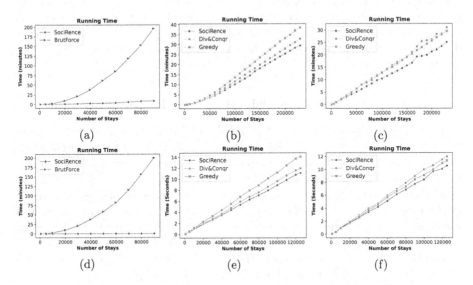

Fig. 4. The performance of *SociRence* in comparison to established approaches for private and public objects datasets. (a) and (d) depict *SociRence*'s performance against *BrutForce*. (b) and (e) demonstrate *SociRence*'s performance against *Div&Conqr* and *Greedy* according to Scenario 1. (c) and (f) illustrate *SociRence*'s performance against *Div&Conqr* and *Greedy* according to Scenario 2.

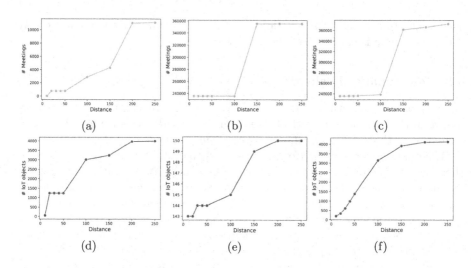

Fig. 5. The effect of the "distance" on the number of meetings (first row) and participated IoT objects (second row) for all datasets private, public, and both, respectively.

be to have an unsorted list of stays. As a result, sorting the data is required, and this is the worst-case scenario when comparing *SociRence* to *Div&Conqr* and *Greedy*. As illustrated in Figs. 4(c) and 4(f), *SociRence* continues to exceed the baselines. The results revealed that *SociRence*'s performance is consistent and stable regardless of whether the stays are sorted or not. In comparison, the other two approaches exhibit inconsistent performance because they require the datasets to be sorted and increase the computation cost while *SociRence* does not require that.

4.4 Effect of "distance" and "duration" on the Social Structure

We investigated the influences of "distance" and "duration" on the social structure establishment among IoT objects to show how to affect social interactions (meetings) and thus the social structure. Our findings indicated that when distance increases, the number of IoT objects interacting with each other increases as well, and accordingly, the number of meetings increases. In this setting, "duration" is not considered, so whenever, any IoT object meets another peer, it is considered as a social interaction as shown in Fig. 5. For example, in the public dataset, there are around 220,000 meetings that occurred among 144 IoT objects when the distance was 50 m, while there are 360,000 meetings that occurred among 149 objects in 150 m as shown in Figs. 5(b) and 5(e).

After exploring how increasing the distance allows more IoT objects to interact, we added the "duration" parameter. Our findings indicated that when the duration increases, the number of social interactions decreases, as shown in Fig. 6. For example, when the meeting duration was 30 min in a distance of 250 m, less than 2,000 meetings occurred among 16,216 objects using both datasets.

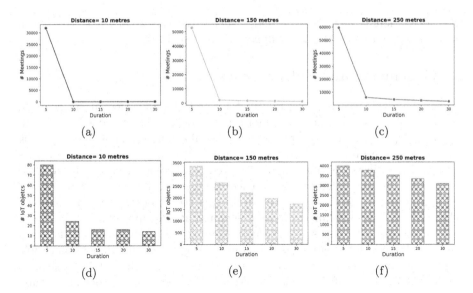

Fig. 6. The effect of the "distance" and "duration" on the resulted meeting numbers (first row) and the number of participated IoT objects (second row) for both datasets.

However, when the duration was decreased to 5 min, there are around 60,000 meetings occurred, as shown in Fig. 6(c).

5 Related Works

The current SIoT research focuses on identifying policies and strategies for forming relationships between smart devices autonomously and without human intervention. This structure can help with network navigation, service discovery, and trust management [2]. Social structure can be established between IoT objects by creating relationships of various types between objects in the network. The social relationship is one of the most crucial relationships in constructing a dynamically built social structure that follows specified rules. However, little work has been done in this vital direction. Consequently, the lack of considering social interactions among IoT objects has inevitably constrained the capacity to construct a social structure under this paradigm. A closer look at the literature reveals some gaps and deficiencies in SIoT-related literature when it comes to mechanisms for developing social structure. Currently, the majority of what we know about establishing a social structure among IoT objects in the context of the SIoT is derived from simulation tools [1]. We, therefore, need to create an efficient algorithm that can build this type of structure. Some studies proposed methods to discover implicit correlations among IoT objects via exploiting their owners' relationships [9,10] or via their fixed locations [6]. However, our work differs from two angles. First, a rapid and accurate method using the sweep line technique is used to determine the social relationships among IoT objects, whether stationary or mobile. Second, a social structure among IoT objects can then be built based on the social dimension idea as in [2].

6   Conclusion and Future Work

One of the overlooked issues in the SIoT is the lack of an adequate mechanism for establishing social structure among IoT objects. We examined and studied the unique and challenging problem of establishing social structure among IoT objects. We propose a novel approach for determining social relationships between IoT objects based on their Spatio-temporal co-occurrences. Our method Social Relationships Inference *(SociRence)* is based on the sweep line technique. Using stay data of IoT objects, this technique tries to determine latent social relationships. The experimental results demonstrate the approach's effectiveness and robustness. Building social structure among IoT objects is a crucial challenge, and it is the first step towards consolidating the social dimension in IoT objects. In future works, we will investigate and analyze how it is possible to predict the evolution of this social structure, given the observed social structure.

References

1. Atzori, L., Iera, A., Morabito, G.: From "smart objects" to "social objects": the next evolutionary step of the internet of things. IEEE Commun. Mag. **52**(1), 97–105 (2014)
2. Atzori, L., Iera, A., Morabito, G., Nitti, M.: The Social Internet of Things (SIoT) - when social networks meet the Internet of Things: concept, architecture and network characterization. Comput. Netw. **56**(16), 3594–3608 (2012)
3. Bentley, J.L., Ottmann, T.A.: Algorithms for reporting and counting geometric intersections. IEEE Trans. Comput. **9**, 643–647 (1979)
4. Marche, C., Atzori, L., Pilloni, V., Nitti, M.: How to exploit the social internet of things: query generation model and device profiles' dataset. Comput. Netw. **174**, 1–13 (2020)
5. Roopa, M., Pattar, S., Buyya, R., Venugopal, K.R., Iyengar, S., Patnaik, L.: Social Internet of Things (SIoT): foundations, thrust areas, systematic review and future directions. Comput. Commun. **139**(1), 32–57 (2019)
6. Shemshadi, A., Sheng, Q.Z., Qin, Y., Alzubaidi, A.: CEIoT: a framework for interlinking smart things in the internet of things. In: Li, J., Li, X., Wang, S., Li, J., Sheng, Q.Z. (eds.) ADMA 2016. LNCS (LNAI), vol. 10086, pp. 203–218. Springer, Cham (2016). https://doi.org/10.1007/978-3-319-49586-6_14
7. Tran, N.K., Sheng, Q.Z., Babar, M.A., Yao, L.: Searching the web of things: state of the art, challenges, and solutions. ACM Comput. Surv. **50**(4), 55 (2017)
8. Tran, N.K., Sheng, Q.Z., Babar, M.A., Yao, L., Zhang, W.E., Dustdar, S.: Internet of things search engine. Commun. ACM **62**(7), 66–73 (2019)
9. Yao, L., Sheng, Q.Z., Ngu, A.H., Gao, B.: Keeping you in the loop: enabling web-based things management in the internet of things. In: Proceedings of the Conference on Information and Knowledge Management (CIKM), pp. 2027–2029 (2014)
10. Yao, L., Sheng, Q.Z., Ngu, A.H., Li, X.: Things of interest recommendation by leveraging heterogeneous relations in the internet of things. ACM Trans. Internet Technol. (TOIT) **16**(2), 9 (2016)

Graph Mining

A Local Seeding Algorithm for Community Detection in Dynamic Networks

Yanmei Hu[✉], Yingxi Zhang, Xiabing Wang, Jing Wu, and Bin Duo

Chengdu University of Technology, Chengdu, China
huyanmei@cdut.edu.cn

Abstract. Discovering communities by seed expansion is a good alternative in large networks as well as dynamic networks, since it only requires exploring the local view of the seeds to uncover communities, rather than the entire network. However, the effectiveness of seed expansion usually depends on the position of the seed. Thus, seeding is necessary to community detection using seed expansion. In this paper, we focus on local seeding because of its efficiency. We first propose three hybrid local centrality measurements to evaluate how good a node is as a seed, and then apply them to a fast local seeding algorithm to select seeds in static networks. Further, based on the static local seeding, we propose a dynamic local seeding algorithm to handle dynamic networks by only considering the nodes that are involved by network change. Experiments on static networks show that the proposed hybrid local centralities have superiority to the existing local centralities and experiments on dynamic networks show that the proposed dynamic local seeding algorithm is very fast.

Keywords: Seeding · Community detection · Dynamic networks

1 Introduction

Community detection is an important task in network analysis, and there have been a large number of work on it [4, 5]. However, with the increase of network data, community detection is challenging since the network as well as the community structure are more and more complicated. Under this scenario, discovering communities from the local view of nodes is a good approach, which only requires local information of nodes, rather than the entire network, and is also suitable for the case where the network is partially accessible. Moreover, many networks always evolve with time, which probably results in the evolution of community structure. Designing dynamic algorithms of community detection from the local view of nodes is also more feasible, since the network usually does not dramatically evolve in a short time period and the community structure may be partially changed at two consecutive timesteps [13, 18]. Local view method can update the communities in the part where network changes, rather than detecting communities from scratch.

Several approaches based on the local view of nodes have been witnessed to community detection. For example, the label propagation algorithm [17] and seed expansion

© Springer Nature Switzerland AG 2022
B. Li et al. (Eds.): ADMA 2021, LNAI 13088, pp. 97–112, 2022.
https://doi.org/10.1007/978-3-030-95408-6_8

(also known as local community detection) [1, 3, 23]. The former one initially assigns each node a unique label and then updates each node's label as the most one among its neighbors. After several iterations, the nodes in one community almost have the same label and the communities are uncovered. The latter one usually starts from a node, which is usually called seed, and expands the community by adding nodes in turn. Each added node is from the neighborhood of nodes in the community and must increase the community quality which is evaluated by a specified score function [23]. The technique of approximate personalized PageRank is also applied to seed expansion, which first performs a truncated random walk starting from the seed, and then obtains the community by a sweep over the nodes visited by the random walk [20, 23]. The seed expansion discovers the community by only exploring the local view of the seed and does not consider the entire network, which is quite suitable for large-scale networks and networks that evolve smoothly.

However, many algorithms of seed expansion cannot uncover a community well if the seed is not a core node of that community [9, 20]. Thus, selecting proper seeds, which is called seeding, is necessary to seed expansion. Several seeding algorithms have appeared in the literature, e.g., the voting based seeding [9], the Spread Hub [15, 20], and local maximum degree [2]. Almost all the seeding algorithms first take a centrality measurement to evaluate how a node is as a seed, and then select the ones with the global or local best centrality as seeds. For instance, Spread Hub sequentially takes the nodes with the highest degree as nodes, while the algorithm of local maximum degree selects the nodes with degree not lower than any neighbor as seeds. Because the latter one only requires the degree information in the neighborhood to decide whether a node is a seed, it is very efficient. Later, degree centrality is replaced by other centrality measurements such as conductance of neighborhood and the similarity to neighbors [15, 20]. In summary, any centrality measurement can be used in this local seeding algorithm. Considering efficiency, here we focus on local centrality measurements that only require nodes' local information. The existing local centrality measurements evaluate nodes according to the degree or the denseness of neighborhood. However, we explore that the degree centrality would miss some seeds and the centralities based on denseness of neighborhood would produce redundant seeds or improper seeds. Based on this exploration, we propose three hybrid local centrality measurements by combining the degree and the denseness of neighborhood, and apply them to the local seeding algorithm and analyze their effectiveness and efficiency by comprehensive experiments on static networks. Experiments show that the hybrid local centrality measurements have superiority to the existing local centrality measurements over large real networks.

Further, to deal with the dynamic evolution of networks, we propose a dynamic local seeding algorithm. Specifically, a fast technique is developed to update the centrality values of nodes involved by network change; and according to the updated centrality values, the neighborhood of nodes involved by network change is checked to update the seed set. Because only the nodes involved by network change are considered in the whole process of seeding, the dynamic local seeding algorithm is very fast when the network evolves smoothly, which is also demonstrated by the experiments over dynamic networks.

The organization of the remained part is as follows. Section 2 presents the notations used in this paper. Section 3 presents the local seeding algorithm used in static networks as well as the local centrality measurements and the proposed hybrid local centrality measurements. The proposed dynamic local seeding algorithm is presented in Sect. 4. Experimental results and analysis are presented in Sect. 5. Finally, Sect. 6 concludes our work.

2 Notations

Let $G = \{G_0, \Delta G_1, \ldots, \Delta G_t, \ldots\}$ be an undirected and unweighted dynamic network. $G_0 = (V_0, E_0)$ is the initial timestep of the network, where V_0 is the set of nodes and E_0 is the set of edges. $\Delta G_t = (\Delta V_t, \Delta E_t)$ is the differential network and indicates the changes between two consecutive timesteps $t - 1$ and t. $\Delta E_t = \{(u, v, sign)|u, v \in \Delta V_t, sign \in \{+, -\}\}$ is the set of edges that change in the interval $(t - 1, t]$, and created edges are indicated by the sign "+" while deleted edges are indicated by the sign "−". ΔV_t is the set of nodes of change due to the creation and deletion of edges. The network data at time t is denoted as $G_t = (V_t, E_t)$ and is constructed as $G_t = G_0 + \sum_{i=1}^{t} \Delta G_i = G_{t-1} + \Delta G_t$. Note that for each timestep we only consider the nodes and edges appearing at that timestep, rather than the cumulative interactions till the current time. For a given timestep G_t, d_u^t denotes the degree of node u, which is the number of u's neighbors at timestep t. N_u^t denotes the set of u's neighbors at timestep t and $N_u^{+t} = N_u^t \cup u$. $vol(S^t)$ denotes the sum of degrees of nodes in S at timestep t and is defined as $vol(S^t) = \sum_{u \in S^t} d_u^t$. $cut(S^t)$ is the number of edges connecting nodes in S and the remained network at timestep t. Neighborhood of node u at timestep t is the subnetwork containing N_u^{+t}. For convenience, we ignore the superscript indicating timestep when the timestep is not specified.

3 Static Seeding by Local Strategy

In this section, we first describe the fast local seeding algorithm, which only requires local information to select seeds. Next, we describe several existing local centrality measurements, which also only require local information, that are used to score each node as a seed. After that, we propose three hybrid local centrality measurements based on the existing local centrality measurements.

3.1 Local Seeding Algorithm

Here we apply a local seeding algorithm originated from [2], which determines a seed only by the centrality values of nodes in its neighborhood. Particularly, for a node u, we check its centrality value and the ones of its neighbors, and take it as a seed if it has the best centrality value. Further, when there are neighbors that also have the best centrality value, we take it as a candidate seed. If a node u is a candidate seed, we further check whether its neighbors have been chosen as seeds. If there is a neighbor that has been chosen, then u is not chosen; otherwise, it is still chosen. In this way, a seed is the "central" node in its local view as well as separated from other seeds.

3.2 Local Centrality Measuring

In the local seeding algorithm presented above, each node should be scored by a centrality measurement which evaluates the node as a seed. There are many centrality measurements, e.g., degree centrality, betweenness centrality, closeness centrality and PageRank centrality [30], in the literature; but here we want to assess the extent to which a node is a core member of its belonging to community. Thus, local centrality measurements which only require local information are more suitable. There are generally two categories of local centrality measurements in the literature. The first one is based on the wisdom that nodes with high degree usually play leading roles in their social circles, which is also demonstrated by the observation that there are hub nodes connecting to many members in communities [22], and so "degree" is naturally taken as a centrality measurement. The second one is based on the idea that core members of a community always have dense neighborhoods, and so measurements that quantify the denseness of a node set, such as conductance, density and local clustering coefficient, can be taken to measure node centrality. Following are the formal descriptions of these local centrality measurements.

Degree centrality. A node u's degree centrality is its degree, i.e., the number of neighbors, and is defined as

$$lc_{degree}(u) = d_u \tag{1}$$

Conductance centrality. A node u's conductance centrality measures the denseness of its neighborhood by the ratio of out-going edges to the total edges induced by nodes in the neighborhood, and is defines as

$$lc_{conductance}(u) = \frac{cut(N_u^+)}{vol(N_u^+)} \tag{2}$$

Local clustering coefficient centrality (lcc centrality). Lcc centrality measures the denseness of a node's neighborhood by the probability that a pair of neighbors are connected. For a node u, its lcc centrality is defined as

$$lc_{lcc}(u) = \frac{|\{v, w \in E \, for \, v, w \in N_u\}|}{\binom{d_u}{2}} \tag{3}$$

Density centrality. Density centrality measures the denseness of a node's neighborhood by the ratio of edges in the neighborhood to the edges in the complete graph containing the same number of nodes. A node u's density centrality is defined as

$$lc_{density}(u) = \frac{|\{(v, w) \in E \, for \, v, w \in N_u^+\}|}{\binom{d_u+1}{2}} \tag{4}$$

3.3 Hybrid Local Centrality Measuring

According to the definitions of local centrality measurements in the previous section, we can see that nodes with higher degree or denser neighborhood than their neighbors should be taken as seeds. However, there are usually a very little fraction of nodes with very high degree, since the distribution of node degree in most real networks shows a power-law form [16]. In addition, high degree nodes are in many nodes' neighborhood since friendship paradox and small-world phenomenon appear in real networks [8, 19].Thus, selecting seeds according to degree centrality can only discover a few communities, which can be also seen from the experimental results of LM-degree in the experimental part. On the other hand, whisker communities, which are small dense subgraphs connected to the largest biconnected component by a single edge, always correspond to relatively good conductance value [12]. This means that nodes at the boundary part of a community may be chosen as seeds according to conductance centrality. Moreover, because real networks often have high average local clustering coefficient [16, 19], many nodes that are not good seeds may score highly over lcc centrality and density centrality and be chosen as seeds. Consequently, many communities of low quality are produced, which can be seen from the experimental results of LM-lcc and LM-density in the experimental part.

Based on the discussions above, we believe that nodes having both high degree and dense neighborhood are better candidate seeds. Thus, we propose to measure local centrality by combining degree and denseness of neighborhood. Consequently, three hybrid local centrality measurements are obtained as follows.

Hybrid local centrality combined by conductance and degree, abbreviated as *hctd* for convenience, is defined as

$$lc_{hctd}(u) = \frac{lc_{conductance}(u)}{d_u} \tag{5}$$

Similarly, hybrid local centrality combined by local clustering coefficient and degree, abbreviated as *hlccd*, and hybrid local centrality combined by density and degree, abbreviated as *hdtd*, are respectively defined as

$$lc_{hlccd}(u) = \frac{lc_{lcc}(u)}{d_u} \tag{6}$$

$$lc_{hdtd}(u) = \frac{lc_{density}(u)}{d_u} \tag{7}$$

4   Dynamic Local Seeding

Real networks are usually dynamic, which probably results in community structure evolves. To discover community structure in dynamic networks, here we propose a dynamic seeding algorithm based on the static local seeding algorithm presented in the previous section to adapt the evolution of network. Particularly, we develop a fast technique to update the centrality values of nodes involved by network change; and according to the updated centrality values we only check the neighborhood of nodes involved by network change to update the seed set. Next, we first introduce the technique of updating centrality values and then present the dynamic seeding algorithm.

4.1 Updating Local Centrality

For a dynamic network $G = \{G_0, \Delta G_1, \ldots, \Delta G_t, \ldots\}$, assuming the centrality value of each node in G_t is known, how to obtained the centrality value of each node in G_{t+1}? From the definitions of lcc centrality and density centrality shown in Eqs. 3 and 4, we have

$$lc_{lcc}(u) = \frac{vol\left(N_u^+\right) - cut\left(N_u^+\right) - 2d_u}{2\binom{d_u}{2}} \tag{8}$$

$$lc_{density}\left(u'\right) = \frac{vol\left(N_u^+\right) - cut(N_u^+)}{2\binom{d_u+1}{2}} \tag{9}$$

This means that all the centralities defined in the previous section can be calculated only if $vol\left(N_u^+\right)$, $cut\left(N_u^+\right)$ and d_u are known. Following, we present how to incrementally calculate the three quantities when an edge is added in or deleted from the network. For convenience, we use $vol'\left(N_u^+\right)$, $cut'\left(N_u^+\right)$ and d_u' to respectively denote the updated quantities.

When an edges is added in the network $G = (V, E)$, we have Corollary 1.

Corollary 1. For an edge (u, v) that is added in network $G = (V, E)$, if $u, v \in V$, then we have:

1) $vol'\left(N_u^+\right) = vol\left(N_u^+\right) + 2 + d_v$, $cut'\left(N_u^+\right) = cut\left(N_u^+\right) + d_v - 2|N_u \cap N_v|$, $d_u' = d_u + 1$,
2) $vol'\left(N_v^+\right) = vol\left(N_v^+\right) + 2 + d_u$, $cut'\left(N_v^+\right) = cut\left(N_v^+\right) + d_u - 2|N_u \cap N_v|$, $d_v' = d_v + 1$,
3) for each $w \in N_u \cap N_v$, $vol'\left(N_w^+\right) = vol\left(N_w^+\right) + 2$, $cut'\left(N_w^+\right) = cut(N_w^+)$,
4) for each $w \in (N_u \cup N_v)/(N_u \cap N_v \cup \{u, v\})$, $vol'\left(N_w^+\right) = vol\left(N_w^+\right) + 1$, $cut'\left(N_w^+\right) = cut\left(N_w^+\right) + 1$;

if $u \in V$ and $v \notin V$, then we have (it is similar for the case where $u \notin V$ and $v \in V$):

1) $vol'\left(N_u^+\right) = vol\left(N_u^+\right) + 2$, $cut'\left(N_u^+\right) = cut\left(N_u^+\right)$, $d_u' = d_u + 1$,
2) $vol'\left(N_v^+\right) = d_u + 2$, $cut'\left(N_v^+\right) = d_u$, $d_v' = 1$;

if $u \notin V$ and $v \notin V$, then we have $vol'\left(N_u^+\right) = 2$, $vol'\left(N_v^+\right) = 2$, $cut'\left(N_u^+\right) = 0$, $cut'\left(N_v^+\right) = 0$, $d_u' = 1$, $d_v' = 1$.

When an edge is deleted from the network $G = (V, E)$, we have Corollary 2.

Corollary 2. For an edge (u, v) that is deleted from network $G = (V, E)$, we have:

1) $vol'(N_u^+) = vol(N_u^+) - (1 + d_v)$, $cut'(N_u^+) = cut(N_u^+) + 2|N_u \cap N_v| + 1 - d_v$,
   $d_u' = d_u - 1$,
2) $vol'(N_v^+) = vol(N_v^+) - (1 + d_u)$, $cut'(N_v^+) = cut(N_v^+) + 2|N_u \cap N_v| + 1 - d_u$,
   $d_v' = d_v - 1$,
3) for each $w \in N_u \cap N_v$, $vol'(N_w^+) = vol(N_w^+) - 2$, $cut'(N_w^+) = cut(N_w^+)$, $d_w' = d_w$,
4) for each $w \in (N_u \cup N_v)/(N_u \cap N_v \cup \{u, v\})$, $vol'(N_w^+) = vol(N_w^+) - 1$, $cut'(N_w^+) = cut(N_w^+) - 1$, $d_w' = d_w$.

Based on Corollary 1 and 2, $vol(N_u^{+t+1})$, $cut(N_u^{+t+1})$ and d_u^{t+1} can be incrementally updated by sequentially dealing with the edges in ΔE_{t+1}. According to $vol(N_u^{+t+1})$, $cut(N_u^{+t+1})$ and d_u^{t+1}, all the centralities, including local centrality and hybrid local centrality, of the nodes involved by change at timestep $t + 1$ can be obtained quickly. It is noted that the nodes that are not involved by ΔE_{t+1}, i.e., the nodes that are not changed or not in the neighborhood of the nodes of change, are not considered since their centrality values are not affected.

4.2 Dynamic Local Seeding Algorithm

Once the centrality value of each node is obtained at timestep $t + 1$, the seed set can be updated. It has been known that whether a node is taken as a seed only depends on its neighborhood. Thus, a node becomes a seed or not only if there are nodes whose centrality value is changed in the neighborhood. Based on this understanding, we can update the seed set by only checking the nodes involved by ΔE_{t+1} and the ones in their neighborhood. See Algorithm 1 for details. Firstly, if a seed at timestep t is deleted at timestep $t + 1$, then we erase it from the seed set, see line 3. Secondly, if a seed at timestep t is not a seed any more at timestep $t + 1$, we erase it from the seed set, and check whether its neighbors become seeds or candidate seeds because of its erasure. If one neighbor becomes a seed, we insert it into the seed set; while we keep it in *candS* if it is a candidate seed, see lines 5–11. Thirdly, if a node becomes a seed at timestep $t + 1$, we insert it into the seed set, see line 13. Further, we erase the neighbor v from the seed set if it is a seed at timestep t (see lines 15–16), and check the neighbors of v to see whether they become seeds. If one of v's neighbors becomes a seed due to v's erasure from the seed set, then we add it into the seed set; while if it is a candidate seed, we record it into *candS* (see lines 17–21). Finally, we further check whether the nodes in *candS* are seeds or not, see lines 27–30.

Algorithm 1 Updating seed set

Input: $G_{t+1} = (V_{t+1}, E_{t+1})$: the network at timestep $t+1$; $lc^{t+1}(u)$: the local centrality for node $u \in V_{t+1}$; V_{t+1}^{in}: nodes involved by ΔE_{t+1}; S^t: seed set at timestep t.

Output: S^{t+1}: the seed seet at timestep $t+1$.

1. Let $S^{t+1} = S^t$, candS = $\emptyset$.
2. For each node $u \in V_{t+1}^{in}$ do:
3.   If $u \notin V_{t+1}$ and $u \in S^t$, then erase u from S^{t+1};
4.   If $u \in V_{t+1}$, then do:
5.   If u is not a seed and $u \in S^t$, then do:
6.   a. $S^{t+1}.erase(u)$, $seed(u) = Flase$;
7.   b. For each node $v \in N_u^{t+1}$, do:
8.   If $v \notin S^t$ and v is a seed, then $S^{t+1}.insert(v)$ and $seed(v) = True$;
9.   Elif $v \notin S^t$ and v is a candidate seed, then $candS.insert(v)$
10.   End for.
11.   End if.
12.   If u is a seed and $u \notin S^t$, then do:
13.   a. $S^{t+1}.isnert(u)$, $seed(u) = True$;
14.   b. For each node $v \in N^{t+1}(u)$ do:
15.   If $v \in S^t$, then do:
16.   a.$S^{t+1}.erase(v)$, $seed(v) = False$;
17.   b. For each node $w \in N^{t+1}(v)$ do:
18.   If $w \notin S^t$ and w is a seed, then do:
19. $S^{t+1}.insert(w)$ and $seed(w) = True$;
20.   Elif $w \notin S^t$ and w is a candidate seed, then $candS.insert(w)$
21.   End for
22.   End If
23.   End for
24.   End if
25. End if
26.End for
27.For each node $u \in candS$ do:
28.   If $seed(v) == False$ for each node $v \in N^{t+1}(u)$, then do:
29. $S^{t+1}.insert(u)$ and $seed(u) = True$
30.End for

Given a dynamic network $G = \{G_0, \Delta G_1, \ldots, \Delta G_t, \ldots\}$, at the initial timestep, we apply the static local seeding algorithm to seeding and obtain the seed set S^0. For each following timestep $t + 1$, we first incrementally update the centrality values of nodes involved by ΔE_{t+1}, by sequentially considering the edges in ΔE_{t+1}. Simultaneously, the network G_{t+1} is also incrementally constructed. After the centrality values and the network G_{t+1} are updated, the seed set at timestep $t + 1$ can be obtained according to Algorithm 1.

5 Experiments

The experiment consists of two parts: one is to evaluate the proposed hybrid local centrality measurements, and the other one is to evaluate the proposed dynamic seeding algorithm. In the first part, the hybrid local centrality measurements are compared with the existing local centrality measurements under the static seeding algorithm; while in the second part, the dynamic seeding algorithm is compared with the static seeding algorithm. To perform seed expansion from each seed to discover communities, we apply the widely used as well as effective technique of approximate personalized PageRank vector, which is referred to [23] for space limitation. All the experiments are done by C++ on a PC with an Intel i7 4.0 GHz and 16 GB RAM. For convenience, we abbreviate the static local seeding algorithm as S-LM and the dynamic seeding algorithm as D-LM, and different suffixes are used to distinguish different local centrality measurements, e.g., S-LM-degree indicates the static local seeding algorithm with degree centrality. Before presenting the experimental results, we first describe the networks and the evaluation metrics.

5.1 Datasets and Evaluation Metrics

In the first part of the experiment, we apply eight real networks with ground-truth communities, which are widely used to test community detection. See Table 1 for the information of these real networks. We also generate three synthetic networks with ground-truth communities by LFR [11], and name them as Network1, Network2, and Network3, respectively. The parameters used to generate the three synthetic networks are as follows: the numbers of nodes are 10,000, 100,000, and 1,000,000, respectively; the average degrees are 50, 60, 70 respectively; the max degrees are 120, 150,180, respectively; the degree exponent is 2 and the mixing parameter is 0.2 for all the networks; the community sizes are in the range of [60, 100], [60, 120] and [60, 150], respectively; the overlapping nodes are 200, 2,000, 20,000, respectively. Further, to construct the dynamic networks for the second part of the experiment, we follow the approach as in [10]. Particularly, we take each of the three synthetic networks as the initial timestep (which is numbered as timestep 0), and generate the following 10 timesteps by randomly choosing a few nodes to change their connections to other nodes, with the aim of changing their community memberships. Details of the three synthetic networks are referred to [10] due to space limitation.

To evaluate the results of seeding, we consider the number of seeds, the coverage and the quality of the resulting communities. To evaluate the quality of the resulting communities, we apply two widely used metrics: F1-score [21], and overlapping modularity [7]. The former one compares the consistence of the detected communities to the ground truth, while the latter one evaluates the cohesiveness in community and the separateness between communities. We also compare the running times consumed by different seeding algorithms.

Table 1. The information of real networks (static).

Networks	Nodes	Edges	Coms	Type	Ref
Karate	34	78	2	Social network	[29]
Dolphin	62	159	2	Social network	[14]
Football	115	613	12	Social network	[6]
Amazon	334,863	925,872	151,039	Co-purchasing network	[23]
DBLP	317,080	1,049,866	13,477	Collaboration network	[23]
YouTube	1,134,890	2,987,624	8,385	Online social network	[23]
LJ	3,997,962	34,681,189	287,512	Online social network	[23]
Orkut	3,072,441	117,185,083	5,043,976	Online social network	[23]

5.2 Experimental Results on Static Networks

See Fig. 1 for the number of seeds chosen by different algorithms. It can be seen that, over the real networks, S-LM-density and S-LM-lcc always select the most seeds that are far more than other algorithms. Following is S-LM-conductance, which generally selects more seeds than the remained algorithms, except that it selects fewer seeds than S-LM-hdtd over Football and S-LM-hlccd over Amazon and DBLP. S-LM-degree selects the least seeds over all the networks except Karate, over which S-LM-hdtd only selects one seed, and Football, over which S-LM-degree selects the most seeds. Moreover, it is obvious that S-LM-hctd (S-LM-hlccd, S-LM-hdtd) selects much fewer seeds than S-LM-conductance (S-LM-hlccd, S-LM-hdtd), especially over large real networks, which demonstrates that the hybrid centrality combining degree and denseness of neighborhood can exclude some seeds with low degree or sparse neighborhood. The result over synthetic networks (the initial timestep) is consistent with the one over real networks, except that S-LM-degree selects more seeds than S-LM-hlccd and S-LM-hdtd. It may be because that degree difference in synthetic networks is much less than the one in large real networks and the former ones are denser, although the former ones are simulated to be power-law distribution.

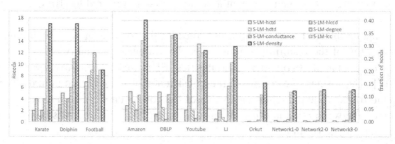

Fig. 1. The number of seeds by different seeding algorithms over small networks (left) and the fraction of seeds by different seeding algorithms over large networks (right).

The coverage of communities expanded from the seeds chosen by different seeding algorithms, which is shown in Fig. 2, is consistent with the number of seeds. That is, the more the seeds are, the higher the corresponding coverage is. For example, S-LM-lcc and S-LM-density select the most seeds, and their corresponding coverages are the highest; S-LM-conductance selects more seeds than S-LM-hlccd and S-LM-hdtd over YouTube, LJ and Orkut, and its corresponding coverage is higher than the latter two; S-LM-hctd (S-LM-hlccd, S-LM-hdtd) always corresponds to lower coverage than S-LM-conductance (S-LM-lcc, S-LM-density).

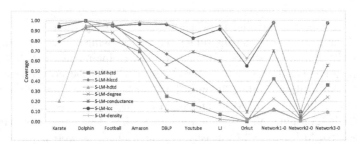

Fig. 2. The coverage of communities resulting from different seeding algorithms.

The quality of the resulting communities from different seeding algorithms is shown in Fig. 3. In terms of F1-score, S-LM-lcc and S-LM-density work best over DBLP, YouTube, LJ, Orkut and the synthetic networks, followed by S-LM-conductance, which further works best over Amazon; S-LM-degree works best over Karate and Football, followed by S-LM-hctd over Karate and S-LM-hdtd over Football; S-LM-hctd works best over Dolphin, followed by S-LM-hlccd; in many cases, S-LM-hctd (S-LM-hlccd, S-LM-hdtd) works worse than S-LM-Conductance (S-LM-lcc, S-LM-density), but works better than S-LM-degree. In terms of modularity, S-LM-hctd generally works best, except that S-LM-hdtd (S-LM-hdtd) obviously works best over Karate (Dolphin); S-LM-conductance, S-LM-lcc and S-LM-density obviously work worse than S-LM-hctd, S-LM-hlccd and S-LM-hdtd, respectively, especially S-LM-lcc and S-LM-density, they work worst over all the networks except Football.

From the results above we can infer: 1) S-LM-conductance, especially S-LM-lcc and S-LM-density, select too many nodes as seeds, but many of them are not proper, which results in relatively good F1-score but obviously bad modularity; 2) S-LM-hctd, S-LM-hlccd and S-LM-hdtd can exclude some improper seeds chosen by S-LM-conductance, S-LM-lcc and S-LM-density, respectively, and the former ones (especially S-LM-hctd) also perform better than S-LM-degree in many cases, which demonstrates that considering both of the degree and the denseness of neighborhood can find more proper seeds. However, S-LM-hlccd and S-LM-hdtd seem missing some good seeds since they produce good modularity but very low F1-score over some networks (especially the synthetic networks). In addition, over synthetic networks S-LM-hctd does not improve S-LM-conductance in terms of modularity, which may be because that in synthetic networks the difference of degrees of nodes is less and the community structure is more obvious compared with real networks, and S-LM-conductance is an excellent seeding algorithm for this kind of networks.

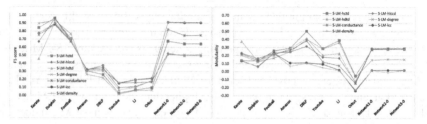

Fig. 3. The quality of the communities resulting from different seeding algorithms.

Next, we compare the running times of different seeding algorithms which are shown in Fig. 4. Because all the seeding algorithms and the following seed expansion are done intermediately over the small networks, i.e., Karate, Dolphin and Football, the corresponding running times are not reported here. It can be seen that the most efficient seeding algorithm is S-LM-degree, while the most time-consuming one over real networks is S-LM-density, followed by S-LM-lcc and S-LM-conductance. S-LM-hctd, S-LM-hlccd and S-LM-hdtd consume more running time than S-LM-degree, but less than S-LM-conductance, S-LM-lcc and S-LM-density. For the synthetic networks, S-hctd costs the most time over Network1, followed by S-LM-hlccd; S-LM-conductance costs the most time over Network2 and Network3, followed by S-LM-hctd, S-LM-hlccd and S-LM-hdtd. However, the difference among different seeding algorithms is relatively little, except S-LM-degree which is much efficient than others. The running time of seed expansion is almost proportional to the number of seeds. That is, the more the seeds are, the more the running time of seed expansion is, e.g., S-LM-degree selects the least seeds over real networks, it leads to the least running time for expansion, followed by S-LM-hctd, S-LM-hdtd and S-LM-hlccd.

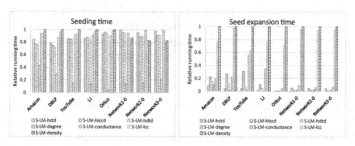

Fig. 4. The relative running times consumed by different seeding algorithms.

5.3 Experimental Results on Dynamic Networks

Here we only present the results of dynamic seeding algorithms with hctd centrality and conductance centrality, because these two centralities obviously perform better than others over synthetic networks (see Fig. 1, 2 and 3). It should be noted that the results of S-LM-hctd and S-LM-conductance are not reported in Fig. 5 and 6, since they produce almost the same results as D-LM-hctd and D-LM-conductance, respectively.

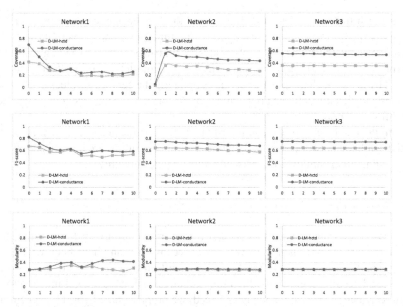

Fig. 5. The coverage, F1-score and modularity of the dynamic seeding algorithm with hctd centrality and conductance centrality.

The coverage, F1-score and modularity resulting from D-LM-hctd and D-LM-conductance are reported in Fig. 5. Overall, D-LM-conductance produces higher coverage than D-LM-hctd over all the three dynamic networks. But the difference is not obvious over Network1 (except the first two timesteps) and the first timestep of Network2. The result of F1-score is consistent with the one of coverage, except that D-LM-conductance produces obviously higher F1-score than D-LM-hctd over the first timestep of Network2. In terms of modularity, D-LM-hctd and D-LM-conductance produce very similar results over Network2 and Network3; and D-LM-hctd performs worse in many cases over Network1.

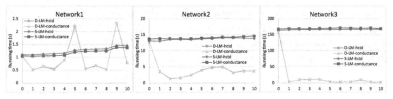

Fig. 6. The running times of static seeding algorithm and dynamic seeding algorithm with hctd centrality and conductance centrality.

We compare the running times of D-LM-hctd (D-LM-conductance) with S-LM-hctd (S-LM-conductance) for each timestep of the three dynamic networks, see Fig. 6. We can see that at the initial timestep, the four seeding algorithms cost almost the same time; for the following timestep, D-LM-hctd is as efficient as D-LM-conductance, and S-LM-hctd costs as much time as S-LM-conductance, and the former two are much efficient than the latter two. But there are two exceptions, see timestep 5 and 9 over Network1, the dynamic seeding algorithms obviously cost more time than the static seeding algorithms. We explore the network and find that at these two timesteps almost all the nodes are involved by network change, which requires updating the centrality values of almost all the nodes and checking almost all the nodes by Algorithm 1. Thus, the dynamic seeding algorithms cost more time.

From the results above, we can infer that: 1) the conductance centrality works best over the synthetic networks; 2) the dynamic seeding algorithms are much faster than the static seeding algorithm over the networks that change smoothly.

6 Conclusions

In this paper, we focus on seeding, which is very important to seed expansion. Deep learning models are promisingly developed in recent years and have been widely used in many application areas [24–28], but to efficiently handle large-scale networks, we apply a local seeding algorithm which only requires each node's local information. In order to evaluate how good a node is as a seed, we propose three hybrid local centrality measurements by combining degree and denseness of neighborhood, which are then used in the local seeding algorithm. Further, we propose a dynamic seeding algorithm for dynamic networks. In the proposed dynamic seeding, only the nodes that are involved by network change are considered to update the seed set, which makes it suitable to the case where network does not change dramatically. Finally, we conduct experiments to evaluate the proposed hybrid local centrality measurements and dynamic seeding algorithm. Experimental results show that the hybrid local centrality measurements have superiority to the existing ones over large real networks and the dynamic seeding algorithm is very fast. However, the hybrid local centrality measurements do not perform as well as the conductance centrality over networks where the difference of degree is little and the community structure is clear, and the dynamic seeding algorithm does not speed up over the networks with many nodes involved by change, which we will further study in future work.

Acknowledgement. This work is supported by Natural Science Foundation of China (No. 61802034), Sichuan Science and Technology Program (No. 2021YFG0333), National Key Research and Development Program of China (No. 2019YFC1509602) and the Digital Media Science Innovation Team of CDUT (Grant 10912-kytd201510).

References

1. Bagrow, J.P.: Evaluating local community methods in networks. J. Stat Mech-Theory E **2008**, P05001 (2008)
2. Chen, Q., Wu, T.T., Fang, M.: Detecting local community structures in complex networks based on local degree central nodes. Phys. A **392**(3), 529–537 (2013)
3. Clauset, A.: Finding local community structure in networks. Phys. Rev. E **72**(2), 26132 (2005)
4. Fortunato, S.: Community detection in graphs. Phys. Rep. **486**, 75–174 (2010)

5. Garza, S.E., Schaeffer, S.E.: Community detection with the label propagation algorithm: a survey. Physica A **534**(15), 122058 (2019)
6. Girvan, M., Newman, M.E.J.: Community structure in social and biological networks. PNAS **99**(12), 7821–7826 (2002)
7. Gregory, S.: Fuzzy overlapping communities in networks. J. Stat. Mech-Theory E, **2011**, P02017 (2011)
8. Hodas, N.O., Kooti, F., Lerman, K.: Friendship paradox redux: your friends are more interesting than you. In: 7th International AAAI Conference on Weblogs and Social Media, Boston (2013)
9. Hu, Y., Hu, K., Yang, B., Zhang, N., Gu X.: Voting based seeding algorithm for overlapping community detection. In: International Conference on Cyber-Enabled Distributed Computing and Knowledge Discovery, pp. 192–199. IEEE, Xi'an (2015)
10. Hu, Y., Yang, B., Lv, C.: A local dynamic method for tracking communities and their evolution in dynamic networks. Knowl.-Based Syst. **110**, 176–190 (2016)
11. Lancichinetti, A., Fortunato, S.: Benchmarks for testing community detection algorithms on directed and weighted graphs with overlapping communities. Phys. Rev. E **80**(1), 016118 (2009)
12. Leskovec, J., Lang, K.J., Dasgupta, A., Mahoney, M.W.: Community structure in large networks: natural cluster sizes and the absence of large well-defined clusters. Internet Math. **6**(1), 29–123 (2009)
13. Lin, Y.R., Chi, Y., Zhu, S., Sundaram, H., Tseng, B.L.: Analyzing communities and their evolutions in dynamic social networks. ACM Trans. KDD. **3**(2), 8 (2009)
14. Lusseau, D., Schneider, K., Boisseau, O.J., Haase, E., Dawson, S.M.: The bottlenose dolphin community of doubtful sound features a large proportion of long-lasting associations. Behav. Ecol. Sociobiol. **54**, 396–405 (2003)
15. Moradi, F., Olovsson, T., Tsigas, P.: A local seed selection algorithm for overlapping community detection. In: ASONAM 2014, Beijing, China, pp. 1–8 (2014)
16. Newman, M.E.J.: Properties of highly clustered networks. Phys. Rev. E **68**, 026121 (2003)
17. Raghavan, U.N., Albert, R., Kumara, S.: Near linear time algorithm to detect community structure in large scale networks. Phys. Rev. E **76**(3), 036106 (2007)
18. Tantipathananandh, C., Berger-Wolf, T., Kempe, D.: A framework for community identification in dynamic social networks. In: KDD, pp. 717–726. ACM (2007)
19. Watts, D.J., Strogatz, S.H.: Collective dynamics of "small-world" networks. Nature **393**(6684), 440–442 (1998)
20. Whang, J.J., Gleich, D.F., Dhillon, I.S.: Overlapping community detection using neighborhood-inflated seed expansion. IEEE Trans. Knowl. Data Eng. **28**(5), 1272–1284 (2016)
21. Yang, J., Leskovec, J.: Overlapping community detection at scale: a nonnegative matrix factorization approach. In: WSDM, Rome, Italy, pp. 587–596 (2013)
22. Yang, J., Leskovec, J.: Structure and overlaps of ground-truth communities in networks. ACM Trans. Intell. Syst. Technol. **5**(2), 26 (2014)
23. Yang, J., Leskovec, J.: Defining and evaluating network communities based on ground-truth. Knowl. Inf. Syst. **42**(1), 181–213 (2013). https://doi.org/10.1007/s10115-013-0693-z
24. Yue, L., Shen, H., Wang, S., et al.: Exploring BCI control in smart environments: intention recognition Via EEG representation enhancement learning. ACM Trans. Knowl. Disc. Data **15**(5), 1–20 (2021)
25. Yue, L., Sun, X.X., Gao, W.Z., et al.: Multiple auxiliary information based deep model for collaborative filtering. J. Comput. Sci. Technol. **33**(4), 668–681 (2018)
26. Yue, L., Tian, D., Chen, W., Han, X., Yin, M.: Deep learning for heterogeneous medical data analysis. World Wide Web **23**(5), 2715–2737 (2019). https://doi.org/10.1007/s11280-019-00764-z

27. Yue, L., Tian, D., Jiang, J., Yao, L., Chen, W., Zhao, X.: Intention recognition from spatio-temporal representation of EEG signals. In: Qiao, M., Vossen, G., Wang, S., Li, L. (eds.) ADC 2021. LNCS, vol. 12610, pp. 1–12. Springer, Cham (2021). https://doi.org/10.1007/978-3-030-69377-0_1

28. Yue, L., Zhao, H., Yang, Y., Tian, D., Zhao, X., Yin, M.: A mimic learning method for disease risk prediction with incomplete initial data. In: Li, G., Yang, J., Gama, J., Natwichai, J., Tong, Y. (eds.) DASFAA 2019. LNCS, vol. 11448, pp. 392–396. Springer, Cham (2019). https://doi.org/10.1007/978-3-030-18590-9_52

29. Zachary, W.W.: An information flow model for conflict and fission in small groups. J. Anthropol. Res. **33**, 452–473 (1977)

30. Zafarani, R., Abbasi, M. A., Liu, H.: Social Media Mining: An Introduction. Cambridge University Press, Cambridge (2014)

Clique Percolation Method: Memory Efficient Almost Exact Communities

Alexis Baudin[1(✉)], Maximilien Danisch[1], Sergey Kirgizov[2],
Clémence Magnien[1], and Marwan Ghanem[1]

[1] Sorbonne Université, CNRS, LIP6, 75005 Paris, France
{alexis.baudin,maximilien.danisch,clemence.magnien,marwan.ghanem}@lip6.fr
[2] LIB, Université de Bourgogne Franche-Comté,
B.P. 47 870, 21078 Dijon Cedex, France
sergey.kirgizov@u-bourgogne.fr

Abstract. Automatic detection of relevant groups of nodes in large real-world graphs, i.e. community detection, has applications in many fields and has received a lot of attention in the last twenty years. The most popular method designed to find overlapping communities (where a node can belong to several communities) is perhaps the clique percolation method (CPM). This method formalizes the notion of community as a maximal union of k-cliques that can be reached from each other through a series of adjacent k-cliques, where two cliques are adjacent if and only if they overlap on $k - 1$ nodes. Despite much effort CPM has not been scalable to large graphs for medium values of k.

Recent work has shown that it is possible to efficiently list all k-cliques in very large real-world graphs for medium values of k. We build on top of this work and scale up CPM. In cases where this first algorithm faces memory limitations, we propose another algorithm, CPMZ, that provides a solution close to the exact one, using more time but less memory.

Keywords: Graphs · Graph mining · Social networks · Community detection · k-clique percolation

1 Introduction

The problem of detecting communities in real networks has received a lot of attention in recent years. Many definitions of communities have been proposed, corresponding to different requirements on the type of communities that are to be detected and/or on some properties of the studied graph: some definitions depend on global or local properties of the graph, nodes can belong to several communities or to a single one, links may have weights, communities may have a hierarchical structure, *etc.* In practice, algorithms also have to be designed to extract the communities from large graphs. Many definitions of communities proposed with their corresponding algorithm already exist [5]. Most real networks are characterized by communities that may overlap, i.e. a node may belong to several communities. In the context of social networks for instance, each person belongs to several communities such as colleagues, family, leisure activities, etc.

© Springer Nature Switzerland AG 2022
B. Li et al. (Eds.): ADMA 2021, LNAI 13088, pp. 113–127, 2022.
https://doi.org/10.1007/978-3-030-95408-6_9

One of the most popular methods designed to find overlapping communities is the clique percolation method (CPM) which produces *k-clique communities* [14].

Definition 1 (*k*-clique). *A k-clique c_k is a fully connected set of k nodes, i.e. every pair of its vertices is connected by a link in the graph.*

For example, in Fig. 2, the set $\{1, 3, 4, 6\}$ is a 4-clique.

Definition 2 (*k*-cliques adjacency). *Two k-cliques are said to be adjacent if and only if they share $k - 1$ nodes.*

For example, in Fig. 2, the two 4-cliques $\{1, 3, 4, 6\}$ and $\{1, 3, 6, 9\}$ are adjacent.

Definition 3 (cpm community). *A k-clique community (or CPM community) is the set of the vertices belonging to a maximal set of k-cliques that can be reached from each other through a series of adjacent k-cliques.*

Though the correspondence between the obtained communities and real-world ones are hard to charactarize in a general manner, the advantages of this definition are well known [8]: it is formally well defined, totally deterministic, does not use any heuristics or function optimizations that are hard to interpret, allows communities to overlap, and each community is defined locally[1].

Despite much effort CPM has not been scalable to large graphs for medium values of k, i.e., values between 5 and 10. We therefore seek in this work to extend the computation of CPM to larger graphs. A bottleneck for most previous contributions is the memory required. Indeed, exact methods need to store in memory either all k-cliques, or all maximal cliques (cliques which are not included in any other clique), which is prohibitive in many cases.

Our contribution is twofold:

1. We improve on the state of the art concerning the computation of CPM communities, by leveraging an existing algorithm able to list k-cliques in a very efficient manner;
2. In cases where this first algorithm faces memory limitations, we propose another algorithm that provides a solution close to the exact one, using more time but less memory.

We will show that these algorithms allow to compute exact solutions in cases where this was not possible before, and to compute a close result of good quality in cases where the graph is so large that our exact method does not work due to memory limitations.

The rest of the paper is organized as follows. In Sect. 2, we present the related work. In Sect. 3, we present our exact and relaxed algorithms. We discuss time and memory requirements in Sect. 4. We then evaluate the performance of our exact algorithm against the state of the art in Sect. 5, and we compare the results and performances of our exact and relaxed algorithms. We conclude in Sect. 6, and present some perspectives for future work.

---

[1] Notice that if a node does not belong to at least one k-clique, it doesn't belong to any community.

2   Related Work

There are many algorithms for computing overlapping communities as shown in a dedicated survey [17]. The focus of our paper is on the computation of the k-clique communities. Existing algorithms to compute k-clique communities in a graph can be split in two categories:

(1) algorithms that compute all maximal cliques of size k or more and use them to compute all k-clique communities. Indeed, two maximal cliques that overlap on $k - 1$ nodes or more belong to the same k-clique community. Most state-of-the-art approaches [8,14,15] belong to this category;
(2) Kumpula *et al.* [9] compute all k-cliques and then compute k-clique communities from them strictly following the definitions of a k-clique community, i.e. detect which k-cliques are adjacent.

Algorithms of the first category differ in the method used to find which maximal cliques are adjacent. However, the first step which consists in computing all maximal cliques is always the same and is done sequentially. While this problem is NP-hard, there exist algorithms scalable to relatively large sparse real-world graphs, based on the Bron-Kerbosch algorithm [1,3,4].

Any large clique, with more than k vertices, will be included in a single k-clique community, and there is no need to list all k-cliques of this large clique. This is the main reason why there are more methods following the approach of listing maximal cliques, category (1), rather than listing k-cliques, category (2). However, it has been found that most real-world graphs actually do not contain very large cliques and that listing k-cliques for small and medium values of k is a scalable problem in practice [2,12], in many cases it is more tractable that listing all maximal cliques. This makes algorithms in the category (2) more interesting for practical scenarios.

The algorithm of [9] proposes a method to list all k-cliques then merges the found k-cliques into k-clique communities using a *Union-Find* [7], a very efficient data structure [6,16] which we describe briefly in Sect. 3.1. In the context of [9] the Union-Find contains all $(k - 1)$-cliques (as elements) and each k-clique c_k triggers the union of the subsets that contain at least one $(k - 1)$-clique of c_k.

Our first contribution builds on the same idea. We first propose to use an efficient algorithm for listing k-cliques [2], which improves the overall performance. Going further, in order to provide an approximation of the community structure for graphs for which it is not possible to obtain the exact result due to memory limits, we propose to perform union of sets of z-cliques, $2 \leq z < k - 1$, instead of $(k - 1)$-cliques. This construction is discussed in details in the next section.

3   Algorithm

A graph $G = (V, E)$ consists of its vertex set V and its edge set E. In the following c_k will always denote a k-clique, from the context it will be clear which one exactly.

3.1 Union-Find Structure

The algorithms we will present rely on the Union-Find structure, also known in the literature as a *disjoint-set data structure*. It stores a collection of disjoint sets, allowing very efficient union operations between them. The structure is a forest, whose trees correspond to disjoint subsets, and nodes correspond to the elements. The operations on the nodes are the following:

- Find(p): returns the root of the tree containing a Union-Find node p.
- Union($r_1, ..., r_l$): performs the union of trees represented by their roots r_i by making one root the parent of all others;
- MakeSet(): creates a new tree with one node p, corresponding to a new empty set, and returns p.

3.2 Exact CPM Algorithm

First we build on the idea introduced in [9]. A CPM community is represented as the set of all the $(k-1)$-cliques it contains. These communities are represented by a Union-Find structure whose nodes are $(k-1)$-cliques. The algorithm then iterates over all k-cliques and tests if the current k-clique belongs to a community, by testing whether it has a $(k-1)$-clique in common with it.

Algorithm 1. Exact CPM algorithm

1: **UF** ← Union-Find data structure
2: **Dict** ← Empty Dictionary
3: **for** each k-clique $c_k \in G$ **do**
4:      $S \leftarrow \emptyset$ ▷ communities of c_k to merge
5:      **for** each $(k-1)$-clique $c_{k-1} \subset c_k$ **do**
6:          **if** $c_{k-1} \in$ Dict.keys() **then**
7:              $p \leftarrow$ UF.Find(Dict$[c_{k-1}]$)
8:          **else**
9:              $p \leftarrow$ UF.MakeSet()
10:             Dict$[c_{k-1}] \leftarrow p$
11:         $S \leftarrow S \cup \{p\}$
12:     UF.Union(S)

Algorithm 1 considers all k-cliques one by one. For every k-clique it iterates over its $(k-1)$-cliques $c_{k-1}^1, c_{k-1}^2, \ldots c_{k-1}^k$. For every $c_{k-1}^i, i \in [1, k]$, it identifies the set p_i to which it belongs in the Union-Find. Then, it performs the union of all sets p_i. Several algorithms exist for efficiently listing k-cliques [12]. We substitute one the best [2] to the one proposed by the authors of [9].

As the number of $(k-1)$-cliques can be very large, this approach is problematic as in some cases it is not possible to store them all in memory. This leads us to a new algorithm which requires less memory but in rare cases incorrectly merges some CPM communities together.

3.3   Memory Efficient CPM Approximation

For relatively small values of k, there are far fewer z-cliques than $(k-1)$-cliques in real-world graphs. To get an intuition for this, consider the case of a large clique of size c. It contains $\binom{c}{z}$ z-cliques and this number increases with z for $z < c/2$. Therefore storing all z-cliques is feasible in cases where it is not possible to store all the $(k-1)$-cliques. We use this idea to propose an algorithm computing relaxed communities.

Definition 4 (cpmz community). *An agglomerated k-clique community (or* CPMZ *community) is the union of one or more* CPM *communities.*

Our memory efficient method, called CPMZ *algorithm*, given a graph G, the size of k-cliques and an integer $z \in [2, k-1)$, returns a set of agglomerated k-clique communities, such that each CPM community is included in one and only one CPMZ community (see Theorem 1).

In the CPM algorithm, a community is represented as a set of $(k-1)$-cliques, and communities correspond to *disjoint* sets of $(k-1)$-cliques. In the following, a community is represented as a set of z-cliques, and CPMZ communities are represented as *non-disjoint* sets of z-cliques.

The main idea of our CPMZ algorithm is to identify each $(k-1)$-clique to the set of its containing z-cliques. The algorithm is very similar to CPM. For each k-clique, all $(k-1)$-cliques are considered. Since we consider that a $(k-1)$-clique is represented by the set of its z-cliques, the community of a $(k-1)$-clique is the one that contains all its z-cliques.

The CPMZ algorithm uses two principal data structures. UF is an Union-Find data structure, whose nodes are identifiers of z-clique sets. We will call these *Union-Find nodes*. The operations defined on this structure are presented in Sect. 3.1. Each z-clique can belong to several Union-Find nodes. This is recorded in the Setz dictionary, which associates to each z-clique the set of Union-Find nodes to which it belongs. See Fig. 1 for an example.

More formally, Setz is a dictionary with z-cliques as keys. For a z-clique c_z:

- Setz$[c_z]$ is a set of Union-Find nodes;
- Setz$[c_z]$.add(q) adds the Union-Find node q to the set of Union-Find nodes of c_z. It can also be seen as the action of adding c_z to the set identified by q.

At the end of the algorithm, every tree corresponds to a CPMZ community represented as a union of sets containing z-cliques.

Note that during the execution of the algorithm, the same z-clique c_z can belong to several Union-Find nodes of the same Union-Find set, which creates redundancies in Setz $[c_z]$. This is the case for instance in the example of Fig. 1 in which Setz[(3,6)] contains both a and b which belong to the same Union-Find set. This situation can occur if a z-clique belongs to two different Union-Find sets which are merged later.

In our CPMZ algorithm (presented below) we eliminate these redundancies when we detect them (see Line 8).

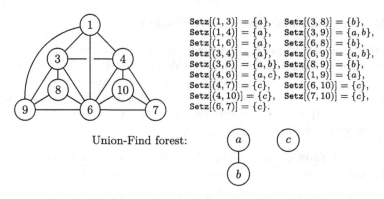

Setz$[(1,3)] = \{a\}$,   Setz$[(3,8)] = \{b\}$,
Setz$[(1,4)] = \{a\}$,   Setz$[(3,9)] = \{a,b\}$,
Setz$[(1,6)] = \{a\}$,   Setz$[(6,8)] = \{b\}$,
Setz$[(3,4)] = \{a\}$,   Setz$[(6,9)] = \{a,b\}$,
Setz$[(3,6)] = \{a,b\}$, Setz$[(8,9)] = \{b\}$,
Setz$[(4,6)] = \{a,c\}$, Setz$[(1,9)] = \{a\}$,
Setz$[(4,7)] = \{c\}$,   Setz$[(6,10)] = \{c\}$,
Setz$[(4,10)] = \{c\}$, Setz$[(7,10)] = \{c\}$,
Setz$[(6,7)] = \{c\}$.

Union-Find forest:

Fig. 1. Example of a graph and the corresponding data structures of the CPMZ algorithm. In this example, we have $k = 4, z = 2$. There are 17 z-cliques belonging to 4 k-cliques, namely $\{1,3,4,6\}$, $\{3,6,8,9\}$, $\{4,7,6,10\}$ and $\{1,3,6,9\}$. The nodes of the Union-Find structure are represented using letters a, b and c. Each z-clique is associated to one or more Union-Find nodes, as shown in the Setz information on the top-right. The Union-Find structure represents two sets because there are two different root nodes: a and c. The first set contains all 2-cliques associated with a or b, the second contains 2-cliques associated with c.

Algorithm 2. CPMZ pseudocode

1: UF ← Empty Union-Find data structure
2: Setz ← Empty Dictionary
3: **for** each k-clique $c_k \in G$ **do**
4:     $S \leftarrow \emptyset$ ▷ Sets of z-cliques to merge
5:     **for** each $(k-1)$-clique $c_{k-1} \subset c_k$ **do**
6:         $P \leftarrow \emptyset$
7:         **for** each z-clique $c_z \subset c_{k-1}$ **do**
8:             Setz$[c_z] \leftarrow \{$UF.Find(p) for $p \in$ Setz$[c_z]\}$
9:             **if** $P == \emptyset$ **then**
10:                 $P \leftarrow$ Setz$[c_z]$
11:             **else**
12:                 $P \leftarrow P \cap$ Setz$[c_z]$
13:         $S \leftarrow S \cup P$
14:     $q \leftarrow NULL$ ▷ Identifier of the resulting set of z-cliques
15:     **if** $S == \emptyset$ **then**
16:         $q \leftarrow$ UF.MakeSet$()$
17:     **else**
18:         $q \leftarrow$ UF.Union(S)
19:     **for** each z-clique $c_z \subset c_k$ **do**
20:         Setz$[c_z]$.add(q)

Algorithm 2 is the pseudo-code of CPMZ. The for loop on Line 3 iterates over each k-clique c_k of a graph G. As in the CPM algorithm, the idea is to identify the communities of each $(k-1)$-clique of c_k and perform their union.

As explained above, the communities of a $(k-1)$-clique are the ones that contain all its z-cliques, which is why we compute their intersection in the set P in Line 12. The set P is computed for all $(k-1)$-cliques in Lines 4–13 and their union is computed in set S. Then all the sets in S are merged in Line 18.

It may turn out that S is empty after the loop of Line 5. This corresponds to the case where none of the $(k-1)$-cliques of c_k were observed before: if a $(k-1)$-clique c_{k-1} has not yet been seen in the algorithm, its z-cliques may not belong to a common Union-Find set, and therefore P computed at Line 12 is empty. If this happens for all $(k-1)$-cliques of c_k S is empty and a new set (Union-Find node) is created on Line 16. The identifier of the resulting (new or merged) set is added to the set of Union-Find nodes for every z-clique of the current k-clique (Line 20).

In some rare cases, Line 12 will consider that a $(k-1)$-clique belongs to a Union-Find set while this is not true in the CPM exact case. Figure 2 gives an example. In that case this causes an incorrect k-clique adjacency detection and results in an incorrect merge of two or more k-clique communities.

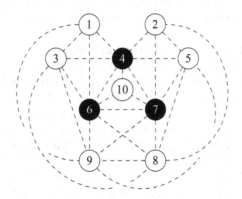

Fig. 2. In this example $k = 4$ and $z = 2$. A k-clique percolation community is formed by the nodes of the following k-cliques: $\{1,3,4,6\}$, $\{1,3,6,9\}$, $\{3,6,8,9\}$, $\{6,7,8,9\}$, $\{5,7,8,9\}$, $\{2,5,7,8\}$, $\{2,4,5,7\}$. The middle $(k-1)$-clique with nodes $\{4,6,7\}$ is formed by the z-cliques (edges) of other k-cliques, whereas it is not itself a part of any k-clique given above. When a new k-clique $\{4,6,7,10\}$ is observed, the CPMZ algorithm will produce one community $\{1,2,3,4,5,6,7,8,9,10\}$, but the exact CPM algorithm gives two communities, namely $\{1,2,3,4,5,6,7,8,9\}$ and $\{4,6,7,10\}$.

Theorem 1 (cpmz validity). *The* CPMZ *algorithm returns a set of agglomerated k-cliques communities, such that each* CPM *community is included in one and only one agglomerated community.*

Proof. If two k-cliques c_k^1 and c_k^2 are adjacent, this means they share a $(k-1)$-clique c_{k-1}. This will be correctly detected by Lines 5–12 of Algorithm 2: after the iteration on c_k^1 in the main loop, all z-cliques of c_{k-1} will belong to a common Union-Find set. The root of this set will belong to S during the iteration on c_k^2, ensuring that the Union-Find sets of both k-cliques will be merged. In other words, CPM communities are never split by CPMZ Algorithm and each CPM community belongs to a single agglomerated community. Conversely, an agglomerated community may contain more than one CPM community.

4   Analysis

We denote the number of k-cliques in graph G by n_k. For each k-clique, the CPM algorithm performs a Find and a Union operation for each of its $(k-1)$-clique (see Algorithm 1). It is well known (see for example [16]) that Union-Find data structure performs operations in $O(\alpha(n))$ amortized time, where α is the inverse Ackermann function, and n is the number of elements. It grows extremely slowly. Therefore, the number of operations is proportional in practice to $k \cdot n_k$. The space complexity of this algorithm is dominated by the tree on the $(k-1)$-cliques and the corresponding cost is proportional to $(k-1) \cdot n_{k-1}$.

CPMZ is a tradeoff between memory and time. Indeed, we will see that the CPMZ has a higher running time than the exact CPM algorithm, but requires less memory.

For the CPMZ algorithm as well, the time required by the Union and Find operations can still be considered as constant, as is the time required for the MakeSet and Add operations. The total number of operations is then dominated by the number of Find operations of Line 8. This line runs on each distinct triplet (c_k, c_{k-1}, c_z), where $c_{k-1} \subset c_k$ and $c_z \subset c_{k-1}$, and there are $\binom{k-1}{z} \cdot k \cdot n_k$ such triplets. Each z-clique c_z of Line 8 belongs to a number of Union-Find nodes $|\mathtt{Setz}[c_z]|$ that depends on the considered clique but also varies during the execution of the algorithm: it can either increase as new Union-Find nodes are added to $\mathtt{Setz}[c_z]$ (on Line 20) or decrease (on Line 8) if some Union-Find trees are merged (on Line 18). This number $|\mathtt{Setz}[c_z]|$ is bounded by the number of k-cliques each z-clique belongs to, which can theoretically be quite high. However, we computed in practice the average number of Find operations performed for each z-clique, and we will see in Sect. 5.3 that it is very often equal to 1 or 2 and never exceeds 6 in our experiments. The main difference in the running time with respect to the exact CPM algorithm is, therefore, the extra $\binom{k-1}{z}$ factor.

Concerning the space requirements, the CPMZ algorithm needs to store all z-cliques, which takes a space proportional to $z \cdot n_z$. Each z-clique c_z then belongs to a number of Union-Find nodes $|\mathtt{Setz}[c_z]|$ that varies during the algorithm execution. Even if the average of this number is low, we are interested now in the maximum space taken at any time of the execution. Finally, the number of nodes in the Union-Find structure is equal to the number of MakeSet operations that have been performed during the execution. In theory this number can also be quite high. However, we will see in Sect. 5 that in practice the memory requirements of the CPMZ algorithm are much lower than those of the CPM algorithm.

Finally, notice that both our algorithms result in the Union-Find structure whose nodes represent sets of cliques. This structure encodes the communities. In order to obtain the actual node list of each community, post-processing is needed. It consists in iterating over all cliques in the Union-Find structure. Then for each clique one must find its root node in the Union-Find and add the clique nodes to the corresponding set. We do not take into account this post-processing in the reported running time and memory usage in the next section.

5   Experimental Evaluation

Machine. We carried out our experiments on a Linux machine DELL PowerEdge R440, equipped with 2 processors Intel Xeon Silver 4216 with 32 cores each, and with 384 GB of RAM.

Datasets. We consider several real-world graphs that we obtained from [11]. Their characteristics are presented in Table 1. We distinguish between three categories of graphs according to their number of k-cliques. For graphs with small core values all algorithms are able to run; for graphs with medium core values, the state-of-the-art algorithms take too long to complete (with the exception of DBLP discussed below) while our CPM algorithm obtains results for small values of k; for graphs with large core values even our CPM algorithm runs out of memory or time except for very small values of k, but we will show that we are able to obtain relaxed results of high quality with our CPMZ algorithm.

Table 1. Our dataset of real-world graphs, ordered by core value c. k_{min} and k_{max} represent the minimum and maximum k on which we could run our CPM algorithm. n_k is the number of k-cliques of the graph.

Network	n	m	c	$k_{min} - k_{max}$	$n_{k_{min}}$	$n_{k_{max}}$
soc-pokec	1,632,803	22,031,964	47	3–15	32,557,458	353,958,854
loc-gowalla	196,591	950,327	51	3–15	2,273,138	201,454,150
Youtube	1,134,890	2,987,624	51	3–15	3,056,386	1,068
zhishi-baidu	2,140,198	17,014,946	78	3–15	25,207,196	1,080,702,188
as-skitter	1,696,415	11,095,298	111	3–6	28,769,868	9,759,000,981
DBLP	425,957	1,049,866	113	3–7	2,224,385	60,913,718,813
WikiTalk	2,394,385	4,659,565	131	3–7	9,203,519	5,490,986,046
Orkut	3,072,627	117,185,083	253	3–5	627,584,181	15,766,607,860
Friendster	124,836,180	1,806,067,135	304	3–4	4,173,724,124	8,963,503,236
LiveJournal	4,036,538	34,681,189	360	3–4	177,820,130	5,216,918,441

Implementation. We implemented our CPM and CPMZ algorithm in C. The implementation is available on the following gitlab repository: https://gitlab.lip6.fr/baudin/cpm-cpmz. For the competitors, we used the publicly available implementations of their algorithms [8,9,14,15].

Computing Domain. For each graph and each algorithm, we performed the computations of CPM for all values of k from 3 to 15, unless we were not able to finish the computation for one of the following reasons:

- the memory exceeded 390 GB of RAM,
- or the computation time exceeded 72 h.

We ran the CPMZ algorithm for $z = 2$ and $z = 3$. It could be computed on all the cases for which CPM works, except for $z = 3$ in graphs zhishi-baidu with $k = 15$ and DBLP with $k = 7$.

The interesting point is that we manage to have results with CPMZ in cases where the computation could not be carried out by the CPM algorithm: for as-skitter $k = 7$, WikiTalk $k = 8, 9$, Orkut $k = 6$ and Friendster $k = 5, 6$.

The detail of all the calculated values, with which the following figures were generated, is available on the following gitlab repository: https://gitlab.lip6.fr/baudin/cpm-supplementary-material.

5.1   Comparison with the State of the Art

The algorithm proposed by Palla *et al.* in the original paper introducing CPM [14] is quadratic in the number of maximal cliques. Given that we are interested in graphs with at least several million cliques, these graphs are too big to be processed by this algorithm. We do not perform experiments with this algorithm.

In addition, our tests have shown that the algorithm by Reid *et al.* [15] has a better performance than that of Gregori *et al.* [8] (sequential version) therefore we do not present the results obtained with the version of Gregori *et al.*

We observed that there are indeed linearity factors:

- in time: for each k-clique, each of its $(k - 1)$-clique is processed in constant time, hence the running time of CPM is indeed linear in $k \cdot n_k$
- in memory: the memory is used to store the Union-Find structure on the $(k - 1)$-cliques: one node per $(k - 1)$-clique encoded on $k - 1$ integers, hence the memory needed by CPM is linear in $(k - 1) \cdot n_{k-1}$.

Figure 3 compares the time and the memory necessary for the computation of the CPM communities by our CPM algorithm and the remaining competitive algorithms in the state of the art, proposed by Reid *et al.* [15] and Kumpula *et al.* [9]. For each competitive algorithm, we plot its running time (resp. memory usage) divided by the running time (resp. memory usage) of our CPM algorithm. We display the results as a function of n_k, where n_k is the number of k-cliques of the input graph. In some cases, our CPM algorithm obtains results whereas one of the state-of-the-art doesn't. This can happen because this algorithm exceeds either the time or memory limit. We display this by placing a symbol on the corresponding horizontal line at the top of the figure.

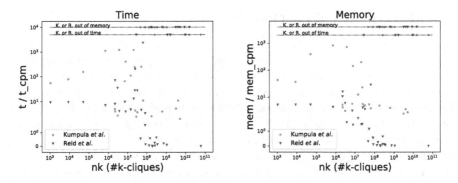

Fig. 3. Comparison between time and memory consumption of the state-of-the-art CPM methods and those from ours. For each competitive algorithm, we plot its running time (resp. memory usage) divided by the running time (resp. memory usage) of our CPM algorithm. We display the results as a function of n_k, where n_k is the number of k-cliques of the input graph. The maximum time is limited to 72 h and the maximum memory to 390 GB. A marker placed at the corresponding line therefore indicates a computation that did not finish, because of either time or memory limit.

First notice that the Reid *et al.* algorithm is better than ours for the four smallest graphs in our dataset (soc-pokec, loc-gowalla, Youtube, zhishi-baidu). Indeed, this algorithm begins by computing the maximum cliques, then processes them to form communities. In the case of these small graphs, the maximum cliques are easily computed. For such graphs, the memory used does not depend on k because in all cases the maximal cliques are stored; interestingly, the time computation time decreases with k as only the maximal cliques of size larger than or equal to k have to be tested for adjacency.

This algorithm is also more efficient than ours in certain configurations, when the graph is already well segmented into large cliques. This is the case with our DBLP graph, for which the Reid *et al.* algorithm manages to compute the communities in 10 s when we need several hours to process the large number of k-cliques.

Notice however that their algorithm does not allow to process the largest graphs of our dataset. The as-skitter intermediate graph contains too many cliques and their algorithm does not provide a result in less than 72 h. For denser graphs (WikiTalk, Orkut, Friendster, LiveJournal), there are too many maximum cliques for RAM, and the algorithm cannot run, while ours is able to compute the result.

Finally, the algorithm of Kumpula *et al.* is systematically less efficient than ours. Our algorithm is also able to obtain results in cases where no other algorithm can provide any (see the points on the two horizontal lines on top of the figures).

5.2   Memory Gain of the CPMZ Algorithm

Figure 4 (right) compares the memory used by our algorithms CPM and CPMZ with $z = 2, 3$. We show the memory used by CPMZ divided by the memory used by CPM, as a function of n_k. As for the previous figure, we represent cases where CPMZ exceeds the time limit on a horizontal line on top of the figure. In addition, cases where we obtain results with CPMZ and not CPM are represented by symbols on a horizontal line at the bottom of the figure. For some small graphs, the number of $(k-1)$-cliques, which are stored by CPM, is smaller than the number of z-cliques. For these graphs CPMZ requires more memory than CPM. In most cases however, we observe a huge memory gain, and in some cases it is even possible to obtain results unachievable by our CPM algorithm.

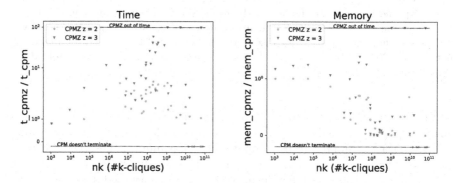

Fig. 4. Comparison between time and memory consumption of the CPMZ algorithm and our CPM. For CPMZ with $z = 2$ and $z = 3$, we plot its running time (resp. memory usage) divided by the running time (resp. memory usage) of our CPM algorithm. We display the results as a function of n_k, where n_k is the number of k-cliques of the input graph. The maximum time is limited to 72 h, and the memory is not limiting in comparison with CPM. A marker placed at the top line therefore indicates a computation that did not finish, because of time limit. A marker placed at the bottom line indicates a computation that finishes for CPMZ but not for CPM.

In addition to this display and to the discussion about memory requirements in Sect. 4, we performed experiments to evaluate the memory associated with each z-clique in the algorithm. To do so, we computed the mean number of Union-Find nodes to which each z-clique belongs. In Algorithm 2, we therefore computed the sum the size of all $\mathtt{Setz}[c_z]$ every time the algorithm reaches Line 8 Then, we divided this sum by the number of times this line is browsed, which is $n_{k-1} \cdot k \cdot \binom{k-1}{z}$. We observed that this factor remains low; for all graphs and all values of k and z it is between 1 and 2, except for the small graphs of Youtube with a value around 4 for $z = 2$ and $k \in [10, 15]$, $z = 3$ and $k \in [11, 15]$, and zhishi-baidu with a value around 5 for $z = 2$ and $k = 5, 6, 7$.

Concerning the running time, as discussed in Sect. 4, there are two factors that cause CPMZ to be slower than CPM. The first one is the fact that a z-clique can belong to several Union-Find nodes. As we just showed, this number is small in practice and therefore it does not play a strong role in the running time. The other factor is the extra $\binom{k-1}{z}$ factor induced by the fact that we consider all z-cliques included in a k-clique. This factor is high and therefore the computation time remains the limiting factor. Figure 4 (left) compares it to the running time of CPM.

5.3   CPMZ Communities Are Very Close to CPM Communities

To measure the precision of our algorithm, we compare the agglomerated communities computed by the CPMZ algorithm with those of the CPM algorithm. To do so, we use an implementation of a Normalized Mutual Information measure for sets of overlapping clusters, called ONMI, provided by McAid et al. [13]. This tool measures how similar two sets of overlapping communities are.

We carried out the similarity comparisons on all the graphs of our dataset, with all the values of k for which we can compute the communities with the CPM algorithm (see Table 1). We observe the following:

- for CPMZ with $z = 2$, the average similarity is 98.6%, the median is 99.4% and all values are larger than 93.8%;
- for CPMZ with $z = 3$, the average similarity is 99.95%, the median is 100% and all values are larger than 99.5%.

This confirms that the incorrect merges between communities performed by the CPMZ algorithm have little influence on the final result: the structure of communities is barely impacted by the CPMZ algorithm.

6   Conclusion and Discussions

In this paper we addressed the problem of overlapping community detection on graphs through the clique percolation method (CPM). Our contributions are twofold: first we proposed an improvement in the computation of the exact result by leveraging a state of the art k-clique listing method; then we proposed a heuristic algorithm called CPMZ that provides agglomerated communities, i.e. communities that are supersets of the exact communities; this algorithm uses much less memory than the exact algorithm, at the cost of a higher running time.

Through extensive experiments on a large set of graphs coming from different contexts, we show that:

- our exact CPM algorithm outperforms the state of the art algorithms in many cases, and we are able to compute the CPM communities in cases where it was not possible before;
- our relaxed CPMZ algorithm uses significantly less memory than the exact algorithm; even though its running time is higher, this allows us to obtain agglomerated communities in cases where no other algorithm can run;

– finally the results provided by the CPMZ algorithm have an excellent accuracy, according to the ONMI method and obtain a score very close to 1 in the vast majority of cases.

Notice however that for the DBLP graph, which is of medium size, the approach proposed in [15] works better than ours. This can be explained because this graph naturally has a strong clique structure. Indeed, a link exists in this graph if two authors have written a paper together, and each paper therefore induces a clique on the set of its authors. In this case computing the maximal cliques and extracting the community out of them is more efficient than detecting adjacent k-cliques. This raises the interesting question of whether it is possible to predict which method will be more efficient on a graph by studying this graph's structure.

Several other interesting perspectives arise from our work. It should be noted that the order in which k-cliques are processed plays an important role in the incorrect community agglomerations performed by the CPMZ algorithm, which we do not yet fully understand. Our experiments show that in practice only a few merges of k-clique communities happen. This gives rise to many interesting graph theoretical questions about the characterisation of the sub-graphs that can produce an incorrect k-clique adjacency detection: how many of them are there in a typical real-world graph? We conjecture that it is possible to construct examples in which no processing order of the k-cliques will lead to the exact solution. However, in many cases including real-world graphs, it is possible that a certain processing order of k-cliques yields results of a higher quality than other orderings. This raises the question of how to design such an ordering. Another interesting possibility would be to run the CPMZ algorithm with two or more different k-cliques ordering and compare their output: since the CPMZ communities are coarser than the exact CPM communities, it is possible to compare the communities of both outputs to obtain a better result that any of the individual runs.

Finally, the linkstream formalism [10] allows to represent interactions that occur at different times, which is a natural framework to represent people meeting at different time during the week or computers exchanging IP packets on the internet. It would be interesting to investigate the community structure and its temporal aspects in such data by extending the definition of k-clique communities to linkstreams.

Acknowledgements. This work was partly supported by projects ANER ARTICO (Bourgogne-Franche-Comté region), ANR (French National Agency of Research) Limass project (under grant ANR-19-CE23-0010), ANR FiT LabCom and ANR COREGRAPHIE project (grant ANR-20-CE23-0002). We would like to greatly thank Lionel Tabourier for insightful discussions, useful comments and suggestions, and Fabrice Lecuyer for his careful proofreading.

References

1. Bron, C., Kerbosch, J.: Algorithm 457: finding all cliques of an undirected graph. Commun. ACM **16**(9), 575–577 (1973)
2. Danisch, M., Balalau, O.D., Sozio, M.: Listing k-cliques in sparse real-world graphs. In: Champin, P.A., Gandon, F.L., Lalmas, M., Ipeirotis, P.G. (eds.) WWW, pp. 589–598. ACM (2018)
3. Eppstein, D., Löffler, M., Strash, D.: Listing all maximal cliques in sparse graphs in near-optimal time. In: Cheong, O., Chwa, K.-Y., Park, K. (eds.) ISAAC 2010. LNCS, vol. 6506, pp. 403–414. Springer, Heidelberg (2010). https://doi.org/10.1007/978-3-642-17517-6_36
4. Eppstein, D., Strash, D.: Listing all maximal cliques in large sparse real-world graphs. In: Pardalos, P.M., Rebennack, S. (eds.) SEA 2011. LNCS, vol. 6630, pp. 364–375. Springer, Heidelberg (2011). https://doi.org/10.1007/978-3-642-20662-7_31
5. Fortunato, S., Castellano, C.: Community Structure in Graphs, pp. 490–512. Springer, New York (2012)
6. Fredman, M., Saks, M.: The cell probe complexity of dynamic data structures. In: Proceedings of the Twenty-First Annual ACM Symposium on Theory of Computing, STOC 1989, pp. 345–354. Association for Computing Machinery (1989)
7. Galler, B.A., Fisher, M.J.: An improved equivalence algorithm. Commun. ACM **7**(5), 301–303 (1964)
8. Gregori, E., Lenzini, L., Mainardi, S.: Parallel k-clique community detection on large-scale networks. IEEE Trans. Parallel Distrib. Syst. **24**(8), 1651–1660 (2013). Implementation available at: https://sourceforge.net/p/cosparallel
9. Kumpula, J.M., Kivelä, M., Kaski, K., Saramäki, J.: Sequential algorithm for fast clique percolation. Phys. Rev. E **78**(2), 026109 (2008). Implementation available at: https://github.com/CxAalto/scp
10. Latapy, M., Viard, T., Magnien, C.: Stream graphs and link streams for the modeling of interactions over time. Soc. Netw. Anal. Min. **8**(1), 61:1–61:29 (2018). https://doi.org/10.1007/s13278-018-0537-7. https://hal.archives-ouvertes.fr/hal-01665084
11. Leskovec, J., Krevl, A.: SNAP Datasets: Stanford large network dataset collection, June 2014. http://snap.stanford.edu/data
12. Li, R.H., Gao, S., Qin, L., Wang, G., Yang, W., Xu Yu, J.: Ordering heuristics for k-clique listing. In: PVLDB (2020)
13. McDaid, A.F., Greene, D., Hurley, N.: Normalized mutual information to evaluate overlapping community finding algorithms (2013). https://arxiv.org/abs/1110.2515
14. Palla, G., Derényi, I., Farkas, I., Vicsek, T.: Uncovering the overlapping community structure of complex networks in nature and society. Nature **435**(7043), 814–818 (2005). Implementation available at: http://www.cfinder.org/
15. Reid, F., McDaid, A., Hurley, N.: Percolation computation in complex networks. In: 2012 IEEE/ACM International Conference on Advances in Social Networks Analysis and Mining (ASONAM), pp. 274–281. IEEE (2012). Implementation available at: https://sites.google.com/site/cliqueperccomp/home
16. Tarjan, R.E., van Leeuwen, J.: Worst-case analysis of set union algorithms. J. ACM **31**(2), 245–281 (1984)
17. Xie, J., Kelley, S., Szymanski, B.K.: Overlapping community detection in networks: the state-of-the-art and comparative study. ACM Comput. Surv. (CSUR) **45**(4), 43 (2013)

Knowledge Graph Embedding Based on Quaternion Transformation and Convolutional Neural Network

Yabin Gao[1], Xiaoyun Tian[1], Jing Zhou[1(✉)], Bin Zheng[2], Hairu Li[2], and Zizhong Zhu[3]

[1] State Grid Financial Technology Group, State Grid Electronic Commerce Co., Ltd., Beijing, China
{gaoyabin,tianxiaoyun,zhoujing}@sgec.sgcc.com.cn
[2] State Grid Ecommerce Technology Co., Ltd., Tianjin, China
[3] College of Intelligence and Computing, Tianjin University, Tianjin, China
zhengbin@sgec.sgcc.com.cn

Abstract. In the cognitive intelligence of machines, more and more researchers use knowledge graphs that represent the structure of entities. The basic idea of knowledge representation learning is to project knowledge (entities and relations) into a vector space. The entities and relationships embedded in the 2-D space use convolutional neural networks to obtain the mutual information between them. However, the feature extraction capabilities of neural networks are limited by the input feature information. Therefore, our model named knowledge graph embedding based on quaternion transformation and convolutional neural network (QCKGE), aims to solve the limitation of input features by riching entities and relations mutual features. Firstly, the entity and relation are expressed as a two-dimensional real number space. Then, these features are mapped to the quaternion space to increase the ability to express entities and relations. Finally, the convolutional neural networks to mine richer interactive information in entities and relationships for link prediction. Besides, this paper also uses multi-layer convolutional neural network to mine deeper information hidden in the features. On the datasets of WN18, FB15k, WN18RR, and FB15k-237, compared with the existing model, our design can show a better result.

Keywords: Quaternion transform · Knowledge graph · Convolutional neural network

1 Introduction

Human beings constantly understand and explore the world through existing knowledge. Knowledge graph can represent the relationship between entities, and it has strong ability of structure representation and relational reasoning.

© Springer Nature Switzerland AG 2022
B. Li et al. (Eds.): ADMA 2021, LNAI 13088, pp. 128–136, 2022.
https://doi.org/10.1007/978-3-030-95408-6_10

For the complex tasks faced by intelligent systems, inspired by humans' problem-solving, they are solved through knowledge representation and knowledge reasoning [1]. Knowledge graphs have important applications in question answering, search, natural language processing and so on. However, knowledge graphs are usually incomplete in our world. Researchers make entities and relations maps into vector space to predict the missing links between entities, and whether the triple is effective using the scoring function. Embedding entities and relations into low-dimensional space is the crucial idea of representation learning. Previous researches mainly embed them into Real Number Space, Complex Number Space, Gaussian Space, and Flow Space [2].

A quaternion is a hypercomplex space, which is constructed of a real number part with three imaginary number parts. Compared with Complex Number Space, it not only has the symmetric relations of the complex space, but also has more degrees of freedom. So the characteristics of entities and relations can be fully expressed. However, most of the existing methods directly use the entity and relations embedding vector for scoring calculation, but use the shallow information of entity and relations, ignoring the implicit interactive information.

Our method projects knowledge (entities and relations) into the quaternion space, and uses convolutional neural networks to enrich mutual information to solve the problem of lack of features. We propose a knowledge graph embedding based on quaternion transformation and convolutional neural network (QCKGE). Its contributions are as follows:

- The entity and relation are converted to quaternion space, and convolution neural network is used for learning the interactive information of entity and relation from quaternion space.
- For extracting more abundant feature information, multi-layer convolutional is used in the algorithm, and residual connection is inserted.
- The proposed model is tested on four public datasets, and good results are obtained.

2 Related Work

Early researchers focused on the translation method, approximating the tail entities embedding to the sum of the head entities embedding and the relations embedding. Such as, TransE [3]. However, TransE is good at one-to-one relations, it is not suitable for Many to-one, one-to-Many, and Many-to-Many relations. Some researchers have made improvements on the basis of the TransE method such as TransH [4], TransR [5], TransD [6], and STransE [7] to deal with the above issue.

Because the deep neural network has strong feature extraction ability, some researchers have introduced it into the triple prediction of knowledge map and achieved good results [9–13]. For example, ConvE [9] firstly embeds the head entities and relations into the reshaping 2D matrix space. Then neural network operates on the 2D matrix through convolution to get the feature maps. Finally, the predicted score is obtained by calculating tail entity vector and normalized feature map. In recent years, some research work focus on complex vector space or even hyper-complex vector space [14,15]. The ComplEx [14] model introduces a complex-valued vector, and calculates the triplet score through the Hermitian dot product.

However, in ConvE model, the input of convolution is a real valued feature space of entities and relations, which can not completely express entities and relations, resulting in the waste of convolution neural network. On the other hand, compared with real space and complex spaces, quaternion space can provide highly expressive calculations through Hamilton products. Zhu et al. [16] projected the image of the RGB channel into the quaternion space. Each channel (R, G, B) corresponds to a dimension (i, j, k) of the quaternion space to form a quaternion convolutional network. Compared with the original neural convolutional network, it is obtained in the image classification task better results. Inspired by this, we conceive a model, named knowledge graph embedding model based on quaternion transformation and convolutional neural network (QCKGE) model, making the quaternion embedded in entity and relation as convolution neural network input, and utilizes multi-layer residual connection to improve the entity prediction results of triples.

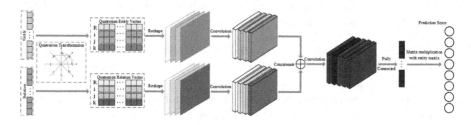

Fig. 1. QCKGE model structure.

3   Method

This paper schemes architecture is shown in Fig. 1, which is Our QCKGE. Firstly, the real valued vectors of entity and relation are mapped to quaternion space to obtain quaternion entities vector and quaternion relations vector respectively. Secondly, reshape each component of the quaternion to obtain the matrix form of a quaternion entity, so that the entities or relations form a four channel two-dimensional matrix. Finally, the four-channel 2-dimensional matrixes are input to the convolutional network to learn the enrich mutual information between entities and relations. Our method utilized the form of convolution to fuse entity and relation through self-learning. This is different from ConvE in fusing entity and related information in a fixed way.

3.1   Quaternion Space

In 1843, Hamilton extended the complex space to the super complex space by using the quaternion containing one real component and three imaginary components to form the quaternion space [17]. Formula 1 is the description of quaternion:

$$q = a + b\mathbf{i} + c\mathbf{j} + d\mathbf{k} \tag{1}$$

Here a, b, c, d denote the real number, a represents real part of quaternion, b, c, d denote the imaginary parts, $\mathbf{i}, \mathbf{j}, \mathbf{k}$ denote the imaginary units. Formula 2 is the most basic algorithm followed by quaternions:

$$\begin{cases} \mathbf{ij} = \mathbf{k}, \mathbf{jk} = \mathbf{i}, \mathbf{ki} = \mathbf{j} \\ \mathbf{ji} = -\mathbf{k}, kj = -\mathbf{i}, \mathbf{ik} = -\mathbf{j} \\ \mathbf{i}^2 = \mathbf{j}^2 = \mathbf{k}^2 = \mathbf{ijk} = -1 \\ \mathbf{i}^0 = \mathbf{j}^0 = \mathbf{k}^0 = 1 \end{cases} \tag{2}$$

The conjugate ($\bar{q}$) and modulus ($|q|$) of quaternions are shown in formulas 3 and 4:

$$\bar{q} = a - b\mathbf{i} - c\mathbf{j} - d\mathbf{k} \tag{3}$$

$$|q| = \sqrt{a^2 + b^2 + c^2 + d^2} \tag{4}$$

3.2   Constructing Quaternions of Entities and Relations

Triples are usually written as (h, r, t) in knowledge graph, and the vectors are denoted as: $h : [h_1, \cdots, h_m], r : [r_1, \cdots, r_m], t : [t_1, \cdots, t_m]$. m is the dimension of the vector. Mapping it to quaternion space can be expressed as follows:

$$h : \begin{bmatrix} h_{R1}, \cdots, h_{Rm} \\ h_{i1}, \cdots, h_{im} \\ h_{j1}, \cdots, h_{jm} \\ h_{k1}, \cdots, h_{kn} \end{bmatrix}, r : \begin{bmatrix} r_{R1}, \cdots, r_{Rm} \\ r_{i1}, \cdots, r_{im} \\ r_{j1}, \cdots, r_{jm} \\ r_{k1}, \cdots, r_{kn} \end{bmatrix}, t : \begin{bmatrix} t_{R1}, \cdots, t_{Rm} \\ t_{i1}, \cdots, t_{in} \\ t_{j1}, \cdots, t_{jm} \\ t_{k1}, \cdots, t_{kn} \end{bmatrix} \tag{5}$$

Among them, the first line is the real component, and the last three lines denote the three directions corresponding to the imaginary components of the quaternion.

This paper uses the initialization algorithm of quaternion network in Parcollet et al. [18]. The specific initialization form is:

$$\begin{aligned} w_{real} &= \varphi \cos(\theta) \\ w_i &= \varphi Q_i \sin(\theta) \\ w_j &= \varphi Q_j \sin(\theta) \\ w_k &= \varphi Q_k \sin(\theta) \end{aligned} \tag{6}$$

Where w_{real}, w_i, w_j and w_k denote the coefficients. θ is an angle in the range $[-\pi, \pi]$. Q_* means a normalized form of quaternion. The value range of φ is $\left[-\frac{1}{\sqrt{2k}}, \frac{1}{\sqrt{2k}}\right]$, reminiscent to the He initialization [19].

3.3 Convolutional Network Designed

For adequately extracting the implicit interactive information in entities and relations, this model framework introduces a convolutional neural network with multi-layer convolutional connections. The convolution operation can be expressed by formula 7:

$$x^{(l)} = f(W^l x^{(l-1)} + b^l) \tag{7}$$

where x^l represents the l layer output, x^{l-1} denotes input of the l layer, W the convolution kernel, b is the bias.

However, deep convolutional neural networks usually generate gradient disappearance and gradient explosion phenomena. Based on the experience of He et al. [20] (as shown in Fig. 2), this paper uses residual connection to solve the above problems. For a convolutional neural network layer, after adding residuals, it can be described as:

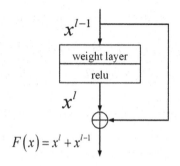

Fig. 2. Residual connection.

$$F(x) = x^{(l)} + x^{(l-1)} = f(W^l x^{(l-1)} + b^l) + x^{(l-1)} \tag{8}$$

$$x^{(l)} = F(x) - x^{(l-1)} \tag{9}$$

In fact, formula 8 can be transformed into formula 9. It can be seen that is convolutional layer output. If such a connection changes slightly to the result $F(x)$, the convolutional layer can get a great perception and make adjustments. Equation 9 is also the reason why Fig. 2 is called residual connection.

3.4 Definition of Loss Function

The binary cross-entropy loss function was utilized to train QCKGE for making the network parameters more effective. As shown in formula 10:

$$\text{loss} = -\frac{1}{N} \sum_i (g_i \log (p_i) + (1 - g_i) \log (1 - p_i)) \tag{10}$$

where p, g denotes the sore of prediction and label. In our paper, the Adam [21] optimization algorithm is used to gradually minimize the loss function and obtain better network model parameters.

4   Experiments

4.1   Experimental Setup

For more comprehensively evaluating the performance, WN18 [3], WN18RR [4], FB15k [3] and FB15k-237 [22] completed this experiment on four public datasets. The CPU model of the experimental platform used in this paper is Intel Core i7 9700K 8 GB, the GPU model is GTX 2080 8 GB video memory, and Ubuntu 16.04 is chosen as the operating system. The algorithm is implemented using the Pytorch = 1.90 deep learning framework. With a learning rate of 0.001 and a batch_size of 128, training 2000 batches on the dataset. At training process, This model that produces better on the validation datasets is saved. When the loss function does not decrease for 5 consecutive batches, it is considered that a good effect has been achieved, and the training is stopped.

4.2   Evaluation Protocol

MR (Mean Rank) and MRR (Mean Reciprocal Rank) are used as metrics with Hit ratio cut-off values $n = 1, 3, 10$, respectively. MR is the predicted correct entities ranking. The better the model predicts, the smaller the MR value. MRR is a general mechanism for evaluating search algorithms, and its evaluation assumption is based on only one relevant result. Hit@n is the correct number ratio of entities n among the top n entities predicted.

Table 1. Comparison results on WN18 and FB15K

Method	WN18					FB15K				
	MR	MRR	hit@10	hit@3	hit@1	MR	MRR	hit@10	hit@3	hit@1
TransE [3]	/	0.495	0.943	0.888	0.113	/	0.463	0.749	0.578	0.297
DistMult [8]	655	0.797	0.946	/	/	42.2	0.798	0.893	/	/
HolE [23]	/	0.938	0.949	0.945	0.930	/	0.524	0.739	0.579	0.599
ComplEx [14]	/	0.941	0.947	0.945	**0.936**	/	0.692	0.840	0.759	0.599
TorusE [24]	/	0.947	0.954	0.950	0.943	/	0.733	0.832	0.771	**0.674**
SimplE [25]	/	0.942	0.947	0.944	0.697	/	0.727	0.838	0.773	0.660
NKGE [26]	336	0.947	0.957	0.949	0.942	56	0.730	**0.871**	0.790	0.650
ConvE [9]	374	0.943	0.956	0.946	0.935	51	0.657	0.831	0.723	0.558
QCKGE (Ours)	**273**	**0.947**	**0.958**	**0.952**	0.933	**47**	**0.734**	0.852	**0.801**	0.611

4.3   Results

The QCKGE is compared with other existing methods on WN18, FB15k, WN18RR, and FB15k-237. Here, we only use this model to sort the prediction scores of triples that do not exist in the datasets, and exclude the known triples in the datasets. On the datasets FB15k, WN18, WN18RR, and FB15k-237, our performance of results are shown in Table 1 and Table 2. The QCKGE model has reached a better performance on these four datasets.

Table 2. Comparison results on WN18RR and FB15K-237

Method	WN18RR					FB15k-237				
	MR	MRR	hit@10	hit@3	hit@1	MR	MRR	hit@10	hit@3	hit@1
TransE [3]	3384	0.226	0.501	/	/	357	0.297	0.465	/	/
DistMult [8]	5110	0.430	0.490	0.440	0.390	254	0.241	0.419	0.263	0.155
ComplEx [14]	5261	0.440	0.510	0.460	0.410	339	0.247	0.428	0.275	0.158
NKGE [26]	4170	0.450	0.526	0.465	0.421	237	0.330	0.510	**0.365**	0.241
ConvE [9]	4187	0.430	0.520	0.440	0.400	244	0.325	0.501	0.356	0.237
ConvKB [27]	**2741**	0.220	0.508	/	/	196	0.302	0.483	/	/
InteractE [13]	5202	0.463	0.528	/	0.430	172	**0.354**	0.535	/	0.263
QCKGE (Ours)	4578	**0.475**	**0.532**	**0.491**	**0.435**	**170**	0.351	**0.536**	0.363	**0.249**

4.4 Ablation Study

In the QCKGE model proposed, when extracting the interactive information of entities and relations, 5 convolutional layers are used, and the residual connection is used in the last layer. This section will evaluate the impact in the final performance with each module in our algorithm. Here $N\{N = 1, 2, 3, 4, 5\}$ convolutional layers are used in the proposed to perform experiments, and the last layer is whether to use residual connection (+res) for experiments. Then we perform these models evaluation in the dataset FB15K-237.

Table 3. Comparison of network layer structure in the model.

N	FB15k-237				
	MR	MRR	hit@10	hit@3	hit@1
1	236	0.323	0.501	0.358	0.236
2	204	0.332	0.516	0.359	0.241
3	187	0.343	0.524	0.362	0.244
4	179	0.347	0.534	0.361	0.247
5	178	0.346	0.531	0.362	0.247
5 + res	170	0.351	0.536	0.363	0.249

In Table 3, with the convolutional neural network layers (N) increasing, the performance of the model is improved, while at the fifth layer, the model effect has little improvement or a decline in some indicators. In addition, the performance is further improved after the residual connection is used in the last layer. The results show that the use of multi-layer convolutional neural networks and residual connections can better extract the interactive information of entities and relations, and then predict more accurate triples.

5 Conclusion

This paper proposes the QCKGE algorithm, which uses convolutional neural networks to rich the mutual information of entities and relations in the quaternion space. The QCKGE proposed in this paper predicts the score from the quaternion space embedded in entities and relations. The model first embeds the entity and relation to quaternion space, then learns feature information and interaction information of the entities and relations by using the convolutional neural network, so as to get prediction results of triples. The results on the four datasets show that QCKGE achieves a better capability. For study of embedding entities and relationships into the quaternion space, we will explore in interpretability of convolutional neural network and the mutual information of entities and relations in the future.

References

1. Newell, A., Shaw, J.C., Simon, H.A.: Report on a general problem solving program. In: Proceedings of the 1st International Conference on Information Processing, pp. 256–264 (1959)
2. Ji, S., Pan, S., Cambria, E.: A survey on knowledge graphs: representation, acquisition and applications. IEEE Trans. Neural Netw. Learn. Syst., 1–21 (2021)
3. Antoine, B., Nicolas, U., Alberto, G.D.: Translating embeddings for modeling multi-relational data. In: Advances in Neural Information Processing Systems, pp. 2787–2795 (2013)
4. Wang, Z., Zhang, J.W., Feng J.L.: Knowledge graph embedding by translating on hyperplanes. In: Proceedings of the 28th AAAI Conference on Artificial Intelligence, pp. 1112–1119 (2014)
5. Lin, Y.K., Liu Z.Y., Sun, M.S.: Learning entity and relation embeddings for knowledge graph completion. In: Proceedings of the 29th AAAI Conference on Artificial Intelligence Learning, pp. 2181–2187 (2015)
6. Ji, G.L., He, S.Z., Xu, L.H.: Knowledge graph embedding via dynamic mapping matrix. In: Proceedings of the 53rd Annual Meeting of the Association for Computational Linguistics and the 7th International Joint Conference on Natural Language Processing, pp. 687–696 (2015)
7. Nguyen, D.Q., Sirts, K., Qu, L.Z.: STransE: a novel embedding model of entities and relationships in knowledge bases. In: Proceedings of the 2016 Conference of the North American Chapter of the Association for Computational Linguistics: Human Language Technologies, pp. 460–466 (2016)
8. Yang, B., Yih, W.T., He, X.D., Gao, J.F.: Embedding entities and relations for learning and inference in knowledge bases. ArXiv preprint arXiv: 1412.6575 (2015)
9. Dettmers, T., Minervini, P., Stenetorp, P.: Convolutional 2D knowledge graph embeddings. In: Proceedings of the 32nd AAAI Conference on Artificial Intelligence, pp. 1811–1818 (2018)
10. Schlichtkrull, M., Kipf, T.N., Bloem, P., van den Berg, R., Titov, I., Welling, M.: Modeling relational data with graph convolutional networks. In: Gangemi, A., et al. (eds.) ESWC 2018. LNCS, vol. 10843, pp. 593–607. Springer, Cham (2018). https://doi.org/10.1007/978-3-319-93417-4_38

11. Nguyen, D.Q., Vu, T., Nguyen, T.D.: A capsule network-based embedding model for knowledge graph completion and search personalization. In: Proceedings of the 2019 Annual Conference of the North American Chapter of the Association for Computational Linguistics: Human Language Technologies, pp. 2180–2189 (2019)

12. Nguyen, D.Q., Nguyen, D.Q., Nguyen, T.D.: Convolutional neural network-based model for knowledge base completion and its application to search personalization. Semantic Web **10**(5), 947–960 (2019)

13. Vashishth, S., Sanyal, S., Nitin, V.: InteractE: improving convolution-based knowledge graph embeddings by increasing feature interactions. In: International Conference on Learning Representations, vol. 34, no. 03, pp. 3009–3016 (2020)

14. Trouillon, T., Welbl, J., Riedel, S.: Complex embeddings for simple link prediction. In: Proceedings of the 33nd International Conference on Machine Learning, pp. 2071–2080 (2016)

15. Sun, Z.Q., Deng, Z.H., Nie, J.Y.: Rotate: knowledge graph embedding by relational rotation in complex space. In: International Conference on Learning Representations, pp. 1–18 (2019)

16. Zhu, X., Xu, Y., Xu, H., Chen, C.: Quaternion convolutional neural networks. In: Ferrari, V., Hebert, M., Sminchisescu, C., Weiss, Y. (eds.) ECCV 2018. LNCS, vol. 11212, pp. 645–661. Springer, Cham (2018). https://doi.org/10.1007/978-3-030-01237-3_39

17. Hamilton, W.R.: Elements of Quaternions. Longmans Green, London (1866)

18. Parcollet, T., Ravanelli, M., Morchid, M.: Quaternion recurrent neural networks. In: International Conference on Learning Representations, pp. 1–19 (2019)

19. He, K.M., Zhang, X.Y., Ren, S.Q., Sun, J.: Delving deep into rectifiers: surpassing human-level performance on ImageNet classification. In: Proceedings of the IEEE International Conference on Computer Vision, pp. 1026–1034 (2015)

20. He, K., Zhang, X., Ren, S.: Deep residual learning for image recognition. In: Proceedings of the IEEE Conference on Computer Vision and Pattern Recognition, pp. 770–778 (2016)

21. Kingma, D.P., Ba, J.: Adam: a method for stochastic optimization. In: International Conference on Learning Representations, pp. 1–15 (2015)

22. Toutanova, K., Chen, D.Q.: Observed versus latent features for knowledge base and text inference. In: Proceedings of the 3rd Workshop on Continuous Vector Space Models and their Compositionality, pp. 57–66 (2015)

23. Nickel, M., Rosasco, L., Poggio, T.: Holographic embeddings of knowledge graphs. In: Proceedings of the 30th AAAI Conference on Artificial Intelligence, pp. 1–7 (2016)

24. Ebisu, T., Ichise, R.: TorusE: knowledge graph embedding on a lie group. In: Proceedings of the 32nd AAAI Conference on Artificial Intelligence, pp. 1–8 (2018)

25. Kazemi, S.M., Poole, D.: Simple embedding for link prediction in knowledge graphs. In: Advances in Neural Information Processing Systems, pp. 4289–4300 (2018)

26. Wang, K., Liu, Y., Xu, X.J.: Knowledge graph embedding with entity neighbors and deep memory network. ArXiv preprint arXiv:1808.03752 (2018)

27. Nguyen, D.Q., Nguyen, T.D., Nguyen, D.Q.: A novel embedding model for knowledge base completion based on convolutional neural network. In: Proceedings of the 2018 Conference of the North American Chapter of the Association for Computational Linguistics: Human Language Technologies, pp. 327–333 (2018)

Text-Enhanced Knowledge Graph Representation Model in Hyperbolic Space

Jiajun Wu, Bohan Li$^{(\boxtimes)}$, Ye Ji, Jiaying Tian, and Yuxuan Xiang

Nanjing University of Aeronautics and Astronautics, Nanjing, China
bhli@nuaa.edu.cn

Abstract. The representation learning of knowledge graph refers to embedding entities and relations in knowledge graph into a low-dimensional dense vector space. Existing knowledge graph embedding models mostly chose Euclidean Space as their vector space and consider each fact triple in knowledge graph independently. However, Euclidean Space is unable to represent knowledge effectively due to its strict constraints and mathematical expression. Besides, entities in knowledge graph are not isolated, while these models ignore the association between entities. To solve the problems above, we proposed a text-enhanced knowledge graph representation learning model in Hyperbolic Space. We utilize rich semantic information of entity description by using Transformer Encoder to enhance the ability of knowledge representation. Besides, we embed entities and relations into Hyperbolic Space, which can better capture hierarchical information of the knowledge graph. Experiments on benchmark dataset show that our method achieves better performance compared with other state-of-art methods.

Keywords: Knowledge graph · Representation learning · Embedding model · Hyperbolic space

1 Introduction

Knowledge graphs such as WordNet (Miller 1995) [15], Freebase (Bollacker et al. 2008) [2], Yago (Suchanek et al. 2007) [19] and Concept Graph (Microsoft Cornered. 2016) store huge numbers of structured data in the form of triples [18]. These triples in knowledge graph are usually represented as (h, r, t), where h represents the head entity, t represents the tail entity, and r represents the relation. More and more people focus on semantic information about entities and relations. Since the semantic information can enhance the representation ability of the entity, it has become a general technology and been widely used in knowledge-based applications, such as intelligent search, Q&A, recommendation system and natural language processing task.

Most knowledge graphs are automatically constructed, therefore they face the problem of lacking integrity. Knowledge graph completion has always been an

© Springer Nature Switzerland AG 2022
B. Li et al. (Eds.): ADMA 2021, LNAI 13088, pp. 137–149, 2022.
https://doi.org/10.1007/978-3-030-95408-6_11

important issue. It is based on the relation between the existing triples in the knowledge graph and predicts new facts from existing facts. Before 2013, most research on knowledge graph completion was based on symbols and logic. In 2013, inspired by word2vec model, Bordes et al. proposed a knowledge graph embedding model TransE [4] based on semantic translation theory. TransE regards the relations of fact triples r as the translation operation between head entity h and tail entity t, as thus it is also called translation distance model, which is shown in Fig. 1(a). Although TransE is efficient, it is hard to model the complex relations. In view of the drawbacks of TransE model, the concept of relation hyperplane was proposed, which is, mapping the head entity vector h and tail entity vector t of fact triples (h, r, t) to the hyperplane of relation r with normal vector W_r. The model diagram is shown in Fig. 1(b). Similar to the idea of TransH [21], TransR [13] projected the head and tail entities into the relation space associated with a specific relation r through the mapping matrix M_r, where the relation is modeled as the translation vector of the space, which is depicted in Fig. 2.

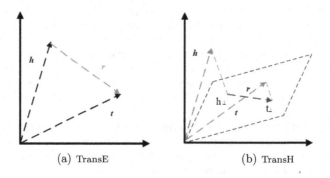

(a) TransE   (b) TransH

Fig. 1. TransE & TransH

In recent years, due to the limitations of knowledge embedding, the performance of various knowledge representation methods has not been improved significantly. Some researchers considered that knowledge representation learning needs to incorporate more semantic information. Ruobing Xie et al. [24] proposed a new learning method of embedded knowledge representation based on entity hierarchical type (TKRL). In TKRL, different entity hierarchy types are regarded as specific entity projection matrix, and designed two types of encoders to model hierarchical type information. Zhigang Wang et al. [22] proposed a text enhanced representation learning method (TEKE) for knowledge graph. TEKE model enhances the effect of knowledge embedding, mainly referring to the text description information of entities. TEKE first constructs entity description text corpus by using entity linking tool, and calculates the co-occurrence frequency between entities or relations, then obtains the context of entities and relations according to the frequency. Finally, TEKE model combines entity and relation representation to design the corresponding context representation method. TEKE model introduces external corpus that greatly enriches

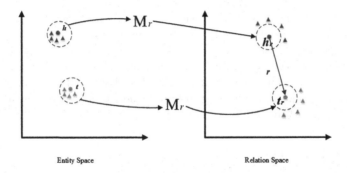

Entity Space   Relation Space

Fig. 2. TransR.

the semantic information of entities and relations, but its essence is still based on semantic translation model. In addition, TEKE model has a simple way to quote text information with high efficiency, while it has no obvious breakthrough in accuracy compared with TransE model.

Besides, although the knowledge representation learning model based on semantic translation theory has achieved good results in Euclidean Space, some researches in recent years have found that the mathematical expressions and overly strict geometric forms in Euclidean Space are not suitable for knowledge embedding. In Euclidean embedding space, the entity is represented as a fixed point, but in the real world, any entity has multi-level and multi-faceted attributes. Therefore, many researches try to find other geometric space that is more suitable for representing knowledge. ManifoldE model [23] relaxed the strict geometric form in Euclidean space, and placed the tail entity t approximately on the manifold of fact triples (i.e. spherical space, hyperplane space, etc.), extending from a point to manifold space such as high-dimensional sphere. The geometric form of ManifoldE model is a hypersphere with $h+t$ as the center and D_r as the radius of the sphere.

Kolyvakis et al. proposed HyperKG model [11], which embeds entities and relations into Hyperbolic Space, and used the self-organization of hyperbolic space to capture hidden information in data to improve the ability of knowledge representation. HyperKG Model defines a group of composite vector representation of head and tail entities and uses a circular permutation matrix to project the object. This introduces non-commutativity into composite vector. The final form of the composite vector is $h + \prod_{\beta} t$, where β is the hyperparameter controlling the number of consecutive cycles.

In this paper, we propose text-enhanced knowledge graph representation learning model in Hyperbolic Space. Our model improves the representation ability by introducing external semantic information. To capture hierarchical information of the knowledge graph, we embed entities and relations in Hyperbolic Space. Our contributions are as follows:

- We solve the problems of knowledge data sparsity and complex relation modeling by introducing the descriptive text information of entities with Transformer encoder.
- We design a knowledge graph representation learning model based on text enhancement and embed Knowledge Graph in Hyperbolic Space.
- We compare our model with state-of-art models and experimental results prove the effectiveness of our model.

2   Related Work

One category of work is to use the translation invariance of word vector in semantic space to model semantic similarity, called the model base on semantic translation theory. In 2013, inspired by the word2vec (T. Mikolov et al. 2013) [14], a method based on representation learning, TransE (Bordes et al. 2013) [4] was proposed. TransE effectively takes semantic information as the only feature learning knowledge representation and uses vector space distance to calculate semantic relations, which greatly alleviates the problem of data sparsity in knowledge graph and the low computational efficiency in traditional representation learning methods. After that, TransH (Wang et al. 2014) [21], TransR (Lin et al. 2017) [13], TransD (Ji et al. 2015) [10] and other models [3] based on semantic translation theory appeared one after another.

In Euclidean Space, the knowledge representation learning model has achieved excessive effective performance. While in recent years, many existing works found that the traditional embedding model based on Euclidean Space still has numerous defects [5] because of the extremely strict geometric constrain and mathematical expression in Euclidean Space. Manifolde et al. [23] placed the tail entities approximately in the spherical space of the factual triple. Since the curvature of Hyperbolic Space is less than zero, under the same number of parameters, the expression ability of Hyperbolic Space is higher than that of Euclidean Space and Spherical Space. Kolyvakis et al. [11] proposed the HyperKG model to embed entities and relationships into the Hyperbolic Space and capture the hidden information in the data by using the self-organization of the Hyperbolic Space.

Apart from finding proper geometry space to model knowledge, the researchers also considered introducing additional information to model knowledge graph. Recently, an increasing number of researchers focused on text information and relation path as additional information of embedded model [12], which can effectively enhance the embedding ability of model. Ruobing Xie et al. [24] proposed a new embedded knowledge representation learning method (TKRL) based on entity hierarchy type. Md Mostafizur Rahman et al. [16] proposed a knowledge graph embedding model TPRC using entity type attributes in relational context. Zhigang Wang et al. [22] proposed TEKE, a textual enhancement representation learning method of knowledge graph. Ito et al. [9] proposed a novel NN architecture called contextual sentiment neural network (CSNN) that can explain its sentiment analysis process and catch up with the summary of the contents. Introducing additional information can improve the performance of knowledge graph embedding. The challenge is how to model the semantic information of different structures in a unified manner.

According to the work of TEKE, the introduction of external information can improve the representation ability of entity. In this paper, we improve the module in TEKE that introduces external information. We use Transformer Encoder to represent the unique description text of the entity, and use this as the vector of the entity. To capture hierarchical information of the knowledge graph, we embed the text-enhanced vector in Hyperbolic Space.

3   Methodology

Given a Knowledge Graph G and Textual Corpus V, we learn the entity and relation embeddings (h, r, t) in Hyperbolic Space. As depicted in Fig. 3, our model includes four basic modules: (1) **Entity Annotation:** we use an entity linking tool to annotate the entities in knowledge graph automatically. (2) **Textual Context Embedding:** based on the entity-annotated text corpus, we construct a Transformer encoder to represent the unique entity description text of the entity and use this vector as the embedding of the entity. (3) **Hyperbolic Space Modeling:** based on the text-enhanced vector of entity and relation, we formulate the embeddings in Hyperbolic Space. (4) **Representation Training:** we use Riemannian Stochastic to optimize the model parameters. In the following parts, We will give a detailed description of each module mentioned above.

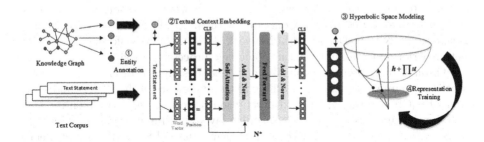

Fig. 3. Text-enhanced representation model in hyperbolic space framework.

3.1   Entity Annotation

Given a Knowledge Graph G and Textual Corpus $V = \{S_1, S_2, \cdots, S_n\}$, where S_i represents the sentence in the textual corpus, we use entity linking tools (AIDA [25], TAGME [8], etc.) to label the entities in knowledge graph. The words in the text corpus compose a text set $D = \{w_1, w_2, \cdots, w_m\}$, where w_i represents the i-th word in the set, m represents the number of the word in the textual corpus. According to the labeling results, the words aligned with the entity are retained, and the unmarked words are deleted. Then we get the entity-annotated text corpus $\boldsymbol{D}' = \{e_1, e_2, \cdots, e_{m'}\}$, where $m' \leq m$. After that, entities in the text corpus are matched to align relevant entities in knowledge graph.

3.2   Textual Context Embedding

Since we get the entity-annotated text corpus $\boldsymbol{D}' = \{e_1, e_2, \cdots, e_{m'}\}$, we calculate the correlation between the text statements and the entity in the text corpus. The calculation of correlation is determined by the sum of co-occurrence frequency of other entities and target entities in the text corpus, where the calculation formula is defined as follows:

$$\mathrm{DESC}\,(S, e_i) = \sum_{e_j \sim w_k \in S} y_{ij} \tag{1}$$

where y_{ij} is defined as the frequency of two entities appearing together in the same text statement. Then we sort the relevance between entity e and text statements in descending order, and the text statement with the highest relevance is regarded as the only text description of entity e. According to the co-occurrence frequency of entity pairs in text corpus, entity context set and relational context set are acquired, which is defined as follows:

$$n\,(e_i) = \{e_j \mid y_{ij} > 0\} \tag{2}$$

$$n\,(e_i, e_j) = \{e_k \mid e_k \in n\,(e_i) \cap n\,(e_j)\} \tag{3}$$

After getting the only text description of entity e, we use Transformer Encoder to obtain the entity representation. Transformer model was proposed by Ashish Vaswani et al. [20]. Compared with the traditional Recurrent Neural Network (RNN) and Deep Neural Network (DNN), the Transformer model has better performance in many natural language processing tasks.

Through data preprocessing, the only text description of entity e is represented as an input sequence. According to the experience of the BERT model [7], we add a [CLS] to the unique text description corresponding to each entity, and then input it into the transformer encoding layer. The input sequence is denoted as $S = (w_0, w_2, \cdots, w_n)$, where w_0 represents the [CLS], and other elements represent the words in the text statement. For each word in the input sequence, the data preprocessing of the transformer encoding layer will convert it into an input vector. The conversion process is defined as follows:

$$\boldsymbol{w}_i^0 = \boldsymbol{w}_i^{w2v} + \boldsymbol{w}_i^{pos} \tag{4}$$

where $\boldsymbol{w}_i^{w2v}$ is the word embedding vector of word $\boldsymbol{w}_i$, and the $\boldsymbol{w}_i^{pos}$ is the position encode of the word to identify the position of the element in the sequence. Multiple transformer encoders are stacked into encoding layers to encode the input sequence. The output of each layer encoder will be used as the input of the next layer encoder until the bottom of the coding layer, which is shown as follows:

$$\boldsymbol{w}_i^l = \mathrm{Transformer} - \mathrm{Encoder}\,\left(\boldsymbol{w}_i^{l-1}\right) l = 1, 2, \cdots, L \tag{5}$$

where w_i^l denotes the output of L-th layer of encoder. Finally, the transformer encoder will learn the corresponding representation of each element in the input sequence, in which the [CLS] is used as the macro representation of the input sequence. Then the vector of [CLS] is the sentence embedding of the unique text description of the entity. Through the text enhancement module, the corresponding feature representation of the entity is obtained. These entities have learned the statement context information and were automatically adapted to the input. For a given fact triple, the corresponding entities and relations are represented as follows by combining semantic information:

$$\hat{h} = h_{\text{Transformer}} \, \boldsymbol{W}_e + h \tag{6}$$

$$\hat{t} = t_{\text{Transformer}} \, \boldsymbol{W}_e + t \tag{7}$$

where $\boldsymbol{W}_e$ represents the transformation matrix of entities. Relation is the words that always appear with the head and tail entities, so we learn the embedding of relation using the relation context. The relation after text enhancement is defined as follows:

$$\hat{r} = \frac{1}{Z} \sum_{e_i \in n(h,t)} \min\left(y_{hi}, y_{ti}\right) e_i \boldsymbol{W}_{\text{rel}} + r \tag{8}$$

where $\boldsymbol{W}_{rel}$ represents the transformation matrix of relations.

3.3 Hyperbolic Space Modeling

Since strict geometric constraints and mathematical expressions, Euclidean Space is not suitable for modeling entities and relations. The curvature of Hyperbolic Space is less than zero, it has a larger accommodating space under the same radius, and its expression capacity is much higher than that of Euclidean Space. In Hyperbolic Space, there are some well-known models include Hyperboloid [17], Klein disk [6] and Poincare-ball [1]. In this paper, we choose Poincare-ball model, due to its feasibility of gradient optimization in knowledge graph representation learning. Poincare-ball is a Riemannian manifold, and its manifold is defined as follows:

$$\mathbb{Q}^{n,c} = \left\{ x \in \mathbb{R}^n \mid \|x\| < \frac{1}{c} \right\} \tag{9}$$

Distance function: $d_{\mathbb{Q}}$ is used to represent the distance function in Hyperbolic Space, for a set of vectors $(\boldsymbol{u}, \boldsymbol{v})$, and the distance function is defined as:

$$d_{\mathbb{Q}}(\boldsymbol{u}, \boldsymbol{v}) = \text{arcosh}\left(1 + 2\frac{\|\boldsymbol{u} - \boldsymbol{v}\|^2}{(1 - \|\boldsymbol{u}\|^2)(1 - \|\boldsymbol{v}\|^2)}\right) \tag{10}$$

Then we carry out vector translation for entities and relations after text enhancement, and the calculation formula is as follows:

$$\hat{h} + \prod_{\beta} \hat{t} \tag{11}$$

where $\prod$ is learnable cyclic permutation matrix, and β is the number of controlling continuous cyclic permutation. In order to restrict all entities to Poincare-ball, the Euclidean norm of vectors represented by all entities is less than 0.5, and the Euclidean norm of vectors represented by relations is less than 1.

The distance between the combined representation of head, tail entities and relation representation is used as the factual triple confidence. According to the definition of distance function of Poincare-ball, the score function of knowledge graph triple in Hyperbolic Space can be expressed as:

$$S(h, r, t) = d_{\mathbb{Q}} \left(\hat{h} + \prod_{\beta} \hat{t}, \hat{r} \right) \tag{12}$$

3.4 Representation Training

We define the training loss function as:

$$Loss = \sum_{(h,r,t) \in G} \sum_{(h',r,t') \in G^-} [\gamma + S(h, r, t) - S(h', r, t')]_+ \tag{13}$$

Since the calculation method of boundary distance of Poincare-ball is similar to the shortest path between two sibling nodes in tree structure, we define the regularized loss function as:

$$R(\boldsymbol{\theta}) = \sum_{i=1}^{|E|+|R|} \left(1 - \|\boldsymbol{\theta}_i\|^2 \right) \tag{14}$$

$\boldsymbol{\theta}$ represents the set of entities and relationships. After introducing the regular term, the objective function is improved as:

$$\text{Loss}'(\boldsymbol{\theta}) = \text{Loss}(\boldsymbol{\theta}) + \lambda R(\boldsymbol{\theta}) \tag{15}$$

λ allocates the influence degree of regular term on the loss function. Finally, we use the Riemann Stochastic Gradient Descent (RSGD) method to optimize the model parameters.

4   Experiment

4.1   DateSet

The model proposed in this paper utilizes external text description information to enhance the ability of knowledge representation. Therefore, we use two kinds of datasets, the knowledge graph dataset containing a large number of factual triples and the text corpus.

Table 1. Knowledge graph data set statistics.

Dataset	#Relations	#Entities	#Triples
WN18	18	40,943	151,442
FB15K	1,345	14,941	592,213

Table 2. Text corpus and knowledge graph entity alignment result statistics.

KG	#Entities	#Annotated entities	#Word stems
WN18	40,943	32,249	1,529,251
FB15K	14,951	14,405	744,983

Knowledge Graph Dataset. A complete knowledge graph contains a large number of fact triples in the open domain, so it needs a large number of time for training. The general approach is to use the subset of the knowledge graph as the dataset to evaluate the model performance. The commonly used subsets are Freebase subset FB13, FB15K, WordNet subset WN11, WN18. In this paper, we select two subsets FB15k and WN18, and detailed statistical data are shown in Table 1.

Text Corpus. We employ Wikipedia as the text corpus, which is commonly used in previous methods. Since the text corpus composing of unstructured natural language documents, our experiment conducts some preprocessing of the original text corpus. We delete the documents containing words "Wikipedia", "WikiProjects" and "Categories". The detailed data after processing is shown in Table 2.

4.2   Evaluation Protocol

We rank each test triple among all possible head entity and tail entity substitutions, and evaluate the quality of this rank. The entity ranking protocol mainly includes Mean Rank and Hits@k. The Mean Rank is the Mean of the sequence ranking of the original factual triples (h, r, t) in all test sets. The smaller the Mean Rank, the better the performance of the model. Hits@k index refers to the proportion of the fact triples in the top K of the test triples. The selection of different parameters k directly affects the severity of evaluation of model performance. Generally, we select k as 10. Hits@k is the opposite of Mean Rank, the larger Hits@k is, the better embedding performance of the model will be.

4.3   Link Prediction

Link prediction task is to predict the missing head and tail entities in triples $(h, r, ?)$ or $(?, r, t)$. It directly reflects the model performance according to the prediction ranking of real triples (h, r, t), which is a very convenient and effective measurement method. We compare the performance of this model with other advanced models in the link prediction task, and the experimental results are shown in Table 3. By comparing the experimental results of the model with HyperKG, we can find that the introduction of external text information can further improve the representation performance of the model in Hyperbolic Space. The experimental results also prove that the Hyperbolic Space can significantly enhance the knowledge representation ability of the model. Compared with other models based on traditional space, the performance of our model is improved by more than 9.26%. Moreover, Mean Rank index does not change significantly in FB15K and WN18 datasets, which reflects the good stability of our model.

Table 3. The link prediction task measures experimental results comparison.

Dataset	WN18		FB15K	
Evaluation	MR	Hits@10	MR	Hits@10
TransE	284	0.721	245	0.331
TransH	307	0.757	226	0.396
TransR	217	0.788	233	0.405
TEKE	221	0.764	217	0.475
HyperKG	193	0.813	202	0.472
Our_Method	**165** (+1.2%)	**0.835** (−1.3%)	**161** (+8%)	**0.519** (+4.4%)

Table 4. Comparison of complex relation link prediction measurement.

Dataset	FB15K (Hits@10)			
Relation	1-1	1-N	N-1	N-N
TransE	43.7	65.7	13.2	32.5
TransH	67.2	**72.6**	22.1	37.2
TransR	**78.8**	72.4	27.8	39.7
TEKE	58.6	71.6	34.6	42.3
HyperKG	66.5	68.7	31.3	40.1
Our_Method	64.8	66.9	**39.2**	**46.4**

In addition, our experiment adds a measure of the model's performance in dealing with complex relations, and the experimental results are shown in Table 4. The experimental results show that compared with other models, the prediction performance of our model in predicting simple relationships, such as 1-1 and 1-N, is not much different from that of other models, and the TransR model has the best performance, which indicates that a better knowledge representation can be obtained when relations are different from entity representation space. However, when dealing with complex relations N-1 and N-N, our model's prediction ability is significantly improved, and the model's performance is stable without great performance fluctuations. This indicates that the cyclic permutation matrix can effectively improve the ability of the model to deal with complex relations. By comparing the model proposed in this paper with state-of-art models, it can be found that the dynamic representation of relationships can solve the modeling problems of complex relationships, but there is still much room for improvement.

5   Conclusion

In this paper, we propose a knowledge graph representation learning model with external semantic information. In this model, we utilize Transformer encoder to introduce descriptive text information of entities, which can solve the problems of knowledge data, namely, sparsity and complex relationship modeling. As Euclidean space cannot represent the multilevel nature of the entity, we try to find other space that can capture hierarchical structure information of the entity like Hyperbolic Space, so we design a knowledge representation learning model based on text enhancement and embedding knowledge in Hyperbolic space. Experimental results prove the effectiveness of our model, and the performance of knowledge representation is significantly improved compared with other advanced methods. In the future, we will improve the efficiency of the model and focus more on the coding of knowledge graph relational schemas, including the coding capabilities of symmetric/antisymmetric, inverse, composite and subrelation schemas.

Acknowledgement. This work was supported partly by National Natural Science Foundation of China (61728204), National Natural Science Foundation of China (62172351), Key Laboratory of Safety Critical Software Ministry of Industry and Information Technology (NJ2018014), Fundamental Research Funds for the Central Universities (NS2019001), CCF-Huawei Database System Innovation Research Plan under Grant CCF-HUAWEIDBIR2020001A

References

1. Benedetti, R., Petronio, C.: Lectures on Hyperbolic Geometry. Springer, Heidelberg (2012)
2. Bollacker, K., Cook, R., Tufts, P.: Freebase: a shared database of structured general human knowledge. In: AAAI, vol. 7, pp. 1962–1963 (2007)
3. Bonner, S., Kureshi, I., Brennan, J., Theodoropoulos, G., McGough, A.S., Obara, B.: Exploring the semantic content of unsupervised graph embeddings: an empirical study. Data Sci. Eng. **4**(3), 269–289 (2019). https://doi.org/10.1007/s41019-019-0097-5
4. Bordes, A., Usunier, N., Garcia-Duran, A., Weston, J., Yakhnenko, O.: Translating embeddings for modeling multi-relational data. In: Neural Information Processing Systems (NIPS), pp. 1–9 (2013)

5. Chamberlain, B.P., Clough, J., Deisenroth, M.P.: Neural embeddings of graphs in hyperbolic space. arXiv preprint arXiv:1705.10359 (2017)
6. Chazal, F., Sun, J.: Proceedings of the Thirtieth Annual Symposium on Computational Geometry, SOCG 2014 (2014)
7. Devlin, J., Chang, M.W., Lee, K., Toutanova, K.: BERT: pre-training of deep bidirectional transformers for language understanding. arXiv preprint arXiv:1810.04805 (2018)
8. Ferragina, P., Scaiella, U.: TAGME: on-the-fly annotation of short text fragments (by Wikipedia entities). In: Proceedings of the 19th ACM International Conference on Information and Knowledge Management, pp. 1625–1628 (2010)
9. Ito, T., Tsubouchi, K., Sakaji, H., Yamashita, T., Izumi, K.: Contextual sentiment neural network for document sentiment analysis. Data Sci. Eng. **5**(2), 180–192 (2020). https://doi.org/10.1007/s41019-020-00122-4
10. Ji, G., He, S., Xu, L., Liu, K., Zhao, J.: Knowledge graph embedding via dynamic mapping matrix. In: Proceedings of the 53rd Annual Meeting of the Association for Computational Linguistics and the 7th International Joint Conference on Natural Language Processing (Volume 1: Long Papers), pp. 687–696 (2015)
11. Kolyvakis, P., Kalousis, A., Kiritsis, D.: HyperKG: hyperbolic knowledge graph embeddings for knowledge base completion. arXiv preprint arXiv:1908.04895 (2019)
12. Li, Z., Wang, X., Li, J., Zhang, Q.: Deep attributed network representation learning of complex coupling and interaction. Knowl.-Based Syst. **212**, 106618 (2021)
13. Lin, H., Liu, Y., Wang, W., Yue, Y., Lin, Z.: Learning entity and relation embeddings for knowledge resolution. Procedia Comput. Sci. **108**, 345–354 (2017)
14. Mikolov, T., Sutskever, I., Chen, K., Corrado, G., Dean, J.: Distributed representations of words and phrases and their compositionality. arXiv preprint arXiv:1310.4546 (2013)
15. Miller, G.A.: WordNet: a lexical database for English. Commun. ACM **38**(11), 39–41 (1995)
16. Rahman, M.M., Takasu, A.: Leveraging entity-type properties in the relational context for knowledge graph embedding. IEICE Trans. Inf. Syst. **103**(5), 958–968 (2020)
17. Reynolds, W.F.: Hyperbolic geometry on a hyperboloid. Am. Math. Mon. **100**(5), 442–455 (1993)
18. Sikos, L.F., Philp, D.: Provenance-aware knowledge representation: a survey of data models and contextualized knowledge graphs. Data Sci. Eng. **5**(3), 293–316 (2020). https://doi.org/10.1007/s41019-020-00118-0
19. Suchanek, F.M., Kasneci, G., Weikum, G.: YAGO: a core of semantic knowledge. In: Proceedings of the 16th International Conference on World Wide Web, pp. 697–706 (2007)
20. Vaswani, A., et al.: Attention is all you need. arXiv preprint arXiv:1706.03762 (2017)
21. Wang, Z., Zhang, J., Feng, J., Chen, Z.: Knowledge graph embedding by translating on hyperplanes. In: Proceedings of the AAAI Conference on Artificial Intelligence, vol. 28 (2014)
22. Wang, Z., Li, J., Liu, Z., Tang, J.: Text-enhanced representation learning for knowledge graph. In: Proceedings of International Joint Conference on Artificial Intelligent (IJCAI), pp. 4–17 (2016)
23. Xiao, H., Huang, M., Zhu, X.: From one point to a manifold: knowledge graph embedding for precise link prediction. arXiv preprint arXiv:1512.04792 (2015)

24. Xie, R., Liu, Z., Sun, M.: Representation learning of knowledge graphs with hierarchical types. In: IJCAI, pp. 2965–2971 (2016)
25. Yosef, M.A., Hoffart, J., Bordino, I., Spaniol, M., Weikum, G.: AIDA: an online tool for accurate disambiguation of named entities in text and tables. Proc. VLDB Endow. **4**(12), 1450–1453 (2011)

Relations Reconstruction in a Knowledge Graph of a Socioeconomic System

Alexander Kalinin$^{(\boxtimes)}$ ⓘ, Danila Vaganov, and Egor Shikov

ITMO University, Saint-Petersburg, Russia
amkalinin@niuitmo.ru, {vaganov,egorshikov}@itmo.ru

Abstract. Data quality, completeness, and consistency are crucial for simulation modeling and predictive tasks in socioeconomic systems. Such systems involve heterogeneous entities and their interrelations, which are becoming available only by combining various data sources. In this study, three different sources were combined in a single knowledge graph (KG). It includes an online social network, an online recruitment system, and a financial bank. The constructed knowledge graph is evaluated on link prediction tasks to obtain complete and consistent data. We try to reconstruct links between users and a) socioeconomic statuses, b) organizations they work for, c) job positions. Knowledge graph embedding models and a graph neural network based on Transformer architecture were applied. We get promising results for reconstruction of User-Employer relations ($MRR = 0.42$, $Hits@10 = 0.74$), as well as for reconstruction of User-Position relations ($MRR = 0.59$, $Hits@10 = 0.88$).

Keywords: Knowledge graph · Ontology · Link prediction

1 Introduction

Socioeconomic systems are complex systems, which connect individuals, industries, and various economic features. In a real-world scenario, the presence of missing data does not allow making a comprehensive representation of the whole system, which, in turn, "loses" its consistency and credibility. Several approaches were developed to solve this problem. For example, some works tried to reconstruct missing occupations of individuals [7,9,14], their incomes [2,6,13,15], and socioeconomic statuses [1,5,10,11,20]. All these studies consider a system as a set of different components located in different spaces.

Recently, *knowledge graphs (KG)*, also known as *ontologies*, have been rapidly used for different application domains [4]. It is a universal structure, which integrates different concepts and relations between them. Using KG, one can represent a whole system in a single, common space. Several studies propose to

The reported study was funded by RFBR according to the research project № 20-37-90126. We are grateful to Artem Petrov for his assistance with text processing tasks and Valentina Guleva for her valuable scientific advice.

B. Li et al. (Eds.): ADMA 2021, LNAI 13088, pp. 150–161, 2022.
https://doi.org/10.1007/978-3-030-95408-6_12

combine classic domain features with big-data observations from related fields and form multi-relational ontology. For instance, Yang et al. [24] introduce a macroeconomic KG that is augmented with relations extracted from news and textual reports. Li et al. [12] propose an ontology-based Web mining method for unemployment rate prediction using knowledge extracted from search queries. Shi et al. [17] reconstruct person-industry relations in private KG "LinkedIn's Economic Graph". LinkedIn is a social network, which is focused on professional entities and relations. However, it is a single collective platform, which encourages users to make relations explicitly. This factor simplifies the reconstruction task since data is less noisy than data combined from many different sources.

In this work, we built a *multi-source* knowledge graph containing information about a) the friendship ties of people in online social network, their communities, occupations, socioeconomic statuses (SES), and b) labor market, namely job vacancies, employers, positions, their industries and professional areas, respectively. Our idea is to reconstruct a complete and consistent high-quality knowledge base of the socioeconomic system using the open and private data sources. Given prior knowledge about existing connections in a system, one can predict the previously unknown connections. Hence, we consider this problem as the link prediction task.

The paper is organized as follows. Section 2 introduces the link prediction problem. Then, Sect. 3 reviews related work. Section 4 describes the process of constructing the socioeconomic knowledge graph from three different sources. In Sect. 5 experimental setup is provided. The result and conclusion are presented in Sects. 6 and 7, respectively.

2   Problem Statement

Link prediction is tightly coupled with knowledge graphs. A fact in knowledge graph is defined as triple <*subject, relation, object*>, where subject node influences on object through some relation. The goal of link prediction is to predict second (first) entity of triple given first (second) one and some relation, e.g., <*Bill Gates, work_in, ?*>. In real-world scenarios, link prediction task is solved under *Open World Assumption, (OWA)*, which states that graph is incomplete. In this case, there are *missing* links, which are not presented in the graph. Due to this problem, a "hard" prediction task is relaxed to ranking, where a model should rank positive triple better than negative ones.

3   Related Work

Link prediction task in multi-relational data could be solved by various techniques. The most common approach is *knowledge graph embedding (KGE)*. The model of this class gives a score for a triple, and thus, can compare plausibility of different facts. Different models define different scoring functions, which are divided on two classes: *distance* functions and *similarity* functions. Usually, the former class is converted to the latter by adding minus to the distance. After that, we assume that the loss function takes plausibility score as an argument.

One of the most representative classes of distance-based models is TransE-family. TransE [3] defines vectors of the same dimensions for both, entities and relations. Relation is considered as translation from subject entity to object, i.e., $\mathbf{s} + \mathbf{r} \approx \mathbf{o}$, where $\mathbf{s}$, $\mathbf{r}$, $\mathbf{o}$ – vectors of subject, relation, and object, respectively. Scoring function is defined as:

$$f_r(s,o) = -\|\mathbf{s} + \mathbf{r} - \mathbf{o}\|_p,$$

where $\|\cdot\|_p$ – is p-norm of a vector. However, this simple model does not distinguish many possible entities for a given (entity, relation)-pair, and embeds them in similar vectors. Moreover, it does not support symmetry relations since $s + r \neq o + r$. Extensions of TransE introduce different techniques to deal with these limitations.

For example, RotatE [18] models relations as rotations from the subject to the object entity in complex vector space, i.e., in case of positive triple, it expects $\mathbf{o} = \mathbf{s} \circ \mathbf{r}$, where $\circ$ means element-wise product, and for each ith element restriction $|r_i| = 1$ is hold. Then, scoring function is:

$$f_r(s,o) = -\|\mathbf{s} \circ \mathbf{r} - \mathbf{o}\|_p.$$

Some similarity-based models represent each relation as a matrix of pairwise interaction between vector elements. For each relation, ComplEx [19] introduces a squared digonal matrix $\mathbf{M}_r = diag(\mathbf{r})$ with dimension d of entity embeddings. Like RotatE, ComplEx moves embeddings in complex space, and the scoring function is defined as:

$$f_r(s,o) = Re(\mathbf{s}^T diag(\mathbf{r})\bar{\mathbf{o}}) = Re(\sum_{i=0}^{d-1}[\mathbf{r}]_i \cdot [\mathbf{s}]_i \cdot [\bar{\mathbf{o}}]_i),$$

where $Re(\cdot)$ is the real part of complex value, $\bar{\mathbf{o}}$ is the conjugate of $\mathbf{o}$.

After defining of scoring function, one has to optimize the loss function. Models could be modified to use different functions. Among others, margin-based losses are naturally suited to OWA since they assume that the negative triple is just less realistic than the positive one. For example, *self-adversarial sampling loss* [18] maximizes the margin between positive and negative triples, at the same time controlling the influence of generated negative samples:

$$\mathcal{L} = -log\,\sigma(\gamma + f_r(s,o)) - \sum_{i=1}^{n} p(s_i',r,o_i')\,log\,\sigma(-f_r(s_i',o_i') - \gamma),$$

where σ is sigmoid function, n is number of negative samples, $<s_i',r,o_i'>$ is an negative triple, and $p(s_i',r,o_i')$ is negative sampling distribution with α as the temperature of sampling:

$$p(s_j',r,o_j' \mid \{(s_i',r,o_i')\}) = \frac{exp\,\alpha f_r(\mathbf{s}_j,\mathbf{o}_j)}{\sum_i exp\,\alpha f_r(\mathbf{s}_i',\mathbf{o}_i')}$$

Recently, deep learning models have been extensively applied for graph structures. *Graph Neural Networks (GNNs)* are designed to address the problem of the irregular nature of relational data. Subclass of GNNs, *convolutional neural networks (CNNs)*, considers node neighborhood as a grid of pixels and defines convolutions on graph structures [22]. Some state-of-the-art solutions exploit the attention mechanism to weigh the importance of "messages" from neighbors. *Heterogeneous Graph Transformer (HGT)* [8] applies Transformer architecture [21] to knowledge graphs. To address the heterogeneity problem, it introduces an attention matrix for each relation. Model parameters are updated during the optimization of a downstream task.

4   Dataset and Preprocessing

To construct a knowledge base of the socioeconomic system, one should use diverse sources. We have collected data from three origins.

1. Online Social Media "VK" [1] is a platform for people communication, where users create friendship ties and communities (groups).

2. Online Recruitment System "HeadHunter" [2] allows to employers share their vacancies with potential workers.

3. Financial partner bank stores depersonalized client debit card transactions and calculates some metrics, e.g., socioeconomic status. The process of data anonymization is presented in our previous studies [10,20].

4.1   Ontology Construction

Table 1 introduces extracted entity types from each source. One can note that different sources have overlapping entity types. Our goal is to construct a common ontology, which integrates all sources. Hence, overlapping entity types are considered the same.

As the starting point, an origin friendship graph from a prior study is used [10,20]. We expand the origin graph with new selected entity types, namely *Group, Employer, Position, Gender,* and *Age*. It's a user-centric graph, where the *User* is connected to all other entity types. We create a link between a user and a group if the former participate in that group. A user is connected to an employer/a position if he/she points it on his/her page.

We also decide to represent demographic attributes as knowledge graph entities. While gender has discrete values (male/female), the age attribute is continuous and, thus, it could not be directly considered as an entity. To solve this problem, we discrete age distribution on 18 parts. Left and right bounds are $(0, 17]$ and $[98; 98+)$, respectively. The rest 16 parts are ranges between bounds, each of them contains four subsequent years.

---

[1] https://vk.com.
[2] https://hh.ru.

In addition, VK provides an opportunity to select a group as an employer, e.g., the official group of "Russian Railways". We connect these employers to their groups.

Then we expand the graph with entities and relations from *HeadHunter*. *Employer* is connected with its *Industry* entities, if they are known. Similar to *Employer*, *Position* is connected to *Professional areas*. If an employer share a vacancy, a link is created between them. *Vacancy* could have salary range, i.e., bounds (floor and ceiling) of possible income. Again, to represent continuous attribute as an entity, we discrete distribution of possible values on several ranges: $\{(i\,t;\,(i+1)\,t],\ldots,(n\,t;\,\infty)\}$, where $t = 10,000$ rubles, $i = \overline{0..n}$, and $n = 20$. Now, each range is an entity in the knowledge graph. *Vacancy* can be connected to *Salary* with two distinct relations, one for floor and one for ceiling bound, respectively.

Bank data is used for revealing the socioeconomic status (SES) of the client. Following prior work [20], SES is defined as average monthly expenses divided with *median value* on two classes, 'low' and 'high'. Ontology restricts a client to links to only one of two statuses. Similar to a VK user, a bank client has connections to gender, age, and an employer.

Table 1. Entity types of different sources with their descriptions

Entity type	VK	HeadHunter	Bank
User	An account in social network	–	A client of the bank
Gender	User gender	–	Client gender
Age	User age	–	Client's age
Group	A community of users	–	–
Employer	An organization, a user works for	An organization	An organization, a client works for
Position	A user's position	An employee's position	–
Vacancy	–	A proposed salary of a vacancy	–
Industry	–	An industry type of organization	–
Professional area	–	A professional area of position	–
Vacancy salary	–	A proposed salary of a vacancy	–
SES	–	–	Client socioeconomic status

Table 2. Entity types of constructed knowledge graph

Entity type	Number of entities	Example
User	1,658,492	https://vk.com/dm
Group	676,113	https://vk.com/rzd_official
Vacancy	64,722	https://spb.hh.ru/vacancy/45822934
Employer	79	Hospital
Position	31	Doctor
Professional area	28	Domestic staff
Industry	27	Car business
Salary	21	(50000; 60000]
Age	18	[28; 32]
Gender	2	Male
SES	2	High

4.2   Entity Matching

Next, we need to match entities within equivalent entity types. For example, *"Teacher"* in both, *VK.com* and *HeadHunter*, is the same entity of *Position* type. After that, the equivalent entities are "collapsed" to a single node, with preserving of relations between origin entities.

Originally, *Employer* and *Position* are the free-string fields in a personal page of the user (except the case when a group is selected as an employer). However, social network data is extremely noisy. Different users write different names for a single position or employer. Hence, one has to process these text fields, cluster them and eliminate noisy elements. This procedure consists of several stages. First, after manually data review, we extract handcrafted rules, which combine employers/positions with similar names or industries/professional areas. For instance, the employer names "School №5" and "School №217" are both schools, so one can rename them to "School". Second, after applying handcrafted rules, we remain only names assigned by at least five users. Third, we use a pre-trained multilingual Sentence Transformer model [23] to get the embedding vector of every unique text name. Then, obtained vectors are clustered by the community detection method[3]. Finally, after review, we manually reform some clusters and remove noisy ones.

On the HeadHunter side, the same handcrafted rules are applied. Then, to match employers/positions between VK and HeadHunter, we find a name from the latter in one of the clusters of the former. Unmatched HeadHunter entities are removed from the graph.

Beside *Employer* and *Position* entity types, we also match *VK* users with clients of our partner bank. The matching procedure are presented in the prior study [10, 20]. After this matching, we should choose gender, age, and an employer of an individual from one of two sources. On one hand, we found that employer

---

[3] We use *community_detection* method from https://github.com/UKPLab/sentence-transformers.

information is outdated for many clients, as they opened accounts during student years, and the bank assigns the "Employer" field to their universities. Taking this into account, we use employer information from bank data to only those VK users who do not point it on the web page. On the other hand, bank data is more confident in case of age and gender. For this reason, we use bank demographic entities for matched clients and VK entities for non-matched users.

The entity types of final knowledge graph are presented in Table 2. Table 3 shows all relations and their statistic. The overall scheme of ontology is illustrated in Fig. 1.

Table 3. Relations of constructed knowledge graph

Relation	Number of triples	Relation type
user/participate_in/group	86,039,460	One-to-many
user/has_friend/user	39,373,278	One-to-many
user/has_gender/gender	1,553,716	One-to-one
user/has_age/age	717,779	One-to-one
user/work_in/employer	111,564	One-to-one
position/has_vacancy/vacancy	62,784	One-to-many
vacancy/salary_floor/salary	43,906	One-to-one
vacancy/salary_ceil/salary	26,363	One-to-one
user/has_ses/ses	10,418	One-to-one
user/has_position/position	8,640	One-to-one
employer/has_vacancy/vacancy	6,609	One-to-many
employer/has_group/group	2,909	One-to-many
position/belong_to/profarea	618	One-to-many
employer/belong_to/industry	112	One-to-many

5   Experiments

To evaluate the quality of constructed graph, we solve three tasks.

1. User-SES link prediction. The aim is to predict the proper user socioeconomic status, i.e., $<user,\ user/has\_ses/ses,\ ?>$. As we have only two SES entities, it is reasonable to evaluate performance as a binary classification task. Moreover, since both SES classes consist of an equal number of users, one could use *accuracy* metric for a fair evaluation.

2. User-Employer link prediction. Due to the Open World Assumption and a relatively large number of possible employers, this task should be evaluated by ranking metrics. We opt for standard *mean rank (MR)*, *mean reciprocal rank (MRR)*, and *Hits@10*. During negative triple generation in the evaluation stage, we corrupt the object of the positive triple, i.e., *Employer* entity. Note that only *Employer* entities are used for corruption.

3. User-Position link prediction. Similar to the previous task, this one is considered as ranking, and only *Position* entities are used for corruption of triples during the evaluation stage.

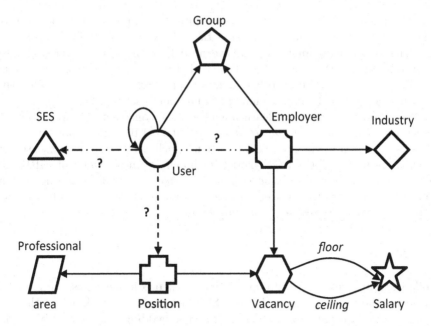

Fig. 1. Overall ontology scheme of the constructed knowledge graph. Dashed lines represent three tasks of link prediction.

For solving the aforementioned tasks, we choose knowledge graph embedding models, namely, TransE, ComplEx, RotatE, and deep learning model HGT. For a fair comparison feature vectors of each model are uniformly initialized.

Due to the large size of the constructed graph, it is infeasible to tune the hyper-parameters of models. To address this issue, we sample a sub-graph of size $\approx 150K$ entities by Metropolis-Hastings algorithm [16]. Triples of sampled graph are split onto *train/test* sets with 0.8/0.2 proportions. Models are trained on *train* set and evaluated on *test*. We apply grid search parameter tuning with next parameter ranges for knowledge graph embedding models: batch size is 128, embedding dimension $d \in \{128, 256\}$, self-adversarial sampling temperature $\alpha \in \{0.5, 1.0\}$, margin $\gamma \in \{1, 5, 10, 15\}$, learning rate $lr \in \{0.01, 0.001\}$. We fix a number of iterations with $100K$, and for each model take the best results among all iterations.

All KGE models are implemented[4] by authors of [18]. Note, that this implementation applies self-adversarial sampling loss. During evaluation in the model selection procedure, we sampled fix set D' of entities for corruptions and compare each positive triple from *test* set with negative triples generated by corruptions with entities from D'. The best model is chosen by the MRR metric.

---

[4] https://github.com/DeepGraphLearning/KnowledgeGraphEmbedding.

HGT model selection was too slow despite sub-graph using. Hence, we use default parameters in author implementation[5]. Note that HGT is optimized for concrete downstream tasks, and we need to train a model for each task separately. Sigmoid activation function with Binary Cross-Entropy loss is set for SES prediction, while for other tasks we apply Softmax layer with Negative Log-Likelihood loss. The maximum epoch number is set to 200.

After model selection, we learn models on the constructed graph. First, its triples are divided on *train/valid/test* sets with 0.65/0.10/0.25 proportions. Valid set is used to stop learning on best iteration/epoch, while results on *test* set are considered as final. Best KGE model is chosen by mean value of MRRs for *user/work_in/employer* and *user/has_position/position* triples. During evaluation, we corrupt triples with entities of appropriate types, e.g., only *Position* entities for *user/has_position/position* relation.

6   Results

Table 4 summarizes the results of all three link prediction tasks. None of the considered models could solve the User-SES link prediction task, where the best *accuracy* = 0.52 is reached by HGT. In graph embeddings case, a possible explanation of low performance is too close vectors of SES entities, and, hence, it is difficult to distinguish between them.

Table 4. Results on link prediction tasks

Model	User-SES	User-employer			User-position		
	Accuracy	MR	MRR	Hits@10	MR	MRR	Hits@10
TransE	0.51	16.4	0.24	0.5	14.6	0.18	0.41
ComplEx	0.51	20.5	0.2	0.46	15.7	0.14	0.34
RotatE	0.5	14.7	0.3	0.61	16.5	0.13	0.33
HGT	**0.52**	**9**	**0.42**	**0.74**	**4.3**	**0.59**	**0.88**

HGT also shows the best result for the User-Employer link prediction task in terms of $MRR = 0.42$ and $Hits@10 = 0.74$. Among graph embedding models, RotatE reaches the highest $MRR = 0.3$. Contrary, the other model based on complex vectors, ComplEx, shows the worst score $MRR = 0.2$.

In terms of MRR metric, TransE is the most powerful model among KGE class in the case of the User-Position link prediction task, $MRR = 0.18$. Again, the highest $MRR = 0.59$ and $Hits@10 = 0.88$ is reached by HGT, and one may conclude that a more sophisticated model can better capture relation patterns in the knowledge graphs.

Next, the investigation of HGT model results is conducted. We calculate the mean reciprocal rank for different groups of users divided by their employer

---

[5] https://github.com/acbull/pyHGT.

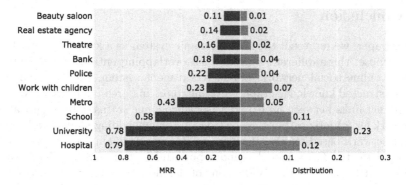

Fig. 2. Correlation between mean reciprocal rank (w.r.t. HGT model) per each employer (test set) and distribution of employers (whole data set). Results are shown for top-10 employers according to MRR.

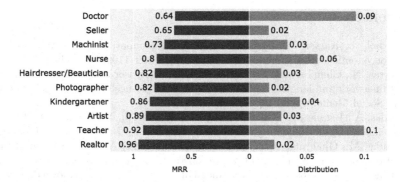

Fig. 3. Correlation between mean reciprocal rank (w.r.t. HGT model) per each position (test set) and distribution of positions (whole data set). Results are shown for top-10 positions according to MRR.

(Fig. 2) and position (Fig. 3). The frequencies of these groups in the whole data set are presented on the right side of the charts. For example, 12% of all users (who indicated their employer) work in the hospital, and for these users $MRR = 0.79$. One can see that the User-Employer model predicts representatives of the majority classes much better than the rare employers, and there is a correlation between MRR and distribution. Possible reason is that the most representative employers belong to social fields, which could be explained by the friendship ties in considered data.

However, the User-Position model breaks this rule completely. The best $MRR = 0.96$ is obtained by realtors who are only 2% of all users pointed their position. Compared to User-Employer relations, the position could be inferred from the local topology structure of social ties, which may include the social links from universities or common professional interests (by evaluating the communities in the online social network).

7   Conclusion

In this paper, we represent the socioeconomic system as a knowledge graph. For this purpose, three different sources with overlapping entities were combined, namely, online social network, online recruitment system, and financial bank. The constructed knowledge graph is evaluated on link prediction tasks. We try to reconstruct links between users and a) socioeconomic statuses, b) organizations, they work for, c) job positions. Knowledge graph embedding models and a graph neural network based on Transformer architecture were applied. As was shown, the sophisticated GNN model is more powerful in terms of standard ranking metrics, MRR and Hits@10. While none of the models could deal with User-SES links, we get promising results for reconstruction of User-Employer relations ($MRR = 0.42$, $Hits@10 = 0.74$), as well as for reconstruction of User-Position relations ($MRR = 0.59$, $Hits@10 = 0.88$).

References

1. Abitbol, J., Karsai, M., Fleury, E.: Location, occupation, and semantics based socioeconomic status inference on Twitter, pp. 1192–1199, November 2018
2. Aletras, N., Chamberlain, B.P.: Predicting Twitter user socioeconomic attributes with network and language information. In: Proceedings of the 29th on Hypertext and Social Media, pp. 20–24. ACM (2018)
3. Bordes, A., Usunier, N., Garcia-Duran, A., Weston, J., Yakhnenko, O.: Translating embeddings for modeling multi-relational data. In: Burges, C.J.C., Bottou, L., Welling, M., Ghahramani, Z., Weinberger, K.Q. (eds.) Advances in Neural Information Processing Systems, vol. 26, pp. 2787–2795. Curran Associates, Inc. (2013)
4. Buchgeher, G., Gabauer, D., Martinez-Gil, J., Ehrlinger, L.: Knowledge graphs in manufacturing and production: a systematic literature review. IEEE Access **9**, 55537–55554 (2021). https://doi.org/10.1109/ACCESS.2021.3070395
5. Ding, S., Huang, H., Zhao, T., Fu, X.: Estimating socioeconomic status via temporal-spatial mobility analysis - a case study of smart card data. In: 2019 28th International Conference on Computer Communication and Networks (ICCCN), pp. 1–9 (2019)
6. Fixman, M., Berenstein, A., Brea, J., Minnoni, M., Travizano, M., Sarraute, C.: A Bayesian approach to income inference in a communication network. In: Proceedings of the 2016 IEEE/ACM International Conference on Advances in Social Networks Analysis and Mining, ASONAM 2016, pp. 579–582. IEEE Press (2016)
7. Han, X., Wang, L., Liu, G., Zhao, D., Xu, S.: Occupation profiling with user-generated geolocation data. In: 2017 2nd International Conference on Knowledge Engineering and Applications (ICKEA), pp. 93–97 (2017)
8. Hu, Z., Dong, Y., Wang, K., Sun, Y.: Heterogeneous graph transformer. In: Proceedings of The Web Conference 2020, WWW 2020, pp. 2704–2710. Association for Computing Machinery, New York (2020)
9. Huang, Y., Yu, L., Wang, X., Cui, B.: A multi-source integration framework for user occupation inference in social media systems. World Wide Web **18**(5), 1247–1267 (2014). https://doi.org/10.1007/s11280-014-0300-6
10. Kalinin, A., Vaganov, D., Bochenina, K.: Discovering patterns of customer financial behavior using social media data. Soc. Netw. Anal. Min. **10**(1), 1–14 (2020). https://doi.org/10.1007/s13278-020-00690-3

11. Lampos, V., Aletras, N., Geyti, J.K., Zou, B., Cox, I.J.: Inferring the socioeconomic status of social media users based on behaviour and language. In: Ferro, N., et al. (eds.) ECIR 2016. LNCS, vol. 9626, pp. 689–695. Springer, Cham (2016). https://doi.org/10.1007/978-3-319-30671-1_54

12. Li, Z., Xu, W., Zhang, L., Lau, R.Y.: An ontology-based web mining method for unemployment rate prediction. Decis. Support Syst. **66**, 114–122 (2014)

13. Matz, S.C., Menges, J.I., Stillwell, D.J., Schwartz, H.A.: Predicting individual-level income from Facebook profiles. PLoS ONE **14**(3), 1–13 (2019)

14. Preoţiuc-Pietro, D., Lampos, V., Aletras, N.: An analysis of the user occupational class through Twitter content. In: Proceedings of the 53rd Annual Meeting of the Association for Computational Linguistics and the 7th International Joint Conference on Natural Language Processing (Volume 1: Long Papers), pp. 1754–1764 (2015)

15. Preoţiuc-Pietro, D., Volkova, S., Lampos, V., Bachrach, Y., Aletras, N.: Studying user income through language, behaviour and affect in social media. PLoS ONE **10**(9), 1–17 (2015). https://doi.org/10.1371/journal.pone.0138717

16. Robert, C.P., Casella, G.: The metropolis-hastings algorithm. In: Robert, C.P., Casella, G. (eds.) Monte Carlo Statistical Methods. STS, pp. 231–283. Springer, New York (1999). https://doi.org/10.1007/978-1-4757-3071-5_6

17. Shi, B., Yang, J., Weninger, T., How, J., He, Q.: Representation learning in heterogeneous professional social networks with ambiguous social connections. In: 2019 IEEE International Conference on Big Data (Big Data), pp. 1928–1937 (2019)

18. Sun, Z., Deng, Z.H., Nie, J.Y., Tang, J.: RotatE: knowledge graph embedding by relational rotation in complex space. In: International Conference on Learning Representations (2019). https://openreview.net/forum?id=HkgEQnRqYQ

19. Trouillon, T., Welbl, J., Riedel, S., Ciaussier, E., Bouchard, G.: Complex embeddings for simple link prediction. In: 33rd International Conference on Machine Learning, ICML 2016, vol. 5, pp. 3021–3032 (2016)

20. Vaganov, D., Kalinin, A., Bochenina, K.: On inferring monthly expenses of social media users: towards data and approaches. In: Cherifi, H., Gaito, S., Mendes, J.F., Moro, E., Rocha, L.M. (eds.) COMPLEX NETWORKS 2019. SCI, vol. 881, pp. 854–865. Springer, Cham (2020). https://doi.org/10.1007/978-3-030-36687-2_71

21. Vaswani, A., et al.: Attention is all you need. In: Guyon, I., et al. (eds.) Advances in Neural Information Processing Systems, vol. 30. Curran Associates, Inc. (2017)

22. Wu, Z., Pan, S., Chen, F., Long, G., Zhang, C., Yu, P.S.: A comprehensive survey on graph neural networks. IEEE Trans. Neural Netw. Learn. Syst. **32**(1), 4–24 (2021). https://doi.org/10.1109/TNNLS.2020.2978386

23. Yang, Y., et al.: Multilingual universal sentence encoder for semantic retrieval. In: Proceedings of the 58th Annual Meeting of the Association for Computational Linguistics: System Demonstrations, pp. 87–94. Association for Computational Linguistics, July 2020. Online

24. Yang, Y., Pang, Y., Huang, G., et al.: The knowledge graph for macroeconomic analysis with alternative big data. arXiv preprint arXiv:2010.05172 (2020)

A Knowledge Enabled Data Management Method Towards Intelligent Police Applications

Hong Jiang[1], Hao Wu[2], Tiexin Wang[1,3(✉)], and Xinhua Yan[1,4]

[1] College of Computer Science and Technology, Nanjing University of Aeronautics and Astronautics, 29#, Jiangjun Road, Jiangning District, Nanjing 211106, China
{jiang1997,tiexin.wang}@nuaa.edu.cn
[2] Sucheng Branch of Suqian Public Security Bureau,
16#, HongZeHu West Road, Suqian 223800, China
[3] Key Laboratory of Safety-Critical Software, Nanjing University of Aeronautics and Astronautics, Ministry of Industry and Information Technology, Nanjing, China
[4] Nanjing DENET System Technology Co. LTD., Nanjing, China
xinhua.yan@njdenet.com

Abstract. The public security bureau masters vast amounts of valuable data. Since the public security bureau faces various types of data and a large number of early warning and judgment tasks, the processing of these data has become a major challenge, which concerns data consistence, data fusion, data association, etc. In this paper, towards the intelligent hotel management of the public security bureau, we propose a knowledge enabled data management method. We build a domain knowledge graph to improve the efficiency of hotel-relevant data management for the public security department. By constructing the domain knowledge graph, the early warning and judgment tasks can be solved based on knowledge reasoning. We carried out experiments to evaluate the feasibility of our proposed method. In the experiment, we use practical data from the Sucheng branch of Suqian Public Security Bureau to construct a knowledge graph. Results show that knowledge reasoning achieved good performance and exhibited the feasibility in early warning and judgment tasks of public security.

Keywords: Public security bureau · Intelligent hotel management · Domain knowledge graph · Knowledge reasoning

1 Introduction

In recent years, with the sustainable development of information techniques such as big data analysis and artificial intelligence, public security informatization has become the current trend and the focus of public security work [1].

The public security bureau masters a large number of data resources, such as data from relatively independent public security business systems, government data, internet data, and social data. We regard all these data as police data. However, due to confidentiality and real-time issues, the management and application of police data have been greatly affected. The effective management and application of police data is an important

B. Li et al. (Eds.): ADMA 2021, LNAI 13088, pp. 162–174, 2022.
https://doi.org/10.1007/978-3-030-95408-6_13

topic worldwide, which concerns data consistence and data fusion management, early warning and violation analysis, etc.

There is a lack of good correlation between various types and sources of police data, which has formed more and more isolated islands of data that has seriously hindered the use of police data. Facing the ever-increasing scale of data, certain information technologies have been used in the management of police data, such as Distributed Data Base (DDB). Although the application of DDB has strengthened the data interaction between different regions, the various connections between data are still not well represented. Furthermore, the lack of governance and integration has caused a large amount of data redundancy.

Building a large-scale knowledge base is one of the effective ways to structured storage and expression of police data [2]. In face of a large number of early warning and judgment tasks, it is necessary to combine the experience of policemen. Knowledge reasoning can complete these tasks by establishing relevant rules.

Focusing on the intelligent hotel management of the public security bureau, we propose a knowledge enabled data management method "SmartHotel". One major challenge of SmartHotel is how to construct an appropriate knowledge graph. We propose a domain knowledge graph, namely SmartHotel domain knowledge graph (ShDKG). Another major challenge is how to realize early warning and judgment tasks. We complete this issue based on knowledge reasoning, so that the workload of decision-makers can be greatly reduced during the decision-making process.

The three main contributions of this paper are as follows:

- We propose a knowledge enabled data management method, which links the corresponding concepts in multi-source heterogeneous data of the public security bureau.
- We apply knowledge reasoning to solve a large number of early warning and judgment tasks, which is helpful for intelligent decision-making in the hotel management of the public security bureau.
- We construct a public security knowledge graph, providing framework support for the expansion of the knowledge graph in the field of public security.

The paper is organized as follows. In Sect. 2, we introduce related concepts and technologies in SmartHotel. A general overview of SmartHotel is given in Sect. 3. Experiments description and results analysis are given in Sect. 4. Section 5 shows the related work. Some concluding remarks are finally given in Sect. 6.

2 Related Concepts and Technologies

2.1 Knowledge Graph

The knowledge graph is a form of knowledge representation proposed by Google in 2012 [3]. As a large-scale semantic network, knowledge graph includes entities, concepts, and the incidence relation between these entities and concepts [4, 5].

SmartHotel is a data management method based on the knowledge graph. It manages data through ShDKG and uses knowledge reasoning to complete reasoning tasks.

As shown in Fig. 1, the whole process of constructing ShDKG can be divided into: ontology construction, knowledge extraction, knowledge fusion, and knowledge representation. Ontology construction is based on existing domain knowledge. Knowledge extraction includes "direct mapping" and "named entity recognition", extracting knowledge from structured data and unstructured data, respectively. Knowledge fusion merges the same entities from the same or different knowledge bases. The detailed process is illustrated in Sect. 3.

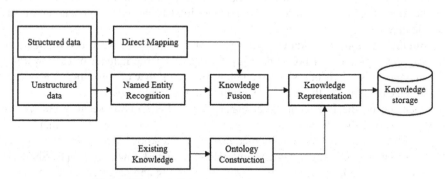

Fig. 1. The overall framework of constructing ShDKG

2.2 Ontology

Ontology is a conceptual model that describes concepts and relationships between concepts in the related fields [6]. Scholars, such as Guarino, analyzed the ontology level and domain dependency, then divided ontology into top-level ontology, domain ontology, task ontology, and application ontology [2]. In this paper, we study concepts and relations in the public security field, so the constructed ontology belongs to domain ontology.

Semantic Web Rule Language (SWRL) is an ontology reasoning language, based on representation rules of the semantic web, combining the advantages of Web Ontology Language (OWL) and Rule Markup Language (RuleML). SWRL can directly use the vocabulary in ontology, and then import it into the reasoning engine for reasoning.

In SmartHotel, we employ existing domain knowledge to build a domain ontology, namely SmartHotel domain ontology (ShDO), the detailed process is shown in Subsect. 3.1. We use SWRL to customize reasoning rules and to implement reasoning tasks; the detailed process is shown in Subsect. 3.4.

3 SmartHotel Overview

In this section, we introduce SmartHotel in detail. The first subsection presents ShDO. The second subsection introduces knowledge extraction from structured and unstructured data. The third subsection illustrates the process of knowledge fusion. The fourth subsection shows reasoning rules.

3.1 ShDO

The most important task of building a knowledge graph is to design ontology [8]. We use a combination of a top-down and bottom-up method [9]: at first, propose an ontology framework based on domain knowledge of public security SmartHotel, and then combine the existing structured data to form a simple graph.

In the field of public security, any case is composed of five basic elements: *person*, *event*, *thing*, *location*, and *organization*. By systematically decomposing cases in the way of five elements, the goal of deep understanding of cases is achieved. Therefore, we designed five top-level classes. As shown in Table 1, we designed subclasses separately for each top-level class.

Table 1. Ontology hierarchy

Top-level class	Subclass
People	Hotel guest
	Hotel staff
	Key person
	Policemen
	Other person
Things	Vehicle
	Drug tools
Events	Drug
	Gambling
	Frequent check-in event
	Minor check-in event
	Inconsistent identity
Organization	Hotel
	Police station
Locations	Province
	Municipality directly under the central government
	Special administrative region

On the basis of classes and class hierarchy, we defined relations between classes as object properties. There are conceptual associations between *person* and *thing*, *event*, *location*, and *organization*. For example, we define an object property *"check in"* between the class *hotel guest* and *hotel*, the domain of the object property is *hotel guest*, and *hotel* is the range of the object property.

We defined the properties of each class, namely data properties. Table 2 shows examples of data properties. For example, data properties for *hotel guest* are: *hasID_number*, *hasCheckInID_number, hasPhoneNumber, hasGender, hasDateOfBirth, hasCheckIn-Time, hasCheckOutTime, hasRoomNumber, hasPassengerCode,* etc.

Table 2. An example of data properties of a class

Class	Data properties
Hotel guest	hasID_Number
	hasCheckInID_number
	hasPhoneNumber
	hasGender
	hasDateOfBirth
	hasCheckInTime
	hasCheckOutTime
	hasRoomNumber
	hasPassengerCode

After defining the object properties and data properties, we use object properties and data properties to constrain the classes in ShDO. As shown in Table 3, ShDO contains 31 classes, 49 object properties and 139 data properties.

Table 3. The number of classes, object attributes, and data attributes in ShDO

Terminology	Class	Object property	Data property
296	31	49	139

The network structure of the ontology model of ShDKG is shown in Fig. 2.

3.2 Knowledge Extraction

Knowledge extraction is an important way of getting data source for building ShDKG. The purpose of knowledge extraction is to extract knowledge from data that are from different sources and in different forms.

Structured Data Extraction. Police data is mostly structured and stored in relational databases. So structured data extraction is a focus of knowledge extraction.

We use a direct mapping method to convert structured data in relational databases into RDF graph data. In a relational database, each row of data represents attributes of one same class, each column represents data values of one same attribute of different subjects. After direct mapping, we reflect data from relational databases in the RDF graph. The rules for direct mapping are as follows.

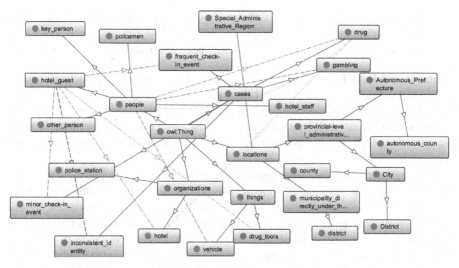

Fig. 2. The ShDO framework

- Tables in relational databases are mapped to RDF classes.
- Columns of tables are mapped to RDF attributes.
- Each row of tables is mapped to an entity.
- The value of each cell in relational database is mapped to an attribute value. When a cell corresponds to a foreign key, we replace it with the entity or attribute pointed to by the foreign key.

Table 4 shows the Key personnel table in a relational database, which includes ID number, type of fugitive, and fugitive date. Due to the confidentiality of police data, the data shown in Table 4 does not refer to the real information of any organization.

Table 4. Key personnel table

ID number	Classification	Fugitive date
111111	Drug-related	2020-05-14
222222	Involved in gambling	2018-11-22

For the two pieces of data shown in Table 4, based on the direct mapping rules, we can output the following RDF data.

<Key person/ID number = 111111> rdf: type <Key person>

<Key person/ID number = 111111> <Key person#ID number> 111111

<Key person/ID number = 111111> <Key person#Classification> "Drug-related"

<Key person/ID number = 111111> <Key person#Fugitive data> "2020-05-14"

<Key person/ID number = 222222> <Key person#ID number> 222222

<Key person/ID number = 222222> <Key person#Classification> "Involved in gambling"

<Key person/ID number = 222222> <Key person#Fugitive data> "2018-11-22"

Unstructured Data Extraction. There are also various forms of unstructured data in the field of public security, including video, audio, pictures, free text, etc. For unstructured data in the form of video, audio, and pictures, we can convert it into free text. For example, video is converted into free text by combining manual recording and SVM algorithms. Therefore, for unstructured data in the field of public security, we only consider free text.

For free text, named entity recognition is an important way of achieving knowledge extraction. The purpose of named entity recognition is to extract entity information from text, including people, things, cases, locations, and organizations. In this paper, we use the BIO labeling system. Where B represents the beginning word of an entity name, I represents the subsequent word of an entity name, O represents the part of the sentence that is not an entity. Furthermore, we not only identify entities but also identify entities types. With BIO labeling system, we set 11 types of labels, namely "O", "B-PEO", "B-THI", "B-CAS", "B-LOC", "B-ORG", "I-PEO", "I-THI", "I-CAS", "I-LOC", "I-ORG". PEO, THI, CAS, LOC and ORG indicating people, things, cases, locations,and organizations, respectively.

Next, we use a named entity recognition method that combines Long Shot-Term Memory Neural Network (LSTM) and Conditional Random Fields (CRF) [10]. As shown in Fig. 3, from bottom to top, a model is divided into Embedding layer, Bi-directional LSTM layer, and CRF layer. The Embedding layer is used as the input of the Bi-directional LSTM layer, which represents sentences as vectors of words. The Bi-directional LSTM layer includes one forward LSTM and one reverse LSTM, which calculate the corresponding vectors of each word considering the left and right words, and then connect the two vectors to form the vector output of the word. The purpose of the CRF layer is to label named entities in one sentence.

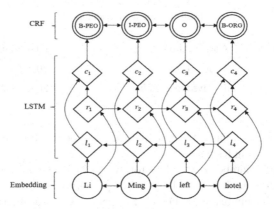

Fig. 3. A named entity recognition model

In Fig. 3, for a sentence "Li Ming left hotel", after being processed with the LSTM-CRF model, we can get the labeling results, which are shown in Table 5.

Table 5. An example of namely entity recognition model

Word	Labeling
Li	B-PEO
Ming	I-PEO
Left	O
Hotel	B-ORG

3.3 Knowledge Fusion

Through the knowledge extraction model, we can extract entities, relationships, and properties from unstructured data (pre-processed as free text). We use Term Frequency-Inverse Document Frequency algorithm (TF-IDF) and cosine similarity to merge the same entities from the same or different knowledge bases [7].

For different entities in free text, we calculate the values of TF and IDF respectively. The TF-IDF value is a feature vector, and we need to use cosine similarity to calculate the similarity between different entities. The cosine similarity of any two entities ranges from 0 to 1. In order to determine whether two entities are similar or not, we set a threshold of 0.9 [7], that is, when the cosine similarity is greater than 0.9, we judge that two entities are the same entity.

3.4 Reasoning Rules

We use SWRL to define reasoning rules. In this paper, we mainly analyze early warning of abnormal persons staying in a hotel. Abnormal persons represent persons with inconsistent identities, fugitives, and minors.

Inconsistent Identity. The inconsistent identity reasoning rule is as follows.

- hotel_guest(?p)^hasID_number(?p,?i)^hasCheckInID_number(?p,?j)^different From(?i,?j)->InconsistentIdentities(?p,inconsistent_identities)

hotel_guest is a subclass of *people*, representing the people staying at hotel. *hasID_number* and *hasCheckInID_number* are two data properties of *hotel_guest*. *hasID_number* represents the real ID number of a person. Through face recognition device (linked with personnel information in public security personnel database), we can obtain the real identity information of a person. *hasCheckInID_number* represents the check-in ID number registered at the front desk of a hotel. *InconsistentIdentities* is an object property between the class *hotel_guest* and *events*, representing people with inconsistent check-in identities. We compare *hasID_number and hasCheckInID_number*, and mark the abnormal personnel with inconsistent identity information.

Fugitives. The reasoning rules for fugitives are as follows.

- key_person(?p)^hotel(?x)^occupant(?x,?y)^hasID_number(?p,?q)^hasCheckInID_number(?y,?i)^sameAs(?i,?q)->PornographyBehavior(?y,pornography)
- key_person(?p)^hotel(?x)^occupant(?x,?y)^hasID_number(?y,?i)^hasID_number(?p,?q)^sameAs(?i,?q)->PornographyBehavior(?y,pornography)
- key_person(?p)^hotel(?x)^occupant(?x,?y)^hasID_number(?p,?q)^hasCheckInID_number(?y,?i)^sameAs(?i,?q)->DrugBehavior(?y,drug)
- key_person(?p)^hotel(?x)^occupant(?x,?y)^hasID_number(?y,?i)^hasID_number(?p,?q)^sameAs(?i,?q)->DrugBehavior(?y,drug)
- key_person(?p)^hotel(?x)^occupant(?x,?y)^hasID_number(?p,?q)^hasCheckInID_number(?y,?i)^sameAs(?i,?q)->GamblingBehavior(?y,gambling)
- key_person(?p)^hotel(?x)^occupant(?x,?y)^hasID_number(?y,?i)^hasID_number(?p,?q)^sameAs(?i,?q)->GamblingBehavior(?y,gambling)

Through these six rules, we compare the identity information registered at the front desk of a hotel and the personnel information recognized by face recognition devices (linked with personnel information in public security Key person database). If there is a consistent identity, the public security bureau will receive an early warning.

Minors. The reasoning rules for minor check-in are as follows.

- minor(?p)^hotel(?x)^occupant(?x,?y)^hasCheckInID_number(?y,?i)^hasID_ number(?p,?q)^sameAs(?i,?q)->MinorCheckIn(?y,minor_check_in_event)
- minor(?p)^hotel(?x)^occupant(?x,?y)^hasID_number(?y,?i)^hasID_number(?p,?q)^sameAs(?i,?q)->MinorCheckIn(?y,minor_check_in_event)

Through these two rules, we compare the identity information registered at the front desk of a hotel and the personnel information recognized by face recognition devices (linked with the personnel information in public security minor database). If there is a consistent identity, we mark the occupant as a minor and trigger an early warning.

4   Experiments

This section uses the reasoning rules defined in Subsect. 3.4 to verify the feasibility of SmartHotel. The first subsection introduces experimental goals. The second subsection illustrates datasets to evaluate SmartHotel. The analysis of experiment results is given in the third subsection. To carry out the experiment, we use Protégé 5.5 and reasoner HermiT 1.4.3.456.

4.1 Purpose

In order to prove the feasibility of our method, we conducted three experiments. They are early warning of fugitives, early warning of minors, and early warning of inconsistent identities. In the experiment, we compare knowledge reasoning rules with SQL statements (currently used in Sucheng branch of Suqian Public Security Bureau) to verify the feasibility of SmartHotel.

The identification of fugitives is an important task of SmartHotel. We compare the ID numbers of passengers with those in Key person database. Passenger represents the people staying at hotel. The Key personnel database contains various data of fugitives from the public security bureau.

Minor check-in is one the most frequent type of incidents. The public security bureau needs to know the status of all minors' occupancies. We compare ID numbers of passengers with those in minor database.

In order to avoid inspection, criminals usually use other people's ID cards to register in hotels. We compare the personnel information recognized by devices with the check-in information registered at the front desk of a hotel.

4.2 Datasets

We use the practical data from the Sucheng branch of Suqian Public Security Bureau, China. In the experiment, we collected three-day hotel occupancy data of Suqian City. On July 12, 2021, we obtained 18,799 passengers data. On July 13, 2021, we obtained 18,837 passengers data. On July 14, 2021, we obtained 18,836 passengers data. Each piece of data includes name, gender, ID number, hotel name, check-in time, check-in room number, etc.

We also used some basic data from the public security bureau, including early warning personnel data, minor data, etc. Considering the confidentiality of police data and to prevent data leakage, we do not display detailed data in experiments.

4.3 Experimental Results and Analysis

We construct 9 reasoning rules, 6 rules related to fugitives, 2 rules related to minor check-in rules, and 1 rule related to inconsistent identity. Table 6 shows the three-day warning results. Regarding three-day warning results, we can find that knowledge reasoning and SQL statements can get the same warning information, which proves that knowledge reasoning is feasible.

For different reasoning tasks, we must write different SQL statements to query different tables in public security database and establish connections between different data. Knowledge reasoning is mainly about reasoning around relations and has strong scalability. For different reasoning tasks, knowledge reasoning only needs to write different reasoning rules.

Table 6. Experimental results

Method	Fugitive			Minor check-in			Inconsistent identity		
	July 12	July 13	July 14	July 12	July 13	July 14	July 12	July 13	July 14
SQL	0	1	0	436	590	450	2	1	0
SmartHotel	0	1	0	436	590	450	2	1	0

5 Related Work

The knowledge enabled data management method in the public security bureau can be divided into two aspects: constructing domain knowledge graph, and analysis of illegal and criminal behaviors.

In [11], Sun proposed a model driven approach based on the Model Driven Architecture (MDA), which automatically constructs knowledge graph from relational databases and realizes high-quality transformation from a relational database to a knowledge graph. In [12], Yu proposed a process for constructing a knowledge graph of government procurement: obtaining the bid-winning announcement information through web crawler technology, constructing the government procurement ontology by combining the professional knowledge of government procurement and professional standards and norms, and using Protégé, D2rq, Neo4j and other software to realize ontology instantiation, entity extraction, N-Triples storage. In [13], a method of constructing a domain knowledge graph is proposed, Lv used information extraction technologies to extract entities and relationships from open web documents. Meanwhile, it mines the multi-dimensional relationships between entities and solves the information conflicts caused by the fusion of multi-source information. However, they fail to consider the data types as structured data and unstructured data.

In [14], Szekely applied the knowledge graph to address the issue of combating human trafficking and deployed it to law enforcement agencies and non-governmental organizations. In [15], Elezaj proposed a framework based on knowledge graph that aims to support crime investigators in solving and preventing crimes, from data collection to inferring digital evidence acceptable to the court. However, the framework has not been fully implemented, and there are no real use cases.

Generally, most of the existing research works are rarely applied in the field of public security. In this paper, we propose SmartHotel, using real structured data and unstructured data from the public security bureau to build ShDKG. Experiment results prove that SmartHotel is a feasible solution.

6 Conclusion

This paper mainly discusses the knowledge enabled data management method SmartHotel. Firstly, based on domain knowledge of public security, we use a combination of top-down and bottom-up method to construct ShDO. Secondly, we extract knowledge in the field of public security hotel management and store it in ShDKG. Then we use the knowledge fusion method based on similarity calculation to merge same entities from same or different knowledge bases. For reasoning tasks of the public security bureau, we adopt rule-based reasoning, which can trigger early warnings. Experimental results show that the method is feasible. Compared with traditional data management and application methods, SmartHotel stores entities and relations, and performs as a foundation for knowledge services in the field of public security.

In future work, we plan to expand the application of our method, and further evaluate and improve the performance of SmartHotel.

Acknowledgement. This work was supported by the Open Fund of the Ministry Key Laboratory for Safety-Critical Software Development and Verification (XCA1816401). The authors would like to thank the policemen from Sucheng branch of Suqian Public Security Bureau for their cooperation and assistance.

References

1. Schwarck, E.: Intelligence and informatization: the rise of the Ministry of Public Security in intelligence work in China. China J. **80**(1), 1–23 (2018)
2. Ren, B., Bu, F., Hou, Z., Fu, Y., Liu, X.: Analysis on the construction of knowledge graph of mass events based on ontology. In: Journal of Physics: Conference Series, vol. 1802, p. 042056. IOP Publishing (2021)
3. Liu, W., et al.: Representation learning over multiple knowledge graphs for knowledge graphs alignment. Neuro-Comput. **320**, 12–24 (2018)
4. Duan, W., Chiang, Y.Y.: Building knowledge graph from public data for predictive analysis: a case study on predicting technology future in space and time. In: Proceedings of the 5th ACM SIGSPATIAL International Workshop on Analytics for Big Geospatial Data, pp. 7–13 (2016)
5. Song, F., Wang, B., Tang, Y., Sun, J.: Research of medical aided diagnosis system based on temporal knowledge graph. In: Yang, X., Wang, C.-D., Islam, M.S., Zhang, Z. (eds.) ADMA 2020. LNCS (LNAI), vol. 12447, pp. 236–250. Springer, Cham (2020). https://doi.org/10.1007/978-3-030-65390-3_19
6. Westerinen, A., Tauber, R.: Ontology development by domain experts (without using the "O" word). Appl. Ontol. **12**(3–4), 299–311 (2017)
7. Qin, H., Yao, Y.: Agriculture knowledge graph construction and application. In: Journal of Physics: Conference Series, vol. 1756, p. 012010. IOP Publishing (2021)
8. Arafeh, M., Ceravolo, P., Mourad, A., Damiani, E., Bellini, E.: Ontology based recommender system using social network data. Future Gener. Comput. Syst. **115**, 769–779 (2021)
9. Zheng, X., Wang, B., Zhao, Y., Mao, S., Tang, Y.: A knowledge graph method for hazardous chemical management: Ontology design and entity identification. Neurocomputing **430**, 104–111 (2021)
10. Lample, G., Ballesteros, M., Subramanian, S., Kawakami, K., Dyer, C.: Neural architectures for named entity recognition. arXiv preprint arXiv:1603.01360 (2016)
11. Sun, S., Meng, F., Chu, D.: A model driven approach to constructing knowledge graph from relational database. In: Journal of Physics: Conference Series, vol. 1584, p. 012073. IOP Publishing (2020)
12. Yaozu, Y., Jiangen, Z.: Constructing government procurement knowledge graph based on crawler data. In: Journal of Physics: Conference Series, vol. 1693, p. 012032. IOP Publishing (2020)

13. Lv, Q., et al.: Research on domain knowledge graph based on the large scale online knowledge fragment. In: 2014 IEEE Workshop on Advanced Research and Technology in Industry Applications (WARTIA), pp. 312–315. IEEE (2014)

14. Szekely, P., et al.: Building and using a knowledge graph to combat human trafficking. In: Arenas, M., et al. (eds.) ISWC 2015. LNCS, vol. 9367, pp. 205–221. Springer, Cham (2015). https://doi.org/10.1007/978-3-319-25010-6_12

15. Elezaj, O., Yayilgan, S.Y., Kalemi, E., Wendelberg, L., Abomhara, M., Ahmed, J.: Towards designing a knowledge graph-based framework for investigating and preventing crime on online social networks. In: Katsikas, S., Zorkadis, V. (eds.) e-Democracy 2019. CCIS, vol. 1111, pp. 181–195. Springer, Cham (2020). https://doi.org/10.1007/978-3-030-37545-4_12

Text Mining

Sparse Generalized Dirichlet Prior Based Bayesian Multinomial Estimation

Fatma Najar$^{(\boxtimes)}$ and Nizar Bouguila

Concordia Institute for Information and Systems Engineering (CIISE),
Concordia University, Montreal, QC, Canada
{fatma.najar,nizar.bouguila}@concordia.ca

Abstract. The popularity of count data is accompanied by its challenging nature such as high-dimensionality and sparsity. Multinomial distribution and extensions are widely applied for modeling data with multivariate count sequences. This paper considers the strength of estimating multinomial parameters based on Bayesian methodology taken into account the sparsity property. Respect of this, we propose a probabilistic approach using a hierarchical generalized Dirichlet prior for sparse multinomial distributions. Our technique builds up on Bayesian knowledge over large discrete domains represented by subsets of feasible outcomes: observed and unobserved. This model allows us to predict the new outcomes based on the preceding data generated from a multinomial distribution. Evaluation over large benchmarks associated with emotion prediction through two different experiments results in competitive performance. The first experiment reveals predicting emotions in poetry context from English and German dictionaries. The second experiment concerns analyzing flow of emotions related to natural disasters.

Keywords: Count data · Generalized Dirichlet prior · Sparse Bayesian multinomial estimation · Emotion prediction

1 Introduction

Data with multivariate count sequences known also as count data abound in many statistical domains including language modeling, political sciences, financial studies, and biology [12,13,17,23]. In this perspective, modeling count data has gained a great attention where the multinomial distribution has been known as the classical model considered for this type of data. However, this distribution was not robust enough to deal with the challenges of count data including sparsity, burstiness, and overdispersion [21]. Improving estimates over multinomial approach leads to incorporating Bayesian knowledge using conjugate priors such as the well-known Dirichlet-compound-multinomial (DCM) [18]. The DCM has been effectively applied in artificial intelligence where it has been considered as a key model in various domains including probabilistic graphical models [15], smoothing methods for language models [27], and topic modeling [19]. While in

© Springer Nature Switzerland AG 2022
B. Li et al. (Eds.): ADMA 2021, LNAI 13088, pp. 177–191, 2022.
https://doi.org/10.1007/978-3-030-95408-6_14

other line of research, methods address the problem of choosing the Dirichlet prior under a mean-squared error criterion [3,6] and additional employments of the Dirichlet prior for the multinomial probabilities [1]. Going beyond the difficulties and the weak properties of the Dirichlet prior, more flexible priors have been introduced in [4] where the generalized Dirichlet has been considered to build the multinomial generalized Dirichlet mixture model. Besides, the Beta-Liouville which belongs to the multivariate Liouville family is a conjugate prior to the multinomial distribution [5]. A recent count data modeling approach has adapted the scaled Dirichlet [25] and the shifted-scaled Dirichlet [26] as conjugate priors to propose statistical frameworks for clustering count data.

Despite all the significant contributions to the modeling of count data, all the above mentioned research works have considered smoothing the multinomial parameters and integrating it out to define a new distribution based on the parameters of the conjugate prior. Unfortunately, there are no considerable research works for modeling sparse count data while keeping the estimation of multinomial cell probabilities. With respect to statistical language processing, in the context of parameter estimation for multinomial cell probabilities [16], Bayesian approaches that employ weak prior knowledge generally face the problem of sparseness and high-dimensionality. In this context, the probability of characters was assigned to subsets of different cardinalities (small, large and moderates size of alphabets) using natural law [22]. Estimating sparse multinomial parameters using Dirichlet prior have been considered in [9,10]. In the work of [9], authors address the problem of large corpora in natural language application when distributions were mostly assigned to words that were not seen in the training set. They propose a Bayesian approach considering a hierarchical Dirichlet prior for multinomial distribution over exponential hypothesis each of which represents a set of feasible outcomes. In [10], the matter of uncertainty in vocabularies was addressed to give more flexibility with regards to the method of Friedman and Singer [9].

Meanwhile, the Dirichlet prior employed in [9] and [10] favors the sparsity due to the definition of proportions in the unit simplex using only one shape parameter. In this regard, sparse outcomes will be assigned low values of shape parameter which leads to prior probabilities located in the corner of the simplex implies to have only small or large probabilities. Consequently, the generalized Dirichlet (GD) distribution defined by [7,20,24] has been proposed to smooth this property through two shape parameters and a more general covariance which shows good capabilities for describing proportional data. The GD distribution was introduced as conjugate prior for multinomial distribution to model count data [4]. This distribution arises in various contexts including: Bayesian life-testing problems [24], medical applications such as analysis of acute lymphoblastic leukemia [2], and computer vision like unusual events prediction [8].

In the context of sparse multinomial estimation, there are no recent works even though the interesting utilities in Bayesian statistics, language modeling, graphical models, etc. Motivated by these facts, we propose a novel sparse generalized Dirichlet prior based Bayesian multinomial estimation over large discrete domains. We define prior over exponential hypothesis using vocabulary knowledge; each of which represents a set of feasible outcomes for seen and unseen words. In this work, we consider two different benchmarks to evaluate our proposed approach. A sparse dictionary of German and English poetry where we predict the emotion revealed by each line and the second database concerns tweets allowing us to analyze the flow of emotions related to natural disasters.

The paper is organized as follows. Section 2 introduces the preliminary definitions used in this work. We present the proposed approach in Sect. 3, experimental results in Sect. 4, and then we conclude in Sect. 5.

2   Preliminary Definitions

With L categories, let $\boldsymbol{X}$ be a vector with cell counts $(N_1, \ldots, N_L)$ that follows a multinomial distribution with parameters $(\theta_1, \ldots, \theta_L)$ where N_d represents the number of times in which the d-th category is observed. The probability density function can be represented as follows:

$$p(\boldsymbol{X}|\Theta) = \frac{N!}{N_1! \ldots N_L!} \prod_{d=1}^{L} \theta_d^{N_d} \tag{1}$$

where N is the total number of observations.

Assuming a Dirichlet distribution as prior over Θ and using Bayes rule, the posterior density function is given by:

$$p(\Theta|\boldsymbol{X}) \propto p(\boldsymbol{X}|\Theta)p(\Theta|\boldsymbol{\alpha}) \propto \prod_{d=1}^{L} \theta_d^{N_d+\alpha_d-1} \tag{2}$$

Using the Dirichlet prior, the expected $\hat{\theta}_d$ is then given by:

$$\hat{\theta}_d = \frac{\alpha_d + N_d}{\sum_{d=1}^{L} \alpha_d + N} \tag{3}$$

From a predictive Bayesian perspective, the posterior predictive distribution describing beliefs about future observations $\tilde{X}$ is given by:

$$p(\tilde{X}|D, M) = \int_{\Theta} p(\tilde{X}|\Theta, M)p(\Theta|D, M)d\Theta \tag{4}$$

where D is the observed data, M is the model described with the parameters Θ and $p(\Theta|D, M)$ is the posterior distribution for the model parameters.

Given that generalized Dirichlet (GD) distribution is conjugate to the multinomial distribution, a GD prior over Θ is characterized with hyperparameters $(\alpha_1, \ldots, \alpha_{L-1}, \beta_1, \ldots, \beta_{L-1})$ as following:

$$p(\Theta) = \prod_{d=1}^{L-1} \frac{\Gamma(\alpha_d + \beta_d)}{\Gamma(\alpha_d)\Gamma(\beta_d)} \Theta_d^{\alpha_d-1} \left(1 - \sum_{j=1}^{d} \Theta_j\right)^{\delta_d} \tag{5}$$

where $\delta_d = \beta_d - \alpha_{d+1} - \beta_{d+1}, d = 1, \ldots, L-2$ and $\delta_{L-1} = \beta_{L-1} - 1$.

Considering this GD prior, the prediction of initial value of X is:

$$p(X_1 = d) = \frac{\alpha_d}{\alpha_d + \beta_d} \prod_{j=1}^{d-1} \frac{\beta_j}{\alpha_j + \beta_j} \tag{6}$$

Given that if the prior is a GD with hyperparameters $\alpha_1, \ldots, \alpha_{L-1}, \beta_1, \ldots, \beta_{L-1}$, then the posterior is a GD with hyperparameters $\alpha_1', \ldots, \alpha_{L-1}', \beta_1', \ldots, \beta_{L-1}'$ (where $\alpha_d' = \alpha_d + N_d$ and $\beta_d' = \beta_d + \sum_{i=d}^{L} N_i$), the prediction for X_{N+1} is as follows:

$$p(X_{N+1} = d) = \frac{\alpha_d + N_d}{\alpha_d + \beta_d + n_d} \prod_{j=1}^{d-1} \frac{\beta_j + n_{j+1}}{\alpha_j + \beta_j + n_j} \tag{7}$$

where $n_d = \sum_{i=d}^{L} N_i$.

3   The Proposed Approach

We present in this work a new Bayesian approach for sparse multinomial distribution. Our technique builds up on proposing a new hierarchical prior namely the generalized Dirichlet for the sparse multinomial distribution. We define the new sparse multinomial estimation on two subsets of outcomes: observed and unobserved. The basic strategy of this work can be stated as predicting a new outcome X_{N+1} given $D = \{X_1, \ldots, X_N\}$ drawn from an unknown multinomial distribution. The Bayesian estimate given a prior over the multinomial distribution can be represented as:

$$p(X_{N+1}|D) = \int_\Theta p(X_{N+1}|\Theta) p(\Theta|X_1, \ldots, X_N) \, d\Theta \tag{8}$$

where $p(\Theta|X_1, \ldots, X_N)$ can be obtained using Bayes theorem:

$$p(\Theta|X_1, \ldots, X_N) \propto p(D|\Theta) \, p(\Theta) \propto p(\Theta) \prod_{d=1}^{L} \theta_d^{N_d} \tag{9}$$

where $p(\Theta)$ is the prior probability of a given Θ.

We note the total vocabulary Σ where a random selection of a subset dictionary $V = \Sigma'$ is consistent with training text data only if it contains all the occurrences d for which $N_d > 0$ where ($\Sigma' \subseteq \Sigma$). Hence, we refer by Σ^o the set of observed words and $k^o = |\Sigma^o|$.

Given now, a GD prior over possible multinomial distributions for only the observed words with the same hyper-parameters α, β for each word in the vocabulary V ($\forall d \; \alpha_d = \alpha, \beta_d = \beta$). Thus, we define the following prior:

$$p(\Theta|V) = \left[\frac{\Gamma(\alpha+\beta)}{\Gamma(\alpha)\Gamma(\beta)} \right]^{|V|} \prod_{d=1}^{L-1} \Theta_d^{\alpha-1} (1 - \sum_{j=1}^{d} \Theta_j)^{-\alpha} \tag{10}$$

where $k = |V|$, $k = 1, \ldots, L - 1$.

Considering the fact that $\theta_d = 0$ for all $d \notin V$ and using Eqs. 5 and 7, we have:

$$p(X_{N+1} = d | X_1, \ldots, X_N, V) = \begin{cases} \frac{\alpha + N_d}{\alpha + \beta + n_d} \prod_{j=1}^{d-1} \frac{\beta + n_{j+1}}{\alpha + \beta + n_j} & \text{If } d \in V \\ 0 & \text{otherwise} \end{cases} \quad (11)$$

Now, if we use the matter of the uncertainty in vocabularies, this will reflect to expect having words outside the vocabulary. Thus, we assume having a specific probability for the unseen words. First, we define two different priors for all the categories of the set V. Let k be the size of V and assuming a prior that gives equal probability to all the sets with same cardinality.

Given Bayesian multinomial estimation properties, the posterior predictive distribution of a new outcome given the training data D is defined as follows:

$$p(X_{N+1} = d | D) = \sum_V p(X_{N+1} = d | D, V) p(V | D) \quad (12)$$

$$= \sum_{V, |V| = k} p(X_{N+1} = d | D, V) p(V = k | D)$$

where, using Bayes theorem, $p(V = k | D)$ is given by:

$$p(V = k | D) = \frac{p(D | V = k) p(V = k)}{\sum_{k'} p(D | V = k') p(V = K')} \quad (13)$$

$$\propto p(D | V = k) p(V = k)$$

$$\propto \sum_{D, |V| = k} p(D | V) p(V | k) p(V = k)$$

Next, we assume that we are given the distribution $p(V | k)$ for $k = 1, \ldots, L-1$. So, the prior over sets is:

$$p(V | k) = \binom{L - 1}{k}^{-1} \quad (14)$$

For simplicity purpose, we suppose $p(V = k)$ is the same for all sets of size k that contains Σ^o. Besides, using Bayes rule we can simplify the prediction of X_{N+1}. As there are two cases where any set V has non-zero posterior probability ($d \in \Sigma^o$)

$$p(X_{N+1} = d|D) = \frac{\alpha + N_d}{\alpha + \beta + n_d} \prod_{j=1}^{d-1} \frac{\beta + n_{j+1}}{\alpha + \beta + n_j} \sum_{V,|V|=k} p(V = k|D)$$

$$= \frac{\alpha + N_d}{k^o \alpha + N} \prod_{j=1}^{d} \frac{\beta + n_j}{\alpha + \beta + n_j} \frac{k^o \alpha + N}{\beta + N}$$

$$\sum_k p(D|V)p(V|k)p(V = k) \text{ If } d \in \Sigma^o$$

$$(15)$$

To simplify the prediction, we move outside the summation terms that don't depend on k. Thus, we need to estimate only:

$$S(D, L) = \frac{k^o \alpha + N}{\beta + N} \sum_k p(D|V)p(V|k)p(V = k) \tag{16}$$

where $S(D, L)$ is considered as the scaling factor and the probability mass assigned to the observed outcomes. Hence, we assign the probability $(1 - S(D, L))$ to unseen words given the training data where $d \notin \Sigma^o$.

Taking advantage of GD properties as a conjugate prior for multinomial distribution for the case of $\Sigma^o \subseteq V$, then we can express the following:

$$p(D|V) = \int_\Theta p(D|\Theta)p(\Theta|V)d\Theta \tag{17}$$

$$= \left[\frac{\Gamma(\alpha + \beta)}{\Gamma(\alpha)\Gamma(\beta)} \right]^{|V|} \prod_{d \in \Sigma^o} \frac{\Gamma(\alpha + N_d)\Gamma(\beta + n_{d+1})}{\Gamma(\alpha + \beta + N_d + n_{d+1})}$$

Therefore, using the previous equations, we conclude:

$$p(D|V)p(V|k) = \binom{L-1}{k}^{-1} \left[\frac{\Gamma(\alpha + \beta)}{\Gamma(\alpha)\Gamma(\beta)} \right]^{|V|=k} \prod_{d \in \Sigma^o} \frac{\Gamma(\alpha + N_d)\Gamma(\beta + n_{d+1})}{\Gamma(\alpha + \beta + N_d + n_{d+1})}$$

$$(18)$$

Sampling a random combination to obtain the possible summation over the subsets V, we have

$$\sum_k p(D|V)p(V|k) = \binom{L-1-k^o}{k-k^o}\binom{L-1}{k}^{-1} \frac{\Gamma(\alpha + \beta)^k}{\Gamma(\alpha)^k \Gamma(\beta)^k}$$

$$\prod_{d \in \Sigma^o} \frac{\Gamma(\alpha + N_d)\Gamma(\beta + n_{d+1})}{\Gamma(\alpha + \beta + N_d + n_{d+1})}$$

$$= \left[\frac{(L-1-k^o)!}{(L-1)!} \prod_{d \in \Sigma^o} \frac{\Gamma(\alpha + N_d)\Gamma(\beta + n_{d+1})}{\Gamma(\alpha + \beta + N_d + n_{d+1})} \right]$$

$$\frac{k!}{(k-k^o)!} \frac{\Gamma(\alpha + \beta)^k}{\Gamma(\alpha)^k \Gamma(\beta)^k} \tag{19}$$

As the term in the square brackets does not depend on the choice of k, we cancel it out to give rise to the proposed equality:

$$p(V = k|D) = \frac{m_k}{\sum_{k' \geq k^0} m'_k} \tag{20}$$

where

$$m_k = p(V = k)\frac{k!}{(k - k^o)!}\frac{\Gamma(\alpha + \beta)^k}{\Gamma(\alpha)^k \Gamma(\beta)^k} \tag{21}$$

Therefore, the scaling factor is expressed as the following:

$$S(D, L) = \Big(\sum_{k=k^o}^{L-1} \frac{k^o \alpha + N}{\beta + N} m_k \Big) \Big(\sum_{k' \geq k^0} m_{k'} \Big)^{-1} \tag{22}$$

Thus, the simplified prediction probability can be defined as:

$$p(X_{N+1} = d|D) = \begin{cases} \frac{\alpha + N_d}{k^o \alpha + N} \prod_{j=1}^d \frac{\beta + n_j}{\alpha + \beta + n_j} S(D, L) \text{ If } d \in \Sigma^o \\ \frac{1}{L - k^o}(1 - S(D, L)) \qquad \text{If } d \notin \Sigma^o \end{cases} \tag{23}$$

4   Experimental Results

Human emotions pose a quite set of challenges that facial expressions are not enough to understand the expressing issues of human being. Concerned about the verbal communication, there is a room for textual information that provides more thoughts about people's opinion and sentiment. So far, limited efforts have focused on sentiment analysis from poetry content for instance poems and books. In this work, we approach the sentiment analysis from various text contents such as poems and messages. Our objectives are to deal with the challenges of text documents that are usually represented with bag-of-words structure (count data) which leads to the sparseness and the high-dimensionality issues. For instance, we consider two challenging applications namely emotion prediction in poetry context and modeling the flow of emotions related to natural disasters.

4.1   Emotion Prediction in Poetry Context

In this section, we evaluate the proposed generalized sparse multinomial (GSM) model on public dataset: PO-EMO [11]. The PO-EMO dataset is a collection of German and English language poems which enables modeling aesthetic emotions in poetry. The German corpus contains 158 poems with 731 stanzas written by 51 authors during the period of 1575–1936. The considered poems are extracted from ANTI-K website[1] which provides a platform for students to help them upload edited poems for class including author names, year of publications,

---

[1] https://lyrik.antikoerperchen.de/.

poetry topic, and literary epochs. Regarding English dataset, it contains 64 poems (174 stanzas) collected from Project Gutenberg[2] which contains a bunch of eBooks freely available sorted by author, title, topic, language, etc. The two poetry corpora consider emotions elicited in the reader rather than expressed in the text or expected by the author. The emotions are annotated within the context of the whole poem by literary graduate students. Each line is annotated with two labels among the set of considered emotions: Beauty/Joy, Sadness, Uneasiness, Vitality, Awe/Sublime, Suspense, Humor, Annoyance, and Nostalgia (not available in the German data) where the frequencies of these emotions are listed in Table 1. We can notice from the Table 1 that "Beauty/Joy" and "Sadness" are the dominant emotions and the remaining are infrequent which makes this dataset more challenging and interesting to explore the effectiveness of the new sparse multinomial model. It is worthy to mention also that there is no major difference in the emotion frequencies regarding the first annotation and the second one. For that, we consider in our experiments only the first annotation.

Table 1. Emotions frequencies for each annotator in the German and English dictionary [11]

Vocabulary	Annotation 1		Annotation 2	
	English	German	English	German
Beauty/Joy	.31	.30	.26	.30
Sadness	.21	.20	.20	.18
Uneasiness	.15	.19	.15	.18
Vitality	.12	.11	.18	.13
Awe/Sublime	.07	.06	.07	.06
Suspense	.04	.07	.07	.08
Humor	.04	.05	.04	.05
Nostalgia	.03	–	.03	–
Annoyance	.03	.04	.02	.02

The experiments were performed on Windows 10, an Intel Xeon E-2144G CPU model with a 32 GB RAM and 64-bit operating system. We implemented in Python 3.7 the GSM approach proposed in Sect. 3, the sparse-multinomials proposed in [9] and [10] for comparison experiments. We consider in our experiments vocabularies with different cardinalities, we give an example of the generated set of words with $L = 300$ for the German and English corpus in Fig. 1.

In view of evaluating the effectiveness of the proposed generalized sparse multinomial model, we target a challenging scenario in terms of predicting emotions in poetry context. We split the data into training/testing sets using different ratios (90/10, 80/20, 70/30, 60/40) where each vector X_i is a line in the

---

[2] https://gutentag.sdsu.edu/.

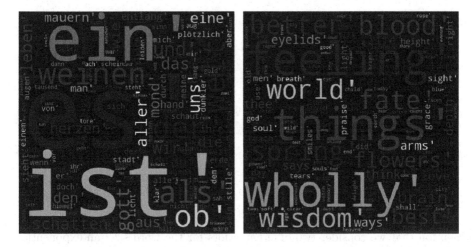

Fig. 1. Generated set of words for German and English poems

poem corpus. First, we train the model on the training data for the purpose of predicting the poems of the testing set. We represent each poem line as the vector of words and we assign a probability for each coming word. If the word is not observed in the context of the previous words, the new word is expected to occur with a specific probability mass. Next, we apply the multinomial mixture clustering on the predicted data to recognize the emotions. We consider the predictive distributions as the multinomial parameters and based on the Bayes rule, we choose the emotion label c corresponding to the poem line $\boldsymbol{X}_i$ given by:

$$p(c|D, \boldsymbol{\theta}_c) = p(\boldsymbol{X}_{N+1}, \ldots, \boldsymbol{X}_{N+T}|c)\pi_c \tag{24}$$

where $\{\pi_c\}_{c=1}^C$ are the mixing weight coefficients, and $p(\boldsymbol{X}_{N+1}, \ldots, \boldsymbol{X}_{N+T}|c)$ is the c-th probability density function (pdf) of the multinomial distribution that corresponds to the emotion c.

We evaluate the impact of the hyperparameters of the proposed approach using as evaluation metric accuracy and F1-micro scores for comparison analysis. We mention that we assumed that parameters α and β are the same for all the d symbols. Thus, the choice of these parameters will be empirical. For that, we consider three hypothesis: when α and β are equals, when $\beta = 2$, $\alpha \in [0.1, 3]$, and when $\alpha = 2$, $\beta \in [0.1, 3]$. From Fig. 2, we can deduce the great impact of the parameters α and β on the generalized sparse multinomial and how to interfere the relations between the two parameters on the resolution of the model. For the German corpus, we reach the highest accuracy performance when $\alpha < \beta$ but for the English data, the better result is achieved when $\alpha = \beta$. Thus, we conclude that there are no strict relation or value for the parameters and the superior performance is achieved through empirical observations.

Other important parameters which affect the results are the size of the vocabulary L and the cardinality of the predicted outcomes set T. Besides, we

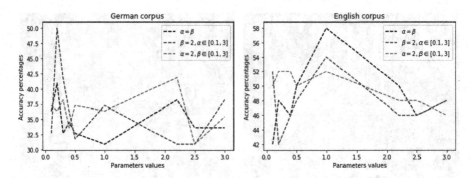

Fig. 2. Impacts of α and β of the effectiveness of the GSM model

mention that we consider two different priors for the word size: an exponential prior $p(S = k) = \epsilon^k$, and a polynomial prior $p(S = k) = k^{-\epsilon}$, where $\epsilon = 0.9$. Figure 3 presents the alteration of the accuracy percentages in terms of L and T. We can see clearly that the performance fluctuates slightly with respect to the size of the vocabulary while it drops quickly with the number of the predicted outcomes. For $L = 200$ and $T = 50$, the GSM achieves the best performance

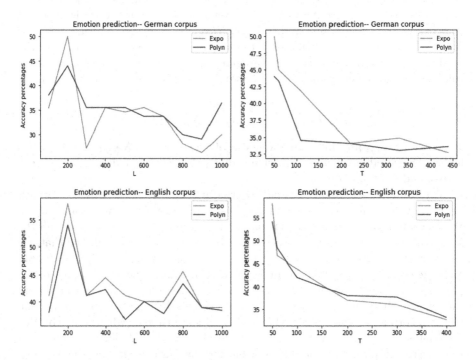

Fig. 3. Illustration of the emotion prediction results within German and English corpus for different values of L (size of the vocabulary) and T (size of the testing set) using two priors: $P(V = k)$ exponential and polynomial.

for the two corpora and it should also be underlined that the proposed model is more capable when the prior for the word size is exponential. We mention also that the best results are obtained on a corpus with the total number of words $N = 14,440$. The difficulty of this model occurs when the number of the future outcomes are important. Indeed, this is due to the fact that the prediction of X_{N+t} is based on the preceding prediction $p(X_{N+t-1})$.

The comparison of our proposed model to the baseline methods are summarized in Table 2. We refer to the Ristad approach: the model proposed in [22], sparse multinomial: Friedman and Singer's method [9], and the Bayesian sparse multinomial: Griffiths's approach [10]. The entire experiments are averaged over 10 times of running the algorithms. We compare also with BERT model (DBMDZ) applied on the German corpus for line-level in [11]. As illustrated in Table 2, the proposed generalized sparse multinomial outperforms all the other related-works on two corpora. The flexibility of the generalized Dirichlet prior gives advantages to the model which results in better performance.

Table 2. Comparative results for Line-level emotion prediction

Model	German		English	
	Accuracy	F1-micro	Accuracy	F1-micro
Ristad approach	.33	.28	.36	.25
Sparse multinomial	.33	.31	.37	.27
Bayesian sparse multinomial	.34	.31	.39	.21
BERT-DBMDZ [11]	–	.420	–	–
Generalized sparse multinomial	.50	.425	.58	.419

4.2   Modeling the Flow of Emotions Related to Natural Disasters

We investigate the performance of the proposed Generalized sparse multinomial (GSM) approach on the second application where we consider, CrisisNLP, a crisis corpora collection [14]. The CrisisNLP corpora contains tweets messages related to different natural disasters like earthquake, floods, and infectious disease. In this work, we consider the 2013-Pakistan earthquake database which contains 156,905 tweets messages related to 9 different emotions categories namely: "Injured or dead people", "Missing, trapped, or found people", "Displaced people and evacuations", "Infrastructure and utilities damage", "Donation needs or offers or volunteering services", "Caution and advice", "Sympathy and emotional support", "Other useful information", "Not related or irrelevant". This corpora presents two important challenges as the datasets have high class imbalance and collected messages are introduced as short texts which increase the sparsity problem. For preprocessing, the bag-of-words approach is used to represent the tweets messages as count vectors. We represent each short text "tweets" as an L-dimensional count vector. We display in Fig. 4 an example of generated vocabulary from the 2013-Pakistan earthquake database with size $L = 600$.

Fig. 4. Vocabulary words of 2013-Pakistan earthquake database

We evaluate the influence of the vocabulary size and the size of testing set on GSM approach and the related works such as Ristard approach (Rt), sparse multinomial (SM), and Bayesian sparse multinomial (BSM). We note from Fig. 5 the outperformance of GSM with regards to other approaches. We mention that in terms of high-dimensionality (high vocabulary size), the GSM model is able to predict emotions with outstanding performance. It is noteworthy to mention also that the more the vocabulary size is important the more the data is sparse. Thus, the proposed approach succeeds to tackle the challenge of sparsity which proofs the effect of including the vocabulary knowledge for the unseen words. In addition, comparing the GSM with approaches that consider the knowledge of unseen words as the SM and the BSM, the GSM achieves the best performance owing to the special characteristics of the generalized Dirichlet prior. Considering the size of testing set, we refer that 200 is 20% of the dataset for testing and 80% for training, 300 represents 30% for testing and 70% for training. We point out that the performance of GSM drops after the size of 600 which is a consequence of the training set is only 30% of the dataset. For that, the performance is affected by the size of the testing-training set of the database.

In Table 3, we compare our proposed method in terms of accuracy percentage with the other related multinomial-based models namely: multinomial distribution, Dirichlet compound multinomial (DCM), generalized Dirichlet multinomial (GDM) that are different to Ristard approach (Rt), sparse multinomial (SM), and Bayesian sparse multinomial (BSM). DCM and GDM considers smoothing the multinomial parameters with Dirichlet and generalized Dirichlet priors respectively without Bayesian vocabulary knowledge. These models are not able

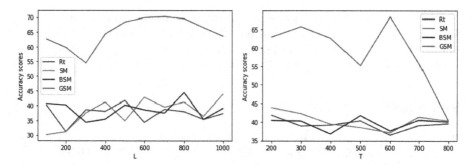

Fig. 5. Evaluation results of the proposed GSM and comparison with related multinomial-based models in terms of L (vocabulary size) and T (size of testing set)

to deal with this nature of data due to the sparsity and the high-dimensionality issues which demonstrate the effectiveness of including a hierarchical prior with vocabulary knowledge to estimate sparse multinomial.

Table 3. Accuracy results on Pakistan earthquake dataset using different multinomial-based models

Models	Accuracy scores
Multinomial	23.81
DCM	28.76
GDM	38.49
Ristard (Rt)	41.79
Sparse multinomial (SM)	43.91
Bayesian sparse (BSM)	44.44
Generalized sparse (GSM)	70.26

5   Conclusion

In this paper, we presented a hierarchical prior for the problem of estimating the sparse multinomial parameters. We proposed a novel sparse model based on the generalized Dirichlet prior which reduces the limitations of Bayesian approaches previously introduced for language model. Our method exploits the knowledge of the structure of the vocabularies in natural language. Explicitly, we employ prior knowledge for two feasible sets of vocabulary of words to be used for the estimation of sparse multinomial distribution. We consider predicting each new word if it is observed/not observed with a specific probability mass. We showed the effectiveness of the proposed approach in predicting emotions in German and English poetry and modeling the flow of emotions related to natural disasters. Different parameters influence the performance of the GSM algorithm, demonstrating that it can be properly considered to more complex applications. Although the proposed model achieved interesting and competitive results, we aim for the future work to investigate its limitations with respect to the size of testing set.

References

1. Agresti, A., Hitchcock, D.B.: Bayesian inference for categorical data analysis. Stat. Methods Appl. **14**(3), 297–330 (2005). https://doi.org/10.1007/s10260-005-0121-y
2. Barcella, W., De Iorio, M., Favaro, S., Rosner, G.L.: Dependent generalized Dirichlet process priors for the analysis of acute lymphoblastic leukemia. Biostatistics **19**(3), 342–358 (2018)
3. Benavoli, A., de Campos, C.P.: Inference from multinomial data based on a MLE-dominance criterion. In: Sossai, C., Chemello, G. (eds.) ECSQARU 2009. LNCS (LNAI), vol. 5590, pp. 22–33. Springer, Heidelberg (2009). https://doi.org/10.1007/978-3-642-02906-6_4
4. Bouguila, N.: Clustering of count data using generalized Dirichlet multinomial distributions. IEEE Trans. Knowl. Data Eng. **20**(4), 462–474 (2008)
5. Bouguila, N.: Count data modeling and classification using finite mixtures of distributions. IEEE Trans. Neural Netw. **22**(2), 186–198 (2011)
6. de Campos, C.P., Benavoli, A.: Inference with multinomial data: why to weaken the prior strength. In: Twenty-Second International Joint Conference on Artificial Intelligence (2011)
7. Connor, R.J., Mosimann, J.E.: Concepts of independence for proportions with a generalization of the Dirichlet distribution. J. Am. Stat. Assoc. **64**(325), 194–206 (1969)
8. Epaillard, E., Bouguila, N.: Variational Bayesian learning of generalized Dirichlet-based hidden Markov models applied to unusual events detection. IEEE Trans. Neural Netw. Learn. Syst. **30**(4), 1034–1047 (2018)
9. Friedman, N., Singer, Y.: Efficient Bayesian parameter estimation in large discrete domains. In: Advances in Neural Information Processing Systems, pp. 417–423 (1999)
10. Griffiths, T.L., Tenenbaum, J.B.: Using vocabulary knowledge in Bayesian multinomial estimation. In: Proceedings of the 14th International Conference on Neural Information Processing Systems: Natural and Synthetic, NIPS 2001, pp. 1385–1392. MIT Press, Cambridge (2001)
11. Haider, T., Eger, S., Kim, E., Klinger, R., Menninghaus, W.: PO-EMO: conceptualization, annotation, and modeling of aesthetic emotions in German and English poetry. In: Proceedings of the 12th International Conference on Language Resources and Evaluation (LREC 2020). European Language Resources Association (ELRA), Marseille, May 2020
12. Harris, T., Hilbe, J.M., Hardin, J.W.: Modeling count data with generalized distributions. The Stata J. **14**(3), 562–579 (2014)
13. Hilbe, J.M.: Modeling Count Data. Cambridge University Press, Cambridge (2014)
14. Imran, M., Mitra, P., Castillo, C.: Twitter as a lifeline: human-annotated Twitter corpora for NLP of crisis-related messages. arXiv preprint arXiv:1605.05894 (2016)
15. Koller, D., Friedman, N.: Probabilistic Graphical Models: Principles and Techniques. MIT Press, Cambridge (2009)

16. Krishnapuram, B., Carin, L., Figueiredo, M.A., Hartemink, A.J.: Sparse multinomial logistic regression: fast algorithms and generalization bounds. IEEE Trans. Pattern Anal. Mach. Intell. **27**(6), 957–968 (2005)
17. Lindén, A., Mäntyniemi, S.: Using the negative binomial distribution to model overdispersion in ecological count data. Ecology **92**(7), 1414–1421 (2011)
18. Madsen, R.E., Kauchak, D., Elkan, C.: Modeling word burstiness using the Dirichlet distribution. In: Proceedings of the 22nd International Conference on Machine Learning, pp. 545–552 (2005)
19. Mimno, D.M., McCallum, A.: Topic models conditioned on arbitrary features with Dirichlet-multinomial regression. In: UAI, vol. 24, pp. 411–418. Citeseer (2008)
20. Ng, K.W., Tian, G.L., Tang, M.L.: Dirichlet and related distributions: theory, methods and applications (2011)
21. Rennie, J.D., Shih, L., Teevan, J., Karger, D.R.: Tackling the poor assumptions of Naive Bayes text classifiers. In: Proceedings of the 20th International Conference on Machine Learning (ICML-2003), pp. 616–623 (2003)
22. Ristad, E.S.: A natural law of succession. Technical report, Department of Computer Science, Princeton University, July 1998
23. Tang, W., et al.: On performance of parametric and distribution-free models for zero-inflated and over-dispersed count responses. Stat. Med. **34**(24), 3235–3245 (2015)
24. Wong, T.T.: Generalized Dirichlet distribution in Bayesian analysis. Appl. Math. Comput. **97**(2–3), 165–181 (1998)
25. Zamzami, N., Bouguila, N.: A novel scaled Dirichlet-based statistical framework for count data modeling: unsupervised learning and exponential approximation. Pattern Recogn. **95**, 36–47 (2019)
26. Zamzami, N., Bouguila, N.: Probabilistic modeling for frequency vectors using a flexible shifted-scaled Dirichlet distribution prior. ACM Trans. Knowl. Discov. Data (TKDD) **14**(6), 1–35 (2020)
27. Zhai, C., Lafferty, J.: A study of smoothing methods for language models applied to ad hoc information retrieval. In: ACM SIGIR Forum, vol. 51, pp. 268–276. ACM, New York (2017)

I Know You Better: User Profile Aware Personalized Dialogue Generation

Wenhan Dong, Shi Feng$^{(\boxtimes)}$, Daling Wang, and Yifei Zhang

School of Computer Science and Engineering, Northeastern University,
Shenyang, China
1901700@stu.neu.edu.cn, {fengshi,wangdaling,zhangyifei}@cse.neu.edu.cn

Abstract. Recently, the response generation for dialogue systems has become a research hotspot both in the academic and business communities. Existing personalized response generation methods mainly stand on the chatbot's perspective, and focus on improving the conversation consistency according to the chatbot's traits. However, for building an emotionally intelligent and human-like chatbot, it is essential to consider the user's profile, such as interests, hobbies, and life experiences, and generate the personalized response from the user-oriented perspective. In this paper, we introduce the user profile aware personalized dialogue generation task. For sparse profile users, we extend Model-Agnostic Meta-Learning (MAML) method to quickly adapt to new profiles by leveraging only a few dialogue samples. Extensive experiments are conducted on a real-world dataset, and the results have validated the superiority of the proposed model over strong baseline methods.

Keywords: Response generation · Personalized dialogue · Meta learning · Dialogue system

1 Introduction

Recently, the open-domain dialogue systems (chatbots) have made great progress towards generating human-like responses, thanks to the development of deep learning models and the accessibility of extremely large conversation corpus. However, the lack of a consistent personality makes it impossible for current dialogue systems to behave coherently and engagingly. How to endow chatbots with a consistent persona is one of the major challenges. The existing methods in building personalized chatbots can learn persona from structured key-value pairs [21,36], semi-structured declarative sentences [3,34], or unstructured tweets [12], and generate personality-coherent responses based on seq2seq learning models.

Qian et al. [21] defined a group of key-value profile pairs as the persona. The authors intended to improve conversation consistency according to the predefined persona, and thus the chatbots could gain the trust of users. As shown in Fig. 1, the chatbot has been assigned the persona/trait including gender, age,

© Springer Nature Switzerland AG 2022
B. Li et al. (Eds.): ADMA 2021, LNAI 13088, pp. 192–205, 2022.
https://doi.org/10.1007/978-3-030-95408-6_15

and location. Therefore, when the user asks persona-related questions, the chatbot can generate consistent responses. Different from key-value persona pairs,
Zhang et al. [34] introduced a dialogue dataset with semi-structured persona by
asking randomly paired crowd workers to chat based on some given persona,
which was further extended in ConvAI2 [3].

Although the previous personalized chatbots have achieved promising results,
these models mainly focused on generating the responses based on the chatbot's
personas/traits, while the user's profile information has been neglected. In fact,
for building an emotionally intelligent and human-like chatbot, it is necessary
to consider the user's personality. Figure 2 demonstrates a motivating example
of a personalized response with user profile awareness. From the user's profile
information, the chatbot can infer that the user's hobby is traveling, thus giving
a more engaging response based on both context and user's profile.

Fig. 1. The chatbot trait grounded personalized dialogue generation.

In this paper, we focus on the task of open domain user profile aware personalized dialogue generation (dubbed as UP-PDG), which is conceptually different
from the chatbot trait grounded personalized dialogue generation (CT-PDG).
Specifically, UP-PDG stands on the perspective of users and thus tends to generate more engaging and smooth responses. To distinguish from the chatbot's
trait, the word "profile" refers to the user's personality information. We observe
that UP-PDG is also a very challenging task.

(i) Unstructured profile. Chatbot's traits can be expressed through predefined
persona categories, such as age, gender, and location [21]. However, humans
are creatures with minds and souls, and human personality exists objec-
tively. The key-value pair persona setting is too idealized to be applied in
practical systems. Moreover, the personality of the human user involved in
the dialogue cannot be set manually. In reality, although some online systems allow users to fill in some personal information, such as gender and
age, this "structured profile" information is an incomplete description of the

Fig. 2. The user profiles aware personalized dialogue generation.

user's personality. Richer personality information needs to be captured from users' dialog histories, such as interests, hobbies, and life experiences.

(ii) Sparse profile. For a practical chatbot, we need to capture the user profile information from dialog histories. Compared with the semi-structured declarative persona sentences in Persona-Chat [34], the personality information UP-PDG task is written unconsciously and implicitly. The chatbot usually needs to learn the user's personality such as preferences and habits from a limited, mixed, and sparse profile.

To tackle these challenges, in this paper we consider learning different user profiles as different tasks via a meta-learning algorithm which is fundamentally distinct from optimizing the model to represent all the user profiles. We expect to learn the parameters of a dialogue model that can quickly adapt to a new profile just by using a few dialogue histories. Moreover, no unstructured user profile dialogue dataset is reported in the previous literature. Therefore, we crawl massive post-comment utterances from microblog platform Weibo[1] to construct a dialogue dataset for the UP-PDG task. In the dataset, the "post-reply" pairs in the microblogs are considered as conversations, and the "post" users' history microblogs are collected as profile information.

In summary, the main contributions of this paper are as follows:

- We propose a user profile aware personalized dialogue generation task. For sparse profile users, we extend the MAML method to quickly adapt to a new profile by leveraging only a few dialogue samples.
- We construct a large-scale user profile dialogue dataset, which contains unstructured user personality information for our task.
- Extensive experiments are conducted on our dataset, and the results have shown that the proposed model outperforms the strong baseline methods.

The rest of this paper is organized as follows. In Sect. 2, we review the related work of our research. In Sect. 3, we formalize our task, introduce the proposed

---

[1] https://weibo.com.

framework with details about its update and propagation components and the approaches to learn model parameters. In Sect. 4, firstly we introduce our personalized dialogue dataset and its construction process, and then we present experimental results with automatic and human evaluation. Finally, we conclude our work in Sect. 5.

2   Related Work

Three types of previous literature are relevant to our work: few-shot learning, meta-learning, and personalized dialogue generation.

2.1   Meta-learning

Deep learning has shown great success in a variety of tasks with large amounts of labeled data in image classification [7], machine translation [31], and speech modeling [19]. These achievements have relied on the fact that optimization of these deep, high-capacity models requires many iterative updates across many labeled examples, which is a so-called few-shot learning problem. This type of optimization breaks down in the small data regime where we want to learn from very few labeled examples. UP-PDG belongs to the few-shot learning task since the profile for each user is very sparse and limited. The key to the few-shot learning is to solve the overfitting problem, the main approach includes data enhancement and meta learning.

Meta-Learning has been suggested as one strategy to overcome the above challenges we mentioned [18,24,28]. The key idea is that meta-learning agents improve their own learning ability over time, or equivalently, learn to learn. The learning process is primarily concerned with tasks (set of observations) and takes place at two different levels: an inner- and an outer-level. Huisman et al. [9] identify three categories of meta-learning approaches: i) metric-, ii) model-, and iii) optimization-based. Meta-learning has been applied in semantic parsing tasks [8], machine translation [5], text classification [33], and personalized dialogue generation [16].

2.2   Personalized Dialogue Generation

Building a "human-like" chatbot has been a research hotspot both in the academic and business communities, where one of the major challenges is to present a consistent persona so that the chatbot can interact with users in a more natural way to gain users' confidence and trust. Li et al. [12] were the first to propose persona based dialogue models for handling the issue of user consistency in neural dialogue generation. Qian et al. [21] defined a group of key-value profile pairs as the persona. Zhang et al. [34] introduced Persona-Chat by asking randomly paired crowed workers to chat based on some given persona, which was further extended in ConvAI2 [3]. The persona information in Persona-Chat was predefined by a series of natural and descriptive sentences with similar patterns, which are categorized as the semi-structured persona. Yavuz et al. [32] explored the effectiveness of the copy mechanism on Persona-Chat. Lian et al. [13] leveraged Posterior Knowledge Selection to guide persona selection.

Several studies improved the persona consistency with various methodologies [6,10,13]. However, all of this previous literature focuses on improving the conversation consistency according to the chatbot's traits and does not consider generating the personalized dialogue responses from the user's perspective. The users are the ultimate concern when designing a dialogue agent. Luo et al. [15] introduced an end-to-end model to improve the effectiveness of the responses with personalized information. This model was implemented for task-oriented dialogue systems, and not for the open-domain chatbot.

3   Personalized Dialogue Generation

3.1   Profile Aware Dialogue Generation

Given a post C and a set of profile texts P as inputs, the model f_θ is to generate a response $Y = \{y_1, y_2, \ldots, y_m\}$ by incorporating the selected profile properly.

$$f_\theta(Y \mid C, P; \theta) = p(y_{1:m} \mid C, p_{1:k}; \theta) \tag{1}$$

The dialogue post is $C = \{x_1, x_2, \ldots, x_n\}$, where x_n denotes the word n in utterance C. The profile set $P = \{p_1, p_2, \ldots, p_k\}$ represents the profile information corresponding to the post microblog, k denotes the number of profiles, where $p_i = \{s_1, s_2, \ldots, s_l\}$ also made up of a series of words and l denotes the length of the profile. The response is $Y = \{y_1, y_2, \ldots, y_m\}$, m denotes the length of response utterance.

The profile aware dialogue generation can be regarded as a kind of knowledge-based dialogue generation task. Therefore, we introduce the base model named CaKe [35] for this task. Firstly, we leverage two encoders to encode post microblog and profile information. The word embeddings are used to map words to high dimensional vector space. The profile and post encoders encode profile and post embeddings into H: $[h_1, h_2, \cdots, h_n]$ and $\mathbf{M}_i : [m_{i1}, m_{i2}, \cdots, m_{il}]$ respectively by bidirectional Recurrent Neural Networks (RNNs), and the outputs of two RNNs are concatenated. Therefore, we get the profile and the post.

Secondly, for profile pre-selection, we select the profile information related to the post microblog. To achieve this, the encoder state of the post is chosen as a query to select the most relevant profile from P. We combine profile-to-post attention and post-to-profile attention to point out the most relevant token position of the profile information sequence. On one hand, profile-to-post (pro2pos) attention reflects which post words are most relevant to each profile. On the other hand, post-to-profile (pos2pro) attention computes which profiles are most relevant to each post word. The pre-selection module forms the post-aware profile distribution.

Thirdly, for the generation part, CaKe generates vocabulary distribution with global attention. Lastly, we combine this preselector part with the generator to generate the final output of each decoding time step. We get the response based on the probability of generating tokens from the vocabulary or copying tokens from the profile information. The CaKe was reported to have promising results for the knowledge based response generation task. However, for UP-PDG the profile information is extremely sparse which brings in a new challenge for response generation.

3.2 Sparse Profile Dialogue Generation

For sparse profile users, instead of conditioning our response on the user's profile sentences, we first adapt θ to the set dialogue made by a profile P and then we only use the dialogue history to condition our response. Equation (1) becomes:

$$f_\theta(Y \mid C; \theta) = p\,(y_{1:m} \mid C; \theta) \tag{2}$$

To mimic the task adaptation stage, Model-Agnostic Meta-Learning (MAML) [4] explicitly trains the parameters of the model so that a small number of gradient steps with a small amount of training data will make rapid progress on new tasks. So here we apply MAML to sparse profile dialogue generation task and refer to the proposed method as Sparse-Profile Meta-Learning (SPML).

Sparse-Profile Meta-Learning (SPML)

Here is how we apply SPML to sparse profile response generation tasks. We define the profile meta-dataset as $\mathcal{M} = \{\mathcal{M}_{p1}, \ldots, \mathcal{M}_{pz}\}$, where z is the number of profiles. Before training, $\mathcal{M}$ is split into $\mathcal{M}_{train}$, $\mathcal{M}_{valid}$, $\mathcal{M}_{test}$. For each training epoch, we sample a batch of profiles $\mathcal{M}_{pi}$ from $\mathcal{M}_{train}$, then from each profile in $\mathcal{M}_{pi}$, we sample a set of dialogues as training $\mathcal{M}_{pi}^{train}$ and another set of dialogues as validation $\mathcal{M}_{pi}^{valid}$. In the simulation of adaptation stage, the model f_θ parameterized θ adapts to this new profile $\mathcal{M}_{pi}^{train}$ using one or more gradient descent updates,

$$\theta'_{p_i} = \theta - \alpha \nabla_\theta \mathcal{L}_{\mathcal{M}_{p_i}^{train}}\,(f_\theta) \tag{3}$$

where α is hyperparameter for the profile-specific learning rate, the cross entropy loss $\mathcal{L}$ can be formulated as:

$$\mathcal{L}_{\mathcal{M}_{p_i}}\,(f_\theta) = -\sum_{\mathcal{M}_{p_i}} \log p\,(u_t \mid u_{1:t-1}; \theta) \tag{4}$$

After that, the model is trained by optimizing the performance of $f_{\theta'_{p_i}}$.

$$\min_\theta \sum_{\mathcal{M}_{p_i} \sim \mathcal{M}_{train}} \mathcal{L}_{\mathcal{M}_{p_i}^{valid}}\left(f_{\theta'_{p_i}}\right) = \\ \sum_{\mathcal{M}_{p_i} \sim \mathcal{M}_{train}} \mathcal{L}_{\mathcal{M}_{p_i}^{valid}}\left(f_{\theta - \alpha \nabla_\theta \mathcal{L}_{\mathcal{M}_{train}^{train}}(f_\theta)}\right) \tag{5}$$

where $\mathcal{L}_{\mathcal{M}_{p_i}^{\text{valid}}}\left(f_{\theta'_{p_i}}\right)$ is the loss evaluated on $\mathcal{M}_{p_i}^{\text{valid}}$. For optimizing Eq. (5), we apply again stochastic gradient descent on the meta-model parameters θ by computing the gradient of $\mathcal{L}_{\mathcal{M}_{p_i}^{\text{valid}}}\left(f_{\theta'_{p_i}}\right)$, which is:

$$\theta \leftarrow \theta - \beta \sum_{\mathcal{M}_{p_i} \sim \mathcal{M}_{\text{train}}} \nabla_\theta \mathcal{L}_{\mathcal{M}_{p_i}^{\text{valid}}}\left(f_{\theta'_{p_i}}\right) \tag{6}$$

Algorithm 1. Sparse-Profile Meta-Learning

Require: $\gamma: \mathcal{M}_{train}$
Require: α, β : step size hyperparameters
1: Randomly initialize θ
2: **while** not done **do**
3:     Sample a batch of tasks $\mathcal{M}_{pi} \sim \mathcal{M}_{train}$
4:     **for all** $\mathcal{M}_{pi}$ **do**
5:         $(\mathcal{M}_{pi}^{train}, \mathcal{M}_{pi}^{valid}) \sim \mathcal{M}_{pi}$
6:         Evaluate $\nabla_\theta \mathcal{L}_{\mathcal{M}_{pi}^{train}}(f_\theta)$ using $\mathcal{M}_{pi}^{valid}$
7:         Compuate adapted parameters with gradient descent: $\theta'_{p_i} = \theta - \alpha \nabla_\theta \mathcal{L}_{\mathcal{M}_{pi}^{train}}(f_\theta)$
8:     **end for**
9:     $\theta \leftarrow \theta - \beta \sum_{\mathcal{M}_{p_i} \sim \mathcal{M}_{\text{train}}} \nabla_\theta \mathcal{L}_{\mathcal{M}_{pi}^{\text{valid}}}\left(f_{\theta'_{p_i}}\right)$
10: **end while**

---

where β is the meta-learning rate across the task. A summary of the training procedure is shown in Algorithm 1.

4   Experiment

In this section, we first induction the construction of the dialogue dataset with user profile information. Then we present the baseline methods and the implementation details of our model. Both the automatic and manual evaluation results are given with discussions. Finally, we conduct case study for our proposed model and baseline methods.

4.1   Dataset

Since there is no off-the-shelf dataset for user profile aware personalized dialogue generation task, we crawl massive user microblogs (post-comment pairs) from Weibo and construct a dialogue dataset (dubbed as UP-Weibo) with user profile information. We consider the user's microblog post and the corresponding comment as a dialog pair and regard the user's historical posts as an unstructured profile.

The UP-Weibo dataset was preprocessed as follows. To obtain dialogue pairs that contain valid speaker's profile information, we limited the length of the posts and corresponding replies to 4–35. In addition, all video sharing links and hashtag tokens were removed. The posts were removed by matching ".*www:*", ".*http:.*" and "@" with regular expressions. After that, we matched the posts and corresponding comments. Since a single post may correspond to multiple comments, we sorted the thumb-up number of comments in descending order, and the comments with the highest number of "likes" were selected as the final comment data. This strategy is based on the intuition that the comment with the most "likes" maybe best matched with the original post. After data preprocessing and screening, we got 1,020K valid dialogue pairs. Finally, we split dataset into three non-overlapping partitions - train set (964,562), validation set (40,000) and test set (20,000). Table 1 shows the statistics of the UP-Weibo dataset after data preprocessing steps.

Table 1. Dataset statistics after preprocessing steps, where the column "Ratio" represents the proportion of valid data in the total dataset.

Total crawled posts	Posts with length 4–35	Valid data	Ratio
4,270K	2,480K	1,020K	0.23

After preprocessing, in the UP-Weibo dataset, the average microblog length is 16.69, and the average length of the comment is 11.78. Each user profile has 19.13 sentences on average, with an average sentence length of 17.89.

4.2 Baselines

For UP-PDG, we consider it as a kind of knowledge-based dialogue generation task, where user profile information is regarded as "knowledge". We compare our proposed SPML with several strong baseline methods.

Seq2Seq maps the context to the response with an encoder-decoder framework based on GRU.

Pro-S2S is an improved variant of the Seq2Seq model that additionally adds a profile encoder used for encoding profile information.

PostKS [13] employs a knowledge selection mechanism where both prior and posterior distributions over knowledge are used to facilitate knowledge selection.

GTTP [25] leverages background information with a coping mechanism to copy a token from the background at the appropriate decoding step.

CaKe [35]: an improved version of GTTP, which introduces a pre-selection process that uses dynamic bi-directional attention to improve knowledge selection.

Among them, Pro-S2S is compared for demonstrating the effect of introducing profiles into dialogue generation while the PostKS is compared to verify that incorporating an appropriate profile is helpful for the quality of the generated responses. GTTP shows that the copy mechanism can contribute to the informativeness of the responses. The CaKe is the backbone of our SPML model that can bring in more coherent and engaging responses.

4.3   Implementation Details

We used Gated Recurrent Units (GRU) [2] as RNN cells with 256-dimensional hidden sizes. We employed pretrained Chinese word embeddings [22] for initialization and the dimension of word embedding was set to 300. The batch size was set to 16 with a learning rate = 0.0001 and applied greedy search for all models. The best model is selected based on the BLEU and Rouge metrics. For the SPML training, we used SGD for the inner loop and Adam [11] for the outer loop with a learning rate = 0.001 and = 0.0003 respectively, and batch size of 16 for both. The same model was tested three times respectively, and the mean value of the three results was taken. All experiments were conducted on a single 11 GB NVIDIA GeForce RTX 2080ti GPU card with the PyTorch framework.

4.4   Evaluation Metrics

Embedding-Based Metrics. These metrics are calculated based on word embeddings, including the semantic similarity between the generated response and the gold standard message by averaging word embeddings (Embed A), the semantic similarity of the most similar words in the generated response, and the gold standard message (Embed G), using the vector extrema method to calculate the semantic similarity between the two sentences (Embed E).

Dist1 and Dist2. The proportions of distinct unigrams and bigrams in the generated responses.

BLEU-1/2 [20]. Word-overlap scores against gold-standard responses. BLEU-1/2 refers to unigram and bigram scores.

Rouge [14]. This metric is originally utilized in the summarization task, which measures the overlap of n-grams between the generated response and the gold standard message.

4.5   Evaluation Results

Automatic Evaluation

We adopted BLEU, Distinct, embedding-based metrics, and Rouge [14] to perform evaluation, and the results are summarized in Table 2 and 3. Among them, Rouge is used for evaluating the co-occurrences of n-grams in the user profile and generated response. Compared with the Seq2Seq model, the decline in BLEU and embedding-metrics of Pro-S2S indicates that simply introducing profile into Seq2Seq without profile selection is not conducive to the informativeness of the response. PostKS outperforms Pro-S2S, and the improvements on BLEU, especially on Distinct metric shows that incorporating both prior and posterior distributions over profile is helpful for the quality of the response. GTTP performs remarkably better on the BLEU metric, which means that copying tokens from the user profile does contribute to generating more informativeness responses. The decrease in the Distinct metric indicates that we can not completely avoid the problem of duplicated response generation even with a coverage mechanism.

CaKe performs better than GTTP in terms of all objective metrics. For sparse profile tasks, we use SPML with CaKe which performs the best on all the metrics except Distinct. The improvement of BLEU and Rouge shows that with SPML, we can generate more engaging responses while ensuring the informativeness of the response.

Table 2. The automatic evaluation results for BLEU and Distinct metrics. The best results are in bold.

Model	BLEU-1	BLEU-2	Distinct-1	Distinct-2
Seq2Seq	0.0301	0.0189	0.1667	0.1667
Pro-S2S	0.0252	0.0161	0.0083	0.0167
PostKS	0.0357	0.0208	**0.4175**	**0.7502**
GTTP	0.3354	0.1941	0.0023	0.0031
CaKe	0.3459	0.2313	0.1727	0.3257
CaKe+SPML	**0.5720**	**0.3825**	0.1421	0.2358

Table 3. The automatic evaluation results for embedding and Rouge metrics. The best results are in bold.

Model	Embed E	Embed A	Embed G	Rouge-1	Rouge-2
Seq2Seq	0.3190	0.4174	0.2372	–	–
Pro-S2S	0.2637	0.3135	0.1798	0.0646	0.0102
PostKS	0.3104	0.4206	0.2476	0.0926	0.0105
GTTP	0.2412	0.3224	0.1641	0.1036	0.0128
CaKe	0.3640	0.4911	0.3045	0.1158	0.0173
CaKe+SPML	**0.3706**	**0.5032**	**0.3276**	**0.1375**	**0.0354**

Manual Evaluation

We conduct a manual evaluation to further compare SPML with two strong baselines. We randomly sample 200 dialogue samples from the test set. Three annotators[2] are asked to read the profile information of each user, and then score the response in terms of the following aspects with a rating of 0, 1, or 2. (i) **Fluency:** whether the generated response is fluent and free of grammatical errors; (ii) **Coherency:** whether the generated response is logically coherent with its context; (iii) **Relevance:** whether the generated response conforms to the user's profile information.

---

[2] All annotators are fluent English speakers and are familiar with annotating rules.

Table 4. Manual evaluation results

Model	Fluency	Coherency	Relevance
GTTP	1.04	1.06	1.03
CaKe	1.20	1.19	1.16
CaKe+SPML	**1.21**	**1.20**	**1.18**

Table 4 depicts the manual evaluation results. For two strong baselines, CaKe performs better than GTTP in terms of all subjective metrics. For sparse profile dialogue generation, CaKe with SPML demonstrates that our approach can achieve better user profile relevance by using only a few dialogues instead of conditioning on the profile information from the user's perspective while ensuring the fluency and coherency of the generated response.

4.6 Case Study

We select two examples from the test set to illustrate the performance of Pro-S2S, PostKS, CaKe, and CaKe+SPML, as shown in Table 5 and 6. We can see that with the SPML method, CaKe can select the right profile unit from the user profile information or generate fluent tokens at the appropriate time and position, resulting in more informative and appropriate responses.

For instance, in the first example, CaKe+SPML copies the right token "Sichuan" and "hot pot" within the user profile to form a more natural and engaging response. In contrast, Pro-S2S tends to generate generic responses in the absence of profile selection. PostKS can select the right profile information "hot pot" with a lower Rouge score and attractiveness. CaKe can not only generate words related to the user profiles but also keep the coherence and informativeness of responses. Compared with PostKS, the decline of the Distinct metric indicates that CaKe can not guarantee the diversity of the generated response well.

In the second example, the response generated by CaKe+SPML shows that, with the right token "Shanghai Wild Animal Park" from the user profile, the response is more natural and engaging. Firstly, Pro-S2S tends to generate generic responses like "Me too" in the absence of profile selection. For PostKS, although the generated response is also not meaningful compared with the Pro-S2S, the response is a way of questioning, which arouses the interest of user interaction. According to CaKe's response, we observe that the response has the advantages of PostKS and GTTP, which can select the appropriate profile and copy the correct token "Shanghai Wild Animal Park". This result is consistent with the automatic evaluation in terms of BLEU and Rouge scores.

There are also failure cases for CaKe+SPML as well as the other baselines: one serious issue is that the models tend to incorporate the same profile units when generating personalized responses. This indicates that a better mechanism is needed to track the already used profile.

Table 5. The first example of the generated responses on ProWeibo dataset.

First example	
Profile	Students don't want to go home in winter vacation, so they find someone to go out with
	Finally, I had an authentic Sichuan hot pot, but it was too oily
	Yunnan travel guide is ready, looking forward to your calling
	Seeking co-renting, the coordinates are near Tongji University
	Please recommend easy to use and cheap brand of lipstick for students
	Waiting for The Voice of China tonight
	How do you watch the live broadcast of the Spring Festival Gala aboard?
Post	Snowy days go best with hot pot
ProS2S	I want it, too
PostKS	Hot pot is delicious
CaKe	What hot pot?
CaKe+SPML	Do you want to eat Sichuan hot pot?

Table 6. The second example of the generated responses on ProWeibo dataset.

Second example	
Profile	Yesterday, I went to Beijing to see the flag ceremony
	Do you have any plans for a quick trip?
	The pandas in Shanghai Wild Animal Park are so cute
	I'm about to graduate and I'm looking for a place to travel
	You have to remember that happiness is the most important thing
	I hope it won't rain tomorrow
	It's a fine day today
Post	It's boring now
ProS2S	Me too
PostKS	What do you want to do?
CaKe	I want to travel
CaKe+SPML	How about go to Shanghai Wild Animal Park?

5 Conclusion

This paper proposes a user profile aware personalized dialogue generation task, which generates personalized responses from the user's perspective. For sparse profile users, we extend the Model-Agnostic Meta-Learning method to quickly adapt to new profiles by leveraging only a few dialogue samples. We construct a large-scale user profile dialogue dataset UP-Weibo, which contains unstructured user personality information. Experiments results by both automatic and manual evaluations have shown that the proposed SPML model outperforms the strong baseline methods. For future work, we plan to apply user profile aware personalized dialogue generation to a multi-turn dialogue system.

Acknowledgments. The work was supported by the National Natural Science Foundation of China (61872074, 61772122, 62172086), and the Fundamental Research Funds for the Central Universities (N180716010, N2116008).

References

1. Bengio, S., Bengio, Y., Cloutier, J., Gecsei, J.: On the optimization of a synaptic learning rule. In: Preprints Conference on Optimality in Artificial and Biological Neural Networks, vol. 2 (1992)
2. Chung, J., Gulcehre, C., Cho, K., Bengio, Y.: Empirical evaluation of gated recurrent neural networks on sequence modeling. arXiv preprint arXiv:1412.3555 (2014)
3. Dinan, E., et al.: The second conversational intelligence challenge (ConvAI2). In: Escalera, S., Herbrich, R. (eds.) The NeurIPS 2018 Competition. TSSCML, pp. 187–208. Springer, Cham (2020). https://doi.org/10.1007/978-3-030-29135-8_7
4. Finn, C., Abbeel, P., Levine, S.: Model-agnostic meta-learning for fast adaptation of deep networks. In: International Conference on Machine Learning, pp. 1126–1135. PMLR (2017)
5. Gu, J., Wang, Y., Chen, Y., Cho, K., Li, V.O.: Meta-learning for low-resource neural machine translation. arXiv preprint arXiv:1808.08437 (2018)
6. Hancock, B., Bordes, A., Mazare, P.E., Weston, J.: Learning from dialogue after deployment: feed yourself, chatbot! arXiv preprint arXiv:1901.05415 (2019)
7. He, K., Zhang, X., Ren, S., Sun, J.: Deep residual learning for image recognition. In: Proceedings of the IEEE Conference on Computer Vision and Pattern Recognition, pp. 770–778 (2016)
8. Huang, P.S., Wang, C., Singh, R., Yih, W., He, X.: Natural language to structured query generation via meta-learning. arXiv preprint arXiv:1803.02400 (2018)
9. Huisman, M., van Rijn, J.N., Plaat, A.: A survey of deep meta-learning. arXiv preprint arXiv:2010.03522 (2020)
10. Joshi, C.K., Mi, F., Faltings, B.: Personalization in goal-oriented dialog. arXiv preprint arXiv:1706.07503 (2017)
11. Kingma, D., Ba, J.: Adam: a method for stochastic optimization. Computer Science (2014)
12. Li, J., Galley, M., Brockett, C., Spithourakis, G.P., Gao, J., Dolan, B.: A persona-based neural conversation model (2016)
13. Lian, R., Xie, M., Wang, F., Peng, J., Wu, H.: Learning to select knowledge for response generation in dialog systems. arXiv preprint arXiv:1902.04911 (2019)
14. Lin, C.Y.: ROUGE: a package for automatic evaluation of summaries. In: Text Summarization Branches Out, pp. 74–81. Association for Computational Linguistics, Barcelona, July 2004. https://www.aclweb.org/anthology/W04-1013
15. Luo, L., Huang, W., Zeng, Q., Nie, Z., Sun, X.: Learning personalized end-to-end goal-oriented dialog. In: Proceedings of the AAAI Conference on Artificial Intelligence, vol. 33, pp. 6794–6801 (2019)
16. Madotto, A., Lin, Z., Wu, C.S., Fung, P.: Personalizing dialogue agents via meta-learning. In: Proceedings of the 57th Annual Meeting of the Association for Computational Linguistics, pp. 5454–5459 (2019)

17. Meng, C., Ren, P., Chen, Z., Monz, C., Ma, J., de Rijke, M.: RefNet: a reference-aware network for background based conversation. In: Proceedings of the AAAI Conference on Artificial Intelligence, vol. 34, pp. 8496–8503 (2020)
18. Naik, D.K., Mammone, R.J.: Meta-neural networks that learn by learning. In: 1992 Proceedings of the IJCNN International Joint Conference on Neural Networks, vol. 1, pp. 437–442. IEEE (1992)
19. van den Oord, A., et al.: WaveNet: a generative model for raw audio. arXiv preprint arXiv:1609.03499 (2016)
20. Papineni, K., Roukos, S., Ward, T., Zhu, W.J.: BLEU: a method for automatic evaluation of machine translation. In: Proceedings of the 40th Annual Meeting of the Association for Computational Linguistics, pp. 311–318 (2002)
21. Qian, Q., Huang, M., Zhao, H., Xu, J., Zhu, X.: Assigning personality/profile to a chatting machine for coherent conversation generation. In: IJCAI, pp. 4279–4285 (2018)
22. Qiu, Y., Li, H., Li, S., Jiang, Y., Hu, R., Yang, L.: Revisiting correlations between intrinsic and extrinsic evaluations of word embeddings. In: Sun, M., Liu, T., Wang, X., Liu, Z., Liu, Y. (eds.) CCL/NLP-NABD -2018. LNCS (LNAI), vol. 11221, pp. 209–221. Springer, Cham (2018). https://doi.org/10.1007/978-3-030-01716-3_18
23. Ravi, S., Larochelle, H.: Optimization as a model for few-shot learning (2016)
24. Schmidhuber, J.: Evolutionary principles in self-referential learning, or on learning how to learn: the meta-meta-... hook. Ph.D. thesis, Technische Universität München (1987)
25. See, A., Liu, P.J., Manning, C.D.: Get to the point: summarization with pointer-generator networks. In: Proceedings of the 55th Annual Meeting of the Association for Computational Linguistics (Volume 1: Long Papers), pp. 1073–1083 (2017)
26. Shum, H.Y., He, X., Li, D.: From Eliza to Xiaoice: challenges and opportunities with social chatbots. Front. Inf. Technol. Electron. Eng. 19(1), 10–26 (2018)
27. Sung, F., Yang, Y., Zhang, L., Xiang, T., Torr, P.H., Hospedales, T.M.: Learning to compare: relation network for few-shot learning. In: Proceedings of the IEEE Conference on Computer Vision and Pattern Recognition, pp. 1199–1208 (2018)
28. Thrun, S.: Lifelong learning algorithms. In: Thrun, S., Pratt, L. (eds.) Learning to Learn. Springer, Boston (1998). https://doi.org/10.1007/978-1-4615-5529-2_8
29. Thrun, S., Pratt, L.: Learning to Learn. Springer, Heidelberg (2012)
30. Vaswani, A., et al.: Attention is all you need. arXiv (2017)
31. Wu, Y., et al.: Google's neural machine translation system: bridging the gap between human and machine translation. arXiv preprint arXiv:1609.08144 (2016)
32. Yavuz, S., Rastogi, A., Chao, G.L., Hakkani-Tur, D.: DeepCopy: grounded response generation with hierarchical pointer networks. arXiv preprint arXiv:1908.10731 (2019)
33. Yu, M., et al.: Diverse few-shot text classification with multiple metrics. arXiv preprint arXiv:1805.07513 (2018)
34. Zhang, S., Dinan, E., Urbanek, J., Szlam, A., Kiela, D., Weston, J.: Personalizing dialogue agents: i have a dog, do you have pets too? (2018)
35. Zhang, Y., Ren, P., de Rijke, M.: Improving background based conversation with context-aware knowledge pre-selection. arXiv preprint arXiv:1906.06685 (2019)
36. Zheng, Y., Chen, G., Huang, M., Liu, S., Zhu, X.: Personalized dialogue generation with diversified traits. arXiv preprint arXiv:1901.09672 (2019)

Label-Value Extraction from Documents Using Co-SSL Framework

Sai Abhishek Sara[1], Maneet Singh[2]([✉]), Bhanupriya Pegu[2],
and Karamjit Singh[2]

[1] Indian Institute of Technology Bombay, Mumbai, India
abhisheksara@ee.iitb.ac.in
[2] AI Garage Mastercard, Mumbai, India
{maneet.singh,bhanupriya.pegu,karamjit.singh}@mastercard.com

Abstract. Label-value extraction from documents refers to the task of extracting relevant values for corresponding labels/fields. For example, it encompasses extracting the *total* amount from receipts, the *date* value from invoices/patents/forms, or *tax* amount from receipts/invoices. Automated label-value extraction has widespread applicability in real-world scenarios of document understanding, book-keeping, reconciliation, and content summarization. Recent research has focused on developing label-value extraction models, however, to the best of our knowledge, limited attention has been given to developing a light-weight compact label-value extraction module generalizable across different document types. Since in real-world deployment, a developed model is often required to process different types of documents for the same label/field type, this research proposes a novel *Context-based Semi-supervised (Co-SSL)* framework for the same. The proposed Co-SSL framework focuses on identifying candidates for each label/field, followed by the generation of their *context* based on spatial cues. Further, novel data augmentation strategies are proposed which are specifically applicable to the problem of information extraction from documents. The extracted information (candidate and context) is then provided to a deep learning based model trained in a novel semi-supervised setting for applicability in real-world scenarios of limited training data. The performance of the Co-SSL framework has been demonstrated on three challenging datasets containing different document types (receipts, patents, and forms).

Keywords: Document parsing · Label-value extraction · Semi-supervised

S.A. Sara—This work was done while Abhishek was interning at AI Garage, Mastercard, India.

B. Li et al. (Eds.): ADMA 2021, LNAI 13088, pp. 206–218, 2022.
https://doi.org/10.1007/978-3-030-95408-6_16

1   Introduction

Information extraction from documents is a common need in many businesses for various purposes. Most of the documents like invoices, scanned forms, and patents have critical information stored in the form of *label-value* pairs. Generally, *label-value* pairs correspond to objective information that can be extracted from documents where each label (such as *date*, *total*, or *tax*) has a corresponding single value (such as *12/06/2020*, *6294*, or *424*). Figure 1 presents sample applications of label-value extraction from a given invoice document. In real world scenarios, it is often important to extract correct information such as *date* or *total* from invoice documents which are generally the official records of a company's purchase transactions. This information is then later used for various purposes such as reconciliation, record keeping, or compliance. Similarly, label-value information is also extracted from other documents (e.g. patents and forms) for downstream tasks in many business applications.

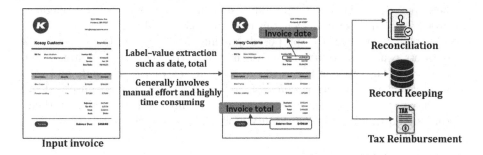

Fig. 1. Label-value extraction from an invoice is used for different purposes such as reconciliation, record keeping, or tax reimbursement.

Until recently, a significant amount of manual effort and time used to be invested in the extraction of such label-value pairs from documents. Further, the enormous volume of data to be processed often leads to higher costs and larger manpower requirement. According to the state of epayables 2019[1], cost of processing a single invoice is over 10 dollars, thus often resulting in large monetary overheads for document processing. To eliminate the need for manual processing and overhead costs, this research focuses on automating the process of label-value extraction with minimal manual intervention.

In literature, most of the initial techniques for label-value extraction from documents were rule-based or utilized hand-crafted features. Such approaches work well on specific documents, however suffer from the challenge of low generalizability to new document layouts. Recently, deep learning techniques have focused on extracting relevant label-value pairs from documents with more variations in the document layout. However, these techniques often require high

---

[1] https://tinyurl.com/3e5x3xt5.

computational resources and a large amount of training data, which is often not available in real-world scenarios. Therefore, this research proposes a novel compact *Context-based Semi-supervised Learning (Co-SSL)* framework for extracting label-value pairs from documents under the real-world constraint of limited training data as well. The proposed algorithm is also shown to be generalizable across different document types. One of the key highlights of the proposed method is its compact learning architecture which can be trained with limited training data as well. Therefore, the key contributions of this research are:

- An end-to-end pipeline has been proposed for label-value extraction from documents which consists of different modules such as candidate generation, context selection, data augmentation, and scoring. The proposed pipeline focuses on extracting textual and spatial cues for accurate field extraction.
- The proposed pipeline is trained with a novel semi-supervised loss function, enabling it to be trained with limited labeled training data, while utilizing a large amount of unlabeled data for effective feature learning.
- As part of the proposed pipeline, novel data augmentation techniques have been proposed which are especially useful in scenarios of natural language processing, and useful in scenarios of limited labeled data.
- The performance of the proposed pipeline has been evaluated on three datasets containing different document types: (i) receipts, (ii) patents, and (ii) forms. The pipeline has been evaluated for extracting the *date* and *total* label-value pairs, where it demonstrates high performance on unseen document types of patents and forms even without any explicit training on them, thus supporting the generalizability of the proposed technique.

2   Related Work

Initial research on information extraction from documents focused heavily on rule-based approaches [3,4,7]. In real-world scenarios, such techniques are often not scalable due to the varying layouts since they require to develop new rules or templates for a new document type. Recent research has focused more on extracting relevant fields from documents with varying formats [5]. The advantage of such techniques is the ability to process unseen layouts, however, most of the algorithms are focused on the textual information only with limited attention to the visual cues present in the document.

Recently, Sarkhel and Nandi [15] proposed extraction of named entities from multi-modal visually rich documents. Parallelly, Liu et al. [12] also proposed using Graph Convolution Networks for extracting relevant information from visually rich documents such as invoices or receipts. Further, Zhao et al. [17] proposed a graph based technique to capture semantic and spatial information of text in documents. Davis et al. [6] proposed extracting information from form fields and the filled text for different document types. Different from other techniques, recently, Majumder et al. [2] presented a novel approach for extracting structured information from form-like documents using representation learning. The proposed framework is most closely related to the work presented by the authors [2], however, the Co-SSL framework extends the state-of-the-art by showing stronger generalizability across different document types, training with limited labeled data, and using novel data augmentation strategies for robust feature learning.

3   Proposed Co-SSL Label-Value Extraction Framework

Figure 2 presents an overview of the proposed framework for label-value extraction. A scanned image is taken as input, which is pre-processed using techniques for noise removal, resizing, erosion, dilation, and binarization. Pre-processing ensures removal of noise from the scanned documents and allows for easier processing via existing text extraction techniques. Text is extracted from the pre-processed image using an Optical Character Recognition (OCR) engine like Tesseract [16]. The OCR engine outputs a bounding box for each detected word in the image. The co-ordinates of the bounding boxes are normalized with respect to the dimensions of the image so that they lie in the range [0, 1]. The extracted text is then used for generating *candidates* for each field based on field-specific rules. Following candidate extraction, for each candidate, *context* information is extracted using the spatial cues. The textual and spatial information of the *context*, along with the position of the candidate is passed to the data augmentation module. During training, augmentation is performed on the context and candidate information followed by an attention-based neural network architecture [2]. Each candidate is scored for the corresponding field, and the highest scoring candidate is assigned as the value for that field. The framework is trained using a novel *semi-supervised* loss, where the unsupervised component focuses on distinguishing between the different data-types of the textual components to introduce an additional level of distinction during feature learning.

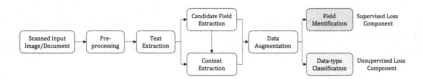

Fig. 2. During training, the Co-SSL framework utilizes a scanned input document (e.g. form, invoice, or receipt), followed by pre-processing and text extraction. The image and extracted text are then used for generating textual and spatial features for identifying the correct value corresponding to a given label (e.g. date, total, and tax).

3.1   Candidate Extraction

Given the text of the document, the first step is to identify candidates for each required field. A strong prevalent characteristic is utilized for candidate generation, wherein candidates of a given field must adhere to the same data type. For example, all currency tokens would be candidates for *total* and *tax* fields, while all date-type text would be candidates for the *invoice date* field. To this effect, we construct field specific regular expressions to generate candidates for each field based on prior knowledge. For example, the regular expression used to identify the *total* field is as follows: "?$[0 - 9] + (? : \.[0 - 9]2,)$". For the extraction of dates, the DateParser[2] tool has been used to capture instances of dates across a variety of formats with high recall. Towards the end of this module, there exists a candidate set for each field for which the correct value needs to be identified.

3.2   Candidate Context Extraction

Given the candidates for each field, the proposed framework next focuses on extracting the corresponding *context* for each candidate (Fig. 2). Context of a candidate is crucial to determine whether the candidate is a true value for that field or not. Here, the context of a candidate is used to capture the textual and spatial information of other related text in the document. Based on the observation that the context of the candidate is generally present in the same row or the same column, we define the *row context* around the candidate spanning the entire width of the page, vertically bounded by a multiple of the candidate height. Similarly, we define the *column context* spanning the entire height of the page, horizontally bounded by a multiple of the candidate width.

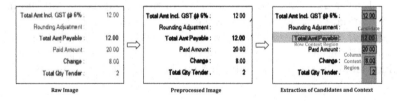

Fig. 3. Sample input receipt image and the pre-processed image provided to Tesseract for text extraction. The processed image is used for identifying the row context and the column context, along with the relevant words for modeling the contextual region.

Given the defined context region (Fig. 3), the words whose bounding boxes overlap by more than half with the context region are assigned to one of the contexts: *left context, right context, top context,* and *bottom context.* Top-k closest words (based on the spatial co-ordinates) are picked from each set, where k is the desired number of words from a region to include in the *context*. It is important to note that k is a hyper-parameter which can be adjusted based on the document and fields, e.g., if a field type for a document has a description spanning multiple words followed by the value in the same row, then one can choose to include more words from the *left context.* For each word selected in the context region, the textual information and relative position of the word

---

[2] https://github.com/scrapinghub/dateparser.

with respect to the candidate is chosen to be further processed by the model. Contextual information provides the model relevant textual and spatial cues to identify the correct candidate from the given set for a particular field.

In the literature, similar to the proposed technique, Majumder et al. [2] have defined a neighbourhood zone around the candidate extending all the way to the left of the page and about 10% of the page height above it. Candidates whose bounding boxes overlap by more than half with the neighbourhood zone are assigned as neighbours for the candidate of interest. We hypothesize that defining the context based on the number of words rather than the dimensions of the document is more generalizable, especially across documents of different sizes, resolutions, and layouts.

3.3 Data Augmentation

As shown in Fig. 2, the candidate and context extraction is followed by the data augmentation module. Label-value pair extraction from documents suffers from the challenge of limited availability of labeled training data. Small size and limited variability in the training set often results in poor generalization of the model to documents from other domains having different layouts. In order to address the above limitation of limited training data, we propose novel data augmentation strategies applied at the spatial and textual level, as opposed to the image level. This is done in order to provide a larger training set to the scoring module as opposed to challenging the OCR for efficient text extraction. To this effect, the following three data augmentation techniques are proposed:

(a) Candidate Transform   (b) Context Transform

Fig. 4. Sample representation of the (a) candidate and (b) context cor-ordinate transform based data augmentation strategies.

(a) Synonym Substituter: While dealing with documents from different domains, even though the fields of interest (label) might be the same, the terminology used to describe the field often varies. For example, a receipt could contain the term "Total" or "Amount" referring to the total amount billed in the receipt. Also, OCR errors where a letter is mistaken as another, is a common scenario especially with scanned/hand-written documents. To handle such cases under the constraint of limited labeled data, during training, we replace an instance of some common key-phrases with a word randomly sampled from its corresponding set of synonyms before passing the text to the model. For example, an instance of *total* would be replaced by a word randomly sampled from the set {*total, totol, totals, amount*} with corresponding assigned probabilities. Mis-spelt words like {*'totol', 'dote', 'cate'*}, have also been included in the set with a small probability to make the model robust to OCR errors. This can also be used to extend the model to multiple languages by adding the translated word in other languages to its synonym set.

(b) **Candidate Co-ordinate Transform**: Beyond the textual information of a candidate, its position could also contain information about the field type of the candidate. For example, an instance of "Date" of a document could often be present in the beginning of a document. Similarly, an instance of "Total" would often be present in the latter half of the document. In order to ensure that the model does not learn the exact locations of the different fields or be specific to certain layouts, we shift the co-ordinates of the candidate by a random fraction of the document dimension horizontally and vertically as shown in Fig. 4(a) before passing the candidate position to the model.

(c) **Context Co-ordinate Transform**: For each word in the context, rather than shifting the position both horizontally and vertically, we only shift along the direction of maximum relative distance with the candidate as shown in Fig. 4(b). This is done since the component with the minimum relative distance would represent if the word belongs to the row-context or the column-context, and we would want to keep this information intact. We hypothesize that such an augmentation would expose our model to a larger distribution of context positions reproducing the effect of having more data with varying spatial information.

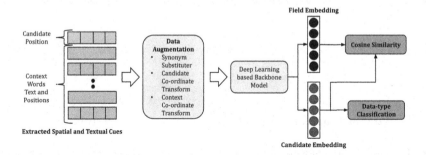

Fig. 5. The Co-SSL framework extracts position/spatial and textual cues from a document (candidate words and contextual regions). Proposed data augmentation techniques are applied on the extracted co-ordinates and text. A deep learning based backbone model is trained with a semi-supervised loss which outputs the field and candidate embedding for predicting the true value for a given label and the candidate data-type.

The above three data augmentation techniques are applied in real-time on the candidate and context information during training. We believe that the augmentation strategies introduces variability in the training data and also results in a regularization effect, thus preventing over-fitting on the training set.

3.4   Semi-supervised Learning for the Co-SSL Framework

Figure 5 presents a diagrammatic overview of the proposed Co-SSL framework. As mentioned previously, the extracted textual and spatial information for the context along with the positional information of the candidate is provided to a deep learning based backbone model [2] for field identification. The model generates a representation for each candidate using the candidate's spatial information (bounding box co-ordinates from Sect. 3.1) and the contextual information (text and spatial co-ordinates from Sect. 3.2). The model utilizes a self-attention mechanism to capture interactions between the words identified in the context. Further, a field encoding is also learned for each field/label to be extracted. The candidate encoding and field encoding are compared using cosine similarity to ensure true candidate embeddings are closer to the field embedding. In the Co-SSL framework, the same backbone has been used with updates to the architecture to incorporate an additional unsupervised loss component. Thus, the model is trained with a novel semi-supervised loss function, as below:

- **Supervised Loss Component:** The supervised loss focuses on calculating the cosine-similarity of the candidate encoding with the field encoding and the then computing the Focal Loss [11] between the cosine-similarity scores obtained and the labels which tell whether each candidate is a true candidate. The cosine similarity (p_c) between the candidate embedding (e_c) and the field embedding (e_f) is given by $p_c = \frac{e_c \cdot e_f}{\|e_c\|\|e_f\|}$. Given the cosine similarity, the probability for ground truth (p_t) is given as:

$$p_t = \begin{cases} p_c, \text{ if } e_c \text{ is an embedding for a true candidate} \\ 1 - p_c, \text{ otherwise} \end{cases} \tag{1}$$

With the above, the Focal Loss [11] acts as the supervised loss for Co-SSL:

$$\mathcal{L}_{Sup.} = \alpha_t(1 - p_t)^\gamma \log p_t + (p_t)^\gamma \log(1 - p_t) \tag{2}$$

where, α_t is the weight given to the *true* class and γ is the shape parameter.
- **Proposed Unsupervised Loss Component:** To tackle the commonly encountered problem of scarce labelled data, we propose a novel unsupervised loss based on the data-type of the candidate. We generate data-type labels for each candidate by writing regular expressions. The candidate encoding learned above is passed to a data-type classifier where the encoding is linearly projected and used to obtain the classification probabilities (p_i) for each data-type class i. The unsupervised loss is calculated by applying weighted binary cross entropy between the data-type classification prediction and the ground-truth labels for each candidate with class weights w_i as follows:

$$\mathcal{L}_{Unsup.} = \sum_{i \in classes} w_i \log p_i \tag{3}$$

As discussed above, the candidate encoding captures its position and context while being agnostic to the candidate text. Thus, predicting the data-type of a candidate solely based on the context and position of the candidate is a non-trivial task. Since the field type and data-type of the candidate are often correlated, we hypothesize that the unsupervised loss component encourages the Co-SSL pipeline to capture the context of the candidate that contains information about the data-type and concomitantly the field type.

The Co-SSL pipeline is thus trained in a semi-supervised manner via a combination of Eq. 2 and Eq. 3. The loss focuses on capturing the spatial and textual cues of the candidates for identifying the relevant *value* for a given *label/field*.

3.5   Implementation Details

The Co-SSL framework has been trained on two fields: *date* and *total* for the supervised loss. For the unsupervised loss component, the model has been trained on three classes: *date*, *currency*, and *other*. A 32-dimensional embedding is obtained from the dense-layer which is used by the cosine similarity function and the data-type classifier consisting of two layers ($[64, 3]$). A weight of 0.01 has been used for the unsupervised loss. The losses of the data-type classifier were weighted to compensate for the imbalance in the data-type counts by using the inverse frequency observed in the training data: 7 (*date*), 0.3 (*currency*) and 0.2 (*other*). For the supervised loss component, Focal Loss [11] with $\alpha = 9$ and $\gamma = 2$ has been used. Adam optimizer [10] has been used with a learning rate of $10^{-6}/10^{-4}$ for the supervised loss/data-type classifier. The proposed model has been implemented using the PyTorch framework [1] and trained for 50 epochs with a batch-size of two images. The model consists of 226,692 parameters.

(a)   (b)   (c)

Fig. 6. Sample images from the datasets used in this research: (a) SROIE dataset (receipts), (b) Ghega dataset (patents), and (c) FUNSD dataset (forms).

4   Datasets and Protocols

Three datasets have been used for evaluations, each containing different document types (receipts, forms, and patents). Details regarding each are as follows:

- **ICDAR2019 Scanned Receipts OCR and Information Extraction (SROIE) Dataset** [8] contains 626 scanned receipts images with variations in receipt layout, quality, and resolution. 20% of the data is used for validation, 20% for testing, and 60% constitute the training partition. The dataset is annotated with fields corresponding to the *total* and *date* labels.

- **Form Understanding in Noisy Scanned Documents (FUNSD) Dataset** [9] contains 199 annotated scanned form documents. The images vary in terms of the scanning quality and the format of the forms. 95 images from the FUNSD dataset with annotations for *date* have been used for evaluating the proposed model for the task of *date* extraction.
- **Ghega Dataset** [14] contains (a) patents and (b) data-sheets of electronic components. As part of this research, we utilize English patents for extraction of *Publication Date* comprising of 45 scanned documents. The dataset also provides the ground-truth text blocks for *Publication Date* obtained via an OCR, which have been used to generate the values for the *date* label.

In order to follow a real-world protocol, data corresponding to the training partition of the SROIE dataset has only been used for training the proposed framework, while evaluations are performed on the test sets of all three datasets.

5 Results and Analysis

Evaluation has been performed on three types of documents: (i) receipts (SROIE dataset), patents (Ghega dataset), and forms (FUNSD dataset). The Co-SSL framework has been used for extracting different fields from each: *total* (receipts) and *date* (patents and forms). It is important to note that a single model has been trained on the SROIE dataset, followed by evaluation on the Ghega and FUNSD datasets for the different fields. The key results and analysis are as follows:

Table 1. Recall (0.00–1.00) obtained by the Co-SSL framework on different datasets for extracting the relevant fields. For FUNSD and Ghega datasets, the date field has been extracted, while the total field has been extracted for the SROIE dataset.

Algorithm	Dataset			Average
	SROIE (Receipts)	Ghega (Patents)	FUNSD (Forms)	
Baseline	0.62	0.02	0.15	0.26
Proposed - {Context}	0.78	0.47	0.31	0.52
Proposed - {Data augmentation}	0.77	0.49	0.68	0.64
Proposed - {Unsupervised loss}	0.40	0.51	0.26	0.39
Proposed Co-SSL	**0.89**	**0.89**	**0.78**	**0.84**

- **Comparison with Baseline Model:** Table 1 presents the recall values obtained by the proposed model for the different datasets and document types. The proposed framework demonstrates a high recall for different document types despite being trained on the receipts images only. Specifically, a recall of 0.89 is obtained on the SROIE dataset, 0.89 is obtained on the Ghega dataset, and 0.78 is obtained on the FUNSD dataset. Across the three datasets and document types, an average performance of 0.84 recall is seen. The proposed model demonstrates a significant improvement from the baseline technique, where the baseline reports an average recall of 0.26. We hypothesize that the low performance obtained by the baseline technique is probably due to the real world setup of limited training data. The high performance on unseen evaluation datasets suggests high generalizability of the model, and suitability for real-world deployment and usage.

– **Ablation Study on the Co-SSL Framework:** Table 1 can also be analyzed to understand the ablation study performed on the Co-SSL framework, where experiments have been performed by removing different components from the framework. The removal of any component results in a drop in the overall performance (and performance across all datasets). Maximum drop in performance is seen upon the removal of the unsupervised loss. Since the unsupervised loss provides an additional level of distinction based on the data type of the candidate, we believe it facilitates learning of a better identification model. A large drop is also observed upon removing the context component and instead of passing the *neighbours* as done in Majumder et al. [2]. It is our belief that since the context component provides additional meaningful information for a candidate, its removal results in lesser meaningful cues for the identification model, thus resulting in reduced performance.

– **Additional Analysis on the Co-SSL Framework:** Figure 7(a) presents the recall obtained on the Ghega dataset (patent documents) for date retrieval when trained with varying number of training samples. It is interesting to note that even with only 300 training images, the proposed framework is able to obtain a recall performance of 0.77, while achieving 0.89 when trained on the entire available training partition. Despite the drop in performance, the framework still reports improved performance as compared to the other model variations seen in Table 1. Further, the recall trend also suggests that higher

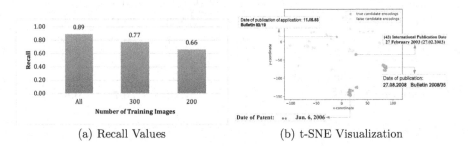

(a) Recall Values   (b) t-SNE Visualization

Fig. 7. (a) Recall values obtained on the Ghega dataset (patent documents) with lesser training images. With only 300 training images, the framework still reports a recall of 0.77, thus supporting its utility in real-world scenarios with limited training data. (b) t-SNE visualization of sample true/positive and false/negative candidate encodings.

performance can be obtained with the framework if more labeled data can be sourced for training. Figure 7(b) presents sample t-SNE [13] visualization of the embeddings learned by the Co-SSL framework. It is interesting to observe that while the embeddings of the negative/false candidates are spread across the feature space, the embeddings of the true/positive embeddings are clustered together. On further analysis, we observed documents with similar layout and text being clustered together. The plot suggests robust feature learning, capable of distinguishing between positive and negative candidates.

6   Conclusion and Future Work

The scarcity of publicly available annotated data for the task of label-value pair extraction necessitates the need for an approach that is generalizable to formats unseen during training while making use of minimal data and preventing over-fitting. This research proposes a novel compact Context-based Semi-supervised Learning (Co-SSL) framework for label-value extraction from scanned documents. To the best of our knowledge, this is the first research to have taken a semi-supervised approach to tackle the problem of label-value extraction. Through this study, we have demonstrated that the proposed semi-supervised loss helps in faster convergence, prevents over-fitting and captures the context of the candidate across documents of domains both seen and unseen during training. The proposed approach allows the model to leverage unlabeled data to assist in the task of label-value pair extraction. Through our ablation study, we have shown that the data-augmentation pipeline increases the robustness of the model to documents from different domains and varying formats while having a regularizing effect on the overall training process. We also showed that our pipeline not only generalizes well to documents from other domains, but also learns an interpretable candidate representation capturing the context of the candidate. This representation can be used in downstream tasks such as classification and clustering of document templates. While in this research we limited our scope to extraction of label-value pairs only, as part of future work, we intend to extend the approach to subjective information extraction from varying document types and extraction of label-value pairs, where the labels are not predefined.

References

1. Paszke, A., et al.: Pytorch: an imperative style, high-performance deep learning library. In: NeurIPS, pp. 8024–8035 (2019)
2. Majumder, B.P., et al.: Representation learning for information extraction from form-like documents. In: ACL, pp. 6495–6504 (2020)
3. Chiticariu, L., Li, Y., Reiss, F.: Rule-based information extraction is dead! Long live rule-based information extraction systems! In: EMNLP, pp. 827–832 (2013)
4. Schuster, D., et al.: Intellix-end-user trained information extraction for document archiving. In: ICDAR, pp. 101–105 (2013)

5. d'Andecy, V.P., Hartmann, E., Rusinol, M.: Field extraction by hybrid incremental and a-priori structural templates. In: IAPR International Workshop on Document Analysis Systems, pp. 251–256 (2018)

6. Davis, B., Morse, B., Cohen, S., Price, B., Tensmeyer, C.: Deep visual template-free form parsing. In: IEEE ICDAR, pp. 134–141 (2019)

7. Esser, D., Schuster, D., Muthmann, K., Berger, M., Schill, A.: Automatic indexing of scanned documents: a layout-based approach. In: Document Recognition and Retrieval XIX, vol. 8297 (2012)

8. Huang, Z., Chen, K., He, J., Bai, X., Karatzas, D., Lu, S., Jawahar, C.: ICDAR2019 competition on scanned receipt OCR and information extraction. In: ICDAR, pp. 1516–1520 (2019)

9. Jaume, G., Ekenel, H.K., Thiran, J.P.: FUNSD: a dataset for form understanding in noisy scanned documents. In: ICDAR Workshops, vol. 2, pp. 1–6 (2019)

10. Kingma, D.P., Ba, J.: Adam: a method for stochastic optimization. arXiv preprint arXiv:1412.6980 (2014)

11. Lin, T.Y., Goyal, P., Girshick, R., He, K., Dollár, P.: Focal loss for dense object detection. In: IEEE ICCV, pp. 2999–3007 (2017)

12. Liu, X., Gao, F., Zhang, Q., Zhao, H.: Graph convolution for multimodal information extraction from visually rich documents. arXiv arXiv:1903.11279 (2019)

13. Van der Maaten, L., Hinton, G.: Visualizing data using t-SNE. J. Mech. Learn. Res. **9**(11), 2579–2605 (2008)

14. Medvet, E., Bartoli, A., Davanzo, G.: A probabilistic approach to printed document understanding. Int. J. Doc. Anal. Recog. **14**(4), 335–347 (2011)

15. Sarkhel, R., Nandi, A.: Visual segmentation for information extraction from heterogeneous visually rich documents. In: ACM SIGMOD, pp. 247–262 (2019)

16. Smith, R.: An overview of the tesseract OCR engine. In: ICDAR, vol. 2, pp. 629–633 (2007)

17. Zhao, X., Niu, E., Wu, Z., Wang, X.: Cutie: learning to understand documents with convolutional universal text information extractor. arXiv preprint arXiv:1903.12363 (2019)

Entity Relations Based Pointer-Generator Network for Abstractive Text Summarization

Tiancheng Huang[1,2], Guangquan Lu[1,2(✉)], Zexin Li[1,2], Jiagang Song[1,2], and Lijuan Wu[1,2]

[1] Guangxi Key Lab of Multi-source Information Mining and Security, Guangxi Normal University, Guilin 541004, Guangxi, China
{huangtcjohn,songjg,wulijuan}@stu.gxnu.edu.cn, lugq@mailbox.gxnu.edu.cn
[2] School of Computer Science Engineering, Guangxi Normal University, Guilin 541004, Guangxi, China

Abstract. The goal of automatic text summarization is to generate a shorter text containing the main ideas and key information of the original text. In recent years, sequence-to-sequence (Seq2Seq) models have made great progress in text summarization task. Many derived models appeared and successfully handled challenges of this task, such as fluency and readability. They also alleviate repetition and out-of-vocabulary (OOV) word problems. However, there remains an important issue to be solved, the factual consistency (also named factual coherency). Since important messages exist in the entities and their relations which appear in the original text sentences, this paper investigates the value of entity relations to boost performance of Seq2Seq abstractive text summarization models. To this end, we present **Entity relations based Pointer-Generator Network** (ERPG) which has 1) **Informative OpenIE Relation Triples Selection Algorithm** that generating non-redundant Open-domain relation triples from plain text by using **Stanford OpenIE** (Open Information Extraction); 2) **Entity Relations Graph Attention network** (ERGAT), a new graph attention neural network is designed to obtain structural features from entity relation triples in the text. 3) **Entity-focused attention**, a modified calculation of attention distribution is introduced to guide Seq2Seq model to focus on the salient words of the text. Experimental results show that ERPG can boost the performance of Pointer-Generator network, ERGAT is the main factor of improvement and the keyinfo attention can enhance the basic attention mechanism. The relation triples have high potential to improve abstractive text summarization models.

Keywords: Abstractive text summarization · Seq2Seq · Entity relations · Graph attention networks · Knowledge graph

This work is partially supported by the Research Fund of Guangxi Key Lab of Multi-source Information Mining & Security (No. 20-A-01-01), Research Fund of Guangxi Key Lab of Multi-source Information Mining & Security (No. 20-A-01-02), Research Fund of Guangxi Key Lab of Multi-source Information Mining & Security (MIMS20-M-01) and the Project of Guangxi Science and Technology (GuiKeAD20159041).

B. Li et al. (Eds.): ADMA 2021, LNAI 13088, pp. 219–236, 2022.
https://doi.org/10.1007/978-3-030-95408-6_17

1 Introduction

Automatic text summarization is a task that summarizing important information automatically from a long text/document into a much shorter text/document. For now, there are two ways of text summarization, extractive and abstractive. Extractive text summarization method obtains the summaries by selecting keywords and sentences from original articles. On the contrast, abstractive text summarization method generates the summaries which has salient information and meanings of original articles. The summaries generated by abstractive way can have different words and different narratives from the reference summaries, resulting in having rich varieties and a good similarity with human-written summaries. Furthermore, abstractive text summarization has abilities of producing summaries with external knowledge in specific application scenarios. In this paper, we study the abstractive method of text summarization.

In the last decade, deep learning has made a great success in computer vision [6,18,29,33]. Meanwhile, natural language process has also gain great progress due to deep learning. The abstractive text summarization models in recent years are mainly designed as neural networks using Seq2Seq framework. Inspired by the neural machine translation [1,28], Rush et al. [24] proposed a Seq2Seq model with attention mechanism to deal with abstractive sentence summarization task, and significantly improved the performance than conventional approaches. Chopra et al. [3] introduced a novel convolutional attention-based encoder and used Recurrent Neural Networks (RNN) as decoder. Generally, LSTM [8,12] or GRU [4] is implemented in encoder and decoder. This model outperforms other state-of-the-art models on Gigaword dataset. Nallapati et al. [22] enhanced the RNN based Seq2Seq model by introducing large vocabulary trick, feature-rich encoder for capturing keywords, switching generator-pointer, and Hierarchical attention for capturing hierarchical document structure. These methods help address some critical problems in attractive text summarization.

RNN based Seq2Seq models have several disadvantages when they are applied to the task of summarizing long documents into multi-sentences, such as accuracy of reproducing salient information, efficiency of handling OOV words, low fluency of summary and repeated words or sentences. To solve the problems above, pointing/copying mechanism was proposed. Actually, pointing/copying mechanism is a class of methods generate target words by switching between generation and copying mode from input sequences. Typical models of pointing/copying mechanism are CopyNet [9], Pointer-Generator [26], Pointer softmax [10] and Switching Generator-pointer [22]. For repetition handling, coverage mechanism [26], distraction mechanism [2], temporal attention [22] and intra-decoder attention [23] are introduced to Seq2Seq models. In order to solve the exposure bias [15,20,30] problem of the Seq2Seq model, reinforcement learning algorithms are applied to the training strategy. Even though reinforcement learning can improve model's performance, but it also brings high cost of training time.

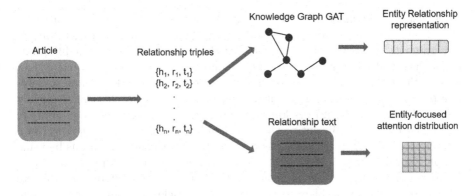

Fig. 1. Illustration of how entities and their relationship information features are extracted and obtained. h_n, r_n and t_n indicate subject, relation and object of a triple, respectively.

Table 1. The illustration of factual inconsistency problem.

Text type	Text
Article	The label on the package claimed that it contained T-shirts and baby toys. But when customs officials in **Sydney** X-ray scanned the parcel, they found instead five pythons and two venomous tarantulas.... The parcel was sent from the **United States** last week, but officials would not say specifically where it had been mailed from. The snakes were wrapped within white calico bags and the spiders were packed in clear plastic containers, the customs agency said. The **creatures** were later killed because they posed a quarantine risk, the **agency** said in a press release.
Factual inconsistency summary	Customs officials in United States find pythons and tarantulas in package. The parcel had been sent from the Australia . The agency were later killed because they posed a quarantine risk.
Reference summary	Customs officials in Australia find pythons and tarantulas in package. The parcel had been sent from the United States. The creatures were later killed because they posed a quarantine risk

Even though now the abstractive text summarization models have successfully deal with many problems, such as saliency, fluency, readability, textual coherence, conciseness, clarity, repetition and OOV words. But the factual consistency between the summaries and original articles is not got enough attention to researchers.

Factual consistency refers to the degree of conformity between the facts that is narrated in summaries and the ones in original text. Apparently, summaries which provide wrong information from original articles could cause unknown consequences and make itself worthless. According to Kryscinski et al. [19], almost 30% abstracted summaries suffer from this problem, resulting in we can not ignore it. Maynez et al. [21] found that the existing models are highly prone to produce factual consistency problem content. Fortunately, researchers now have noticed that Factual consistency is a critical issue and attempt to solve this problem by exploring different approaches. A few researchers have already proposed entity driven [27] or knowledge driven [17] approaches, but there are still no effective and efficient methods to handle factual inconsistency problem. Therefore, resolving factual inconsistency problem with entity relations by using Graph Neural Networks (GNNs) [25] is still an open issue in exploration [14].

In this paper, potential of relation triples in text is explored to alleviate factual inconsistency problem. By observing the articles, we found that the main information of the article is contained in the entities and their relations. Relation triples together can build a knowledge graph of the original article. To utilize the entities align features and help Seq2Seq models improve performance,

(1) The Informative OpenIE Triples Selection Algorithm which obtains relation triples by using Stanford CoreNLP OpenIE is introduced. The algorithm aims to select the non-redundant and informative triples.
(2) A modified GAT [32] model is introduced, named ERGAT which can extract entity relationship features from a knowledge graph. The knowledge graph is constructed to a directed graph, the subjects and objects are denoted as nodes, relations are denoted as edges. ERGAT can also handling the situation of multiple relations between the same subject and object.
(3) Using an entity relation-focused method to lead the model only calculate the attention distribution over the entities and relation words in the sequence of original text. keyinfo attention distribution method and ERGAT can be easily implemented on any Seq2Seq framework models.

2   Related Work

According to the research of Patrick et al. [7], integrating graph neural networks to Seq2Seq models can improve performance of both pure Seq2Seq models and pure graph models on text summarization tasks. To solve factual inconsistency problem, some researchers proposed new architectures [11,13,34] that the encoder and decoder are both equipped with transformers-based [31] or BERT-based [5] to deal with this challenge. Zhu et al. [34] proposed FASum (Fact-Aware Summarization model), which extracts factual relations from article to build a knowledge graph and integrates it into the decoding process. In this model, knowledge graph takes the factual relations triples as nodes and utilize GAT and LSTM to obtain original article's knowledge representation. FASum constructs the knowledge graph to an undirected graph. Different from FASum, Huang et al. [13] proposed ASGARD, which constructs knowledge graph to a directed graph and each node has self-loops.

FASum and ASGARD have similarities on model structure. Their encoders both consist of text sequence encoder module and knowledge graph encode module. The text sequence encoder module is implemented by Transformer-based model or BERT-based model. The knowledge graph encoder module encodes relation triples information and then fuses the graph hidden states with text sequence hidden states. In addition, a LSTM layer or an attention layer is implemented on one of the two modules above. In the knowledge graph of FASum and ASGARD, relation triples which extracted by OpenIE have redundant and overlap triples. Furthermore, subjects, relation and objects are all treated as nodes, resulting in the final graph embedding contains unnecessary noise, because the factual inconsistency is mainly manifested in that entities appear in a wrong place but less correlation with relations.

On the other hand, Gunel et al. [11] utilize relation triples from Wikidata to construct a commonsense knowledge graph helping the model enhance the representation of facts in the source article. But it can also bring in noise data and additional computational costs.

Inspired by the potential ability of hybrid sequence-graph models and considering shortages of other related models, we propose an Entity Relations based Pointer-Generator network (ERPG). ERPG needs non-redundant triples, which obtained by using Informative triples selection algorithm, to build knowledge graph. Informative triples are extracted by OpenIE on data preprocess stage, and then build directed knowledge graph for training. During training, a Bi-GRU layer encodes text sequence and a knowledge graph encoder module ERGAT encodes the knowledge graph. The ERGAT can learn correlations of entities with simple node embeddings, and the entity-focused attention can help Seq2Seq model improve ROUGE scores in some extent.

3   Preliminaries

In this section, we describe Pointer-Generator model and graph attention network. The proposed model is built under the structure of the two models.

3.1   Pointer-Generator Network

The data flow and structure of Pointer-Generator [26] is displayed in Fig. 2. The original article texts are tokenized to a word sequence by $S = \{word_1, word_2, word_3, ..., word_J\}$, J is the number of word sequence. The word sequence will be transformed to word sequence embeddings as the input of the model's encoder $x^e = \{x_1^e, x_2^e, x_3^e, ..., x_J^e\}$, which the superscript e indicates encoder. The encoder (a single layer bidirectional LSTM) takes as the word sequence embeddings input one by one, and produces a sequence of encoder hidden states $h^e = (h_1^e, h_2^e, h_3^e, ..., h_J^e)$. The decoder is a single layer unidirectional LSTM and the decoder LSTM's hidden state h_0^d is initialized by the final hidden states h_J^e from encoder, where superscript d indicates decoder. On each decode step t, the decoder is fed with the concatenation embedding of context vector and word embedding of the previous word (in training phrase, the previous word is from target summary on step $t-1$ while in test phrase it is the previous output word of decoder), and outputs summary word y_t and the decoder state h_t^d. y_t

belongs to $y = (y_1, y_2, y_3, ..., y_T)$, T is the maximum decode steps. And then the attention distribution α is calculated as below:

$$s_{jt} = v^T tanh(W_h h_j^e + W_\sigma h_t^d + W_c c_t + b_{attn}), \tag{1}$$

$$\alpha_{jt} = \text{Softmax}(s_{jt}) = \frac{\exp(s_{jt})}{\sum_{k=1}^J \exp(s_{kt})}, \tag{2}$$

$$c_t = \sum_{t'=0}^{t-1} \alpha_{jt'}, \tag{3}$$

where v, W_h, W_σ and b_{attn} are learnable parameters. s_{jt} indicates the attention score of the t-th decoder input word with the j-th encoder input word. α_{jt} indicates the attention of the t-th decoder input word pay to the j-th source word. c_t is the sum of attention distributions of all previous decoder steps, and represents the coverage degree of the previous output words, called coverage vector. Taking coverage vector as input of attention distribution score function makes the decoder can aware of the previous attention distribution on each decode step. Next, the attention distribution is used to compute the context vector z_t (the weighted sum of encoder hidden states):

$$z_t = \sum_{j=1}^J \alpha_{jt} h_j. \tag{4}$$

The context vector can be viewed as the historical representation of the source text on the current step. It is concatenated with decoder hidden state s_t and then fed through two linear layers and a SoftMax layer to obtain a probability distribution over all words in the vocabulary, known as vocabulary distribution P_{vocab}:

$$P_{vocab} = \text{Softmax}(U'(U[h_t^d \oplus z_t] + b) + b'), \tag{5}$$

where U, U', b and b' are learnable parameters. During decoding, the input of decoder x^d is produced by a feedforward network using the concatenated of previous word embedding y_{t-1} and context vector z_{t-1}, superscript d indicates 'decoder'. At each decode step, the LSTM layer takes x_t^d and the decoder hidden state of previous step h_{t-1}^d as input. On training stage, the previous word y_{t-1} at step t is the $(t-1)$-th word from reference summary. On the other hand, y_{t-1} is the current output of decoder on testing stage.

$$x_t^d = [y_{t-1} \oplus z_{t-1}], \tag{6}$$

$$h_t^d = \text{LSTM}(h_{t-1}^d, x_t^d). \tag{7}$$

Soft Switch Generate/Copy Mechanism. To enhance the model's ability of handling OOV words, a soft switch generate/copy mechanism is implemented to calculate the final distribution to predict words w. To implement this mechanism,

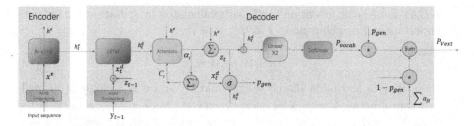

Fig. 2. Illustration of Pointer-Generator model's structure and data flow [26]. * indicates multiply operation. $\oplus$ indicates concatenation operation. σ indicates sigmoid function. $\sum_0^{t-1}$ indicates sum of vector α from step 0 to $t-1$. $\sum *$ indicates the sum of multiplication of h^e and α_t.

un extended vocabulary $V_{ext} = V \cup X \cup <UNK>$, needs to be build, V and X represent the unique tokens in vocabulary and source sequence respectively. The final vocabulary distribution over the extended vocabulary at step t to predict target word y_t is calculated as:

$$p_{gen} = \sigma(w_z^T z_t + w_h^T h_t^d + w_x^T x_t + b_c), \tag{8}$$

$$P_c(y_t) = \sum_{j:x_j=y_t} \alpha_{jt}, \tag{9}$$

$$P_{v_{ext}}(y_t) = p_{gen}P_{vocab}(y_t) + (1 - p_{gen})P_c(y_t), \tag{10}$$

where w_z^T, w_h^T, w_x^T are learnable parameters, y_t indicates the target word at step t, and σ is a sigmoid function. p_{gen} is a generation probability that helps the model to decide to generate a word from vocabulary or copying a word from the input sequence.

On the training stage, the negative log likelihood of the target word is the loss function. Additionally, in order to alleviate the repetition problem of Seq2Seq models, a coverage loss is added as penalization to the primary loss function. The loss function for all text sequence is calculated as below, λ is a hyperparameter and is set to 1:

$$loss = -\frac{1}{T}\sum_{t=0}^{T}(\log P_{v_{ext}}(y_t) - \lambda \sum_j \min(\alpha_{jt}, c_{jt})). \tag{11}$$

3.2 Graph Attention Network

The graph attention network's main idea is to learn relatively importance of each node in an arbitrary graph by using self-attention mechanism. Different from Graph Convolution Network (GCN) [16] model, GAT model has three advantages: (1) Be applicable to both transductive and inductive problems, (2) Can be used in arbitrary graph without costly matrix operation, and (3) Be able to assign different weights to nodes according to the graph's structure.

In GAT model, the attention coefficients calculated by self-attention indicate the importance of neighbor node j to the node i:

$$e_{ij} = a(W \vec{h}_i, W \vec{h}_j), \tag{12}$$

where W is a learnable shared weight matrix, and a is a single-layer feedforward neural network with a learnable vector $\vec{\theta}$. Node $j \in N_i$, and N_i is the set of the first-order neighbors of node i in the graph. Next, the weight between node i and node j is computed as :

$$
\begin{aligned}
\beta_{ij} &= \text{Softmax}(e_{ij}) \\
&= \frac{\exp(e_{ij})}{\sum_{k \in N_i} \exp(e_{ik})} \\
&= \frac{\exp(\text{LeakyReLU}(\vec{\theta}^T(W \vec{h}_i \oplus W \vec{h}_j)))}{\sum_{k \in N_i} \exp(\text{LeakyReLU}(\vec{\theta}^T(W \vec{h}_i \oplus W \vec{h}_k)))},
\end{aligned}
\tag{13}
$$

where $\oplus$ represents concatenation operation. Finally, the model employs multi-head attention to update the feature of node i by aggregating the weight sum of neighbor nodes' features.

$$\vec{h}_i^* = \sigma(\frac{1}{K} \sum_{k=1}^{K} \sum_{j \in N_i} \beta_{ij}^k W^k \vec{h}_j). \tag{14}$$

4 The Proposed Model

In this section, we describe the Informative OpenIE triples selection algorithm, the proposed model ERPG with ERGAT and Entity-focused attention method. ERGAT and Entity-focused attention method can be implemented in any Seq2Seq attention models.

ERPG's encoder consists of two modules: ERGAT and Bi-GRU. ERGAT is response of encoding knowledge graph information, and Bi-GRU encodes source text sequence information. The decoder has a GRU layer, two feedforward layer and a SoftMax layer. We do not use coverage mechanism because we want to remove irrelevant elements of knowledge graph encoding since coverage mechanism is mainly to solve repetition problem.

4.1 Informative OpenIE Triples Selection Algorithm

In order to utilize entity relations features to improve performance of the model, we firstly use an informative OpenIE triples selection algorithm to obtain nonredundant triples. The triples are then constructed to a knowledge graph and the graph is used to learn entity relations representations with an entity relations graph attention network model. Moreover, a modified calculation of attention distribution is implemented to help model focus on the key information on text.

The proposed ERPG model is based on the architecture of Pointer-Generator network.

To utilize the entity relationships features in text, the entity relationship triples need to be extracted first. Since the triples varied in different texts, the Stanford OpenIE tool is the best choice. This tool can extract relation tuples without specified schema in advance, more importantly the subject and object are text from original text, and the relation's name is the text linking subject and object.

However, the OpenIE tool will generate redundant triples. For example, when OpenIE process sentence "Beijing, the imperial and modern capital of China, is the front door to China's history and China today. It has some of the finest remnants of China's imperial past and its cityscapes showcase modern China's prestige.", the triples generated will be like:

Triple 1, {'Beijing', 'is door to', 'China's history'} Triple 2, {'Beijing', 'is front door to', 'China's history'} Triple 3, {'Beijing', 'is', 'door to China's history'} Triple 4, {'Beijing', 'is', 'front door to China's history today'} Triple 5, {'Beijing', 'capital of', 'China'} Triple 6 ,{'Beijing', 'imperial capital of', 'China'}

Apparently, these triples have redundant and overlap problem, and tripe 2, 6 are the ideal ones. To solve this problem, the Informative OpenIE Triple Selection Algorithm is proposed here. Details are introduced at experiment section. The Informative OpenIE Triples Selection Algorithm's psecudocode is show at Sect. 5.2.

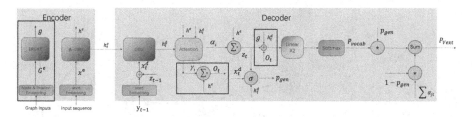

Fig. 3. The ERPG model. The red box areas denote new module or changes compared with Pointer-Generator network. (Color figure online)

4.2   Entity Relations Graph Attention Network

Entity relations are naturally and easily represented as a directed knowledge graph that consisting of entity nodes and relation edges. Since GAT can learn each neighbor nodes' importance to a specific linked node, it is suitable to be applied to the knowledge graph built with entity relations, and learn the aligns of entities. Accordingly, we make two minor adjustments to the GAT, so that it is able to receive relation embedding and making entity nodes not only capable to aggregate information of neighbor nodes but also the relation edges' information.

The first adjustment is generating embeddings of entity nodes and relation edges. Usually, nodes and edges in the graph need a unique embedding represent their features. In our experiment, the entity relation triples are extracted by

Stanford OpenIE, and the triple elements are consisted of multiple words. Hence, we use the sum of word embeddings to represent entity nodes and relation edges.

The second adjustment is injecting relation features to a temporal node together with the subject nodes. Step one, each node and relation features will be fed to a feedforward neural network. Step two, the feature of subject nodes concatenates the relation node feature to produce a temporal neighbor node of the connected object node. The key step three, the temporal neighbor node's feature and the corresponding objective node feature are fed to a bilinear layer and a feedforward layer. So, the formulation of attention score is:

$$e_{irj} = \text{LeakyReLU}(\vec{\theta}^T([W_h \vec{h_j} \oplus W_v \vec{v_r}]W_r(W_h \vec{h_i}))), \tag{15}$$

where $W_h, W_v, W_r, \vec{\theta}^T$ are learnable parameters. $r \in R_{ij}$, and R_{ij} is the total number of relations between node i and node j. v_r is the r-th relation embedding of node i and node j. Considering there may be multiple relations between the same pair entities, there exists multiple edges between a same pair entity. The weights on each edge are calculated as:

$$\beta_{irj} = \frac{\exp(\text{LeakyReLU}(\vec{\theta}^T([W_h \vec{h_j} \oplus W_v \vec{v_r}]W_r(W_h \vec{h_i}))))}{\sum_{k \in N_i} \sum_{m \in R_{ij}} \exp(\text{LeakyReLU}(\vec{\theta}^T([W_h \vec{h_k} \oplus W_v \vec{v_m}]W_m(W_h \vec{h_i}))))}, \tag{16}$$

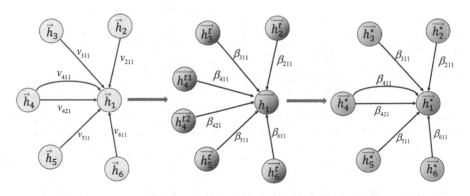

Fig. 4. Knowledge graph nodes representation update process. v denotes relations between subjects and objects, it is also edges of the knowledge graph. β denotes weights between nodes, which is neighbor node's importance to an object node. $\vec{h_i}$ denotes the initial node embedding, $\vec{h_i^t}$ denotes the temporal neighbor node, superscript t means 'temporal'. $\vec{h_i^*}$ denotes node representation after updating. When the node updates, a temporal neighbor node is created by concatenating subject feature and the relation feature.

The node's update formulation is the same as GAT. In this paper, ERGAT runs 3 iterations and outputs the graph feature g by averaging all nodes features.

The graph feature is then used to calculate vocabulary distribution by being concatenated with decoder hidden states h_t^d and context vector z_t. Formulation (5) is modified as:

$$P_{vocab} = \text{Softmax}(U'(U[h_t^d \oplus z_t \oplus g] + b) + b'). \tag{17}$$

The ERGAT model, as a component, is added to the encoder of Pointer-Generator network. On the other side, the LSTM model is replaced with GRU model because the GRU model has almost the same ability to process sequence data but is faster than LSTM. As display in Fig. 3, the GRU and ERGAT modules can run parallelly.

4.3   Entity-Focused Attention Method

Since the entities and their relations include the main information of the source text, the attention distribution on each decode step can be calculated with decoder hidden state and encoder hidden states which corresponds to the sequence indicis of entities and relations, named entity-focused attention. Next, we obtain keyinfo context vector with the same calculation way of context vector. The keyinfo context vector o_t will together with decoder hidden state h_t^d, context vector z_t and graph feature g get the vocabulary distribution. This operation helps the decoder generating words from more precise information and avoiding unnecessary computation. To implement this method, the sequence indicis need to be prepared firstly on data preprocessing. The attention distribution formulation is modified as:

$$s_{lt} = v^T tanh(W_h h_l^e + W_\sigma h_t^d + b_{attn}) \qquad l \in L, \tag{18}$$

$$\gamma_{lt} = \text{Softmax}(s_{lt}), \tag{19}$$

$$o_t = \sum_{l=1}^{L} \gamma_{lt} h_l^e, \tag{20}$$

where l is the index of entities and relations corresponding words of encoder hidden states, $L = \{n_1, n_2, n_3, ..., n_I\}$, I is the number of entities and relations corresponding words extracted from source article. γ_t is the keyinfo attention distribution, o_t represents the keyinfo context vector. When the Entity-focused attention method and ERGAT are both implemented, the vocabulary probability calculation is modified as:

$$P_{vocab} = \text{Softmax}(U'(U[h_t^d \oplus z_t \oplus o_t \oplus g] + b) + b'). \tag{21}$$

As mentioned before, the coverage mechanism is not used in ERPG model, then the final loss function of ERPG model for overall text sequence is:

$$
\begin{aligned}
loss &= -\frac{1}{T} \sum_{t=0}^{T} \log P_{v_{ext}}(y_t) \\
&= -\frac{1}{T} \sum_{t=0}^{T} (p_{gen} P_{vocab}(y_t) + (1 - p_{gen}) P_c(y_t)).
\end{aligned}
\tag{22}
$$

5   Experiments

5.1   Datasets

We use **CNN/Daily Mail** dataset to train, validate and test our model. Abstractive summaries (3.75 sentences and 56 words on average) are written by human from news articles (781 tokens on average) in CNN and Daily Mail websites. This corpus has 287,226 training pairs, 13,368 validation pairs and 11,490 test pairs.

5.2   Data Preprocessing

As mentioned at Sect. 4.1, we need data preprocessing to generate non-redundant and non-overlap relation triples. Due to the OpenIE's limitation of the performance, we have to abandon the samples that OpenIE cannot generate triples. The training set abandons 6,287 samples, remains 280,940 samples; validation set abandons 179 samples, remains 13,189 samples; test set abandons 765 samples, remains 10,725 samples.

5.3   Impementation Details

We follow previous works of See et al. [26], the encoder input text words, decoder input text words and generated abstracts lengths are set to 400, 100 and 100 respectively (including start and end flag <SOS>, <EOS>). Word embedding dimension size is 128, encoder and decoder hidden size is 256. The source texts and target texts share the same vocabulary of size 50k.

On training stage, we train the model on Nvidia GeForce RTX 2080Ti GPU with a batch size of 8 by using Adagrad optimizer with learning rate of 0.15 and initial accumulate value of 0.1. The magnitude for GRU cells random uniform initialization is 0.02. Other parameters' standard of truncated norm initialization is 1e-4. The gradient clipping is maximum gradient norm of 2. As the ERGAT graph iteration number, we found that setting it to 3 can improve our model's performance without too much calculation cost after trying different number of 1, 2, 4, 5 and 6. Similar to graph iteration, we set the ERGAT's multi-head number to 3. The total training iterations are 500k.

On testing stage, we set the minimum decoded length to 60 and the maximum 100, and produced summaries using beam search with beam size 4. We use pyrouge package (ROUGE-1.5.5) to measure generated summaries.

Algorithm 1. Informative OpenIE triples selection

```
input: Triples ← {Triple₁, Triple₂, ...Tripleₙ}
output: newTriples
  function MAIN(Triples)
    lenTriples ← len(Triples)
    choosenIdxs ← {}
    excludeIdxs ← {}
    for i ← 0 < lenTriples do
      idxLongest ← i
      if find i in choosenIdx or excludeIdx then continue
      end if
      for idx ← i + 1 < lenTriples do
        idxLongest ← Examine(checkItems ← {subject, relation, object})
      end for
      if idxLongest == idx then
        newTriples.update(Triples[idxLongest])
      else if idxLongest! = idx and newTriples is not None
        if newTriples[lastOne]! = Triples[idxLongest] then
          newTriples.update(Triples[idxLongest])
        end if
      else newTriples.update(Triples[idxLongest])
      end if
      choosenIdxs.update(idxLongest)
    end for
    return newTriples
  end function

  function EXAMINE(checkItems, idxLongest, idx)
    item ← checkItems.pop()
    if Triple[idxLongest]['item']! = Triplse[idx]['item'] then
      idxLongest, idxExcluded          ←          getLongest&exlcludedIdx(Triples[idxLongest]['item'],
Triples[idx]['item'])
      excludeIdxs.update(idxExcluded)
    elseif checkItems is not None
      idxLongest ← Examine(checkItems)
    end if
    return idxLongest
  end function
```

5.4   Quantitative Results

The results are given in Table 2, the proposed model outperforms all other compared models. Our model is compared with Seq2Seq [28], Seq2Seq + attn [24], Seq2Seq + intra attn [23], CopyNet [9], Pointer-Generator [26] models. As our goal is to investigate the penitential value of entity relations, we do not need complex models to be experimented and we choose the basic Seq2Seq models and the Seq2Seq Pointer-Generator framework models to compare with. Noted that our dataset has been preprocessing and abandons a small part of data, resulting in metric scores of the compared models decreasing in some extend (about –1.5 to –2 ROUGE F1 points).

The standard ROUGE metric is used to evaluate the models. We report the F_1 scores and average F_1 scores for ROUGE-1, ROUGE-2 and ROUGE-L which measure the word overlap, bigram overlap and longest common sequence (LCS) between the reference summary and the generated summaries. The F_1 scores and average F_1 scores are different. When the ROUGE measurement is applied, the F_1 scores are calculated after all reference summary and generated summary pairs are packaged to the pyrouge, on the other hand, average F_1 scores are calculated overall F_1 scores of single testing samples' summary pairs.

The experimental results show that ERPG model outperforms all other compared models except for Pointer-Generator model at ROUGE-1 and ROUGE-2 metric. Even though, ERPG still has an advantage at ROUGE-L metric compared with Pointer-Generator model.

Table 2. The performance comparisons with Seq2Seq [28], Seq2Seq+attn [24], Seq2Seq+intra attn [23], CopyNet [9], Pointer-Generator [26] models on CNN/Daily mail dataset.

Model	ROUGE-1		ROUGE-2		ROUGE-L	
	F1	AVG	F1	AVG	F1	AVG
Seq2Seq	15.91	16.6	2.53	2.59	14.5	15.15
Seq2Seq+attn	27.2	29.87	10.07	11.25	24.78	27.27
Seq2Seq+intra attn	34.12	34.41	13.92	13.98	31.54	31.78
CopyNet	32.56	32.66	13.20	12.97	29.93	30.02
Pointer-Generator (no coverage)	**34.20**	**34.26**	**14.36**	**14.09**	31.01	31.06
ERPG	33.73	33.84	13.83	13.58	**31.26**	**31.36**

5.5   Ablation Studies

In this section, we study the effectiveness of ERPG's two pivotal approaches: ERGAT and Entity-focused attention method. Table 3 shows the effectiveness of ERGAT and Entity-focused attention of the ERPG model, and Table 4 shows the effectiveness of ERGAT and Entity-focused attention when they are implemented on other models.

Apparently, ERGAT can boost the model's performance at ROUGE-1 and ROUGE-2 metrics. Meanwhile, Entity-focused attention method and ERGAT together can boost the model's performance at ROUGE-L metric but get less improvement at ROUGE-1 and ROUGE-2 compared with only keyinfo attention method is implemented.

When Entity-focused attention is implemented on Seq2Seq model without basic attention, the performance gets deteriorated. However, when it is implemented on Seq2Seq model with basic attention, the performance gets improved. This phenomenon indicates that Entity-focused attention enhances the attention mechanism but it cannot work well without basic attention. The explanation of this phenomenon is probably the Entity-focused attention sequence is not fluent and coherent, and the keyinfo context vector produced leads to influent and incoherent summary without basic attention because the Seq2Seq+attn model's context vector does not lead to these metric scores decreasing.

On the other hand, the ERGAT proves its positive effects. However, its improvement to the model is not significant enough. This is probably because lacking of a proper embedding method for entity relations. In this paper,

ERGAT's nodes and edges embeddings are simply designed as the sum of words embeddings. For instance, subject node "a well dressed gentleman" has four words, and its embedding is the sum of four words' embeddings. Even though the node embedding contains semantic information, there may be other more suitable and effective representations for entity and relations while learning their connections. In other words, ERGAT can boost performance of the Seq2Seq frame work models even using simple representations of nodes and edges. So, the entity relation triples still have potentials to improve performance of abstracted summarization models.

Table 3. Effectiveness of ERPG's two pivotal approaches: ERGAT and keyinfo attention.

Model	ROUGE-1		ROUGE-2		ROUGE-L	
	F1	AVG	F1	AVG	F1	AVG
Non-ERGAT	32.90	33.00	13.36	13.10	30.48	30.57
Non-keyinfo attn	**33.85**	**33.92**	**14.24**	**13.98**	30.70	30.77
Complete-model	33.73	33.84	13.83	13.58	**31.26**	**31.36**

Table 4. The performance comparisons between original models and models with ERGAT and keyinfo context respectively.

Model	ROUGE-1		ROUGE-2		ROUGE-L	
	F1	AVG	F1	AVG	F1	AVG
Seq2Seq	15.91	16.6	2.53	2.59	14.5	15.15
Seq2Seq+keyattn	15.68	16.49	2.35	2.41	14.25	15.02
Seq2Seq+ERGAT	**16.56**	**17.34**	**2.66**	**2.72**	**15.13**	**15.83**
Seq2Seq+attn	27.2	29.87	10.07	11.25	24.78	27.27
Seq2Seq+attn+keyattn	**27.82**	**30.60**	**10.40**	**11.64**	**25.41**	**27.91**
Seq2Seq+attn+ERGAT	27.73	30.37	10.23	11.38	25.27	27.64

6   Conclusion

We propose an Informative OpenIE triples selection algorithm and an ERPG model with ERGAT module and Entity-focused attention method to explore the potential of entity relations in text for abstractive summarization. The experimental results shows that keyinfo attention can enhance the basic attention mechanism but cannot work well independently. The ERGAT can boost Seq2Seq models performance with simple knowledge graph embedding solution. The experimental results have showed that leveraging graph neural networks to encode knowledge graph information worth for further study.

References

1. Bahdanau, D., Cho, K.H., Bengio, Y.: Neural machine translation by jointly learning to align and translate. In: 3rd International Conference on Learning Representations, ICLR 2015 (2015)
2. Chen, Q., Zhu, X.D., Ling, Z.H., Wei, S., Jiang, H.: Distraction-based neural networks for modeling document. In: IJCAI, vol. 16, pp. 2754–2760 (2016)
3. Chopra, S., Auli, M., Rush, A.M.: Abstractive sentence summarization with attentive recurrent neural networks. In: Proceedings of the 2016 Conference of the North American Chapter of the Association for Computational Linguistics: Human Language Technologies, pp. 93–98 (2016)
4. Chung, J., Gulcehre, C., Cho, K., Bengio, Y.: Empirical evaluation of gated recurrent neural networks on sequence modeling. In: NIPS 2014 Workshop on Deep Learning, December 2014 (2014)
5. Devlin, J., Chang, M.W., Lee, K., Toutanova, K.: Bert: pre-training of deep bidirectional transformers for language understanding. In: Proceedings of the 2019 Conference of the North American Chapter of the Association for Computational Linguistics: Human Language Technologies, vol. 1 (Long and Short Papers), pp. 4171–4186 (2019)
6. Dosovitskiy, A., et al.: An image is worth 16x16 words: transformers for image recognition at scale. In: International Conference on Learning Representations (2020)
7. Fernandes, P., Allamanis, M., Brockschmidt, M.: Structured neural summarization. In: International Conference on Learning Representations (2018)
8. Gers, F.A., Schmidhuber, J., Cummins, F.: Learning to forget: continual prediction with lSTM. Neural Comput. **12**(10), 2451–2471 (2000)
9. Gu, J., Lu, Z., Li, H., Li, V.O.: Incorporating copying mechanism in sequence-to-sequence learning. In: Proceedings of the 54th Annual Meeting of the Association for Computational Linguistics (vol. 1: Long Papers), pp. 1631–1640 (2016)
10. Gulcehre, C., Ahn, S., Nallapati, R., Zhou, B., Bengio, Y.: Pointing the unknown words. In: Proceedings of the 54th Annual Meeting of the Association for Computational Linguistics (vol. 1: Long Papers), pp. 140–149 (2016)
11. Gunel, B., Zhu, C., Zeng, M., Huang, X.: Mind the facts: knowledge-boosted coherent abstractive text summarization. In: 33rd Conference on Neural Information Processing Systems (2019)
12. Hochreiter, S., Schmidhuber, J.: Long short-term memory. Neural Comput. **9**(8), 1735–1780 (1997)
13. Huang, L., Wu, L., Wang, L.: Knowledge graph-augmented abstractive summarization with semantic-driven cloze reward. In: Proceedings of the 58th Annual Meeting of the Association for Computational Linguistics, pp. 5094–5107 (2020)
14. Huang, Y., Feng, X., Feng, X., Qin, B.: The factual inconsistency problem in abstractive text summarization: a survey. arXiv preprint arXiv:2104.14839 (2021)
15. Keneshloo, Y., Shi, T., Ramakrishnan, N., Reddy, C.K.: Deep reinforcement learning for sequence-to-sequence models. IEEE Trans. Neural Netw. Learn. Syst. **31**(7), 2469–2489 (2019)
16. Kipf, T.N., Welling, M.: Semi-supervised classification with graph convolutional networks. In: 5th International Conference on Learning Representations (2017)

17. Koncel-Kedziorski, R., Bekal, D., Luan, Y., Lapata, M., Hajishirzi, H.: Text generation from knowledge graphs with graph transformers. In: Proceedings of the 2019 Conference of the North American Chapter of the Association for Computational Linguistics: Human Language Technologies, vol. 1 (Long and Short Papers), pp. 2284–2293 (2019)

18. Krizhevsky, A., Sutskever, I., Hinton, G.E.: Imagenet classification with deep convolutional neural networks. Adv. Neural Inf. Process. Syst. **25**, 1097–1105 (2012)

19. Kryściński, W., Keskar, N.S., McCann, B., Xiong, C., Socher, R.: Neural text summarization: a critical evaluation. In: Proceedings of the 2019 Conference on Empirical Methods in Natural Language Processing and the 9th International Joint Conference on Natural Language Processing (EMNLP-IJCNLP), pp. 540–551 (2019)

20. Li, P., Bing, L., Lam, W.: Actor-critic based training framework for abstractive summarization. arXiv preprint arXiv:1803.11070 (2018)

21. Maynez, J., Narayan, S., Bohnet, B., McDonald, R.: On faithfulness and factuality in abstractive summarization. In: Proceedings of the 58th Annual Meeting of the Association for Computational Linguistics, pp. 1906–1919 (2020)

22. Nallapati, R., Zhou, B., dos Santos, C., Gulçehre, Ç., Xiang, B.: Abstractive text summarization using sequence-to-sequence RUNs and beyond. In: Proceedings of The 20th SIGNLL Conference on Computational Natural Language Learning, pp. 280–290 (2016)

23. Paulus, R., Xiong, C., Socher, R.: A deep reinforced model for abstractive summarization. In: International Conference on Learning Representations (2018)

24. Rush, A.M., Chopra, S., Weston, J.: A neural attention model for abstractive sentence summarization. In: Proceedings of the 2015 Conference on Empirical Methods in Natural Language Processing, pp. 379–389 (2015)

25. Scarselli, F., Gori, M., Tsoi, A.C., Hagenbuchner, M., Monfardini, G.: The graph neural network model. IEEE Trans. Neural Netw. **20**(1), 61–80 (2008)

26. See, A., Liu, P.J., Manning, C.D.: Get to the point: summarization with pointer-generator networks. In: Proceedings of the 55th Annual Meeting of the Association for Computational Linguistics (vol. 1: Long Papers), pp. 1073–1083 (2017)

27. Sharma, E., Huang, L., Hu, Z., Wang, L.: An entity-driven framework for abstractive summarization. In: Proceedings of the 2019 Conference on Empirical Methods in Natural Language Processing and the 9th International Joint Conference on Natural Language Processing (EMNLP-IJCNLP), pp. 3280–3291 (2019)

28. Sutskever, I., Vinyals, O., Le, Q.V.: Sequence to sequence learning with neural networks. Adv. Neural Inf. Process. Syst. **27**, 3104–3112 (2014)

29. Tang, H., Xiao, B., Li, W., Wang, G.: Pixel convolutional neural network for multi-focus image fusion. Inf. Sci. **433**, 125–141 (2018)

30. Van Hasselt, H., Guez, A., Silver, D.: Deep reinforcement learning with double q-learning. In: Proceedings of the AAAI Conference on Artificial Intelligence, vol. 30 (2016)

31. Vaswani, A., et al.: Attention is all you need. In: Advances in Neural Information Processing Systems, pp. 5998–6008 (2017)

32. Veličković, P., Cucurull, G., Casanova, A., Romero, A., Liò, P., Bengio, Y.: Graph attention networks. In: International Conference on Learning Representations (2018)

33. Xiao, B., et al.: PAM-DenseNet: a deep convolutional neural network for computer-aided covid-19 diagnosis. IEEE Trans. Cybern. (2021). IEEE
34. Zhu, C., et al.: Enhancing factual consistency of abstractive summarization. In: Proceedings of the 2021 Conference of the North American Chapter of the Association for Computational Linguistics: Human Language Technologies, pp. 718–733 (2021)

Linguistic Dependency Guided Graph Convolutional Networks for Named Entity Recognition

Ximin Sun, Jing Zhou$^{(\boxtimes)}$, Shuai Wang, Xiaoming Li, Bin Zheng, and Dan Liu

35th Floor, Maoye Building, No. 78 Haihe East Road,
Guangfu Road Street, Hebei District, Tianjin, China

Abstract. The GCN model used for named entity recognition (NER) tasks reflects promising results by capturing the long-distance syntactic dependency between words in sentences. However, existing models focus on the syntactic relations, we study the usefulness of linguistic, including semantic and syntactic dependency types information for NER. Through experiments on the OntoNotes 5.0 data set and ConLL2003 data set, we have demonstrated the significant improvement of our new SDP-GCN NER model.

Keywords: Named entity recognition · Linguistic dependency · Graph neural network

1 Introduction

NER is an indispensable and important task in natural language processing (NLP). The focus of this task is to recognize rigid indicators in texts of pre-defined semantic classes [37,40]. On the one hand, a lot of semantic-related information useful for NLP tasks can be obtained from named entities, including multiple tasks such as coreference resolution, relationship extraction, and semantic analysis [12]. On the other hand, it is also possible to obtain relevant semantic information from natural language sentences through the dependency tree.

At the same time, research on language dependence theory shows that the master-slave relationship is common between words in sentences, and the dependence structure between them shows the semantic level information, which is a considerable boost for NER. With the support of these studies, later generations have done a lot of work on improving the performance of the NER model by grammatical dependence and syntactic dependence [19,20,41]. As highlighted in [19], There is a close relationship between entity types and dependencies, which can be used to improve the prediction effect of named entities containing various dependencies, but how to use the long-distance word interaction in complex sentences and the integrity of the named entity It is still an unsolved problem to improve NER based on the dependency structure.

© Springer Nature Switzerland AG 2022
B. Li et al. (Eds.): ADMA 2021, LNAI 13088, pp. 237–248, 2022.
https://doi.org/10.1007/978-3-030-95408-6_18

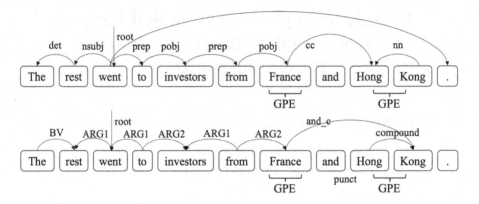

Fig. 1. Two sentences annotated with dependencies and named entities.

Figure 1 contains two sentences adapted from the OntoNotes 5.0 English dataset [37], and it illustrates the relationship between language dependency structures and named entity types. The first example in Fig. 1 illustrates that the long-distance dependency has been found valuable for capturing non-local structural information [14], and distributed hybrid representation deep learning models have been used to obtain semantic and syntactic dependencies. The long-distance dependency relationship from "go" to "." reflects the direct relationship between them, and is also a way to describe the existence of named entities. However, the current NER model based on linear chain structure is not good at capturing this long-distance relationship, which is non-local structure. From the two sentences in picture 1, we can seen that the noun "Hong Kong" composed of two words of the GPE type entity instance is characterized by its dependent arc. The arc in the figure is the expression of a certain degree of semantic role played by words in sentences.

As mentioned earlier, the connection and syntactic dependence between grammatical dependence and named entities have been used to enhance the performance of NER, but little work has been done on the use of semantic dependence and syntactic dependence. Therefore, the usefulness of semantic dependence and the role of syntactic dependence in NER have not been explored clearly. How to use this information to enhance word embedding in NER is still an open question.

In this work, we present on leveraging syntactic and semantic dependency characteristics for NER. It's a NER model based on BiLSTM-CRF [23] with a GCN [30] on top of it to obtain the long-distance relationship of words in sentences through processing syntactic and semantic dependency. We conducted many experiments on multiple data sets in different languages, and finally proved that our model is effective and achieved the most advanced performance. Our large number of experimental results on these corpora show the effectiveness of the model and the advantages of semantic dependence and syntactic dependence in enhancing the NER model.

2   Related Work

NER is an enduring topic about NLP, and its importance is evident. A lot of recent research works [2,11,35] have focused on enhancing NER by finding excellent contextual word representations.

Sasano and Kurohashi [41] take advantage of the syntactic dependency of NER in Japanese and achieve better performance through a SVM classifier. Similarly, Ling et al. [27] include the first word in the edge of the dependency, it can be used as a feature of fine-grained entity recognition. Their method is a pipeline in which they use linear-chain conditional random fields (CRF) [22] to extract entity mentions, and use classifiers to predict entity types. [20] proposed an effective semi-Markov CRF-based dependent guidance NER model.

Some works focus on learning distributed representations to capture the semantic and syntactic characteristics of words. In addition to word-level (e.g., ELMo [35], GloVe [34]) and character-level [2] representations, additional information is often incorporated into the representation before they are input into the context coding layer. For example, the BiLSTM-CRF model uses four types of features: spelling, context and place name index features, and word embedding.

Some recent works make use of linguistic dependency information as an additional feature [20,27]. In 2017, in order to maintain non-Markovian features while meeting the requirements of reducing time complexity, Jie et al. [20] proposed an efficient dependent guidance model based on semi-Markov CRF. They observe the relationship between named entities and the edges of dependencies. This relationship can define a descending search space for their model. Based on previous research, Jie et al. in 2019 [19] incorporate syntactic dependency structures to capture long-distance syntactic interactions between words. Aguilar et al. [1] also considered the syntactic tree structure and gave relevant and global attention, while Nie et al. [32] incorporated syntactic information into the neural model. These methods all make use of grammatical dependence information, but do not consider semantic dependence.

Since we did not find any data sets containing artificially annotated named entities and their semantic dependencies, we need to use the existing SDP model to obtain semantic dependencies. By comparing the performance of existing models such as SemEval 2015 task 18 [33] and SemEval 2016 task 9 [5] on the SDP corpus, we selected two SDP models provided by the NLP toolkit Hanlp and SuPar.

Using dual-lexicalized dependency grammar [47], the syntax and semantic dependencies can be extracted through dependency analysis. Syntactic dependency analysis reveals the shallow semantic information in the sentences. Syntactic and semantic dependency can be extracted by dependency parsing, using bi-lexicalized dependency grammar. Syntactic dependency parsing reveals shallow semantic information in sentences. On the contrary, we can regard semantic dependency analysis (SDP) based on dependency graph analysis as an extension of syntactic dependency analysis, which has more features of semantic relations. Therefore, this paper studies the NER model with semantically dependent information.

3 Model

In this part, we explained our NER model SDP-BiLSTM-GCN-CRF model in detail, which is a result obtained from the BiLSTM-CRF model [23]. Unlike [4], which also uses BiLSTM-GCN-CRF model, but we leverage the dependency relations in GCN.

3.1 BiLSTM-CRF

CRF [3, 16, 36] is a commonly used sequence tagging algorithm that can be used for many tasks in NLP. BiLSTM-CRF [6, 18, 26, 28] is currently a very commonly used sequence labeling algorithm. It not only uses BiLSTM [42, 44], but also combines CRF. This allows the combined model not only to make full use of the correlation between any sequence before and after CRF, but also to have the same fitting and feature extraction capabilities as LSTM.

The process of named entity recognition task is to input a sentence x = x1, x2,...,xn, and then use this sentence to predict a label sequence y = y1, y2,...,yn, n is The number of words in the sentence, y1, y2,...yn are labels defined according to the BIO, IOB or IOBES tagging schemes [31, 39, 45]. The CRF layer calculates the probability of the label sequence y predicted according to x:

$$P(\mathbf{y} \mid \mathbf{x}) = \frac{\exp(\text{score}(\mathbf{x}, \mathbf{y}))}{\sum_{\mathbf{y}'} \exp(\text{score}(\mathbf{x}, \mathbf{y}'))} \tag{1}$$

According to the research of Lample et al. [23], the label prediction sequence has the highest output score, that is, the predicted result is the sequence with the highest score among all output label sequences. Then the output score can be obtained by summing the migration score and the emission score of BiLSTM:

$$\text{score}(\mathbf{x}, \mathbf{y}) = \sum_{i=0}^{n} F_{y_i, y_{i+1}} + \sum_{i=1}^{n} G_{\mathbf{x}, y_i} \tag{2}$$

Where F is the transition matrix and $F_{y_i, y_{i+1}}$ is the transition parameter of $F_{y_i, y_{i+1}}$, G is the emission matrix obtained from the BiLSTM hidden layer, $G_{\mathbf{x}, y_i}$ are the scores of the tag y_i which is the i-th word in the sentence.

3.2 GCN

GCN (Graph Convolution Network) [9, 21] exquisitely designed a method to extract features from graph data. Relative to displacement, scaling and distortion, it has the characteristics of stability and invariance, so it is a very useful way to extract image features. However, the graph structure is very different from the picture. For example, the graph structure has no translation invariance. As a result, we cannot use the traditional convolution method.

At present, there are mainly two ways to extract structural features by GCN: one is to define the order of local receptive fields or nodes and neighbor nodes, such as specifying the edges of nodes Direction [7,43,46,49]; the other is to process the graph structure through the eigenvectors and eigenvalues of the Laplacian matrix [10,24,29].

3.3 SDP-BiLSTM-GCN-CRF

Our model turns the NER problem into a sequence labeling problem. To guide the BiLSTM-CRF model with syntactic and semantic dependency information, we use GCN to process such dependency information. Unlike [48], which uses only adjacency matrices to capture dependency edges between words, our model also processes dependency tag information. Our model combines BiLSTM with directed GCN, using CRF as the final layer in place of a softmax function. The GCN captures the dependency structure as shown in Fig. 2. To represent the input, each word is represented by a concatenation of word embedding, its context-based word vector from ELMO [35], and its character-based representation from GloVe [34] for English and FastText [17] for Chinese. The input will be sent to the BiLSTM layer, from which we can get the context information of the word.

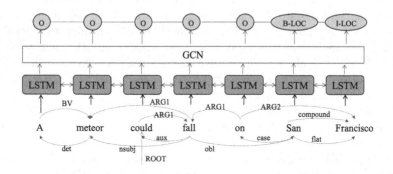

Fig. 2. BiLSTM-GCN-CRF. Dashed connections mimic the dependency edges.

Following most of the implementation for context-based GCN [30,48], we stack the GCN layer on top of the LSTM. This method can help extract the semantic dependencies between words to enrich the representation of words. Using GCN allows our model to effectively capturing global information. We treat the dependency graph as directed and build a symmetric adjacency matrix during the GCN update. The final syntactic GCN computation is formulated as:

$$\mathbf{h}_i^{(l)} = ReLU\Big(\sum_{j=1}^{n} A_{ij}(\mathbf{W}_1^{(l)}\mathbf{h}_j^{(l-1)} + \mathbf{W}_2^{(l)}\mathbf{h}_j^{(l-1)}w_{r_{ij}})\Big) \qquad (3)$$

where $\mathbf{h}_i^{(l)}$ represents the hidden state at the i-th position of the l-th layer, $w_{r_{ij}}$ is the weight of the dependency relation $r_{i,j}$. We use different parameter matrices $\mathbf{W}_1$ and $\mathbf{W}_2$ for self-connection and dependent connection respectively. For L layers of GCN in the model, $\mathbf{h}_1^{(L)}, \ldots, \mathbf{h}_n^{(L)}$ are the output word representations. Finally, the last layer is CRF.

4   Experiment

In this part, We will compare our model with the best-performing NER model based on grammatical dependence and syntactic dependence information to evaluate the performance of our model on certain commonly used datasets.

4.1   Datasets

We adopted the Chinese and English OntoNotes 5.0 datasets [37]. We finally decided to use it because this dataset not only has syntax dependency annotations, but also named entity annotations, so that we can compare our model with models that use this information. However, we do not yet know that this type of open data set has annotated semantic dependencies. Therefore, in our experiment, we must use "SuPar"[1] to generate syntax-dependent comments. This toolkit can evaluate the impact of different semantic dependent information predicted by different models on performance. Meanwhile, the OntoNotes 5.0 dataset includes 18 types of entities. Then for Chinese, the split result provided by Pradhan et al. [38] can be used; At the same time, for English, Pradhan et al. [37] also provide a well-performing split, and some previous works have already used this split [8,15,25].

In addition to the OntoNotes 5.0 dataset, the CoNLL 2003 English dataset was also used in this experiment [40]. This data set can be used as early training data for testing named entity recognition. Its text source is newspaper news. CoNLL 2003 NER is composed of news line data set from Reuters RCV1 corpus, marked with four different entity types (PER, LOC, ORG, MISC). The model is evaluated and tested based on the F1 of the span on this dataset. It consists of eight documents, covering two languages: English and German. Each language includes: training set, development set, test set and unlabeled data.

4.2   Experiment Setup

We implemented all the models with PyTorch including BiLSTM-CRF and GCN. These models are used as baseline models and are responsible for providing

---

[1] A Python package that includes many state-of-the-art syntactic/semantic parsers, https://github.com/yzhangcs/parser/.

BiLSTM-GCN-CRF with related information such as grammatical dependence and syntactic dependence. We call it the SDP-BiLSTM-GCN-CRF model, which can be used to compare the benefits of grammatical dependence and syntactic dependence. The dimension of the hidden layers of LSTM and GCN models is set to 200. Our model uses mini-batch stochastic gradient descent (SGD) for optimization, and the learning rate is 0.01. The L2 regularization parameter is 1e–8.

4.3 Results

In a series of experiments, we compare our model with existing models on the three datasets, OntoNotes 5.0 Chinese (OntoNotes CN), English (OntoNotes EN), and CoNLL-2003 English (CoNLL). For each compared model, we used the numbers of LSTM/GCN layers that gave the best performance; for instance, BiLSTM(1)-GCN(1)-CRF has 1 LSTM lay and 1 GCN layer. All the inputs are concatenated with the ELMo representations. The Dependency column shows whether dependency information is not included (–), or it is provided with the datasets (gold), or it is generated. If the dependency is generated, we record the F1 score of the generating models and the text corpus they are trained on. Table 1 shows the results, where those for BiLSTM-CRF and Syn-BiLSTM-GCN-CRF are from [19, 23].

Table 1. Comparison on OntoNotes 5.0 Chinese/English and CoNLL-2003 English.

Dataset	Model (+ELMo)	Dependency	Prec.	Rec.	F1
OntoNotes CN	BiLSTM(1)-CRF	-	**79.20**	79.21	**79.20**
	SDP-BiLSTM(1)-GCN(1)-CRF	80.41 (TEXT)	78.25	**79.52**	78.88
	Syn-BiLSTM(1)-GCN(1)-CRF [19]	gold	78.71	79.29	79.00
OntoNotes EN	BiLSTM(2)-CRF	-	88.25	89.71	88.98
	SDP-BiLSTM(1)-GCN(1)-CRF	92.32 (DM)	88.86	89.69	89.27
	SDP-BiLSTM(1)-GCN(1)-CRF	93.43 (PAS)	<u>89.14</u>	**89.96**	**89.55**
	SDP-BiLSTM(1)-GCN(1)-CRF	82.64 (PSD)	87.59	88.62	88.10
	BiLSTM-GCN-CRF [4]	-	84.3	80.1	82.0 ± 0.4
	Syn-BiLSTM(1)-GCN(1)-CRF [19]	gold	**89.40**	<u>89.71</u>	**89.55**
CoNLL	BiLSTM(2)-CRF	-	**92.10**	**92.30**	**92.20**
	SDP-BiLSTM(1)-GCN(1)-CRF	92.32 (DM)	91.64	91.40	91.41
	Syn-BiLSTM(1)-GCN(1)-CRF [19]	95.86 (LAS)	91.93	92.26	92.09

On the Ontonote 5.0 EN datasets, SDP-BiLSTM-GCN-CRF outperforms the baseline BiLSTM-CRF. Compared to Syn-BiLSTM-GCN-CRF, our model SDP-BiLSTM-GCN-CRF gave a close performance. The result is not good enough, it is because of using the prediction dependency not gold annotation. This may also prompt us to continue to study effective semantic-dependent NER models. However, the accuracy of BiLSTM-GCN-CRF (L = 1) is lower than that of DGLSTM-CRF, which uses syntax dependency to achieve the best performance. There is still a slight gap. This also shows that the semantic dependency introduced by BiLSTM-GCN-CRF has errors and has not reached the gold standard. This may also prompt us to continue to study effective semantic-dependent NER models.

OntoNotes English. Table 2 demonstrates the performance contradistinction between our work and previous models on the OntoNotes English dataset. The best-performing baseline BiLSTM-CRF (with ELMo) LSTM layer is 2 (that is, L = 2) and achieves an F1 score of 88.98. The performance gap is noticeable by compared with the model BiLSTM-GCN (with semantic dependency)-CRF model (with ELMO). The performance of the BiLSTM-GCN (with semantic dependency)-CRF model (with ELMO) reached 89.65, which is also exceeded the same model BiLSTM-GCN (with syntactic dependency)-CRF (with ELMO), the model DGLSTM under the prediction syntactic dependency dataset. The exceed performance is not noticeable compared to the F1 of the Chinese dataset. It indicates that the semantic dependency of English may be less evident than Chinese. However, we believe that semantic dependent features play a more critical role in named entity recognition than syntactic dependent information.

Table 2. Performance contradistinction on the OntoNotes 5.0 English dataset.[2]

Model	Predict	Prec.	Rec.	F1
BiLSTM-CRF (L = 1) + ELMo	Gold	88.25	89.71	88.98
BiLSTM-GCN(syn)-CRF + ELMo(L = 1)	Gold	89.40	89.71	89.55
BiLSTM-GCN(sem)-CRF + ELMo(L = 1)	92.2(DM)	89.22	90.10	89.65
BiLSTM-GCN(sem)-CRF + ELMo(L = 2)	92.2(DM)	88.78	89.90	89.34
BiLSTM-GCN(sem)-CRF + ELMo(L = 1)	94.38(PAS)	89.18	90.04	89.61
BiLSTM-GCN(sem)-CRF + ELMo(L = 2)	94.38(PAS)	88.98	89.77	89.37
BiLSTM-GCN(sem)-CRF + ELMo(L = 1)	79.6(PSD)	88.73	90.25	89.49
BiLSTM-GCN(sem)-CRF + ELMo(L = 2)	79.6(PSD)	88.00	89.10	88.55
DGLSTM-CRF (L = 2) + ELMo(Predicted)	95.86	89.35	90.14	89.74
DGLSTM-CRF (L = 2) + ELMo(Gold)	Gold	89.59	90.17	89.88

ConLL-2003 English. Table 3 demonstrates the performance of the CoNLL-2003 English dataset. Since there is no syntactic dependency in CoNLL-2003, we used the Supar toolkit to add the syntactic dependency relationship in the dataset. The dependency LAS of syntactic prediction performance F1 is 95.86, which model is based on the Biaffine [13]. Furthermore, the semantic dependency prediction F1 score is 92.2 (DM), which is the same model used in Ontonotes 5.0 dataset as well. We can see more clearly, that the F1 score based on the semantic is better than the syntactic dependency in the absence of the gold standard for syntactic dependencies. The experiment once again shows that semantic dependency has a more important value in NER than syntactic dependency.

Table 3. Performance contradistinction on the ConLL2003 English dataset.

Model	Predict	Prec.	Rec.	F1
BiLSTM-CRF (L = 2) + ELMo	—	92.1	92.3	92.2
BiLSTM-GCN(syntactic)-CRF (L = 1) + ELMo	95.86(PTB)	91.93	92.26	92.09
BiLSTM-GCN(semantic)-CRF (L = 1) + ELMo	92.2(DM)	92.21	92.49	92.35
DGLSTM-CRF (L = 2) + ELMo (predicted)	95.86(PTB)	92.27	92.63	92.45

5   Analysis

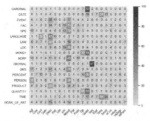

(a) Heap map on training data.

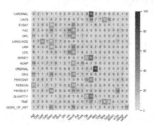

(b) Heap map on NER prediction.

Fig. 3. Correlations and Percentage between the entity types (y axis) and the of semantic dependency relations (x axis) in the OntoNotes Chinese dataset. For brevity, columns with percentages less than 5% will be ignored.

In Fig. 3, we can see that their densities are similar. They all show a consistent relationship between dependencies and entity types. Their confrontation shows that this improvement is partly due to the influence of dependencies. We also found from the predictions of the model that some entity types are strongly related to dependency pairs.

We can see that most entities are related to Desc, Nmod, Quan dependencies. In particular, the dependency relationship Quan (Quantity) has more than 80% of the entity type CARDINAL associated with 58% of the entity type Quantity, indicating that there is a semantic association.

6 Conclusion

Motivated by the relationships between syntactic dependency and name entities, we propose a new BiLSTM-GCN-CRF model to encode linguistic information and then enhance the word representation of the NER task. Through a lot of experiments on multiple datasets, it is proved that the proposed model can be used effectively and we can use the model to find the long-distance dependency relationships between the words for improving NER performance. We leave studying a more effective multi-feature fusion mechanism of syntactic and semantic of full dependencies for NER as future work.

References

1. Aguilar, G., Solorio, T.: Dependency-aware named entity recognition with relative and global attentions. arXiv preprint arXiv:1909.05166 (2019)
2. Akbik, A., Blythe, D., Vollgraf, R.: Contextual string embeddings for sequence labeling. In: Proceedings of COLING-2018, pp. 1638–1649 (2018)
3. Bale, T.L., Vale, W.W.: CRF and CRF receptors: role in stress responsivity and other behaviors. Annu. Rev. Pharmacol. Toxicol. **44**, 525–557 (2004)
4. Cetoli, A., Bragaglia, S., O'Harney, A.D., Sloan, M.: Graph convolutional networks for named entity recognition. In: TLT (2018)
5. Che, W., Shao, Y., Liu, T., Ding, Y.: SemEval-2016 task 9: Chinese semantic dependency parsing. In: Proceedings of the 10th International Workshop on Semantic Evaluation (SemEval-2016), pp. 1074–1080 (2016)
6. Chen, T., Xu, R., He, Y., Wang, X.: Improving sentiment analysis via sentence type classification using BiLSTM-CRF and CNN. Exp. Syst. Appl. **72**, 221–230 (2017)
7. Chen, W., Chen, L., Xie, Y., Cao, W., Gao, Y., Feng, X.: Multi-range attentive bicomponent graph convolutional network for traffic forecasting. In: Proceedings of the AAAI Conference on Artificial Intelligence, vol. 34, pp. 3529–3536 (2020)
8. Chiu, J.P., Nichols, E.: Named entity recognition with bidirectional LSTM-CNNs. Trans. Assoc. Comput. Linguist. **4**, 357–370 (2016)
9. Defferrard, M., Bresson, X., Vandergheynst, P.: Convolutional neural networks on graphs with fast localized spectral filtering. Adv. Neural Inf. Proces. Syst. **29**, 3844–3852 (2016)
10. Deng, C., Zhao, Z., Wang, Y., Zhang, Z., Feng, Z.: GraphZoom: a multi-level spectral approach for accurate and scalable graph embedding. arXiv preprint arXiv:1910.02370 (2019)
11. Devlin, J., Chang, M., Lee, K., Toutanova, K.: BERT: pre-training of deep bidirectional transformers for language understanding. In: Proceedings of NAACL-HLT-2019, pp. 4171–4186 (2019)
12. Dong, L., Lapata, M.: Coarse-to-fine decoding for neural semantic parsing. In: Proceedings of ACL-2018, pp. 731–742 (2018)
13. Dozat, T., Manning, C.D.: Deep biaffine attention for neural dependency parsing. In: Proceedings of ICLR-2017 (2017)
14. Finkel, J.R., Grenager, T., Manning, C.D.: Incorporating non-local information into information extraction systems by Gibbs sampling. In: Proceedings of ACL-2005, pp. 363–370 (2005)

15. Ghaddar, A., Langlais, P.: Robust lexical features for improved neural network named-entity recognition. arXiv preprint arXiv:1806.03489 (2018)
16. Gillies, G., Linton, E., Lowry, P.: Corticotropin releasing activity of the new CRF is potentiated several times by vasopressin. Nature **299**(5881), 355–357 (1982)
17. Grave, E., Bojanowski, P., Gupta, P., Joulin, A., Mikolov, T.: Learning word vectors for 157 languages. In: Proceedings of LREC-2018 (2018)
18. Huang, Z., Xu, W., Yu, K.: Bidirectional LSTM-CRF models for sequence tagging (2015)
19. Jie, Z., Lu, W.: Dependency-guided LSTM-CRF for named entity recognition. In: Proceedings of EMNLP-2019, pp. 3860–3870 (2019)
20. Jie, Z., Muis, A.O., Lu, W.: Efficient dependency-guided named entity recognition. In: Proceedings of AAAI-2017, pp. 3457–3465 (2017)
21. Kipf, T.N., Welling, M.: Semi-supervised classification with graph convolutional networks. arXiv preprint arXiv:1609.02907 (2016)
22. Lafferty, J.D., McCallum, A., Pereira, F.C.N.: Conditional random fields: probabilistic models for segmenting and labeling sequence data. In: Proceedings of ICML-2001, pp. 282–289 (2001)
23. Lample, G., Ballesteros, M., Subramanian, S., Kawakami, K., Dyer, C.: Neural architectures for named entity recognition. In: Proceedings of NAACL-HLT-2016, pp. 260–270 (2016)
24. Li, C., Qin, X., Xu, X., Yang, D., Wei, G.: Scalable graph convolutional networks with fast localized spectral filter for directed graphs. IEEE Access **8**, 105634–105644 (2020)
25. Li, P.H., Dong, R.P., Wang, Y.S., Chou, J.C., Ma, W.Y.: Leveraging linguistic structures for named entity recognition with bidirectional recursive neural networks. In: Proceedings of the 2017 Conference on Empirical Methods in Natural Language Processing, pp. 2664–2669 (2017)
26. Lin, B.Y., Xu, F.F., Luo, Z., Zhu, K.: Multi-channel LSTM-CRF model for emerging named entity recognition in social media. In: Proceedings of the 3rd Workshop on Noisy User-generated Text, pp. 160–165 (2017)
27. Ling, X., Weld, D.S.: Fine-grained entity recognition. In: Proceedings of AAAI-2012 (2012)
28. Luo, L., et al.: An attention-based BILSTM-CRF approach to document-level chemical named entity recognition. Bioinformatics **34**(8), 1381–1388 (2018)
29. Ma, Y., Hao, J., Yang, Y., Li, H., Jin, J., Chen, G.: Spectral-based graph convolutional network for directed graphs. arXiv preprint arXiv:1907.08990 (2019)
30. Marcheggiani, D., Titov, I.: Encoding sentences with graph convolutional networks for semantic role labeling. In: Proceedings of EMNLP-2017, pp. 1506–1515 (2017)
31. Nayel, H.A., Shashirekha, H., Shindo, H., Matsumoto, Y.: Improving multi-word entity recognition for biomedical texts. arXiv preprint arXiv:1908.05691 (2019)
32. Nie, Y., Tian, Y., Song, Y., Ao, X., Wan, X.: Improving named entity recognition with attentive ensemble of syntactic information. arXiv preprint arXiv:2010.15466 (2020)
33. Oepen, S., et al.: SemEval 2015 task 18: broad-coverage semantic dependency parsing. In: Proceedings of the 9th International Workshop on Semantic Evaluation (SemEval 2015), pp. 915–926 (2015)
34. Pennington, J., Socher, R., Manning, C.D.: Glove: global vectors for word representation. In: Proceedings of EMNLP-2014, pp. 1532–1543 (2014)
35. Peters, M.E., et al.: Deep contextualized word representations. In: Proceedings of NAACL-HLT-2018, pp. 2227–2237 (2018)

36. Plotsky, P.M., Meaney, M.J.: Early, postnatal experience alters hypothalamic corticotropin-releasing factor (CRF) mRNA, median eminence CRF content and stress-induced release in adult rats. Mole. Brain Res. **18**(3), 195–200 (1993)
37. Pradhan, S., et al.: Towards robust linguistic analysis using ontonotes. In: Proceedings of CoNLL-2013, pp. 143–152 (2013)
38. Pradhan, S., Moschitti, A., Xue, N., Uryupina, O., Zhang, Y.: CoNLL-2012 shared task: Modeling multilingual unrestricted coreference in ontonotes. In: Joint Conference on EMNLP and CoNLL-Shared Task, pp. 1–40 (2012)
39. Ratinov, L., Roth, D.: Design challenges and misconceptions in named entity recognition. In: Proceedings of CoNLL-09, pp. 147–155 (2009)
40. Sang, E.F.T.K., Meulder, F.D.: Introduction to the CoNLL-2003 shared task: Language-independent named entity recognition. In: Proceedings of CoNLL-2003, pp. 142–147 (2003)
41. Sasano, R., Kurohashi, S.: Japanese named entity recognition using structural natural language processing. In: Proceedings of IJCNLP-2008, pp. 607–612 (2008)
42. Siami-Namini, S., Tavakoli, N., Namin, A.S.: The performance of LSTM and BiLSTM in forecasting time series. In: 2019 IEEE International Conference on Big Data (Big Data), pp. 3285–3292. IEEE (2019)
43. Wu, Z., Pan, S., Long, G., Jiang, J., Zhang, C.: Graph wavenet for deep spatial-temporal graph modeling. arXiv preprint arXiv:1906.00121 (2019)
44. Xu, G., Meng, Y., Qiu, X., Yu, Z., Wu, X.: Sentiment analysis of comment texts based on BiLSTM. IEEE Access **7**, 51522–51532 (2019)
45. Yaghoobian, N., Kleissl, J.: An indoor-outdoor building energy simulator to study urban modification effects on building energy use-model description and validation. Energy Build. **54**, 407–417 (2012)
46. Yan, S., Xiong, Y., Lin, D.: Spatial temporal graph convolutional networks for skeleton-based action recognition. In: Thirty-second AAAI Conference on Artificial Intelligence (2018)
47. Zhang, M.S.: A survey of syntactic-semantic parsing based on constituent and dependency structures. Sci. China Technol. Sci. **63**(10), 1898–1920 (2020). https://doi.org/10.1007/s11431-020-1666-4
48. Zhang, Y., Qi, P., Manning, C.D.: Graph convolution over pruned dependency trees improves relation extraction. In: Proceedings of EMNLP-2018, pp. 2205–2215 (2018)
49. Zhao, L., et al.: T-GCN: a temporal graph convolutional network for traffic prediction. IEEE Trans. Intell. Transp. Syst. **21**(9), 3848–3858 (2019)

Multimedia and Time Series Data Mining

CS-Siam: Siamese-Type Network Tracking Method with Added Cluster Segmentation

Xuming Han[1], Qi Qin[2], Yuwei Wang[2(✉)], Yihang Zhang[2], Hanlin Li[2], and Zihe Liu[2]

[1] College of Information Science and Technology, Jinan University, Guangzhou 510632, China
[2] School of Computer Science and Engineering, Changchun University of Technology, Changchun 130012, China

Abstract. In the visual target tracking, the template image often contains background information because of manual box selection, which increases the difficulty of feature extraction and the complexity of calculation when the image goes through feature extraction. The existing method has achieved satisfactory results by optimizing the internal of the Siamese network model. However, it fails to consider pre-processing the template image, which is an important process to improve the performance of the target tracking model. Thus, we use image segmentation to extract the target from the template image and then propose a method that introducing the clustering segmentation into the Siamese network to reduce the background information on the tracker. Introducing our present into SiamFC, SiamRPN, SiamRPN++, and SiamFC++ frameworks, we achieve performance improvements on both OTB2015 and VOT2018 challenging benchmarks.

Keywords: Target tracking · Siamese network · Clustering

1 Introduction

Visual target tracking, one of the fundamental computer vision tasks, has been adopted for a wide range of vision applications, such as security surveillance [23] and robot navigation [19]. Although a lot of efforts were put into the visual target tracking model in recent years, it still is considered a challenging task because of the illumination variations, occlusions and background clutter [32,41].

Among these efforts, Siamese network-based trackers [11,12,20,21,26,33,34] is considered as one of the widely used approaches for tackling visual target-tracking task. Siamese network itself is a neural network architecture, not a specific network, which differs from specific deep learning models widely used in multiple fields [5,6,30,31,35–39]. In specific, Siamese network trackers formulate the target tracking task as learning a general similarity map by cross-correlation between the feature representations which learned for the target template and the search region. In order to ensure the efficiency of the Siamese network method, when the Siamese network is trained on large-scale image pairs

© Springer Nature Switzerland AG 2022
B. Li et al. (Eds.): ADMA 2021, LNAI 13088, pp. 251–262, 2022.
https://doi.org/10.1007/978-3-030-95408-6_19

offline, the similarity function is usually fixed during the run-time. Inspired by Siamese Network, SiamRPN [21] tracker introduces a regional proposal network for joint classification regression tracking, and SiamMask [29] tracker introduces mask branches to achieve target segmentation. DaSiamRPN [40] further introduces a distractor-aware module to improve the recognition capability of the model. SiamRPN++ [20] tracker uses ResNet as the backbone network instead of the regular Alexnet to get a performance improvement.

The above-mentioned Siamese network-based trackers are mainly focused on improving either the backbone of the network or the mapping of similar images to improve the performance of the model. However, they did not consider improving the input of the Siamese network by reducing unnecessary noise. It is widely accepted that pre-processing is an effective and efficient approach for performance improvement [14]. Therefore, we proposed using pre-processing for clustering segmentation of the template image. By K-means clustering method, the pixels of the image are taken as data points that are clustered according to the specified number of clusters and replaced with its corresponding centroid. The clusters except the target cluster are filled with a solid color to achieve effective separation of the target from the background. After applying the clustering method, the new template image is obtained and used as the input of the Siamese network. The intensive experiments (as shown in Sect. 4) illustrated that the proposed approach is capable of effectively separating the target from the background, which improves the accuracy of the input side of the Siamese-type network model, thus improving the accuracy of the whole network and reducing the computational complexity of the overall model.

Our contributions can be summarized in three perspectives:

- The proposed CS-Siam pre-processing method can reduce the noise of input to model so that more accurate template images can be used for model training, reducing the overall model's computational complexity.
- The proposed CS-Siam is a well-generalized approach; it can be adopted for various Siamese-type networks.
- Through experimental validation analysis, the Siamese class network with the introduction of the clustered image segmentation method achieves improved performance on both the OTB2015 and VOT2018.

The rest of the paper is organized as follows. We review related work in Sect. 2. The method is introduced in Sect. 3, followed by the experiment implementation, evaluation results, and performance analysis in Sect. 4. Finally, we conclude the paper.

2 Related Works

Since the main contribution of this paper is to introduce clustering image segmentation into Siamese network, we give a brief review on two aspects related to our work: Siamese network based object trackers and image segmentation based on clustering.

2.1   Siamese Network Based Trackers

Due to the Universality of the Deep learning, researchers have begun to apply deep neural networks to target tracking tasks. Tao et al. [27] propose a new method SINT (Siamese INstance search Tracker), which trains a Siamese network to identify candidate image locations that match the appearance of the initial object. Although this method achieves a great improvement in accuracy, it is time-consuming. SiamFC, proposed by Bertinetto et al. [4], further defines the tracking problem as a similarity learning problem that has drawn much attention from researchers because of its fast tracking speed and high accuracy.

Apart from these initial approaches, there are many improvements based on the Siamese network architecture. Li et al. [21] propose SiamRPN, introducing regional proposal network (RPN) into Siamese network. In which, Siamese network is used to extract image features and RPN is used to predict the location and Reliability of the target. Wang et al. [29] propose SiamMask, which performs both target tracking and segmentation on the basis of Siamese network by adding the mask branch of heat map prediction, achieving the improvement of tracking accuracy.

The problem of positional bias occurs when researchers use deeper convolutional networks for feature extraction suggesting that earlier work could only perform feature extraction through shallow networks. Li et al. [20] discuss the above problem. They analyze the existing Siamese trackers and found that the reason for the accuracy degradation is the destruction of the strict translation invariance. To solve this problem, Li et al. present a simple and convenient sampling strategy to break restriction of twin trackers, and successfully train a SiamRPN-based tracker using ResNet as the backbone network. SiamRPN++ [20] achieves excellent results in terms of accuracy and robustness.

2.2   Image Segmentation Based on Clustering

Image segmentation divides an image into several disjoint regions based on features such as gray scale, color, spatial texture, and geometry shape, making these features show similarity in the same region and significant differences in different regions. In this paper, we process the template image with the aim of effectively separating the target from the background information.

Image segmentation methods include threshold-based segmentation methods [9], edge detection based segmentation methods [3,24] and clustering based segmentation methods [1,7]. Although the threshold-based segmentation method is simple to calculate, it only considers the gray value features of pixel points and ignores spatial features, so it is more sensitive to noise and less robust. The edge detection-based method has the advantages of fast speed and accurate edge positioning, but it has drawbacks that be sensitive to noise. Even if the amplitude of noise is small, as long as its frequency is large enough, it will produce wrong detection results.

Clustering, as a representative of unsupervised learning, can be applied to the field of image segmentation because of its ability to classify data similarly without relying on instances with labels. Clustered image segmentation is to represent pixels in the image space with corresponding feature space points and segment the feature space according to their clustering condition in the feature space. We then map the pixels to the original image space to get the segmentation result. It can well avoid other image segmentation methods neglect of spatial features. The methods of clustering include various kinds, such as division-based clustering methods [22,25], density-based clustering algorithms [8], hierarchy-based clustering algorithms [10], model-based clustering algorithms [16], and so on.

In conclusion, Siamese network architecture is a better solution for target tracking task. Siamese network architecture approach makes full use of the advantages of deep learning methods to improve the tracking accuracy by extracting deeper features. We think that interference can be reduced by pre-eliminating the background in the template image. Therefore, we choose the image segmentation method based on clustering algorithm, which has better segmentation effect on dense samples.

3   CS-Siam

In this section, we will describe our CS-Siam framework in detail. The framework focuses on the pre-processing work of template image for clustering image segmentation. The overall framework is shown in Fig. 1, and the framework is composed of two parts: clustering image segmentation and Siamese network.

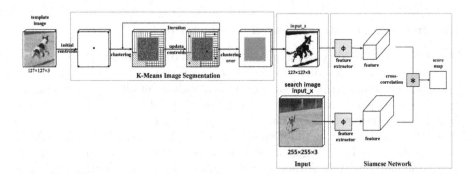

Fig. 1. Illustration of CS-Siam: The left side is the process of K-Means clustering and segmentation of the template image. And then, using new template image (donated by input_z) and search image (denoted by input_x) as input to Siamese Network. The right side is a Siamese sub-network with cross-correlation operation (denoted by *).

3.1   Clustering Image Segmentation and Input

The input side of Siamese network has two parts, template image and search image, in which the background information contained in the template image can interfere with the tracker. Therefore, we perform a clustering image segmentation operation on the template image to effectively separate the target from the background and reduce the interference of the background to the tracker.

K-means [13,28], as a representative algorithm of clustering, has the advantages of low time complexity, good scalability in dealing with large datasets, and adjustable number of clusters and convenient operation. Therefore, in this paper, we choose K-Means clustering method to perform segmentation operation on template image.

The operation of clustering segmentation on the template image can be described as follows:

1. Choosing K initial centroids $\mu_k(k = 1, .., K)$ on the template image.
2. Calculating the Euclidean distance between each pixel $x^{(i)}(i = 1, ..., N)$ and each centroid and classify it into the nearest cluster:

$$c^{(i)} := \arg \min_k ||x^{(i)} - \mu_k||_2 \tag{1}$$

where $c^{(i)}$ donates the cluster closest to $x^{(i)}$ among K clusters, and the value of it is one from 1 to K.
3. Recalculating the positions of the K centroids: At the end of one classification process, take the mean of all samples in each cluster as the new centroid:

$$\mu_k := \frac{\sum_{i=1}^{N} 1\{c^{(i)} = k\}x^{(i)}}{\sum_{i=1}^{N} 1\{c^{(i)} = k\}} \tag{2}$$

4. The clustering is updated by continuously iterating step 2–3 until centroid no longer changes. After the clustering is over, the cluster closest to the centroid of the image is used as the target, and the rest of the clusters are regarded as the background.

The background part is replaced by the color that is more different from the target, and the new template image $input\_z$ is obtained and input into the Siamese network. We consider the particularity of the template image, that is, the target is at the centroid of the image, so the centroid point of the image and the four vertices are set as the centroids.

3.2   Siamese Network Structure

The tracking algorithms based on the Siamese network formulate the target tracking task as a cross-correlation problem, and use the Siamese network models to learn a similarity map. A Siamese network consists of two branches, one branch is used to learn the feature presentation of the tracking target, the template image is usually given in the first frame of the video sequence and in our work it is the segmented template image $input\_z$. The other branch for learning the features of the search region, it is usually using the search image as the input x in the current frame. The Siamese backbone shares the parameters between two branches, and performs the same transformation on the input $input\_z$ and x. The two branches are embedded into a common feature space for subsequent tasks. The template branch and search branch which embedded in the space ϕ need to perform a cross-correlation operation:

$$f(z, x) = \phi(z) * \phi(x) + b \tag{3}$$

Where $*$ denotes the cross-correlation operation, b is used to model the offset of the similarity value.

4 Experimental Results

4.1 Implementation Details

The proposed CS-Siam is implemented in Python on the Ubuntu operating system with PyTorch, and trained on a single GPU. For fair comparison, the input size of template patch and search regions are set to 127 pixels and 255 pixels, respectively. For different Siamese-type tracking models, we use Alexnet [15] and ResNet-50 [2] as the backbone network, they are pre-trained on ImageNet [18], which has been proven practical for tracking task. Our method is evaluated on the OTB2015 [32] and VOT2018 [17], and the test data are challenging.

4.2 Dataset

Various databases have been established to evaluate visual tracking tasks, such as OTB2015 [32] and VOT2018 [17]. The state-of-the-art methods are tested on both of them.

- **OTB2015:** OTB2015 is one of the most commonly used datasets to test the performance of tracking algorithms. The sequences in OTB2015 are 100 sequences from a paper [32] which published in Transactions on Pattern Analysis and Machine Intelligence (TPAMI). Since most image sequences are not properly annotated, it is collected from common tracking sequences for fair performance evaluation, and the different data is tagged with different attributes. These attributes can represent common difficulties in the field of target tracking. For example, IV refers to changes in illumination, SV refers to changes in scale, and OCC refers to occlusion.
- **VOT2018:** The VOT Challenges provide a well-defined and reproducible way to compare short-term trackers, and a general platform for discussing assessments and progress in the field of visual tracking. The goal of the challenges is to establish a repository of considerable benchmarks to facilitate development and research in the field of visual tracking. VOT paper was accepted at Transactions on Pattern Analysis and Machine Intelligence. VOT2018 is the standard dataset for visual tracking competitions, and is one of the most recent

datasets for evaluating online model-free single object trackers. It includes 60 public sequences with different challenging factors, such as fast motion, occlusion.

4.3 Comparison Model

We implemented four state-of-the-art methods using suggested setting. These models were evaluated under same settings. The selected comparable methods are as the following:

- Bertinetto et al. [4]: Fully-convolutional siamese networks for object tracking.
- Li et al. [21]: High performance visual tracking with siamese region proposal network.
- Li et al. [20]: SiamRPN++: Evolution of siamese visual tracking with very deep networks.
- Xu et al. [33]: SiamFC++: Towards robust and accurate visual tracking with target estimation guidelines.

4.4 Evaluation Metrics

We show more details and evaluate the metrics. We evaluate our tracker on several widely used tracking benchmarks: OTB2015 and VOT2018.

- **OTB2015:** Two standard evaluation metrics on OTB are success rate and precision. For each frame, we need to calculate the IoU (intersection over union) between the tracking target and the ground truth bounding boxes, and the distance between their centroids. By evaluating the success rate under different IoU thresholds, a success plot can be achieved, and the area-under-curve (AUC) of the success plots is reported. The same is true for the precision plots, but the representative precision (P) at the 20-pixel threshold is usually reported.
- **VOT2018:** Following the evaluation protocol of VOT2018, we adopt the Accuracy (A), Robustness (R) and Expected Average Overlap (EAO) to compare different trackers.
  1. Accuracy
     Accuracy is used to evaluate the accuracy of the tracking target. The higher the value, the higher the accuracy. Define the per-frame averaged accuracy:

$$\Phi_t(i) = \frac{1}{N_{rep}} \sum_{k=1}^{N_{rep}} \Phi_t(i, k) \tag{4}$$

where $\Phi_t(i, k)$ denotes the accuracy of i-th tracker at frame t at repetition k, and N_{rep} denotes the number of repetitions. And then calculate the average accuracy of the video sequence:

$$\rho_A(i) = \frac{1}{N_{valid}} \sum_{t=1}^{N_{valid}} \Phi_t(i) \tag{5}$$

where N_{valid} denotes the number of valid frames.

2. Robustness

Robustness is used to evaluate the stability of the tracker in tracking the target. The smaller the value, the better the stability. Define the function F(i, k) to be the number of times the i-th tracker fails during the k-th algorithm repeated measurement, and then the average robustness of the video sequence is calculated as follows:

$$\rho_R(i) = \frac{1}{N_{rep}} \sum_{i=1}^{N_{rep}} F(i, k) \tag{6}$$

3. Expected Average Overlap (EAO)

First, we define the average of per-frame overlaps Φ_{N_s} for the N_s of the video frame:

$$\Phi_{N_s} = \frac{1}{N_s} \sum_{i=1} \Phi_i \tag{7}$$

Then, the calculation formula of EAO is as follows:

$$EAO = \frac{1}{N_{hi} - N_{lo}} \sum_{N_s = N_{lo}:N_{hi}} \hat{\Phi}_{N_s} \tag{8}$$

4.5   Result on OTB2015

The results of our comparative experiment are shown in Table 1. On the OTB2015, we compare and analyze the experimental results based on the AUC score and precision. The experiments demonstrate the Siamese-type network model, which uses the template image after clustering image segmentation as input, has improved in terms of success rate and precision. For example, compared with SiamRPN++, CS-SiamRPN++ improves the AUC score and precision by 4.1% and 4.6%, respectively. Compared with SiamFC++, both evaluation metrics of CS-SiamFC++ are improved by 4.2%. The performance improvement proves the effectiveness of using the clustering method to separate the target from the background in the template image.

Table 1. Experimental comparison with the original algorithm after adding clustering to the OTB2015

Model	AUC	AUC(↑)	P	P(↑)
SiamFC	0.589		0.794	
CS-SiamFC	0.611	0.022	0.810	0.016
SiamRPN	0.603		0.820	
CS-SiamRPN	0.641	0.038	0.862	0.042
SiamRPN++	0.623		0.837	
CS-SiamRPN++	0.664	0.041	0.883	0.046
SiamFC++	0.629		0.830	
CS-SiamFC++	0.671	0.042	0.872	0.042

4.6   Result on VOT2018

Table 2. Experimental comparison with the original algorithm after adding clustering to the VOT2018

Model	A	A($\uparrow$)	R	R($\downarrow$)	EAO	EAO($\uparrow$)
SiamFC	0.501		0.534		0.233	
CS-SiamFC	**0.553**	**0.052**	**0.481**	**0.053**	**0.235**	**0.002**
SiamRPN	0.490		0.460		0.244	
CS-SiamRPN	**0.520**	**0.030**	**0.410**	**0.050**	**0.267**	**0.023**
SiamRPN++	0.563		0.375		0.300	
CS-SiamRPN++	**0.571**	**0.008**	**0.301**	**0.074**	**0.351**	**0.051**
SiamFC++	0.584		0.342		0.308	
CS-SiamFC++	**0.596**	**0.012**	**0.285**	**0.057**	**0.351**	**0.043**

As shown in Table 2, we use the three evaluation indicators of A, R, and EAO to carry out experimental comparative analysis. Experimental results show that the model after introducing our method has improved accuracy and EAO. The decrease in robustness proves one thing, compared with the original tracking model, the Siamese network model using the template image after clustering segmentation as input is more stable. Specifically, compared with SiamFC, the accuracy of the CS-SiamFC model is increased by 5.2%, and the EAO gains 0.2%, and the robustness is reduced by 5.3%. For SiamRPN, the accuracy and EAO of CS-SiamRPN have gains of 3% and 2.3%, respectively. In terms of robustness, the value drops by 5%, which means that the stability of CS-SiamRPN is better than original method.

In summarize, all experimental results prove that clustering image segmentation of template images can effectively improve the performance of the Siamese-type tracking model.

5   Conclusion

In this paper, we aim at the deficiencies of the Siamese network architecture in the pre-processing of template images, and introduce the k-means into the overall architecture to reduce the interference of redundant backgrounds on target features. The Siamese network model that introduces our method has improved tracking accuracy, and it is verified that improving the accuracy of the template image has a positive effect on the Siamese-type network model. In the future, more advanced image segmentation methods can be used to optimize the Siamese network structure.

References

1. Achanta, R., Shaji, A., Smith, K., Lucchi, A., Fua, P., Süsstrunk, S.: Slic super-pixels compared to state-of-the-art superpixel methods. IEEE Trans. Patt. Anal. Mach. Intell. **34**(11), 2274–2282 (2012)
2. Akiba, T., Suzuki, S., Fukuda, K.: Extremely large minibatch SGD: training resnet-50 on imagenet in 15 minutes. arXiv preprint arXiv:1711.04325 (2017)
3. Al-Amri, S.S., Kalyankar, N., Khamitkar, S.: Image segmentation by using edge detection. Int. J. Comput. Sci. Eng. **2**(3), 804–807 (2010)
4. Bertinetto, L., Valmadre, J., Henriques, J.F., Vedaldi, A., Torr, P.H.S.: Fully-convolutional Siamese networks for object tracking. In: Hua, G., Jégou, H. (eds.) ECCV 2016. LNCS, vol. 9914, pp. 850–865. Springer, Cham (2016). https://doi.org/10.1007/978-3-319-48881-3_56
5. Chen, W., Long, G., Yao, L., Sheng, Q.Z.: AMRNN: attended multi-task recurrent neural networks for dynamic illness severity prediction. World Wide Web **23**(5), 2753–2770 (2020)
6. Chen, W., Yue, L., Li, B., Wang, C., Sheng, Q.Z.: DAMTRNN: a delta attention-based multi-task RNN for intention recognition. In: Li, J., Wang, S., Qin, S., Li, X., Wang, S. (eds.) ADMA 2019. LNCS (LNAI), vol. 11888, pp. 373–388. Springer, Cham (2019). https://doi.org/10.1007/978-3-030-35231-8_27
7. Comaniciu, D., Meer, P.: Mean shift: a robust approach toward feature space anal-ysis. IEEE Trans. Patt. Anal. Mach. Intell. **24**(5), 603–619 (2002)
8. Ester, M., Kriegel, H.P., Sander, J., Xu, X., et al.: A density-based algorithm for discovering clusters in large spatial databases with noise. In: KDD, vol. 96, pp. 226–231 (1996)
9. Goh, T.Y., Basah, S.N., Yazid, H., Safar, M.J.A., Saad, F.S.A.: Perform. Anal. Image Thresh. Otsu Techn. Measurement **114**, 298–307 (2018)
10. Guha, S., Rastogi, R., Shim, K.: CURE: an efficient clustering algorithm for large databases. ACM SIGMOD Record **27**(2), 73–84 (1998)
11. Guo, D., Wang, J., Cui, Y., Wang, Z., Chen, S.: Siamcar: Siamese fully convo-lutional classification and regression for visual tracking. In: Proceedings of the IEEE/CVF Conference on Computer Vision and Pattern Recognition, pp. 6269–6277 (2020)
12. Guo, Q., Feng, W., Zhou, C., Huang, R., Wan, L., Wang, S.: Learning dynamic Siamese network for visual object tracking. In: Proceedings of the IEEE Interna-tional Conference on Computer Vision, pp. 1763–1771 (2017)
13. Hamerly, G., Elkan, C.: Learning the k in k-means. Adv. Neural Inform. Proces. Syst. **16**, 281–288 (2004)
14. Han, H., Shan, S., Chen, X., Gao, W.: A comparative study on illumination pre-processing in face recognition. Patt. Recogn. **46**(6), 1691–1699 (2013)
15. Iandola, F.N., Han, S., Moskewicz, M.W., Ashraf, K., Dally, W.J., Keutzer, K.: Squeezenet: Alexnet-level accuracy with 50x fewer parameters and< 0.5 mB model size. arXiv preprint arXiv:1602.07360 (2016)
16. Kohonen, T.: The self-organizing map. Proc. IEEE **78**(9), 1464–1480 (1990)
17. Kristan, M., et al.: The sixth visual object tracking vot2018 challenge results. In: Proceedings of the European Conference on Computer Vision (ECCV) Workshops (2018). https://doi.org/10.1007/978-3-030-11009-3_1
18. Krizhevsky, A., Sutskever, I., Hinton, G.E.: ImageNet classification with deep con-volutional neural networks. Adv. Neural Inf. Process. Syst. **25**, 1097–1105 (2012)

19. Kumar, B.A., Sirisha, K., Kumar, R.U.: Development of robot navigation system. In: IOP Conference Series: Materials Science and Engineering, vol. 1057, p. 012022. IOP Publishing, Osaka (2021)

20. Li, B., Wu, W., Wang, Q., Zhang, F., Xing, J., Yan, J.: Siamrpn++: evolution of Siamese visual tracking with very deep networks. In: Proceedings of the IEEE/CVF Conference on Computer Vision and Pattern Recognition, pp. 4282–4291 (2019)

21. Li, B., Yan, J., Wu, W., Zhu, Z., Hu, X.: High performance visual tracking with Siamese region proposal network. In: Proceedings of the IEEE Conference on Computer Vision and Pattern Recognition, pp. 8971–8980 (2018)

22. MacQueen, J., et al.: Some methods for classification and analysis of multivariate observations. In: Proceedings of the fifth Berkeley Symposium on Mathematical Statistics and Probability, vol. 1, pp. 281–297. Oakland (1967)

23. Marois, A., Lafond, D., Williot, A., Vachon, F., Tremblay, S.: Real-time gaze-aware cognitive support system for security surveillance. In: Proceedings of the Human Factors and Ergonomics Society Annual Meeting, vol. 64, pp. 1145–1149. SAGE Publications, Los Angeles (2020)

24. Muthukrishnan, R., Radha, M.: Edge detection techniques for image segmentation. Int. J. Comput. Sci. Inf. Technol. **3**(6), 259 (2011)

25. Park, H.S., Jun, C.H.: A simple and fast algorithm for k-medoids clustering. Expert systems with applications **36**(2), 3336–3341 (2009)

26. Shen, J., Tang, X., Dong, X., Shao, L.: Visual object tracking by hierarchical attention Siamese network. IEEE Trans. Cybern. **50**(7), 3068–3080 (2019)

27. Tao, R., Gavves, E., Smeulders, A.W.: Siamese instance search for tracking. In: Proceedings of the IEEE Conference on Computer Vision and Pattern Recognition, pp. 1420–1429 (2016)

28. Wagstaff, K., Cardie, C., Rogers, S., Schrödl, S., et al.: Constrained k-means clustering with background knowledge. In: ICML, vol. 1, pp. 577–584 (2001)

29. Wang, Q., Zhang, L., Bertinetto, L., Hu, W., Torr, P.H.: Fast online object tracking and segmentation: a unifying approach. In: Proceedings of the IEEE/CVF Conference on Computer Vision and Pattern Recognition, pp. 1328–1338 (2019)

30. Wang, Y., Chen, W., Pi, D., Yue, L.: Adversarially regularized medication recommendation model with multi-hop memory network. Knowl. Inf. Syst. **63**(1), 125–142 (2020). https://doi.org/10.1007/s10115-020-01513-9

31. Wang, Y., Chen, W., Pi, D., Yue, L., Wang, S., Xu, M.: Self-supervised adversarial distribution regularization for medication recommendation. In: Proceedings of the Thirtieth International Joint Conference on Artificial Intelligence Main Track, pp. 3134–3140 (2021)

32. Wu, Y., Lim, J., Yang, M.: Object tracking benchmark. IEEE Trans. Pattern Anal. Mach. Intell. **37**(9), 1834–1848 (2015)

33. Xu, Y., Wang, Z., Li, Z., Yuan, Y., Yu, G.: Siamfc++: towards robust and accurate visual tracking with target estimation guidelines. In: Proceedings of the AAAI Conference on Artificial Intelligence, vol. 34, pp. 12549–12556 (2020)

34. Yang, K., He, Z., Zhou, Z., Fan, N.: Siamatt: Siamese attention network for visual tracking. Knowl.-based Syst. **203**, 106079 (2020)

35. Yue, L., et al.: Exploring BCI control in smart environments: intention recognition via EEG representation enhancement learning. ACM Trans. Knowl. Discov. Data **15**(5), 1–20 (2021)

36. Yue, L., Sun, X.X., Gao, W.Z., Feng, G.Z., Zhang, B.Z.: Multiple auxiliary information based deep model for collaborative filtering. J. Comput. Sci. Technol. **33**(4), 668–681 (2018)

37. Yue, L., Tian, D., Chen, W., Han, X., Yin, M.: Deep learning for heterogeneous medical data analysis. World Wide Web **23**(5), 2715–2737 (2019). https://doi.org/10.1007/s11280-019-00764-z
38. Yue, L., Tian, D., Jiang, J., Yao, L., Chen, W., Zhao, X.: Intention recognition from spatio-temporal representation of EEG signals. In: ADC, pp. 1–12 (2021)
39. Yue, L., Zhao, H., Yang, Y., Tian, D., Zhao, X., Yin, M.: A mimic learning method for disease risk prediction with incomplete initial data. In: Li, G., Yang, J., Gama, J., Natwichai, J., Tong, Y. (eds.) DASFAA 2019. LNCS, vol. 11448, pp. 392–396. Springer, Cham (2019). https://doi.org/10.1007/978-3-030-18590-9_52
40. Zhu, Z., Wang, Q., Li, B., Wu, W., Yan, J., Hu, W.: Distractor-aware Siamese networks for visual object tracking. In: Proceedings of the European Conference on Computer Vision (ECCV), pp. 101–117 (2018)
41. Zhu, Z., Wu, W., Zou, W., Yan, J.: End-to-end flow correlation tracking with spatial-temporal attention. In: Proceedings of the IEEE Conference on Computer Vision and Pattern Recognition, pp. 548–557 (2018)

On Group Theory and Interpretable Time Series Primitives

Athanasios Tsitsipas$^{(\boxtimes)}$ and Lutz Schubert

Institute of Information Resource Management, Ulm University, Ulm, Germany
{athanasios.tsitsipas,lutz.schubert}@uni-ulm.de

Abstract. A time series in its numeric form remains vulnerable to its nature, being highly dimensional. To be machine- and human- interpretable, a time series should be abstracted in a form to accommodate further computational tasks. As such, the form of abstraction may continue to be numerical (e.g., an aggregation feature) or lexical (i.e., text-based), which might increase the level of their interpretability (In machine learning and data mining communities, *interpretability* is the ability to explain or to present in understandable terms to a human [1].). In this paper, we propose the concept of extracting primitive lexical constructs, called *shapeoids*, which offers the ability to abstract a time series curve in natural language (i.e., interpretable), enabling tasks such as reasoning and information retrieval to occur on a later step. The definition of a *shapeoid* remains unchanged for any input time series. We provide formal evidence, using group theory, that our method will always enable us to extract *shapeoids* from a time series.

Keywords: Group theory · Verification · Symbolic aggregate approximation · Shapeoids · Interpretable patterns · Data mining

1 Introduction

A time series is a construct where a sequence of data points exhibits a temporal ordering. Many real-world applications mandate the use of pattern recognition tasks in time series analysis. Biomedical signals (e.g., Electrocardiogram (EKG) and Electroencephalography (EEG)), financial data (e.g., stock market), safety devices (e.g., air quality sensors, smoke sensors), industrial cases (e.g., wind power generation), image processing, and music analysis are some examples with a time series nature [2–5].

Numerous studies on time series analysis use various forms of time series representations employing dimensionality reduction techniques to cope with the high-dimensionality of data while preserving the characteristics of the original time series. One will find many different time series representation methods in the literature [6,7]. Our work focuses on a symbolic representation method named Symbolic Aggregate Approximation (SAX) [8], a simplistic but yet with high computational efficiency in transferring a real-valued time series to its symbolic representation. Many works employ SAX successfully in data mining tasks,

© Springer Nature Switzerland AG 2022
B. Li et al. (Eds.): ADMA 2021, LNAI 13088, pp. 263–275, 2022.
https://doi.org/10.1007/978-3-030-95408-6_20

such as classification, clustering, and anomaly detection. For more information, we point the interested reader to this survey [9]. The symbolic representations are appealing for the user as they are low-dimensional and interpretable [10]. However, different types of data result in various levels of *interpretability* for a human [11,12].

SAX is essentially a sequential string-based description of the time series, with a predefined set of symbols for its description (cf. Sect. 2). However, symbolic techniques, such as SAX rely on fixed parameters that significantly impact the resulting time series representation and accuracy. Many works tried to tackle this problem by finding the optimal fixed parameters [13], which is costly or employing techniques that allow representations at multiple resolutions [14] and multiple domains [10]. Nonetheless, such techniques are susceptible to the definition of these parameters for extracting a possible interesting subsequence, including the burden to adjust them for different time series, without verifying the possible outcome. Moreover, the refutation of trend changes (uptrend and downtrend) in the time series is not covered explicitly by SAX. For example, such information is vital for discovering significant connections between predefined known patterns in applications, such as biomedical data [2]. Another work [15] introduces trend indicators for SAX but encoded directly on the SAX representation raising its complexity. The final result remains obscure and does not increase the level of interpretability. Interpretable data supporting and enabling interpretable models towards explainability of black-box systems is a demanding research area [12].

Our contribution towards extracting interpretable data from time series is two-fold. First, we introduce a primitive concept named *shapeoid*, which describes the time series curve using lexical representations. They raise the interpretability of a time series without introducing any additional burden in the underlying technology of SAX. Using a segmentation technique and string-based methods for their extraction, we lift the representation from SAX's obscure symbolic letter sequence to a representation in natural language. As such, the extracted temporal descriptions of the time series will be used for reasoning tasks [16] employing logic-based methods to express the discovery of complex organizations of patterns (e.g., anomaly detection, information retrieval). Secondly, we provide evidence via *group theory* the verification of our method for extracting a *shapeoid*. As such, we stay agnostic to the underlying time series.

Section 2 contains a basic introduction to group theory to grasp the significance of this mathematical structure and a brief overview of the previously mentioned technique of SAX. Section 3 elaborates on the concept of *shapeoid* and describes the different types while using an example from a real dataset. Next, Sect. 4 elaborates the proof of how the elements of possible *shapeoids* belong to a group. Finally, in Sect. 5, we revisit our contributions while discussing limitations and future work.

2   Preliminaries

Group Theory. It is a wealthy branch of mathematics and one of the building blocks of modern algebra. Moreover, it plays an essential role in many mathematics and other sciences (e.g., biology, chemistry, computer science), as it is an appropriate conceptual framework for studying symmetries. In this section, we will introduce the concept of group and its characteristics briefly, as they are helpful for us in the paper. Then, for background material for the reader, we point to introductory textbooks on group theory [17,18].

A *group* G is a set equipped with an operation $G \star G \to G$ satisfying certain axioms:

1. For any $x, y \in G$, $x \star y$ is also an element of G (closure).
2. There is a unique element $e \in G$, called the *empty* or *identity element*, such that $e \star x = x \star e = x$ for any $x \in G$.
3. For any $x \in G$, there exists an element $x' \in G$, called the *reverse* or *inverse element* of x, such that $x \star x' = x' \star x = e$.
4. The operation $\star$ is associative, that is, for any $x, y, z \in G, x \star (y \star z) = (x \star y) \star z$.

Example 1. The set of integers ($\mathbb{Z}$), real numbers ($\mathbb{R}$), rational numbers ($\mathbb{Q}$) and complex numbers ($\mathbb{C}$), endowed with the operation of addition ($+$), form a group. In contrast, the pairs ($\mathbb{N}, +$) and ($\mathbb{N}_0, +$) do not constitute a group under addition; for the operation $\ll + \gg$ there is no *identity* element in the set $\mathbb{N}$, and for a positive natural number n there is no inverse element in the set $\mathbb{N}_0$. We point out that $\mathbb{N}_0 = \mathbb{N} \cup \{0\}$.

Example 2. Group theory does not consider only classic algebraic sets but also abstract ones. Some known examples are the following: (i) the "game with two coins", in which given a set of allowed moves between the coins and their successive movements, form a group [19]; (ii), solving the Rubik's cube within a group, by making a set of all possible moves (i.e., permutations of the cube's face) with the rotation operation [20,21].

The abstract applications of group theory is a form of verification of applying a method in a domain, where one cannot calculate the result beforehand for all the possible outcomes. Still, there is a theoretical backbone that supports its mechanics. Therefore, we focus on the last statement and apply it in a data mining technique.

SAX. We present the basics of this time series representation method and refer the reader to [8] for the original description of the method. The main result of SAX is the transformation of a time series to a sequence of symbolic letters forming the so-called SAX *word* of the time series. A raw *time series* T consists of a set of timed data points $\{t_1, t_2, \ldots, t_l\}$, where l denotes the length. The T in SAX is *finite*. As such, the length of a time series scopes its size. The static nature of T is a fundamental characteristic of performing the initial normalisation step, as we will showcase. As such, the normalised time series set is

$\hat{T} = \{\hat{t}_1, \hat{t}_2, \ldots, \hat{t}_l\}$, with a mean of *zero* and a standard deviation of *one*. The next step of dimensionality reduction using the Piecewise Aggregate Approximation (PAA) method, over $\hat{T}$, is defined as $\bar{T}$ containing ω equal partitions t_i:

$$\bar{t}_i = \frac{\omega}{n} \sum_{l=\frac{n}{\omega}(i-1)+1}^{\frac{n}{\omega}i} \hat{t}_l \tag{1}$$

To reduce the initial normalised time series from its current dimension n (i.e., its length), the data is split into equal-sized partitions ω; each partition represents the mean value of the data falling into it.

The final discretisation step is the conversion of the numerical set $\bar{T}$ to a string-based SAX *word* W of length ω. The number of letters α constitutes the level of smoothness of the initial time series. The higher the value, the more features are visible. To determine the distribution of letters, SAX uses the partitions in $\bar{T}$ and assigns the letters based on breakpoints $B = \{\beta_1, \ldots, \beta_{\alpha-1}\}$. In the Gaussian distribution $\mathcal{N}(0,1)$, the probabilities of a split region $[\beta_i, \beta_{i+1}]$ are equal to $1/\alpha$, with $\beta_0 = -\infty$ and $\beta_\alpha = +\infty$. The lower partition assigns to the letter 'a', the next passing a breakpoint, to 'b', and so on. Table 1 enumerates the breakpoints for the number of characters in the alphabet A.

Table 1. A statistical lookup table containing the breakpoints in B for splitting the Gaussian distribution into several equiprobable regions.

β_i	α			
	3	**4**	**5**	**6**
β_1	−0.43	−0.67	−0.84	−0.97
β_2	0.43	0	−0.25	−0.43
β_3		0.67	0.25	0
β_4			0.84	0.43
β_5				0.97

3   Extracting Shapeoids in SAX

In this section, we introduce the abstracted time series primitive, named *shapeoid*. We define the key terms for its extraction with a mathematical notation and introduce the different lexical *shapeoids* we may find in a time series.

Definition 1 (SAX Word). *A SAX word W is a sequence of letters w_0, $w_1, \ldots, w_\omega$ from the alphabet $A, |A| = 26$, with length ω.*

We provide a global definition of the term. The definition applies to the *global* view of the original time series T, which forms a single big word and the *local* view, considering a subsequence in the single SAX word.

Definition 2 (Subsequence). *Given a word $\mathcal{W}$, a subsequence $\mathcal{S}$ of $\mathcal{W}$, is a sampling of length $\sigma \leq \omega$ of successive positions in $\mathcal{W}$, that is $w_p, \ldots, w_{p+\sigma-1}$ for $1 \leq p \leq \omega - \sigma + 1$.*

Remark 1. A subsequence also forms a word, as it is a local snapshot of a larger element.

Definition 3 (Sliding Window). *Given a $\mathcal{W}$ of length ω and a defined subsequence $\mathcal{S}$ length of σ with a sliding period ρ, all possible subsequences can be extracted by sliding a window of size ω across $\mathcal{W}$ and considering each subsequence $\mathcal{S}_\rho^\sigma$ of $\mathcal{W}$. Here the superscript σ is the length of the subsequence, and subscript ρ indicates the initial position of the window after sliding it through $\mathcal{W}$.*

In modern data processing frameworks, windowing techniques have a central role. Following Definition 3, it is a standard technique to select data based on a fixed amount of time. It has also been used for accommodating the need of finding motifs and discords in a time series [22]. Based on it and combining it with SAX, numerous works produced significant results, notably classification techniques such as BOP [23] and SAX-VSM [13]. Such works resemble our approach for extracting patterns, but we create a more abstract definition of the pattern, turning it into an interpretable representation.

Definition 4 (Multiset of words). *The multiset of all subsequences of length σ extracted from $\mathcal{W}$ is defined as $S_\mathcal{W}^\sigma = \langle S_\rho^\sigma$ of $\mathcal{W}$, for $1 \leq \rho \leq \omega - \sigma + 1 \rangle$.*

Remark 2. We put forward that a time series translates to a *multiset of words* as an abstract symbolic representation of its curve.

Definition 5 (Shapeoid). *Let $s \in S_\mathcal{W}$ be a word of length σ. The s forms a shapeoid if and only if $|s| = 3$.*

The *shapeoid* is a lexical characterisation of a word as interpretable applied to any domain. We define four individual shapeoids FLAT, ANGLE, HOP and HORN. On top of them, there exist also orientation classes or trends, named as *upward* and *downward*. The step of dimensionality reduction in SAX and its discretisation process lifts the computation from the numerical real-valued elements to symbolic interrelations.

Example 3. As a leading example, we introduce the following time series T^M. It contains findings from an installed air quality sensor in a room [24]. The results measure the carbon dioxide levels in the environment. We consider a snapshot of the continuous data stream and apply the technique of SAX. Figure 1 provides an overview of the initial time series and the extracted SAX word.

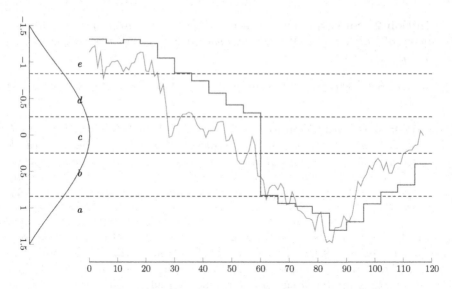

Fig. 1. A time series of 120 data points (grey line) transforming it to a SAX word with 20 PAA partitions and five ordered letters (from a to e). The dotted line represents the breakpoints (cf. Table 1) for splitting the curve into equiprobable partitions. Using the aggregated time series (red line), the resulting word is *eeeeeeddddbaaaaaabbb*. (Color figure online)

3.1   Lexical Shapeoids

Next, we will elaborate on the definitions of the individual lexical *shapeoids* (FLAT, ANGLE, HOP, HORN) and their trends (*upward* and *downward*). We define a word $w \in W$ of a *shapeoid* as w^s. The word w^s forms a FLAT if $w_1^s = w_0^s$ and $w_1^s = w_2^s$. The FLAT has no trend values for obvious reasons.

The FLAT is an almost sturdy line with minor variations in the curve. Figure 2 illustrates, for the sake of homogeneity with the figures above, three variations of the shapeoid using each of the described letters (e.g., *aaa*, *bbb*, *ccc*). It is a straightforward pattern, as, after the dimensionality reduction, the data remain in the same probabilistic boundary and do not exceed any breakpoint to get another letter assignment. Although its extraction is not complex, it might be interesting for the use case in focus.

The word w^s forms an ANGLE if ($w_1^s = w_0^s + 1$ or $w_1^s = w_0^s$) and ($w_2^s = w_1^s + 1$ or $w_2^s = w_1^s$). The w^s defines an *upward* ANGLE. The word w^s has a *downward* trend of the same shapeoid, if ($w_1^s = w_0^s - 1$ or $w_1^s = w_0^s$) and ($w_2^s = w_1^s - 1$ or $w_2^s = w_1^s$).

An ANGLE is a gradual and continuous increase or decrease in the original time series T. In Fig. 3, we illustrate variations of the same shapeoid where Fig. 3(a) and 3(b) are two possibilities of the *upward* trend using the words *abc* and *bbc*, respectively. Figure 3(c) depicts an example of the *downward* trend using the word *cba*.

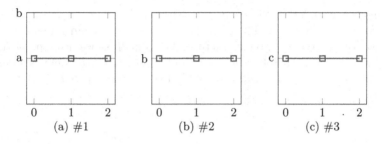

Fig. 2. Variations of the FLAT shapeoid using a sequence of three letters in w.

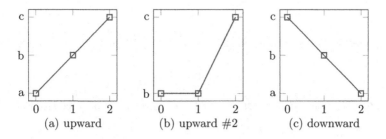

Fig. 3. Variations of the ANGLE shapeoid using a sequence of three letters in w.

The word w^s forms a HOP if $(w_1^s > w_0^s + 1$ or $w_1^s = w_0^s)$ and $(w_2^s > w_0^s + 1$ or $w_2^s = w_1^s)$. The w^s defines an *upward* HOP. The word w^s has a *downward* trend of the same shapeoid, if $(w_1^s < w_0^s - 1$ or $w_1^s = w_0^s)$ and $(w_2^s < w_1^s - 1$ or $w_2^s = w_1^s)$.

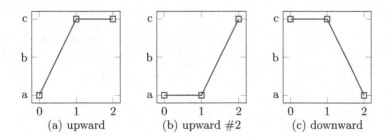

Fig. 4. Variations of the HOP shapeoid using a sequence of three letters in w.

A HOP describes a distinctive phase shift in the original time series T, leading to an overall visible change. The pattern extraction resembles the ANGLE shapeoid; however, we do not opt for a successive change in the characters of the word, but an instantaneous change which translates to omitting the successive character in the alphabet A. We may observe that in the samples from Fig. 4, where in Fig. 4(a), the word acc shows an upward trend of the shapeoid; as per its definition, the second position letter in the word is not the successive letter of the first position letter. Similarly, Fig. 4(b) and 4(c) have an *upward* shapeoid and a *downward* shapeoid. The third character in w^s should remain constant; otherwise, the pattern will be characterised as a HORN as we describe next.

The word w^s forms a HORN if $w_1^s > w_0^s$ and $w_1^s > w_2^s$. The w^s defines an *upward* HORN. The word w^s has a *downward* trend of the same shapeoid, if $w_1^s < w_0^s$ and $w_1^s < w_2^s$.

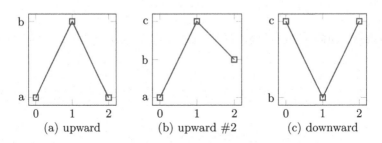

(a) upward   (b) upward #2   (c) downward

Fig. 5. Variations of the HORN shapeoid using a sequence of three letters in w.

The HORN is an ephemeral increase or decrease in the time series T. Thus, a short-term effect fades quickly, as the end of the pattern returns almost to the initial point. An illustration of this is in Fig. 5, where two variation examples of the upward trend are in Fig. 5(a) and 5(b), using *aba* and *acb*. Interestingly, the shapeoid in Fig. 5(b) is almost a HOP, but the third position in the word does not satisfy the conditions of its definition above. Figure 5(c) illustrates a variation of the *downward* trend using the word *cca*.

Example 4 (cont'd). Now that we have introduced the different *shapeoids* and their trends, we continue the description of our example using the extracted SAX representation of the illustrated time series. The word *eeeeeeddddbaaaaaabbb* needs to be traversed using a sliding window of length three and a period of one, which means that at every one point, there is a new window. Hence, the above word will result in a multiset of smaller words S_W^σ. For the sake of the example, we enumerate the multiset as:

$$S_W^\sigma = \{eee, eee, eee, eee, eed, edd, ddd, ddd, ddb, dba, baa, aaa, aaa, aaa, aaa, aab, abb, bbb\}$$

S_W^σ is a symbolic representation of the time series. Now, lifting the SAX words to lexical *shapeoids*, we describe the curve in a natural language as a narrative. We present the matching *shapeoids* in Table 2.

The *shapeoid* extraction results in a time series vocabulary for reasoning tasks in the individual use case. The curve of a time series may be used for tasks like anomaly detection and event recognition. The *shapeoids* are unrelated to the number of letters in a SAX word. However, the number of word subsequences for their extraction grows exponentially with the increase in the selected sequence of letters. Nonetheless, the method of extracting *shapeoids* from a time series is

Table 2. A table containing the matchmaking between the SAX words and the lexical *shapeoids*.

s_i	Shapeoid
eee, ddd, aaa	**FLAT**
eed, baa	*downward* **ANGLE**
abb	*upward* **ANGLE**
ddb, dba	*downward* **HOP**

always valid for solving the interpretability of a time series. We may test that by either examining every possible time series out there or supporting it with some proof. As we will demonstrate in the next section, we can support the claim via group theory that all possible combinations of subsequences will always result in a new subsequence which we translate to a known *shapeoid*.

4   Group Theory and Shapeoid Extraction

The purpose of this section is to provide evidence that the set of window slides for *shapeoid* extraction on any time series of any length belongs to an algebraic group, which we denote as $(G, \star)$.

The elements of G will be the possible slides on any extracted SAX word $\mathcal{W}$, which are unknown beforehand. Therefore, we equip it with the group operation $\star : G \times G \mapsto G, (x, y) \mapsto x \star y$, the result of which is the running of the sliding window L across $\mathcal{W}$. Now, we start with the general theorem we want to expose, and then we work out the individual properties from Sect. 2, for a set to be a group.

Theorem 1. *The shapeoid extraction process for any time series T forms a group G.*

Lemma 1 (closure). *G is closed under the operation $\star$.*

Proof. It is certainly true, since if L_1 and L_2 are slides, then $L_1 \star L_2$ is a slide as well.

Lemma 2 (identity element). *There exists an element $e \in G$, such that $g \star e = g$ for all $g \in G$.*

Proof. Let e be the "empty" slide (a slide that does not change the extracted result), then $L \star e$ translates to "initially execute L, then do nothing". It is exactly the same to just run L, hence $L \star e = L$. As such, $(G, \star)$ always has a right identity element.

Lemma 3 (inverse element). *For each $g \in G$, there exists $g' \in G$ such that $g \star g' = e$.*

Proof. If L is a slide across the timeline, we can reverse the steps of L to get a slide L'. As such, the slide $L \star L'$ translates to "initially execute slide L, then reverse all the steps of slide L". Therefore, we consider this as doing nothing at the end, so $L \star L' \equiv e$, with L' being the inverse of L. Therefore, every element of G has a right inverse.

Lemma 4 (associativity). *The operation $\star$ in G is associative.*

Proof. The slide L of the window is defined by the change in the letters of a word $\mathcal{W}$. So we will denote as $L(\mathcal{W})$ the sliding function and the result of the slide after its execution. So that is, the initial characters of $\mathcal{W}$ should be the result of the initial slide $L(\mathcal{W})$.

Let us begin with sequencing two slides on the word. If L_1 and L_2 denote two slides, then the $L_1 \star L_2$ is also a slide where we initially do L_1 and then L_2. The slide L_1 extracts from the word $\mathcal{W}$ the resulting subsequence $L_1(\mathcal{W})$; the slide L_2 shifts it to $L_2(L_1(\mathcal{W}))$. Hence, the equality is as follows:

$$(L_1 \star L_2)(\mathcal{W}) = L_2(L_1(\mathcal{W})) \tag{2}$$

To prove that the operation $\star$ is associative, we need to demonstrate that $(L_1 \star L_2) \star L_3 = L_1 \star (L_2 \star L_3)$ for every slide L_1, L_2, and L_3. It is the same as proving that $(L_1 \star L_2) \star L_3$ and $L_1 \star (L_2 \star L_3)$ have the same outcome for every word. We want to verify that $[(L_1 \star L_2) \star L_3](\mathcal{W}) = [L_1 \star (L_2 \star L_3)](\mathcal{W})$ for every $\mathcal{W}$.

Using the equation in (2) we want to validate that $[(L_1 \star L_2) \star L_3](\mathcal{W}) = L_3([L_1 \star L_2](\mathcal{W})) = L_3(L_2(L_1(\mathcal{W})))$.

Furthermore, we want to apply the same equation to show that $[L_1 \star (L_2 \star L_3)](\mathcal{W}) = (L_2 \star L_3)(L_1(\mathcal{W})) = L_3(L_2(L_1(\mathcal{W})))$. As such, $(L_1 \star L_2) \star L_3 = L_1 \star (L_2 \star L_3)$. Therefore, we prove that $\star$ is associative.

Thus, $(G, \star)$ is effectively a group.

Proposition 1. *The group operation $(G, \star)$ in the shapeoid extraction process is not commutative (abelian).*

Proof. Again to prove that an operation is not commutative, we need to demonstrate that for $L_1 \star L_2 \neq L_2 \star L_1$. Effectively using the equation in (2), $L_2(L_1(\mathcal{W})) \neq L_1(L_2(\mathcal{W}))$. Let $L_1(\mathcal{W}) = eee$ and $L_2(\mathcal{W}) = eed$. Computing the $L_2(L_1(\mathcal{W}))$ results to eee and $L_1(L_2(\mathcal{W}))$ to dde, and $eee \neq dde$. Thus, the operation $\star$ is not commutative.

A triplet subsequence in a SAX word will always map to a *shapeoid* according to the above proof. Each of the group elements via a projection function f, the string-based computation described in Sect. 3.1, maps to an element in the set of the described lexical *shapeoids*.

Note 1. The group of shapeoids resembles the family of the "3-transposition" groups instituted by Bernd Fischer [25], wherein our case, we use the set of the alphabet A in SAX to conjugate 3-transpositions.

Example 5 (cont'd). The forming group of a shapeoid extraction using a SAX alphabet of five letters results in a group G with 5^3 — 125 possible "3-transpositions". Each 3-transposition word is a shapeoid. For the sake of complexity and space, we will not enumerate all the elements of the group. However, with any input time series, we provided evidence above that the resulting multiset $S_\mathcal{W}^\sigma$, from Example 4, will always contain a valid element from the shapeoid extraction group G.

5   Conclusion and Discussion

Our paper presented a concept of time series primitives which are lightweight, interpretable and easy to understand. The direct connection with an algebraic *group* translates the feasibility of extracting a *shapeoid* from possible time series. The *shapeoid* preserves its structure while sliding the window on a SAX word representation of a time series. Finding *shapeoids* in a time series is a step towards its direct interpretation. However, it does not interpret the algorithm, leading to its explainability, as the latest requirements in the topic [10] propose. Due to the transformation of a time series to an abstracted representation, it is evident that it contains a minor level of information loss. This is tightly connected with selected parameters of SAX; i.e., the length of the SAX word or the size of the alphabet. Finding the optimal parameters for a time series is highly interwoven with the use case and the application at hand. Selecting a class of time series or a known set of time series with background knowledge (e.g., what kind of patterns one wants to extract and how they look like) will assist the initial configuration. Our proposal remains agnostic to the time series, and we assume optimal initial parameters for the extraction of appropriate *shapeoids* for a given task at hand. Moreover, the window size over the SAX word must remain on the size of three to accommodate the string-based extraction logic. Finally, the extraction order is sequential, and therefore this implies a temporal order preserving the morphology of the time series.

In the paper, we provide a theoretical evaluation for extracting the concept of *shapeoids* (cf. Sect. 4). As future work, we plan to develop our technique and evaluate it against real datasets. Moreover, we want to consider another symbolic representation similar to SAX, named Symbolic Fourier Approximation (SFA) [26] considering an improvement in accuracy and efficiency. The *shapeoid* extraction will remain intact, as the result of SFA is an equal symbolic representation to that of SAX. Concerning the use of group theory, we consider it an enlightening way to verify our approach, and we will pursue no further research.

Acknowledgements. The research leading to these results has received partial funding from Germany's Federal Ministry of Education and Research (BMBF) under HorME (01IS18072).

References

1. Doshi-Velez, F., Kim, B.: Towards a rigorous science of interpretable machine learning. arXiv preprint arXiv:1702.08608 (2017)

2. Yin, H., Yang, S., Zhu, X., Ma, S., Chen, L.: Symbolic representation based on trend features for biomedical data classification. Technol. Health Care **23**(s2), S501–S510 (2015)
3. Barnaghi, P.M., Bakar, A.A., Othman, Z.A.: Enhanced symbolic aggregate approximation method for financial time series data representation. In: 2012 6th International Conference on New Trends in Information Science, Service Science and Data Mining (ISSDM2012), pp. 790–795. IEEE (2012)
4. Kolozali, Ş., Puschmann, D., Bermudez-Edo, M., Barnaghi, P.: On the effect of adaptive and nonadaptive analysis of time-series sensory data. IEEE Internet Things J. **3**(6), 1084–1098 (2016)
5. Bifet, A.: Adaptive Stream Mining: Pattern Learning and Mining from Evolving Data Streams, vol. 207. IOS Press, Amsterdam (2010)
6. Fu, T.C.: A review on time series data mining. Eng. Appl. Artif. Intell. **24**(1), 164–181 (2011)
7. Wang, X., Mueen, A., Ding, H., Trajcevski, G., Scheuermann, P., Keogh, E.: Experimental comparison of representation methods and distance measures for time series data. Data Min. Knowl. Disc. **26**(2), 275–309 (2013)
8. Lin, J., Keogh, E., Lonardi, S., Chiu, B.: A symbolic representation of time series, with implications for streaming algorithms. In: Proceedings of the 8th ACM SIGMOD Workshop on Research Issues in Data Mining and Knowledge Discovery, pp. 2–11 (2003)
9. Bagnall, A., Lines, J., Bostrom, A., Large, J., Keogh, E.: The great time series classification bake off: a review and experimental evaluation of recent algorithmic advances. Data Min. Knowl. Disc. **31**(3), 606–660 (2016). https://doi.org/10.1007/s10618-016-0483-9
10. Nguyen, T.L., Gsponer, S., Ilie, I., Ifrim, G.: Interpretable time series classification using all-subsequence learning and symbolic representations in time and frequency domains. arXiv preprint arXiv:1808.04022 (2018)
11. Huysmans, J., Dejaeger, K., Mues, C., Vanthienen, J., Baesens, B.: An empirical evaluation of the comprehensibility of decision table, tree and rule based predictive models. Decis. Support Syst. **51**(1), 141–154 (2011)
12. Guidotti, R., Monreale, A., Ruggieri, S., Turini, F., Giannotti, F., Pedreschi, D.: A survey of methods for explaining black box models. ACM Comput. Surv. (CSUR) **51**(5), 1–42 (2018)
13. Senin, P., Malinchik, S.: SAX-VSM: interpretable time series classification using SAX and vector space model. In: 2013 IEEE 13th International Conference on Data Mining, pp. 1175–1180. IEEE (2013)
14. Large, J., Bagnall, A., Malinowski, S., Tavenard, R.: On time series classification with dictionary-based classifiers. Intell. Data Anal. **23**(5), 1073–1089 (2019)
15. Zhang, K., Li, Y., Chai, Y., Huang, L.: Trend-based symbolic aggregate approximation for time series representation. In: 2018 Chinese Control And Decision Conference (CCDC), pp. 2234–2240. IEEE (2018)
16. Tsitsipas, A., Schubert, L.: Modelling and reasoning for indirect sensing over discrete-time via Markov logic networks. In: Proceedings of the Twelfth International Workshop Modelling and Reasoning in Context (MRC 2021). CEUR-WS.org (2021)
17. Dummit, D.S., Foote, R.M.: Abstract Algebra, vol. 3. Wiley, Hoboken (2004)
18. Lang, S., et al.: Algebra. Springer, New York (2002)
19. Pinter, C.C.: A Book of Abstract Algebra. Courier Corporation, New York (2010)
20. Zassenhaus, H.: Rubik's cube: a toy, a Galois tool, group theory for everybody. Phys. A **114**(1–3), 629–637 (1982)

21. Joyner, D.: Adventures in Group Theory: Rubik's Cube, Merlin's machine, and Other Mathematical Toys. JHU Press, Baltimore (2008)
22. Keogh, E., Lin, J., Fu, A.: Hot SAX: efficiently finding the most unusual time series subsequence. In: Fifth IEEE International Conference on Data Mining (ICDM 2005), pp. 8-pp. IEEE (2005)
23. Lin, J., Khade, R., Li, Y.: Rotation-invariant similarity in time series using bag-of-patterns representation. J. Intell. Inf. Syst. **39**(2), 287–315 (2012)
24. Birnbach, S., Eberz, S.: Peeves: physical event verification in smart homes (2019)
25. Fischer, B.: Finite groups generated by 3-transpositions. I. Inventiones Mathematicae **13**(3), 232–246 (1971)
26. Schäfer, P., Högqvist, M.: SFA: a symbolic Fourier approximation and index for similarity search in high dimensional datasets. In: Proceedings of the 15th International Conference on Extending Database Technology, pp. 516–527 (2012)

Target Detection in Infrared Image of Transmission Line Based on Faster-RCNN

Shifeng Yan, Peipei Chen, Shili Liang$^{(\boxtimes)}$, Lei Zhang, and Xiuping Li

School of Physics, Northeast Normal University, Changchun 130024, China
lsl@nenu.edu.cn

Abstract. Compared with the visual image, the infrared image of the transmission line has lost some image characteristics and the image resolution is lower. In this paper, an improved Faster-RCNN method is used to locate the target in the infrared image of the transmission line. We first construct the infrared image data set of the transmission line and extract the image features by comparing different network models; then we increase the scale and candidate frame when generating target candidate regions in the region proposal network according to the small target features of the infrared image data set. The accuracy of the insulator string (AP) is improved by about 8.4%, and the average accuracy (mAP) is improved by about 3%. Experiments show that this method has higher recognition accuracy when detecting infrared image targets with lower resolution.

Keywords: Transmission line · Infrared image · Faster-RCNN · Target detection · Feature extraction network · Candidate box

1 Introduction

With the widespread application of unmanned aerial vehicle technology, the disadvantages of traditional manual methods have become more and more obvious, and it is becoming more and more convenient to use aircraft to check [10]. Infrared thermal imaging temperature measurement technology is widely used in the fields of power equipment detection and fault identification due to its characteristics such as small influence by electromagnetic fields, high detection efficiency, and safety in temperature measurement. Infrared detection technology is also widely used in the detection of transmission line faults.

The complexity of the transmission line environment makes it difficult to locate and identify the components of the transmission line. Zou [22] proposed a method for identifying and detecting bird's nests on transmission towers that integrates corner points, straight lines, colors, and shapes. Yan et al. [15] proposed an improved Otsu algorithm based on morphological methods to segment transmission line images, and then used a new filtering method to remove tiny noises according to the geometric characteristics of power lines. Zhu et al. [21] used color space conversion, Otsu segmentation algorithm and edge detection methods to mark the connected domain of the insulator string. Zhao et al. [20] used NSCT's gray entropy model to realize the automatic positioning of insulator

© Springer Nature Switzerland AG 2022
B. Li et al. (Eds.): ADMA 2021, LNAI 13088, pp. 276–287, 2022.
https://doi.org/10.1007/978-3-030-95408-6_21

strings in complex backgrounds. Liu et al. [8] used the relative position relationship between the power tower and the inspection aircraft as a priori information to roughly locate the power tower and then used machine learning to further locate it. Yetgin et al. [16] and others used a new strategy based on discrete cosine transform to detect power lines in visible light images or infrared images. Tong et al. [12] proposed a segmentation and identification method for insulators based on aerial images, which can effectively identify insulators operating online with high accuracy.

The traditional method of target detection method is more complicated, and the recognized target is relatively single. Deep learning has made great contributions in many applications [1, 19], such as Yue et al. [2, 3, 17, 18] proposed a series of deep learning-based models that effectively recognize human intentions via EEG signals analysis and have achieved brilliant recognition results. Deep learning theory is widely used in the fields of image recognition and target detection. Wang et al. [13] and others constructed a spiking neural network and designed a new infrared image edge detection method using the characteristics of spiking neurons. In 2014, Girshick et al. [4] first proposed the Region-CNN algorithm. First, the selective search algorithm (Selective Search, SS) extracts the target candidate area, then the deep convolutional network extracts the features, and finally the target category and location are output. In the continuous optimization based on Fast-RCNN [5], Faster-RCNN [9] has been proposed successively. Faster-RCNN algorithm uses RPN to complete the extraction of target candidate regions instead of SS algorithm, which realizes end-to-end training and detection. With the development of deep learning, deep learning methods have gradually been applied to the detection of transmission lines. Wang et al. [14] realized the positioning and identification of low-power components through the RCNN algorithm. Lin et al. [6] can maintain high recognition accuracy and speed in detecting images with different resolutions and different position angles by using the improved Faster-RCNN algorithm. Liu et al. [7] used Faster-RCNN algorithm to locate heating faults in infrared images of power transmission based on the image library of heating faults of power transmission. Tao et al. [11] and others proposed a new type of deep convolutional neural network cascade architecture, which can effectively detect insulator defects under various conditions.

Faster-RCNN is not widely used in power equipment, and there are few studies on using Faster-RCNN to detect the fault of power equipment in infrared images. Therefore, this paper adopts the improved Faster-RCNN algorithm, first establishes a database through infrared images of infrared video clips obtained by infrared cameras, and then realizes the identification and positioning of transmission line components.

2 Target Detection Algorithm Based on Infrared Image

2.1 Transmission Line Target Detection Algorithm

The combination of RPN and Fast-RCNN can be regarded as Faster-RCNN. RPN realizes the selection of target candidate regions, and Fast-RCNN realizes the classification and positioning of candidate regions. The two neural networks share the convolutional layer, and the feature maps of the convolutional layer are paired. By adjusting the two neural networks, the target detection and positioning of the infrared image are finally realized. The algorithm flow chart is shown as in Fig. 1.

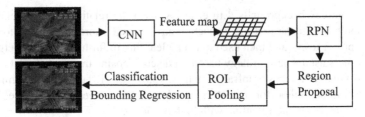

Fig. 1. Faster-RCNN algorithm flowchart

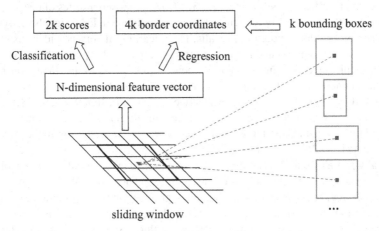

Fig. 2. RPN network

The RPN network searches for all target candidate regions on the feature map. The RPN network is shown in Fig. 2. For the feature map, the RPN generates 9 anchor boxes according to different proportions and different areas, and finally the sum of the anchor boxes generated by all pixels is k. The feature map is convolved with the 3×3 convolution kernel and sliding convolution, and then the category judgment and position determination are performed through two fully connected layers. The regression layer outputs the coordinates of k boxes; the classification layer outputs the probability of whether there is a target in the anchor box.

When the RPN network generates the candidate area, it uses the non-maximum suppression algorithm to remove the redundant candidate frame, and finally outputs the target candidate area with a higher score as the suggested area to the Fast-RCNN network; Finally, the fully connected layer calculates the classification score and boundary regression to realize the positioning in the recognition.

2.2 Faster-RCNN Structure Parameter Selection Optimization

Feature Extraction Network Model

The VGG16 is practical and performs well in the field of image recognition. They designed a residual module to train a deeper network. The residual module establishes a direct connection between input and output. MobileNet consists of two independent modules, 3 × 3 depthwise Conv (3 × 3 Depthwise Conv) and 1 × 1 convolution (1 × 1 Conv). The batch normalization unit BN and the nonlinear activation unit RELU are added to the output result. We compared the effects of three different feature extraction network models on the results.

Optimize RPN

All target candidate regions can be found on the feature map through the RPN network, which is composed of convolutional layers, etc. In the RPN network of the Faster-RCNN algorithm, there are preset 9 kinds of anchors corresponding to 3 kinds of scales and 3 kinds of aspect ratios. It can improve the accuracy to choose the appropriate scale and aspect ratio for different datasets. In the infrared image dataset produced in this article, the recognition rate of some insulator strings and other objects is low due to the small area occupied in the image. To solve the problem of low recognition rate caused by the small area occupied in the image, we have added a set of scales of 64^2 to the RPN network and added the candidate boxes' number from 9 to 12; the results show that the recognition rate has been significantly improved.

3 Experiment

3.1 Dataset Establishment

To obtain the dataset required for deep learning training, we made the dataset through the video collected by the infrared thermal imaging camera. The flow chart of our dataset's production is shown in Fig. 3. In this article, we intercepted the pictures in the transmission line video collected by the infrared thermal imaging camera, and then selected 850 clear pictures and marked the transmission lines, towers, and insulator strings in the pictures, and finally produced the VOC2007 dataset. During the labeling process, areas where the image is too blurry are not labelled. Deep learning often requires a lot of data training. To solve the insufficient of image data, we have expanded it by flipping and rotating the image. Then the data set was expanded to 3400 sheets, of which 3060 sheets were used as the training set and 340 sheets were used as the test set through data enhancement. An example of dataset annotation is shown in Fig. 4.

Fig. 3. Dataset production's flow chart.

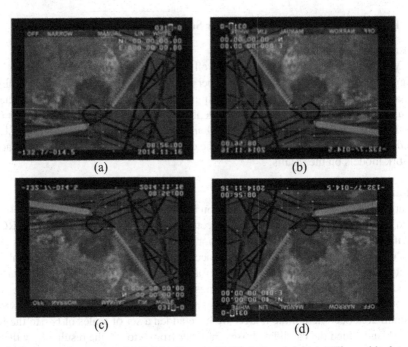

Fig. 4. Dataset enhancement. (a) Original image (b) Flip left and right (c) Flip upside down (d) Rotate 180°

Evaluation Index

To evaluate the effectiveness of Faster-RCNN in infrared image target detection, the mean Average Precision (mAP) is used as the evaluation standard. The mAP can effectively characterize the global performance of the algorithm.

Intersection over Union (IoU) is an important index to measure the coincidence degree of different regions on the same image. For the model prediction area D and the real labeled area G, the intersection ratio represents the ratio of their intersection and union. Specifically, it can be defined as:

$$IoU = \frac{D \cap G}{D \cup G} \tag{1}$$

When the IoU of the model predicted area D and the real labeled area G > 0.5, the predicted area is considered correct. True Positive (TP), False Positive (FP), and False Negative (FN) are basic indicators commonly used in machine learning. For a certain type of target in target detection, TP represents and marks The number of prediction regions with IoU > 0.5 (if there are multiple detection results that match the same labeled region, it will only be calculated once); FP means the number of prediction regions with IoU <= 0.5 in the labeled region and redundant detection results that match the same labeled region Quantity; FN represents the number of marked areas that have no matching results.

The mAP is calculated by precision (Precision, P) and recall (Recall, R). The expressions of precision rate and recall rate are as Eqs. (2) and (3).

$$Precision = TP/(TP + FP) \tag{2}$$

$$Recall = TP/(TP + FN) \tag{3}$$

3.2 Analysis of Results

Compare Different Convolutional Network Models

The VGG16, Resnet101, and MobileNet networks were selected for feature extraction, and different iterations were performed on the training data set. Table 1, Table 2, and Table 3 respectively represent the three network training results.

Table 1. Extracting network results based on VGG16 features.

Iters	Transmission line	Tower	Insulator	mAP
80000	0.899	0.9091	0.8136	0.8739
70000	0.8972	0.9091	0.8142	0.8735
60000	0.8971	0.9091	0.814	0.8734
50000	0.8854	0.9091	0.8135	0.8693
40000	0.8712	0.9091	0.8114	0.8639
30000	0.8326	0.9085	0.8057	0.8489
20000	0.7933	0.9061	0.8007	0.8333
10000	0.6229	0.9018	0.762	0.7622

Table 2. Extracting network results based on Resnet101 features.

Iters	Transmission line	Tower	Insulator	mAP
80000	0.8893	0.9091	0.8167	0.8717
70000	0.8891	0.9058	0.8167	0.8705
60000	0.8908	0.9071	0.8156	0.8712
50000	0.8553	0.9031	0.8134	0.8573
40000	0.8553	0.893	0.8117	0.8533
30000	0.8336	0.9091	0.7978	0.8468
20000	0.7092	0.9057	0.7978	0.8042
10000	0.6849	0.8979	0.7127	0.7652

Table 3. Extracting network results based on MobileNet features.

Iters	Transmission line	Tower	Insulator	mAP
80000	0.7924	0.9082	0.7772	0.8259
70000	0.7952	0.9082	0.7958	0.8331
60000	0.7853	0.9063	0.7731	0.8216
50000	0.7603	0.9037	0.7842	0.8161
40000	0.6869	0.9052	0.7155	0.7692
30000	0.6098	0.8957	0.7571	0.7542
20000	0.5845	0.8994	0.6483	0.7207
10000	0.5143	0.8704	0.6094	0.6647

The results show that the VGG16 network and Resnet101 network are better than the MobileNet network for target recognition in the transmission line. Therefore, we optimize the Faster-RCNN algorithm based on the VGG16 network and the Resnet101 network to improve the accuracy.

Parameter Optimization

When the proportion of the recognized object in the picture is relatively low, the recognition rate of the object will be significantly reduced. To solve the problem of the decline in the recognition rate caused by the low proportion, we have added a set of 64 × 64 scales to the Faster-RCNN based on VGG16 and ResNet101 to improve the recognition rate. The precision-recall curve of these networks before and after the improvement is shown in Fig. 5, and its statistical table is shown in Table 4.

We can see that Resnet101 performs slightly better than the VGG16 model after improvement from the above table. After adding a set of scales, the accuracy of the insulator string has been greatly improved, by about 8.4%, and the overall accuracy by about 3% which showing that the improved method has certain effectiveness.

To further reflect the improvement of network fine-tuning for classification, we show the change of the loss value when training the network with the number of iterations in Fig. 6.

We set the total number of iterations to 80,000, and then conducted four sets of experiments with VGG16 and ResNET101 as the feature extraction network and controlling whether to fine-tune as a condition.

It can be seen from the figure that whether VGG16 or ResNET101 is used as feature extraction, the fine-tuned network can converge at a faster speed and converge to a lower loss value.

From the perspective of different feature extraction networks, the ResNET101 network can converge at a smaller loss value than the VGG16 network. ResNET101 is more suitable for use as a feature extraction network in this study. This conclusion is consistent with what we have obtained from Table 4.

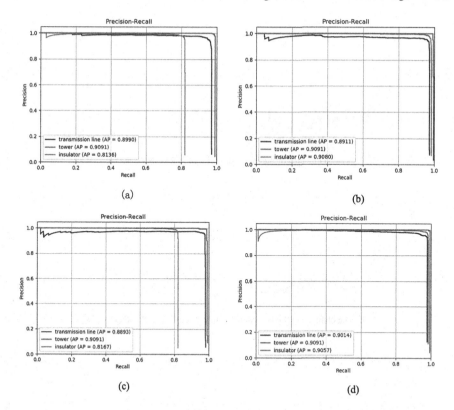

Fig. 5. The precision-recall graph. (a) Faster-RCNN (VGG16) precision-recall curve. (b) Improved Faster-RCNN (VGG16) precision-recall curve. (c) Faster-RCNN (ResNet101) precision-recall curve. (d) Improved Faster-RCNN (ResNet101) precision-recall curve.

Table 4. Comparison before and after parameter optimization

Neural networks	Number of candidate boxes	Target detection AP value/%			mAP/%
		Power line	Tower	Insulator	
Faster-RCNN (VGG16)	9	0.899	0.9091	0.8136	0.8739
Faster-RCNN (ResNet101)	9	0.8893	0.9091	0.8167	0.8717
Faster-RCNN (VGG16)	12	0.8911	0.9091	0.908	0.9027
Faster-RCNN (ResNet101)	12	0.9014	0.9091	0.9057	0.9054

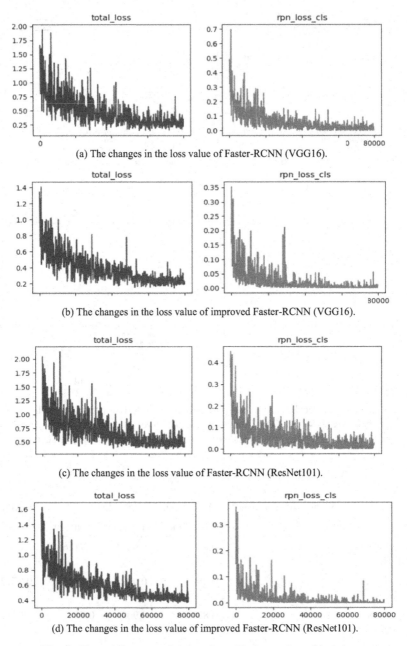

(a) The changes in the loss value of Faster-RCNN (VGG16).

(b) The changes in the loss value of improved Faster-RCNN (VGG16).

(c) The changes in the loss value of Faster-RCNN (ResNet101).

(d) The changes in the loss value of improved Faster-RCNN (ResNet101).

Fig. 6. The training network loss value with the number of iterations.

3.3 Experiment

According to the above improvement method, the Faster RCNN algorithm based on ResNet101 after adding a set of scales is finally selected and tested on the untrained data set. The testing effect is shown in Fig. 7. We can see that the algorithm accurately identifies transmission lines, insulator strings, and towers.

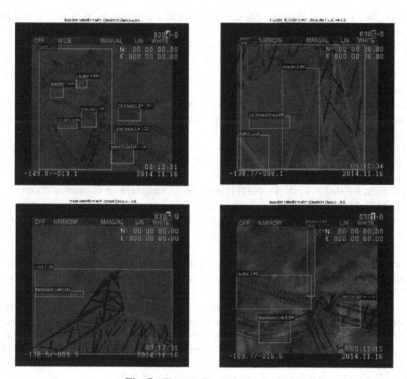

Fig. 7. The results on the test set.

4   Conclusion

For the difficult positioning of transmission line components under infrared image conditions, the Faster-RCNN algorithm is used to compare the target recognition effect of different feature extraction networks; we add a set of scales to solve the target area being too small.

The recognition accuracy of the insulator string is increased by about 8.4%, and the average recognition accuracy of the overall category is increased by about 3%, which verifies the effectiveness of the method. In future research, we will train the faulty equipment pictures of the transmission line and identify and locate the faulty device category and location.

Acknowledgements. This work was supported by the Jilin Provincial Science and Technology Department (NO.20190303016SF) and the 13th Five-year Plan for Science and Technology Project of the Education Department of Jilin Province (JJKH20170913KJ).

References

1. Chen, W., Long, G., Yao, L., Sheng, Q.: AMRNN: attended multi-task recurrent neural networks for dynamic illness severity prediction. World Wide Web **23**(5), 2753–2770 (2020)
2. Chen, W., Yue, L., Li, B., Wang, C., Sheng, Q.Z.: DAMTRNN: a delta attention-based multi-task RNN for intention recognition. In: Li, J., Wang, S., Qin, S., Li, X., Wang, S. (eds.) ADMA 2019. LNCS (LNAI), vol. 11888, pp. 373–388. Springer, Cham (2019). https://doi.org/10.1007/978-3-030-35231-8_27
3. Chen, W., et al.: EEG-based motion intention recognition via multi-task RNNs. In: Proceedings of the 2018 SIAM International Conference on Data Mining, Society for Industrial and Applied Mathematics, pp. 279–287 (2018)
4. Girshick, R., Donahue, J., Darrell, T., Malik, J.: Rich feature hierarchies for accurate object detection and semantic segmentation. In: IEEE International Conference on Computer Vision and Pattern Recognition, pp. 580–587 (2014)
5. Girshick, R.: Fast R-CNN. In: IEEE International Conference on Computer Vision (ICCV), pp. 1440–1448 (2015)
6. Lin, G., Wang, B., Peng, H., Wang, X., Chen, S., Zhang, L.: Multi-target detection and location of transmission line inspection image based on improved Faster-RCNN. Electr. Power Autom. Equipment **39**(5), 213–218 (2019)
7. Liu, Y., Pei, S., Wu, J.: Deep learning based target detection method for abnormal hot spots infrared images of transmission and transformation equipment. South. Power Syst. Technol. **13**(2), 27–33 (2018)
8. Liu, C., Wen, Y., Hua, W., Yang, G.: Detection of power poles based on fusion of geographical location information. J. Huazhong Univ. Sci. Technol. (Nat. Sci. Edn.) **41**(41), 208–210 (2013)
9. Ren, S., He, K., Girshick, R., Sun, J.: Faster R-CNN:towards real time object detection with region proposal networks. IEEE Trans. Pattern Anal. Mach. Intell. **39**(6), 1137–1149 (2017)
10. Tang, M., Dai, L., Lin, C., Wang, F., Song, F.: Application of unmanned aerial vehicle in inspecting transmission lines. Electr. Power **46**(3), 35–38 (2013)
11. Tao, X., Zhang, D., Wang, Z., Liu, X., Zhang, H., Xu, D.: Detection of power line insulator defects using aerial images analyzed with convolutional neural networks. IEEE Trans. Syst. Man Cybern. Syst. **50**(4), 1486–1498 (2018)
12. Tong, W., Li, B., Pei, L.: Extraction and recognition of insulator based on aerial image. In: 2011 International Conference on Electric Information and Control Engineering, Wuhan, pp. 4195–4198 (2011)
13. Wang, B., Chen, L., Zhang, Z.: A novel method on the edge detection of infrared image. Optik Int. J. Light Electr. Opt. **180**, 610–614 (2019)
14. Wang, W., Tian, B., Liu, Y., Liu, L., Li, J.: Study on the electrical devices detection in UAV images based on region based convolutional neural networks. J. Geo Inf. Sci. **19**(2), 256–263 (2017)
15. Yan, S., Jin, L., Duan, S., Zhao, L., Yao, C., Zhang, W., Power line image segmentation and extra matter recognition based on improved Otsu algorithm. In: 2013 2nd International Conference on Electric Power Equipment - Switching Technology (ICEPE-ST), Matsue, pp. 1–4 (2013)
16. Yetgin, Ö., Gerek, Ö.N.: Automatic recognition of scenes with power line wires in real life aerial images using DCT-based features digit. Sig. Process **77**, 102–119 (2018)

17. Yue, L., Shen, H., Wang, S.: Exploring BCI control in smart environments: intention recognition via EEG representation enhancement learning. ACM Trans. Knowl. Discov. Data (TKDD) **15**(5), 1–20 (2021)
18. Yue, L., Tian, D., Jiang, J., Yao, L., Chen, W., Zhao, X.: Intention Recognition from Spatio-Temporal Representation of EEG Signals. In: ADC, pp. 1–12 (2021)
19. Yue, L., Tian, D., Chen, W., Han, X., Yin, M.: Deep learning for heterogeneous medical data analysis. World Wide Web **23**(5), 2715–2737 (2020)
20. Zhao, Z., Wang, L.: Aerial insulator string image automatic location method. Chin. J. Sci. Instrum. **35**(3), 558–565 (2014)
21. Zhu, S.: Insulator Identification and Location of High Voltage Transmission Line Image. Anhui University (2018)
22. Zou, D.: Research on Recognition of Key Components and Detection of Anomaly in Transmission Line. School of Electrical and Electronic Engineering, North China Electric Power University (2017)

Automatic Quality Improvement of Data on the Evolution of 2D Regions

Rogério Luís de C. Costa[1]([⊠])[iD] and José Moreira[2][iD]

[1] CIIC, Polytechnic of Leiria, 2411-901 Leiria, Portugal
`rogerio.l.costa@ipleiria.pt`
[2] DETI - IEETA, University of Aveiro, 3810-193 Aveiro, Portugal
`jose.moreira@ua.pt`

Abstract. This work deals with data cleaning and quality improvement when representing the evolution of 2D regions extracted from real-world observations. It presents a method that combines quadtrees and time series to identify inconsistencies and poor-quality data in a sequence of 2D regions. Our algorithm splits a 2D space recursively into buckets and creates time series using spatial functions on bucket-delimited subregions. Smaller buckets represent the subregions with a higher number of inconsistencies over time. Then, it uses time series outlier detection methods and consistency metrics to identify polygons that are poor-quality representations and remove them from the original sequence. The proposed method identifies errors and inaccuracies even if they occur in several consecutive observations. We evaluated our strategy using a dataset extracted from real-world videos and compared it with another method from the literature. The results prove the effectiveness of this proposal.

Keywords: Spatio-temporal data · Quadtree · Time series · Data quality · Prophet

1 Introduction

Using spatio-temporal data to represent real-world phenomena is a promising approach with application in several areas, including geosciences and microbiology. These data can be modelled using abstractions such as moving points and moving regions. The latter can represent the spatial evolution of objects or events such as icebergs, forest fires, and cells, over time. In this approach, the position and shape of the regions are captured at several timestamps (e.g., photos and videos), the region of interest in each observation is segmented and simplified, and the resulting polygons can be loaded into a database for subsequent analysis.

The accurate representation of the data extracted from raw sources can be a challenging task due to noise, the presence of obstacles and other issues related to the acquisition process, the characteristics of the events of interest and the surrounding environment, among others. Previous work on spatio-temporal databases and data mining assumes that the data was prepossessed and that

© Springer Nature Switzerland AG 2022
B. Li et al. (Eds.): ADMA 2021, LNAI 13088, pp. 288–300, 2022.
https://doi.org/10.1007/978-3-030-95408-6_22

there are sequences of geometries representing the phenomena accurately. However, very few works exist on transforming raw data (e.g., aerial images and videos) into good quality spatio-temporal data.

One of the key challenges is identifying data (or features) that exhibit abnormal behaviour, either spatially or temporally [5,8]. Research in this area mainly focuses on spatio-temporal clustering, and its goal is to find whether an instance behaves abnormally regarding its spatial neighbors [2] or to quantify the so-called outlierness of an instance [8]. Most of the existing work deals with point data and does not considers that the instances or phenomena of interest may have a spatial extension (shape) that changes over time. In such a situation, values are not singular, and inconsistencies may be partial (local), e.g., a part of the region of interest may behave abnormally. The use of global measures such as the area, perimeter or Haussdorf distance is not enough to detect these kinds of issues because some local inconsistencies can be mitigated or even cancelled out by other inconsistencies in the same instance, or some instances can be consistent with neighbouring instances, but inconsistent regarding the time series as a whole. Thus, in addition to handling noisy data, it is also necessary to drill down and analyze specific parts of the input data either spatially and temporally.

This work deals with spatio-temporal data cleaning and presents an approach that automatically identifies and removes poor-quality data. The data are sequences of spatial objects with extension, and the aim is to find the observations (snapshots) that best represent a phenomenon of interest along time. It is assumed that behavioural patterns exist, allowing to assess the quality of the data. We present a method that splits the evolution of a region of interest into buckets and evaluates the spatial evolution of the subregion in each bucket. Buckets are parts of a quadtree. Their number and size vary according to the spatial evolution of the region of interest in each bucket. Then, we define a time series for each bucket. We employ spatial functions on the subregions delimited by each bucket to calculate the time-series values. Consistency checks are applied to select the best (or worst) observations using a time series forecasting method to determine a trend on the spatial behaviour of the phenomenon in each bucket and to identify deviations from the expected behaviour (i.e., outliers).

The proposed method is automatic and does not need user intervention, which is especially useful when dealing with videos with thousands of frames. The basic principle is that behavioural patterns can be used to assess whether the representation of a spatio-temporal phenomenon is coherent. For instance, a moving region representing the spread of a forest fire or the expansion/retraction of glaciers should increase/decrease monotonously during a certain time. The quality of the input data is a key factor in representing real-world phenomena in spatio-temporal databases and data mining.

2   Data Quality Improvement

Data quality can be measured according to several dimensions, like accuracy, consistency, completeness and validity. For instance, consider a set of polygons representing the extent of a glacier over time, extracted from a sequence of satellite images. As the source images may contain clouds covering part of the glacier, polygons representing the glacier over time may be much larger (e.g., the polygons may include clouds as part of the glacier) or smaller (e.g., the polygons do not represent parts of the glacier hidden by clouds) than expected. Determining whether the spatial representation of a phenomenon at a given moment is good or poor is difficult or even impossible in some cases. However, since the behavior of real-world phenomena is not random, it is possible to assume certain patterns of evolution over time and space, for instance, the extent (size) of a glacier should decrease monotonously during the summer and increase monotonously during the winter.

2.1   Creating Quadtree-Based Time Series

The input data consists of a series of n observations representing the geometry (position and shape) of a real-world object or event (moving region) over time. Let p_i be the polygon that represents the moving region at timestamp t_i and P the set of all polygons defined as follows.

$$P = \{p_i \mid 1 \leq i \leq n\} \tag{1}$$

The problem that arises is how to automatically identify which geometries should be used (or rejected) to represent the moving region. The proposed method uses consistency checks and spatial functions to compare the geometry of the polygons with each other. We want to use only implicit information in the time series and so, there are no user input during the data selection process. Let $g(p_i)$ be a spatial function returning a real value, e.g., the area or the perimeter of a polygon (p_i), or a measure (Hausdorff distance, Jaccard Index, etc.) between p_i and another polygon in P,

$$U = f(g(P)) \tag{2}$$

be a function that computes a quality value (U) denoting the number of inconsistencies in P, and f a function that performs user-defined consistency checks on the values of $g(P)$. For instance, considering that g is a function returning the area of a polygon p_i at time t_i, and assuming that the area of a glacier must be a monotonously decreasing function (due to melting), then $f(g(P))$ would return the number of cases such that $g(p_{i+1}) > g(pi)$.

The decomposition of the space is defined as follows. Let $BB(p_i)$ be the bounding box of a polygon p_i. The region of interest RI (Eq. 3) is the union of all bounding boxes obtained when applying BB to each polygon in P.

$$RI = \bigcup_{i=1}^{n} BB(p_i) \tag{3}$$

We recursively split the RI space into quadrants (buckets) to create the quadtree R. The intersection of a polygon p_i with the boundary of each bucket b_k ($1 \leq k \leq q \mid q$ is the number of buckets in R) defines a subregion $s_{i,k}$. Note that $s_{i,k}$ can be an empty polygon. Let $S(k)$ be the set of moving subregions for a given bucket k, as defined in Eq. 4.

$$S(k) = \{s_{i,k} \mid 1 \leq i \leq n\} \tag{4}$$

From the above, the quality metric for each quadrant is $U(k) = f(g(S(k)))$. If the value of $U(k)$ is greater than a threshold value δ, the bucket k is split again into four quadrants. The quality evaluation and bucket splitting continue recursively until $U(k) \leq \delta$, or a bucket is too small (i.e., bucket size $\leq \alpha$).

2.2 Identifying and Removing Inconsistent Data

Algorithm 1 outlines how to detect and remove poor-quality data from the dataset. The first step is to choose a bucket b_k ($1 \leq k \leq q$) (line 6). $SelectBucket$ gets k as input to prevent that the same bucket keeps being selected several times in a row. The algorithm can converge more or less quickly to the desired result depending on the order in which the buckets are selected. The alternatives considered in this work are listed in Sect. 3.4.

Algorithm 1. Removing poor-quality polygons

1: **Input:** P, R, S
2: **Output:** set of consistent p_i
3: **Method:**
4:    $ConsistentP \leftarrow P; \ k \leftarrow -1; \ U \leftarrow f(ConsistentP);$
5:    **while** $(U > 0) \wedge len(ConsistentP) > \tau)$ **do**
6:       $k \leftarrow SelectBucket(R, k)$
7:       $TimestampsList \leftarrow LookForOutliers(S(k))$
8:       $U' \leftarrow f(ConsistentP - P_{TimestampsList})$
9:       **if** $(U - U') > (\epsilon * len(TimestampsList))$ **then**
10:          $ConsistentP \leftarrow ConsistentP - P_{TimestampsList}; \ U \leftarrow U'$
11:       **end if**
12:    **end while**
13:    **return** $ConsistentP$

The next step (line 7) is to build a feature-based time series and identify outliers. As the geometries in $S(k)$ represent the temporal evolution of a moving subregion, we can apply a spatial function (g), e.g., perimeter or area, on each $s_{i,k}$ to create a time series for a bucket k ($g(S(k))$). The polygons of the timestamps in $TimestampsList$ are considered inaccurate and removed from the dataset (lines 8–11) if their removal significantly increases the quality of the representation of the moving region. To verify this, we compare the decrease in the U metric with the number of polygons removed (ϵ controls the minimum required percentage of

U decrease). Bucket selection, outlier identification, and the quality evaluation stop when there are no inconsistencies or the number of remaining polygons is smaller than a predefined threshold (τ in Algorithm 1).

3   Experimental Evaluation

The method proposed in this paper assumes that spatio-temporal behavioural patterns exist in some use cases, and this knowledge can be used to assess the quality of the data representing real-world phenomena. The application example in this work uses data on the evolution of a controlled forest fire extracted from a video. In this case, the assumption is that the coverage of the burned area over time should grow monotonously, i.e., zones that are given as burned at a certain time cannot be considered not burned at a later time. This kind of data can be used, for instance, in studies on the propagation of forest fires or the emission of pollutants into the atmosphere.

3.1   Datasets and Tools

The case study consists of extracting data about the evolution of a controlled forest fire from a video captured at Pinhão Cel, Portugal, using UAVs. The video is available at [13]. The duration is 15 min and the frame rate is 25 fps. First, we used a segmentation algorithm to obtain a representation of the burned area in each video frame, as exemplified in Fig. 1.

The frames in Figs. 1a and 1b consist of two aerial images near the beginning and the ending of the video, respectively. The polygon in Fig. 2b represents the burned area extracted from a frame using segmentation and simplification [12,14] algorithms. The definition of the polygon representing the burned area is loaded into a database. This process may be applied over all the frames in a video, thus building a spatio-temporal dataset.

(a) Near the beginning of the video   (b) Near the end of the video

Fig. 1. Sample frames

The dataset consists of an ordered sequence of 22,500 observations. Each observation comprises a polygon (p_i) representing the shape of the burned area at a certain time (t_i). Polygons are represented in WKT (Well-Known Text format). The main challenges consist of dealing with noisy data (the height of the flames is highly variable, and the shape of the fireline in consecutive frames is erratic) and identifying outliers due to occlusion of the region of interest by smoke. Several polygons include part of the smoke with the burned area, while others are affected by the occlusion of the area of interest by smoke.

As these obstacles may remain during several video frames, there may exist sequences whose observations are consistent with each other, but they are poor quality representations regarding the whole phenomenon. For instance, Fig. 2 presents a sequence with three (consistent) frames in which the segmentation of the burned area (wrongly) incorporated part of the smoke. On the other hand, there also are sequences in which the segmented burned area does not include part of the burned area due to dense smoke. These are clusters of outliers, and their presence makes the identification of poor quality data more challenging [7]. If the data resulting from the segmentation and simplification processes are not filtered to remove inaccurate representations, the resulting temporal sequence will be inconsistent (e.g., a zone marked as burned at a given time cannot be marked as not burned at a later time) and unrepresentative of the phenomenon under study. This is why it is necessary to define consistency rules and methods to determine which are the observations in a time series that best represent the phenomenon to be modelled.

We used PostgreSQL 11, PostGIS 2.5.3, and GEOS 3.7.2 to store the polygons, create the quadtree, compute quality metrics, choose the bucket to be evaluated, and store selected geometries. Polygons were stored using PostGIS's geometry data. Facebook's Prophet [9] was used for time series outlier detection. We used a Jupyter Notebook to control the overall algorithm execution, running Facebook's Prophet and accessing PostgreSQL to get and update data.

3.2   Quadtree Generation

The quadtree creation routine has two main parameters: (i) α, which represents the lowest area allowed for a bucket, and (ii) δ, which represents the highest allowed value for U. We used $\alpha = 6,400$ (which represents approximately 2,0% of the area burned in the first frame, 1,5% of the area burned in the last frame, and 1,2% of the area of the root bucket) and $\alpha = 81$, (approximately 12% of the initial value of U). We experimentally tuned those parameters to avoid creating too many small buckets. Equation 5 presents the definition of the spatial function g. In our experiments, U represents the number of observations in which any polygon generated by $p(i) - p(i+1)$ is greater than a certain percentage (μ) of $p(i)$ ($1 \leqslant i \leq n - 1$).

$$U = Count(\frac{A(DUMP(p(t) - p(t+1)))}{A(p(t))} > \mu) \tag{5}$$

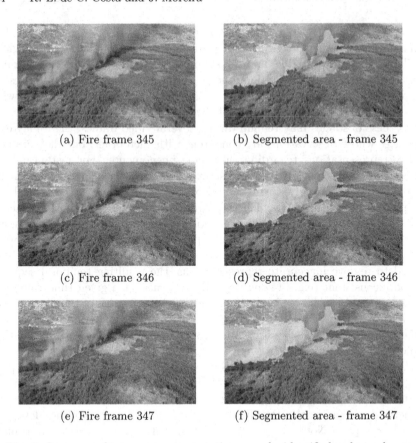

(a) Fire frame 345

(b) Segmented area - frame 345

(c) Fire frame 346

(d) Segmented area - frame 346

(e) Fire frame 347

(f) Segmented area - frame 347

Fig. 2. Sequence of inaccurate segmentation - smoke identified as burned area

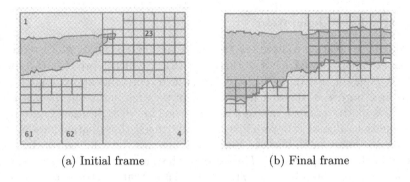

(a) Initial frame

(b) Final frame

Fig. 3. Quadtree over burned areas (Color figure online)

The final quadtree has 82 buckets and a depth of 5. Figure 3a presents the quadtree and the burned area at the first frame, while Fig. 3b presents the quadtree and the burned area at the last video frame. Figure 3a also presents the identification number (in red) of some large buckets. Bucket 1 (in the upper-left of Fig. 3a) comprises almost all the burned area identified in the initial polygon.

As the number of inconsistencies found in the subregion defined by that bucket for all observations is smaller than the threshold value, the bucket was not split. Indeed, the inconsistencies occurred mostly in the area that burned during the video recording. As the fire propagates mostly from left to right, and the smoke propagates mostly to the upper-right, most of the buckets of depth 5 are in the top-right (Fig. 3a, near bucket 23). Buckets 61 and 62 do not limit a burned area at any frame. All other buckets (including the ones that do not limit any burned area in the first and final polygons - e.g. bucket number 4) limit a sub-region identified as burned in some polygons of the temporal series. Indeed, the buckets that do not limit a subregion burned at Fig. 3b are in areas that didn't burn during the forest fire. Any observations with polygons that intersect these buckets are inaccurate representations and should be filtered out.

3.3   Building the Time Series

We need to choose a spatial function (g) to create the time series. A straightforward approach is to use the area of the polygons in the time series. Although the area of the polygons should grow over time (as the polygons represent the area burned by a fire), there is another important geometric characteristic to be considered: the polygon (p_i) representing the burned area at a given time t_i should be contained in the polygon representing the burned area at the subsequent time t_{i+1} ($p_i \subseteq p_{i+1}$). This property does not hold in every case if we consider functions like the area of the polygons. Thus, to create the time series, we used the Jaccard Index (JI) between the polygons p_i and p_n (where n represents the last polygon in the time series) as defined in Eq. 6.

$$JI(p_n, p_i) = \frac{|p_n \cap p_i|}{|p_1 \cup p_i|} \mid 1 \leq i \leq n \tag{6}$$

This feature is suitable to be used in this context because it depends not only on the size of the polygons but also on their shape and position over time. Ideally, the value of $JI(p_i, p_n)$ should be monotonically increasing. Its value may start in any range between 0 and 1, depending on if the (sub)region area was initially burned or not. The final value of JI for any burned subregion should be 1. As depicted in Fig. 4a, the JI for the original time series is far from being a monotonically increasing function.

After creating the quadtree and choosing the spatial function, we created the time series. For each bucket k, we computed the temporal evolution of the JI ($s_{i,k}$). Figures 4b and 4c present the time series created for the subregions delimited by buckets 1 and 23, respectively (see Fig. 3a for bucket number and position). Both series should be monotonically increasing, as discussed in the previous section, but that is still not the case. Note that the JI series for bucket 23 is very erratic (this bucket is in the upper right corner of the area captured by the video, where there is heavy smoke in most of the frames).

Some buckets do no intersect the final polygon in the time series. As the burned area in a forest fire always grows, buckets without intersecting polygons in the last timestamp representation should not intersect polygons in previous timestamps representations. Hence, the observations on which such an intersection is not empty (more than 5,000) correspond to inaccurate data and must be removed from the time series. Recalculating the JI for the reminder observations, the time series is still far from being a monotonically increasing function.

3.4   Consistent Data Selection

We used Facebook's Prophet to look for outliers in time series. It is a time series forecasting tool based on an additive model that is robust to missing data, which means that we can remove inconsistent polygons from the dataset and still use Prophet to detect outliers over the remaining polygons in the time series. Besides fitting a trend (named $yhat$) to a time series, Prophet also provides uncertainty intervals delimited by upper and lower values (named $yhat\_upper$ and $yhat\_lower$, respectively).

We considered that any (JI) value outside the uncertainty interval is an outlier. The width of the uncertainty intervals is configurable. Although the default value is 0.8, we got better results when using values close to 1. For instance, when executing our algorithm with a given configuration (bucket-selection based on the highest value of U and $\epsilon = 0.5$), a change on the uncertainty interval width from 0.98 to 0.99 results in an increase of almost 25% on the number of selected good quality polygon representations at the end of the algorithm's execution.

At this point, we have several time series created (one per bucket) and the order in which they would be evaluated could influence the number of evaluations needed to reach the final result. We experimentally evaluated some alternatives, like starting with the time series related to buckets closest to the first polygon's centroid, starting with the ones of buckets faraway to the centroid of the first polygon, etc. We obtained the best results when choosing, at each round, the time series of the bucket with the highest value of U.

After each outlier selection execution, the algorithm tests if removing the outliers from the dataset would improve consistency. Some alternatives were evaluated for the value of ϵ (inconsistency reduction factor in Algorithm 1). The best results were obtained when starting with a relatively high value of ϵ, and then decreasing ϵ's when all the buckets have been analyzed at least one time. This way, the algorithm initially removes the extreme JI values at each bucket. Then, at each reevaluation step, the algorithm becomes less demanding and allows the removal of a certain number of polygons to have a lower effect in reducing dataset inconsistency.

Starting with $\epsilon = 0.96$, an uncertainty interval width of 0.99, and reducing the value of ϵ by 0.02 after all buckets are verified, the algorithm identified a consistent dataset composed of 4.594 polygons. Figure 4d presents the JI evolution at the end of the process (consistent dataset). The trend is near-optimal, with small inconsistencies (that would be considered adequate for this kind of data) and the monotonically increasing behaviour is represented in Fig. 4d by the exponential moving average of the JI evolution.

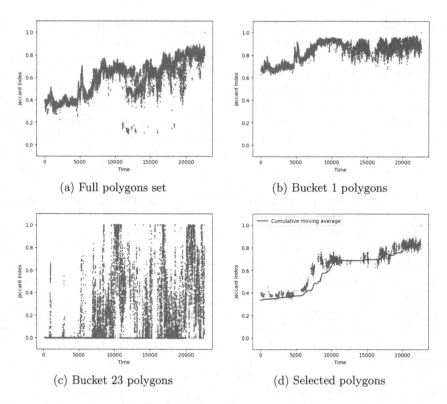

(a) Full polygons set

(b) Bucket 1 polygons

(c) Bucket 23 polygons

(d) Selected polygons

Fig. 4. JI evolution for full polygons set, bucket-based polygons and final polygons set

To build the consistent dataset, the algorithm processed each bucket 7 times and executed Prophet 792 times. In 92% of Prophet executions, the quality improvement achieved by removing the proposed outliers (candidates) was below a predefined threshold. In such cases, the algorithm didn't remove the corresponding polygons from the dataset, which confirms the importance of the quality improvement check. Finally, the number of consistent polygons identified by the proposed algorithm is 27% higher than the number of polygons selected in [6].

4   Related Work

Outliers generally refer to misrepresentations of real-world objects or phenomena [7]. They usually result from anomalies, noise, and unusual events [5].

In [15], the authors use spatio-temporal data mining on precipitation data. First, the algorithm finds the top-k highest discrepancy regions at a time. Then, it stretches each of the top-k outliers by a threshold factor, resulting in several stretched regions per period. For each period (e.g., year), the algorithm compares the stretched regions with other regions. Any region framed into a stretched region is considered an outlier. Finally, outliers are organized in a tree, which keeps track of when the outlier occurred and the order of outlier identification.

Cheng and Li [5] present an approach for outlier detection in spatio-temporal data with application to coastal geomorphological studies. The first step consists of the classification and clustering of the input data to create regions that have a semantic meaning, e.g., foreshore, beach or foredune. In the second step, the spatial scale of the identified objects is changed to make the smaller ones disappear. Finally, results obtained from steps 1 and 2 are compared and the objects identified in step 1 that are missing in step 2 are potential outliers. This strategy presupposes the identification of several objects of interest in a single image and removing those that are considered outliers, which is different from the case we are dealing with in this work.

There are also works specialized on detecting outliers in data streams. They are mainly focused on generating change alerts, and two types of data changes are considered: gradual change (drift) and abrupt change (shift) [3]. In addition, [16] considers that there may exist multiple data series that co-evolve over time. Other work on outlier identification in time series and data streams includes [1,4, 10,11]. The latter presents surveys on anomaly and outlier detection techniques. However, all these works deal only with point data and do not consider that the event or phenomena of interest may have a spatial extension (geometry) that evolves over time.

In [6], Costa et al. use consistency rules and geometric operations to remove outliers from a spatio-temporal data series. First, two key representations are selected, visually verified and manually adjusted. Then, geometric operations are applied to compare the verified representations with the other representations between them. Consistency checks are applied over the resulting set and outliers are identified. Then, the process restarts with the selection of a new key representation, and continues until a required consistency level is achieved. The goal is similar to the one proposed in this work, however, the method described in [6] requires the user to select by visual inspection, the key (good quality) observations in the time series until reaching the desired result.

5   Conclusions and Future Work

Transforming real-world data (e.g., videos and images) into spatio-temporal data is a challenging task, as they usually present several types of issues, e.g., noise and occlusions. In this work, we deal with finding inconsistent data in a series of polygons used to represent the spatio-temporal evolution of a moving region. As inconsistencies do not spatially affect the polygons uniformly, the first step in our method is to split the phenomenon representation into buckets, thus creating subregions and multiple (series of) polygons (delimited by a quadtree). The number and size of buckets depend on the quality of the region representation over time. We build time series on the evolution of spatial features of bucket-delimited regions. Then, our proposal uses time-series outlier detection techniques to identify timestamps with inaccurate polygons.

We experimentally use Facebook's Prophet for such a purpose. Then, we evaluate if the removal of outlier candidates from the time series would increase the dataset's quality. We tested our proposals using a real-world dataset and obtained better results than previous approaches from the literature.

As future work, we plan to evaluate our approach in other real-world videos and use the identified high-quality phenomena representations (i.e., polygons) to represent real-world objects and phenomena in a spatio-temporal database.

Acknowledgments. This work is partially funded by National Funds through the FCT (Foundation for Science and Technology) in the context of the projects UIDB/04524/2020, UIDB/00127/2020 and POCI-01-0145-FEDER-032636, and under the Scientific Employment Stimulus - Institutional Call - CEECINST/00051/2018.

References

1. Adam, N.R., Janeja, V.P., Atluri, V.: Neighborhood based detection of anomalies in high dimensional spatio-temporal sensor datasets. In: Proceedings of the 2004 ACM Symposium on Applied Computing, pp. 576–583. SAC 04 (2004)
2. Aggarwal, C.C.: An introduction to outlier analysis. In: Outlier Analysis, pp. 1–34. Springer, Cham (2017). https://doi.org/10.1007/978-3-319-47578-3_1
3. Appice, A., Guccione, P., Malerba, D., Ciampi, A.: Dealing with temporal and spatial correlations to classify outliers in geophysical data streams. Inf. Sci. **285**, 162–180 (2014)
4. Birant, D., Kut, A.: Spatio-temporal outlier detection in large databases. In: 28th International Conference on Information Technology Interfaces, pp. 179–184 (2006)
5. Cheng, T., Li, Z.: A multiscale approach for spatio-temporal outlier detection. Trans. GIS **10**(2), 253–263 (2006)
6. Costa, R.L.C., Miranda, E., Dias, P., Moreira, J.: Experience: quality assessment and improvement on a forest fire dataset. J. Data Inf. Q. **13**(1), 1–13 (2021). https://doi.org/10.1145/3428155
7. D'Urso, C.: Experience: glitches in databases, how to ensure data quality by outlier detection techniques. J. Data Inf. Q. **7**(3), 1–22 (2016)
8. Duggimpudi, M.B., Abbady, S., Chen, J., Raghavan, V.V.: Spatio-temporal outlier detection algorithms based on computing behavioral outlierness factor. Data Knowl. Eng. **122**, 1–24 (2019)
9. Facebook: Prophet: forecasting at scale (2017). https://research.fb.com/blog/2017/02/prophet-forecasting-at-scale/
10. Gupta, M., Gao, J., Aggarwal, C.C., Han, J.: Outlier detection for temporal data: a survey. IEEE Trans. Knowl. Data Eng. **26**(9), 2250–2267 (2014)
11. Kwon, D., Kim, H., Kim, J., Suh, S.C., Kim, I., Kim, K.J.: A survey of deep learning-based network anomaly detection. Cluster Comput. **22**(1), 949–961 (2017). https://doi.org/10.1007/s10586-017-1117-8
12. Miranda., E., Costa., R.L.C., Dias., P., Moreira., J.: Matching-aware shape simplification. In: Proceedings of the 15th International Joint Conference on Computer Vision, Imaging and Computer Graphics Theory and Applications - GRAPP, pp. 279–286. INSTICC, SciTePress (2020). https://doi.org/10.5220/0008969402790286
13. MoST-Team: Most forest fire dataset (2020). http://most.web.ua.pt/Video15minImagesWKT.zip

14. Visvalingam, M., Whyatt, J.D.: Line generalisation by repeated elimination of points. The cartographic J. **30**(1), 46–51 (1993)
15. Wu, E., Liu, W., Chawla, S.: Spatio-temporal outlier detection in precipitation data. In: Gaber, M.M., Vatsavai, R.R., Omitaomu, O.A., Gama, J., Chawla, N.V., Ganguly, A.R. (eds.) Sensor-KDD 2008. LNCS, vol. 5840, pp. 115–133. Springer, Heidelberg (2010). https://doi.org/10.1007/978-3-642-12519-5_7
16. Yi, B., Sidiropoulos, N.D., Johnson, T., Jagadish, H.V., Faloutsos, C., Biliris, A.: Online data mining for co-evolving time sequences. In: Proceedings of 16th International Conference on Data Engineering, pp. 13–22 (2000)

Cross-modal Data Linkage for Common Entity Identification

Pragya Prakash[1], Jay Rawal[1], Snehal Gupta[1], Deepak P[2(✉)],
and Mukesh Mohania[1]

[1] IIIT Delhi, New Delhi, India
{pragya16067,jay17240,snehal16201,mukesh}@iiitd.ac.in
[2] Queen's University Belfast, Belfast, UK
deepaksp@acm.org

Abstract. Multi-modal data is becoming pervasive in the digital era, providing compelling scenarios that require cross-modal linkage such as linking image data with databases. We outline a critical matching/linking task within that space, which we call cross-modal common entity identification. This involves linking images with structured databases with the aid of available unstructured information. We propose a framework and method, *ICE*, which embodies a structured approach for the same involving information extraction from images and person matching followed by identifying a common entity that unites people represented in the image. We curate data sources from the entertainment domain, upon which we illustrate the effectiveness of our method. We hope *ICE* will generate interest in other tasks within the realm of multi-modal data processing in the intersection of image processing, NLP and databases.

1 Introduction

The pervasive nature of digital data has enabled several technologies, making data-driven AI technologies a mainstay in our everyday lives. Digital data appears in a variety of different forms: images, videos, text, numeric data and what not. Mixed-modality data has also become quite common in this era; for example, social media posts routinely contain text in the company of images and videos. The same phenomenon manifesting in a variety of different modalities, such as the same information in a social media post being covered through text as well as images and video, has inspired much interest in the discipline of multi-modal data fusion [9]. Techniques from the family, such as those for multi-view clustering [5] and others [4], often assume the existence of *parallel* data, where there is a linkage between the different modalities. This is most often the case; the text and image in a social media post are linked through belonging to the same social media post, whereas the results of multiple medical tests (e.g., X-ray images, structured results from blood tests etc.) that belong to the same individual are linked through the unique id associated with the individual.

P. Prakash, J. Rawal and S. Gupta—Contributed equally to this research.

© Springer Nature Switzerland AG 2022
B. Li et al. (Eds.): ADMA 2021, LNAI 13088, pp. 301–313, 2022.
https://doi.org/10.1007/978-3-030-95408-6_23

However, in a number of modern day scenarios, such linkages are often missing or complex. For example, a photograph from an all-hands meeting in an organization may involve several employees in the organization, thus conceptually linking the photograph with a plurality of records in an organizational HR database. To enable effective organization and search over such media records, it would be necessary to identify such linkages and make them explicit. The analogous task in text data processing is that of *entity linking* [13] which involves identifying mentions of entities in text, and collectively disambiguating a set of such entity mentions to form linkages with a structured knowledge base such as Wikipedia. The corresponding task in the image domain, that of learning cross-linkages between images and structured databases, is neither straightforward nor well-defined. However, aided by the availability of image analytics APIs that can identify information nuggets from within images, there is an opportunity to address cross-modal tasks without delving into the nuances of image processing, a significantly different task from text and relational data mining.

We address a particular task in the realm of forming linkages between images and structured databases with the aid of external unstructured data. Consider an image that contains information about multiple real-world people whose information is held within a structured data source. With the aid of limited high-level image analytics and image tagging information, we would like to identify the *common entity* in the structured information source which unifies the multiple people in the image. For example, an image from a historic world cup football game could, through the (possibly imprecise) identification of players and (reasonably accurate) linking to player databases, be matched to the record corresponding to the edition of the world cup involved, or better, to the record corresponding to the precise game. In other words, the collective information embodied across the different individuals in the image is used together to pinpoint the common entity of interest. The task is of utility in multiple domains where images may need to be contextualized using a common entity. Our core contribution is a framework and method, codenamed *ICE*, that we develop to address the task. We evaluate its effectiveness over a curated dataset from the entertainment domain.

2   Related Work

Our task in this paper involves making use of image analytics APIs (as black-boxes), leveraging them in order to identify common entities to be associated with images in an image dataset. We now cover pertinent related work across: (i) image analytics, and (ii) knowledge management literature related to record linkage and entity identification.

Image Analytics: Our work is motivated by the availability as well as proliferation of image analytics APIs which do a good job of identifying attributes of individuals in an image with quite good accuracies. There are many advanced tools and multiple readily available APIs present for the task of facial recognition. One such highly expressive API is Face++ [1]; for every image as input, it provides face landmarks (bounding boxes), along with attributes like age and gender for the faces present in it. There are also other services provided for the same, such as Google Vision API [2] and Kairos Face Recognition [3].

Linking Records to Entities: While our task of linking imprecise records to common entities in a knowledge base through linkages to person entities is novel in formulation, there have been similar tasks explored in literature. Record Linkage [12], the task of linking records across different sources, has been explored in multiple variants, such as semi-supervised settings [8]. Entity Linking [7] is the task of identifying mentions of entities within text documents and collectively disambiguating the mentions of such entities within a document against a structured knowledge base. As mentioned earlier, our task may be positioned as being analogous to entity linking, especially in the first part of linking ambiguous records to person entities in a database. Using databases for information retrieval, as explored in [6], is another related task. SCORE [11] provides the integration between relational queries and unstructured documents through identifying keywords. Overall, linking imprecise data from images to a structured data source is a task for which we have not seen prior explorations.

3   Problem Definition

Consider a dataset of images, $\mathcal{I} = \{\ldots, I, \ldots\}$ with potential linkages to a structured database containing a number of tables, $\mathcal{D} = \{\ldots, T, \ldots\}$. There are two designated tables of interest within $\mathcal{D}$; the person table T_p and the common entity table T_e. T_p contains information about people who could potentially have appeared within images in $\mathcal{I}$ and T_e contains information about potential common entities. As an example, $\mathcal{I}$ could be a collection of movie posters, T_p a table with information about actors, and T_e a table containing information about movies. T_p, T_e and other tables in $\mathcal{D}$ are linked together through foreign key relationships. The task of *common entity retrieval* is a per-image task, that of scoring entities within T_e based on their relevance to the chosen image.

For each image I, we assume the existence of an image analytics API (e.g., Face++, Google Vision) which produces a collection of records.

$$I \xrightarrow[\text{Extraction}]{\text{Record}} R(I) = \{\ldots, [(a_1 : v_{i1}), \ldots, (a_k : v_{ik})], \ldots\} \qquad (1)$$

In other words, the image analytics is expected to produce a set of records, $R(I)$, containing one record per individual person who appears in the image. Each such record takes on specific values for person's attributes, $[a_1, \ldots, a_k]$. These attributes match to appropriate columns within the schema for table T_p. An example of such attributes that are identifiable from an image would be *age*, *gender*, *ethnicity* and in certain cases such as the case of celebrities, even *names*. The sequence of values taken on by the ith record is denoted as $[v_{i1}, \ldots, v_{ik}]$ as indicated in Eq. 1. While some of these values would be *null* (e.g., the image analytics API may not return an age in certain cases), all of these are expected to be imprecise and required to be considered with a level of uncertainty. For example, even if the image analytics API returns $age = 40$, we may need to interpret it as $age = 40 \pm 5$ to account for the impreciseness.

Our task, in this paper, is that of using the collective information across records in $R(I)$ along with the structured database $\mathcal{D}$, to arrive at a relevance score for entities in T_e to be the *common entity* for the image I.

$$R(I) \xrightarrow[Scoring]{CommonEntity} \{(e, s)|e \in T_e\} \tag{2}$$

In other words, the common entity scoring task uses $R(I)$ and $\mathcal{D}$ to associate each entity $e \in T_e$ with a score s. A practical way of using such scores would be to choose the top-k scored entities in T_e to be output as the common entity.

Common Entity-Based Caption Generation: Once the listing of common entities is identified, a useful next step is to generate a caption based on the top common entity in a domain-specific manner. For example, in the case domain we use in this paper, that of identifying common entities as movies, a meaningful movie caption would be one that covers details of the main cast in the movie, along with key personnel such as movie genre, director and producer.

4   ICE: Proposed Method

We call our method for **I**mage-based **C**ommon **E**ntity identification as *ICE*. ICE comprises two distinct phases, that of starting with an image, I, to extract a record, $R(I)$, and then using $R(I)$ to score common entities:

$$I \xrightarrow[Extraction]{Record} R(I) \xrightarrow[Scoring]{Entity} \{(e, s)|e \in T_e\} \tag{3}$$

To ensure that the narration is relatable to a usage domain, we use aspects of our experimental domain, that of images from movie posters to identify common entities as movies from the IMDB database. However, ICE is a general-purpose method that can be used in any appropriate domain.

4.1   Record Extraction

The input image I, with its associated name tags and year of origin, is passed to an appropriate image analytics engine - we use Face++ [1] - to extract pertinent information about people from the image. In our case of movie poster/red carpet images, the Face++ outputs are useful to match against IMDB attributes, *gender* and *age*. In addition to such information about each person appearing in the image, the Face++ API also outputs the location of the face for each person for which it provides the gender and age information. This face location/landmark is essentially a bounding box. We use the face location and Google Image Search in order to identify a *name tag* to fill in the $R(I)$ record. The name tag is simply the most common name in the captions of images that are related to the face location extract pointed to by Face++; our name tag thus typically contains the first name of the person. Examples of records are $[(gender : male), (age : 45), (nametag : chris)]$ and $[(gender : female), (age : 35), (nametag : sophia)]$.

We observed that the age was often identified approximately. Thus, we interpret the age as being within a window of 10 years centered on the identified age; the window size could be set as appropriate for particular domains. This leads to the above records being interpreted as $[(gender : male), (age : 45 \pm 5), (nametag : chris)]$ and $[(gender : female), (age : 35 \pm 5), (nametag : sophia)]$ respectively. The set of records, denoted as $R(I)$ forms the input to the next phase.

4.2 Entity Scoring

The goal of the entity scoring phase is that of scoring records from the common entity table T_e in the context of $R(I)$. This involves *Person Matching*, matching each record in $R(I)$ against entities in T_p, followed by *Common Entity Matching*, that of scoring entities in T_e using $R(I)$ and person matching results.

Person Matching. Each record in $R(I)$ is converted to a SQL query to be applied over the person table, T_p. This involves identifying the columns associated with the attributes in the record, and appropriately formulating the query using simple rules to handle ranges, exact matches and regex matches. As an example, the first record would yield the following query: *SELECT * FROM PERSON WHERE NAME LIKE '%chris%' AND GENDER = 'male' AND AGE $\geq$ 40 AND AGE $\leq$ 50;*.

All rows from the table retrieved using the query are then scored based on the similarity between the entity names and the nametag in $R(I)$, using the *fuzzywuzzy* string matching framework[1]. In this way, the person matching phase provides a scored set of potential personal records for each person record in $R(I)$.

Common Entity Matching. Each entity/row in the common entity table T_e may be associated with multiple person entities from the T_p table. For our setting where T_e contains movies, it involves following a number of foreign key connections. As an example, using the *movie id* foreign key that links tables corresponding to *directors, actors, producers* and other kinds of film crew enables one to associate each movie with a list of people associated with the movie. In other scenarios, one may need to traverse appropriate foreign keys. In short, we associate each entity in T_e with a set of associated people:

$$\forall e \in T_e, A(e) = \{p|p \in T_p \land Associated(p, e)\} \qquad (4)$$

where the function $Associated(p, e)$ is defined in a domain-specific manner as outlined above. Using the results from the person matching phase over all records in $R(I)$, we associate each entity $e \in T_e$ with an affinity score as follows:

---

[1] https://github.com/seatgeek/fuzzywuzzy.

$$Aff(e) = \sum_{r \in R(I)} \sum_{p \in Matched(r)} Vote(p, r) \tag{5}$$

where $Matched(r)$ is the set of person records from T_p matched with the record $r \in R(I)$. In other words, $Aff(e)$ simply aggregates the votes from all person entities matched with records in $R(I)$. The $Vote(p, r)$ is directly related to the string matching similarity score employed in the person matching phase. We additionally incorporate a constant factor to incorporate the credit for p's membership in $Matched(r)$. Thus, $Vote(p, r)$ is constructed as:

$$Vote(p, r) = \mathbb{I}(p \in Matched(r)) + SimScore(p.name, r.nametag) \tag{6}$$

where $\mathbb{I}$ is the indicator function, and $SimScore(.,.)$ stands for the match between the name in p and the nametag in r. Having associated an affinity score with each $e \in T_e$, we could simply take the top-k common entities and output, completing the common entity retrieval process in ICE.

4.3   Caption Generation

Once a common entity is chosen to associate with the image, we may like to associate the image with a suitable caption using the choice of the common entity. Based on whether the domain is a public one or not, one could employ different strategies for caption generation. For ICE applied over public domains (e.g., celebrities, financial markets) with much contemporary interest in the media, suitable captions could be harvested from the social media streams. For a domain that is not public or caption harvesting from social media is not suited for other reasons, a bespoke caption generation method could be devised.

Caption Generation from Social Media. Mining suitable captions from social media streams relies on an information retrieval approach whereby social media such as Twitter will be searched using a set of keywords. The set of keywords are generated as follows:

- *Keyword Generation from Person Entities:* We employ a set of queries SQL(r) over a structured database in the person matching phase. These queries would be *'translated'* to keywords by means of context-oriented information retrieval systems; we employ SCORE [11] for this purpose.
- *Keyword Generation from Common Entities:* The appropriate text fields in the row corresponding to the highly scored common could be merged in order to find a set of keywords from the common entity.

For caption generation from social media, ICE makes use of the combination of the keywords from the two sources above to retrieve suitable social media posts to be used as captions for an image I.

Bespoke Domain-Specific Caption Generation. In certain domains where social media captions may be unavailable or unsuitable (e.g., due to being informal in nature), it would be desirable to generate captions that are of a specified format. Accordingly, ICE generates captions using a template-based process. First, a template a determined, which may be the following for a movie set:

- [ACTORS] star together in [MOVIE].
- The cast includes [OTHERS].
- The movie was directed by [DIRECTOR] and produced by [PRODUCER].

The words in upper case will be filled in the next steps. ICE first determines the set of top-scored persons for each record in $R(I)$ as $People(I)$. Among $People(I)$, those that are related to the common entity $CE(I)$ through an actor foreign key are added to the $ACTOR$ set, and similarly for $DIRECTOR$ and $PRODUCER$. The leftover people in $People(I)$ are then associated with $OTHERS$. Finally, the $MOVIE$ is set to the movie name associated with the common entity $CE(I)$. A general cross-domain framework for the above follows:

- Determine a structure for the caption, with placeholders for various roles.
- Determine the top-matched person associated with each record in $R(I)$, to form a set of people to be covered in the caption as $People(I)$. Associate each person in $People(I)$ with one of the roles in the caption.
- Fill roles in the caption that need to be filled with information from the chosen common entity $CE(I)$.
- Output the completed caption with roles filled as above.

Algorithm 1: *ICE: The Overall Technique*

Input. Image I
Output. Scored list of common entities in T_e, and optionally a caption.

1. *Perform Image Analytics and Image Caption Search to form $R(I)$.*
2. *Match each record in $R(I)$ with records in T_p to identify persons, using SQL queries and string matching.*
3. *Use the person matching results to perform affinity scoring over entities in T_e to arrive at a scored set of entities for I.*
4. *Optionally, generate a caption using both the top-scored person entities from (2) and the common entities in (3) using social media scoring and/or template filling. 5. Output scored entity list from (3) and optionally, caption from (4).*

4.4   Overall Approach

The overall approach employed by *ICE* is outlined in Algorithm 1, with an illustration in Fig. 1. The flow proceeds in phases sequentially, first identifying the structured record from the image as $R(I)$, and using it in order to identify people, and then common entities, finally producing an optional caption to accompany the common entity scoring. All of these steps, as obvious, are linear in their time complexity, and some, such as database querying, could be sped up by employing suitable indexes.

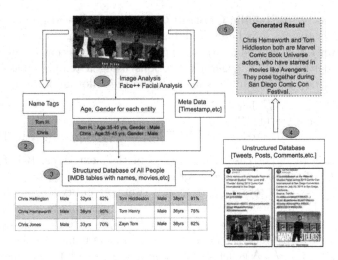

Fig. 1. ICE pipeline. (1) API information calls (age & gender), (2) Name tagging using image search, (3) Record search & linkage in structured DB (person & common entity matching), (4) Unstructured DB search, (5) Caption generation.

5   Case Study and Experimental Analysis

We now present the details of our implementation of the *ICE* framework over the movie data scenario referenced abundantly above. We start by describing our data settings, followed by empirical results on accuracy and performance.

Data Sources. The main data sources for ICE are the set of images and the relational database. We manually curated an Image dataset of Hollywood celebrities by collecting 100 images from the internet, which consisted of group photos of the cast and crew of popular Hollywood movies and TV shows like The Avengers, The Big Bang Theory, Friends, Harry Potter etc. We annotated each image with the names and ages of people who appear in the image, to be used as ground truth in the evaluation. There were an average of 3.17 people in each image, 1.94 males and 1.23 females. These images contain actors, directors, screenwriters, producers and other cast members who appear in the IMDB relational dataset. For the structured database, we used the publicly available IMDB dataset.

Experimental Setup. *ICE* requires several external calls, viz., image analytics and social media querying. We use Face++ [1] as our image analytics API. For each image, Face++ [1] API outputs a list of face location coordinates along with the predicted gender and age. We use google image search using the extracted face in order to get nametags, which happen to be combinations of initials, parts of the first and last names of the person in question. For caption generation, we use the template-based approach, given that our movies are not all recent, and social media streams are not good with entities that do not have real-time relevance.

Table 1. Average MRR

Technique	MRR
all	0.526
nogender	0.510
noage	0.373
nogenderage	0.298

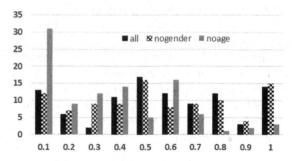

Fig. 2. MRR histogram

Table 2. #Successes in movie identification in our 100 image dataset

Technique	Success@1	Success@5
all	59	68
nogender	16	38
noage	31	56
nogenderage	22	36

5.1   Experimental Results and Analysis

Evaluation of Person Matching. The first part of the common entity matching is the matching of records in $R(I)$ to personal information in T_p. The person matching makes use of three kinds of information, *gender* and *age* from the image api, and the *nametag* to produce a list of person entities ordered based on probabilistic name matching. While the nametag is quite crucial for the process, given the large database we use, we would like to analyze the additional utility of the image analytics outputs, *gender* and *age* through an ablation analysis. We compare using all information, *ICE-all*, against dropping each of them in turn, called *nogender* and *noage* respectively. MRR [10], the mean reciprocal rank, is an evaluation measure that measures the accuracy as the reciprocal of the rank at which the correct answer was found. The correct answer (our ground truth) from manual labelling, which is not available to *ICE*, is available to us in this evaluation stage. We plot the average MRR achieved across the 100 images in Table 1; this table also includes *nogenderage* which excludes both *gender* and *age* from consideration. As may be seen, *all* performs the best, as expected, scoring an MRR above 0.5; this indicates that it is able to rank the correct person at either rank 1 or rank 2, on an average, which is quite promising to note. The exclusion of *gender* does not affect much; this may be intuitive since the nametag is likely to contain gender correlated information, given that male and female names often come from reasonably distinct vocabularies. Exclusion of the *age* attribute is seen to cause a significant dip in MRR; this indicates that the *age* is quite crucial for accurate matching. Further dips are observed when both *gender* and *age* are excluded, as on expected lines. This also highlights that the extra information extracted via the image API had a significant contribution in improving the quality of results. The distribution of MRR across the $[0-1]$ range divided into 10 equi-sized buckets is shown in Fig. 2. As may be seen therein, the dip for *noage* is caused due to people records appearing very far down the list (at $MRR < 0.1$, which is Rank > 10). This analysis indicates that the combination of *nametag* with *gender* and *age* in *ICE* are very useful to accomplish fairly accurate matching.

Evaluation of Movie (Common Entity) Matching. We now analyze the accuracy of movie matching, movies being the common entity in our setting. As outlined earlier, the common entity matching process associates each entity in T_e with an affinity score using a voting process from matched persons. Similar to the case of person matching, we use the correct movie, from the manual labelling, in evaluating the accuracy of *ICE* common entity matching. In the ideal case, we would like to have the correct movie as the top-scored entity in the list. Thus, *Success@1* is a pertinent measure of interest. Even in cases where the correct entity is not top-ranked, it would be useful for it to be among the top few. Thus, we additionally measure *Success@5*, which counts each scenario where the correct answer appears among the top-5 as a success. We simply count the number of successes among the 100 images in our dataset, for *ICE* (denoted as earlier, as *all*) and its variants as used in the person matching evaluation; the results are listed in Table 2. As may be seen therein, the full *ICE* (i.e., *all*) outperforms all others by huge margins. On an absolute level, it is seen that *all* gets the movie right at the top-spot around 3 out of 5 times, and the correct movie is left out of the top-5 only in 32% of occasions. The differences in accuracies between *all* and others are sharper than for person identification, as may be expected since a combination of errors across records in $R(I)$ could be highly misleading.

Qualitative Analysis. Having analyzed person identification and movie identification quantitatively, we now provide some example results in Table 3. We used a slightly more expressive caption template than outlined in Sect. 4.3 by incorporating the year and genre values from the movie identified; with those details being minor and unrelated to the task accomplished by *ICE*, we do not go into details for brevity. From Table 3, we can observe that the results from *ICE* are meaningful, indicating the effectiveness of our methodology.

Efficiency. The main time-consuming part of the core *ICE* logic, outside database and image analytics querying, is that of doing the affinity scoring of common entities, which depends on the number of person records retrieved in

Table 3. Sample pictures with identified persons and generated captions

Persons

- Chris Hemsworth, Male, 36
- Chris Evans, Male, 38
- Robert Downey Jr., Male, 55
- Scarlett Johansson, Female, 35
- Jeremy Renner, Male, 49
- Mark Ruffalo, Male, 52

Common Entity: *The Avengers: Assembling the Ultimate Team*

Caption: "Chris Hemsworth, Robert Downe Jr., Scarlett Johansson and Mark Ruffalo star together in The Avengers: Assembling the Ultimate Team, a Short film that was released in 2012.The cast includes distinguished actors like Clark Gregg, Scarlett Johansson, Robert Downey Jr., Chris Hemsworth, Mark Ruffalo, Tom Hiddleston, Chris Evans and Samuel L. Jackson, writers Clark Gregg and Joss Whedon, with Clark Gregg, Joss Whedon and Mark Ruffalo as directors. The film was produced by Kevin Feige."

Persons

- David Schwimmer, Male, 53
- Matt LeBlanc, Male, 52
- James Michael Tyler, Male, 58
- Jennifer Anniston, Female, 51
- Courteney Cox, Female, 55
- Lisa Kudrow, Female, 56

Common Entity: *Friends*

Caption: "David Schwimmer, Matt LeBlanc, James Michael Tyler, Jennifer Anniston, Courteney Cox; Lisa Kudrow star together in Friends, a popular American sitcom which first aired in 1994. The cast includes distinguished actors like David Schwimmer, Matt LeBlanc, James Michael Tyler, Jennifer Anniston, Courteney Cox; Lisa Kudrow, Paul Rudd, and Cole Sprouse with writers and producers David Crane and Marta Kauffman."

Persons

- Matthew McConaughey, Male, 50
- Christopher Nolan, Male, 49
- Jessica Chastain, Female, 43
- Anne Hathaway, Female, 37

Common Entity: *Interstellar*

Caption: "Matthew McConaughey, Christopher Nolan, Jessica Chastain star together in Interstellar, a Sci-Fi movie that was released in 2014. The cast includes distinguished actors like Matthew McConaughey, Timothy Chamalet, Jessica Chastain, Anne Hathaway, and Matt Damon, with Christopher Nolan and Jonathan Nolan as writers and directors. The film was produced by Christopher Nolan and Emma Thomas."

the person matching phase. The information from the image analytics API (*gender* and *age*) plays an important role in restricting the person records involved in affinity scoring. We obtained running times of the order of 1–2 s for *ICE all* which was also similar for *nogender* (given our observation that gender usually implicit in the nametag). This indicates that *ICE* is quite fast and suitable for practical scenarios. On the other hand, *noage* and *nogenderage* recorded running times of ≈10 s and ≈60 s respectively, due to many more related person records.

6   Conclusions and Future Work

We outlined the novel problem of cross-modal common entity identification in order to establish linkages between images and structured databases. We proposed a structured framework and method that leverages off-the-shelf image analytics for the task, *ICE*, whereby images are linked to a common entity they are likely to be associated with, through an intermediate person matching phase. Our approach also includes an optional caption generation phase. We instantiated the method over a real-world dataset derived from the movie domain, and illustrated its effectiveness in the task. For future work, we are considering extending *ICE* to work with more expressive multi-modal data scenarios such as those involving videos. Further, we are considering crowdsourcing of data combinations involving labelled images with associated structured data from diverse scenarios including healthcare and enterprise knowledge bases.

References

1. Face++ API for facial recognition. https://console.faceplusplus.com/documents/5679127
2. Google Vision API. https://cloud.google.com/vision
3. KariosAPI for Facial Recognition. https://rapidapi.com/KairosAPI/api/kairos-face-recognition
4. Bhadra, S.: Multi-view data completion. In: Deepak, P., Jurek-Loughrey, A. (eds.) Linking and Mining Heterogeneous and Multi-view Data. USL, pp. 1–25. Springer, Cham (2019). https://doi.org/10.1007/978-3-030-01872-6_1
5. Deepak, P., Jurek-Loughrey, A. (eds.): Linking and Mining Heterogeneous and Multi-view Data. USL, Springer, Cham (2019). https://doi.org/10.1007/978-3-030-01872-6
6. DeFazio, S., Daoud, A., Smith, L.A., Srinivasan, J.: Integrating IR and RDBMS using cooperative indexing. In: SIGIR (1995)
7. Gupta, N., Singh, S., Roth, D.: Entity linking via joint encoding of types, descriptions, and context. In: EMNLP, pp. 2681–2690 (2017)
8. Jurek-Loughrey, A., Deepak, P.: Semi-supervised and unsupervised approaches to record pairs classification in multi-source data linkage. In: Deepak, P., Jurek-Loughrey, A. (eds.) Linking and Mining Heterogeneous and Multi-view Data. USL, pp. 55–78. Springer, Cham (2019). https://doi.org/10.1007/978-3-030-01872-6_3
9. Lahat, D., Adali, T., Jutten, C.: Multimodal data fusion: an overview of methods, challenges, and prospects. Proc. IEEE **103**(9), 1449–1477 (2015)

10. Radev, D.R., Qi, H., Wu, H., Fan, W.: Evaluating web-based question answering systems. In: LREC (2002)
11. Roy, P., Mohania, M., Bamba, B., Raman, S.: Towards automatic association of relevant unstructured content with structured query results. In: CIKM (2005)
12. Sayers, A., Ben-Shlomo, Y., Blom, A.W., Steele, F.: Probabilistic record linkage. Int. J. Epidemiol. **45**(3), 954–964 (2016)
13. Shen, W., Wang, J., Han, J.: Entity linking with a knowledge base: Issues, techniques, and solutions. IEEE TKDE **27**(2), 443–460 (2014)

Modeling of the Digital Class-D Amplifier Based on Deep Double Feedback Elman Neural Network

Zeqi Yu[✉], Bingbing Jiang, and Haokai Liu

Zhengzhou University of Light Industry, Zhengzhou, China

Abstract. This paper presents a double feedback Elman neural network (DFENN) based on restricted Boltzmann machine (RBM), which we call RBM-DFENN, for modeling of the digital class-D Amplifier. RBM is the basic module of constructing deep learning networks, and the precision of the deep learning network is higher than that of the general network. The Elman neural network (ENN) was first proposed for speech signals, which has memory effect compared with the back propagation neural network (BPNN). Compared with the traditional ENN, the DFENN has stronger memory effect. Therefore, the RBM-DFENN proposed in this paper models the digital class-D amplifier. Experimental results show that the proposed model can accurately describe the memory effect of the system, and the modeling accuracy is higher.

Keywords: Digital class-D amplifier · Restricted Boltzmann machine · Nonlinear modeling · Double feedback Elman neural network

1 Introduction

Under the background of energy shortage in today's society, the digital class-D amplifier has become the research hotspot of many scholars because of it's high power efficiency. However, in the process of amplifying audio signals, due to the characteristics of various components, the final output produces nonlinear distortion, which reduces the audio quality. As a disadvantage of the digital class-D amplifier, it is necessary to study the distortion phenomenon. At present, the most common method is to accurately model of the digital class-D amplifier to analyze its nonlinear distortion phenomenon.

For a nonlinear system, the input and model parameters of the system are subject to nonlinear to the output [1]. Modeling of nonlinear systems has become a common method of system analysis. It can accurately and conveniently predict the system-level performance, and avoid the complex computation of the physical-level analysis [2]. The digital class-D amplifier is a typical nonlinear system with memory effect. Researchers have proposed many methods to model the amplifier with memory effect accurately. Among them, the most commonly used methods are the Volterra series model and its simplified model [3, 4] and the neural network [5, 6]. The Volterra series models, which can be implemented in digital circuits, can model amplifiers [4]. However, the Volterra

This work was supported by the Science and Technology Project of Henan Province (Grant Nos. 222102210039 and 222102210103).

B. Li et al. (Eds.): ADMA 2021, LNAI 13088, pp. 314–325, 2022.
https://doi.org/10.1007/978-3-030-95408-6_24

series model contains a large number of coefficients, so the calculation is relatively large in the process of realization. The ability of the neural network to deal with nonlinearity is higher than that of Volterra series, and it can approximate any nonlinear function with arbitrary accuracy, so it is favored by more scholars.

The Elman neural network (ENN) was proposed in 1990. It is a dynamic recurrent neural network with the function of dynamic feedback [7]. It performs well in dealing with problems with memory effect. This paper presents a double feedback Elman neural network (DFENN) based on restricted Boltzmann machine (RBM), which we call RBM-DFENN. The RBM-DFENN model, which overcomes the trapping of traditional neural network algorithms into local optimum, further enhances the memory effect of the model and improves the accuracy of the model.

This paper is organized as follows. Section 2 describes the characteristics of the digital class-D amplifier. Section 3 introduces the RBM. Section 4 introduces the traditional ENN model and DFENN mode. The new model proposed in this paper and simulation results are described in Sect. 5. Section 6 is the conclusion of this paper.

2   Characteristics of the Digital Class-D Amplifier

Digital class-D amplifier is a nonlinear system for connecting speakers with other parts of the system and amplifying audio signals. Figure 1 shows the general structure diagram of the digital class-D amplifier, where F_s is the sampling frequency of the input signal, M is the multiple of the digital interpolation filter and N is the level of the PWM generator. The digital class-D amplifier firstly oversamples and re-quantizes the input digital audio signal through the digital interpolation filter and the Sigma-Delta modulator to reduce the influence of quantization noise. Then, the output of the Sigma-Delta modulator is converted into the binary continuous-time signal by the PWM generator. The binary continuous-time signal is amplified through the H-bridge power stage or the single-ended power stage. Finally the amplifier uses the analog low-pass filter to filter out high-frequency components of the amplified signal to drive the speaker.

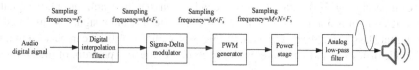

Fig. 1. General structure diagram of the digital class-D amplifier.

However, in the process of amplifying the digital audio signals, the coefficient bit-width of the interpolation filter can't be infinite, so the quantization error caused by its bit-width limitation will produce signal distortion in circuit implementation. The Sigma-Delta modulator is an efficient implementation of the quantization noise shaping technology, which introduces quantization noise in the process of re-quantization of input signal. The PWM generator produces harmonic distortion in the process of signal modulation. The power stage is not ideal in the working status, and the error will be caused by components in the analog low-pass filter. From the description above, it can be known that all the blocks in the digital class-D amplifier will produce distortion in the process of signal amplification.

When the frequency, amplitude and sampling frequency of the input signal are 1 kHz, 0 dB and 48 kHz, respectively, a digital class-D amplifier shown in Fig. 2 is tested. The time domain diagram and the frequency spectrum of the input signal are shown in Fig. 3(a) and (b), respectively. The time domain diagram and the frequency spectrum of the amplifier output signal are shown in Fig. 4(a) and (b), respectively.

Fig. 2. Structure diagram of a digital class-D amplifier.

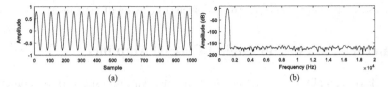

Fig. 3. (a) Time domain diagram and (b) frequency spectrum of the input signal.

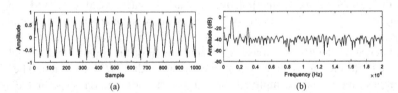

Fig. 4. (a) Time domain diagram and (b) frequency spectrum of the amplifier output signal.

Comparing Fig. 3(a) with Fig. 4(a), it can be seen that the amplifier output signal in the time domain is not a smooth sinusoidal signal after the input signal is amplified by the digital class-D amplifier. Comparing Fig. 3(b) with Fig. 4(b), it can be seen that the harmonic distortion and noise are produced in the frequency spectrum of the amplified output signal.

3   RBM

The RBM is an energy-based model. The energy in the RBM is used to represent the stable state of the system [8]. It is a bidirectional neural network model with visible and hidden layers of neurons. The RBM is an important part of the deep neural network. Its structure is shown in Fig. 5. In Fig. 5, v is the visible layer, h is the hidden layer. u and o are the number of neurons in the visible layer and the hidden layer, respectively. W is the weight matrix between the two layers, representing the energy conversion within the

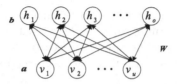

Fig. 5. Structure of the RBM

system. a and b are the bias vectors of the visible layer and the hidden layer, respectively, representing the energy exchange between the system and the outside world.

The neurons of the RBM commonly used in the visible layer and the hidden layer are randomly equal to 0 or 1. The energy function of the RBM is defined as:

$$E(v, h; \theta) = -\sum_{m=1}^{u}\sum_{n=1}^{o} W_{mn}v_m h_n - \sum_{m=1}^{u} a_m v_m - \sum_{n=1}^{o} b_n h_n \tag{1}$$

where $\theta = \{W, a, b\}$ are the parameters.

The energy function value can be converted into the probability value by the Gibbs distribution [9]. Therefore, we can get the joint probability distribution as follows:

$$p(v, h; \theta) = \frac{1}{Z(\theta)} \exp(-E(v, h; \theta)) \tag{2}$$

$$Z(\theta) = \sum_v \sum_h \exp(-E(v, h; \theta)) \tag{3}$$

where $Z(\theta)$ is the partition function, which is the sum of all the energies corresponding to $[v, h]$. The states of neurons in visible and hidden layer are conditionally independent of each other [10]. Therefore, the conditional distributions of neurons in visible layer and hidden layer are defined respectively as:

$$p(v_m = 1|h; \theta) = \sigma\left(a_m + \sum_n W_{mn}h_n\right) \tag{4}$$

$$p(h_n = 1|v; \theta) = \sigma\left(b_n + \sum_m W_{nm}v_m\right) \tag{5}$$

In addition, the RBM uses maximum likelihood estimation to maximize the distribution of original data, and uses gradient ascending method to calculate parameters θ. The calculation formulas of the parameters ΔW_{mn}, Δa_m and Δb_n are as follows:

$$\Delta W_{mn} = \frac{\partial \log p(v; \theta)}{\partial W_{mn}} = [v_m h_n]_{\text{data}} - [v_m h_n]_{\text{model}} \tag{6}$$

$$\Delta a_m = \frac{\partial \log p(v; \theta)}{\partial a_m} = v_m - \sum_v p(v; \theta)v_m \tag{7}$$

$$\Delta b_n = \frac{\partial \log p(v; \theta)}{\partial b_n} = p(h_n = 1|v; \theta) - \sum_v p(v; \theta)p(h_n = 1|v; \theta) \tag{8}$$

where $[\cdot]_{\text{data}}$ represents the expectation of observation data in the training set, $[\cdot]_{\text{model}}$ represents the expectation on the distribution determined by the model.

Finally, the RBM adopts contrast divergence (CD) algorithm to optimize the reconstruction model. The reconstruction error function is expressed as:

$$E_{\text{reconst}} = \{[v_m]_{\text{data}} - [v_m]_{\text{model}}\}^{\text{T}}\{[v_m]_{\text{data}} - [v_m]_{\text{model}}\} \tag{9}$$

W_{mn}, a_m, b_n in θ are expressed respectively as:

$$W_{mn}(p) = W_{mn}(p-1) + \lambda\Delta W_{mn} \tag{10}$$

$$a_m(p) = a_m(p-1) + \lambda\Delta a_m \tag{11}$$

$$b_n(p) = b_n(p-1) + \lambda\Delta b_n \tag{12}$$

where λ is the learning rate of the RBM, and p is the number of iteration.

4   Elman Neural Network

4.1   Traditional Elman Neural Network

The ENN has added a feedback from the hidden layer to the input layer in the BPNN structure. This feedback keeps the information inside the network well, and enhances the ability of the network to deal with the dynamic information. Therefore, the ENN is more suitable for the systems with memory effect.

The feedback of the ENN is reflected in the context layer. The context layer stores the feedback data from the hidden layer. In the next iteration, these feedback data are transmitted to the hidden layer together with the data of the input layer. Therefore, it reflects the memory effect of the ENN. The structure diagram of the ENN is shown in Fig. 6. The input layer has N nodes. The number of nodes in the hidden layer and the context layer is L. The output layer has M nodes. The dynamical equations of the ENN model are as follows:

$$y(s) = g[W^2(s)H(s)] \tag{13}$$

$$H(s) = f[W^1(s)x + W^3(s)X_C(s)] \tag{14}$$

$$X_C(s) = \alpha H(s-1) \tag{15}$$

where x is the input of the ENN, s is the number of iteration, $y(s)$ is the s-th iteration output of the model, $H(s)$ is the output of the hidden layer and $X_C(s)$ is the output of the context layer. W^1 is the $N \times L$ dimensional weight matrix from the input layer to the hidden layer. W^2 is the $L \times M$ dimensional weight matrix from the hidden layer to the output layer. W^3 is the $L \times L$ dimensional weight matrix from the hidden layer to the

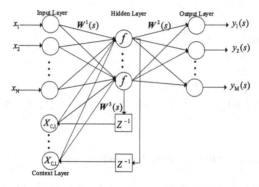

Fig. 6. Structure diagram of the ENN

context layer. $f(x)$ is the activation function of the hidden layer, and usually represents the Sigmoid function. $g(x)$ is the linear activation function of the output layer, α is the coefficient of the context layer.

Generally, $g(x)$ is equal to x, so (13) is changed to:

$$y(s) = W^2(s)H(s) \tag{16}$$

If the s-th iteration actual output of the system is $y_d(s)$ and the output of the model is $y(s)$, the objective function can be defined as:

$$E(s) = \frac{1}{2}[(y_d(s) - y(s))^T(y_d(s) - y(s))] \tag{17}$$

The ENN uses gradient descent algorithm to adjust weights so that the objective function achieves the minimum value [11].

According to the gradient descent algorithm, the correction formula for calculating the weights among layers are as follows:

$$\Delta W_{nl}^1(s) = -\eta_1 \frac{\partial E(s)}{\partial W_{nl}^1(s)} = \eta_1 \delta_l^h(s) \frac{\partial H_l(s)}{\partial W_{nl}^1(s)} \tag{18}$$

$$\Delta W_{lm}^2(s) = -\eta_2 \frac{\partial E(s)}{\partial W_{lm}^2(s)} = \eta_2 \delta_m^o(s) H_l(s) \tag{19}$$

$$\Delta W_{il}^3(s) = -\eta_3 \frac{\partial E(s)}{\partial W_{il}^3(s)} = \eta_3 \delta_l^h(s) \frac{\partial H_l(s)}{\partial W_{il}^3(s)} \tag{20}$$

with

$$\delta_l^h(s) = \sum_{m=1}^{M} (\delta_m^o(s) W_{lm}^2(s)) \tag{21}$$

$$\delta_m^o(s) = y_{d,m} - y_m(s) \tag{22}$$

$$\frac{\partial H_l(s)}{\partial W_{nl}^1(s)} = f_l'(.)[x_n + \alpha. W_{il}^3(s) \frac{\partial H_l(s-1)}{\partial W_{nl}^1(s-1)}] \tag{23}$$

$$\frac{\partial H_l(s)}{\partial W_{il}^3(s)} = f_l'(.)[\alpha.H_i(s-1) + \alpha.W_{il}^3(s)\frac{\partial H_l(s-1)}{\partial W_{il}^3(s-1)}] \tag{24}$$

where n represents the n-th neuron in the input layer, l represents the l-th neuron in the hidden layer, i represents the i-th neuron in the context layer, m represents the m-th neuron in the output layer. η_1, η_2 and η_3 are the learning rates of W^1, W^2 and W^3, respectively.

4.2 Double Feedback Elman Neural Network

The gradient descent algorithm is slow in learning and easy to fall into the local minimum. Therefore, the traditional ENN model has a large error [12, 13]. Compared with the traditional ENN model, the DFENN model adds the feedback of the output layer. Hence, the DFENN model has better dynamic characteristics and memory function. The structure of the DFENN is shown in Fig. 7.

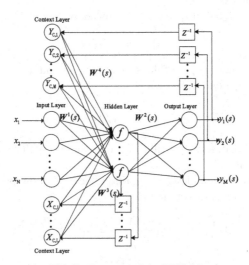

Fig. 7. Structure of the DFENN

The dynamical equations of the DFENN are as follows:

$$y(s) = g[W^2(s)H(s)] \tag{25}$$

$$H(s) = f[W^1(s)x + W^3(s)X_C(s) + W^4(s)Y_C(s)] \tag{26}$$

$$X_C(s) = \alpha H(s-1) \tag{27}$$

$$Y_C(s) = \beta y(s-1) \tag{28}$$

The DFENN uses the same training algorithm and objective function as the ENN. The correction formulas for calculating the weights among layers of the DFENN are as follows:

$$\Delta W_{nl}^1(s) = -\eta_1 \frac{\partial E(s)}{\partial W_{nl}^1(s)} = \eta_1 \delta_l^h(s) \frac{\partial H_l(s)}{\partial W_{nl}^1(s)} \tag{29}$$

$$\Delta W_{lm}^2(s) = -\eta_2 \frac{\partial E(s)}{\partial W_{lm}^2(s)} = \eta_2 \delta_m^o(s) H_l(s) \tag{30}$$

$$\Delta W_{il}^3(s) = -\eta_3 \frac{\partial E(s)}{\partial W_{il}^3(s)} = \eta_3 \delta_l^h(s) \frac{\partial H_l(s)}{\partial W_{il}^3(s)} \tag{31}$$

$$\Delta W_{jm}^4(s) = -\eta_4 \frac{\partial E(s)}{\partial W_{jm}^4(s)} = \eta_4 \delta_l^h(s) \frac{\partial H_l(s)}{\partial W_{jm}^4(s)} \tag{32}$$

with

$$\delta_l^h(s) = \sum_{m=1}^M (\delta_m^o(s) W_{lm}^2(s)) \tag{33}$$

$$\delta_m^o(s) = y_{d,m} - y_m(s) \tag{34}$$

$$\frac{\partial H_l(s)}{\partial W_{nl}^1(s)} = f_l'(.)[x_n + \delta_h^o \frac{\partial H_l(s-1)}{\partial W_{nl}^1(s-1)}] \tag{35}$$

$$\frac{\partial H_l(s)}{\partial W_{il}^3(s)} = f_l'(.)[\alpha H_i(s-1) + \delta_h^o \frac{\partial H_l(s-1)}{\partial W_{il}^3(s-1)}] \tag{36}$$

$$\frac{\partial H_l(s)}{\partial W_{ml}^4(s)} = f_l'(.)[\beta y_m(s-1) + \delta_h^o \frac{\partial H_l(s-1)}{\partial W_{ml}^4(s-1)}] \tag{37}$$

$$\delta_h^o = \alpha W_{il}^3(s) + \beta W_{ml}^4(s) W_{lm}^2(s) \tag{38}$$

5   Principle of New Model and Analysis of Simulation Results

5.1   Deep Double Feedback Elman Neural Network

The deep learning model is composed of a lot of machine learning models. It has more hidden layers and data to fully learn useful features. Therefore, the precision of the deep learning model is higher than that of the machine learning model [14]. Based on the strong memory effect of the DFENN, the RBM-DFENN is proposed in this paper. The new model increases the depth of the network and makes the learning of the model more accurate. The learning process of the RBM-DFENN is as follows:

Step 1 According to Sect. 3, train the RBM to get the weight matrix between the visible layer and the hidden layer.

Step 2 Normalize the input and output data. Batch the input data. The sum of squared error (SSE) threshold of the RBM-DFENN is set to 10^{-3}, and the maximum iteration number is set to 100.

Step 3 Initialize the weight matrices $W^3(0)$ and $W^4(0)$ of the DFENN according to the weight matrix obtained in step 1. $W^2(0)$ is a zero matrix. $W^1(0)$ is a random matrix that obeys the normal distribution. Set $\partial H_l(0)/\partial W_{nl}^1 = 0$, $\partial H_l(0)/\partial W_{il}^3 = 0$, $\partial H_l(0)/\partial W_{jm}^4 = 0$. The initial value of the context layers are $X_C(0) = 0$ and $Y_C(0) = 0$. Set the coefficients α and β of the two context layers respectively. Set learning rates η_1, η_2, η_3 and η_4.

Step 4 According to (25)–(28), calculate the output $y(s)$. Use $y(s)$ and y_d to calculate the SSE. If the SSE is larger than the threshold, go to step 5. If the SSE is smaller than the threshold or the number of iteration steps reaches 100, go to step 6.

Step 5 According to (29)–(38), update the weight matrices $W^1(s)$, $W^2(s)$, $W^3(s)$ and $W^4(s)$ of the RBM-DFENN. Save the updated weight matrices and go to step 4.

Step 6 Save the value of $y(s)$, which is the final output of the RBM-DFENN. End the RBM-DFENN training.

The structure diagram of the RBM-DFENN is shown in Fig. 8:

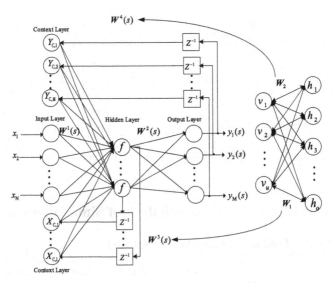

Fig. 8. Structure of the RBM-DFENN

5.2 Simulation Result Analysis

In this section, five models are used to model the digital class-D amplifier to evaluate the advantages of the proposed RBM-DFENN model. The comparison models are the BPNN model, the ENN model, the DFENN model, the RBM-ENN model and the RBM-DFENN model. A signal with frequency, amplitude and sampling frequency of 1 kHz, 0 dB and 48 kHz, respectively, is used as the input signal of the models. The desired output is generated by the digital class-D amplifier shown in Fig. 2. MATLAB is used for simulation experiment. Because there is a random matrix in the initialization weight matrix of these models, the final results were compared by arithmetically averaging the values obtained from a number of experiments. The evaluation indexes are the mean square error (MSE) and the maximum error. The smaller the calculated values of the MSE and the maximum error, the higher the accuracy of the model.

The number of the batch data in the input layer is 30. The number of neurons in the hidden layer is 40. The learning rates $\eta_1 = \eta_2 = \eta_3 = \eta_4 = 0.05$. The coefficients $\alpha = \beta = 0.01$. Table 1 shows the comparison results of the MSE and the maximum error for these models. In Table 1, the MSE-T and MSE-F represent the MSE in the time domain and the frequency domain, respectively. The Max error-T and Max error-F represent the maximum error in the time domain and the frequency domain, respectively. Figure 9(a)–(e) are the time domain diagrams of the outputs of these five models with the desired output, respectively. Figure 10(a)–(e) are the output frequency spectra of these five models with the desired output frequency spectrum.

Table 1. Comparison results of the five models.

Model	MSE-T	Max error-T	MSE-F	Max error-F
BPNN	0.137871	0.326272	0.000678	0.050642
ENN	0.132544	0.324833	0.000664	0.043663
DFENN	0.132100	0.324177	0.000660	0.042784
RBM-ENN	0.126379	0.324076	0.000592	0.040174
RBM-DFENN	0.125889	0.323931	0.000577	0.037981

From Table 1, it can be seen that the MSE-T, the Max error-T, the MSE-F and the Max error-F of the proposed RBM-DFENN model are all smaller than those of other models. Comparing Fig. 9(a)–(e), it can be seen that the output of the model proposed in this paper is closer to the desired output. Comparing Fig. 10(a)–(e), it can be seen that the output frequency spectrum of the proposed RBM-DFENN model is closer to the desired output frequency spectrum. Therefore, the proposed RBM-DFENN can model the digital class-D amplifier well.

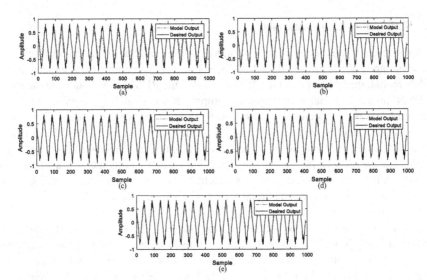

Fig. 9. Time domain diagram of those models output and the desired output. (a) BPNN, (b) ENN, (c) DFENN, (d) RBM-ENN, (e) RBM-DFENN.

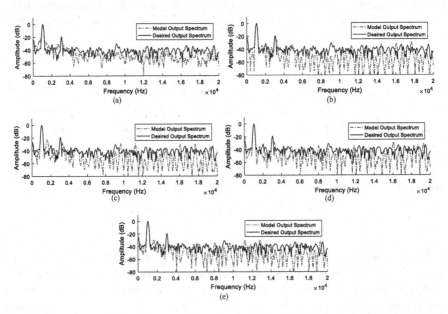

Fig. 10. Frequency spectra of those models output and the desired output. (a) BPNN, (b) ENN, (c) DFENN, (d) RBM-ENN, (e) RBM-DFENN.

6 Conclusion

In this paper, the RBM-DFENN is studied, which can be used to model nonlinear systems. The digital class-D amplifier system is used for experimental verification, and the experimental results show that the proposed model has higher modeling accuracy. Parameter initialization plays an important role in the convergence speed and modeling accuracy of a neural network. Therefore, how to initialize each parameter of the neural network model to make the network performance better is worth further studying.

References

1. Zhu, Q.M., Wang, Y.J., Zhao, D.Y., Li, S.Y., Billings, S.: Review of rational (total) nonlinear dynamic system modelling, identification, and control. Int. J. Syst. Sci. **46**(12), 2122–2133 (2013)
2. Jin, X., Shao, J., Zhang, X., An, W., Malekian, R.: Modeling of nonlinear system based on deep learning framework. Nonlinear Dyn. **84**(3), 1327–1340 (2015). https://doi.org/10.1007/s11071-015-2571-6
3. Wei, W.T., Ye, P., Song, J.P., Zheng, H., Gao, J., Zhao, Y.: A behavioral dynamic nonlinear model for time-interleaved ADC based on Volterra series. IEEE Access **7**, 41860–41873 (2019)
4. Zhu, A.D.: Behavioral modeling for digital predistortion of RF power amplifiers: from Volterra series to CPWL functions. In: 2016 IEEE Topical Conference on Power Amplifiers for Wireless and Radio Applications (PAWR), Austin, Texas, USA, pp. 1–4 (2016)
5. Liu, Z.J., Hu, X., Liu, T., Li, X.H., Wang, W.D., Ghannouchi, F.M.: Attention-based deep neural network behavioral model for wideband wireless power amplifiers. IEEE Microwave Wirel. Compon. Lett. **30**(1), 82–85 (2020)
6. Zhang, Y.K., Li, Y., Liu, F.L., Zhu, A.D.: Vector decomposition based time-delay neural network behavioral model for digital predistortion of RF Power amplifiers. IEEE Access **7**, 91559–91568 (2019)
7. Elman, J.L.: Finding structure in time. Cogn. Sci. **14**(2), 179–211 (1990)
8. Chen, X., Wan, Z.P., Wang, J.T.: A Study of unmanned path planning based on a double-twin RBM-BP deep neural network. Intell. Autom. Soft Comput. **26**(4), 1531–1548 (2020)
9. Guo, S., Zhou, C.J., Wang, B., Zheng, X.D.: Training restricted Boltzmann machines using modified objective function based on limiting the free energy value. IEEE Access **6**, 78542–78550 (2018)
10. Qiao, J., Wang, L.: Nonlinear system modeling and application based on restricted Boltzmann machine and improved BP neural network. Appl. Intell. **51**(1), 37–50 (2020). https://doi.org/10.1007/s10489-019-01614-1
11. Gao, S.Z., Zhang, Y.M., Zhang, Y.M., Zhang, G.G.: Elman neural network soft-sensor model of PVC polymerization process optimized by chaos beetle antennae search algorithm. IEEE Sens. J. **3**(21), 3544–3551 (2020)
12. Singh, U.P., Mittal, A.K., Dwivedi, S., Tiwari, A.: Predictability study of forced Lorenz model: an artificial neural network approach. History **40**(181), 27–33 (2015)
13. Zhang, W., Xiao, R., Deng, J.: Research of traffic flow forecasting based on the information fusion of BP network sequence. In: He, X., et al. (eds.) IScIDE 2015. LNCS, vol. 9243, pp. 548–558. Springer, Cham (2015). https://doi.org/10.1007/978-3-319-23862-3_54
14. Altaher, A.: Hybrid approach for sentiment analysis of arabic tweets based on deep learning model and features weighting. Int. J. Adv. Appl. Sci. **4**(8), 43–49 (2017)

A Novel Face Detection Framework Based on Incremental Learning and Low Variance Directions

Mohamed Khalil Ben Salah[1]([✉]), Takoua Kefi-Fatteh[1], and Adel Bouhoula[2]

[1] Digital Security Research Lab, Higher School of Communication of Tunis,
University of Carthage, Tunis, Tunisia
`MohamedKhalil.BenSalah@insat.u-carthage.tn`, `takoua.kefi@supcom.tn`
[2] Department of Next-Generation Computing, College of Graduate Studies,
Arabian Gulf University, Manama, Kingdom of Bahrain
`a.bouhoula@agu.edu.bh`

Abstract. Face detection has gained an ever increasing importance since it has a direct implication in several security systems and devices. Actually, several challenges related to visual variations have been associated with face detection. They can be attributed to many factors, such as occlusion, imaging conditions, illumination, image orientation and pose. Such factors may lead to the performance degradation of the face detectors. Therefore, developing a classifier able to adjust automatically its parameters according to the visual variations has become a fundamental topic for face detection in dynamic settings. In this paper, we investigate the potency of incrementally projecting data in low variance directions, after extracting useful facial information. In fact, Several feature extraction methods have shown high performance in real world applications, and particularly Human Face Detection. Besides, in one-class classification, the low variance directions in the training data carry crucial information to build a good model of the target class. On the other hand, incremental learning is known to be powerful, when dealing with dynamic data. Extensive tests on human faces, and comparative experiments need to be carried out to find the best combination for an accurate human face detection framework.

Keywords: Face detection · Feature extraction · Incremental one-class classification

1 Introduction

For the past few decades, Human Face Detection (HFD) has been a hot topic in machine learning and computer vision. It has been considered as a fundamental step for face understanding and analysis tasks, particularly for security and privacy issues.

In fact, face detection is a keystone in all authentications and security systems. It has brought many benefits to users, such as, improving security

© Springer Nature Switzerland AG 2022
B. Li et al. (Eds.): ADMA 2021, LNAI 13088, pp. 326–337, 2022.
https://doi.org/10.1007/978-3-030-95408-6_25

and automated identification. For example, thanks to HFD, transactions have become more secure than using credit. HFD has an impact in fighting crimes, by allowing the detection and identification of criminals within a crowd, and tracking them. Besides, HFD is an important phase to be used in airports to check travelers' identities by using face-scanning. Thus we can easily and reliably control access to sensitive areas.

The main contribution of our research project is to build a novel framework for HFD based on an incremental Covariance-guided One-class Support Vector Machine (iCOSVM) for data classification. The used classifier takes advantage of the incremental strategy while emphasizing the low variance directions in order to minimize target dispersion and improve classification performance. This phase is preceded by a feature extraction process. Besides, it is not trivial to find the most convenient model for feature extraction. Thus, we intend to study the effectiveness of Histogram of Oriented Gradients (HOG) and Local Binary Pattern (LBP) for human features extraction.

The remaining paper is structured as follows: Sect. 2 presents a brief literature review of the different proposed methods for face detection on single images. Section 3 discusses the phases of our framework. An experimental evaluation is conducted on different databases and presented in Sect. 4. Finally, conclusion and future directions are outlined in Sect. 5.

2   Related Works

HFD is one the research focuses on computer vision. It has been applied to solve several critical problems related to face analysis, such as, face verification and recognition, target tracking, etc... Works on automated HFD can be traced back to more than 50 years ago [1]. Yet, researchers have successfully worked for the improvement of the proposed algorithms and techniques.

In [2], it has been shown that applying HOG with SVM classification performance achieves the highest results in terms of accuracy, precision and sensitivity. These results were strengthened in [3] where different types of images were used to compare HOG against other state-of-the-art feature extractors. HOG was proven to be fast and accurate in detecting human faces in images.

Another face detector scheme was introduced [4]. The proposed model is based on LBP feature extraction method. The fundamental contribution of the method is the relative position of the threshold pixel to the coding pixel of the original LBP are spaced on a circle or an ellipse that is centered at a threshold pixel. However, there are no similar constraints on the threshold pixel and coding pixel of the newly proposed method.

A fusion of HOG and LBP was successfully performed in [5] and [6]. In spite of the challenging conditions from one used dataset to another, the method showed a high efficiency.

Once useful features are extracted from face images, a classification algorithm has to be applied. For instance, we can use Convolutional Neural Network (CNN), Artificial Neural Network (ANN), Random Forests, Support vector

Machines (SVM) and many other algorithms. Yet, SVM has become widely and successfully used for human face detection.

Yet, SVM [7] is an outperforming classifier, that has been successfully used in a wide range of applications. It has been known with its better generalization performance, especially when compared to the traditional Neural Networks [8]. While Neural Networks, such as Multiple Layer Perceptrons (MLPs), can produce on low error rate on training data, there is no guarantee that this will translate into better performance on test data. MLPs minimize the mean squared error over the training data (empirical risk minimization), whereas SVM uses an additional principle called structural risk minimization. The purpose of structural risk minimization is to give an upper bound on the expected generalization error.

Besides, One-class SVM was outperforming, compared to binary or multi-class SVM. Especially, when applied on massive data or a class with an atypical distribution. In fact, including additional class needs to expand a pre-trained multi-class classification model, which requires retraining the entire model. This leads to increasing the computational complexities of retraining, storing and testing/using the model, since it grows after including more and more classes [10].

In [9] an incremental Covariance-guided One-class Support Vector Machine (iCOSVM) was applied for face detection. It is commonly implemented using the advantage of incrementally emphasizing the low variance direction to improve classification performance, which is not the case for classical one-class models. Actually, classical One-Class Classification techniques assume that all the training data are provided in advance, which is referred to a batch learning. Hence, such techniques may lead to performance degradation in a real-world application. Therefore, incremental learning is more effective when dealing with a dynamic or large amount of data. On the other side, the iCOSVM considers data spread information using a covariance matrix.

3   Proposed Framework

As shown in Fig. 1, our model is composed of three main parts: (1) face extraction, (2) feature extraction, (3) data classification. Each phase will be described in the following subsections.

3.1   Face Extraction

Naturally, image contains different objects such as cars, trees, pets, etc. Our objective is to extract human faces, using Viola Jones face detector with high-level image processing and high accuracy. As introduced in [12], this technique is based on the computation of simple features to encode some universal properties of the human face. Three kinds of features were used and, for each one, we compute the sum of the pixels within rectangular regions. The value of the darker region will be smaller than the value of the lighter region and it may be for example an edge of an eyebrow or sometimes the middle portion may be shinier than the surrounding boxes, which can be interpreted as a nose.

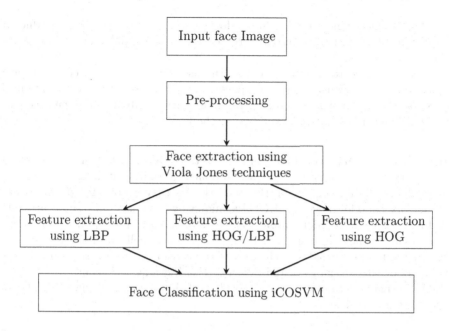

Fig. 1. The flowchart of the our face detection framework

These values can be determined quickly using an integral image. Mathematically, each point (x, y) in the integral image is given by the sum of all points above and to the left of this point in the image as follows:

$$ii(x, y) = \sum_{x' \leq x, y' \leq y} i(x', y'), \tag{1}$$

where ii(x, y) was the integral image at location x, y and i(x′, y′) was the pixel value at the original image location.

Then, AdaBoost [13], a machine learning algorithm is used to generate the weight and size of each computed feature. Hence it allows the selection of the most relevant ones.

Finally a Cascaded classifier is applied to eliminate non-face and prevent computation imagery areas out of the region of interest. The cascaded classifier is composed of stages each containing a strong classifier. The job of each stage is to determine whether a given sub-window is definitely not a face or maybe a face. When a sub-window is classified to be a non-face by a given stage it is immediately discarded. Conversely a sub-window classified as a maybe-face is passed on to the next stage.

3.2 Feature Extraction

When dealing with unconstrained scenarios such as video surveillance or images captured by hand-held devices, classic face detectors, even the most performing like Viola Jones, tend to fail. This performance degradation is, mainly, due to important illumination variations, large pose variations, different facial expressions and motions, etc.

Thus, we need to re-enforce it with the use of a feature extraction method applied to the previously extracted images. Many Feature Extraction techniques were used in different fields, among the most successfully applied ones, we can cite HOG and LBP feature extraction methods.

Histogram of Oriented Gradients HOG. (HOG) is a fast and an effective feature extraction method. It has been applied in a different areas of computer vision especially face detection. Based on the distribution of intensity gradients of each pixel and local texture, HOG technique divides images into small sub cells and extract accurate information. The steps of HOG as presented in [14], start with dividing image into small cells like 4×4. These cells are used to compute the edge direction. Besides, each pixel of the considered region is assumed as a variable for edge orientation and associated with gradient element.

After that we calculate the magnitude and the direction of the gradients by using these formulas:

$$g = \sqrt{g_x^2 + g_y^2} \tag{2}$$

$$\theta = \arctan \frac{g_y}{g_x} \tag{3}$$

where, g_x and g_y represent calculated gradients in both x and y direction separately. The next step in HOG is to create histogram from these gradients, using the orientation and direction of each cell. Each histogram gives distribution frequency through using gradient magnitude to fill the values in the matrix where we have bins on the x-axis. Since lighting can affect the image and make brightness difference at a region of image. It would be better to normalize the gradients. Then, after grouping the cell together into connected blocks and normalizing them, are concatenated in order to obtain HOG features.

Local Binary Pattern LBP. (LBP) is a powerful feature extractor. It has been used as texture analysis also as local structures descriptor, it was widely applied in different areas such as remote sensing, biomedical analysis and face recognition. LBP method dictates that every block of 3×3 window processed separately and every pixel of an image is labeled using threshold of the centre of matrix block compared to 8 neighbors. In matrix of 3×3 window, every neighbor of threshold will take a binary value for example, the neighbor takes 1 if his values are equal or higher than the central value otherwise 0.

Due to problems related to scale structures, LBP operator was extended to take different sizes of neighborhoods. We assign for every block a circle with a radius R from the center, which is considered as threshold, and a size P presents sampling points, in general for every pixel (x_c, y_c) decimal value will compute using the following formulas:

$$LBP_{P,R}(x_c, y_c) = \sum_{P=0}^{P-1} s(i_p - i_c)2^P \tag{4}$$

$$s(x) = \begin{cases} 1 & if \ x \geq 0 \\ 0 & otherwise \end{cases} \tag{5}$$

where i_c and i_p represent respectively the values of the central pixel and P surrounding pixels in the circle with gray-level. Based on new generated image we extract the histogram of each region then create a new and bigger histogram through concatenating each histogram of each grid.

3.3 Classification

The main idea of iCOSVM is to take into consideration the covariance matrix Δ and add it to the dual optimization problem, a key value used $\eta \in [0, 1]$ to get the balance between the contribution of the kernel matrix $\mathbf{K}$ and the covariance matrix to the objective function. The optimization problem will be:

$$\min_{\alpha} W(\alpha, b) = \frac{1}{2}\alpha^T(\eta K + (1 - \eta)\Delta)\alpha - b(1 - \sum_{i=1}^{N}\alpha_i) \tag{6}$$

$$s.t. \quad 0 \leq \alpha_i \leq \frac{1}{vN} = C, \quad \sum_{i=1}^{N}\alpha_i = 1, \tag{7}$$

where, $\Delta = K(I - 1_N)K^T$, η is a key parameter used in order to control the contribution of the kernel matrix K and the covariance matrix Δ, $v \in (0, 1]$ represents a key that controls the fraction of outliers, C penalty weight, $K(x_i, x_j) =< \phi(x_i), \phi(x_j) >, \forall i, j \in \{1, 2, ..., N\}$ is a kernel matrix and α are the Lagrange multipliers.

Herein, We aim to build our model recursively by getting new data added at one time and retraining the Karush-Kuhn-Tucker Conditions on all previously acquired data and we will have a global optimum solution. Let's note Γ matrix as a combination of the kernel and covariance matrices controlled by η parameter: $\Gamma = (\eta K + (1 - \eta)\Delta)$.

Using KKT conditions we can divide the target data into three major subsets:

- $S = \{i/0 < \alpha_i < C\}$ represents the unbounded support vectors,
- $E = \{i/0 < \alpha_i < C\}$ represents the bounded support vectors,
- $O = \{i/0 < \alpha_i < C\}$ represents non-support vectors,

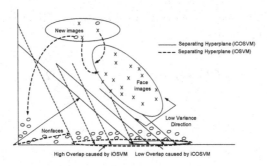

Fig. 2. The illustration of the possible separating hyperplanes for iOSVM and for iCOSVM when ($0 < \eta < 1$). The linear projection direction for iOSVM (depicted by dotted arrows) results in higher overlap between the example target and hypothetical outlier data (circled by dotted boundary) than the iCOSVM projection direction (depicted by solid arrows and the overlap circled by solid boundary).

Since support vectors summarize all the needed information for new data points classification, we would rather focus on the changes that may occur in the subset $\mathcal{S}$.

In real-world cases, the optimal decision boundary scarcely follows a specific variance direction. Therefore, we introduce a trade-off parameter, η, that controls the contribution of our kernel matrix $\mathbf{K}$ and the covariance matrix $\mathbf{\Delta}$. Hence, the value of the parameter η needs to be correctly adjusted so that we lessen the overlap while linearly projecting target objects and outliers. This assumption is outlined in Fig. 2. We can see that the iOSVM, when projecting data linearly (direction depicted by dotted arrows), leads to an expansion of the overlap (the area circled by dotted boundary) between target data objects and the assumed outliers.

4   Experimental Results

In this section, we present detailed experimental analysis and evaluation to validate our proposed method using real world dataset. The rest of this section is presented as follows: at first, we present datasets used, then a description of experimental protocol the same classifiers used for comparison and we finish with a discussion of the results of our experiments.

4.1   Datasets Used

We have employed a publicly available dataset, which has been widely adopted in relevant work in face detection, namely:

- BioID: The BioID consists of 1521 gray level face images, forming the target class. Each one shows the frontal view of a face of one out of 23 different persons.

- Olivetti-Oracle Research Lab (ORL) face database: This database contains 400 frontal face images of 40 different subjects. There are 10 images of each individual with different poses, illumination conditions, facial expressions (open/closed eyes, smiling/not smiling) and facial details (glasses/no glasses).
- MIT-CBCL: It contains 2901 images of faces and 28121 images of non-faces of size 19 × 19 pixels. The dataset is divided into a training set containing 2429 faces and 4548 non-faces and a test set containing 472 faces and 23573 non-faces.
- Face Detection Dataset and Benchmark (FDDB) database: The FDDB includes 2845 images. It is known for a wide variation in backgrounds, appearance, poses and lighting. We used Viola Jones algorithm to extract the annotated faces. The obtained dataset contains 5171 faces, which were considered as target class, and 175 non-faces, considered as outliers.

The BioID and the ORL databases are originally intended for face recognition, and they have been used for several applications throughout the literature from emotion recognition to specific facial feature recognition, etc. However, our purpose is to build a Face Detection framework that can act as a "proof-of-concept" system for comparison purposes among contemporary SVM-based incremental classifiers. Therefore, 500 non-face images were added to each one of them.

4.2   Experimental Protocol

In order to evaluate the performance of our framework, we performed two different experiment sets. First study the rate performance of different feature extraction methods, leading us to decide which features of the facial images have to be extracted. In the second experiment set, we compare the performance of iCOSVM, using proposed feature extraction techniques, against Incremental One-Class Support Vector Machine (iOSVM) and Incremental Support Vector Data Description (iSVDD). We have evaluated the performance of our proposed method using a cross-validation process, which consists of splitting dataset into 10 subsets of equal size. Then, to build a model, one of the 10 subsets was removed, and the rest was used as the training data. The previously removed subset was added to the outliers and this whole set was used for testing. Finally the 10 performance measures are averaged to provide the accuracy over all the models of a dataset. This guarantees that the achieved results were not a coincidence or biased.

As performance metrics we have considered the F-score, the precision and the recall. To better illustrate our interpretation we used the confusion matrix and the ROC curves.

The performance of the iCOSVM was compared to the following incremental One-Class classifiers:

- Incremental One-Class Support Vector Machine (iOSVM) [15]: Based on One-Class SVM, this method tries to find, recursively, the maximum margin hyperplane that separates targets from outliers.

- Incremental Support Vector Data Description (iSVDD) [16]: This method is based on Support Vector Data Description and it tries to give the sphere boundary description of the target data points with minimum volume.

The radial basis function (RBF) was used for kernelization. This kernel is calculated as $\mathcal{K}(x_i, x_j) = e^{-\|x_i - x_j\|^2 / \sigma}$.

Here, σ represents the positive "width" parameter. For η value optimization, the value of σ was set to 1. But, when compared with other methods σ is optimized first. The parameter ν for iOSVM and iCOSVM, also called *fraction of rejection* in the case of iSVDD was set to 0.2.

While optimizing η, the lowest threshold for the fraction of outliers (f_{OL}) was set to 0.1. However, it is too difficult, and even not possible to define optimal values for the parameters f_{OL} and ν in real cases, where data points are unknown at the beginning of the classification process. Therefore, we have set both of the two parameters to 0.2.

It is important to note that setting different ν and f_{OL} values for different datasets can result in better performance for these particular experiments. And they can be adjusted if necessary.

4.3 Results and Discussion

Tables 1 and 2 show the performance metrics for the different classifiers using HOG and LBP feature extraction methods respectively.

iCOSVM provides almost the highest F-score, and lowest FNR. It has a high recall (sensitivity) which means that there is barely few false negatives. However, the precision can be improved.

Table 1. Average performance metrics of each method for 4 face datasets (best method in **bold**, second best *emphasized*), using HOG Feature extraction method.

Dataset	Classifier	F-score	Precision	Recall	FNR	FPR
ORL	iSVDD	*78.1*	**100**	*64.2*	36.0	**00.0**
	iOSVM	**100**	**100**	**100**	**00.0**	**00.0**
	iCOSVM	**100**	*97.3*	**100**	**00.0**	5.5
BioID	iSVDD	51.1	**100**	*34.3*	65.7	**00.0**
	iOSVM	**100**	99.0	**100**	**00.0**	*0.2*
	iCOSVM	*98.8*	*97.6*	**100**	**00.0**	5.0
MIT-CBL	iSVDD	*65.8*	**100**	49	*51.0*	**00.0**
	iOSVM	**100**	**100**	**100**	**00.0**	**00.0**
	iCOSVM	**100**	*99.9*	*99.9*	**00.0**	*0.2*
FDDB	iSVDD	*40.3*	**100**	25.2	74.8	*00.0*
	iOSVM	*97.1*	*99.2*	*95.2*	*4.80*	*1.60*
	iCOSVM	**97.8**	95.6	**100**	**00.0**	9.20

In fact, precision indicates what fraction of the positive predictions made were actually correct. Recall, or sensitivity indicates the fraction of actual positive predictions that were correctly classified by the classifier. Hence, a classifier is outperforming when it has high precision and recall values.

Besides, with 0% FNR, it is assumed that iCOSVM is a good candidate for face detection purposes. Let's note that the FPR has notably increased when using LBP feature extraction method.

Table 2. Average performance metrics of each method for 4 face datasets (best method in **bold**, second best *emphasized*), using LBP Feature extraction method.

Dataset	Classifier	F-score	Precision	Recall	FNR	FPR
ORL	iSVDD	90.4	**100**	00.0	**17.5**	**00.0**
	iOSVM	*92.7*	86.4	**100**	00.0	31.5
	iCOSVM	**98.6**	*97.3*	**100**	17.5	*5.5*
BioID	iSVDD	89.6	**100**	*81.2*	*18.8*	**00.0**
	iOSVM	*95.3*	91.1	**100**	**00.0**	32.1
	iCOSVM	**98.3**	*96.6*	**100**	**00.0**	*11.5*
MIT-CBL	iSVDD	0.875	**100**	*77.7*	*22.3*	**0.0**
	iOSVM	*99.2*	98.4	**100**	**0.0**	3.2
	iCOSVM	**99.5**	*98.9*	**100**	**0.0**	*2.2*
FDDB	iSVDD	**87.6**	**98.9**	*78.7*	*21.3*	**1.8**
	iOSVM	81.5	68.1	**100**	**00.0**	91.0
	iCOSVM	*82.5*	*70.3*	**100**	**00.0**	*84.6*

Comparing the overall performance metrics obtained when applying HOG and LBP feature extraction methods, we can estimate that HOG method combined with iCOSVM classifier is a good solution for face detection tasks.

In Table 3, we provide performance measures using the combination HOG-LBP feature extraction method. Once again, iCOSVM outperforms the other classifiers an practically all the used datasets.

Considering the overall feature extraction techniques applied with the iCOSVM technique, it is assumed that HOG method provides the best F-score. Nevertheless HOG-LBP abates the FPR significantly. Actually, the fusion HOG-LBP combines two different processes in a different manner, and produces a different output, even though they are both based on the gradient information. HOG proves very effective when it comes to capturing the outlines and angles. LBP on the other hand uses 8 directions for each pixel and generates a 256 bin histogram representing the pixel distribution of the input image. The concatenation of the LBP and HOG generated vector is a solution to form a single feature pool, but a curse of dimensionality appears and needs to be resolved.

Table 3. Average performance metrics of each method for 4 face datasets (best method in **bold**, second best *emphasized*), using HOG-LBP Feature extraction method.

Dataset	Classifier	F-score	Precision	Recall	FNR	FPR
ORL	iSVDD	73.2	**100**	*57.7*	*42.2*	**00.0**
	iOSVM	*93.3*	87.5	**100**	**00.0**	14.2
	iCOSVM	**99.75**	*99.5*	**100**	**00.0**	*0.5*
BioID	iSVDD	69.7	**100**	*53.5*	*46.5*	**0.00**
	iOSVM	*98.7*	97.5	**100**	**00.0**	5.00
	iCOSVM	**99.9**	*99.8*	**100**	**00.0**	*0.4*
MIT-CBL	iSVDD	79.3	**100**	*65.8*	*34.2*	**00.0**
	iOSVM	*99.1*	*98.1*	**100**	**00.0**	4.0
	iCOSVM	**100**	**100**	**100**	**00.0**	**00.0**
FDDB	iSVDD	63.3	**100**	46.4	53.6	**00.0**
	iOSVM	*97.1*	*99.1*	*95.2*	*4.8*	*1.8*
	iCOSVM	**97.7**	95.4	**100**	**00.0**	9.6

5   Conclusion

A novel learning-classification framework using local and global facial descriptors has been proposed for face detection. Our main contribution is the introduction of an incremental learning process, which effectively improves classification accuracy. We have, indeed, proposed a framework containing 3 major phases, i.e. (1) data extraction, (2) feature extraction and (3) data classification. Our framework takes advantage of the state-of-the-art incremental One-Class Support Vector Machine, where the covariance matrix, estimated in the kernel space, is incorporated. Since we are dealing with a minimization problem, we can exploit the information carried out by the low variance directions. We performed rigorous experiments on various face datasets, in order to identify the most convenient feature extraction method. We compared Histogram of Oriented Gradients (HOG), Local Binary Patterns (LBP) and the fusion of both methods HOG and LBP. We proved that HOG method provides the bets F-score measure, but HOG-LBP lessens the False Positive Rate. We compared our iCOSVM against incremental SVM-based methods in terms of F-score, Precision, Recall, False Negative Rate and False Positive Rate. Results show the superiority of our method.

The proposed framework can be used as the first component of a reliable surveillance system, used to identify faces and track targets and improve national security.

References

1. Zafeiriou, S., Zhang, C., Zhang, Z.: A Survey on Face Detection in the wild: past, present and future. Comput. Vis. Image Underst. **138**, 1–24 (2015)
2. Sriman, K.P.N., Raj Kumar, P., Naveen, A., Saravana Kumar, R.: Comparison of Paul Viola - Michael Jones algorithm and HOG algorithm for Face Detection. In: IOP Conference Series: Materials Science and Engineering, First International Conference on Circuits, Signals, Systems and Securities (ICCSSS 2020), vol. 1084. IOP Publishing (2021). https://doi.org/10.1088/1757-899X/1084/1/012014. 012014
3. Mohammed, M.G., Melhum, A.I.: Implementation of HOG feature extraction with tuned parameters for human face detection. Int. J. Mach. Learn. Comput. **10**, 654–661 (2020)
4. Chen, J., Wang, J., Zhao, L., He, J.: Branch-structured detector for fast face detection using asymmetric LBP features. SIViP **14**(8), 1699–1706 (2020). https://doi.org/10.1007/s11760-020-01710-7
5. Islam, B., Mahmud, F., Hossain, A.: High performance facial expression recognition system using facial region segmentation, fusion of HOG & LBP features and multiclass SVM. In: 2018 10th International Conference on Electrical and Computer Engineering (ICECE), pp. 42–45. https://doi.org/10.1109/ICECE.2018.8636780
6. Santosh, M., Sharma, A.: Fusion of multi representation and multi descriptors for facial expression recognition. In: IOP Conference Series: Materials Science and Engineering, International Conference on Research and Advances in Mechanical Engineering (ICRAME 2020), Hyderabad, India, vol. 1057. https://doi.org/10.1088/1757-899X/1057/1/012093
7. Farmanbar, M., Toygar, Ö.: Spoof detection on face and palmprint biometrics. SIViP **11**(7), 1253–1260 (2017). https://doi.org/10.1007/s11760-017-1082-y
8. Shao, Y., Lunetta, R.S.: Comparison of support vector machine, neural network, and CART algorithms for the land-cover classification using limited training data points. ISPRS J. Photogram. Rem. Sens. **70**, 78–87 (2012)
9. Kefi-Fatteh, T., Ksantini, R., Kaâniche, M.-B., Bouhoula, A.: Human face detection improvement using incremental learning based on low variance directions. In: Advanced Concepts for Intelligent Vision Systems (ACIVS), pp. 170–179 (2017)
10. Kefi-Fatteh, T., Ksantini, R., Kaâniche, M.-B., Bouhoula, A.: A novel incremental covariance-guided one-class support vector machine. In: Joint European Conference on Machine Learning and Knowledge Discovery in Databases (ECML-PKDD), pp. 17–32
11. Gu, Q., Chang, Y., Li, X., Chang, Z., Feng, Z.: A novel F-SVM based on FOA for improving SVM performance. Expert Syst. Appl. **165** (2021). https://doi.org/10.1016/j.eswa.2020.113713
12. Viola, P., Jones, M.: Rapid object detection using a boosted cascade of simple features. In: ACVPR, no. 1, pp. 511–518. IEEE Computer Society (2001)
13. Dascoudhary, R.N., Tripathy, R.: Real time face detection and tracking using Haar classifier on SOC. Int. J. Psychosoc. Rehabil. **22**(4), 16–28 (2018)
14. Dalal, N., Triggs, B.: Histograms of oriented gradients for human detection. In: 2005 IEEE Computer Society Conference on Computer Vision and Pattern Recognition, CVPR 2005 (2005)
15. Davy, M., Desorby, F., Gretton, A., Doncarli, C.: An online support vector machine for abnormal events detection. Signal Process. **86**, 2009–2025 (2005)
16. Hua, X., Ding, S.: Incremental learning algorithm for support vector data description. J. Softw. **6**, 1166–1173 (2011)

Classification, Clustering
and Recommendation

Supervised Contrastive Learning for Product Classification

Sahel Azizi, Uno Fang$^{(\boxtimes)}$, Sasan Adibi, and Jianxin Li

Deakin University, Burwood, VIC 3125, Australia

Abstract. Contrastive learning has shown great results in image classification. It is primarily applied for semi-supervised or unsupervised representation learning. Contrastive learning has recently shown high accuracy results in supervised environments where fully labeled images were utilized for image classification. In the e-commerce field, product image datasets tend not to have a large number of instances which make the classification of new products more difficult. Thus, a model that can classify product images needs to utilize all the existing labeled images in a detailed manner. This paper adopts supervised contrastive learning to explicitly classify products based on their images. This is done by using Optical Character Recognition (OCR) as an auxiliary input and by fine-tuning pre-trained models. OCR takes advantage of the fact that product images have distinct features over standard images. Labels or texts that appear on product images are captured and fed into the projection network along with their corresponding images. This simplifies the classification of the images for the classifier. The use of the auxiliary input with the fine-tuning has shown a noticeable and promising increase in classification accuracy. Experiments have demonstrated that our proposed framework has achieved over a 15% top-1 accuracy increase over the existing methods on three different datasets.

Keywords: Contrastive learning · Supervised image classification · Optical character recognition

1 Introduction

The e-commerce field has grown rapidly in the last few years. A successful e-commerce platform enables potential buyers to navigate through its website effortlessly to find their desired products [29]. These products often need to be classified manually. Additionally, different shopping websites have different standard product taxonomies [17,29]. This makes the manual product classification time-consuming and prone to mistakes. However, misclassifying products will lead to the loss of sales by directing customers to irrelevant and unwanted results. This also will have a negative impact on the shopping website [13]. Therefore, recommendation applications (e.g., product image retrieval and product taxonomy browsing) have been increasingly leveraged to benefit product classification [30].

© Springer Nature Switzerland AG 2022
B. Li et al. (Eds.): ADMA 2021, LNAI 13088, pp. 341–355, 2022.
https://doi.org/10.1007/978-3-030-95408-6_26

Recent studies [4,11,15] have applied contrastive learning to image classification. Contrastive learning aims to learn effective representations by maximizing the mutual information (MI) by contrasting positive pairs (i.e., two images from the same class) and negative pairs (i.e., two images from different classes). [23] compare 34 image classification methods, and observe that the outstanding methods, FixMatch and SimCLRv2, exceed the threshold of scientific usage and are applicable in high resolution and complex image classification tasks. The two methods achieved 71.46% and 80.9% top-1 accuracy scores respectively on the ILSVRC-2012 dataset as per [23].

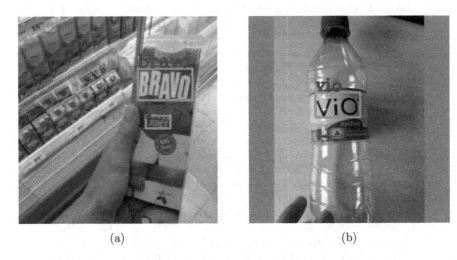

(a)   (b)

Fig. 1. Sample of detected and recognized texts Source: [13,16]

In general, the amount and the diversity of product images tend to be insufficient to meet the data-hunger of deep learning [26]. Also, products from different classes may have similar shapes and appearances [22]. Hence, a robust product classifier is expected to make good use of all the existing images. [15] propose a supervised contrastive learning framework, which can effectively leverage insufficient images to classify images. However, contrastive learning only focuses on the visual information of images, while textual information would be essential for accurate classification. Therefore, Optical Character Recognition (OCR) [20] has been considered to detect and recognize the texts of those product images, which will enhance image classification with additional distinctive information. Figure 1 shows detected and recognized texts from a sample image.

The key contributions of this paper can be summarized as follows:

– We propose a product image classifier under the framework of contrastive learning.
– We implement InceptionV3 [28] and OCR to extract visual information and textual information from product images as embeddings for contrasting.

– We conduct experiments on three product datasets to evaluate our proposed model, which achieves over a 15% top-1 accuracy improvement on each
dataset compared to baseline methods.

The rest of the paper is structured as follows: Sect. 2 reviews the literature
and related work. Section 3 presents the proposed model. Section 4 describes the
experiment, datasets used, and achieved results. Section 5 concludes this work.

2   Related Work

2.1   Deep Learning for Product Classification

In computer vision, Convolutional Neural Networks (CNN) are the best at predicting performance for several image classification tasks [26]. CNN is a common
deep learning technique that was firstly stimulated by the visual cortex of ani-
mals [1]. Unlike traditional image classification techniques, CNN extracts deep
features from images and automatically learns domain-specific features [32]. In
CNN's, features from images are extracted directly via tuning the convolutional
layer(s) and the pooling layer(s) [14]. CNN has also been used in fine-grained
classifications where the categories or classes of images are visually similar to
each other [26]. Chen et al. [3] presented a smart search engine for online shopping where the customer inputs an image of the product that he/she wants to
buy. Then a CNN classifies the product into a relative category. The input vector
of the last layer is then used to feed into a similarity measurement CNN model to
find and recommend similar products in the database. Fengzi et al. [8] performed
a product image classification task on a fashion dataset using VGG19 which is
a convolutional neural network architecture developed by the Visual Geometry
Group, they also performed an image search task using cosine similarity and
autoencoders to recognize similar images.

On the other hand, Wagh and Mahajan [30] stated that text-tagging is relied
on heavily in most product classifications accuracy. Dumais and Chen [6] used
Support Vector Machine (SVM) classifiers and approached product classifications as a text classification task. Chavaltada et al. [2] conducted an experiment
where product name and category data were collected from shopping websites,
text was pre-processed, an n-gram model was used for feature extraction, and
different classification models were built. It was concluded that the Naïve Bayes
model performed the best in the experiment. Other works have implemented
a hybrid system of both which yielded interesting results. Others have used
some auxiliary data such as knowledge graphs to increase the accuracy of the
classifications. And more recently, transfer learning has also been heavily and
successfully implemented in Natural Language Processing (NLP) and Computer
vision streams which have solved many of the encountered issues [21].

2.2   Contrastive Learning

Contrastive methods have been mainly used in the fields of unsupervised
and semi-supervised learning [15]. Most of the time, unsupervised learning is

accomplished by creating pseudo labels which was the reason it is referred to as self-supervised. This type of learning needs to use labeled data to fine-tune the training [23]. Chen et al. [5] exemplified contrastive learning as a dictionary lookup scenario. The contrastive loss aims to differentiate between the positive pairs, which could be an augmented view of the same image, and negative pairs, which could be all the other images in the batch from other classes. Falcon and Cho [7] set a five-phase framework for contrastive self-supervised learning which comprises an encoder, a data augmentation channel, a feature extraction, and a loss function on similarity scores.

More recently, the contrastive learning methods have been used on fully supervised datasets and have shown great and promising results. Khosla et al. [15] applied contrastive learning in computer vision and reported consistent outperformance over the cross-entropy loss in multiple datasets. Their proposed model has also shown more stability and robustness to noise. [31] proposed a hybrid network structure based on contrastive learning to solve the issue of data imbalance and long-tailed image classification. In NLP, Gunel et al. [10] implemented contrastive learning for fine-tuning pre-trained language models and illustrated a more robust model to corruptions and a better generalization to related tasks with few labeled data.

2.3   Optical Character Recognition (OCR)

Optical character recognition is a discipline that transforms different types of documents and images into meaningful and interpretable data through feature extraction and classification [19]. However, OCR can be negatively impacted by the image quality, lighting conditions or visual obstructions. It also suffers from high variability of length, size, font, and language which makes recognition difficult [9]. Yet, it can provide useful information and be applied in different types of applications. In the text detection phase, the purpose is to segment or create bounding boxes of all text occurrences in a given image. Zhou et al. [34] has introduced a scene text detector using a solo neural network that quickly and promptly generates word or line-level projections from full-sized images. In the text recognition phase, the purpose is to decipher or decode those detected occurrences into a readable or editable status. Convolutional Recurrent Neural Network (CRNN) was presented as an end-to-end text recognition system that combines CNN with Recurrent Neural Network (RNN) [24]. CRNN can cope with sequences of random lengths and does not rely on an additional glossary.

3   Proposed Model

The proposed model caters to e-commerce products such as groceries and cosmetics. Figure 2 illustrates the flow of the model starting with the product image and ending with product classification. The model starts by detecting structured or unstructured text in each image using an Efficient and Accurate Scene Text Detector (EAST) model presented by Zhou et al. [34]. Once a text is detected, a

CRNN model [24] is applied to recognize this text into a readable status. Words per each image are then tokenized and encoded into a 32-dimensional vector through a Long short-term memory (LSTM) network [12].

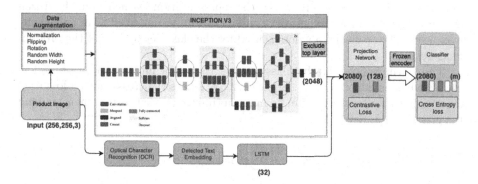

Fig. 2. A diagram showing the flow of the proposed model using the InceptionV3 architecture depicted by [18]

On the other hand, the input images are randomly augmented (e.g., flipping, rotating and re-sizing), then extracted as feature vectors by a designed InceptionV3 [28]. InceptionV3 architecture is fully convolutional, and it has lower computational costs compared to other architectures [27]. We exclude the last layer of InceptionV3, which outputs normalized 2048-dimensional feature vectors. Next, the feature vector of each image is concatenated with the 32-dimensional vector which was encoded earlier through the text detection and recognition step.

The above concatenated vector is fed into a projection network where it gets converted into a normalized 128-dimensional vector. The projection network is trained using the Adamax optimizer and the supervised contrastive loss as per Eq. 1 [15].

$$\mathcal{L}_{out}^{sup} = \sum_{i \in 1} \mathcal{L}_{out,i}^{sup}$$

$$= \sum_{i \in 1} \frac{-1}{|P(i)|} \sum_{p \in P(i)} \log \frac{exp(z_i \cdot z_p / \tau)}{\sum_{a \in A(i)} exp(z_i \cdot z_a / \tau)} \tag{1}$$

Where $P(i)$ refers to all positive samples to the anchor i, z_i represents the projected vector of the input image, z_p is the projected vector of an image of the same class of the input image, z_a denotes the projected vector of any other image, and τ is a scalar temperature parameter used to control the randomness of predictions.

The loss function maximizes the dot products of the normalized vectors for the product images of the same class and minimizes the dot products for product images belonging to different classes. This way the representation vectors of product images and detected texts of the same are brought together and those are of different classes are pushed apart.

After the completion of the training using the contrastive loss, the projection network can be abandoned, and the learned weights are frozen. A new classification network is trained where it uses the representation learned from the frozen encoder. The classification network consists of a fully connected layer and a softmax layer. The cross-entropy loss is used for the classifier to predict the product image class.

The softmax layer in the classifier has the same number of the products classes which is denoted as M. Equation 2 [25] shows the cross-entropy loss used for training the classifier. The Adamax optimizer is used again when training the classification network.

$$\mathcal{L}_{CE} = -\sum_{c=1}^{M} y_c \log p(y = c|\mathbf{x}) \tag{2}$$

M represents the number of classes, y_c is a binary indicator where it is equal to 1 if the class label is c or equal to 0 if not, $p(y = c|x)$ indicates the predicted probability that the label is of class c.

The concatenation of the encoded detected texts to the encoded images gives the model additional important features that assist and make it easier for the classifier to predict the right class.

4   Experiment

4.1   Datasets

Freiburg Groceries Dataset. Freiburg Groceries Dataset [13] was collected in real-world settings consisting of 5,000 images of 25 classes of groceries. The images have a variety of backgrounds in terms of lighting conditions, clutter, and perspectives. 5 classes were chosen randomly for the experiment which are Beans, Cake, Candy, Tea, and Water. The total number of images used for the experiment was 1,643. The sample images of Freiburg Groceries Dataset are shown in Fig. 3.

Grocery Store Dataset. Grocery Store Dataset [16] consists of over 5,000 real-world images of fruits, vegetables, and packaged products. Our experiment focuses on the packaged products where informative texts (e.g., product brand, size and type) can be seen on the packages. The texts can be effectively utilized in the classification task. The dataset has 1,743 images across 9 classes which are Juice, Milk, Oatghurt, Oat-Milk, Sour-Cream, Sour-Milk, Soyghurt, Soy-Milk, Yogurt. The sample images of Grocery Store Dataset are shown in Fig. 4.

Fig. 3. A random sample from different classes of The Freiburg Groceries Dataset
Source: [13]

Fig. 4. A random sample from different classes of the Grocery Store Dataset
Source: [16]

Grozi-3.2K Dataset. Grozi-3.2K Dataset [33] has 80 different product classes containing 8,350 images in total. Random samples have been demonstrated in Fig. 5. We adopt the class of House Products, which is made of 989 images. This class has 9 sub-classes (i.e., Bathroom, Batteries, Candles, Cooking, Lighting, Office Supplies, Others, Storage, and Textiles). The sample images of Grozi-3.2K Dataset are shown in Fig. 5.

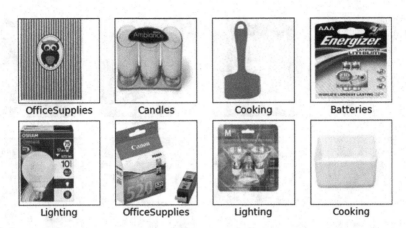

OfficeSupplies   Candles   Cooking   Batteries

Lighting   OfficeSupplies   Lighting   Cooking

Fig. 5. A random sample from different classes of the Grozi-3.2K Dataset Source: [33]

4.2 Training the Model

All datasets used were randomly split into 80% for training and 20% for testing. The training started with detecting texts using EAST [34] and recognizing them using CRNN [24] from images in the training set. The extracted texts from an image are encoded into a 32-dimensional vector through an LSTM network [12]. In addition, image augmenting operations, including normalizing, re-sizing, flipping and rotating, are randomly applied on images. Then, the augmented images are fed into InceptionV3 architecture to output 2048-dimensional feature vectors. The batch size is set to 32 for the training.

Both above inputs (input images and detected texts) are trained for 10 epochs using the contrastive loss (see Eq. 1) and the Adamax optimizer through the projection network. The learning rate is set to 0.001 and the temperature parameter τ is set to 0.05. After training the model, the encoder is frozen, and the projection network is abandoned. The classification network is trained using the encoded fixed weights. The classifier has one dense layer using the Relu function and another Softmax layer with an output of the number of classes required. The classifier was trained for another 10 epochs, which are found to be sufficient but can be changed depending on the dataset and requirements.

4.3 Evaluation

Compared Models. One of the Baseline models, **InceptionV3-based Classifier**, is a CNN that uses the pre-trained InceptionV3 [28] architecture for the encoding and uses a fully connected layer and a SoftMax layer for the classification. Another baseline method, **CL-based Classifier**, is the supervised contrastive learning model proposed by a state-of-the-art study [15] with only images as the input. The proposed model is a fine-tuned supervised contrastive learning model with images and OCR as inputs. Our results are also compared to the top-1 accuracy results achieved by FixMatch 71.46% and SimCLRv2 80.9%

on the ILSVRC-2012 dataset which was deemed applicable to real-world image classification applications as concluded by Schmarje et al. [23]. The following sections demonstrate the results achieved by the proposed model on each dataset and compare the top-1 accuracy results with the other models.

The Freiburg Groceries Dataset Results. The proposed model has a significant improvement in both the training and testing classification accuracy over the other two models as shown in Table 1. The achieved accuracy also exceeds the reported rates [23] of FixMatch 71.46% and SimCLRv2 80.9% on the ILSVRC-2012 dataset by over 13%.

Table 1. Accuracy results for the Freiburg Groceries Dataset

Model	Training accuracy	Testing accuracy
InceptionV3-based classifier [28]	93.31%	61.40%
CL-based classifier [15]	90.11%	82.46%
Proposed model	99.72%	94.3%

Figure 6 shows the training and validation accuracy over 10 Epochs of training for the proposed model. The validation accuracy noticeably increased up till the third epoch where it stayed almost steady afterwards. The training accuracy reached 99.72% by the end of the 10 epochs of training.

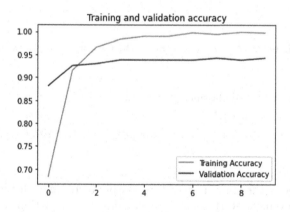

Fig. 6. Training and validation accuracy for the Freiburg Groceries Dataset

Table 7a shows a classification summary including precision, recall, and F1-Score using the proposed model. The support column shows the number of samples used during testing for each class.

The confusion matrix illustrated in Fig. 7b shows that the cake photos were most confused with tea during the classification. This is believed to be due to having the lowest number of images for training for that category.

Class	Precision	Recall	F1-score	Support
Beans	1.00	0.92	0.96	25
Cake	1.00	0.79	0.88	28
Candy	0.91	0.99	0.95	70
Tea	0.90	0.96	0.93	54
Water	1.00	0.96	0.98	51
accuracy			0.94	228
macro avg	0.96	0.92	0.94	228
weighted avg	0.95	0.94	0.94	228

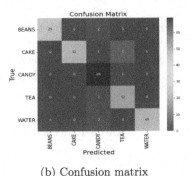

(a) Classification summary   (b) Confusion matrix

Fig. 7. Classification summary and confusion matrix for the Freiburg Groceries Dataset

The Grocery Store Dataset Results. The proposed model outperformed the other 2 models in both the training and testing accuracy. There is a significant improvement in the testing accuracy with over 37% increase in accuracy over the baseline model and over 16% over the supervised contrastive learning model as shown in Table 2. The achieved accuracy also exceeds the reported rates [23] of FixMatch 71.46% and SimCLRv2 80.9% on the ILSVRC-2012 dataset by over 18%.

Table 2. Accuracy results for the Grocery Store Dataset

Model	Training accuracy	Testing accuracy
InceptionV3-based classifier [28]	97.32%	62.06%
CL-based classifier [15]	81.02%	83.24%
Proposed model	99.44%	99.71%

Figure 8 shows the training accuracy sharply increasing till the fourth epoch then the improvement starts to slow down while the validation accuracy almost peaking around the second epoch and remains almost stable till the end of the 10 epochs.

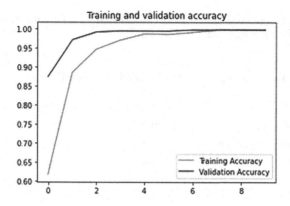

Fig. 8. Training and validation accuracy for the Grocery Store Dataset

The precision scores were 100% for all classes except for the Yoghurt class. The recall scores were 100% for all classes except for the Sour-Cream class. This can all also be seen reflected in the F1-Score shown in Table 9a.

Class	Precision	Recall	F1-score	Support
Juice	1.00	1.00	1.00	95
Milk	1.00	1.00	1.00	73
Oatghurt	1.00	1.00	1.00	14
Oat-Milk	1.00	1.00	1.00	13
Sour-Cream	1.00	0.95	0.97	19
Sour-Milk	1.00	1.00	1.00	10
Soyhghurt	1.00	1.00	1.00	23
Soy-Milk	1.00	1.00	1.00	20
Yoghurt	0.99	1.00	0.99	73
accuracy			1.00	340
macro avg	1.00	0.99	1.00	340
weighted avg	1.00	1.00	1.00	340

(a) Classification summary

(b) Confusion matrix

Fig. 9. Classification summary and confusion matrix for the Grocery Store Dataset

Only one image was incorrectly classified where it can be seen in the confusion matrix (see Fig. 9b). The model predicted an image of a Yoghurt while it was a Sour-Cream image.

The Grozi-3.2k Dataset Results. The proposed model also outperformed the other 2 models in both the training and testing accuracy. The increase in accuracy for the testing set was 27% over the baseline model and 24% over the supervised contrastive learning model as shown in Table 3. The achieved accuracy also exceeds the reported rates [23] of FixMatch 71.46% and SimCLRv2 80.9% on the ILSVRC-2012 dataset by over 4%.

Table 3. Accuracy results for the Grozi-3.2k Dataset results

Model	Training accuracy	Testing accuracy
InceptionV3-based classifier	90.91%	58.08%
CL-based classifier	66.40%	61.11%
Proposed model	94.84%	85.35%

Figure 10 shows the training accuracy kept gradually increasing till the tenth and last epoch. The validation accuracy had also an increasing trend till the last epoch.

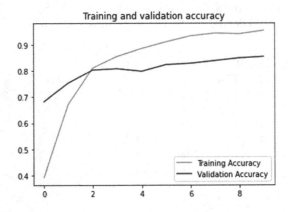

Fig. 10. Training and validation accuracy for the Grozi-3.2k Dataset results

The classification summary (See Table 11a) shows lower precision and recall scores than the other two datasets. This can be referred to the small number of samples used for the classification task.

The confusion matrix in Fig. 11b shows the "others" class and the "cooking" class were the most interchangeably miss-classified. This can be due to not having specific features that the model can extract to define the "others" category.

The results achieved above by the proposed model for all datasets show a significant improvement in the classification accuracy. The number of samples impacted the results for the Grozi-3.2k dataset as it was much smaller than the other two. The accuracy results are believed to be reliable and practical for the use of e-commerce platforms in addition to the small number of epochs needed for the training.

Class	Precision	Recall	F1-score	Support
Bathroom	1.00	0.60	0.75	10
Batteries	1.00	0.80	0.89	5
Candles	1.00	0.29	0.44	7
Cooking	0.81	0.74	0.77	34
Lighting	0.96	0.96	0.96	25
OfficeSupplies	0.81	0.98	0.89	49
Others	0.61	0.74	0.67	19
Storage	0.87	0.81	0.84	16
Textiles	1.00	1.00	1.00	33
accuracy			0.85	198
macro avg	0.90	0.77	0.80	198
weighted avg	0.87	0.85	0.85	198

(a) Classification summary

(b) Confusion matrix

Fig. 11. Classification summary and confusion matrix for the Grozi-3.2k Dataset

5 Conclusion

In this paper, we introduce a product image classifier which leverages visual information and textual information. The proposed model uses Optical Character Recognition (OCR) as an auxiliary input and applies fine-tuned supervised contrastive method to increase the classification task accuracy. The model has achieved significant improvement in top-1 classification accuracy over three product datasets. The accuracy rates achieved were 94.3%, 99.71%, 85.35% which have over 15% improvement over the baseline models. During the experiment it was noticed there was some noise in the detected and recognized text. This is an area for investigation and future work as it is directly connected to the product classification outcome.

References

1. Aloysius, N., Geetha, M.: A review on deep convolutional neural networks. In: 2017 International Conference on Communication and Signal Processing (ICCSP), pp. 0588–0592. IEEE (2017)
2. Chavaltada, C., Pasupa, K., Hardoon, D.R.: A comparative study of machine learning techniques for automatic product categorisation. In: Cong, F., Leung, A., Wei, Q. (eds.) ISNN 2017. LNCS, vol. 10261, pp. 10–17. Springer, Cham (2017). https://doi.org/10.1007/978-3-319-59072-1_2
3. Chen, L., Yang, F., Yang, H.: Image-based product recommendation system with convolutional neural networks (2017)
4. Chen, T., Kornblith, S., Norouzi, M., Hinton, G.: A simple framework for contrastive learning of visual representations. In: International Conference on Machine Learning, pp. 1597–1607. PMLR (2020)
5. Chen, X., Fan, H., Girshick, R., He, K.: Improved baselines with momentum contrastive learning. arXiv preprint arXiv:2003.04297 (2020)

6. Dumais, S., Chen, H.: Hierarchical classification of web content. In: Proceedings of the 23rd Annual International ACM SIGIR Conference on Research and Development in Information Retrieval, pp. 256–263 (2000)
7. Falcon, W., Cho, K.: A framework for contrastive self-supervised learning and designing a new approach. arXiv preprint arXiv:2009.00104 (2020)
8. Fengzi, L., Kant, S., Araki, S., Bangera, S., Shukla, S.S.: Neural networks for fashion image classification and visual search. SSRN 3602664 (2020)
9. Georgieva, P., Zhang, P.: Optical character recognition for autonomous stores. In: 2020 IEEE 10th International Conference on Intelligent Systems (IS), pp. 69–75. IEEE (2020)
10. Gunel, B., Du, J., Conneau, A., Stoyanov, V.: Supervised contrastive learning for pre-trained language model fine-tuning. arXiv preprint arXiv:2011.01403 (2020)
11. He, K., Fan, H., Wu, Y., Xie, S., Girshick, R.: Momentum contrast for unsupervised visual representation learning. In: Proceedings of the IEEE/CVF Conference on Computer Vision and Pattern Recognition, pp. 9729–9738 (2020)
12. Hochreiter, S., Schmidhuber, J.: Long short-term memory. Neural Comput. **9**(8), 1735–1780 (1997)
13. Jund, P., Abdo, N., Eitel, A., Burgard, W.: The freiburg groceries dataset. arXiv preprint arXiv:1611.05799 (2016)
14. Kaur, T., Gandhi, T.K.: Deep convolutional neural networks with transfer learning for automated brain image classification. Mach. Vis. Appl. **31**(3), 1–16 (2020). https://doi.org/10.1007/s00138-020-01069-2
15. Khosla, P., et al.: Supervised contrastive learning. arXiv preprint arXiv:2004.11362 (2020)
16. Klasson, M., Zhang, C., Kjellström, H.: A hierarchical grocery store image dataset with visual and semantic labels. In: 2019 IEEE Winter Conference on Applications of Computer Vision (WACV), pp. 491–500. IEEE (2019)
17. Kozareva, Z.: Everyone likes shopping! Multi-class product categorization for e-commerce. In: Proceedings of the 2015 Conference of the North American Chapter of the Association for Computational Linguistics: Human Language Technologies, pp. 1329–1333 (2015)
18. Mahdianpari, M., Salehi, B., Rezaee, M., Mohammadimanesh, F., Zhang, Y.: Very deep convolutional neural networks for complex land cover mapping using multi-spectral remote sensing imagery. Remote Sens. **10**(7), 1119 (2018)
19. Memon, J., Sami, M., Khan, R.A., Uddin, M.: Handwritten optical character recognition (OCR): a comprehensive systematic literature review (SLR). IEEE Access **8**, 142642–142668 (2020)
20. Mori, S., Nishida, H., Yamada, H.: Optical Character Recognition. Wiley, Hoboken (1999)
21. Pan, S.J., Yang, Q.: A survey on transfer learning. IEEE Trans. Knowl. Data Eng. **22**(10), 1345–1359 (2009)
22. Peng, J., Xiao, C., Li, Y.: RP2K: a large-scale retail product dataset for fine-grained image classification. arXiv preprint arXiv:2006.12634 (2020)
23. Schmarje, L., Santarossa, M., Schröder, S.M., Koch, R.: A survey on semi-, self- and unsupervised learning for image classification. arXiv preprint arXiv:2002.08721 (2020)
24. Shi, B., Bai, X., Yao, C.: An end-to-end trainable neural network for image-based sequence recognition and its application to scene text recognition. IEEE Trans. Pattern Anal. Mach. Intell. **39**(11), 2298–2304 (2016)
25. Sosnovshchenko, O., Baiev, O.: Machine Learning with Swift: Artificial Intelligence for IOS. Packt Publishing Ltd., Birmingham (2018)

26. Srivastava, M.M.: Bag of tricks for retail product image classification. In: Campilho, A., Karray, F., Wang, Z. (eds.) ICIAR 2020. LNCS, vol. 12131, pp. 71–82. Springer, Cham (2020). https://doi.org/10.1007/978-3-030-50347-5_8
27. Szegedy, C., Vanhoucke, V., Ioffe, S., Shlens, J., Wojna, Z.: Rethinking the inception architecture for computer vision. In: Proceedings of the IEEE Conference on Computer Vision and Pattern Recognition, pp. 2818–2826 (2016)
28. Szegedy, C., Vanhoucke, V., Ioffe, S., Shlens, J., Wojna, Z.: Rethinking the inception architecture for computer vision. CoRR arXiv:1512.00567 (2015)
29. Umaashankar, V., Prakash, A., et al.: Atlas: a dataset and benchmark for e-commerce clothing product categorization. arXiv preprint arXiv:1908.08984 (2019)
30. Wagh, D., Mahajan, S.: Product image classification techniques. Int. J. Innov. Technol. Explor. Eng. (IJITEE) **8**, 389–393 (2019)
31. Wang, P., Han, K., Wei, X.S., Zhang, L., Wang, L.: Contrastive learning based hybrid networks for long-tailed image classification. In: Proceedings of the IEEE/CVF Conference on Computer Vision and Pattern Recognition, pp. 943–952 (2021)
32. Wang, Y., Wang, Z.: A survey of recent work on fine-grained image classification techniques. J. Vis. Commun. Image Represent. **59**, 210–214 (2019)
33. Xie, J., Girshick, R., Farhadi, A.: Unsupervised deep embedding for clustering analysis. In: International Conference on Machine Learning, pp. 478–487. PMLR (2016)
34. Zhou, X., et al.: EAST: an efficient and accurate scene text detector. In: Proceedings of the IEEE Conference on Computer Vision and Pattern Recognition, pp. 5551–5560 (2017)

Balanced Spectral Clustering Algorithm Based on Feature Selection

Qimin Luo[1,2], Guangquan Lu[1,2], Guoqiu Wen[1,2], Zidong Su[1,2], Xingyi Liu[3(✉)], and Jian Wei[1,2(✉)]

[1] Guangxi Key Lab of Multi-Source Information Mining and Security,
Guangxi Normal University, Guilin 541004, Guangxi, China
{lugq,guoqiuwen}@mailbox.gxnu.edu.cn
[2] School of Computer Science and Engineering, Guangxi Normal University,
Guilin 541004, Guangxi, China
[3] Guangxi Vocational and Technical Institute of Industry, Nanning 530001, China

Abstract. High dimensional data clustering faced some problems such as sparse samples, difficulty in calculating similarity and so on. In addition, the clustering results sometimes be extremely unbalanced with too many or too few category samples. Therefore, we propose a novel algorithm, that is a balanced spectral clustering algorithm based on feature selection. Firstly, the least square method is used to calculate the target loss error. Secondly, the method of feature selection is used to reduce the influence of noise and redundant features. Thirdly, a balanced regularization term exclusive lasso is introduced to balance the clustering results. Finally, the locality preserving projection is used to maintain the feature structure of the samples. A large number of experimental results show that the proposed algorithm outperformed the comparison algorithms on the two indicators (accuracy and normal mutual information) in most cases, which proves the effectiveness of the proposed spectral clustering algorithm.

Keywords: Spectral clustering · Locality preserving projection · Feature selection · Exclusive lasso

1 Introduction

Clustering analysis is a technology for static data analysis, which is widely used in many fields, including machine learning, data mining, pattern recognition, image analysis and biological information [5, 7, 20, 26, 29, 31, 34, 35]. Clustering is a process of classifying data into different subsets. Each subset is called a cluster,

This work is partially supported by the Project of Guangxi Science and Technology (GuiKeAD20159041); the Research Fund of Guangxi Key Lab of Multi-source Information Mining & Security (No. 20-A-01-01); the Research Fund of Guangxi Key Lab of Multi-source Information Mining & Security (MIMS20-M-01), the Innovation Project of Guangxi Graduate Education (No. YCSW2021095, No. JXXYYJSCXXM-2021-010).

© Springer Nature Switzerland AG 2022
B. Li et al. (Eds.): ADMA 2021, LNAI 13088, pp. 356–367, 2022.
https://doi.org/10.1007/978-3-030-95408-6_27

so that the samples in the same cluster are as close to each other as possible, and the samples among the different clusters are as far away as possible [10]. In the past few decades, many clustering algorithms have been proposed [6,11,28]. Among these algorithms, k-means and min-cut have become the most popular choices for real-world applications due to their simplicity and effectiveness [6]. Recently, spectral clustering [22,30,36,38] has gained a lot of attention, and has been successfully applied to many practical situations, such as constrained laplacian rank [18], image clustering which includes content based on image retrieval, graph annotation and graph indexing and so on [4,8,25,33,39].

Although traditional clustering methods have achieved good performance in many applications, they still have some problems. Firstly, with the development and application of balanced clustering [1,2,12], the method described in the literature [15] is a spectral clustering method that does not balance the clustering results. Then we made improvements on the basis of the literature [15], so that it can balance the clustering results. Secondly, ordinary clustering methods are difficult to deal with non-convex datasets and when the given data samples are too many or the dimensionality is too high, there are usually many irrelevant redundant features which makes the algorithm suffer from the disaster of dimensionality.

In order to solve these problems, firstly, since literature [1,2,12] uses an exclusive lasso to obtain balanced clustering results, the paper also applies the exclusive lasso which was first proposed by Zhou et al. [12]. Secondly, in order to deal with high dimensional data clustering problems, the paper uses $\ell_{2,1}$-norm for feature selection [21,23,32,37] to reduce dimensionality. Based on the above two points, the paper proposes a balanced spectral clustering algorithm based on feature selection for processing balanced non-convex high-dimensional datasets.

The rest of the paper is organized as follows. First, the paper reviews the exclusive lasso and spectral clustering in Sect. 2, and then describes the proposed algorithm in detail in Sect. 3. Then, the paper gives the experimental results in Sect. 4. Finally, the proposed algorithm is summarized in Sect. 5.

2 Related Work

The theories involved in this paper include exclusive lasso, spectral clustering, feature selection and etc., and we briefly review exclusive lasso and spectral clustering in this section.

2.1 Notations

The paper denotes matrices, vectors, and scalars, respectively, as boldface uppercase letters, boldface lowercase letters, and normal italic letters. The notation $||\mathbf{X}||_F^2$ is the square of the Frobenius norm of $\mathbf{X}$, $||\mathbf{X}||_{2,1}$ is the $\ell_{2,1}$-norm of $\mathbf{X}$, i.e., $||\mathbf{X}||_{2,1} = \sum_j \sqrt{\sum_i |\mathbf{x}_{ij}|^2}$, $\mathbf{X}^T$ is the transpose of $\mathbf{X}$, $tr(\mathbf{X})$ is the trace of $\mathbf{X}$, $\mathbf{X}^{-1}$ is the inverse of $\mathbf{X}$.

2.2   Exclusive Lasso

Let $\mathbf{Y} \in \mathbb{R}^{n \times c}$ be a clustering indicator matrix. Zhou et al. [12] proposed exclusive lasso is originally applied to multi-task feature selection to obtain good performance. Exclusive lasso is defined as

$$||\mathbf{Y}||_b = \sum_{j=1}^{c} \left(\sum_{i=1}^{n} y_{ij} \right)^2 = Tr(\mathbf{Y}^T \mathbf{1}_n \mathbf{1}_n^T \mathbf{Y}). \tag{1}$$

By using the exclusive lasso, if a feature of a group is given a large weight, it will assign a small weight to other features in the same group. It can be seen from Eq. (1) that the value of exclusive lasso is equal to the sum of the squares of the number of data points of each cluster. The following theorem minimizes the exclusive lasso can ensure that $||\mathbf{Y}||_b$ can be used to obtain the most balanced division.

Theorem 1. *Suppose* $\mathbf{Y} \in \mathbb{R}^{n \times c}$ *is a cluster indicator matrix, and* $\sum_{i=1}^{n} y_{ij}$ *is equal to* $\frac{n}{c}$. *If* $\frac{n}{c}$ *is an integer,* $||\mathbf{Y}||_b$ *gets its minimum value. Otherwise, it equals to* $\{\lfloor \frac{n}{c} \rfloor, \lceil \frac{n}{c} \rceil\}$ $(j \in [1, c])$.

Proof. Let $\mathbf{u} \in \mathbb{R}^{c \times 1}$ be a column vector, where $u_j = \sum_{i=1}^{n} y_{ij}$ and $\sum_{j=1}^{c} u_j = n$. Let $\mathbf{v} \in \mathbb{R}^{c \times 1}$ be a constant column vector, where $v_j = \frac{1}{c}$, according to the CauchySchwarz inequality, $|\mathbf{u}, \mathbf{v}|^2 \leq ||\mathbf{u}||^2 ||\mathbf{v}||^2$, which can be expressed as:

$$\sum_{j=1}^{c} u_j^2 \geq \frac{n^2}{c}. \tag{2}$$

For all $j \in [1, c]$, when $u_j = \frac{n}{c}$, the inequality holds. Therefore, when $\sum_{i=1}^{n} y_{ij} = \frac{n}{c}$ $(j \in [1, c])$, $||\mathbf{Y}||_b$ gets its minimum value. If $\frac{n}{c}$ is not an integer, we can prove that when $\sum_{i=1}^{n} y_{ij} = \{\lfloor \frac{n}{c} \rfloor, \lceil \frac{n}{c} \rceil\}$, $||\mathbf{Y}||_b$ can get its minimum value.

According to the above theorem, we can obtain the most balanced division by minimizing the exclusive lasso. Therefore, this paper integrates the exclusive lasso as a regularization term into the proposed framework to obtain balanced spectral clustering results.

2.3   Spectral Clustering

Spectral clustering [14,16] is a clustering method based on graph theory. Compared with traditional clustering algorithms, spectral clustering can perform clustering in arbitrary sample space and converge to the global optimum. It can be understood as mapping data from high-dimensional space to low-dimensional space, and then uses other clustering algorithms (such as k-means [6]) to cluster in low-dimensional space.

The basic idea of the spectral clustering algorithm [22]. Firstly, we calculate the similarity matrix according to the sample points, secondly, we calculate the degree matrix and adjacency matrix according to the similarity matrix; thirdly, we calculate the laplacian matrix according to the degree matrix and adjacency matrix; fourthly, we calculate the corresponding eigenvectors according to the first k small eigenvalues of the laplacian matrix. Finally, the eigenvectors corresponding to the k eigenvalues, which can form the eigenmatrix $\mathbf{U} \in \mathbb{R}^{n \times k}$, and each row of $\mathbf{U}$ becomes a newly generated sample point. K-means clustering is performed on these newly generated sample points, the newly generated sample points are clustered into k categories, then it outputs the clustering results.

3 The Proposed Method

In this section, we depict the proposed method, balanced spectral clustering algorithm based on the exclusive lasso, and describe an iterative solution method to solve the original problem.

3.1 The Details of Our Algorithm

Given sample $\mathbf{X} = \{\mathbf{x}_1, \mathbf{x}_2, ..., \mathbf{x}_n\} \in \mathbb{R}^{d \times n}$, where n is the number of samples, and d is the dimension. The clustering task has no class labels, so that the paper gives a class indicator matrix $\mathbf{Y} \in \mathbb{R}^{n \times c}$. The purposed algorithm is to find a suitable $\mathbf{W} \in \mathbb{R}^{d \times c}$ that makes the error between $\mathbf{X}^T \mathbf{W}$ and the indicator matrix $\mathbf{Y}$ smaller. According to the least square method, the loss term of the proposed method can be expressed as $\min_{\mathbf{W}} \sum_{i=1}^{n} (\mathbf{x}_i^T \mathbf{W} - \mathbf{y}_i)^2$. In machine learning, the sample dimension is multi-dimensional, so the loss function of the optimization objective in the paper can be expressed as:

$$\min_{\mathbf{Y}, \mathbf{W}} ||\mathbf{X}^T \mathbf{W} - \mathbf{Y}||_F^2. \tag{3}$$

When there are too many sample features and the number of samples is relatively small, Eq. (3) is easily falling into overfitting. In order to alleviate the overfitting problem, we introduce the $\ell_{2,1}$-norm to make it easier to obtain a sparse solution, and apply orthogonal constraints on $\mathbf{W}$ for subspace learning. Through subspace learning and feature selection [23] for dimensionality reduction, which can effectively remove redundant features, reduce the risk of overfitting and retain important features. Consequently, the objective function can be written as:

$$\min_{\mathbf{Y}, \mathbf{W}} ||\mathbf{X}^T \mathbf{W} - \mathbf{Y}||_F^2 + \beta ||\mathbf{W}||_{2,1}$$
$$s.t. \ \mathbf{W}^T \mathbf{W} = \mathbf{I}, \tag{4}$$

the regularization term parameter $\beta > 0$, called the adjustment factor, is used to adjust the sparsity of the entire row of the matrix $\mathbf{W}$. $\mathbf{I}$ is the identity matrix, that is, a square matrix with diagonal elements of 1 and other elements of 0, $\mathbf{W}^T\mathbf{W} = \mathbf{I}$ is used to perform subspace learning to improve model performance. At present, there are some clustering algorithms that cluster few samples into one category. This situation should be avoided when the target data set is balanced. We know that exclusive lasso has the ability to introduce competition in different categories. Therefore, in order to obtain a more balanced clustering result, the paper introduces exclusive lasso to the clustering model. Therefore, the objective function is further written as,

$$\min_{\mathbf{Y},\mathbf{W}} ||\mathbf{X}^T\mathbf{W} - \mathbf{Y}||_F^2 + \beta||\mathbf{W}||_{2,1} + \gamma||\mathbf{Y}||_e$$
$$s.t. \ \mathbf{W}^T\mathbf{W} = \mathbf{I}, \tag{5}$$

among them, γ is the parameter of the balance regularization term. Replace $||\mathbf{Y}||_e$ with Eq. (1), the objective function can be rewritten as:

$$\min_{\mathbf{Y},\mathbf{W}} ||\mathbf{X}^T\mathbf{W} - \mathbf{Y}||_F^2 + \beta||\mathbf{W}||_{2,1} + \gamma Tr(\mathbf{Y}^T\mathbf{1}\mathbf{1}^T\mathbf{Y})$$
$$s.t. \ \mathbf{W}^T\mathbf{W} = \mathbf{I}. \tag{6}$$

Finally, the locality preservation projection is introduced who can maintain the consistency of the local structure of the data after dimensionality reduction. The final objective function is expressed as:

$$\min_{\mathbf{Y},\mathbf{W},\mathbf{W}^T\mathbf{W}=\mathbf{I}} Tr(\mathbf{Y}^T\mathbf{L}\mathbf{Y}) + \alpha||\mathbf{X}^T\mathbf{W} - \mathbf{Y}||_F^2$$
$$+ \beta||\mathbf{W}||_{2,1} + \gamma Tr(\mathbf{Y}^T\mathbf{1}\mathbf{1}^T\mathbf{Y}) \tag{7}$$

where α is the parameter of the loss function, which is used to adjust the role of the loss term in the entire algorithm framework, where $\mathbf{L} \in \mathbb{R}^{n \times n}$ is the laplacian graph matrix, $\mathbf{L} = \mathbf{D} - \mathbf{W}$, where $\mathbf{D}$ is the diagonal matrix, $d_{ii} = 1/2\sqrt{\sum_{i=1}^{d} |w_{i,j}|^2}$.

3.2 Optimization of the Algorithm

Since the objective function is convex and non-smooth, in order to obtain the optimal solution, the value of the objective function must be minimized. It is usually difficult to directly solve the optimal $\mathbf{Y}$ and $\mathbf{W}$ at the same time. Therefore, this paper proposes an iterative optimization method to settle the objective function. Since the objective function has two variables to be solved, and $\mathbf{W}$ has an orthogonal restriction, it cannot be solved directly, so this paper choose to optimize $\mathbf{Y}$ first, and then optimize $\mathbf{W}$. First, the objective function Eq. (7) can undergo the following equivalent transformation:

Algorithm 1. The pseudo code of optimization to solve Eq.(7)

Input: training sample $\mathbf{X} = [\mathbf{x}_1, \mathbf{x}_2, ..., \mathbf{x}_n] \in \mathbb{R}^{d \times n}$, control parameter α, β, γ;
Output: $\mathbf{Y} \in \mathbb{R}^{n \times c}$, $\mathbf{W} \in \mathbb{R}^{n \times c}$.
1. Initialize $t = 1$;
2. Randomly initialize $\mathbf{W}^{(0)}$ and satisfy $\mathbf{W}^T \mathbf{W} = \mathbf{I}_c$;
3. **repeat:**
   3.1 Update the relationship matrix $\mathbf{Y}^{(t)}$ through Eq.(11);
   3.2 Update the value on the diagonal of $\mathbf{D}^{(t)}$, which is related to each row of $\mathbf{W}^{(t)}$,

and it can be defined by the formula: $d_{ii} = 1/2 \sqrt{\sum_{i=1}^{d} |w_{i,j}|^2}$;

   3.3 Update $\mathbf{A}^{(t)}$ via Eq.(13);
   3.4 Update $\mathbf{B}^{(t)}$ via Eq.(14);
   3.5 Update $\mathbf{W}^{(t)}$ via GPI;
   3.6 Update $t = t + 1$;
   until Eq.(7) convergence
4. Perform k-means clustering on the obtained indication matrix $\mathbf{Y}$;
5. Get the final cluster label.

$$\min_{\mathbf{Y}, \mathbf{W}, \mathbf{W}^T \mathbf{W} = \mathbf{I}} Tr(\mathbf{Y}^T \mathbf{L} \mathbf{Y}) + \alpha ||\mathbf{X}^T \mathbf{W} - \mathbf{Y}||_F^2 + \beta ||\mathbf{W}||_{2,1}$$
$$+ \gamma Tr(\mathbf{Y}^T \mathbf{1} \mathbf{1}^T \mathbf{Y})$$
$$\Leftrightarrow \min_{\mathbf{Y}, \mathbf{W}, \mathbf{W}^T \mathbf{W} = \mathbf{I}} Tr(\mathbf{Y}^T \mathbf{L} \mathbf{Y}) + \alpha Tr(\mathbf{W}^T \mathbf{X} \mathbf{X}^T \mathbf{W}$$
$$- 2\mathbf{Y}^T \mathbf{X}^T \mathbf{W} + \mathbf{Y}^T \mathbf{Y}) + \beta Tr(\mathbf{W}^T \mathbf{D} \mathbf{W}) + \gamma Tr(\mathbf{Y}^T \mathbf{1} \mathbf{1}^T \mathbf{Y})$$

$$(8)$$

– Fix $\mathbf{W}$ and optimize $\mathbf{Y}$.
  When $\mathbf{W}$ is fixed, $\mathbf{Y}$ is obtained by solving the following problems

$$\min_{\mathbf{Y}} Tr(\mathbf{Y}^T \mathbf{L} \mathbf{Y}) + \alpha Tr(-2\mathbf{Y}^T \mathbf{X}^T \mathbf{W} + \mathbf{Y}^T \mathbf{Y})$$
$$+ \gamma Tr(\mathbf{Y}^T \mathbf{1} \mathbf{1}^T \mathbf{Y})$$

$$(9)$$

the paper takes the derivative of $\mathbf{Y}$ and make the derivative equal to zero, then

$$2(\mathbf{L} + \alpha \mathbf{I}_n + \gamma \mathbf{1} \mathbf{1}^T) \mathbf{Y} - 2\alpha \mathbf{X}^T \mathbf{W} = 0, \qquad (10)$$

$\mathbf{Y}$ is obtained

$$\mathbf{Y} = (\mathbf{L} + \alpha \mathbf{I}_n + \gamma \mathbf{1} \mathbf{1}^T)^{-1} \alpha \mathbf{X}^T \mathbf{W}, \qquad (11)$$

– Fix $\mathbf{Y}$ and optimize $\mathbf{W}$.
  Since $\mathbf{W}$ has the constraint of orthogonal restriction, it cannot be differentiated like $\mathbf{Y}$. Therefore, this paper has found another way to optimize it. According to the GPI in [19], this paper turns the term containing $\mathbf{W}$ in the objective function into the form of $\max_{\mathbf{W}^T \mathbf{W} = \mathbf{I}} tr(\mathbf{W}^T \mathbf{A} \mathbf{W} + 2\mathbf{W}^T \mathbf{B})$, and get

$$\min_{\mathbf{W}^T\mathbf{W}=\mathbf{I}_c} \alpha tr(\mathbf{W}^T\mathbf{X}\mathbf{X}^T\mathbf{W} - 2\mathbf{W}^T\mathbf{X}\mathbf{Y}) + \beta tr(\mathbf{W}^T\mathbf{D}\mathbf{W})$$

$$\Leftrightarrow \min_{\mathbf{W}^T\mathbf{W}=\mathbf{I}_c} tr(\mathbf{W}^T(\alpha\mathbf{X}\mathbf{X}^T + \beta\mathbf{D})\mathbf{W}) - 2\mathbf{W}^T\mathbf{X}\mathbf{Y} \qquad (12)$$

$$\Leftrightarrow \max_{\mathbf{W}^T\mathbf{W}=\mathbf{I}_c} tr(\mathbf{W}^T(\lambda\mathbf{I}_d - \alpha\mathbf{X}\mathbf{X}^T - \beta\mathbf{D})\mathbf{W}) + 2\mathbf{W}^T\mathbf{X}\mathbf{Y},$$

at this time, the $\mathbf{A}$ and $\mathbf{B}$ of the algorithm are:

$$\mathbf{A} = \lambda\mathbf{I}_d - \alpha\mathbf{X}\mathbf{X}^T - \beta\mathbf{D}, \qquad (13)$$

$$\mathbf{B} = \mathbf{X}\mathbf{Y}. \qquad (14)$$

According to the above, the specific steps of the proposed method can be described by Algorithm 1.

4   Experimental Analysis

In the experiment, the paper compares the proposed algorithm with several different clustering algorithms on 12 benchmark datasets. The paper focuses on the datasets used in the experiment and the results of the analysis and comparison.

4.1   Datasets and Evaluation Metrics

The paper downloads the datasets from UCI Machine Learning Repository [27] and the website of Feature Selection Data sets [24]. The 12 data sets used in the article are MSRA, Movements, ORL, Prostate-GE, QSAR, RELATHE, Sonar, Statlog, Urbanlandcover, Yale, Binalpha, WarpAR10P. This paper lists the details of the used datasets in Table 1.

The paper uses the clustering Accuracy (ACC), Normalized Mutual Information (NMI) to evaluate the clustering performance for all methods [3].

4.2   Analysis and Comparison of the Experiment Results

In the experiment, we compare our algorithm with six algorithms. Our proposed algorithm includes Proposed with a balanced regularization term, and Proposed-0 without a balanced regularization term is similar to CSP [15], that is the parameter of the balanced regularization term is 0. The comparison algorithms are the classic k-means clustering algorithm [6], the balanced clustering algorithm BCLS for unprocessed data sets and ProBCLS algorithm for processed data sets [13], the CLR [18], SSC [9] and KMM [17]. In order to reduce the contingency of the algorithms, for each comparison algorithm, we run the algorithm 20 times and take the average value as the final clustering result, and

Table 1. Details of the used datasets.

Datasets	Samples	Features	Classes
MSRA	1799	256	12
Movements	360	90	15
ORL	400	1024	40
Prostate-GE	102	5966	2
QSAR	1055	41	2
RELATHE	1427	4322	2
Sonar	208	60	2
Statlog	6435	36	6
Urbanlandcover	168	147	9
Yale	165	1024	15
Binalpha	1404	320	36
WarpAR10P	130	2400	10

Table 2. ACC (%) of all methods on different data sets.

Data sets	k-means	SSC	KMM	CLR	ProBCLS	BCLS	Proposed-0	Proposed
MSRA	50.47	48.84	55.77	53.81	30.87	43.26	56.11	**57.40**
Movements	43.47	47.60	44.21	48.33	6.67	27.50	56.39	**57.78**
ORL	55.34	65.10	52.35	64.50	38.62	16.10	68.75	**70.00**
Prostate-GE	58.82	56.86	58.28	58.82	59.04	53.14	69.45	**71.18**
QSAR	58.86	53.93	62.55	62.18	62.83	58.79	61.96	**64.77**
RELATHE	54.66	56.27	54.56	54.87	51.45	50.53	55.78	**56.95**
Sonar	55.29	53.85	50.53	50.48	56.71	52.69	65.14	**68.67**
Statlog	61.93	40.85	55.25	60.33	23.82	23.82	57.09	**75.29**
Urbanlandcover	34.20	30.95	30.65	35.12	17.27	28.81	62.65	**65.59**
Yale	40.39	52.52	35.30	43.64	32.30	20.97	65.81	**70.22**
Binalpha	44.44	43.63	35.53	37.96	3.87	10.01	46.82	**48.82**
WarpAR10P	21.88	33.00	17.62	20.77	39.02	22.31	63.08	**65.38**

Table 3. NMI (%) of all methods on different data sets.

Data sets	k-means	SSC	KMM	CLR	ProBCLS	BCLS	Proposed-0	Proposed
MSRA	57.81	55.73	63.26	**69.20**	29.35	41.59	63.51	65.96
Movements	57.10	60.37	58.31	65.73	0.00	26.76	72.62	**74.61**
ORL	75.57	81.44	72.14	80.05	55.65	40.07	86.94	**87.91**
Prostate-GE	2.35	1.34	3.18	4.22	3.85	0.52	18.18	**20.17**
QSAR	0.02	3.76	2.48	**3.92**	1.25	3.01	2.01	2.17
RELATHE	0.08	**1.95**	0.33	0.32	0.09	0.01	0.64	0.62
Sonar	0.88	0.37	2.44	2.68	2.04	0.33	13.82	**13.89**
Statlog	54.82	26.67	43.30	46.06	0.00	0.00	48.57	**64.64**
Urbanlandcover	28.22	25.82	25.68	29.18	0.01	18.40	73.53	**73.74**
Yale	48.32	56.79	39.38	48.79	35.26	25.91	81.05	**83.70**
Binalpha	58.94	57.65	49.68	53.92	1.15	15.67	72.69	**72.88**
WarpAR10P	17.27	33.40	11.67	19.29	37.66	16.35	75.75	**76.90**

the proposed algorithm uses the method of 10 fold cross validation and takes the average of these 10 results as the final balanced clustering result. The paper lists the results of ACC and NMI of all methods in Tables 2 and 3, where the bold number stands for the best clustering performance in that row.

From the two tables, the observation is as follows.

- Tables 2 and 3 shows the average ACC and NMI values obtained with several clustering algorithms on 12 real data sets. It can be seen that the result of our experiment is the best in most cases. On the Urbanlandcover dataset, the ACC value of the proposed algorithm improves about 30% compared to the comparison algorithm CLR. On the ORL dataset, the NMI value of our proposed algorithm improves about 6% compared to the comparison algorithm SSC. In most cases, the Proposed is better than Proposed-0, so it can be seen that the algorithm with balanced regularization term is more effective.
- Compared with SSC, the average value of our proposed method is 15.72% and 19.32% higher than the average of all datasets on the two evaluation indicators, respectively.
- From Tables 1, 2, and 3, it can be seen that the algorithm performs better on the five datasets Movements, ORL, Yale, Binalpha and WarpAR10P, which are small sample multi-classification balanced data sets. It can be seen that the algorithm is more suitable for small sample multi-classification balanced data sets.

Obviously, from these comparison results, it can be seen that the results obtained by the proposed algorithm are relatively effective.

4.3 Convergence Analysis

The convergence of each dataset in Fig. 1 shows that how the target value changes with the number of iteration increases in Algorithm 1. In Algorithm 1, the paper sets the convergence condition as $|\frac{obj(t+1)-obj(t)}{obj(t)}| \leq 10^{-5}$ or $t = 100$, where $obj(t)$ represents the value of the objective function during the t-th iteration. According to Fig. 1, the horizontal axis and the vertical axis respectively present the number of iterations and the value of the objective function, as the number of iterations increases, the value of the objective function decreases until the Algorithm 1 converges. It shows that the proposed algorithm can reach convergence, which further proves the effectiveness of the proposed algorithm.

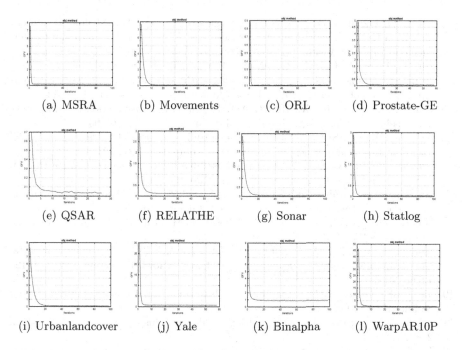

(a) MSRA	(b) Movements	(c) ORL	(d) Prostate-GE
(e) QSAR	(f) RELATHE	(g) Sonar	(h) Statlog
(i) Urbanlandcover	(j) Yale	(k) Binalpha	(l) WarpAR10P

Fig. 1. The convergence of each data set.

5   Conclusion

In order to solve the problem of dimensional catastrophe and clustering few points into a subset, the paper proposes a new clustering method, namely, balanced spectral clustering algorithm based on feature selection. In the experiments, the paper adjusts each hyperparameter to make the proposed algorithm have better performance. By comparing the validation of each algorithm with different datasets, the two evaluation metrics show that the ACC and NMI of the algorithm proposed in this paper is better than the comparison algorithm in most cases.

Compared with some algorithms that perform spectral clustering on the original dataset, the algorithm in this paper is performed in a low-dimensional space, which reduces the computation time and memory, meanwhile, reduces the complexity of the proposed algorithm. However, there exist a few datasets where the NMI of running on the proposed algorithm is relatively low. In the future, we will focus on developing more spectral clustering algorithms to make them suitable for more applications and have better robustness.

References

1. Chen, X., Hong, W., Nie, F., Huang, J.Z., Shen, L.: Enhanced balanced min cut. Int. J. Comput. Vis. **128**(7), 1982–1995 (2020)

2. Chen, X., Zhexue Haung, J., Nie, F., Chen, R., Wu, Q.: A self-balanced min-cut algorithm for image clustering. In: Proceedings of the IEEE International Conference on Computer Vision, pp. 2061–2069 (2017)
3. Du, T., Wen, G., Cai, Z., Zheng, W., Tan, M., Li, Y.: Spectral clustering algorithm combining local covariance matrix with normalization. Neural Comput. Appl. **32**(11), 6611–6618 (2018). https://doi.org/10.1007/s00521-018-3852-z
4. Gan, J., Peng, Z., Zhu, X., Hu, R., Ma, J., Wu, G.: Brain functional connectivity analysis based on multi-graph fusion. Med. Image Anal. **71**, 102057 (2021)
5. Guo, Y., Wu, Z., Shen, D.: Learning longitudinal classification-regression model for infant hippocampus segmentation. Neurocomputing **391**, 191–198 (2020)
6. Hartigan, J.A., Wong, M.A.: Algorithm as 136:a k-means clustering algorithm. J. Roy. Stat. Soc. Ser. C (Appl. Stat.) **28**(1), 100–108 (1979)
7. Hu, R., et al.: Multi-band brain network analysis for functional neuroimaging biomarker identification. IEEE Trans. Med. Imaging **40**, 3843–3855 (2021)
8. Hu, R., Zhu, X., Zhu, Y., Gan, J.: Robust SVM with adaptive graph learning. World Wide Web **23**(3), 1945–1968 (2020)
9. Huang, D., Wang, C.D., Wu, J.S., Lai, J.H., Kwoh, C.K.: Ultra-scalable spectral clustering and ensemble clustering. IEEE Trans. Knowl. Data Eng. **32**(6), 1212–1226 (2019)
10. Jain, A.K., Dubes, R.C.: Algorithms for Clustering Data. Prentice-Hall Inc., Upper Saddle River (1988)
11. Kang, Z., et al.: Partition level multiview subspace clustering. Neural Netw. **122**, 279–288 (2020)
12. Li, Z., Nie, F., Chang, X., Ma, Z., Yang, Y.: Balanced clustering via exclusive lasso: A pragmatic approach. In: Thirty-Second AAAI Conference on Artificial Intelligence (2018)
13. Liu, H., Han, J., Nie, F., Li, X.: Balanced clustering with least square regression. In: Thirty-First AAAI Conference on Artificial Intelligence (2017)
14. Lucińska, M.: A spectral clustering algorithm based on eigenvector localization. In: Rutkowski, L., Korytkowski, M., Scherer, R., Tadeusiewicz, R., Zadeh, L.A., Zurada, J.M. (eds.) ICAISC 2014. LNCS (LNAI), vol. 8468, pp. 749–759. Springer, Cham (2014). https://doi.org/10.1007/978-3-319-07176-3_65
15. Luo, Q., Wen, G., Zhang, L., Zhan, M.: An efficient algorithm combining spectral clustering with feature selection. Neural Process. Lett. **52**(3), 1913–1925 (2020)
16. Ng, A.Y., Jordan, M.I., Weiss, Y.: On spectral clustering: analysis and an algorithm. In: Advances in Neural Information Processing Systems, pp. 849–856 (2002)
17. Nie, F., Wang, C.L., Li, X.: K-multiple-means: a multiple-means clustering method with specified k clusters. In: Proceedings of the 25th ACM SIGKDD International Conference on Knowledge Discovery and Data Mining, pp. 959–967 (2019)
18. Nie, F., Wang, X., Jordan, M.I., Huang, H.: The constrained Laplacian rank algorithm for graph-based clustering. In: AAAI, pp. 1969–1976. Citeseer (2016)
19. Nie, F., Zhang, R., Li, X.: A generalized power iteration method for solving quadratic problem on the Stiefel manifold. Sci. China Inf. Sci. **60**(11), 112101 (2017)
20. Shen, H.T., et al.: Heterogeneous data fusion for predicting mild cognitive impairment conversion. Inf. Fusion **66**, 54–63 (2021)
21. Shen, H.T., Zhu, Y., Zheng, W., Zhu, X.: Half-quadratic minimization for unsupervised feature selection on incomplete data. IEEE Trans. Neural Netw. Learn. Syst. **32**, 3122–3135 (2020)
22. Von Luxburg, U.: A tutorial on spectral clustering. Stat. Comput. **17**(4), 395–416 (2007)

23. Xie, G., et al.: SRSC: selective, robust, and supervised constrained feature representation for image classification. IEEE Trans. Neural Networks Learn. Syst. **31**(10), 4290–4302 (2020)
24. Yang, Y., Duan, Y., Wang, X., Huang, Z., Xie, N., Shen, H.T.: Hierarchical multi-clue modelling for poi popularity prediction with heterogeneous tourist information. IEEE Trans. Knowl. Data Eng. **31**(4), 757–768 (2018)
25. Yuan, C., Zhong, Z., Lei, C., Zhu, X., Hu, R.: Adaptive reverse graph learning for robust subspace learning. Inf. Process. Manage. **58**(6), 102733 (2021)
26. Zhang, S., Li, X., Zong, M., Zhu, X., Cheng, D.: Learning K for KNN classification. ACM Trans. Intell. Syst. Technol. (TIST) **8**(3), 1–19 (2017)
27. Zhang, Y., Zhao, Q., Jin, J., Wang, X., Cichocki, A.: A novel BCI based on ERP components sensitive to configural processing of human faces. J. Neural Eng. **9**(2), 26018 (2012)
28. Zhang, Z., Liu, L., Shen, F., Shen, H.T., Shao, L.: Binary multi-view clustering. IEEE Trans. Pattern Anal. Mach. Intell. **41**(7), 1774–1782 (2018)
29. Zhou, Y., Tian, L., Zhu, C., Jin, X., Sun, Y.: Video coding optimization for virtual reality 360-degree source. IEEE J. Sel. Top. Sig. Process. **14**(1), 118–129 (2019)
30. Zhu, X., Gan, J., Lu, G., Li, J., Zhang, S.: Spectral clustering via half-quadratic optimization. World Wide Web **23**(3), 1969–1988 (2019). https://doi.org/10.1007/s11280-019-00731-8
31. Zhu, X., Li, X., Zhang, S.: Block-row sparse multiview multilabel learning for image classification. IEEE Trans. Cybern. **46**(2), 450–461 (2016)
32. Zhu, X., Li, X., Zhang, S., Ju, C., Wu, X.: Robust joint graph sparse coding for unsupervised spectral feature selection. IEEE Trans. Neural Netw. Learn. Syst. **28**(6), 1263–1275 (2017)
33. Zhu, X., Li, X., Zhang, S., Xu, Z., Yu, L., Wang, C.: Graph PCA hashing for similarity search. IEEE Trans. Multimedia **19**(9), 2033–2044 (2017)
34. Zhu, X., et al.: Joint prediction and time estimation of COVID-19 developing severe symptoms using chest CT scan. Med. Image Anal. **67**, 101824 (2021)
35. Zhu, X., Yang, J., Zhang, C., Zhang, S.: Efficient utilization of missing data in cost-sensitive learning. IEEE Trans. Knowl. Data Eng. **33**, 2425–2436 (2019)
36. Zhu, X., Zhang, S., Li, Y., Zhang, J., Yang, L., Fang, Y.: Low-rank sparse subspace for spectral clustering. IEEE Trans. Knowl. Data Eng. **31**(8), 1532–1543 (2018)
37. Zhu, X., Zhang, S., Zhu, Y., Zhu, P., Gao, Y.: Unsupervised spectral feature selection with dynamic hyper-graph learning. IEEE Trans. Knowl. Data Eng., 1 (2020)
38. Zhu, X., Zhu, Y., Zheng, W.: Spectral rotation for deep one-step clustering. Pattern Recogn. **105**, 107175 (2020)
39. Zhu, Y., Ma, J., Yuan, C., Zhu, X.: Interpretable learning based dynamic graph convolutional networks for Alzheimer's disease analysis. Inf. Fusion **77**, 53–61 (2022)

Multi-domain and Context-Aware Recommendations Using Contextual Ontological User Profile

Aleksandra Karpus$^{(\boxtimes)}$ and Krzysztof Goczyła

Faculty of Electronics, Telecommunications and Informatics,
Gdańsk University of Technology, Gdańsk, Poland
{alekarpu,krissun}@pg.edu.pl

Abstract. Recommender Systems (RS) became popular tools in many Web services like Netflix, Amazon, or YouTube, because they help a user to avoid an information overload problem. One of the types of RS is Context-Aware RS (CARS) which exploits contextual information to provide more adequate recommendations. Cross-Domain RS (CDRS) was created as a response to the data sparsity problem which occurs when only a few users can provide reviews or ratings for many items. One of the kinds of CDRS is Multi-domain RS which use user information from at least two domains to recommend items from all these domains. In this paper, we investigate how Contextual Ontological User Profile can be used for making multi-domain and context-aware recommendations. We show the improvement of accuracy and diversity of recommendations while combining CARS with CDRS.

Keywords: Recommender systems · Context-awareness · Multi-domain recommendations · Ontology · Personalization

1 Introduction

In the past few decades, Recommendation Systems (RS) became popular tools in many Web services like Netflix, Amazon, or YouTube, because they help a user to avoid an information overload problem. However, few users can provide reviews or ratings for many items which leads to another problem i.e. data sparsity. This is one of the reasons why Cross-Domain RS (CDRS) was created [11,26]. A cross-domain algorithm can deal with items from different domains. One of the kinds of CDRS is Multi-domain RS which uses user information from at least two domains to recommend items from all these domains.

In parallel, Context-Aware RS (CARS) was developed. CARS exploits contextual information to provide more adequate recommendations. For example, a restaurant recommendation for a Saturday evening with friends should be different from one suggested for a workday lunch with co-workers [22].

Karpus et al. [16] proposed Contextual Ontological User Profile (COUP) which allows to intuitively store user preferences in a context. The authors show

© Springer Nature Switzerland AG 2022
B. Li et al. (Eds.): ADMA 2021, LNAI 13088, pp. 368–380, 2022.
https://doi.org/10.1007/978-3-030-95408-6_28

the usefulness of this profile for recommendation in a single domain by proposing the Ontology-Based Contextual Pre-filtering method [17] (preOnto). The user representation and the approach have a big potential to create a bridge between CARS and CDRS.

An important issue in recommendation systems is an accuracy-diversity trade-off [14]. Many recent works focus on increasing the diversity of recommendations [4,28]. However, with the growing amount of information, products and other items on the Web, users more than ever need relevant recommendations.

In this paper, we investigate how COUP, introduced by us elsewhere, can be used for making multi-domain and context aware recommendations. We show that combination of CARS and CDRS extended with preOnto and COUP improves the balance between relevance and diversity of recommendations.

The rest of the paper is organized as follows. Section 2 provides background knowledge and is followed by the related work in Sect. 3. Section 4 explains how context-aware and multi-domain recommendations are generated. Datasets used for evaluation are described in Sect. 5 while results and discussion are placed in Sect. 6. Conclusions and future work close the paper.

2   Background

2.1   Recommendation Systems

Recommendation Systems (RS) were created as a response to the information overload problem, which we suffer from nowadays. These software tools aim at suggesting new items that may possibly be of interest to a user [15].

Cremonesi et al. [8] distinguish three types of CDRS: linked-domain, cross-domain and multi-domain. For simplicity, we use only two domains in the following explanations. Linked-domain CDRS uses information (e.g. user ratings) from both domains to make predictions in only one of them. Cross-domain CDRS uses information from one domain to make predictions in another domain. The third kind, multi-domain CDRS, recommends items from both domains using all possible information. The biggest advantage of CDRS is that it offers added value to recommendations, i.e. diversity, novelty, and serendipity [7].

Adomavicius and Tuzhilin [2] distinguish three main types of CARS, i.e. contextual pre-filtering, contextual post-filtering and contextual modeling. The paradigms differ in the way they incorporate context in the recommendation process. In contextual pre-filtering, we first do a selection of preferences taking into account only relevant context. After this preparation, any traditional recommender algorithm can be applied on the data. In contrast, contextual post-filtering applies context after traditional recommendation process. Contextual modeling differs radically from previously described paradigms. In this kind of recommenders, we do not filter anything, but we incorporate a context in a prediction model. The recommendations are achieved directly from the model, taking into account the current user-context situation. Contextual pre- and post-filtering have a big advantage that they can be used with every known two-dimensional recommendation algorithm.

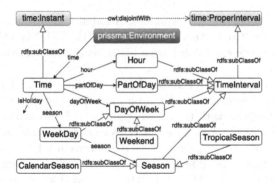

Fig. 1. Concepts and relations of RSCtx representing the time dimension (from [16]).

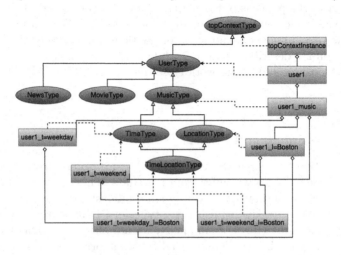

Fig. 2. An example of the contextual ontological user profile.

2.2 Recommender System Context Ontology

Recommender System Context (RSCtx) ontology [16] was designed to model context parameters that can be used in RS. The main goal in this contextual model is the possibility to express different levels of granularity for different context parameters. Figure 1 illustrates how time is represented.

2.3 Contextual Ontological User Profile

Contextual ontology [12] enables us to model different situations in which a user could find himself as a set of ontological modules. As an ontology we mean here a Description Logics ontology which consists of a terminology (TBox) and a world description (ABox). As a *context type* we understand a part of TBox defined by values of a set of contextual parameters. The contexts are arranged in an inheritance hierarchy. More specialized terminologies may "see" more general ones, but more general terminologies are unaware of the existence of more specialized ones. To deal with possible different assertional parts of the knowledge base we can create many ABoxes for one terminology. These ABoxes are called *context instances*. To allow for a flow of conclusions between context instances, they are connected by the relation of aggregation. This approach to modularization is called *Structured-Interpretation Model* (SIM) [12].

Contextual Ontological User Profile (COUP) [17] is a user model that is based on the SIM approach. It supports storage of preferences from multiple domains, which is done by adding context types related to different domains. Context types and context instances related to contextual parameters are added to COUP in a dynamic way. Thus, we can use as many variables as needed. Also, many user profiles can be stored in one SIM ontology. An example of a contextual profile for one user is shown in Fig. 2.

Three modules in the example in Fig. 2 are fixed: `UserType`, `topContextType` and `topContextInstance`. All the others are configurable or can be added dynamically. Modules `topContextType` and `topContextInstance` are obligatory in the SIM model. `UserType` is artificial and is present in the SIM ontology to enable adding many user profiles to the ontology. In `topContextType`, the concept `Rating` and its corresponding roles, e.g. `isRatedWith` and `hasValue`, are defined. In the next level of the hierarchy, there are context types that describe domains of interests related to the RS which will use the profile. At this level existing domain ontologies can be reused. At the next levels, all context types and instances are added to the contextual user profile during the creation of profile (e.g. from a rating matrix) or later, when a new contextual situation occurs. User preferences are stored in these lower context instances.

3 Related Work

In this section, we briefly review existing context-aware and ontology-based RS. We also show an overview of cross-domain RS and highlight those which utilize contextual information in the process of recommendation.

3.1 Ontology-Based Recommender Systems

Several ontology-based and context-aware RS have been proposed. AMAYA [21] allows management of contextual preferences and contextual recommendations and uses an ontology-based content categorization scheme to map user preferences to entities to recommend. News@hand [6] is a hybrid personalized and context-aware recommender system, which retrieves news via RSS feed and annotates by using system domain ontologies. User context is represented by a weighted set of classes from the domain ontology. Rodriguez et al. [23] proposed a CARS which recommends Web services. They use a multi-dimensional ontology model to describe Web services, a user context, and an application domain. The multi-dimensional ontology model consists of three independent ontologies: a user context ontology, a Web service ontology, and an application domain ontology, which are combined into one ontology by some properties between classes from different ontologies. The recommendation process consists in assigning a weight to the items based on a list of interests in the user ontology. Our work is somehow similar to this approach because we also use more than one ontology and one of them represents the context dimensions. However, all these works focus on a specific domain and an ad-hoc algorithm, while our approach is multi-domain and can be combined with different recommendation algorithms.

Hawalah et al. [13] suggest that each context dimension should be described by its taxonomy. Default context parameters in the movie domain are time, date, location, and device. It is possible to add other domain-specific context variables as long as they have clear hierarchical representations. Moreover, this approach uses a reference ontology to build contextual personalized ontological profiles. The key feature of this profile is the possibility of assigning user interests in groups if these interests are directly associated with each other by a direct relation, sharing the same super-class, or sharing the same property. Similarly to this approach, we model context-dependent user preferences using ontology. They are kept in the form of modules, which represent specific context situations, so we could say that we also group user interests. However, we have one ontology for all context dimensions, in contradiction to one taxonomy per each dimension.

Other works use ontologies and taxonomy to improve the quality of recommendations. Su et al. proved that ontological user profile improves recommendation accuracy and diversity [25]. Middleton et al. [19] use an ontological user profile to recommend research papers. Mobasher et al. [20] proposed a measure that combines semantic knowledge about items and user-item rating, while Anand et al. [3] inferred user preferences from rating data using an item ontology. A detailed description of ontology-based techniques is available in [9,18].

3.2   Cross-domain Recommender Systems

Braunhofer et al. [5] developed a mobile application that selects music content that fits a point of interest (POI) visited by a user. The application use location and emotional tags assigned to both music tracks and POIs. However, this solution is not truly contextual, because a user context is used to check in which POI a user is located. Thus, users in the same location would obtain the same recommendations. On the contrary, our approach is truly context-aware.

Singh and Bedi [24] introduced a parallel approach in CDRS using a graphic processing unit. The authors developed a prototype in the tourism domain using four subdomains (restaurant, tourist places, shopping places, and hotels). The proposed RS stores user preferences and contextual information (user's location and device) for all of those subdomains and recommends items for anyone of them. The main limitation of this approach is that it relies on the recommendation algorithm adopted, i.e., single-domain collaborative filtering.

Véras et al. [27] proposed pre- and post-filtering techniques for incorporating context in the CDRS. They tested their solution on two-domain datasets, i.e., (Book and Television) and (Book and Music). Although this approach is similar

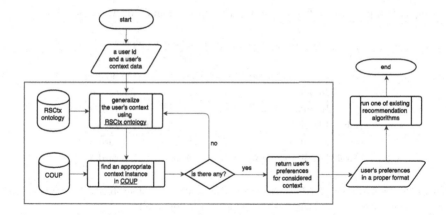

Fig. 3. The schema of the preOnto.

Table 1. Sample user preferences in the movie domain of Alice, Bob and Carol.

User	Item (Movie)	Rating	Companion	Day
Alice	Girl interrupted	2	Friend	Sunday
Alice	How to hook up your home theater	4	Family	Saturday
Alice	The imaginarium of doctor parnassus	5	Friend	Sunday
Bob	City of angels	2	Girlfriend	Saturday
Bob	Inception	1	Friend	Tuesday
Bob	Green mile	5	Friend	Saturday
Carol	The curse of the black pearl	5	Friend	Sunday
Carol	The fellowship of the ring	5	Alone	Tuesday
Carol	Cast away	2	Alone	Saturday

to the one proposed in the paper, it belongs to the linked-domain CDRS, while our approach is multi-domain. Moreover, our approach uses ontologies for making recommendations which allows us to better handle a user context.

4   Context-Aware and Multi-domain Recommendations

The general recommendation process of the preOnto is presented in Fig. 3 and proceeds as follows. Given a user and his current contextual situation, a proper generalization of values for his contextual parameters is generated by using the RSCtx ontology [17]. By a generalization of the contextual parameters, we mean mapping of raw user context data into some desired granularity level from the RSCtx ontology. Then, an appropriate context instance from COUP is identified by using the generalized context information. If a context instance is not found in the user profile, the generalization step is repeated to search for a module that corresponds to the new values of contextual parameters. If it is found, relevant

Table 2. Sample user preferences in the restaurant domain of Alice, Bob and Carol.

User	Item (Restaurant)	Rating	Companion	Day
Alice	Fish bar	4	Friend	Sunday
Alice	Italian restaurant	5	Family	Sunday
Alice	Noodle bar	3	Family	Saturday
Bob	Russian cuisine	2	Friend	Saturday
Bob	Pizzeria	1	Girlfriend	Tuesday
Carol	Noodle bar	5	Friend	Saturday
Carol	Italian restaurant	1	Alone	Saturday

Table 3. Preferences of Alice, Bob and Carol after ontology-based contextual pre-filtering for Alice on saturday with a friend (both domains).

User	Item	Rating
Alice	Girl interrupted	2
Alice	The imaginarium of doctor parnassus	5
Alice	Fish bar	4
Bob	Green mile	5
Bob	Russian cuisine	2
Carol	The curse of the black pearl	5
Carol	Noodle bar	5

preferences (for considered user and all other users who have the context instance with the same value for the same contextual parameters) are prepared to be used with a recommendation algorithm.

Let us consider an example to explain the process of the preOnto for the multi-domain ranking task. We will not show the final ranking list, but we will stop after returning a set of ratings on which any traditional algorithm can be applied. Users ratings from two different domains: movies and restaurants, are presented in Tables 1 and 2. Let us assume that we want to generate a list of the top 3 recommendations for Alice for a Saturday with a friend. The initial values of contextual parameters are not raw data, so we can skip the first generalization step of the preOnto. We have to find context instance corresponding to the specific contextual situation (`companion` = *friend*, `time` = *Saturday*). However, this is the first occurrence of such a contextual situation for Alice. Thus, we have to do the generalization step. It is hard to generalize `companion`, but `time` has a natural hierarchy. The upper level for `time` granularity will be a division into *weekday* and *weekend*. The value of the `time` is equal to *weekend*. In Alice COUP there exists such a context instance. The same happens for Bob and Carol. The returned set of ratings is presented in Table 3.

Note how easy it was to obtain ratings from different domains. The reason for that is how modules in COUP are connected. Because context types that represent contextual parameters can inherit from context types that describe domains, context instances related to certain contextual situations will contain

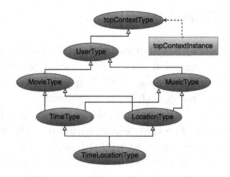

Fig. 4. Connections between context types in COUP for multi-domain RS.

preferences from different domains. Of course, it is not obligatory to have this inheritance relation. Everything depends on the desired application of COUP and the decisions of RS designers.

It should be noticed that if we considered any other user than Alice, i.e. Bob or Carol, we would not have to perform any generalization of contextual parameters. Both users, Bob and Carol, have their COUP with context instances corresponding to the contextual situation *on Saturday with a friend*. It is one of the biggest advantages of the approach. For each user, we allow (and can obtain) different level of granularity for values of contextual parameters. It enables us to better model and deal with context-aware user preferences.

5 Datasets

The `ConcertTweets` dataset [1] was collected from publicly available and well-structured tweets shared on Twitter. The dataset contains user feedback that refers to musical shows and concerts of various artists and bands. In this paper, we use only explicit user ratings in the range [0.5, 5.0].

The `MovieTweetings` dataset [10], similarly to `ConcertTweets`, consists of ratings extracted from Twitter. The dataset contains basic information about movies, ratings in a 0–10 scale and an exact time when a user rated a movie which we assumed was done just after watching it. Thus, we used the `timestamp` as a contextual parameter that represents the time of watching a movie.

`MovieTweetings` and `ConcertTweets` datasets are created based on publicly available tweets from Twitter. We found 296 Twitter users that appear in both datasets and therefore can be used for testing multi-domain recommendations with COUP. We divided their ratings into training and test sets using a 4:1 ratio. However, in a test set we put only positive ratings of users. All ratings from users that appeared only in one dataset were used for training.

The most important thing for the preOnto is how context types are connected in COUP. Here, we have two domains: music and movies, and two contextual parameters: time and location, which appear in at least one of the datasets. Figure 4 presents terminological part of COUP and connections between modules.

6   Results and Discussion

We performed several series of experiments to confirm usability of the proposed methods for recommending good items. For evaluation we chose four baseline algorithms: BPR, FISM, LDA, and WRMF from LibRec library and we used four measures: *precision, recall, nDCG*, and *diversity*.

In the following tables, a prefix *onto*-denotes the algorithm applied on the data returned by preOnto. The best results within one algorithm pair (with and without preOnto) are marked in bold while globally best results are in italic.

Results for single domain recommendations are collected in Table 4. As expected, adding contextual information into the recommendation process increases *precision* and *recall* values for all algorithms and datasets that were used. For all of the methods on `MovieTweetings` dataset the preOnto increases *diversity* of recommendations.

Results obtained for multi-domain recommendations are shown in Table 5. It is hard to compare them with other methods since, to the best of our knowledge, there is no other context-aware method for multi-domain recommendation. However, comparing the results with those obtained by the method for single domain on the same datasets, we can observe improvement of *diversity*. The preOnto with BPR algorithm obtained *diversity* values for single domain equal to 0.3002 and 0.2773 on `MovieTweetings` and `ConcertTweets` datasets, respectively (see Table 4), while for multi-domain *diversity* is equal to 0.3696 (see Table 5). *Diversity* value obtained for multi-domain recommendations with WRMF algorithm is equal to 0.3450 in comparison to values 0.3156 and 0.2764 obtained for single domain on `MovieTweetings` and `ConcertTweets` datasets, respectively.

Table 4. Single-domain recommendations on `MovieTweetings` and `ConcertTweets` datasets.

Dataset	MovieTweetings				ConcertTweets			
Algorithm	Precision	Recall	nDCG	Diversity	Precision	Recall	nDCG	Diversity
ontoBPR	**0.0261**	**0.2607**	**0.0400**	**0.3002**	**0.0853**	**0.8533**	**0.4894**	0.2773
BPR	0.0075	0.0271	0.0275	0.2964	0.0003	0.0031	0.0016	*0.4510*
ontoFISM	**0.0094**	**0.0942**	0.0105	*0.3824*	**0.0853**	**0.8533**	**0.5096**	0.2741
FISM	0.0049	0.0320	**0.0147**	0.3273	0.0031	0.0299	0.0132	**0.4234**
ontoLDA	**0.0267**	**0.2670**	**0.0425**	0.2866	**0.0233**	**0.2328**	**0.2313**	**0.4351**
LDA	0.0094	0.0628	0.0327	**0.2986**	0.0009	0.0079	0.0024	0.3613
ontoWRMF	*0.0305*	*0.3046*	*0.0707*	**0.3156**	*0.0867*	*0.8667*	*0.5430*	0.2764
WRMF	0.0086	0.0581	0.0305	0.2963	0.0016	0.0142	0.0067	**0.3922**

Figure 5 shows a trade-off between relevance, measured with F1 score, and diversity of recommendations obtained by considered baselines on single domain datasets (algorithm names), and baselines combined with preOnto: on single domain datasets (names with the *onto-* prefix) and the multi-domain dataset

Table 5. Results obtained for multi-domain recommendations with the preOnto.

Algorithm	Precision	Recall	nDCG	Diversity
BPR	0.0172	0.1724	0.0374	0.3696
FISM	0.0161	0.1609	0.0418	0.3566
LDA	0.0241	0.2414	0.0437	0.3015
WRMF	0.0230	0.2299	0.0617	0.3450

(names with *multi-* prefix). Please note that results obtained on single domain datasets are averaged.

It should be noticed that traditional baselines obtained best diversity values, while traditional preOnto gained best F1 score values. Still, multi-domain pre-Onto achieved the best trade-off between relevance and diversity of recommendations. An exception is the LDA algorithm, for which preOnto returned more diverse recommendations for a single domain than for a multi-domain dataset.

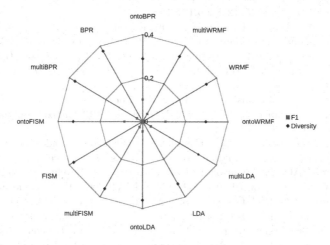

Fig. 5. The relevance-diversity trade-off of the preOnto.

7   Conclusions and Future Work

In this paper, we proved that preOnto with COUP can be successfully applied as a context-aware and multi-domain recommendation method. We compared our approach with four single-domain baselines, i.e., BPR, FISM, LDA, and WRMF, and showed that it can improve a balance between relevance and diversity of recommendations. We did not perform a comparison with other context-aware and multi-domain methods since, to the best of our knowledge, this is the first truly context-aware and multi-domain recommendation approach.

The next step that needs to be taken is a comparison of the method with existing non-context-aware multi-domain RS. Moreover, this paper allows further investigation in multiple research directions such as: checking if the method can be applied in other kinds of CDRS, e.g., for linked-domain recommendations, as well as developing new or testing existing semantic recommendation algorithms in combination with preOnto method.

References

1. Adamopoulos, P., Tuzhilin, A.: Estimating the value of multi-dimensional data sets in context-based recommender systems. In: 8th ACM Conference on Recommender Systems (RecSys 2014) (2014)
2. Adomavicius, G., Tuzhilin, A.: Context-aware recommender systems. In: Ricci, F., Rokach, L., Shapira, B., Kantor, P.B. (eds.) Recommender Systems Handbook, pp. 217–253. Springer, Boston, MA (2011). https://doi.org/10.1007/978-0-387-85820-3_7
3. Anand, S.S., Kearney, P., Shapcott, M.: Generating semantically enriched user profiles for web personalization. ACM Trans. Internet Technol. 7(4), 22–es (2007). https://doi.org/10.1145/1278366.1278371
4. Anelli, V.W., Di Noia, T., Di Sciascio, E., Ragone, A., Trotta, J.: The importance of being dissimilar in recommendation. In: Proceedings of the 34th ACM/SIGAPP Symposium on Applied Computing, pp. 816–821. SAC 2019, Association for Computing Machinery, New York, NY, USA (2019). https://doi.org/10.1145/3297280.3297360
5. Braunhofer, M., Kaminskas, M., Ricci, F.: Location-aware music recommendation. Int. J. Multimedia Inf. Retrieval 2(1), 31–44 (2013). https://doi.org/10.1007/s13735-012-0032-2
6. Cantador, I., Bellogín, A., Castells, P.: Ontology-based personalised and context-aware recommendations of news items. In: Proceedings of the 2008 IEEE/WIC/ACM International Conference on Web Intelligence and Intelligent Agent Technology, vol. 01, pp. 562–565. WI-IAT 2008, IEEE Computer Society, Washington, DC, USA (2008). http://dx.doi.org/10.1109/WIIAT.2008.204
7. Cantador, I., Fernández-Tobías, I., Berkovsky, S., Cremonesi, P.: Cross-domain recommender systems. In: Ricci, F., Rokach, L., Shapira, B. (eds.) Recommender Systems Handbook, pp. 919–959. Springer, Boston, MA (2015). https://doi.org/10.1007/978-1-4899-7637-6_27
8. Cremonesi, P., Tripodi, A., Turrin, R.: Cross-domain recommender systems. In: 2011 IEEE 11th International Conference on Data Mining Workshops, pp. 496–503 (2011). https://doi.org/10.1109/ICDMW.2011.57
9. Di Noia, T., Ostuni, V.C.: Recommender systems and linked open data. In: Faber, W., Paschke, A. (eds.) Reasoning Web 2015. LNCS, vol. 9203, pp. 88–113. Springer, Cham (2015). https://doi.org/10.1007/978-3-319-21768-0_4
10. Dooms, S., De Pessemier, T., Martens, L.: Movietweetings: a movie rating dataset collected from twitter. In: Workshop on Crowdsourcing and Human Computation for Recommender Systems, CrowdRec at RecSys 2013 (2013)
11. Fernández-Tobías, I., Cantador, I., Kaminskas, M., Ricci, F.: Cross-domain recommender systems: a survey of the state of the art. In: Proceedings of the 2nd Spanish Conference on Information Retrieval, pp. 187–198 (2012)

12. Goczyła, K., Waloszek, A., Waloszek, W., Zawadzka, T.: Modularized knowledge bases using contexts, conglomerates and a query language. Intell. Tools Build. Sci. Inf. Platform **390**, 179–201 (2012)
13. Hawalah, A., Fasli, M.: Utilizing contextual ontological user profiles for personalized recommendations. Exp. Syst. Appl. **41**(10), 4777–4797 (2014). https://doi.org/10.1016/j.eswa.2014.01.039
14. Isufi, E., Pocchiari, M., Hanjalic, A.: Accuracy-diversity trade-off in recommender systems via graph convolutions. Inf. Process Manag. **58**, 102459 (2021). https://doi.org/10.1016/j.ipm.2020.102459
15. Jannach, D., Zanker, M., Felfernig, A., Friedrich, G.: Recommender Systems: An Introduction, 1st edn. Cambridge University Press, New York, NY, USA (2010)
16. Karpus, A., Vagliano, I., Goczyła, K., Morisio, M.: An ontology-based contextual pre-filtering technique for recommender systems. In: 2016 Federated Conference on Computer Science and Information Systems (FedCSIS), pp. 411–420 (2016)
17. Karpus, A., Vagliano, I., Goczyła, K.: Serendipitous recommendations through ontology-based contextual pre-filtering. In: Kozielski, S., Mrozek, D., Kasprowski, P., Małysiak-Mrozek, B., Kostrzewa, D. (eds.) BDAS 2017. CCIS, vol. 716, pp. 246–259. Springer, Cham (2017). https://doi.org/10.1007/978-3-319-58274-0_21
18. Lops, P., de Gemmis, M., Semeraro, G.: Content-based recommender systems: state of the art and trends. In: Ricci, F., Rokach, L., Shapira, B., Kantor, P.B. (eds.) Recommender Systems Handbook, pp. 73–105. Springer, Boston, MA (2011). https://doi.org/10.1007/978-0-387-85820-3_3
19. Middleton, S.E., Shadbolt, N.R., De Roure, D.C.: Ontological user profiling in recommender systems. ACM Trans. Inf. Syst. **22**(1), 54–88 (2004). https://doi.org/10.1145/963770.963773
20. Mobasher, B., Jin, X., Zhou, Y.: Semantically enhanced collaborative filtering on the web. In: Berendt, B., Hotho, A., Mladenič, D., van Someren, M., Spiliopoulou, M., Stumme, G. (eds.) EWMF 2003. LNCS (LNAI), vol. 3209, pp. 57–76. Springer, Heidelberg (2004). https://doi.org/10.1007/978-3-540-30123-3_4
21. Rack, C., Arbanowski, S., Steglich, S.: Context-aware, ontology-based recommendations. In: SAINT-W 2006: Proceedings of the International Symposium on Applications on Internet Workshops. pp. 98–104. IEEE Computer Society, Washington, DC, USA (2006). http://dx.doi.org/10.1109/saint-w.2006.13
22. Ricci, F., Rokach, L., Shapira, B.: Introduction to recommender systems handbook. In: Ricci, F., Rokach, L., Shapira, B., Kantor, P.B. (eds.) Recommender Systems Handbook, pp. 1–35. Springer, Boston, MA (2011). https://doi.org/10.1007/978-0-387-85820-3_1
23. Rodríguez, J., Bravo, M., Guzmán, R.: Multidimensional ontology model to support context-aware systems. In: AAAI Workshops (2013). http://www.aaai.org/ocs/index.php/WS/AAAIW13/paper/view/7187
24. Singh, R., Bedi, P.: Parallel proactive cross domain context aware recommender system. J. Intell. Fuzzy Syst. **34**, 1521–1533 (2018). https://doi.org/10.3233/JIFS-169447
25. Su, Z., Yan, J., Ling, H., Chen, H.: Research on personalized recommendation algorithm based on ontological user interest model. J. Comput. Inf. Syst. **8**(1), 169–181 (2012)
26. Taneja, A., Arora, A.: Cross domain recommendation using multidimensional tensor factorization. Exp. Syst. Appl. **92**, 304–316 (2018). https://doi.org/10.1016/j.eswa.2017.09.042

27. Véras, D., Prudêncio, R., Ferraz, C.: Cd-cars: cross-domain context-aware recommender systems. Exp. Syst. Appl. **135**, 388–409 (2019). https://doi.org/10.1016/j.eswa.2019.06.020

28. Wasilewski, J., Hurley, N.: Incorporating diversity in a learning to rank recommender system. In: Markov, Z., Russell, I. (eds.) Proceedings of the Twenty-Ninth International Florida Artificial Intelligence Research Society Conference, FLAIRS 2016, Key Largo, Florida, USA, May 16–18, 2016, pp. 572–578. AAAI Press (2016). http://www.aaai.org/ocs/index.php/FLAIRS/FLAIRS16/paper/view/12944

A Relevance Feedback-Based Approach for Non-TI Clustering

Sanjit Kumar Saha[(✉)] and Ingo Schmitt

Brandenburg University of Technology Cottbus-Senftenberg, Cottbus, Germany
{sahasanj,schmitt}@b-tu.de

Abstract. Homogeneity of persons in a social network is based on the similarity of their attributes. Traditional clustering algorithms like hierarchical (agglomerative) clustering or DBSCAN take distances between objects as input and find clusters of objects. Distance functions need to satisfy the triangle inequality (TI) property, but sometimes TI is violated and, in addition, not all attributes do have the same influence on the network and thus may affect the network and compromise the quality of resulting clusters. We present an *adaptive clustering-based quantitative weighting* approach that is completely embedded in logic. To facilitate the user interaction with the system, we exploit the concept of relevance feedback. The approach takes user feedback as input to improve the quality of clusters and finds meaningful clusters where TI does not hold. In addition, it has the capability of providing the user alternative possible feedbacks that can be fulfilled. To test the approach, we evaluate a *clustering distance* regarding an ideal solution. Experiments demonstrate the benefits of our approach.

Keywords: Social network clustering · Quantitative weighting · Relevance feedback · Clustering distance · Similarity measure · Clique

1 Introduction

Social networks can be seen as graphs consisting of a set of social actors (such as individuals or organizations) and a set of dyadic ties. More specifically, the actors can be represented by nodes, and ties between pairs of nodes can be regarded as edges if the nodes are related by the relationship that characterizes the network.

Clustering a network is a process of grouping actors into disjoint clusters where intra-cluster similarities among actors are significantly higher than inter-clusters similarities. The greater the similarity within a group and the smaller the similarity between groups, the better is the clustering. Technically, traditional clustering techniques like *k-medoids* and *hierarchical* use distance functions like Euclidean distance function or Manhattan distance function and take distances of object pairs as input. Distance functions must satisfy amongst others the triangle inequality (TI) $d(x,y) \leq d(x,z) + d(y,z)$ property but sometimes there are functions that fulfil all distance properties except TI. We will call them non-TI functions. The violation of TI may compromise the quality of the resulting

© Springer Nature Switzerland AG 2022
B. Li et al. (Eds.): ADMA 2021, LNAI 13088, pp. 381–393, 2022.
https://doi.org/10.1007/978-3-030-95408-6_29

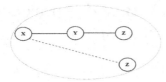

(a) TI violation in $k-medoids$ clustering: due to the problem of visualizing non-TI in a plane object Z appears twice

(b) Non-TI Clustering

Fig. 1. Clustering scenarios.

clusters. For example in Fig. 1a, consider three objects X, Y and Z within a cluster with two edges between them. If there are edges (X, Y) and (Y, Z), but no edge (X, Z), then the distance from X to Z exceeds the sum of the distances from X to Y to Z. The cohesion of Z may be seriously impacted because X is close to Y but very far away from Z and thus violates TI property.

But meaningful clustering is possible in the way that X and Z reside in different cluster and Y can reside in more than one cluster at the same time as shown in Fig. 1b. Newman [8] proposed an approach for discovering community structure in networks using modularity function. Considering the ill-effects of bridge vertices in a network, Scripps et al. [9] presented an overlapping clustering algorithm. Using graph coloring method, Tantipathananandh et al. [10] presented a community finding algorithm for dynamic networks. Saha and Schmitt [3] proposed a commuting quantum query language (CQQL) based clique-guided approach for Non-TI clustering. Though these approaches offer some satisfying results it causes a new issue: sometimes it does not meet user satisfaction.

Example 1. In a social network of alumni of a school, let $P = \{p_1, p_2, ..., p_n\}$ be a set of n people and the similarity among people can be sufficiently expressed by relying on their admission year and graduation year. The similarity value between two people p_1 and p_2 can be expressed as a CQQL condition $q(p_1, p_2)$:

$$\underbrace{\underbrace{school(p_1, p_2)}_{(p_1.school=p_2.school)\in\{0,1\}}}_{Boolean\ condition} \wedge \underbrace{\underbrace{admission(p_1, p_2)}_{(p_1.adm\approx p_2.adm)\in[0,1]}}_{similarity\ condition} \wedge \underbrace{\underbrace{graduation(p_1, p_2)}_{(p_1.grad\approx p_2.grad)\in[0,1]}}_{similarity\ condition} \quad (1)$$

The similarity of persons can be sufficiently expressed by relying on their admission and graduation year but it is obvious that friends can complete their graduation in different class year but their admission year is the same. Because of their different graduation year, their corresponding similarity values should have less influence on the result. Regarding this issue, Saha and Schmitt [4] proposed an idea of a *quantitative weighting* approach. They presented a quantitative weighting approach called "adaptive clustering" that is capable of assigning query weights to atomic conditions. In addition to their approach, we propose a relevance feedback concept with user interaction. In user interaction, the approach includes feedback in every round to a feedback set that must be fulfilled.

In addition, it provides the user alternate feedbacks that can be fulfilled if no weight(s) is found that satisfies the corresponding constraints of the feedback set. To test the quality of clustering of the approach, we evaluate a *clustering distance* regarding an ideal solution.

The paper is organized as follows. Section 2 outlines the theoretical concepts of the query language CQQL. The following section discusses initial weighting schemes. Section 4 shows a flow diagram of our approach and gives a motivating example. Section 5 introduces the core idea of our relevance feedback approach. Section 6 gives a detailed explanation of the transformation of feedback into weights. Section 7 presents some clustering properties. Section 8 describes the quality measure to test our approach. The following section presents experimental results. Finally, the paper concludes with Sect. 10.

2   Theoretical Concepts of CQQL

Traditional Boolean-logic-based database system typically returns the Boolean value *true* for perfect match and *false* otherwise. If vague aspects are part of the query or a complete match is nearly impossible, Boolean logic does not always meet the requirements. Thus, there is a need for integrating vague or imprecise predicates into a logic-based query language. For such a scenario, many proposed query languages use concepts from fuzzy logic. But fuzzy set theory suffers from weaknesses during the set operations such as union ($\cup$), intersection ($\cap$) and complement ($\neg$). For example, if X is a collection of objects denoted generically by x and $\mu(x)$ is the membership function of x, Zadeh [12] suggests the usage of *max* for union, *min* for intersection and $1 - \mu(x)$ for complement. But the binary *min/max* functions return only one value and thus lead to a value dominance of one of the two input values while the other one is completely ignored and can not express grades of importance of both values on a result. That means $max(0.01, 1)$ gives the same result as $max(0.95, 1)$, although both pairs do differ very much from a human points of view.

Substituting *min/max* by other *t-norms/t-conorms* cause another violations of the Boolean algebra described in [11]. To overcome this, Schmitt [1] presented a quantum logic based query language (CQQL). CQQL allows the formulation of logic-based queries incorporating both Boolean and similarity conditions. Similarities from the interval [0, 1] are commonly used to test how close attribute values between two objects are.

Let AC be a set of atomic conditions on database tuples (objects) where every $ac(o_1, o_2) \in AC$ is a binary condition on two objects that measures the closeness of two given objects based on the values of an attribute. Let $eval(\varphi(o_1, o_2))$ be the evaluation of a condition φ on two objects o_1 and o_2. A CQQL condition can be evaluated by means of simple and straightforward arithmetics. It forms the base case for the evaluation of a condition and results in a similarity value from the interval [0, 1] for an object pair o_1 and o_2 with the fulfillment of the following properties: (*i*) *Reflexivity:* $\varphi(o_1, o_1) = 1$ and (*ii*) *Symmetric:* $\varphi(o_1, o_2) = \varphi(o_2, o_1)$.

Subsequently, the evaluation of a CQQL condition in a special syntactical normal [1] form is performed by recursively applying the succeeding formulas until the base case is reached: (i) $eval(\varphi_1 \wedge \varphi_2) = eval(\varphi_1) \cdot eval(\varphi_2)$, (ii) $eval(\varphi_1 \vee \varphi_2) = eval(\varphi_1) + eval(\varphi_2) - eval(\varphi_1) \cdot eval(\varphi_2)$, (iii) $eval(\varphi_1 \dot\vee \varphi_2) = eval(\varphi_1) + eval(\varphi_2)$, and (iv) $eval(\neg\varphi_1) = 1 - eval(\varphi_1)$.

where (i) and (ii) applies when φ_1 and φ_2 are not exclusive and (iii) applies when φ_1 and φ_2 are exclusive (i.e. $eval(\varphi_1 \wedge \varphi_2) = 0$). For simplification, the objects o_1 and o_2 are dropped here. The dot (.) over disjunction operator ($\vee$) signals an exclusive disjunction ($\dot\vee$).

3   Weighting of CQQL Conditions

CQQL incorporates weights in order to express different importances of sub-conditions within a query while staying consistent with a Boolean algebra. Weights $\Theta = \{\theta_i\}$ are assumed to be values from the interval $[0,1]$. They can be used to give operands of a conjunction or a disjunction differently strong impacts on the evaluation result. The idea is to transform a weighted conjunction or a weighted disjunction into a logical formula without weights:

$\varphi_1 \wedge_{\theta_1,\theta_2} \varphi_2 = (\varphi_1 \vee \neg\theta_1) \wedge (\varphi_2 \vee \neg\theta_2)$ and $\varphi_1 \vee_{\theta_1,\theta_2} \varphi_2 = (\varphi_1 \wedge \theta_1) \vee (\varphi_2 \wedge \theta_1)$

Two extreme cases will be considered to clarify the understanding of the weight semantics. A zero-weighted operand ($\theta_i = 0$) means that such a condition has no impact on the overall result. In contrast, a one-weighted operand ($\theta_1 = \theta_2 = 1$) cause a result equivalent to unweighted conditions. The arithmetic evaluation of the weighted conjunction and weighted disjunction is:

$$eval(\varphi_1 \wedge_{\theta_1,\theta_2} \varphi_2) = (\varphi_1 + \neg\theta_1 - \varphi_1 \cdot \neg\theta_1) \cdot (\varphi_2 + \neg\theta_2 - \varphi_2 \cdot \neg\theta_2) \qquad (2)$$

$$eval(\varphi_1 \vee_{\theta_1,\theta_2} \varphi_2) = (\varphi_1 \cdot \theta_1) + (\varphi_2 \cdot \theta_2) - (\varphi_1 \cdot \varphi_2 \cdot \theta_1 \cdot \theta_2) \qquad (3)$$

where $\neg\theta_x = 1 - \theta_x$.

We present an interesting special case of a weighting q^Θ when connected weights are used. It is simply a complemented form of weight of object o_1 against o_2 and the formulation requires less weighting variables than the previous weighting concept: $\varphi_1 \wedge_\theta \varphi_2 = (\varphi_1 \vee \neg\theta) \wedge (\varphi_2 \vee \theta)$ and $\varphi_1 \vee_\theta \varphi_2 = (\varphi_1 \wedge \theta) \dot\vee (\varphi_2 \wedge \neg\theta)$

The arithmetic evaluation of the weighted disjunction is the weighted sum:

$$eval(\varphi_1 \dot\vee_\theta \varphi_2) = \varphi_1 \cdot \theta + \varphi_2 \cdot (1 - \theta) \qquad (4)$$

Very surprisingly, logical transformation based on Boolean algebra shows that connected weights in a conjunction equals exactly connected weights in a disjunction.

$$(\varphi_1 \vee \neg\theta) \wedge (\varphi_2 \vee \theta) \rightarrow (\varphi_1 \wedge \varphi_2) \vee (\varphi_1 \wedge \theta) \vee (\varphi_2 \wedge \neg\theta) \vee (\theta \wedge \neg\theta) \rightarrow$$

$$(\varphi_1 \wedge \varphi_2 \wedge \theta) \vee (\varphi_1 \wedge \varphi_2 \wedge \neg\theta) \vee (\varphi_1 \wedge \theta) \vee (\varphi_2 \wedge \neg\theta)$$

$$\rightarrow (((\varphi_1 \wedge \varphi_2) \vee \varphi_1) \wedge \theta) \dot\vee (((\varphi_1 \wedge \varphi_2) \vee \varphi_2) \wedge \neg\theta) \rightarrow (\varphi_1 \wedge \theta) \dot\vee (\varphi_2 \wedge \neg\theta)$$

Therefore the arithmetic evaluation of the weighted conjunction is also the weighted sum:

$$eval(\varphi_1 \wedge_\theta \varphi_2) = \varphi_1 \cdot \theta + \varphi_2 \cdot (1 - \theta) \qquad (5)$$

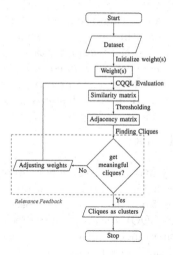

Fig. 2. Flowchart of Non-TI clustering.

4   Social Network Clustering

The flow diagram in Fig. 2 illustrates our approach to finding clusters. It first calculates the similarity values between pairwise objects to form a similarity matrix, after that derives an adjacency matrix based on threshold value th and finally find clusters based on clique approach. We incorporate weights $\theta \in [0, 1]$ on each atomic condition. A user can provide a feedback for re-constructing a cluster. If the system fulfils the feedback, it infers the weight value for a weighted CQQL, otherwise it notifies the user of some alternate solutions if available.

For example, we recall the Example 1 and consider a weighted CQQL query $q^{\Theta}(p_1, p_2)$ with weight variables $\Theta = \{\theta_i\}$. A weighting function w assigns every weight variable $\theta_i \in \Theta$ a value from $[0, 1]$. Therefore, following Schmitt [2], we reformulate the query by assigning a weight to each atomic condition in a complimented form of one against other.

$$q^{\Theta}(p_1, p_2) = school(p_1, p_2) \wedge \Big(admission(p_1, p_2) \wedge_{\theta} graduation(p_1, p_2) \Big) \quad (6)$$

Using Eq. 4 the arithmetic evaluation of $q^{\Theta}(p_1, p_2)$ yields:

$$school(p_1, p_2) \cdot \Big(admission(p_1, p_2) \cdot \theta + graduation(p_1, p_2) \cdot (1 - \theta) \Big)$$

The query condition is executed on $P \times P$. The evaluation of $q^{\Theta}(p_1, p_2)$ is realized by the function $eval(q^{\Theta}(p_i, p_j), w)$ which calculates a similarity value from $[0, 1]$ for every pair of objects $(p_i, p_j) \in P \times P$ and hence provides a similarity matrix $S = (s_{ij})$. An adjacency matrix $Adj = \{a_{ij}\}$ can be derived from S by applying Eq. 7 with threshold value th.

$$a_{ij} = \begin{cases} 1 & \text{if } s_{ij} \geq th \\ 0 & \text{otherwise} \end{cases} \quad (7)$$

The adjacency matrix *Adj* is then used to build an undirected graph G. By using the Bron-Kerbosch algorithm [6] in G, maximal cliques can be found that lists all subsets of vertices with the two properties that each pair of vertices in one of the listed subsets is connected by an edge, and no listed subset can have any additional vertices added to it while preserving its complete connectivity. We regard cliques as clusters. Be aware, clusters can overlap.

5   Relevance Feedback

The core idea is to modify and to learn weights through user interactions that rely completely on feedback. The user is given the opportunity to modify sample clusters by moving objects from one cluster to another one.

We assume a weighted CQQL query q^Θ on paired objects with weight variables $\Theta = \{\theta_i\}$. A weighting function w assigns a value from $[0, 1]$ to the weight variable $\theta_i \in \Theta$. Let w^I denote an initial weighting function that set the weight variable(s) to an initial value of either 0.5 or 1. The query is executed on pairs from n objects. The evaluation of q^Θ is realized by function $eval(q^\Theta(o_i, o_j), w)$. The execution of $eval(q^\Theta(o_i, o_j), w)$ yields a similarity value from $[0, 1]$ for every pair of objects $(o_i, o_j) \in O \times O$ and hence provides a similarity matrix $S = (s_{ij})$. Initially w^T is usually unknown. This leads to the issue that the initial weighting scheme w^I often finds clusters which are seldom compliant with the user's expectations. As a result, it is necessary to approximate the target clusters that would be found by w^T gradually based on user feedback.

Definition 1 (Feedback). *Let C be a set of clusters of objects O, $th \in [0, 1]$ be a threshold, $c \in C$ be a cluster and $co \subseteq O$ be a set of objects. Depending on the user interaction, every feedback falls into one of the two feedback categories:*

(i) Feedback for constructing a new cluster: A feedback f^{co} requires all objects $o \in co$ to reside in a same cluster i.e. $co \subseteq c \in C$ produced by a weighted query q^Θ. A weighting scheme w fulfills the feedback f^{co} if and only if
$$\forall_{o_1, o_2} \in co : eval(q^\Theta(o_1, o_2), w) \geq th \text{ holds.}$$
That is there are edges between all objects.

(ii) Feedback for removing an object from a cluster: A feedback $f^{o,c}$ requires an object $o \in c$ should be outside of the cluster c i.e. $o \notin c$ produced by a weighted query q^Θ. A weighting scheme w fulfills the feedback $f^{o,c}$ if and only if
$$\exists_{o_1} \in c : eval(q^\Theta(o_1, o), w) < th \text{ holds.}$$

For example, considering the complemented form of Eq. 5, Fig. 3a visualizes the results of an evaluation of $q^\Theta(p_1, p_2)$ of Eq. 6 w.r.t. different weight values for θ. Let, similarities of two friends p_1 and p_2 is $s_{p_1, p_2}(1, 0.3, 0.6)$ where $school(p_1, p_2) = 1$, $admission(p_1, p_2) = 0.3$ and $graduation(p_1, p_2) = 0.6$ and threshold th is 0.5 (red horizontal line). Considering feedback $f^{\{p_1, p_2\}}$, it is clearly visible that for the initial weight value 0.5, there is no edge between p_1 and p_2 (yellow circled) that means they cannot reside in the same cluster. If user provides a feedback of requiring them residing within the same cluster, the feedback can be fulfilled with some weight with $w(\theta) \leq 0.33$.

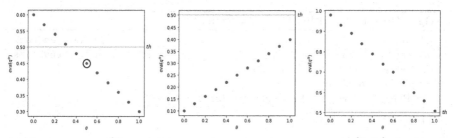

(a) Evaluation of $q^{\Theta}(p_1, p_2)$ with respect to θ (b) Inconsistent case of feedback $f^{\{p_1, p_2\}}$ (left) and $f^{p_1, \{p_1, p_2, \ldots\}}$ (right)

Fig. 3. Feedback scenarios.

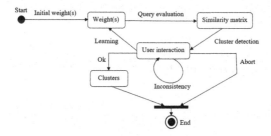

Fig. 4. State diagram of relevance feedback.

Every feedback with respect to a weighted query can be: (*i*) *Inconsistent:* If no $w(\Theta) \in [0, 1]$ can satisfy f^{co} or $f^{o,c}$ (see Fig. 3b) and (*ii*) *Consistent:* Otherwise, the feedback is called consistent (see Fig. 3a).

As an example of an *inconsistent* feedback, $f^{\{p_1, p_2\}}$ can be easily shown by setting $th = 0.5$ and the similarities of two friends p_1 and p_2 with respect to attributes *school*, *admission* and *graduation* as $s_{p_1, p_2}(1, 0.4, 0.1)$ and $f^{p_1, \{p_1, p_2, \ldots\}}$ can be shown by setting $th = 0.5$ and the similarities as $s_{p_1, p_2}(1, 0.51, 0.98)$. The feedback $f^{\{p_1, p_2\}}$ and $f^{p_1, \{p_1, p_2, \ldots\}}$ cannot be fulfilled because no weight can be found as illustrated in Fig. 3b.

During relevance feedback, clusters are presented to the user that can be modified according to their subjective need. Starting point of the relevance feedback is a structured query - a weighted CQQL query. Figure 4 shows the state diagram of relevance feedback. After modification of the clusters, they have to be examined regarding inconsistencies based on Definition 1. The modification of one or more cluster leads usually to new clusters. As a consequence, old clusters may disappear while new clusters may emerge. If the user stops altering because of satisfaction or abortion, the system reaches a fixed point and cluster does not develop any further.

Algorithm 1: Algorithm for a new feedback.

    Data: f `// new feedback`

1   $isPossible := true,\ F := F \cup f$ `// F is the set of feedbacks`

2   $isPossible :=$ check if F is satisfiable

3   **if** $\neg isPossible$ **then**

4   Report "no weight(s) is found that fulfills the feedbacks F"

5      $k := |F| - 1$

6   **do**

7          $F_{alt} := \{\}$ `// alternate feedbacks`

8          $S :=$ generate all k-subsets of F containing f

9   **for** *every subset F_s in S* **do**

10             $isPossible :=$ check if F_s is satisfiable

11   **if** $isPossible$ **then**

12                 $F_{alt} := F_{alt} \cup F_s$

13   **end**

14   **end**

15   **if** $F_{alt} \neq \emptyset$ **then**

16   Report "F_{alt} can be fulfilled"

17   **end**

18          $k := k - 1$

19   **while** $k \neq 1$

20 **end**

21 **else**

22   Report "weight(s) $w(\Theta)$ fulfills the feedback F"

23 **end**

---

6   Weight Learning

In every round each feedback must be added to a feedback set: a set of feedbacks means a set of constraints and the complete set must be satisfied. If no weight(s) can be found that satisfies the set of constraints, then the system checks subsets of constraints and returns the user a member of alternate possible feedbacks sets that can be fulfilled. The procedure is summarized in Algorithm 1.

As an example, consider a set of feedbacks $F = \{f_1, f_2\}$ provided by a user and a weight(s) value $w(\Theta) \in [0, 1]$ is found that already satisfies the corresponding set of constraints. Suppose, the user provides a new feedback f_3. The system checks and does not find a weight(s) value that satisfies the corresponding set of constraints of the set of feedbacks $F = \{f_1, f_2, f_3\}$. Therefore, the system checks the corresponding constraints of *2-subsets* containing feedback f_3 ($\{f_1, f_3\}$ and $\{f_2, f_3\}$) and provides the user alternate feedbacks F_{alt} that can be fulfilled.

It becomes obvious that we have to deal with a non-linear optimization problem because a CQQL query evaluation can be expressed as a sum of products of atomic conditions and weight variables. We use SLSQP method implemented by Dieter Kraft [7] that uses Sequential Least Squares Programming to minimize an objective function of several variables with any combination of bounds, equality and inequality constraints.

Table 1. Contingency matrix.

	Predefined (cluster)	
	Pairs in C_I	Pairs not in C_I
Predicted (cluster)		
Pairs in C	$T_{11} = \lvert T_{C_I} \cap T_C \rvert$	$T_{10} = \lvert T_C \setminus T_{C_I} \rvert$
Pairs not in C	$T_{01} = \lvert T_{C_I} \setminus T_C \rvert$	$T_{00} = \lvert T_P \setminus (T_{C_I} \cup T_C) \rvert$

7   Clustering Properties

Let $S = \{p_{ij}\}$ be a similarity matrix which consists of a finite set of actors (objects) $P = \{p_1, p_2, ..., p_n\}$ having two attributes *"admission"* and *"graduation"*. For simplicity, we use A for *admission* and G for *graduation*. Hence an adjacency matrix $Adj = \{a_{ij}\}$ can be derived from the similarity matrix S by applying Eq. 7 with threshold th where $a_{ij} = 1$ means there is an edge (similar) between p_i and p_j and $a_{ij} = 0$ means no edge (dissimilar).

Property 1 (Set Operation). If $E_A \subseteq P \times P$ be a set of edges based on A and $E_G \subseteq P \times P$ be a set of edges based on G, then $E_{A \wedge_\theta G}$ be a set of edges of weighted conjunction of A and G with weighted variable $\theta \in [0, 1]$ so that $E_{A \wedge_\theta G} \subseteq E_A \cup E_G$ holds.

Using Eq. 5 it can be demonstrated easily that if $\theta = 1$ then $E_{A \wedge_\theta G} = E_A$ and if $\theta = 0$ then $E_{A \wedge_\theta G} = E_G$ and for other values of θ within $[0, 1]$, $E_{A \wedge_\theta G} \subseteq E_A$ or $E_{A \wedge_\theta G} \subseteq E_G$ or $E_{A \wedge_\theta G} \subseteq E_A \cap E_G$.

8   Quality Measure for Social Network Clustering

As clustering is an unsupervised technique, assessment based on quantitative performance measures is not possible due to missing ground truth data. However, for testing our approach, we assume a human generated clustering (a clustering of objects that is considered to be "correct" in some sense) as an ideal solution and use it in our approach for evaluating a ***clustering distance***: a measure for the dissimilarity between two clusterings. To avoid confusion, we distinguish between cluster (data points of a group) and clustering (the set of clusters that result from a clustering process). An interesting approach of comparing clusterings is counting pairs of objects that are "grouped" in the same way in both clusterings.

Given a predefined clustering C_I and a clustering C predicted by our approach of the data set $P = \{p_i\}_{i=1}^n$ with n peoples, we first define data set pairs $T_P = \{(p_i, p_j) \lvert p_i, p_j \in P \text{ and } i < j\}$ as all the pairs realizable from the complete data set. Second, clustered pairs $T_{C_I} = \{(p_1, p_2) \in T_P \lvert (p_1, p_2) \subseteq c_I \in C_I\}$ and $T_C = \{(p_1, p_2) \in T_P \lvert (p_1, p_2) \subseteq c \in C\}$ that cluster together in C_I and C respectively. Using T_{C_I}, T_C and T_P the values of the four quadrants of the contingency matrix is shown in Table 1. Note that $\lambda = \lvert T_P \rvert = T_{11} + T_{10} + T_{01} + T_{00} = \frac{n(n-1)}{2}$.

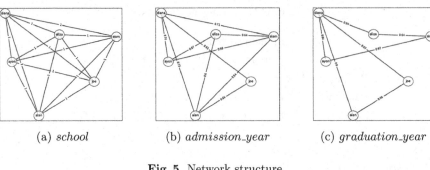

(a) *school* (b) *admission_year* (c) *graduation_year*

Fig. 5. Network structure.

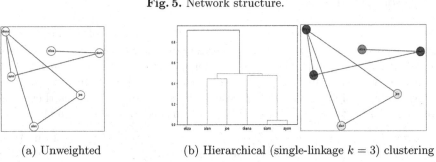

(a) Unweighted (b) Hierarchical (single-linkage $k = 3$) clustering

Fig. 6. Traditional clustering.

The *Accuracy* $\mathcal{A}$ for a clustering C concerning a certain predefined clustering C_I indicates how "good" the clustering C describes the clustering C_I. It can be defined as: $\mathcal{A}(C_I, C) = \frac{T_{11} + T_{00}}{\lambda}$, *where* $\mathcal{A}$ ranges from 0 (no pair classified in the same way under both clusterings) to 1 (identical clusterings).

We can derive the **clustering distance** $d(C_I, C)$ from the similarity measure $\mathcal{A}(C_I, C)$ by applying $s(x, y) = e^{-d(x,y)}$ *where* d ranges from 0 (identical clusterings) to ∞ (no pair classified in the same way under both clusterings) as: $d(C_I, C) = -\ln(\mathcal{A}(C_I, C))$.

9   Experiments

To validate the utility of our approach, we perform experiments on social networks of different sizes. For a better understanding, we consider a small social network of 6 people in this paper. All experiments were run on a modern desktop computer and algorithms were implemented with Python.

In our experiment, we obtain the similarity matrix $S = (s_{ij})$ by applying a simple conjunctive weighted query q^Θ with weight variable $\theta = 0.5$ on attributes *school*, *admission_year* and *graduation_year* of people pairs and derive an adjacency matrix $Adj = (a_{ij})$ from S with threshold value $th = 0.5$. Figure 5 illustrates the network structure of three attributes of a small social network. We use the Fruchterman-Reingold algorithm [5] to produce two-dimensional pictures of graphs using the adjacency matrix Adj.

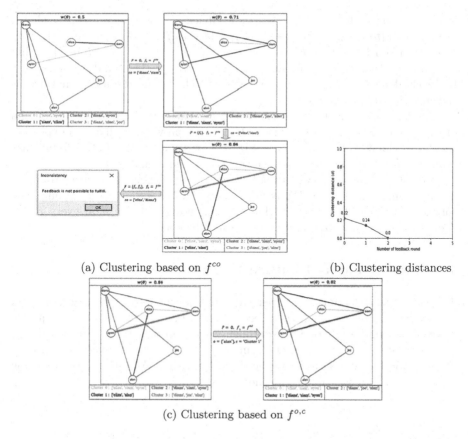

(a) Clustering based on f^{co} (b) Clustering distances

(c) Clustering based on $f^{o,c}$

Fig. 7. Non-TI clustering based on user feedback.

The first experiment in Fig. 6 analyzes how clusters can be found by applying traditional clustering techniques. Figure 6a shows the network structure constructed by unweighted query. Applying single-linkage ($k = 3$) hierarchical clustering algorithm on the network, three clusters $\{'diana', 'ayon', 'siam'\}$, $\{'alan', 'joe'\}$ and $\{'eliza'\}$ can be found as shown in Fig. 6b. But the cluster $\{'diana', 'ayon', 'siam'\}$ violates the TI property because there is no edge within the pair $\{'diana', 'siam'\}$ which is visible in Fig. 6b(right).

The next experiment analyzes how meaningful clusters can be found using our proposed approach with user interaction. The experiment is initialized by considering that both attributes have the equal influence (by setting $\theta = 0.5$) while performing conjunction ($\wedge$) (see Fig. 7a (*top left*)). If a user provides a feedback $F_1 = f^{co}$ of requiring $co = \{'diana', 'siam'\}$ within the same cluster, Fig. 7a (*top right*) shows that $w(\theta) = 0.71$ is found that fulfills the feedback by satisfying the constraint and finding clusters. The feedback is added to the set $F = \{F_1\}$. The user provide a second feedback $F_2 = f^{co}$ of requiring $co = \{'eliza', 'alan'\}$ within the same cluster and $w(\theta) = 0.84$ is found that fulfils the feedback along with the set of previous feedbacks F and finds clusters as shown in Fig. 7a (*bottom right*). The feedback is added to $F = \{F_1, F_2\}$. Next, the user provides a third feedback $F_3 = f^{co}$ of requiring $co = \{'eliza', 'diana'\}$ within the same cluster. In this scenario, no weight $w(\theta) \in [0, 1]$ is found that fulfils the feedback along with the set of previous feedbacks F and the user is notified as shown in Fig. 7a (*bottom left*).

The last experiment shows user feedback (category $f^{o,c}$) requiring that an object should be outside of a cluster. If the user provides feedback of expecting $o = 'alan'$ outside of $c = cluster$ 1, Fig. 7c shows that $w(\theta) = 0.82$ is found that fulfils the feedback by satisfying the constraint and it finds clusters.

To test our approach, we evaluate a clustering distance d in every round of our experiment in Fig. 7a. We assume that Fig. 7a (*bottom right*) is our ideal solution. It is visible in Fig. 7b that the clustering distance d in every round decreases and finally converges to the ideal solution.

10   Conclusion and Future Work

To meet user satisfaction, this paper presents a novel approach to reform network in user interaction based on their feedback and find clusters. As a consequence of the promising results of our experiments, we plan to develop a graphical user interface that supports the user during the refinement of a query. One future challenge poses the complexity of the clique algorithm. We will consider reducing the complexity by weakening the clique condition.

References

1. Schmitt, I.: QQL: a DB&IR query language. VLDB J. **17**(1), 39–56 (2008)
2. Schmitt, I.: Incorporating weights into a quantum-logic-based query language. In: Aerts, D., Khrennikov, A., Melucci, M., Toni, B. (eds.) Quantum-Like Models for Information Retrieval and Decision-Making. SSTEAMH, pp. 129–143. Springer, Cham (2019). https://doi.org/10.1007/978-3-030-25913-6_7
3. Saha, S.K., Schmitt, I.: Non-TI clustering in the context of social networks. Procedia Comput. Sci. **170**(2020), 1186–1191 (2020)
4. Saha, S.K., Schmitt, I.: Quantitative weighting approach for Non-TI clustering. Procedia Comput. Sci. **184**, 966–971 (2021)
5. Fruchterman, T.M.J., Reingold, E.M.: Graph drawing by force-directed placement. Softw. Pract. Exp. **21**(11), 1129–1164 (1991)
6. Bron, C., Kerbosch, J.: Algorithm 457: finding all cliques of an undirected graph. Commun. ACM **16**(9), 575–577 (1973)
7. Kraft D.: A software package for sequential quadratic programming. Technical Report DFVLR-FB 88-28, Institut für Dynamik der Flugsysteme, Oberpfaffenhofen (1988)
8. Newman, M., Girvan, M.: Finding and evaluating community structure in networks. Phys. Rev. E **69**(2), 26113 (2004)
9. Scripps, J., Tan, P.: Constrained overlapping clusters: minimizing the negative effects of bridge-nodes. Stat. Anal. Data Min. **3**(1), 20–37 (2010)

10. Tantipathananandh C., Berger-Wolf T., Kempe D.: A framework for community identification in dynamic social networks. In: Proceedings of the 13th ACM SIGKDD International Conference on Knowledge Discovery and Data Mining, vol. 726 (2007)
11. Fagin, R., Wimmers, E.L.: A formula for incorporating weights into scoring rules. Theor. Comput. Sci. **239**(2), 309–338 (2000)
12. Zadeh, L.A.: Fuzzy sets. Inf. Control **8**, 338–353 (1965)

Scalable Nonlinear Mappings for Classifying Large Sparse Data

Xiang Li[1,2] and Xiao Li[3(✉)]

[1] Academy of Military Science, Beijing 100091, China
lixiang41@nudt.edu.cn
[2] Advanced Institute of Big Data (AIBD), Beijing 100195, China
[3] National University of Defense Technology, Changsha 410073, China
xiaoli@nudt.edu.cn

Abstract. Classifying very large sparse data is important in many real-world applications, such as to predict users' gender and profitability based on product ratings. Traditionally, such datasets are often classified with linear models (logistic regression and linear SVM) for scalability, but the predictive accuracy may suffer. Existing applications demonstrate that large sparse datasets often have a low-rank structure. By computing a polynomial approximation to the low-rank data space, a previous work [9] has developed a kernelized classifier, KARMA, to improve the performance on sparse data. However, such method does not scale well to large datasets. In this paper, we develop scalable feature mappings to efficiently approximate the kernels used in KARMA. In experiments, our method inherits the good predictive performance of KARMA on small to medium sized data while showing a significantly better scalability on large datasets.

Keywords: Sparse data · Classification · Feature mapping · Scalability

1 Introduction

Many user-item datasets in real-world applications are extremely sparse and very high in dimensionality. For example, the Flickr dataset [4], as one of the datasets used in our experiment section has a feature dimensionality of $d = 497,470$ and sparsity $s = 99.9994\%$. Classifying such large sparse data is important in many applications, such as to predict users' gender and profitability based on the product ratings.

Traditionally, linear models (such as logistic regression and linear SVM) are preferred in such a learning task because of the efficiency in dealing with sparsity. However, linear models do not have a rich learning capacity, and the predictive accuracy may suffer.

In recent years, large sparse datasets have been the focus of collaborative filtering research. Many popular algorithms in this field rely on the assumption that the dataset is of a low rank. This assumption is also intuitive as items/users

© Springer Nature Switzerland AG 2022
B. Li et al. (Eds.): ADMA 2021, LNAI 13088, pp. 394–405, 2022.
https://doi.org/10.1007/978-3-030-95408-6_30

can often be well-described by a small number of latent factors. For classification problems, there are also research efforts to take advantage of this low-rank property. For example, [7] attempt to treat the classification label as an additional column to the input feature matrix, and assume that the augmented matrix is of low rank. This formulation allows the use of matrix completion algorithms to solve the classification problem. However, optimizing the matrix completion loss function is neither necessary nor sufficient for ensuring good classification performance [9].

More recently, [9] have developed a classification framework for low-rank and missing *input* data. Compared to [7], the new framework considers the lowrank property of the input features only, which is more natural for practical classification tasks. By using polynomial approximation of the low-rank input space, they demonstrate that the framework is possible to compete with the oracle linear classifiers which have access to the full input data (i.e., without missing) during training. Based on the framework, the authors provide a learning algorithm, KARMA (Kernelized Algorithm for Risk-minimization with Missing Attributes), which is a kernel classifier and is optimized with stochastic gradient descent. While KARMA outperforms previous methods on medium-sized sparse data, it does not scale well to larger datasets because of the expensive kernel computation; see Sect. 2.2.

In this paper, we develop a scalable learning algorithm based on KARMA [9]. Instead of using kernels which are computationally expensive, we propose to use feature mappings that satisfy the following criteria:

- **Compactness.** The feature mapping can be computed and stored efficiently.
- **Expressiveness.** Similar to the KARMA kernels, the feature mapping should capture the linear and also non-linear (low rank) structures in the sparse data.

To achieve this goal, we first study the empirical performance of KARMA with different degrees of polynomial approximation. We find that degree-two polynomial approximation often leads to the best generalization performance in most cases, even though the KARMA kernel supports approximation of an arbitrary degree. It represents a good tradeoff between model expressiveness and complexity, while higher degree approximations often over-fit the data. Based on this, we propose three novel feature mappings to efficiently approximate the degree-two polynomials; see Sect. 3.

Our methods are evaluated on several real-world large sparse datasets. When classifying medium-sized sparse data (with $<10^5$ instances), our method can achieve similar accuracy to that of the KARMA kernel classifier. For large scale classification problems where it is too expensive to compute the KARMA kernel, our methods scale efficiently to datasets of 10^7 data points with over 105 sparse features. Compared to the original KARMA algorithm, our method is also much more efficient in terms of memory usage. Training such large scale datasets can be done within several hours on a normal desktop PC Most importantly, as our methods can learn from both the linear and non-linear (low-rank) structures in the data, it leads to significant accuracy improvement over the linear classifiers;

see Sect. 4. For the above reasons, our method is well-suited for classifying large sparse datasets in real-world applications.

The rest of the paper is organized as follows. In Sect. 2, we describe the problem setting and review previous works of classifying sparse data. In Sect. 3, we provide empirical studies on the KARMA classifier with real-world large sparse datasets. We further describe our novel feature mappings in details. Section 4 describes our experiments. Section 5 concludes this paper.

2   Classify Large Sparse Data

In this section, we introduce the problem setting of classifying large sparse data. We review several techniques of classifying datasets with missing values.

2.1   Problem Formulation

Suppose $p(\mathbf{x}, y)$ is the underlying distribution for a fully observed dataset $\mathcal{S}_{dense} = \{\mathbf{x}^{(i)}, y^{(i)}\}_{i=1...N}$, where $\mathbf{x} = [x_1, x_2, \ldots, x_d] \in \mathbb{R}^d$ is the input vector and $y \in \mathcal{Y}$ is a one-dimensional label. We study the case where the majority of the feature values in $\mathbf{x}$ are missing. In other words, instead of learning from the dataset $\mathcal{S}_{dense}$, the learner is only given an extremely sparsified dataset $\mathcal{S}_{sparse} = \{\mathbf{x_o}^{(i)}, y^{(i)}\}_{i=1...N}$ where $\mathbf{o} = [o_1, o_2, \ldots, o_d] \in [0, 1]^d$ a is a d-dimensional observability vector indicating whether each feature is missing or not.

Using $*$ to denote a missing value, we have that $\mathbf{x_o} \in \{\mathbb{R} \cup \{*\}\}^d$, in particular,

$$(\mathbf{x_o}^{(i)})_j = \begin{cases} x_j^{(i)} & \text{if } o_j^{(i)} = 1 \\ * & \text{if } o_j^{(i)} = 0 \end{cases} \tag{1}$$

Given a Lipschitz loss function $l(\cdot)$, the goal of classifying large sparse data is to learn from $\mathcal{S}_{sparse}$ and induces a solution f^* that has small risk on future (sparse) data:

$$f^* = \min_{f \in \mathcal{H}} \mathbb{E}_{(\mathbf{x_o}, y) \sim p(\mathbf{o}, \mathbf{x}, y)} \left[l\big(f(\mathbf{x_o}), y\big) \right] \tag{2}$$

We denote the distribution $p(\mathbf{o}|\mathbf{x}, y)$ as the *data missing mechanism*. According to the missing data theory [13], the dataset is MCAR (Missing Completely At Random) when the observability does not depend on the feature values, i.e., $p(\mathbf{o}|\mathbf{x}, y) = p(\mathbf{o})$; MAR (Missing At Random) if observability only depends on the observed feature values $p(\mathbf{o}|\mathbf{x}, y) = p(\mathbf{o}|\mathbf{x_o}, y)$, and MNAR (Missing Not At Random) in all other cases. The study in this paper does not restrict the data missing mechanism. It is applicable to any of MAR, MNAR or MCAR.

2.2   Previous Works

To classify data with missing values, one can simply skip the missing values if using a generative classifier such as naive Bayes. For (discriminative) linear classifiers such as support vector machines, one of the common strategy is to use 0-imputation where all $*$s are replaced with 0s. For 0-imputation, we have

$$(\mathbf{x_o}^{(i)})^{\text{0-imp}} = \mathbf{x}^{(i)} \circ \mathbf{o}^{(i)} \tag{3}$$

$\circ$ denotes element-wise product. Apart from imputation, [5] propose to maximize the classifier margin computed according to geometries of the non-missing dimensions of a particular instance, i.e.:

$$\max_{\mathbf{w}} \left(\min_i \frac{y^{(i)} \mathbf{w} \mathbf{x}^{(i)}}{||\mathbf{w} \circ \mathbf{o}^{(i)}||} \right) \tag{4}$$

However, this method has not been tested on the classification tasks of large sparse user-item datasets where the sparsity could be extremely high. In the field of budgeted learning, there are also many works on learning from data with a limited number of observed features [2,3,8,12]. However, they all assume that the learner can actively choose which features to observe, which is different from our setting.

The success of low-rank matrix factorization algorithms [17] on many collaborative filtering tasks suggest that many large sparse datasets have a low rank structure. To leverage this low-rank property, [7] formulate missing data classification as a matrix completion task where the class label is treated as an additional column to the sparse input matrix. This formulation can handle multi-label classification, semi-supervised classification and matrix completion at the same time. However, instead of optimizing the classification loss, this model needs to optimize the matrix completion loss as an indirect step.

To address this challenge, [9] have proposed a learning framework that only assumes the input $\mathbf{X}$ is of low-rank. By studying the polynomial approximation of the linear models in the low-rank data space, authors provide a learning framework for classifying low-rank data that directly optimizes classification loss. As described in Theorem 1 of [9], when distribution $\mathcal{D}$ is of low rank, let $\Gamma = \sum_{j=1}^{\gamma} d^j$ be the number of unique sequences s of feature index $\{1, 2, \ldots, d\}$ with length $1 \leq |s| \leq \gamma$. Using γ-degree polynomial approximation to the inner product $(\mathbf{w} \cdot \mathbf{x})$ in the low-rank space, authors have proved that a certain feature mapping $\phi_\gamma : \{\mathbb{R} \cup \{*\}\}^d \to \mathbb{R}^\Gamma$ can be constructed, such that there exists a classifier $\mathbf{v}^*$ in the ambient space $\mathbb{R}^\Gamma$ which satisfies

$$\mathbb{E}[l(\mathbf{v}^* \cdot \phi_\gamma(\mathbf{x_o}), y)] \leq \min_{\mathbf{w}} \mathbb{E}[l(\mathbf{w} \cdot \mathbf{x}, y)] + \epsilon \tag{5}$$

In other words, the classifier $\mathbf{v}^*$ can compete with the best linear classifier that accesses the full data during training.

Instead of computing ϕ_γ directly which is extremely high-dimensional, its inner product can be computed using the following kernel trick (Theorem 2 of [9]):

$$\langle \phi_\gamma(\mathbf{x_o}^{(i_1)}), \phi_\gamma(\mathbf{x_o}^{(i_2)}) \rangle = k_\gamma(\mathbf{x_o}^{(i_1)}, \mathbf{x_o}^{(i_2)})$$

$$:= \frac{|\mathbf{o}^{(i_1)} \cap \mathbf{o}^{(i_2)}|^\gamma - 1}{|\mathbf{o}^{(i_1)} \cap \mathbf{o}^{(i_2)}| - 1} \langle \mathbf{x_o}^{(i_1)}, \mathbf{x_o}^{(i_2)} \rangle \tag{6}$$

where $|\mathbf{o}^{(i_1)} \cap \mathbf{o}^{(i_2)}|$ denotes the size of common non-missing features of $\mathbf{x_o}^{(i_1)}$ and $\mathbf{x_o}^{(i_2)}$. Based on this kernel trick, [9] further provide a kernelized stochastic gradient descent learning algorithm, KARMA, to find the optimal solution in the space of ϕ_γ.

Restricted by the time and space complexity of kernel computation, KARMA is not scalable on large sparse datasets. Meanwhile, notice that Eq. (6) is essentially a dot product kernel in the ultra-high dimensional ($\Gamma = \sum_{j=1}^{\gamma} d^j$) space. It is too expensive even to compute its random feature approximation [16]. For example, to get N random features for a dot-product kernel, we need to generate $d \times N$ random numbers [11].

Next, we describe our method which benefits from the theoretic results of [9] while skipping the kernel computation step. Our approach is motivated by the following thought:

Since the dimensionality of ϕ_γ is too high to compute directly, is it possible to approximate ϕ_γ using relatively lower dimensional feature mappings which we can compute and store explicitly?

3   Approximate Feature Mappings

To approximate ϕ_γ, we first review its definition (Definition 4 in [9]). Given γ, each dimension of ϕ_γ encodes a unique sequence s of feature index $\{1, 2, \ldots, d\}$, $1 \leq |s| \leq \gamma$:

$$(\phi_\gamma(\mathbf{x_o}))_s = \begin{cases} \mathbf{x}_{s_{end}} & \text{if } s \in \mathbf{o} \\ 0 & \text{else} \end{cases} \tag{7}$$

where s_{end} denotes the last element of s. We could see that when $\gamma = 1$, $\phi_\gamma(\mathbf{x_o}) = (\mathbf{x_o})^{0\text{-imp}}$; while ϕ_2 is the concatenation of $\phi_1(\mathbf{x_o})$ and the co-occurrence information of each feature pair:

$$\phi_2(\mathbf{x_o}) = [\phi_1(\mathbf{x_o}), A(\mathbf{x_o})] \tag{8}$$

where the operator $A : \{\mathbb{R}\cup\{*\}\}^d \to \mathbb{R}^{d^2}$ denotes the flattening of outer-product:

$$A(\mathbf{x_o}) := ((\mathbf{x_o})^{0\text{-imp}} \otimes \mathbf{o})_{\text{flatten}} \tag{9}$$

which encodes the second order (co-occurrence) information among the non-missing features. For example, for data point $\mathbf{x_o} = [2 * 3]$, we have $\phi_2(\mathbf{x_o}) = [203202000303]$. where $\phi_2(\mathbf{x_o})_{[1:3]} = (\mathbf{x_o})^{0\text{-imp}}$ and $\phi_2(\mathbf{x_o})_{[4:12]}$ equals to flattening of $[203] \otimes [101]$. It is obvious that larger γ provides higher learning capacity but also increases the risk of over-fitting.

To see how the polynomial degree γ affects classification performance on sparse data, we use several real-world benchmark datasets for empirical evaluation. The task is to classify user gender from movie rating vectors (*ml100k, ml1m*[1], *ymovie*[2]) or age according to grocery shopping records (*tafeng*[3]). We use hinge loss with $l2$-regularization in our experiments. For fast optimization, we use the kernelized

---

[1] http://grouplens.org/datasets/movielens/.
[2] http://webscope.sandbox.yahoo.com.
[3] http://recsyswiki.com/wiki/Grocery_shopping_datasets.

Table 1. Dataset information

Datasets	n	d	Sparsity	Label
ml-100k	943	1,682	0.937	Gender
ml-1m	6,040	3,952	0.958	Gender
ymovie	7,620	11,914	0.998	Gender
tafeng	32,266	23,812	0.999033	Age
book	61,308	282,700	0.99996	Age
epinions	113,629	318,114	0.999969	Trustworthy
flickr	11,195,143	497,470	0.99999	Commented

Table 2. Best test performance with different γ values. Each dataset is split as 4:1 for training and testing. The last column indicates the percentage of hyper-parameters visited when using the path tracking method for hyperparameter selection.

Data	$\gamma = 1$	$\gamma = 2$	$\gamma = 3$	$\gamma = 4$	$\gamma = 5$	Solved
ml100k	0.8349	**0.8459**	0.8202	0.8183	0.8018	19/150
ml1m	0.8416	**0.8501**	0.8457	0.8407	0.8348	18/150
ymovie	0.7883	**0.8383**	0.8380	0.8353	0.8328	44/150
tafeng	0.7423	**0.7680**	0.7567	0.7391	0.7306	150/150

version of Stochastic Dual Coordinate Ascent [18]. We compute the generalization performance under a series of parameter settings, i.e., $\gamma = \{1.0, 2.0, 3.0, 4.0, 5.0\}$ and regularization parameter $C = \{2^{-15}, 2^{-14}, \ldots, 2^{14}, 2^{15}\}$. This is a parameter grid of 150 vertices. To speed up the exhaustive grid search process, we use the approximate parameter path tracking approach [1]. The basic idea is that when a dual solution α found by SDCA is optimal (with a duality-gap less than ϵ) at regularization parameter C_1, then $\frac{C_2}{C_1}\alpha$ will also be an optimal solution for the problem at C_2 if C_2 is in the vicinity of C_1. With this approximate tracking procedure, we only need to solve the SDCA problems for a small number of grid vertices; see the last column of Table 2.[4]

An important observation from these real-world experiments is that $\gamma = 2.0$ gives significant performance boost compared to 0-imputation ($\gamma = 1.0$). Meanwhile, in many of our experiments, $\gamma > 2.0$ leads to over-fitting rather than better generalization performance. While it is too early to conclude that $\gamma = 2.0$ is always the best setting, it is likely that ϕ_2 could help improve classification accuracy in many tasks. Besides, as introduced in the previous section, higher γ corresponds to a more complex model structure and thus is harder to compute or approximate efficiently. Because of the above reasons, we focus on degree-two polynomial approximation, which is promising to provide a good trade-off between model expressiveness and complexity. However, even ϕ_2 is still $d + d^2$ dimensional which is intractable for large datasets where the feature dimension $d > 10^5$.

---

[4] The *tafeng* dataset is an exception, for which the approximate path does not lead to any speedup.

Next we discuss several practical strategies to construct a sufficiently compact feature mapping to approximate ϕ_2. Notice that the first d-dimensions in ϕ_2 equals to the 0-imputation of the original feature vector, which needs no computation and is tractable for storage. We only need to approximate the d^2 dimensions that encode the second-order terms in the polynomial (feature co-occurrence information). We propose the following strategies.

Density-Based Strategy. For many real-world large sparse data, an important observation is that density often follows a long-tailed distribution, so that a small fraction of features contribute a majority of non-missing values. Naturally, a large number of co-occurrence information are contributed only by the small number of dense features. Let $F \subseteq \{j_1, j_2, \ldots, j_k\}$ be the top-k features in terms of density. We approximate the second order terms $A(\cdot)$ in $\phi_2(\cdot)$ by only representing the co-occurrence among these k dense features, i.e., we approximate ϕ_2 (see Eq.(8)) with

$$\tilde{\phi}_2(\mathbf{x_o}) = [(\mathbf{x_o})^{0\text{-imp}}, A((\mathbf{x_o})_F)]$$
$$= [(\mathbf{x_o})^{0\text{-imp}}_{-F}, \phi_2((\mathbf{x_o})_F)] \tag{10}$$

where $-F$ denotes features except for F, and $\phi_2((\mathbf{x_o})_F) = [(\mathbf{x_o})^{0\text{-imp}}_F, A((\mathbf{x_o})_F)]$ is the degree-two polynomial approximation to the low rank space F. The intuition is that we care more about the low-rankness in the denser features because learning from the extremely sparse features may not be worthwhile in terms of information gain v.s. computational cost. The procedure is also described in Algorithm 1.[5]

Algorithm 1. Feature Mapping with Density-based Strategy

Require: $\mathbf{x_o}$, the original input vector (sparse);
Require: k, the dimensionality of the selected subspace;
　Select top-k dense features to form the subspace F;
　Compute $A((\mathbf{x_o})_F)$ and $\tilde{\phi}_2(\mathbf{x_o})$ using (9) and (10);
　Use $\tilde{\phi}_2(\mathbf{x_o})$ to train / test with a linear classifier;

According to Theorem 1 and 2 in [9], the classifier trained with $\tilde{\phi}_2(\mathbf{x_o})$ can still compete with the semi-oracle classifier that can observe all feature values in the subspace F without any missing. (the subspace of the less dense features $-F$ are handled with 0-imputation.) With this strategy, the overall dimension of $\tilde{\phi}_2$ will be $d + k^2$ and can be computed efficiently in $O(k^2_{nnz})$ time using simple outer product operations, where k_{nnz} denotes the average number of non-zeroes in the selected k features. The memory consumption will be $O(d_{nnz} + k^2_{nnz})$. When $k \ll d$, it is possible to directly compute and store $\tilde{\phi}_2$.

---

[5] The algorithm for the other two feature-mapping strategies are very similar. We omit for brevity.

Feature-Selection Strategy. Alternatively, we could also select the subspace F using feature selection algorithms [19]. In our current implementation, we simply rank the feature importance according to $|w_j|$, where $\mathbf{w}$ is the weight vector of a pre-trained linear SVM. More advanced feature selection algorithm is possible to lead to better performance, which can be studied in future work.

Clustering-Based Strategy. Finally, instead of selecting a small subspace for low-rank learning, we could also aggregate the sparse and high dimensional data space to form the more compact subspace [6]. In this clustering-based strategy, we use K-means clustering [10] to aggregate the d features into k feature clusters, which forms the space F of cluster-level features. We set the value of each cluster-level feature as the mean of its member features; see Fig. 1. This method is also intuitive because latent item clusters do exist in many large sparse data (e.g., different episodes of a TV opera), several previous methods [15,20] have successfully exploited this observation. With this strategy, F is no longer a subspace of the original feature space. However, same as the previous two strategies, using $\tilde{\phi}_2$ (Eq. (10)) can still take advantage of the low-rank structure of space F according to the framework of [9].

Combining Feature Mapping Strategies. The aforementioned strategies use feature selection or clustering to form a low-dimensional space F and approximate the second-order information $A(\mathbf{x_o})$ with $A((\mathbf{x_o})_F)$. It is possible that the space formed by different strategies can capture complementary information. For this reason, we also propose to combine different feature mapping strategies, which could be implemented simply by concatenating their corresponding subspaces. In our experiments, we will show that combining the density-based strategy with the clustering-based strategy helps improve classification performance. In the next section, we compare the predictive performance of these different strategies.

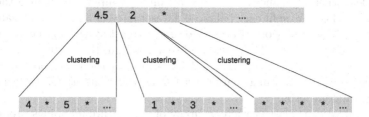

Fig. 1. A graphical illustration of the clustering-based feature mapping strategy. $*$ denotes missing. We set the value of each cluster-level feature as the mean of its member features.

Table 3. Testing accuracy on different large sparse datasets. The best accuracy is in **bold** while the second best is marked with *. <u>Underlined</u> results indicate significantly better than linear classification under McNemar's test ($p = 0.05$). '–' means unable to compute the KARMA kernel with given resource and time.

Datasets	0-imp	Geom	KARMA	DenseFM	WeightFM	ClusterFM	MixFM
ml-100k	0.7806	0.7667	<u>0.7885</u>*	0.7739	0.7752	**0.7909**	0.7703
ml-1m	0.8150	0.8156	**0.8219**	0.8216*	0.8146	0.8160	0.8161
ymovie	0.7736	0.7484	**0.7976**	<u>0.7913</u>	<u>0.7826</u>	0.7732	<u>0.7956</u>*
tafeng	0.7158	0.7038	<u>0.7333</u>	<u>0.7390</u>*	**0.7391**	0.7192	<u>0.7354</u>
book	0.7276	0.6881	**0.7355**	<u>0.7308</u>	<u>0.7297</u>	<u>0.7309</u>	<u>0.7337</u>*
epinions	0.7211	0.6960	–	<u>0.7308</u>	<u>0.7301</u>	<u>0.7548</u>*	**0.7664**
flickr-500k	0.6645	0.6278	–	<u>0.6657</u>	<u>0.6659</u>	<u>0.6873</u>*	**0.6937**
flickr-5m	0.7090	0.6455	–	<u>0.7231</u>*	<u>0.7209</u>*	<u>0.7191</u>	**0.7447**
flickr-all	0.7164	0.6477	–	<u>0.7480</u>*	<u>0.7437</u>	<u>0.7263</u>	**0.7659**

4 Experiments

We use several large and sparse real-world datasets, as shown in Table 1. For simplicity, all datasets address binary classification tasks. Apart from *ymovie*, *ml-1m*, *ml-100k* and *tafeng* datasets introduced in a previous section, we use *book* [21] dataset to predict user age from highly-sparse book rating records. For *epinions* [14] dataset, we classify each user as trustworthy or not based on the rating records. For the *flickr* [4] dataset, we classify whether a photo is heavily commented according to the likes given by a large population of users. Apart from the whole *flickr* data, we also populate the *flickr-5m* and *flickr-500k* data using random subsampling.

To deal with imbalanced data, we use under-sampling to reduce the over-represented class. We split each balanced dataset into 6:1:3 as training, validation and test set. The validation set is used to tune the best hyper-parameters. For the regularization parameter C, we use grid search within $[10^{-5}, 10^{-4}, \ldots, 10^4, 10^5]$ and we tune the best γ within $[1, 2, 3, 4, 5]$. We repeat the whole process (under-sampling, splitting, training, parameter-tuning and testing) for 10 times with different random seeds.

We evaluate the classification accuracy of the feature mappings proposed in Sect. 3, which include *DenseFM*, *WeightFM*, *ClusterFM* and a mixed strategy (*MixFM*) that combines *DenseFM* and *ClusterFM*[6]. For the baseline methods, we consider linear classification with 0-imputation, geometric margin adjustment (geom) [5] and the KARMA kernel classifier [9].

All our experiments are carried on a desktop PC with 24 GB of memory. Since the feature selection strategies are simple and efficient, we try to make

---

[6] Notice that we have also tried combining *ClusterFM* and *WeightFM*, the accuracy and time/space complexity is similar.

k as large as possible so long as it fits into the memory. For *DenseFM* and *WeightFM* strategies we select the dimension of F to be $k = 40000$. For the *ClusterFM* strategy the number of clusters is set as 1000 for efficient clustering.

The averaged test accuracy[7] is shown in Table 3. For the KARMA experiments, we only record the best performance among different settings of γ. Notice that all classifiers are trained by the SDCA optimizer [18], and duality gap $\epsilon < 10^{-4}$ is used as the stopping condition. For smaller datasets, we evaluate all classification methods mentioned above. For datasets with more than 10^5 instances, we cannot compute and store the KARMA kernels in limited time and resources.

With the above settings, the memory and time consumption on the larger datasets ($>10^5$) is given in Table 4. For KARMA, we need to store the kernel matrix which is $O(n^2)$. For other methods, we only need to store the non-zero entries in the features or feature mapping vectors.

From the above results, we have the following observations:

Table 4. Training time (feature mapping computation included) in seconds. '–' means unable to compute KARMA kernel with given resource and time. The statistics in brackets are theoretic memory consumption in millions of nonzero entries.

Datasets	0-imp	Geom	KARMA	DenseFM	WeightFM	ClusterFM	MixFM
book	0.1 (0.3)	0.1 (0.3)	– (605)	30 (54)	30 (11)	280 (1.7)	310 (55)
epinions	0.3 (0.95)	0.3 (1.0)	– (2179)	90 (71.5)	70 (42)	1000 (11)	1000 (82)
flickr-500k	2 (1.8)	1 (1.8)	– (1150)	190 (40)	200 (40)	3500 (5)	3600 (45)
flickr-5m	25 (18)	12 (18)	– (1.2e7)	1900 (358)	2000 (369)	5300 (46)	6400 (405)
flickr-all	46 (32)	33 (32)	– (3.6e7)	3100 (635)	3200 (654)	7000 (82)	8200 (716)

Observation 1. On the small to medium-sized data (*ml100k, ml1m, ymovie* and *tafeng*) where it is possible to compute a KARMA kernel, the proposed feature mapping strategies can achieve similar performance to that of KARMA. For large scale classification tasks where we cannot compute the KARMA kernel matrix (*book, epinions, flickr*), all our feature mapping strategies significantly outperform 0-imputation and the Geom algorithm, especially for the *MixFM* strategy.

Observation 2. Comparing different feature mapping methods, we notice that *DenseFM* and *WeightFM* have very similar behavior in terms of classification accuracy, runtime and space complexity. This is no surprise, as both of them select subsets of features to form the low dimensional space. Meanwhile, *ClusterFM* does behave differently. Finally, *MixFM* leads to the best performance especially on the larger datasets. This indicates that *DenseFM* and *ClusterFM* do provide complementary information. For this reason, we recommend *MixFM* to be the first-choice in real-world applications.

---

[7] The test accuracy for KARMA is different from the results in Table 2. The reason is different data splitting strategies.

Observation 3. As shown in Table 4, the proposed feature mapping methods need far less memory than the KARMA kernels, which makes them tractable on a normal desktop PC even for large dataset *flickr-all* with $> 10^7$ instances.

Observation 4. All competing methods can use a stochastic linear optimizer such as SDCA and SGD who scales linearly with the number of non-zeroes. Though the proposed methods do need some extra time to pre-compute the feature mappings, they could efficiently train the largest data *flickr-all* within several hours.

Observation 5. Comparing different feature mapping strategies, the *ClusterFM* method uses a much smaller k value than the *DenseFM* and *WeightFM* while achieving comparable results. This indicates that the subspace constructed from clustering is more informative than simply selecting subsets of features. However, *ClusterFM* requires a clustering step which involves a considerable amount of computation.

5   Conclusion

In this paper, we have developed an efficient and effective method for classifying large sparse datasets. Our method efficiently approximates the KARMA kernel [9] which can learn from the low-rank structure of a large sparse dataset but does not scale well to very large datasets. To achieve this, we first analyze the empirical performance of KARMA, and find that the degree-two polynomials often lead to superior performance. We then propose several novel scalable feature mappings to efficiently approximate the degree-two polynomials. In experiments, our method is comparable with KARMA on medium-sized data and scales well to larger datasets that KARMA does not. Our method also significantly outperforms linear classifiers on datasets of various sizes. Overall, our method is well-suited for classifying large sparse datasets in real world applications.

Acknowledgements. This work is supported by the National Key Research and Development Program of China (No. 2020AAA0108800), the National Natural Science Foundation of China (61702532).

References

1. Blechschmidt, K., Giesen, J., Laue, S.: Tracking approximate solutions of parameterized optimization problems over multi-dimensional (hyper-) parameter domains. In: Proceedings of The 32nd International Conference on Machine Learning, pp. 438–447 (2015)
2. Bullins, B., Hazan, E., Koren, T.: The limits of learning with missing data. In: Advances in Neural Information Processing Systems, pp. 3495–3503 (2016)
3. Cesa-Bianchi, N., Shalev-Shwartz, S., Shamir, O.: Efficient learning with partially observed attributes. J. Mach. Learn. Res. (JMLR) **12**, 2857–2878 (2011)
4. Cha, M., Mislove, A., Gummadi, K.P.: A measurement-driven analysis of information propagation in the flickr social network. In: Proceedings of the 18th International Conference on World Wide Web, pp. 721–730. ACM (2009)

5. Chechik, G., Heitz, G., Elidan, G., Abbeel, P., Koller, D.: Max-margin classification of data with absent features. J. Mach. Learn. Res. **9**, 1–21 (2008)
6. Gao, H., Jian, S., Peng, Y., Liu, X.: A subspace ensemble framework for classification with high dimensional missing data. Multidimension. Syst. Signal Process. **28**(4), 1309–1324 (2016). https://doi.org/10.1007/s11045-016-0393-4
7. Goldberg, A., Recht, B., Xu, J., Nowak, R., Zhu, X.: Transduction with matrix completion: three birds with one stone. In: Advances in Neural Information Processing Systems, pp. 757–765 (2010)
8. Hazan, E., Koren, T.: Linear regression with limited observation. In: Proceedings of the 29th International Conference on Machine Learning (ICML), pp. 807–814 (2012)
9. Hazan, E., Livni, R., Mansour, Y.: Classification with low rank and missing data. In: Proceedings of the 32nd International Conference on Machine Learning (ICML 2015), pp. 257–266 (2015)
10. Kanungo, T., Mount, D.M., Netanyahu, N.S., Piatko, C.D., Silverman, R., Wu, A.Y.: An efficient k-means clustering algorithm: analysis and implementation. IEEE Trans. Pattern Anal. Mach. Intell. **24**(7), 881–892 (2002)
11. Kar, P., Karnick, H.: Random feature maps for dot product kernels. In: Proceedings of The 15th International Conference on Artificial Intelligence and Statistics (AISTATS) (2012)
12. Kukliansky, D., Shamir, O.: Attribute efficient linear regression with distribution-dependent sampling. In: Proceedings of the 32nd International Conference on Machine Learning (ICML), pp. 153–161 (2015)
13. Little, R.J., Rubin, D.B.: Statistical Analysis with Missing Data. Wiley, New York (2014)
14. Meyffret, S., Guillot, E., Médini, L., Laforest, F.: RED: a rich epinions dataset for recommender systems. Technical report. RR-LIRIS-2012-014, LIRIS UMR 5205 CNRS/INSA de Lyon/Université Claude Bernard Lyon 1/Université Lumière Lyon 2/École Centrale de Lyon, October 2012. http://liris.cnrs.fr/publis/?id=5787
15. Mirbakhsh, N., Ling, C.X.: Clustering-based factorized collaborative filtering. In: Proceedings of the 7th ACM conference on Recommender systems. pp. 315–318. ACM (2013)
16. Rahimi, A., Recht, B.: Random features for large-scale kernel machines. In: Advances in Neural Information Processing Systems, vol. 20, pp. 1177–1184 (2007)
17. Salakhutdinov, R., Mnih, A.: Bayesian probabilistic matrix factorization using Markov chain Monte Carlo. In: Proceedings of the 25th International Conference on Machine Learning, pp. 880–887. ACM (2008)
18. Shalev-Shwartz, S., Zhang, T.: Stochastic dual coordinate ascent methods for regularized loss. J. Mach. Learn. Res. **14**(1), 567–599 (2013)
19. Tang, C., et al.: Feature selective projection with low-rank embedding and dual Laplacian regularization. IEEE Trans. Knowl. Data Eng. **32**(9), 1747–1760 (2020)
20. Xu, B., Bu, J., Chen, C., Cai, D.: An exploration of improving collaborative recommender systems via user-item subgroups. In: Proceedings of the 21st international conference on World Wide Web. pp. 21–30. ACM (2012)
21. Ziegler, C.N., McNee, S.M., Konstan, J.A., Lausen, G.: Improving recommendation lists through topic diversification. In: Proceedings of the 14th International Conference on World Wide Web (WWW), pp. 22–32. ACM (2005)

Constrained Energy Minimization for Hyperspectral Multi-target Detection Based on Ensemble Learning

Qinggang Wu[✉] and Zhongchi Liu

Zhengzhou University of Light Industry, Zhengzhou 450002, China

Abstract. The traditional hyperspectral target detection usually recognizes a single type of object at one time. However, there are usually various categories of targets in real scenarios, and it is necessary to simultaneously detect multiple types of targets. Although some detection methods have been proposed, most of them suffer from the limited non-linear spectral expression ability to distinguish different types of hyperspectral targets. To overcome this problem, we propose an ensemble learning-based multi-objective constrained energy minimization (E-IMTCEM) for hyperspectral multi-target detection in this paper. Specifically, E-IMTCEM combines ensemble learning to improve both the non-linear spectral expression ability and detection ability in the task of hyperspectral multi-target detection. The experimental results on simulated hyperspectral images show the effectiveness of the proposed method.

Keywords: Hyperspectral target detection · Constrained energy minimization (CEM) · Multi-target detection · Ensemble learning

1 Introduction

Hyperspectral images have been widely used in many areas such as military and civil fields for the abundant spectral information. Generally, a hyperspectral image can be regarded as a three-dimensional array [1–3], where the first two dimensions record the spatial information and the third dimension means the spectral band. As is known, the spatial resolution of a hyperspectral image often goes smaller, while the spectral resolution becomes larger and the spectrum characteristics are able to distinguish different targets which are made up of various materials. Hence, the pixel values will come into an approximately continuous spectral curve covering a large range of spectral bands. However, the spectral curve is non-linear in most real cases, and results in more challenges for many tasks including hyperspectral multi-target detection.

The target detection in hyperspectral images is still a hot topic in the fields of remote sensing image processing and interpretation. In recent years, abundant algorithms have been developed and validated to perform well on simulated hyperspectral images, including SAM (Spectral Angle Mapping) [5, 6], SID (Spectral Information divergence) [7], CEM (Constrained Energy Minimization) [8], MF (Matched Filter) algorithm [11], and

© Springer Nature Switzerland AG 2022
B. Li et al. (Eds.): ADMA 2021, LNAI 13088, pp. 406–416, 2022.
https://doi.org/10.1007/978-3-030-95408-6_31

ACE (Adaptive Contrast Enhancement) [12]. Unfortunately, the hyperspectral images captured in real environments are often affected by atmospheric turbulence, noise, spectral mixing, and other factors, which completely differs from the spectral priors as in the simulated scenarios and often shows strong nonlinear distribution characteristics. As a result, the aforementioned methods tend to perform worse in real cases, which are interfered by adverse factors. To solve this problem, the algorithms of CEM and ACE are improved by [9, 10] and [12], respectively. Although some improvements have been achieved in [9, 10], it is still in need of further discussing the robust detection of the diverse targets in hyperspectral images with non-linear distribution characteristics. For example, although the methods of CEM, ACE and MF could generalize well in certain hyperspectral applications, the abilities are still weak in expressing the spectral data under nonlinear distributions. The reason mainly lies in the fixed kernels which are carefully designed in these approaches.

To avoid the disadvantage of the traditional algorithms that are limited to detect a single type of target, several methods are proposed to perform multi-target detection in hyperspectral images. For instance, Chang et. al propose three different types of energy minimization methods to simultaneously detect multiple targets in an input hyperspectral image: multiple-target constrained energy minimization (MTCEM, Multiple-Target CEM), summation constrained energy minimization (SCEM), and Winner-Take-All constrained energy minimization (WTACEM) [12, 13]. Meanwhile, as is reported in [9], the QCEM (Quadratic CEM) algorithm uses a quadratic term in the optimization objective to model the nonlinear property of hyperspectral data for improving the noise robustness. Inspired by these literatures, we propose a new method by embedding QCEM into MTCEM based on ensemble learning to simultaneously detect multiple targets as well as to enhance the robustness of detection results to undesired noises.

As for the ensemble learning, the main idea is to integrate multiple weak supervised models into a more comprehensive strong supervised model for improving the expression ability and generalization ability of the whole algorithm. Generally, there are two different lines in ensemble learning. One is Boosting, which keeps the generalization performance of weakly supervised models unchanged and improves their expression ability. A typical algorithm is Adaboost [21]. The other is Model Combination, which improves the generalization performance while ensuring the strong expression ability of the weakly supervised models. An example algorithm is Bagging [22]. In this paper, we follow the second research line and propose a new method based on QCEM and MTCEM to improve both the multi-target detection performance and the robustness to nonlinear noises. The contributions of the paper can be summarized as follows:

(1) A multi-target detection method of E-IMTCEM is proposed by combing the multiple IMTCEMs and ensemble learning to recognize the interested objects in a hyperspectral image.
(2) We embed the parameter of lambda into the basic constrained energy minimization models to increase the feature representation ability by constructing a multi-layer cascade detector.

2 Constrained Energy Minimization (CEM)

The CEM algorithm is designed to suppress the background and detect targets by solving an optimization problem [15]. The key of this algorithm is an impulse response filter, which is capable of adjusting the target spectrum properly, i.e., suppressing the background information and reserving the target pixels with larger values. Therefore, the target spectrum and the background spectrum can be separated effectively.

A hyperspectral image is usually denoted by $X = \{x_1, x_2, \cdots, x_N\}$, where x_i is the i-th pixel, N means the number of all pixels, $x_i = \{x_{i1}, x_{i2}, \cdots, x_{iL}\}^T$, and L is the number of spectral bands. The signature of the target spectrum is represented by $d = (d_1, d_2, \cdots, d_L)^T$. With these preparations, the CEM problem is to design an impulse response filter $w = (w_1, w_2, \cdots, w_L)^T$, through which the target spectral information is maintained to produce a large output and the background spectrum is suppressed to generate a small output. Therefore, the filter should satisfy the following constraint:

$$d^T w = \sum_{i=1}^{L} d_i w_i = 1. \tag{1}$$

For a hyperspectral image, the average energy of a filter output can be represented by the sum of squared filter responses at all pixels. As a consequence, the energy objective function can be formulated as

$$E\{y^2\} = E\left\{\left(w^T x\right)^2\right\} = w^T R w. \tag{2}$$

$$R = \frac{1}{N}\left(\sum_{i=1}^{N} x_i x_i^T\right) \tag{3}$$

where y is a test result, w denotes the unknown filter, and R means the auto-correlation matrix of size $L \times L$ computed on the sample set. Finally, the optimization of the filter coefficient w is to solve the following minimization problem:

$$\begin{cases} \min_w w^T R w \\ d^T w = 1 \end{cases}. \tag{4}$$

To find w by solving (4), the Lagrange multiplier method is considered and the solution reads as below.

$$w^{CEM} = \frac{R^{-1} d}{d^T R^{-1} d}. \tag{5}$$

where w^{CEM} represents the optimal filter coefficient. As this coefficient could effectively inhibit the background output while keeping the target output unchanged, the target can be detected from the background. For an input vector x_i, the output response y_i of CEM is

$$y_i = w_{CEM}^T x_i = \left(\frac{R^{-1} d}{d^T R^{-1} d}\right)^T x_i = \frac{d^T R^{-1} x_i}{d^T R^{-1} d}. \tag{6}$$

3   Improved Multi-target Constrained Energy Minimization Algorithm (IMTCEM)

Suppose that $D = \{d_1, d_2, \cdots, d_q\}$ is a matrix that contains the spectral information of q targets. Hence, the scalar constraint for a single d in (1) could be extended to a vector constraint for multiple ds in D:

$$D^T w = 1. \tag{7}$$

where $1 = [1, 1, \cdots, 1]^T$ is a column vector. By replacing (1) using (7), the formula (4) is modified accordingly as

$$\begin{cases} \min_w w^T R w, \\ D^T w = 1. \end{cases} \tag{8}$$

The solution of (8) can be obtained as in (5) and the final form is:

$$w^{MTCEM} = \frac{R^{-1} D}{D^T R^{-1} D}. \tag{9}$$

Given an input r, the output of MTCEM takes the form of

$$MTCEM(r) = w^T r = (\frac{R^{-1} D}{D^T R^{-1} D} \times 1)^T r. \tag{10}$$

As the real hyperspectral image often contains noises, the auto-correlation matrix R is irreversible. To make the MTCEM filter more stable and stronger in generalization, the unit matrix I is introduced with the same size of R, and a scalar parameter λ is also introduced to adjust the predictor (10) appropriately. Hence, an improved version of (10) is formulated as follows [16]:

$$IMTCEM(r) = w^T r = (\frac{(R + \lambda I)^{-1} D}{D^T (R + \lambda I)^{-1} D} \times 1)^T r. \tag{11}$$

The reasons for the introduction of parameter λ are as follows. First, the correlation matrix R can be a singular matrix in real cases. For example, when the band number D is less than the pixel number N, R will be a singular matrix and thus is irreversible. The regularization of R is an effective tool to improve the numerical stability and ensure the reversibility of R [9, 10]. Second, the MTCEM algorithm is regarded as a constrained least square regression problem as reviewed previously, and the regularization of MTCEM means to add a L_2 norm penalty $\lambda \|\omega\|_2^2$ to the objective function (7). So, the above operation plays a role similar to the "Tickhornoff regularization" in statistical analysis, which is a classical method for solving the under-conditioned regression problem. For these reasons, we select the regularized MTCEM as the basic detector in this paper.

4 Hyperspectral Target Detection via Ensemble Learning Based Multi-objective Constrained Energy Minimization

On the basis of ensemble learning [14], we construct a cascade detector by integrating the methods of cascade detection [23], stochastic averaging [24] and nonlinear transformation [25, 26] to improve the nonlinear expression ability and generalization ability of the proposed algorithm. As shown in Fig. 1, the input of the proposed cascade detector is the spectrum vector from the original hyperspectral image at a pixel, and the output is the final detection accuracy measured by AUC (Area Under Curve). A higher AUC value suggests a greater possibility that the current pixel is the target. In each cascade of our detector, we use multiple I-MTCEMs independently and the commonly-used Sigmoid function to improve the robustness and the nonlinear expression ability of the detector, respectively. Figure 1 shows the schematic diagram of the proposed E-IMTCEM detector.

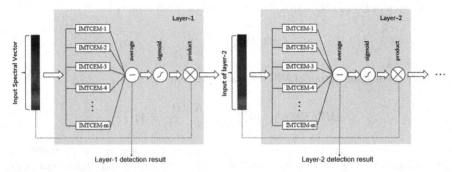

Fig. 1. Structure of the proposed E-IMTCEM method. The input spectral vector keeps nearly unchanged or becomes smaller through the process of the first layer, and are then fed to the second layer.

Our proposed cascaded detector consists of multiple layers in series. In each layer, the input of a cascade is an initial or a processed spectrum vector. Specifically, the initial input spectral vector is passed through multiple IMTCEM filters subsequently. The IMTCEM filter in each layer is designed to include a random group of regularization coefficients $\lambda_1, \cdots, \lambda_m$ for improving the generalization ability of the proposed method. The final output $\bar{u}$ is a vector of size $q \times 1$, and contains the average values of CEM with respect to q targets [17]

$$\bar{u} = \frac{1}{m} \sum_{i=1}^{m} w(\lambda_i)^T \tilde{r}_t$$

$$= \frac{1}{m} \sum_{i=1}^{m} \frac{D^T (R + \lambda_i I)^{-1} \tilde{r}_t}{D^T (R + \lambda_i I)^{-1} D} \qquad (12)$$

With the result of (12), we have the following summation

$$\tilde{s} = \bar{u} \times [1, \cdots, 1]^T. \qquad (13)$$

The result of Eq. (13) is adjusted by the nonlinear Sigmoid function, and the output is further multiplied by the input spectral vector. These operations are formulated as below

$$\tilde{r}_{t+1} = \tilde{r}_t h(\tilde{s}) \tag{14}$$

where the Sigmoid function takes the form of [18]

$$h(x) = 1/(1 + e^{-x}) \tag{15}$$

The mechanism of (15) is to suppress smaller $\tilde{s}$ values while retaining larger ones. Based on this property, the background areas of the input hyperspectral image are suppressed, and the targets are well preserved by each layer of the proposed detector. Finally, the last layer outputs the detection results of our E-IMTCEM.

It should be noted that the multiplication operation (14) is used at the end of each layer. The reasons are two-folded. Firstly, although the output of each layer contains the information of input hyperspectral vector, it just reflects the probability scores and does not contain the input hyperspectral information, which cannot be directly fed to the next layer. Secondly, the multiplication operation in each layer acts as the attention mechanism. Specifically, the features of background areas are further suppressed, and those of the targets tend to be salient. Thus, the targets produce the highest responses, which are beneficial to the final detection results.

5   Experimental Results and Analysis

To evaluate the proposed E-IMTCEM algorithm, we perform extensive experiments on synthetic hyperspectral data. For fair comparisons, we select the MTCEM algorithm [16] as a baseline, and run both of them by using Python 3.8 on the same platform, i.e., a PC host with CPU frequency of 3.4 GHz. The detection performance of our method is robust to the parameter λ when randomly select from $(\alpha/(1 + \alpha))$ to α, where α is empirically set to $1 \times e^{-12}$. In the following experiments, we use 4 layers of cascades in our method.

5.1   Dataset

As in most publications, we select the Digital Spectral Library of the Geological Survey [19] dataset to compare different multi-target detection methods. The dataset contains plenty of synthetic hyperspectral images. More details of the dataset are elaborated as below.

The Digital Spectral Library of the Geological Survey [19] includes various spectrum bands of pure materials [20]: Neodymium oxide GDS34, Basalt HS17.3B, Monazite HS255.3B, Axinite HS342.3B, Rhodochrosite HS67, Chrysocolla HS297.3B, Niter GDS43 (K-Saltpeter), Anthophyllite HS286.3B, Neodymium Oxide GDS34, Monazite HS255.3B, Samarium Oxide GDS36, Pigeonite HS199.3B, Meionite WS700.HLsep, Spodumene HS210.3B, Labradorite HS17.3B, Grossular WS484, Zoisite HS347.3B, and Wollastonite HS348.3B. For the limited memory of our test platform, we randomly choose two types of materials with different spectrum bands, i.e., Basalt HS17.3B and Samarium Oxide GDS36. Thereafter, the target implantation method [19] is used to generate the synthetic hyperspectral data for evaluating the proposed multi-target detection method E-IMTCEM. Each synthetic image carries 224 bands and 64 × 64 pixels, and the spectrum bands at each pixel record only one kind of ground cover. In addition, 20 dB and 25 dB Gaussian white noises are added to the final synthetic images for evaluating the robustness of our algorithm to spectral perturbations. An example of these images is shown in Fig. 2. As observed from the first spectral band in (a), the small squares including those at bounds stand for the materials of different spectrum bands. Figure 2(b) shows the ground-truth positions of five interesting targets, which are marked by ourselves to prepare multiple targets for comparing E-IMTCEM with MTCEM. Specifically, the upper two and the left one brighter dots/blocks belong to Basalt HS17.3B, while the below two dots are Samarium Oxide GDS36. Darker pixels represent the background area, while the brighter ones are the targets to detect.

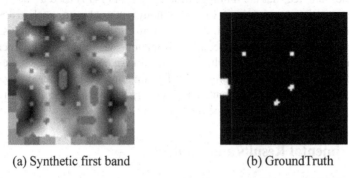

(a) Synthetic first band   (b) GroundTruth

Fig. 2. An example of synthetic data. (a) Synthetic first band. (b) GroundTruth

5.2 Detection Results and Evaluations

The detection results of our E-IMTCEM detector with one to four layers are provided in Fig. 3. As shown, the detection results of E-IMTCEM are indicated by different levels of brightness which stand for different substances. It can be easily observed that our detection results become more accurate as the number of layer increases. Meantime, they are also more accurate than MTCEM by comparing with the ground truth. It's disappointing that MTCEM only vaguely detects the target.

Quantitative evaluations are reported in Table 1, which provides the AUC values and running time of MTCEM and E-IMTCEM on synthetic data with different levels of white Gaussian noises. It should be noted that the AUC values and running time in this table are averaged from 10 times of repeated experiments for fair comparisons. As observed, the proposed E-IMTCEM algorithm with four layers achieves the best object detection performance compared with other layers.In addition, the AUC values of the MTCEM and the fourth layer of E-IMTCEM algorithms are 1.0000 and 1.0000, 0.8674 and 0.9780, 0.9691 and 0.9954 for 0 dB, 20 dB, and 25 dB noises, respectively. Our E-IMTCEM method is slower than the original MTCEM, and it will need more running time as the number of layers in E-IMTCEM is increasing due to the multiple IMTCEM detectors and the additional operations of stochastic averaging and nonlinear

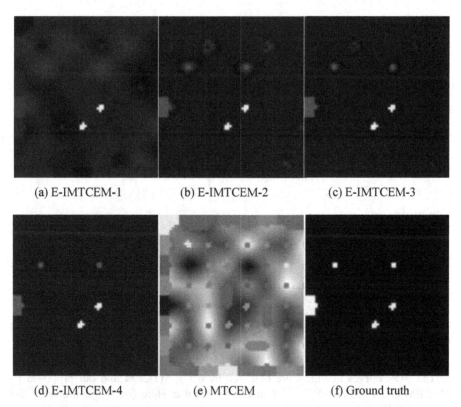

(a) E-IMTCEM-1   (b) E-IMTCEM-2   (c) E-IMTCEM-3

(d) E-IMTCEM-4   (e) MTCEM   (f) Ground truth

Fig. 3. Target detection results by different methods for comparison. (a)–(d) The outputs of the first to fourth layers of the E-IMTCEM algorithm on the image in Fig. 2, respectively. (e) The output by MTCEM algorithm. (f) The ground truth

Table 1. Comparisons of different algorithms in terms of AUC values and running time(s) on synthetic data with white Gaussian noises of 0 dB, 20 dB and 25 dB.

Method	Syn data			
	w/o noise	20 dB SNR	25 dB SNR	Time(s)
MTCEM	1.00000	0.8674	0.9691	0.0897 s
E-IMTCEM: layer 1	1.00000	0.8746	0.9683	0.2652 s
E-IMTCEM: layer 2	1.00000	0.9413	0.9908	0.3380 s
E-IMTCEM: layer 3	1.00000	0.9566	0.9935	0.4411 s
E-IMTCEM: layer 4	1.00000	0.9780	0.9954	0.4945 s
E-IMTCEM: layer 5	1.00000	0.8807	0.9092	0.5992 s

transformation. However, the AUC values achieved by our E-IMTCEM are all equal or higher than those by MTCEM, which demonstrates the superiority of our proposed method.

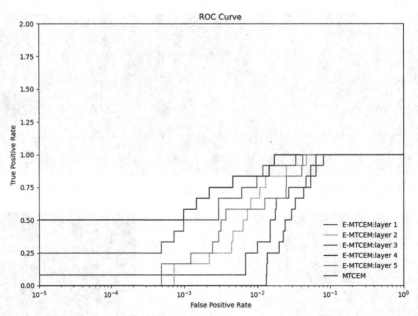

Fig. 4. The ROC curves generated by MTCEM and our E-IMTCEM on the image in Fig. 2 under 25 dB white Gaussian noise.

The ROC curves in Fig. 4 are obtained by using MTCEM and our proposed E-IMTCEM under 25 dB SNR of white Gaussian noise. Here five layers are set in the proposed E-IMTCEM algorithm. As observed, the area enclosed by the ROC curve of E-IMTCEM is obviously larger than that enclosed by the ROC curve of MTCEM in noisy cases. The proposed E-IMTCEM algorithm with four layers obtains the maximum areas. This result is consistent with the AUC values in Table 1.

6 Conclusion

This paper introduces a multi-target detection method (i.e., E-IMTCEM) to process an input hyperspectral image. Inspired by the idea that the original MTCEM is improved by incorporating the parameter of lambda to enhance the stability of the whole detection algorithm, we embed this parameter (lambda) into the widely-used technique of ensemble learning to increase the expression ability of features by constructing a multi-layer cascade detector. Then, the effectiveness of the proposed method is verified by performing extensive experiments on synthetic images.

References

1. Manolakis, D., Marden, D., Shaw, G.A.: Hyperspectral image processing for automatic target detection applications. Linc. Lab. J. **14**(1), 79–116 (2003)
2. Shaw, G.A., Burke, H.K.: Spectral imaging for remote sensing. Linc. Lab. J. **14**(1), 2–28 (2003)

3. Shi, Z., Qin, Z., Yang, S.: Spatial multiple materials detection in hyperspectral imagery. In: IEEE 3rd International Conference on Awareness Science and Technology (iCAST), pp. 76–80 (2011)
4. Zhao, R., Shi, Z., Zou, Z.: Ensemble-based cascaded constrained energy minimization for hyperspectral target detection. Remote Sens. **11**(11), 1310 (2019)
5. Winter, E.M., Miller, M.A., Simi, C.G.: Mine detection experiments using hyperspectral sensors. Int. Soc. Opt. Photonics **5415**, 1035–1041 (2004)
6. Chang, C.I.: An information-theoretic approach to spectral variability, similarity, and discrimination for hyperspectral image analysis. IEEE Trans. Inf. Theory **46**(5), 1927–1932 (2000)
7. Kay, S.M.: Fundamentals of Statistical Signal Processing: Practical Algorithm, vol. 3. Pearson Edducation, Westford (2013)
8. Harsanyi, J.C., Chang, C.I.: Hyperspectral image classification and dimensionality reduction:an orthogonal subspace projection approach. IEEE Trans. Geosci. Remote Sens. **13**(4), 779–785 (1994)
9. Zou, Z., Shi, Z., Wu, J.: Quadratic constrained energy minimization for hyperspectral target detection. In: IEEE International Geoscience and Remote Sensing Symposium (IGARSS), pp. 4979–4982 (2015)
10. Zou, Z., Shi, Z.: Hierarchical suppression method for hyperspectral target detection. IEEE Trans. Geosci. Remote Sens. **54**(1), 330–342 (2016)
11. Kraut, S., Scharf, L.L., Mcwhorter, L.T.: Adaptive subspace detectors. IEEE Trans. Signal Process. **49**(1), 1–16 (2001)
12. Ren, H., Du, Q., Chang, C.I., Jensen, J.O.: Comparison between constrained energy minimization based approaches forhyperspectral imagery. In: IEEE Workshop on Advances inTechniques for Analysis of Remotely Sensed Data, pp. 244–248 (2003)
13. Chang, C.I.: Hyperspectral Imaging: Techniques for Spectral Detection and Classification, 1st edn. Springer, Boston (2003). https://doi.org/10.1007/978-1-4419-9170-6
14. Zhou, Z.H.: Ensemble Methods: Foundations and Algorithms. Chapman and Hall/CRC, New York (2012)
15. Freund, Y., Schapire, R., Abe, N.: A short introduction to boosting. J.-Jpn. Soc. Artif. Intell. **14**, 771–780 (1999)
16. Jihao, Y., Yan, W., Yisong, W.: An improved multi-small target detection algorithm in hyperspectral image. Acta Electronica Sinica **38**(9), 1975–1978 (2010)
17. Zhou, Z.H.: Ensemble learning, Encyclopedia of Biometrics, pp. 270–273. Springer, Berlin (2009)
18. Goodfellow, I., Bengio, Y., Courville, A.: Deep Learning, 1st edn. MIT Press, Cambridge (2016)
19. Clark, R.N., Swayze, G.A., Gallagher, A.J.: The US geological survey, digital spectral library: version 1 (0.2 to 3.0 um); Technical report. Geological Survey (US), Reston (1993)
20. Chang, Y.C.C., Ren, H., Chang, C.I.: How to design synthetic images to validate and evaluate hyperspectral imaging algorithms. Int. Soc. Opt. Photonic **6966**, 69661 (2008)
21. Solomatine, D.P., Shrestha, D.L.: AdaBoost. RT: a boosting algorithm for regression problems. In: IEEE International Joint Conference on Neural Networks, vol. 2, no. 4, pp. 1163–1168 (2004)
22. Tuysuzoglu, G., Birant, D.: Enhanced bagging (eBagging): a novel approach for ensemble learning. Int. Arab. J. Inf. Technol **17**(4), 515–528 (2020)
23. Behroozi, M., Boostani, R.: Presenting a new cascade structure for multiclass problems. In: IEEE International Conference on Electronics, pp. 192–195 (2013)
24. Karimireddy, S.P., Kale, S., Mohri, M.: Scaffold: stochastic controlled averaging for federated learning. In: International Conference on Machine Learning, pp. 5132–5143 (2020)

25. Wanto, A., Windarto, A.P., Hartama, D.: Use of binary sigmoid function and linear identity in artificial neural networks for forecasting population density. Int. J. Inf. Syst. Technol. (IJISTECH) **1**(1), 43–54 (2017)
26. Dai, Z., Wang, P., Wei, H.: Signal detection based on Sigmoid function in Non-Gaussian noise. J. Electron. Inf. Technol. **41**(12), 2945–2950 (2019)

Author Index